PEOPLE, PLACES AND PASSIONS

PEOPLE, PLACES AND PASSIONS

'Pain and Pleasure': A Social History of Wales and the Welsh, 1870–1945

Russell Davies

www.uwp.co.uk

British Library Cataloguing-in-Publication Data.
A catalogue record for this book is available from the British Library.

ISBN 978-1-78316-237-6
eISBN 978-1-78316-238-3

Typeset in Wales by Eira Fenn Gaunt, Pentyrch, Cardiff
Printed by CPI Antony Rowe, Chippenham, Wiltshire

i dri hanesydd, meistri eu crefft, a geisiodd ddysgu hanes fy ngwlad a'm pobl i mi:

John Davies
Geraint Jenkins
Ieuan Gwynedd Jones

pe bawn ond wedi mynd i fwy o ddarlithoedd . . .

ac i bedair cenhedlaeth o Gymry sydd wedi cyfoethogi fy nhaith:

fy nhad John Haydn Davies, Dai a Beryl
Nerys
Betsan a Dylan, Ffion ac Udara
Cati a Beca

Contents

List of Illustrations

Prologue: Sources for a 'Sullen Art'

> Nes na'r hanesydd at y gwir di-goll, ydyw'r dramodydd, sydd yn gelwydd oll.
>
> (Closer than the historian to the lost truths is the dramatist who deals in lies).
>
> R. Williams Parry, 'Gwae Awdur Dyddiaduron'

Historians, especially those working on the earliest historical periods, often bemoan their lack of sources. Others, with an echo of British Rail's excuse that the 'wrong type of snow' caused train delays, complain that the material available does not allow them to answer the particular questions they wish to ask. Anyone who has worked on the late nineteenth and early twentieth centuries, is aware of another difficulty – there is too much material for teams of academics, let alone an individual, to read and comprehend. Thus the historian of modern Wales must have considerable sympathy for the hero of Laurence Sterne's eighteenth-century novel Tristram Shandy, who worries that, since he has spent two years chronicling the first two days of his life, material will accumulate faster than he can cope with it and, as time goes by, he will be further and further from the end of his history.

The shelves of the libraries, museums and archives of Wales groan under the weight of autobiographies, biographies, census reports, diaries, family and personal papers, journals, letters, official government papers, newspapers, hymn books, novels and poems, each of which is relevant to our study. Many of these documents are now available on internet sites, providing the historian with unbroken and unlimited access to the sources. In this respect a priceless resource is the *Gathering the Jewels* project, which enables the historian to browse the treasures of the Welsh archives from desk – or laptop.[1]

It is almost axiomatic for many historians that the 'facts' of the past are to be found in the 'official' documents created by a society. The stately and staid volumes of the reports of 'official' bodies appointed by governments, to inquire and enquire into specific events or to observe and preserve society's attitudes, are often regarded as if they possess an almost biblical prescience and infallibility. But we need to remember that official documents are not exempt from the problems and pitfalls of all historical sources. They too contain bias, opinion and prejudice and many are as much creative works as they are factual testimonies. Official sources do not always reveal the entire story. Public records such as court papers and the Registrar General's statistics provide skeletal details that hint at vivid tales of illegitimacy, forced marriages, infant mortality, enforced separations of warring partners and entire families and neighbourhoods locked in moral decline. Other sources are needed to tease out the detail of these tragic tales.

A people's literature, in contrast to official records, reveals much of what actually concerned people. Fiction is often as useful as fact in revealing their innermost and intimate obsessions. Writers often offer unique viewpoints into their worlds, while historical novelists operate in the no-man's-land between history and fiction where historians fear to tread. They walk with the dead unfettered by footnotes. To those with a historiographical training, such indiscipline appears to provide an unfair liberation. But in reality this is a terrible kind of freedom as, ironically, the writer of fiction is actually firmly fettered by credibility, whereas the writer of 'facts' is not. Not all creative writing was, or is, make-believe.[2] The sleuthing of literary detectives such as John Harris into the dark background of Caradoc Evans and J. Elwyn Hughes into the darker upbringing of Caradog Prichard have uncovered the real individuals involved in their nightmare fictions.[3] Ballads, novels, poems and short stories can be read historically by a historian without venturing unduly into the field of literary criticism. Swansea University's Centre for Research into the English Literature and Language of Wales (CREW) has published several detailed studies which provide novel insights into the inner lives of the Welsh people.[4] The Welsh Assembly Government also deserves considerable praise for funding Parthian Press's project of republishing the out-of-print classics of the Library of Wales, as does Honno's campaign to republish classic works by women authors.[5]

But the legacy of this age is not only in print. The historian of modern Wales has another considerable advantage over those of earlier periods. A vast range of artistic, audio, aural, dramatic, cinematic and photographic material has been lovingly preserved in the archives. Such sources need to be interpreted with care and caution. The superb collections of photographers, such as those of David Harries of Llandeilo and John Thomas of Liverpool, reveal an animated world of bucolic business and industry.[6] Their studio portraits of workers in the clothes of their trade are intimate character sketches, from which one can almost still smell the stench of night-breath, underarm sweat and over-worn clothes. Stare long enough at these photographs and some of the reality sinks in – the pervasive dirt, the clothing gone to shreds and holes, the seams and furrows of worry on faces and foreheads. Every picture told, and tells, a story. But these studies in sepia also reflect the desire to pose, or be posed, in the style of contemporary aesthetic norms rather than according to social reality. Sailor-suited siblings, dressed for the event, play inattentively with dolls, sailing ships and model steam-engines, the toys provided by the photographer rather than their own personal favourites. Even from its earliest origins, the camera lied. A historian must learn to question the image which meets the eye.[7]

Anyone interested in the history of war and warfare will be familiar with the pasty faces of the fallen, forever frozen in time. Those who died young, who never grew old, their candles burning out long before their legends, stare at us from countless thousands of photographs taken in now forgotten studios. So powerful are these images that they create the impression that this was a duotone world of black and white or at best a permafrost world of grey on grey. We should not, because of the limitations of technology, forget that people's lives were lived in colour. One of the most frustrating problems is that we do not know who many of the people staring and smiling out at us are. Familiarity dictated that the photographs contained within the double-cardboard covers of the family photograph albums carried no names. Everyone knew that Dad was Dad, that Mam was Mam, and that the fourteenth child, 'little M.', was the apple of their eyes. Even later, when time and war and the shortening of skirts and hair had shattered the Victorian dream, no-one had the foresight to name the people in the photographs. Today, these people are unknown and, probably, unknowable.

Photography, for all its technological advantages of immediacy and apparent veracity, never replaced painting in the visual world of the Welsh people. Artists such as Augustus and Gwen John, John Elwyn, Christopher Williams and countless others painted Wales and the Welsh for their present but also with an eye towards posterity. Art historians like Peter Lord and Robert Meyrick have been tireless in their efforts to recover the images of the nation. Painting, they have shown, was not merely a private source of pleasure for rich connoisseurs but also undertook a public function in creating a national iconography and imagery. The work of Welsh painters presents a rich portrait of the people in farm and field, mill and mine, prison and poorhouse.[8]

The work of Welsh cartoonists also provides a fascinating visual insight into the working of society. The Swansea and Newport cartoonist Herbert Samuel Thomas (1883–1966) raised over £250,000 for tobacco for the troops in 1916 through sales of his cartoon 'Arf a Mo Kaiser', a feat he repeated in the Second World War with the self-plagiarised 'Arf a Mo Hitler'. His book, *Fun at the Seaside,* reveals a much less fastidious view of Wales and the world.[9] J. M. Staniforth, Ronald Niebour (NEB) and Leslie Illingworth also satirised their society in caricatures which provide the historian with visual clues to society's real obsessions.[10] As well as creating a number of military insignia, John Kelt Edwards (1875–1934) produced war cartoons of an irreverent nature that provide a satirical corrective to the dominant image of heroism. One of his characters was that rare feminine representation of national identity, Dame Wales – the beautiful and bounteous consort, who would out-rule Britannia and become the perfect partner for the bellicose and brutal John Bull. Cartoons are not just comic ephemera. They provide clues to areas of tension and trauma in society, provide an effective weapon of social and political invective and issue a corrective to behaviour which society found abhorrent. *Y Punch Cymraeg* provides ample evidence that Welsh cartoonists were just as effective as their English-speaking colleagues in bursting the bubbles of pomp and pretence.

Contemporaries stare at us silently from the patina of paintings and faded photographs, but they also address us directly on flickering celluloid. Early cinema provides a phantasmagoria of people engaged in their hobbies and habits, their trades and transports, their parades and pageants. Lives appear as fragile as the film and glass on which they were captured. Once again the historian should not take everything at face value in this world of staccato-paced people, for the secret is that although that world seems to represent what is, it is not what it seems. In the 1960s, when the BBC still believed that its function was to 'elevate and educate', a landmark history series was produced on *The Great War*. Amongst those interviewed are several Welsh soldiers including the remarkable and redoubtable Frank Richards, who saw action in virtually every major British campaign on the Western Front, without suffering any injury. Many of these images are now available on the internet sites of libraries and museums and on the all-pervading YouTube.[11]

G. M. Young famously advised historians 'to go on reading until you can hear the people talk'. Given the wealth of audio and visual evidence available, historians of the late nineteenth and early twentieth centuries could be forgiven if they unwisely chose to ignore this sage advice. The temptation to do so is even greater when we remember that for many people these years were all their yesterdays. Oral history is therefore an important source for the historian of modern Wales. In the 1970s the South Wales Miners' Library and the St Fagan's National History Museum interviewed elderly people on a bewildering array of topics. More recently, the National Library of Wales has gathered the reminiscences of Welsh people from the 'age of austerity' that reigned between 1940–50.[12] Many Welsh people also provided their observations to the social observers in the Mass Observation project in the 1930s, 1940s and 1950s.[13] Those who were spared amnesia as they aged let their nostalgia run free. The old tales and unreliable memoirs present a web of paradox and several decades of memory have added to the confusion, yet these memory mines remain a priceless resource to the historian. When you listen to the tape-recordings and read the transcripts, some seem startlingly alive, almost Proustian – detailed memories triggered by the madeleines from the time of the mind. One of the joys of oral history is that the past talks back, debates, corrects.[14]

Oral history and the manufacturing of myths, legends and rumour are all useful in creating a human portrait, however elusive. The nation is a mystery-generating engine and the deeper one delves the more questions emerge. Oral history and individual experience help one to become aware that there is no one single story and that there are many different angles from which a story can unfold. National identity can be fissile, malleable and mercurial. The challenge for the historian is to capture the particular experiences of individuals without losing sight of the general forces which changed society. In *Hitler's Willing Executioners*, Daniel Goldhagen uncovered countless examples of how individual 'ordinary Germans' were involved in atrocities against the Jews, but the overall effect was to cloud the enormity of the Holocaust.[15] Richard Cobb, Olwen Hufton and David Cressy appear to have been more successful and skilful in producing masterpieces of historical reconstructions in which the lives of the poor and the downtrodden are given the front of the stage.[16] They realised that not all historical events or evidence have an equivalent call on the historian's attention. The danger of an indiscriminate celebration of the humdrum is that history will dissolve into a random aggregate of disconnected episodes, anecdotally related. The evidence has to be evaluated, compared, selected, interpreted. Unlike the social anthropologist, the historian needs to explain as well as to describe phenomena. The historian also has the difficult task of choosing which approach to take. At the opposite extremes are the 'microcosmic vision' of a Carlo Ginzberg, who considered the cosmology of a seventeenth-century miller as a means of seeing the world, and the equally unattainable *histoire totale* of Febvre and Braudel, in which everything was considered as grist to the historian's mill.[17] This study has benefitted from the approach and insights offered by several historiographical schools. If, however, one had to categorise the historical approach of a study which adopts the modus operandum of a thieving magpie, then one would have to say that this is a narrative history of Wales and the Welsh that attempts to consider evidence from across as broad a range as possible in order to present a different portrait of a country and a people, of a land and a nation. It is to be hoped that this will enable us to realise that Welsh national identity was far more complex and contradictory than it has traditionally been regarded.

In addition to contemporary material, a historian must also be aware of what colleagues have written about a period. Since the 1970s there has been a remarkable renaissance in Welsh history which has produced countless monographs on a whole range of topics. Each county boasts its historical society transactions and family history journals, publishing the results of detailed research. The history departments within the universities of Wales have produced magisterial and doctoral theses of startling originality and a torrent of books has been published by the presses of Wales. Some historians have skilfully and sympathetically evoked the spirit of an age, others have etched the character of shorter periods. There are thus detailed studies of certain decades (the *fin de siècle* of the 1890s, the Roaring Twenties, the 'Years of the Locust' in the 1930s, evocations of individual years (1914, 1939, 1940), certain key months (July 1910, May 1926), particular days (4 August 1914, Christmas Day 1915) and even substantial studies of a single hour (11 a.m. on 11 November 1918). Added to it all is the work of specialists in other fields – demography, economics, geography, anthropology, ethnology, sociology and all the other 'ologies' – which can provide valuable insights into the past lives of Wales and the Welsh.

Confronted with all this material, the historian cannot but feel inadequate to the burdens of a 'sullen art'. This is perhaps why Welsh history has, over the past few years, become more specialist. Ever more material is being produced on ever narrower subjects. Welsh history is today more vigorous, ingenious and skilful than it has ever been. There appears to be no aspect of life in Wales that is not being studied by a historian – class, death, gender, happiness, humour, literature, music, national identity, race, sex, sport. Unfortunately, the material is so specialised in some cases that it has created barriers of incomprehension. Demography and economics, for example, appear to have become more like branches of mathematics than historical enterprises. Though they often yield highly original insights and results, one sometimes gets the feeling that the statistics are used in the same way as a drunkard uses a lamp post – for support rather than illumination. Similarly, those who enjoy conceptualising and theorising have been busily at work. Welsh history has now, it seems, passed through its Marxian, Gramscian, Derridean and Foucaultian phases and entered a brave new post-colonial, post-modern, post-nationalist, post-structuralist world.[18]

The vast mass of material available to the historian calls not for despair, but perhaps for a new approach. General studies of modern Wales have tended to use politics and religion as the means of unlocking the secrets of society. These are, of course, forces of profound importance in modern societies, affecting several aspects of peoples' lives. Since the publication of K. O. Morgan's seminal *Rebirth of a Nation: Wales 1880–1980* (1980), many historians have pursued this path.[19] Yet there are whole layers of human experience which are not affected by either politics or religion. There are levels of peoples' lives which are too deep for the political historian's plumb-line. In *People, Places and Passions* and the related volume *Sex, Sects and Society*, we will seek to venture along some paths less travelled in the social history of Wales 1870–1945. Straying from the beaten track might not be much of a methodology, but a detour off the highways and down the byways creates the possibility of enjoying some unusual views, and sometimes they can be the most revealing.

Studying people's emotions and passions might be an equally insightful way of investigating the experiences of Welsh people. At the core of this study is the individual, with all her and his contradictions and complexities. It seems sad that historians so often avoid the eccentric and embrace the average; much of the evidence evaluated in this study simply shows that one cannot calculate the mean of meaning. *People, Places and Passions* examines the structures of everyday life and the tumultuous changes that took place in the years between 1870–1945. It traces the drift from Victorian prosperity to Elizabethan austerity, looks at the rise of consumer cultures and how mankind attempted to conquer time and space, and follows the wandering stars of Wales around the world. *Sex, Sects and Society* looks at the individual experiences of the Welsh people, using emotions such as anxiety, anger, avarice, fear, hatred, joy, love, lust, loathing, melancholy, pride, and several others to provide a different perspective on the lives of the Welsh. It attempts to show the complexity and contradictions of the national identity and also looks at the way in which death's dark shadow lightened and the effect that this had on religion and superstition. Though they can be seen as freestanding volumes, they are intended to be part of a coherent whole. The first volume sets out the structures and systems of the backcloth against which the emotional dramas of the Welsh were enacted. *People, Places and Pleasures* considers the material worlds of Wales, whilst *Sex, Sects and Society* looks at the mentalities of the Welsh.

Our approach is not that of 'history from below', which was so fashionable at the end of the twentieth century. Neither is it what could be termed Gettysberg history – of the people, for the people, by the people. Rather it attempts to use the experience of individuals to give a top down, bottom up, and in all directions across the middle view of social and emotional life in the years 1870–1945. Despite the dictates of demography, which would insist that this be another analysis of south Wales, or in reality Glamorgan, an attempt is made to pay attention to every part of Wales – north, south, east and west. Though Wales is treated as an unity, this study also brings local cultures under scrutiny and tries to be sensitive to regional variations and to reveal the complexities of circumstances and context. Although our focus will be on the sedentary stay-at-home Welsh, we will also venture after those rainbow chasers who fled their 'father's land' in search of freedom, gold, glory or God.

In this pursuit, my debt to the pathfinders who have written on the period will become obvious. The footnotes attempt to acknowledge my sources in as comprehensive a manner as has been possible. Undoubtedly there will be omissions, for which I present sincere apologies. I remain fearful that when I look over my shoulder I will see a thief's shadow. During the thirty or so years that I have been working on the books, I have received a constant flow of support from the Trustees of the Sir David Hughes Parry Awards at Aberystwyth University. I am deeply grateful to the Trustees for entrusting their resources to me. I am also grateful to Mrs Kylie Evans for help with the typescript.

That the two volumes have taken so long to complete is probably due to the author's tendency to spend too much time enjoying too many of the more dissipated topics covered in this work. I might have, I should have read much more, talked to more people, attempted a more comprehensive survey. But even if I had, the study would have been incomplete, its conclusions still tentative, like those of these books – an ant's attempt to build a pyramid.

Notes

1 *Casglu'r Tlysau / Gathering the Jewels* website provides a wealth of valuable material at *www.gtj.org.uk*. For a discussion of the value of digital and virtual sources in the 'recreation' of a past society, see Stephen Robertson, *Digital Harlem: Everyday Life 1915–1930* (Sydney, 2012).

2 Deborah O'Keefe, *Readers in Wonderland: the Literary Worlds of Fantasy Fiction* (London, 2004), pp. 42–3, makes valuable suggestions regarding the factual basis of fantasy in the work of Cardiff-born Roald Dahl and other writers. On the relevance of literature as a historical source, see Keith Thomas, *History and Literature: the Ernest Hughes Memorial Lecture* (Swansea, 1988) and Natalie Zemon Davis, *Fiction in the Archives: Pardon Tales and their Tellers in Sixteenth-century France* (London, 1988). In 2011, the Institute of Historical Research organised a virtual conference on the theme of 'Novel approaches: from academic history to historical fiction'. Amongst the most interesting were a series of articles that compared the literary treatment of war with standard historical works; for the First World War, Pat Barker's fictional *Regeneration* was contrasted with *Dismembering the Male: Men's Bodies, Britain and the Great War* by Joanna Bourke, whilst for the Second World War, A. L. Kennedy's novel *Flyer* was assessed with *The Flyer: British Culture and the Royal Air Force*,

1939–45 by Martin Francis. See *www.history.ac.uk/reviews* – reviews 1172 and 1173.

3 See, for example, John Harries. 'A biographical introduction', in *Fury Never Leaves Us: A Miscellany of Caradoc Evans* (Bridgend, 1985), pp. 9–46, and 'Introduction: the banned, burned book of war', in *Caradoc Evans, My People* (Bridgend, 1987), pp. 7–48; see also J. Elwyn Hughes, *Byd a Bywyd: Caradog Prichard 1904–80* (Swansea, 2005) and *Byd Go Iawn Un Nos Ola Leuad* (Swansea, 2008).

4 Amongst the titles published thus far are: Stephen Knight, *One Hundred Years of Welsh Fiction* (Cardiff, 2004); Chris Wigginton, *Modernism from the Margins: the 1930s Poems of Dylan Thomas and Louis MacNeice* (Cardiff, 2006); Barbara Prys-Williams, *Twentieth-century Welsh Autobiography* (Cardiff, 2004); and M. Wynn Thomas, *In the Shadow of the Pulpit* (Cardiff, 2010).

5 For the Library of Wales titles, see *www.thelibraryofwales.com/catalog/1* (accessed 10 September 2013); for Honno's republished classic titles, see *www.honno.co.uk/chiviler.php?func=pori_advanCadran=Classic* (accessed 1 September 2013).

6 There have been excellent published studies of these photographers' work. The most accessible are probably R. Iestyn Hughes, *Casgliad o Ffotograffau: D. C. Harries: A Collection of Photographs* (Aberystwyth, 1996); Iwan Meical Jones, *Hen Ffordd Gymreig o Fyw: A Welsh way of life* (Aberystwyth, 2008). The Geoff Charles collection in the National Library of Wales provides valuable collections of photographs of cultural and rural life dating from the 1940s; see Ioan Roberts, *Cefn Gwlad Geoff Charles: Cip yn ôl ar yr Hen Ffordd Gymreig o Fyw* (Talybont, 2001). There is also valuable material in Elfyn Scourfield, *Welsh Rural life in Photographs* (Barry, 1979). In the 1970s and 1980s, Stewart Williams Publishers produced many collections of photographs of Welsh towns and their environs. On war photography, see Catherine Moriaty, 'Through a picture only: portrait photography and the First World War', in Gail Braybon (ed.), *Evidence, History and the Great War: Historians and the Impact of 1914–18* (London, 2007), pp. 101–17.

7 For an interesting discussion on the establishment of a 'visual school of history', see Roy Porter, 'Seeing the Past', *Past and Present*, 118 (1988), 186–205. See also John Berger, *Ways of Seeing* (London, 1972) and Bruno Latour, 'Visualisation and Cognition: Thinking with Eyes and Hands', *Knowledge and Society*, vi (1986), 1–40.

8 Especially Peter Lord, *The Visual Culture of Wales: Imaging the Nation* (Cardiff, 2004); *Winifred Coombe Tenant: a life through art* (Aberystwyth, 2007); 'Winifred Coombe Tennant: a retrospective', Glynn Vivian

Art Gallery, Swansea, 13 December 2008–15 February 2009; Robert Meyrick, *John Elwyn* (London, 2000); 'Famous amongst the Barns: the Cardiganshire Landscapes of John Elwyn', *Ceredigion*, 15 (2002), 89–104; 'Wealth, wise and culture kind: Gregynog in the 1920s and 1930s', in *Things of Beauty: what two sisters did for Wales* (National Museum, Cardiff, 2007); *Christopher Williams: an Artist and Nothing Else*, (Aberystwyth, 2012); 'John Elwyn: a Retrospective', National Library of Wales, Aberystwyth, 1996; and 'Christopher Williams: a Retrospective', National Library of Wales, Aberystwyth, 2012.

9 On Herbert Samuel Thomas, see P. V. Bradshaw, *Bert Thomas and his Work* (London, 1918) and *Who's Who in Art* (London, 1929).

10 On Leslie Illingworth, see Mark Bryant, *World War II in Cartoons* (London, 1995). Professor Chris Williams of Cardiff University has lectured and published on J. M. Staniforth. See *www.gtj.org.uk/small/item/GTJ62414*, 'Cartoons of the Welsh Coal Strike' (accessed 2 June 2009). Useful biographies can be found in M. Bryant and S. Heneage (eds), *A Dictionary of Cartoonists and Charicaturists 1730–1980* (London, 1994) and Roy Douglas, *The Great War 1914–18: the Cartoonist's View* (London, 1995). There are also useful images and information in *www.llgc.org.uk/illingworth/index_s.htm* (last accessed 1 February 2009). On the value of cartoons, see Michael Duffy et al., *The English Satirical Print*, 7 vols (Cambridge, 1986); V. A. C. Gatrell, *City of Laughter: Sex and Satire in Eighteenth-century London* (London, 2006).

11 Frank Richards published two remarkable volumes of autobiography – *Old Soldier Sahib* (Eastbourne, n.d.) and *Old Soldiers Never Die* (Eastbourne, n.d.).

12 'Maes y gad i lles y wlad 1939–59: from warfare to welfare 1939–59', *www.tpyf-wales.com*. For an interesting assessment of the rural traditions of Wales, see Robin Gwyndaf, 'Memory in Action: Narration, Communication and the Repertoire of a Passive Tradition-bearer', *Folklife*, 33 (2000–1), 49–65.

13 Sussex University has established a superb website which gives access to much of the Mass Observation material: *http://www.massobs.org.uk* (accessed 21 July 2010).

14 Paul Thompson pioneered oral history, especially in *The Voice of the Past: Oral History* (Oxford, 1978) and *The Edwardians* (London, 1978). In the latter study, Thompson recounts the experiences of Harriet Vincent, whose family kept a boarding house in Cardiff's Tiger Bay (pp.121–9) and Gwen Davies (pp. 139–48). See also Joan Tumblety, *Memory and History: Understanding Memory as Source and* Subject (Abingdon, 2013). The Mass Observation archive has been well quarried by a number of

historians; see, for example, A. Calder and D. Sheridan (eds), *Speak for Yourself: A Mass Observation Anthology 1937–49* (London, 1984); J. Gardiner, *Wartime Britain 1939–45* (London, 2004); S. Garfield, *Our Hidden Lives: the Everyday Diaries of a Forgotten Britain 1945–48* (Sussex, 2004); J. Hinton, *Nine Wartime Lives: Mass Observation and the Making of the Modern Self* (London, 2010); N. Hubble, *Mass Observation and Everyday Life: Culture, History, Theory* (London, 2005); M. Snape, *God and the British Soldier: Religion and the British Army in the First and Second World Wars* (London, 2005); and L. Stanley, *Sex Surveyed, 1949–94: from Mass Observation's 'Little Kinsey' to the National Survey and the Hite Reports* (London, 1995). In the Welsh context, see B. Browning, *EKCO's of Cowbridge: House and War Factory* (Cowbridge, 2005). See also D. Smith, 'What does History Know of Nailbiting?', *Llafur* 1 (1972–5), 34–41.

15 Daniel G. Goldhagen, *Hitler's Willing Executioners: Ordinary Germans and the Holocaust* (London, 1996); see also Jeremy Popkin, 'Holocaust Memories, Historians, Memoirs: First Person Narrative and the Memory of the Holocaust', *History and Memory* 49/5 (2003), 49–84.

16 Richard Cobb, *Paris and its Provinces, 1792–1802* (Oxford, 1975) and *The Police and The People: French Popular Protest, 1789–1820* (Oxford, 1972); Olwen Hufton, *The Poor of Eighteenth-century France, 1750–1789* (Oxford, 1975); David Cressy, *Birth, Marriage and Death: Ritual,Religion and the Life-cycle in Tudor and Stuart England* (Oxford, 1999). Also noteworthy in this respect are the works of Eric Hobsbawm, *Captain Swing* (London, 1968) and *Bandits* (London, 1969). In the Welsh context, David Jones's *Rebecca's Children: a Study of Rural Crime and Protest* (Oxford, 1989), and David W. Howell's *The Rural Poor in Eighteenth-century Wales* (Oxford, 1989; Cardiff, 2002) are probably the closest in spirit to these works, especially Olwen Hufton's.

17 Carlo Ginzberg, *The Cheese and the Worms: the Cosmology of a Sixteenth-century Miller* (Baltimore, MD, 1980); Fernand Braudel, *The Mediterranean in the Age of Phillip II* (London, 1949) and 'Sensibility and history: how to reconstitute the emotional life of the past', in Peter Burke (ed.), *A New Kind of History from the Writings of Febvre* (London, 1973), pp. 12–26. Some historians have taken the biographical approach to history to its illogical conclusion and have focussed upon autobiography in their work, a tendency which Pierre Nora termed 'ego-histoire'. See Richard Vinen, 'The Prisoned Madeleine: the Autobiographical Turn in Historical Writing', *Journal of Contemporary History*, 46/3 (2011), 531–54. For a discussion on these themes, see Simon Schama, *Scribble, Scribble, Scribble: Writing on Ice Cream, Obama, Churchill and my Mother* (London, 2011), pp. 391–5.

18 Daniel Williams has argued for a more 'liberating' and 'all embracing approach' to a post-colonial Welsh identity in 'Back to a National Future? Wales and Postcolonialism', *Planet* (April, May 2006), 78–85. See also Andy Croll, 'Holding onto History: Modern Welsh Historians and the Challenge of Postmodernism', *Journal of Contemporary History*, 38 (2003), 323–32 and 'People's Remembrancers in a Postmodern Age: Contemplating the Non-crisis of Welsh Labour History', *Llafur: the Journal of Welsh Labour History*, 8/1 (2000), 5–17; see also Chris Williams, 'A post-national Wales', *Agenda* (Winter 2003/4). For a brief discussion of postmodernism and Wales, see Harold Carter, *Yr Iaith Gymraeg mewn Oes Ôl-fodern* (Cardiff, 1992). See also Kirsti Bohata, *Postcolonialism Revisited: Writing Wales in English* (Cardiff, 2004).

19 K. O. Morgan, *Rebirth of a Nation: Wales 1880–1980* (Oxford and Cardiff, 1980).

Introduction: Private Lives, the Individual and Society

Morgrug ydym ac esgid fawr Ffawd byth bythol yn hofran uwch ein pennau bach dibwys; morgrug . . . morgrug ar domen hanes.'

(We are ants and the big foot of Fate forever hovers above our tiny unimportant heads; ants . . . ants on the dunghill of history).

Emyr Humphreys, *Y Tri Llais* (1958)

'She ate the food of angels': after the death of a fasting girl

For me neglect and world-wide fame were one.
I was concerned with those the world forgot,
In the tale's ending saw its life begun;

And I was with them still when time was not.'

Vernon Watkins, 'Fidelities', quoted in Roland Mathias, *Vernon Watkins: Writers of Wales* (Cardiff, 1974), p. 119

Tread softly, whoever you are. History is always an intrusion, but it is late. It is 3.00 a.m. on Friday, 15 December 1869. Sarah is lying in this 'Welsh December dark bedroom', adorned by her mother with flowers in her hair and coloured ribbons cascading on to the pillows – a pre-pubescent, Pre-Raphaelite Ophelia. But the flowers, like Sarah, are fading. Sarah is dying. She has twelve hours left on earth. She is twelve years old. Her body, emaciated by a slow suicide from hysteria, is drifting away into unconsciousness. Sarah's breath, no stronger than a lark's, has an 'offensive' sepulchral stench. Her life has been a victory for religious credulity and superstitious gullibility more fitting to the medieval world of miracles and marvels than the late nineteenth century. Sarah's death will be a triumph for rational, scientific, modern medicine.

Sarah Jacob of Llethr-neuadd, Llanfihangel-ar-arth, became famous throughout Wales as the 'Welsh Fasting Girl'.[1] Her remarkable story occurred at one of those periods of transition and transformation when old ways coincide without yet yielding to the new. Technologies, such as the newspaper, the telegraph and the railway, still relatively new and novel during Sarah's brief, truncated life, played a key role in her fate. The press told her story far and wide. Having read all about it, the curious and the credulous decided to see for themselves and so, their desire aroused, they boarded specially chartered trains bound for the small rail station at Pencader. On the platform, 'hundreds of visitors' were greeted by men and boys emblazoned with placards displaying the bold words 'Guide to the Fasting Girl' or 'Guide to Llethr-neuadd'.

The Great Western Railway and the guides were not the only people to prosper from the travellers. Coins, notes and trinkets often decorated Sarah's chest to suggest to the pilgrims that they should be neither reluctant nor embarrassed to present gifts to the 'wondrous girl'. Her family boasted that Sarah had lived for over two years without any sustenance crossing her lips and fervently believed that she was one of God's wonders. She had, they said, lived on 'bwyd yr angylion' – the food of angels. The local doctor, Dr Evan Davies, was baffled. The local vicar, the Revd Evan Jones BD, professed, as befitted his profession, to believe the family's stories of supernatural support. His letter to the local newspaper, *The Welshman,* published on 19 February 1869, eventually resulted in a bizarre medical experiment.[2] In order to prove that a person could not live without food or water, four nurses from Guy's Hospital, London, were posted on an around-the-clock guard in Sarah's bedroom, to ensure that she could neither eat nor drink. After eight days, the death watchers' vigil became a wake. On Christmas Eve 1869 a carillon of bells tolled, not in celebration but in lamentation, as the famished corpse of Sarah Jacob was laid to rest in the quiet earth of Llanfihangel-ar-arth churchyard – 'pridd i'r pridd, llwch i'r llwch' ('dust to dust, ashes to ashes').

Sarah Jacob's death is one of the most shameful and stupid episodes in the history of belief and medicine in Wales. Her curtailed life had an element of mystery which left both the spiritualists and the scientists puzzled. The private tragedy was not without public significance. The events that took place in her dank and dark bedroom reveal much about the complex nature of Welsh society in the late nineteenth century. The medical journal *The Lancet* and English newspapers sought to present the tragic events as the natural product of the unnatural lives of rural Welsh people locked by their language behind the door that separated the medieval from the modern age, a people enwombed within their tiny horizon, suffering an uncommon hysteria. In contrast the medical authorities were portrayed as reasoned, respectable and responsible. But the supreme event of Sarah's life – her death – reflected as badly upon the doctors and the medical professionals as it did upon the parents and local people. Sarah was not so much their patient as their prey. The London medical establishment initiated the most extreme experiment in order to prove the material foundations of life itself. In 1869 medicine, it seemed, had not yet acquired the confidence, prestige or knowledge to disprove or discount the challenges presented to it by the claims of a hysterical girl.[3] During those last agonising twelve hours, there was only one voice of reason in Llethr-neuadd. Nurse Sarah Jones, a Welsh speaker, felt Sarah's body loosen, unravel. Touching the rawness of life itself, Nurse Jones disobeyed her superiors and valiantly, but sadly vainly, remonstrated with the parents to allow her to give Sarah a little food and some water mixed with brandy.

The events at Llethr-neuadd have been interpreted in books and the press, on stage and screen, as confirmation of the oppression of women and children in Victorian society. Yet the attention lavished on Sarah, the press reports of her evangelical erudition and the astonished recounting of precocious wisdom, revealed that this twelve-year-old girl was remarkably voluble and resourceful in telling her tale. One conclusion that could be drawn is that perhaps women and children in Welsh society had more agency than contemporaries could allow, and much more than some modern historians would credit. This little child was not only seen, she was also heard.

Sarah's story also suggests that the worlds of religion and superstition were not diametrically opposed to each other, but interrelated and interconnected in myriad ways. People in Wales acknowledged the earthly presence of unearthly beings such as angels, cherubs, seraphs and demons. Some of these supernatural creatures were generous, for angels shared their food with Sarah Jacob. Such beliefs were not the flotsam of superstitious minds, but fundamental to religious faith. Preacher after preacher, hymn after hymn, sermon after sermon, warned that somewhere in the cloud-strewn skies of Wales, grim-faced angels, eagle-eyed, spied for a God, ever ready to swoop and punish any indiscretion or immorality. Indeed, the astral planes above Wales appeared congested in that heady year 1869. Further east, in Llanthony, several children, enchanted by Father Ignatius's High Church, Judaic mysticism, saw supernatural lights, angels and visions of the Virgin Mary.[4] Some things had to be believed to be seen.

Individuals appear to have been remarkably capable of incorporating conflicting and contradictory ideas and ideals into their lives. Beliefs supposedly discredited and dismissed during the Reformation and the Renaissance had a secure and safe refuge in many personal cosmologies in late nineteenth century Wales. This is not surprising as people had, and have, remarkable longevity. Lives do not conform to the confines of the artificial and arbitrary boundaries of historical periods created by historians.[5]

Upset by the unfavourable press attention which west Wales had received, outraged at the incompetence and insensitivity of the medical authorities and angered by the superstition and stubbornness of the parents, Carmarthenshire magistrates initiated enquiries into whether there had been any criminal activity at Llethr-neuadd. The magistrates bitterly condemned the medical staff involved in the death of Sarah Jacob, but in 1871, in a gross miscarriage of justice, they imprisoned Evan and Hannah Jacob for their daughter's manslaughter. The court proceedings revealed a society characterised by several competing narratives. It appeared that every witness could tell a tale, plausible or implausible, about the 'wonderful little girl'. The tales told by doctors, nurses, vicars, farmers, parents or neighbours differed markedly from each other. The testimony is so diverse that there could have been several fasting girls in this verdant corner of west Wales in 1869. It is this diversity of experience and evidence which makes history such a fascinating, but often frustrating pursuit. The truth is often hard to pin down. People tell us in the clearest terms what happened to them, but we can never know with certainty. The historian is often stranded in the position of the much-maligned wife in one of Rhys Davies's short stories. When her philandering husband promises her that he will tell her what happened the previous night, she replies 'you will tell me what happened, but I will never know'.[6] However much historians have aspired to believe that the secrets of the past may be laid open, we are often left with a pedlar's pack of mysteries, a fardel or farrago of fictions, much of which may never be fully untangled. Evidence from one person therefore needs to be set against that provided by another, different world views need to be evaluated in order to recreate some of the complexity of the world we have lost.

Perchance to dream?: private lives, public witnesses

'Mal llong yr ymollyngais – i fôr byd,
Dros ei ferw byw hwyliais;
Ni ellir gweld, er llwyr gais,
Fy ôl, y ffordd drafaeliais.'

(Like a ship I cast myself – to the world's sea,
Over its live ferment I sailed;
You cannot see, however you seek,
My route, the trail I travelled).

'Bywyd', Evan Evans (Ieuan Glan Geirionydd)

Before, during and after the Second World War the Swansea philosopher Rush Rhees (1905–89), who had escaped the academic and theological conservatism of New York for the intellectual freedom of his great-great-grandfather's land, not only explained the opaque theories of Wittgenstein, but mused on the complex nature of society. Human society, he argued, was composed of 'countless conversations which interrelated and interacted with each other according to circumstances and events'. Rhees suggested that philosophy was the most appropriate mechanism to eavesdrop on and evaluate these conversations and explain 'messy human reality'.[7] This study of Wales between the years 1870 and 1945 utilises a similar approach in that it tries to portray the experience of the wider society through the prism of an individual's life story. Like the Bible, the book that was probably read most often by Welsh people in the years 1870–1945, history is an amalgam of biographies. The ambitions and emotions which drove individuals – anxiety, ambition, aspiration, envy, fear, greed, happiness, hate, jealousy, loneliness, love, lust, pride – will feature strongly in this study. We will seek to examine evidence from people who pursued the rational and reasonable pursuits of politics and religion, but also the experiences of others who were anxious and alarmed, confused and distressed, unreasonable and irrational, traumatised and terrified. The evidence of the mad, the deranged and the damaged, those people who could not escape their incessant inner monologues, reveals much of a society's fears and phobias.

Such particular experiences are not wholly representative of society's general experience, indeed they might not even be wholly representative of an individual's life story. Very often what the historian has to examine are the experiences of brittle individuals. People in distress, confined in court, or in police custody, or a mental hospital, or individuals trapped in a moment of crisis, caught up in the anarchic chaos of a religious revival or a riot, tossed about by anxiety and grief, or locked in by the intensities which our insecurities can inspire. Such experiences might have been wholly out of character. There are pictures of Sarah Jacob's parents, Evan and Hannah, in that terrifying ledger of human depravity, Carmarthen Gaol's Felons Register. On almost the same page is a photograph of 74-year-old Daniel Griffiths, of 'healthy complexion', from Laugharne. As far as is known, it is Daniel's only appearance in the historical record. He was charged with having 'committed buggery with an ass'.[8] The stark facts of the startling accusation and some personal details about Daniel are all we have. Surely, there must have been more to his life than this? What about his role as worker, friend, family member or neighbour? Unfortunately, there is no more evidence, confirmation that a 'total past' is not accessible because all that our historical research could ever recover consists of no more than traces, remains or fragments of times gone by. No other driftwood from Daniel's life has found its way to the shores of the archives. Thus, there is silence.

The experiences of such lonely, extreme, isolated people, often on the edges of madness or suicide, can produce only a partial account of the history of Wales. Superficially such experiences might not reveal much about the forces that have dominated modern Welsh historiography – the decline and fall of the Welsh aristocracy, the rise of 'Y Werin', the strange, slow death of Liberal Wales, the decline of religion, the growth of labour, the 'reawakening' or 'rebirth' of national aspirations. But the fundamental fact of their common humanity demands that the experiences of marginalised people should be considered alongside the histories of the great and the good. The social and cultural history of modern Wales is incomplete and impoverished without consideration of life at the margins. Exclude such people from Welsh history and unreality sets in; restore them, and the drama gains a fully human cast of characters – men and women whose foibles, fears and failings help to enrich and enliven the story.

General histories, by their very nature, have to offer a compressed and schematic account, compounding into one all social classes, all geographical areas, and cramming the diversity of reality and the uniqueness of individuals into averages. By focussing on individuals, it is to be hoped that a more complex picture of life in Wales and the lives of the Welsh can be offered. Not everyone perceives situations and circumstances in the same way. To give only a few examples, many people, especially in mining communities, expressed their support of the Bolsheviks during and after the Russian Revolution, support which in the case of David Ivon Jones was rewarded by burial amongst the 'heroes of the revolution' in Moscow's Novodevichy monastery.[9] But Anglesey-born Sir Max Kennedy Horton (1883–1951), the first captain to sink a ship from a submarine and 'a bit of a pirate', was active in countering Bolshevik agression in the Baltic States in the early 1920s.[10] Major John Fitzwilliams and his brother Duncan of Cilgwyn, Newcastle Emlyn, witnessed the brutalities of the Russian Civil War at first hand when fighting against the Bolsheviks in the Ukraine and Archangel.[11] A decade later, in the 1930s, not all the Welsh people who allowed themselves to be involved in the Spanish Civil War were engaged in the republican cause. Some, such as Frank Thomas, paid homage to a very different Catalonia and fought for the Fascists.[12]

One problem with using the life stories of individuals is that the story often acquires the appearance of unavoidability and predictability. The tales are often chronicles of deaths foretold. Past lives are laid out in linear retrospect and told with the doomed inevitability of a coroner's report. Sarah Jacob, throughout the recountings of her story, appears predestined to suffer. Others appear equally doomed. The life story of Marie Jeanette (Mary) Kelly follows a terrible trajectory. For over a year she walked and worked the streets of Carmarthen as a prostitute. Hoping for a better future in the east, she moved to work in Cardiff, then London. Despite her hopes, the capital's streets were not lined with gold, but with blood; Mary's blood. On 9 November 1888 Mary Kelly's disembowelled body was discovered, the final blood-splattered victim of Jack the Ripper.[13] Another innocent at large was the self-fantasist Timothy Evans, an illiterate van driver of Merthyr Tydfil. In 1949 he was the victim of a fearful miscarriage of justice. Timothy was hanged for the murder of his wife Beryl, who had actually been brutally slain by the sadistic John Christie at the infamous 10 Rillington Place.[14] The glacially good-looking Ruth Ellis of Rhyl, the last woman to be hanged in Britain – in 1955, at the order of Gwilym Lloyd George – also appears to have been set on an unavoidable path to destruction. Photographs of the young Ruth, in the Rhyl of her youth, before she had either stripped or teased in the London clubs, show an innocent, unaware of the misery that was yet to come – wartime romance, illegitimate child, marriage to a violent and vengeful drunkard, descent into affairs, alcoholism and her impassioned drink-and-drugs-driven revenge.[15] Yet Ruth's and many other people's destinies seem preordained and predetermined.

The lives of such tragic figures have often been told in such a way that the end is the beginning. All's well that ends badly. Yet these insights are the results of the foresight of hindsight. We look at the 1930s, for example, through the lens of the Second World War and all its horrors. But it is a poor sort of memory that only works backwards, as the White Queen says to Alice. Contemporaries were not enchained to their fate, they went through life unaware of the denouement to come, hoping above all for happiness. The historian thus has to be especially vigilant of chronology, of not reading back into the past aspects of the story that are yet to unfold. At the dawning of each year people celebrated and ventured bravely into what would surely be the *annus mirabilis*, the golden year of 1869, 1898, 1910, 1914, 1915, 1917, 1921, 1926, 1929, 1933 or 1939.[16] Hope springs more eternal than infernal. People lived their lives unaware of the destiny that would be forced on them by the iron claw of European politics or the brutal capriciousness of the global economy.

The historian must also guard against the hubris of those who claimed to have a clear plan of their personal development. However much some sought to forge a future for themselves, people were often the helpless and hapless victims of forces beyond their control or comprehension. Even those who had reached positions of power and prestige did not have a clear perception of how their lives would unfold. David Lloyd George's life story is perhaps the best example of how hindsight has obscured contemporary reality. The 'cottage-bred boy's' 'tempestuous journey' to 'the greatest office in the land' is the *locus classicus* of the opportunities available to Welsh people in the period 1870–1945. Each small step of the pilgrimage has been lovingly recounted in several hagiographic biographies. In 1917 a book was published with the arrogant title *The Early Life of Lloyd George together with a Short History of the Welsh People*. The title's implication was clear enough. To reorder one of his slogans of 1911 – '*trech arglwydd na gwlad*' (a lord is mightier than his land). Such writers were strongly influenced by Lloyd George's own interpretation of his life's story. No other author, apart perhaps from his friend, rival and colleague Churchill, was so obsessed with the need to control the past. To ensure that his version of events would hold sway, Lloyd George wrote his *War Memoirs* with the assistance of the sinister A. J. Sylvester. These wrist-breaking six volumes had an almost biblical ambition to force posterity to interpret early twentieth-century world history according to the perspectives, if not of Llanystumdwy, then certainly of Churt. This was history as a retrospective, introspective monologue. Lloyd George knew that winning the First World War was not just a matter of fighting, but of writing.[17]

'Ac eto nid myfi': individual experience, emotional expression and society

> I was in prison
> Until you came: your voice was a key
> Turning in the enormous lock
> Of hopelessness. Did the door open
> To let me out or yourselves in?
>
> R. S. Thomas, 'A Welsh Testament', in *Tares* (London, 1961)

Accepting the complexity of historical situations will hopefully help us to gather new insights into Welsh society. The intention is not to write a historiographical polemic, but some of the suggestions contained within this book are at odds with several well-entrenched historical views. General histories of Wales often base their conclusions on assumptions as much as analysis and still hold to the old traditional framework of Welsh historiography. Quite often, the story has the feeling of that old déjà vu all over again, as many generalisations have held on with the tenacity of a barnacle.

The period under study here, 1870–1945, witnessed some of the key transitions in the history of emotions.[18] These transitions correlate and perhaps are in some measure caused by changes in social, economic, cultural and structural transformations in Wales: the emergence of a more democratic form of government, an egalitarian social ethos, the market revolution, the spread of urbanisation, the growth and importance of larger companies, the spread of a consumer society and its attendant ethos, the rise and fall of a worldwide empire. In such a changing environment, it became imperative not simply to control emotions and their expression, but to suppress some whilst releasing others.[19] In some social contexts it was vital to contain certain emotions, in particular passion and anger. But in other areas of life, such as business or military and sporting endeavours, a determined and passionate approach was much vaunted and valued. In the world of commerce, success came to the brave and he or she who ventured.[20] In 1914, Wales experienced not just an outpouring of jingoism, but an outburst of honour, duty and love – emotions and character traits that had a strong biblical pedigree and were vital for onward marching Christian soldiers.[21] Emotions were both internalised and externalised depending on changing social and cultural circumstances.[22] Social rage was usually contained but on occasion, as during the riots across south Wales in 1898, at Tonypandy in 1910 and Llanelli in 1911, it was no longer contained but exploded in traumatic violence.

Twentieth-century Wales is often portrayed as a patriarchal society in which the 'Victorian paterfamilias' still ruled wife and child with a rod of iron. However, read the children's literature of the period and it becomes clear that the mother was the most influential figure within the family. Rural communities were dominated by women, as many young, able men had been drawn away to work in mill and mine. The salt-dashed coastal towns were also matriarchal societies, for the men were either away for long periods or forever lost at sea. Eiluned Lewis's novel *The Captain's Wife*, a tale of seafaring Wales set at the time when sail yielded to steam, reveals that sailor's children barely knew their fathers.

Some historians argue that in these years, people were hardened to death and consequently made little emotional investment in their families, especially in their children. Yet the evidence of gravestones, hymns and poems and the mute crowds who gathered at funerals suggest the opposite. Far from there being an absence of emotional warmth in the Welsh people, this study suggests that emotional lives were intense and intimate, especially affected by grieving and loving. It is a common, but false claim made by some historians that poverty deadened emotional sensitivity to grief. The fact that the poor were buried without the ceremonial trappings of mourning, should not blind us to the fact that they were emotionally involved.[23] Grief was as severe and sincere in the cottage as it was in the castle. This was a society of religious zeal and high morality, yet love letters and poems reveal that emotional bonds were warm. At the dawn of the twentieth century, customary courtship rites and rituals, traditional merriment and mirth continued to trouble pious saints and pompous sabbatarians, just as they had in the years of 'Y Diwygiad Mawr' (the Great Revival) of the eighteenth century.[24]

The history of late nineteenth- and early twentieth-century Wales has often been told in terms of conflict and confrontation. The years down to the First World War saw conflict in almost every sphere of life. Industrial relations were tense. Serious rioting linked to industrial disputes took place across south Wales in 1898, in north Wales during 1900–3, at Tonypandy in 1910 and in Llanelli in 1911. In 1911 riots against the Irish and Jewish communities suggested that there was no welcome kept either on hillside or in vale. The militant wing of the suffragette movement was active across Wales. Several women, such as Margaret Haig Mackworth (later Lady Rhondda), Sybil Haig Thomas and Amy Dillwyn, were involved in illegal and violent activities.[25] The 1902 Education Act, which provided funding for church educational establishments, provoked the ever-over-sensitive 'Nonconformist conscience' into open rebellion.

In the light of the above, it appears remarkable that some could portray the period before the First World War, as one of contentment, a golden age, 'the endless summer'. The portrayal was made even less credible by the weather. The summers were damp and dismal, the winters glacially cold – the harsh winter of 1913–14 only thawed, reluctantly, in April 1914. Yet cooperation and compromise were just as frequent as conflict or out-and-out intransigence. The South Wales Miners' Federation, the much loved 'Fed', is seen as the key institution in the lives of people in the mining communities, but for many people the cooperative movement was more relevant.

By the early 1950s this retail movement had a combined membership of around 250,000 people, more than 300 branches, a turnover of £17 million and employed 8,000 staff.[26] Of course, there were uncompromising bigots as well as determined disciplinarians in the industrial, religious and political lives of Wales who generated lots of noise and paper, but often more moderate voices prevailed. The miners' trades unions, those much vaunted leaders of industrial militancy, probably spent more time defending individual miners' compensation and insurance cases than on strike. For every 'little Moscow' that subscribed to the view that Wales would be a better place if it were run from another country, there were several Little Genevas where it was considered that Wales would be a better place if it were run from another dimension.

There is a strong tradition in Welsh historiography of idolising the heroes of the long march of labour. Those on the left who saw salvation in the red light of a Soviet dawn are lionised. The 'fellow travellers of the right', such as the Merthyr Tydfil-born newspaper magnate, William Ewart Berry, first Viscount Camrose (1879–1954), who met Hitler in 1939, and Newport-born Winifred Wagner – Hitler's 'beloved Winnie'– who gave him the paper on which he wrote *Mein Kampf*, have been rightly castigated and condemned for their support of a murderous tyranny. Yet the people of the political left seem to have escaped censure for supporting an equally murderous ideology.[27] People in the late 1920s and 1930s could, perhaps, be excused for greeting the events in Russia with all the self-deception and rapture with which the Young Romantics had greeted the French Revolution before the Terror set in. Historians have no excuse.

It is a fact not often noted, and even less frequently stated, that there was a strong Conservative element in Welsh life. The traditional view is that decades of depression, degradation and deprivation followed by the experience of total war were part of the road to 1945 and Labour's landslide election victory, when Wales became a 'Tory-free zone'. Some commentators have suggested that 'sightings of Tories were so rare that they were recorded in wildlife magazines'.[28] Yet their lack of success at parliamentary and local elections and the views of contemporary radicals and subsequent historians should not blind us to the existence of those exotic creatures – Welsh Conservatives. Even on the extreme right of the Tory party, people could be found who were proud of their Welsh ancestry. They developed and defined their Welsh identity on the basis of genealogy, anthropology and wealth. The journalist Howell Arthur Gwynne (1865–1950) was one of ten children born in 'genteel poverty' in Swansea. His career took him into the editorial chairs of some of the most extreme right-wing journals. Gwynne's response to the economic and social crises of the 1930s was to campaign clandestinely for a military *coup d'état*. He was one of the key figures in the far-right group of Tory 'Die-Hards' who became influential in the years leading up to the Second World War.[29] The 'Glamour Boys', the followers of Anthony Eden, who all resigned because of the conduct of foreign policy in 1938, featured amongst their number J. P. L. Thomas and Paul Vychan Emrys-Evans (1894–1967). In 1945, 220,780 people in Wales voted Conservative at the general election. There were more Conservatives than colliers amongst the Welsh. To ignore them in historical works is to disinherit a substantial number of the Welsh people.

It is a sad fact that the aristocracy is often dismissed from Welsh history. In the Welsh context, it is the aristocracy, not the people, which has suffered the terrible fate of, in E. P. Thompson's evocative phrase, being forgotten by the 'enormous condescension of posterity'. The historians of Wales have often happily followed the teachings and taunts of rural and urban radicals that this was an alien group and not part of Welsh society. However refined and cut-glass their assumed accents and social pretences, the barons, earls and viscounts of Aberdare, Cilcennin, Cleddau, Gwaenysgor, Harlech, Islwyn, Merthyr Tydfil, Ogmore, Pembroke, Penrhyn, Rhondda, Rhyl, St Davids, Tenby or Treowen could not deny their origins. Their names were forever tied to Wales. Incorporating them into Welsh history restores some of the complex character of the national identity.

Ages and events, like individuals, are an amalgam of opposites. The 1870s and 1890s are rightly described as periods of considerable social discontent and dislocation. Yet, for some people, these were the *fin de siècle* years of decadence and ostentatious display. The

1920s were another decade of depression and decline, but they too had their lighter side. Thus the 'age of anxiety', the nail-bitten years of war-broken men and heartbroken women was also the 'Roaring Twenties' which saw the fripperies of the Bright Young Things and the Flappers. It is hoped that this study will provide an insight into both aspects of Welsh society. Certain historic events have also acquired a particular prominence in our historiography. The Reform Acts of 1832 and 1867, as we have seen in a previous volume (*Hope and Heartbreak: a social history of Wales and the Welsh, 1776–1870*), loom large on the Welsh historical landscape. In contrast, the Reform Acts of 1918 and 1929, which extended the vote to women and created a modern democracy, have received scant attention. The Welsh electorate increased from 425,744 in December 1910 to 1,172,048 in 1918 – the largest single increase since 1688. Allowing women over twenty-one years of age the vote in 1929 further broadened the nascent democracy of Wales to 1,602,138 voters. Another seminal piece of legislation was the 1919 Sex Discrimination (Removal) Act, which made it unlawful to bar from public office a person on the basis that she was a woman. But these reforms receive little attention in the history books.

The First World War has similarly captured the attention of historians because of the barbarous and barbaric slaughter on a previously unimaginable scale. The dominant images are still coloured by our emotions and horror at the mud, the blood, the guts, the gas, the graveyards, the 'death of innocence' and the 'squander of a nation's youth' of too many youths dying too young, too soon in 1914. Yet in terms of mortality, the war was eclipsed by the flu pandemic which swept over the world in 1918 killing over 50 million and perhaps as many as a 100 million people. This contagion, which caused panic and fear on a scale not seen since the ravages of cholera in the mid nineteenth century, killed more than 9,000 people in Wales. Yet there is almost no echo of a cough in the history books.[30]

The Welsh involvement with the British Empire is similarly complex and contradictory. The Welsh claimed that they provided the spiritual core of empire. They converted people to Christianity, rather than conquered them militarily. The strength of their faith was one of the most impressive but also one of the most terrifying things about Welsh missionaries. The evangelists stole people's greatest possession – their innocence. Roger Price (1834–1900) of Llandyfaelog braved incredible hardships in the heart of Africa. Roger could not conceive of defeat. In Makololo, Tanganyika, Zanzibar, Bechuanaland and Matabeleland he tried, tried, tried, tried and tried again to convert the heathen, irrespective of cost. He translated the Old Testament into local languages, but never realised that, for his wife and daughter, Roger's was a 'poisonwood bible'. Both died, sacrificial victims of a selfless, selfish crusader. The role of the Welsh in the Empire was far more varied than that presented by writers such as Fred Morgan. They were not only well-meaning foot soldiers in Christianity's long battle for the soul of Africa. They were merchants and mercenaries, as well as missionaries. Trade followed theology and terror. The teaching of the gospels was often forgotten as the Welsh also 'sleepwalked to dominion of palm and pine'. Welsh people willingly shouldered the 'white man's burden' and acted as field agents for manifest imperial destiny. As one African bitterly complained 'we had the land and they had the Bible. They told us to close our eyes and pray. When we opened them, they had the land and we had the Bible'.[31]

Hen wlad fy mamau – our mothers' land – women and Welsh society

> She's the sort of woman who lives for others, and you can tell the others by their hunted expression.
>
> *C. S. Lewis*

Throughout the course of the nineteenth century Welsh national sentiment created an iconography and a symbolism. Motifs such as dragons, harps, Celtic crosses and sunbursts and figures of bards and druids (dead and alive, but preferably dead) became associated with patriotic feeling. Literature, folklore, history and art primarily affirmed the heroic traditions of the Welsh people, directing their attention to the mythological tales of their once-upon-a-time long ago, when heroes enacted brave deeds. Perhaps the clearest expression of such sentiments was the song 'Mae Hen Wlad fy Nhadau', written in 1872 by the father and son musical duo, Evan James (1809–78) and James James (1833–1902). Gradually, by century's end, the song was adopted as the national anthem. Against a jaunty beat the words describe Wales as a land of rejoicing bards, poets, minstrels and always defeated, always brave warriors.[32]

This was the masculine imagery of a fatherland. Rarely did the women of Wales feature in this romantic and romanticised iconography. Only a few artists portrayed the heroines of Wales alongside her heroes. Sidney Herbert Sime evoked the spirit of *Bronwen*, whilst both Willy Pogany and Margaret Lindsay Williams painted the mythical figure of the *Lady of the Van Lake* (in 1907 and 1910). Curnow Vosper, in *Market Day in Wales* (*c*.1910) and *Salem* (*c*.1908) the most widely sold Welsh picture, portrayed the pious spirit of Dame Wales.[33] Stove-pipe-hatted, dressed in the 'traditional' costume which had been invented by Lady Llanover in the 1840s, this fragile, aged figure supposedly represented an unbroken link with established Welsh virtues and values. Most remarkable of all, in terms of their use of ancient myths to 'inspire and elevate life', were the works *Ceridwen* (1910), *Wales Awakening* (1911), and *Blodeuwedd* (*c*.1925–30) by Christopher Williams. These paintings seem to have been as much about titillation as elevation. In *Wales Awakening*, the sleep-roused nation is symbolised by a nearly naked nymph of impressive physique, draped in flimsy, gossamer muslin. Had the folds of the material been an inch lower, then this Amazon would have lost what little modesty she so obviously had left. Curnow's *Salem* and Williams's *Blodeuwedd* appear to be inhabitants of different worlds. But they both, God-botherer and goddess, represent figures which were often ignored – the women of Wales.

Women could be regarded as the greatest victims in the history of Wales. They worked and lived under serious disadvantages. Until 1919 they were wholly disenfranchised from the political world. They had fewer legal rights than men. When they did work, which was against the ideals of a paternalistic society and the idea of 'separate spheres', they were paid less than men. Medical authority advised that women were frail and fragile creatures ravaged by mental illness and emotional insecurities. While individuals may have conformed to the image of the long-suffering female, the majority were too busy for such self-dramatisation. Any number of activities – cooking, cleaning, washing, caring for children, planting gardens, milking cows, gathering food and fuel, labouring in mines, fields, brickworks, quarries, seaports, dockyards – took priority over brooding. Women were beasts of burden, even when pregnant they carried and they carted – water from fountains and streams, firewood from woods and forests, stones and mortar for buildings. They worked as clerks and secretaries, using large Remington typewriters with bells at the end of the carriage return which rang louder than those on a district nurse's bicycle. Such activities provided greater opportunities for women to integrate with each other and in a broader society than is usually portrayed in historical studies. Women mixed freely with each other, were the guardians of children and attendants of childbirth, and enjoyed mixed company at tavern and pub, church and chapel. Servants had freedom to fall in love or get into trouble, wives had business and pleasure interests outside the home. It is remarkable in a society which supposedly placed a strong emphasis on moral rectitude and the domestic responsibilities of women that so many public houses were kept by women.

Marriage and childbearing was the lot of many, perhaps most women, but it is salutary to note that single women were more plentiful than is generally assumed. Modernisation, westernisation, globalisation and industrialisation were all linked to increasing numbers of women delaying marriage or never marrying. Communities along the coast and in rural Wales were predominantly feminine. The well-educated chose to delay marriage and entered professions as administrators, writers, teachers, even politicians and activists for women's equality. Because of her unhappy love affair with the French artist Rodin, Gwen John is often viewed as a victim, but she was in reality obdurately self-willed. She once said 'I think if we are to do beautiful pictures, we ought to be free from family conventions and ties. I think the family has had its day. We don't go to Heaven in families now but one by one.'[34]

Others had no choice. They were 'singled out' as a result of war. One of them was May Jones, a Welsh carpenter's daughter who, aged eighty-five, wrote her autobiography in biro on scraps of coloured paper. Her sweetheart Philip, a young Quaker intellectual, had gone to France with an ambulance unit in 1915 and was killed. 'I knew then', May wrote, 'that I should die an old maid'. Then she added, in pencil, 'I was only twenty years old.' The rest of the page is blank. It speaks volumes.[35]

Through the Primrose League and the Suffrage movement, on School Boards and Poor Law Authorities, the women of Wales proved that they could be just as effective politicians as men. At times of profound crises for their communities, Welsh women could be decisive. On 3 February 1935, Ceridwen Brown of Aberdare and her friends organised the largest mass demonstration ever seen in Wales. More than 300,000 people marched in protest at the government's decision to implement the Means Test and reduce unemployment benefit.[36]

The 1904–5 religious revival is often considered to have been the creation of one man, Evan Roberts, with, perhaps, a little help from his friends at the *Western Mail*. But others too, in that 'year of wonders', were equally Christ-ravaged. Roberts, that strange combination of St Paul and Phineas T. Barnum, was accompanied by five women on his mission of salvation across Wales. When his fire flickered, theirs burnt bright. The voices of these angels descended, lyrical, emotional, hysterical, drew thousands to salvation. In crisp contralto and sharp soprano they convinced thousands that apocalypse was now. In a photograph that became a best-selling postcard, taken at the height of religious fervour, the girls surround Roberts, bonneted agents of redemption. These nubile young ladies were a potent reminder that religion was a gateway to bliss. The God-focussed eyes of these crazed saints stare accusingly at the viewer – 'ydyw dy enw di lawr?' (is your name listed?). In 1905, few would have dared to answer, 'na' (no).[37]

In their letters of faith, love and loss, women often showed themselves to be superior to men. In the record of their words and actions, the women of Wales provide a clear statement that they do not need any special handling by the historian. The history of the women of Wales encompasses a broad range of emotion, from weak to wilful, and a broader range of experience, from virago to virgin. The role models include not only the 'angel at the hearth', mother, nursemaid, working girl, martyr, captive, but also adventuress, happy hooker and siren.[38] Some were vulnerable victims, others vicious villains, who could exploit and extort as effectively as men. They were saints and sinners. What the women of Wales in our period deserve from the historian is an attempt to provide a framework which is not dominated by masculine preserves such as politics but a more creative structure which will enable their ambitions, anxieties and aspirations to be studied on an equal basis. Perhaps then Welsh history will cease to be what it has been for too long – his story.

1

The Structures of Everyday Life: Endurance and Endeavour

O wynfa goll! O wynfa goll!
Ai dim ond breuddwyd oeddet oll?

(O paradise lost! O paradise lost!
Were you just a dream?)

Cynan (Albert Evans-Jones), 'Mab y Bwthyn'
quoted in Alan Llwyd, *Rhyfel a Gwrthryfel*
(Llandybïe, 2003), p. 179

People and places: vital statistics

Hapus dyrfa
Sydd â'u trigfan yno mwy.

(Happy throng
Have their dwelling there evermore.)

Islwyn (William Thomas: 1838–78),
in O. M. Edwards (ed.), *Gwaith Islwyn* (1903)

The population of Wales rose throughout the period 1870–1931. Within the legally defined geographical boundaries of the country, in 1871, there lived 1,412,583 people. Their number increased to 1,571,780 in 1881 and rose again to 2,420,921 in 1911. In 1921, despite death's diligent harvesting in the First World War and the 1918 influenza pandemic, 2,656,474 people lived in Wales. During the late 1920s and the 1930s, the corrosive and erosive experience of economic decline and depression dislocated population growth so that in 1939, on the eve of the Second World War, the number of people living in Wales had declined to 2,487,000.[1] Despite war, austerity and rationing, by 1951 the population had increased slightly to 2,598,675. The increase was far from uniform over the country. There were zones of stagnation and even of regression, in sharp contrast to zones of dynamic expansion and, from area to area, the chronological patterns varied. The population, as we shall see, was not just increasing, but moving.

The national figures conceal as much as they reveal about the markedly different demographic experience of each county. Anglesey, Breconshire, Cardiganshire, Merioneth, Montgomeryshire, Pembrokeshire and Radnorshire experienced continuous decline in population. A few examples are indicative, if not wholly representative, of the general trend. The western, coastal county of Cardiganshire had its peak of population in 1871 when 73,441 people lived within its borders. Thereafter, each successive census recorded a decrease until 1951, when only 53,278 people lived in Cardiganshire.[2] In remote and rural Radnorshire, time seemed to have been at anchor since the days of George Herbert and the metaphysical poets, for the number of people gently dwindled, from 25,430 in 1871 to 19,993 in 1951. Far from the madding crowd, this part of the 'green desert' of mid Wales had more sheep than people.[3] The chief ambition of many young people in rural Wales was simply to leave. They yearned to escape from the morose countryside, on foot and by donkey-cart, to avoid poverty, stilted ambition and strangled aspirations. In marked contrast to these counties was the general experience of Carmarthenshire, Caernarfonshire, Denbighshire, Flintshire, Glamorgan and Monmouthshire, in which population grew significantly. Glamorgan, in particular, witnessed spectacular growth. In 1871, some 397,859 people lived within the county's boundaries. By 1901 the population had more than doubled to 859,931 and rose again to 1,252,481 in 1921. Thereafter, the county's population entered a period of decline, so that by 1951 around 1,202,581 people lived in Glamorgan.[4]

It is important to emphasise that the rates of growth or decline were neither uniform across each Welsh county, nor consistent down the decades. In the eastern and northern parishes of Cardiganshire, for example, where lead mining had declined to a ghostly echo of a hammer, the population was in serious decline. In contrast, the western coastal town of Aberystwyth, thanks to tourism and the fledgling university, experienced gradual growth from 6,899 people in 1871 to 9,315 in 1951.[5] Glamorgan's predominantly rural and agricultural parishes experienced a slow, mouldering population decline. In contrast, especially in the years down to 1921, population growth in other parts of Glamorgan was breakneck. Neath grew from 9,319 people in 1871 to 32,284 in 1951; Maesteg from 7,667 to 28,917; Mountain Ash from 17,826 to 43,287. Within the old town boundaries of Cardiff there lived 39,536 people in 1871. Ten years later, 82,761 people existed within the new boundaries of the municipal borough. Thereafter the population grew and grew again, until by 1951 there were 243,632 citizens in the city of Cardiff. The Rhondda urban district, in 1871, was still a relatively bucolic area where 'an agile squirrel could make its way up the valley without placing a paw on the ground'. By 1921, an estimated 162,717 people had packed along the valley floor and the slopes above.[6] As the historian studies the census across the decades, new towns suddenly emerge with the arbitrariness of the creative process of Genesis. In 1861, the census had no entry for Briton Ferry. In 1871, 26,112 people lived hugger-mugger in the 'Giant's Grave' there. Barry was a small, gull-infested hamlet of 484 people in 1881. By 1921, thanks largely to David Davies's decision to construct his own docks there to circumvent the Bute monopoly at Cardiff, 38,945 people had been attracted to the town.[7] Ten years, or even three or four years, were time and tide enough for some communities, such as Croesderw in the Afan valley, to grow, flourish and vanish, so that they never appeared in the census enumerator's records. In 1902 the hell-roaring mining camp boomed; by 1910 it was a ghost town.[8]

The census statistics reveal patterns of real human interest. The distribution of men and women across the counties of Wales reflected the patterns of population increase and decrease. Those counties which had experienced demographic decline tended to have higher numbers of women than they did of men.[9] Anglesey, Breconshire, Caernarfonshire, Cardiganshire, Merioneth, Pembrokeshire, Radnorshire, even Carmarthenshire, were effectively matriarchal societies. In Cardiganshire in 1871, 33,396 men lived alongside

40,045 women. In contrast in Glamorgan, as the 1871 census revealed, men outnumbered women by 205,660 to 192,199. Marriage prospects and, presumably, choice, for men were usually better in the rural and western counties. In contrast, women in want of a partner, were advised to 'go east young girl' to Glamorgan, Flintshire, Denbighshire or Monmouthshire.[10] Economic forces must have created profound emotional frustration.

The age profile of different counties also differed significantly. Those counties which grew in population had high percentages of young, unmarried men. In contrast, those areas of Wales which experienced population decline tended to be principally comprised of middle-aged and of elderly women. Indeed, the census statistics reveal that, between 1871 and 1951, the number of Welsh people who survived into old age increased markedly. In 1871, only 21 people in Wales lived to be over 100 years of age. In 1951, there were 397 centenarians. Again, the disparity between the survival of the sexes was apparent. Only 5 men in 1871, and 63 men in 1951 managed to survive to receive birthday greetings from their sovereign. Above 50 years of age, women outnumbered men. Wales was a land of widows - there were always more widows than widowers. In 1891, to take just one date at random, 33,060 widowers outlived their wives, whereas 76,891 widows outlasted their husbands.[11]

Historians have expended considerable industry in explaining the growth of population. From the multitude of variations it is clear that all sorts of factors are involved in population ebb and flow – details of local circumstances, of weather and crops, the ups and downs of manufacturing and trading, local pressures concerning the age of marriage and sexual conduct, opportunities for social and geographical mobility and, more mysteriously, the changes in the virulent force of particular epidemics. Yet a satisfactory answer is elusive, for the reasons are lost in the mysterious interface between biology and behaviour. To simplify the complexity, it can be stated that, in its essence, a population can grow for one of two reasons. Firstly, more people need to be cradled by the midwife than are carried away by the undertaker. Births need to outnumber deaths. Therefore, it was significant that, for a host of reasons, death's sting was softened in the period 1871–1951. Secondly, more people need to live in and move into an area than leave it.[12] Between 1871 and 1921, the population increased because Wales was able to retain a significant portion of her natural increase in population, but it was only that 'Black Gold Rush' decade of 1901–11 that witnessed an absolute increase in population. Thus, the 1911 census revealed that significant numbers of foreign born people had moved into Wales. Cardiff, with 4,786 'foreigners' was second only to London as a centre for immigration, whilst Swansea was in fourth position and Newport in eighth place with regard to the number of foreign-born people who had recently moved in. There were also, on occasion, communities of immigrants in remote places, such as the large numbers of Irish people settled along the coast in Anglesey and Pembrokeshire, and a group of over 200 Italians drawn to north Cardiganshire in an ill-fated attempt to reopen the Frongoch leadmine.[13]

Despite the ability of Wales to draw in immigrants, the emigrant's experience of heartbreak and *hiraeth* was a significant aspect of the Welsh experience. The emigrants created an absence, a sense of communities hollowed out and deprived of men and women. As T. Rowland Hughes lamented in his poem to the deserted homestead, 'Y tyddyn': 'Mae "nhw" wedi mynd i gyd: 'Does 'na ddim o'u hôl, dim byd.' (They have all gone. There is no trace of them, nothing).[14] In 1891, the American census revealed that 100,079 Welsh-born people resided in the United States, the majority of whom, 17,767, had gone off to Pennsylvania in the morning.[15] Others departed Welsh borders and shores to London, Liverpool, Australia, South America, India or South Africa. In the 1880s, W. O. Thomas travelled around the world twice, recounting his adventures in print in *Dwywaith o amgylch y Byd* (Utica, 1882). Wherever he went, he sought out local Welsh people. Shamelessly, he played and preyed upon their homesickness and conned them into providing him with free board and lodging. His book is a remarkable testimony to native generosity and gullibility but also to the global spread of the Welsh diaspora.[16]

Her ability to retain most of her own people had profound implications for the linguistic character and composition of Wales.[17] In 1891, the census enumerators, for the first time, included a question in the census as to the linguistic preferences and practices of the Welsh. The results, despite reservations about the reliability of the statistics, indicate that roughly 54.4 per cent of the people of Wales spoke Welsh. This percentage declined gradually as the combined effects of Anglicisation, education, globalisation, commercialism, emigration and migration generally worked to the detriment of the Welsh language. From 1901, when 49.9 per cent of the people could speak it, the situation of Welsh became parlous. By 1951, the percentage had decreased further to 28.9 per cent. As with all statistics, the levels vary markedly across Wales, but speaking generally and compressing the experiences of particular communities into averages, the percentage of people who spoke Welsh was at its highest the further west one travelled. In Anglesey, Caernarfonshire, Carmarthenshire and Merioneth in 1951, over 70 per cent of the people still spoke Welsh. In 1931, despite the detrimental impacts of education, the First World War and the ravages of economics, a significant number of the people of Anglesey (23.9 per cent), Caernarfonshire (21.4 per cent), Cardiganshire (20 per cent) and Merioneth (29.7 per cent) were monoglots whose sole language was Welsh.[18]

In eastern border counties, where the integration with England was stronger and longer, the percentage who spoke Welsh was substantially lower. Only 4.5 per cent of the people scattered around Radnorshire could speak Welsh. The percentages of Welsh speakers in Flintshire (21.1 per cent), Glamorgan (20.3 per cent) and Monmouth (4.5 per cent) were a cause of serious concern for lovers of the language. This situation led some to argue that the process of industrialisation killed the Welsh language. But others have countered, arguing that even if the percentage of, for example, the total population of Glamorgan who spoke Welsh was comparatively low, the actual total number of speakers was significant. The number of people in Glamorgan who could speak Welsh rose from 320,072 in 1871, to 368,692 in 1921. This figure was far higher than the combined total of people who could speak Welsh in the four counties where the percentage of Welsh speakers was highest. Such facts led the economist Brinley Thomas to argue that industrialisation did not slay, but rather saved, the Welsh language. Carmarthenshire's

Aman and Gwendraeth valleys, Glamorgan's Tawe and Neath valleys and Caernarfonshire's slate-quarrying and Flintshire's coal-mining regions, were significant industrial areas in which Welsh was the community's chosen language.[19]

'Ill fares the land': the failures and fortunes of Welsh agriculture

> Lle dôi gwenith gwyn Llanrhiain
> Derfyn haf yn llwythi cras,
> Ni cheir mwy ond tres o wymon
> Gydag ambell frwynen las.
>
> (Where once came Llanrhiain's white corn,
> At summer's close in loaded carts,
> Now there is just a trace of seaweed
> And a few brambles).

Crwys (William Williams), 'Melin Trefin',
Cerddi Crwys (Wrexham, 1935)

Crwys wrote his sad lines of lament for Melin Trefin after a visit to the derelict mill on the north Pembrokeshire coast. This miller's tale is an eloquent reminder that the history of rural Wales is often told as a saga of decline, despair and doom, where two thing are certain; firstly, it rains, and secondly, with the persistence of rain on the rolling badlands of Pumlumon, farmers complain that times are dire. Yet pessimistic tales of half-empty barns obscure the fact that the period 1870–1945 saw a profound transformation in the functions and fortunes of Welsh agriculture.

By the 1870s Wales had already witnessed remarkable change in the nature and extent of the agriculture practiced. A significant number of farms, depending on their location and the quality of their land, were already heavily commercial in their orientation. Not all farmers planted and picked their forefathers' traditional crops. Some experimented, producing wheat for breadstuffs, cheese and butter, livestock for local and English slaughterhouses and hay for horse fodder. The fertile vales of Clwyd and Glamorgan and Carmarthenshire's Towy valley were linked by rail to urban areas, so that a profitable milk business flourished. In 1871, there were 265,286 cattle being milked on Welsh farms, a figure which increased to 377,346 by 1950. On many farms, the move towards more specialised and market-driven agriculture was well developed. Close to towns the lessons of the marketplace, that farmers needed to produce to sell and should not divert resources into the creation of materials which could be obtained more economically from others, had been learned. In other areas where circumstances allowed, market gardening flourished.

There was a remarkable increase in the number of animals reared on Welsh farms between 1871 and 1948. The number of poultry increased to 4,683,946 in 1948 as people realised that a fowl was not just for Christmas. The number of sheep increased from 2,895,119 in 1871 to 3,286,272 in 1950, with the 1930s being a golden age for sheep, when over 4,000,000 roamed Welsh mountains. Yet perhaps the greatest gains were in the numbers of cattle reared, which increased from 635,145 in 1871 to 1,011,218 in 1950.[20] Carmarthen, with over 900,000 grazing on its pastures, was in Rhys Davies's phrase, 'the cow's capital of Wales . . . prosperously lactic'.[21] Despite the impact of rail and road transport, 81,462 horses were bred on Welsh farms in 1950 and Wales remained an equine world until well into the twentieth century. The demand for land for house building, industrial development and mining actually led to a decrease in the total area given over to agriculture, from 2,831,000 acres in 1871, to 2,696,000 in 1939. Thus famers had to work more efficiently and effectively to cater for the market's needs.[22]

The late 1860s and early 1870s were periods of 'high farming' in Wales which saw considerable investment in buildings, drainage schemes and the use of fertilisers. But as the 1870s progressed, increased competition from foreign producers in Australia, New Zealand and the United States of America darkened the prospects for Welsh farmers. The effect of this competition was not as severe in Wales as it was in the corn- and cereal-growing regions of England, but a general awareness of depression in rural Wales can be perceived in the magazines and periodicals of these years. The agricultural depression was especially acute from 1879 until the mid

1 The powerhouse of the rural economy were the fairs and markets which took place amid 'a sea of human and animal waste'. This one, at Llanidloes, was held in 1881. John Thomas Collection, National Library of Wales.

1890s. Between 1877–80 and 1894–7, the price of store cattle fell by 25 per cent and that of fattened sheep and pigs by 18 per cent, whilst land values dropped by 5.1 per cent. In 1886–91, tithe riots broke out in Denbighshire and Flintshire and the Llandysul area on the border of Carmarthenshire and Cardiganshire. To investigate the disturbances, the Prime Minister, William Gladstone, himself a major landowner at Hawarden in north Wales, set up a Royal Commission. The commissioners gathered evidence from all over Wales and eventually reported in 1896. The published reports reveal a society torn by savage economic pressures. All social groups voiced their concerns, but it is clear that owner-occupiers with mortgages were most hard pressed as mortgagees were less ready to allow postponements or reductions of payments than were the much maligned landlords.[23] These years saw several farm auctions, the saddest and most poignant spectacles of rural Wales. The scenes soon became familiar: the leaden-hearted family, watching as their past was laid out for everyone to inspect, knowing that their future depended on a few hours; the men trying not to cry, but failing, the women, stronger, trying not to bid for some worthless item which was impregnated with priceless memories; the friends and neighbours willing to bid more to help the stricken family; the portly auctioneer corralling and co-ordinating the vultures who had gathered in the yard.

Whether these were years of recession or depression has been much discussed by economic historians. Whatever the phenomenon, it is clear that the effect upon farm servants, was devastating. To survive lean years, farmers had to exercise thrift and economise.[24] There was thus less capacity to employ others, and from the 1870s to the eve of the First World War there was a decline in the number of labourers employed in agriculture and an exodus of people from rural Wales. Here the railways were influential, for in addition to extending the market for certain specialised items, they also relieved the pressure on rural communities, transporting not only farm produce but also people.[25] In 1851, 38 per cent of men employed in Wales worked in agriculture or related trades. By 1911, only 14 per cent of employed men laboured on the land. Only in Radnorshire and Montgomeryshire did the majority of men still work in agriculture. In the late 1890s and again in the 1910s, labourers and farm workers organised themselves into the Farm Labourers Union in order to protect their rights and privileges.[26] During the First World War labourers were further enraged at farmers' willingness to give work to cut-price labour in the shape of land girls and even prisoners of war. Led by poet, minister and communist T. E. Nicholas, they expressed their anger and frustration in a series of 'revolts'.

The pace of change in agricultural practices varied from parish to parish and area to area. The most instructive illustration of the varied experiences of different areas can be seen, perhaps, in a comparative study of the literary works of D. J. Williams (1885–1970) and Caradoc Evans (1878–1945).[27] Ostensibly, they had much in common. They were born around the same time, in roughly the same area – Caradoc in Troed-yr-aur in south Cardiganshire, D.J. in Llansawel, north Carmarthenshire. Both had to leave their rural homes to find employment. D.J. found work as a miner, then a teacher. Caradoc became a tailor, then a journalist in London. Both derived considerable joy and pleasure from literature, but their literary creations were worlds apart. In *Hen Dŷ Ffarm*, *Storïau'r Tir*, *Hen Wynebau*, *Yn Chwech ar Hugain Oed* and *Y Gaseg Ddu*, D. J. Williams walked again amongst those loved and loving people who had given such warmth and pleasure to the early years of his pilgrimage.[28] He evoked a community which was self-supportive and respectful of all members (male, female and animal) – an Eden. In contrast, in his powerful collections of stories, *My People*, *My Neighbours* and *Capel Seion*, Caradoc Evans presented a portrait of a dark, Satanic netherworld which made him the 'most hated man in Wales'.[29]

The explanation for the contrasting literature created by Caradoc Evans and D. J. Williams, is enshrined within the character of the communities in which they were raised. Although Llansawel and Troed-yr-aur were and are separated by only fifteen miles as a crow flew and flies, they were effectively worlds apart. Llansawel was relatively close to Llandeilo, which had, since 1857, been linked by railway to the mining and tinplating districts around Llanelli. D. J. Williams writes glowingly of the butter, cheese, eggs and poultry taken along the 'llwybr lleithog' (milky way) to Llandeilo market. His fond recollections are of a 'land flowing with milk and with the honey of memories'. The parish, according to the 1889 agricultural reports, also had relatively large farms and holdings. Out of 72 holders of land who held 5 acres or more, only 16 (22 per cent) held fewer than 50 acres each, while 33 (46 per cent) held 100 acres or more. The majority, 40 holders, held 75 acres or more. D. J. Williams's family were themselves owners who farmed large holdings. His father, Jaci Williams, farmed Penrhiw (over 200 acres) and leased Trawscoed (300 acres), whilst his uncles, Bili and James, farmed Cwm Du Bach (100 acres) and Cilwennau Uchaf (500 acres).[30]

In contrast, Troed-yr-aur, in 1870, was still reeling from the impact of the agricultural depression which had set in during the 1850s. The holdings were small, over 60 per cent were under 30 acres, and capital was scarce. The 'lle un buwch' (the one-cow farm), where the farmer's wife was often seen leading her entire stock on a string, was commonplace. The parish was principally a cattle-rearing and cheese-producing area which had, until the arrival of the railways, been dependent upon the drovers. The problem for Troed-yr-aur was that the railway never arrived. It got to Crymych in 1874, Cardigan in 1886 and Newcastle Emlyn in 1895. This was far too late for and too far from Troed-yr-aur. The cattle-raisers had already lost whatever advantages they may have had in long-distance markets. Troed-yr-aur was actually isolated by the rail-roads. Like the 'cartless people of Manteg' in Caradoc Evans's bleak story, 'The Way of the Earth', its people were imprisoned by geography and topography. It was as remote as it had been in the middle ages. People still needed to journey out by pony and trap or walk for hours. David Jenkins, that astute historian of rural Wales, reveals that the parish was suffering a social catastrophe.[31]

The tension of rural economics is clear when we compare the evidence given at two sittings of the Royal Commission on Land – at Llansawel on 19 April 1894, and at Newcastle Emlyn on 24 August 1894. At Llandysul, people voiced vague complaints but at Newcastle Emlyn, the relations between landlords and tenants were obviously venomous. Documented details of evictions, rent increases, reprisals, victimisation and intimidation were given.[32] Occupiers who bought their holdings from cash-strapped landlords did themselves little favours, for the mortgages were far in excess of the land's value. In order to obtain help at times of high work demand, farmers used a system of bartering, providing rows of potatoes in their fields in return for labour at the harvest. Such debts were often imprecise, and the cause of further tension. Widows were the most vulnerable people within such communities. In 1882, when her auctioneer husband, William, died of pneumonia in Carmarthen, 35-year-old Mary Evans, the mother of five children, was left with next to nothing.[33] The family's sole source of income was a smallholding of nine or ten acres at Rhydlewis. Some of the humiliations the family suffered from kith, kin and neighbours, as they scratched a living from their 'scorched earth', are savagely detailed in *My People*.

It is important to note that despite all the poetic clichés describing rural idylls, life on the land was a remorseless drudge. Labourers and farmers worked under conditions which Sisyphus would not have tolerated. Work was not driven by the clock, but by the task to be completed. Harvesting was a daylight-long battle to finish before bad weather could ruin crops. Men and women assembled early in the morning, at daybreak, or even before, 'i dorri'r gwair tra bo'r gwlith arno' (to cut grass while the dew is on it), when it was easiest to cut. One after the other they moved across the field, the blades of their long-handled scythes flashing as they swung them in unison, leaving broad swaths or 'windows' of cut grass. Custom and practice noted the best workers. A new hand with the scythe might suffer friendly derision, or risk having his ankles nicked by the blade of the following man. Once dried, the grass was raked, turned and stacked and hauled into barns. Darkening, threatening rain clouds served to accelerate the pace of work so that the precious crop could be gathered. Once these tasks were complete others, equally physical and depending on the season dreary, followed. On some lunar occasions, workers would labour 'all the moon long' for eighteen to twenty hours, bringing in the crop. This was hard physical labour.[34] Gradually, from the 1890s, a few of the more prosperous farmers across Wales purchased machines to ease the work. William Titley of Cowbridge became well known as a maker or corn and turnip drills. In 1885, Joseph Darby remarked on the widespread use of a steam plough near Llantwit Major in Glamorgan and steam-driven machinery was in general use for the preparation of winter fodder. In the early twentieth century, the use of machinery increased substantially. In 1914, the company J. Hibbert of Cardiff sold 242 agricultural machines. By 1919, they were selling 765 items of equipment.[35]

The opening decades of the twentieth century saw a continuing haemorrhage of people from rural Wales. Agriculture continued to be in a dire condition down to the First World War, but in many respects the crisis of war was the making of Welsh agriculture. The guns of August 1914 heralded a brief, precious taste of prosperity for Welsh farmers. The German blockade of British ports and naval trade dictated that the nations must feed themselves or starve. There was a 300 per cent rise in agricultural prices between 1914–20, and a 200 per cent increase in the wages paid to labourers. Yet even this failed to keep pace with inflation.[36] In the words of Avner Offer, one of several 'official historians' of the war, 'the First World

War was not only a war of steel and gold, but a war of bread and potatoes'.[37] Britain's victory was the result not only of superior military forces on the battlefield, but also of her ability to feed and maintain her population.[38] In this, the coal owner D. A. Thomas, newly enobled as Lord Rhondda, played a crucial role in his post of food controller from 1916. His measures to distribute food effectively and efficiently were as important as any changes in agricultural practices. Mundane changes introduced by Thomas made significant differences in reducing waste and increasing production.[39]

Peace ended agricultural prosperity. The lifting of the government's control of prices in 1921 increased competition from foreign producers which, together with a worsening economic environment, created severe pressures on Welsh farmers. The drift of people away from the land continued so that the 1921 peak of 33,400 full-time farm labourers was never seen again. Profits declined, markets contracted, capital was scarce and the misery of rural Wales knew no relief. Many farmers, who had bought their land at sales in the 1920s found themselves carrying massive debts and were owners in name only. Following the financial collapse of 1929 and the depression of the 1930s, conditions were such that R. S. Thomas's description of Wales as 'pain's landscape, a savage agriculture is practised here', appears an understatement.[40]

One of the most notable aspects of Welsh agriculture in the 1920s and 1930s was the substantial transformation in the ownership of Welsh farms. J. A. Venn coined the term 'the Green Revolution' to describe this phenomenon.[41] As agricultural profit margins declined and death duties took a significant portion of family income, an increasing number of landowners put remote sections or whole estates up for sale. The effects of death duties can be seen in the experience of the de Rutzens of Slebech in Pembrokeshire. Two wartime deaths between 1914 and 1918 brought death duties of £100,000 on an estate worth £4,000 a year. Often farms were purchased by their occupiers at terms which were crippling. This process has been described as 'the end of the great estates and the rise of freehold farming in Wales' and has been chronicled with characteristic detail by Dr John Davies.[42] Remarkably, the proportion of the land of Wales owned by the occupier rose from 10.2 per cent in 1904 to 39 per cent in 1941–3. Yet despite the transformation, it is worth noting that all of the twenty very great estates of Wales, which in 1883 had exceeded 20,000 acres, were still in existence in 1922. The reasons why farmers were so keen to purchase were often rooted in social, familial and personal considerations deeper than the purely economic. There was, as the poet William Roberts wrote so eloquently, a sense of a people gaining and regaining their rightful inheritance.[43] At farm sales, sentiment often overrode the bank statement.

The period following the First World War witnessed some remarkable developments in agriculture in Wales. In 1919, a Welsh Section of the Ministry of Agriculture was established. More significantly perhaps, in the same year, the Welsh Plant Breeding Station began work under the guiding genius of Sir George Stapledon.[44] The station, a development of the pioneering work undertaken at the University College of Wales in Aberystwyth, produced new strains of grass which extended and improved the quality of hill farming in Wales. Also in that remarkable *annus mirablis* of 1919, a new Forestry Commission was established, which further enhanced the work of the college at Bangor.[45] In a relatively short period, wood, not wool, became a major product of parts of the uplands of Wales, to the despair of the poet D. Gwenallt Jones, who saw his beloved Rhydcymerau ravaged:

Coed lle bu cymdogaeth, fforest lle bu ffermydd.
Ac ar golfenni, fel ar groesau,
Ysgerbydau beirdd, blaenoriaid, gweinidogion ac athrawon Ysgol Sul,
Yn gwynnu yn yr haul,
Ac yn cael eu golchi gan y glaw a'u sychu gan y gwynt.[46]

(Trees where once were communities, forests instead of farms.
And on trees, as on crosses,
The bones of bards, deacons, ministers and Sunday School teachers,
Whitening in the sun,
And washed by the rain and dried by the wind).

Of all the developments in agriculture in the 1930s, perhaps the one closest to the hearts of Welsh farmers was the establishment of the Milk Marketing Board in 1933.[47] The board safeguarded the purchase price of their milk and thus provided them, for the first time, with a guaranteed market. By the outbreak of war in September 1939, more than 20,000 Welsh farmers produced milk for the board. This was made possible by the remarkable transformation which had taken place in transportation. Motor lorries with their clanking churns linked local farms with the milk factories and thence to the railways for faster further distribution. The distance between cow and consumer was the same, but the speedier journey ensured that at least some milk, if not fresh, was not sour on arrival. Milk factories were established in some previously remote places. In October 1937, the new milk factory at Pont Llanio on the Tregaron to Lampeter railway line brought an alien 'industrial' dimension into one of the heartlands of rural Wales.

The Second World War, proved a boon to Welsh agriculture as had the First. Between 1938 and 1942, farmers' income increased by 207 per cent.[48] Given the extent of the so called 'black economy' of rural Wales, it is probable that the official figures were an underestimate. County committees were established across Wales to set ploughing and production targets for farmers and the land in cultivation increased from 215,000 ha in 1939 to 500,000 ha in 1944 – the highest extent ever of ploughed land. In this process, the pioneering work of Sir George Stapledon was of paramount importance. His experiments enabled cereals and other crops to be grown at altitudes which had previously been too high. The investment in machinery was also dramatic. In 1938, there were only 1,932 tractors at work on Welsh farms; by 1946 there were 13,652. Before the war, many farmers followed ponderous horses and ill-tempered oxen as they ploughed the land. In 1946, the majority sat atop chugging self-propelled tractors as they corrugated the fields. 'Cynddylan on his tractor . . . a new man now, part of the machine . . . oil in his veins' became a common sight across Wales. The Agriculture Act of 1947 safeguarded many of these wartime gains for farmers, providing grants and guaranteeing payments in times of shortages. For the first time, the Welsh farmer was no longer wholly at the mercy of the weather.[49]

Heavy metal: 'the age of steel'

> Moses struck rock and brought forth water, but Sidney Gilchrist Thomas struck the useless phosphoric ore and transformed it into steel, a far greater miracle. Farewell then Age of Iron, all hail King Steel.
>
> Andrew Carnegie

It is now generally appreciated that Britain saw not one, but two industrial revolutions.[50] Like the first, the second 'rather unhappy conjunction of adjective and noun' was not a unitary or integrated phenomenon. Some trace its roots to the late 1840s, a few to the 1850s, others to the period after 1870. The causes, like the chronology, are also contradictory and conflicting. All that can be ventured for certain is that underpinning most of the developments of the late nineteenth and early twentieth centuries was one wondrous material – steel. The industries which characterised this second great period of industrial development included railways, steam ships, motor automobiles, steam and electric machines, weapons, rotary printing presses, mass produced consumer goods, the canning industry, mechanical refrigeration and other food preservation techniques, and the development of the telephone. All made use of the wondrous material of the age of 'King Steel'.

Wales played a notable part in the history of steel, especially through the development of the Siemens open-hearth process which used cast and wrought iron, heated by gas and oxygen, to create exceptionally high-quality metal in special hearths lined with silica bricks. The process resulted in steel that was far stronger and more flexible, and in 1878 Percy Gilchrist and Sidney Thomas perfected the technique of adding limestone to the mix, which enabled iron ores of all quality to be used, even those with a high phosphoric content. The Siemens technique rapidly became the industry's standard production method.[51]

Transformations in production techniques led to transformations in the location of iron and steel production. The Welsh ironworks had long imported iron ore from overseas but from the 1880s, as local stocks dwindled, they switched almost exclusively to foreign ores. By the end of the nineteenth century more than 800,000 tons of ore from Spain were imported annually into Cardiff, an additional 340,000 tons into Newport and 170,000 tons into Swansea. The result was the abandonment of the inland ironworks. At Nantyglo, Treforest, Gadlys, Abercarn, Plymouth (at Dowlais), Blaenavon, Rhymney and Cyfarthfa, mills cooled and foundries crumbled.[52] These behemoths abandoned to the wind and rain became melancholy reminders that courage, determination and all the ancient human values were as nothing in the face of the slightest shift in the tectonic plates of the global economy. Penydarren became the haunt of shooting galleries and a circus, while a contemporary lamented, 'Llwydcoed is a ruin, Gadlys is a wreck. Treforest rusting to decay, Abernant more forlorn than Nineveh, Hirwaun more desolate than the cities of the Plain'.[53]

To operate profitably and economically, steelworks had to be sited close to the ports. Across south Wales at Newport, Cardiff, Swansea and Llanelli and on the north Wales coast at Shotton, new steelworks were built close to coastal waters. By 1914, the Shotton works, which had opened in 1898, gave employment to more than 3,500 people.[54] The most spectacular development was the decision of the Dowlais Company to transfer production to a new works on the East Moors in Cardiff. The move was only partial. Lord Wimborne (great-grandson of John Guest, the firm's original guiding spirit) decided, in order to lessen the social dislocation which would have resulted from total closure, to keep the plant's rail-rolling at the old site in Dowlais. So strong was the work's monopoly on rail production that Merthyr Tydfil's most charismatic historian boasted and jested that Tolstoy's tragic heroine, Anna Karenina, who committed suicide on a Russian railway line, 'would have had Dowlais stencilled on her body'.[55]

Iron and steel manufacturing were heavily affected by the collapse of the world economy in 1929 and then the economic catastrophe of the 1930s. Faced with the harsh, cold winds of economic depression, the fires of the forges cooled. Dowlais closed in 1930, whilst the closure of Brymbo in 1931 caused an unemployment rate of 90 per cent amongst the area's insured adult male workforce. Hawarden Bridge works closed for two and a half years, but it managed to restructure and reopen in 1933, specialising in roofing sheets and motor car body shells.[56] The decision of Richard Thomas and Co. to locate the world's first continuous strip mill at Ebbw Vale in 1937 was taken, not so much on economic grounds, as in order to avoid a catastrophe similar to that which had occurred at Brymbo. To survive these harsh times, iron and steel companies amalgamated and merged with each other. In 1930 the large conglomerate Guest, Keen and Nettlefod (GKN) merged with Baldwins, creating G.K. Baldwins. This company, in its turn, merged in 1945 with Richard Thomas to create Richard Thomas and Baldwin, which eventually became part of the Welsh Steel Company in 1957.[57]

During the 'first industrial revolution' the demand for weapons of war produced a constant demand for the products of ironworks. The international situation and the need for weapons of mass destruction from the 1870s onwards produced an even stronger demand for Welsh steel. In 1875–6, Landore steelworks produced the steel for Admiral Barnaby's 3,720 ton all-steel cruisers *Iris* and *Mercury*. The battle to build the dreadnoughts of the 1900s and the insatiable need for tanks, small weapons, guns, cannons, submarines and ships in the First and then the Second World War resulted in a lucrative demand for the products of the new coastal steelworks of Wales.[58] The naval yards of Pembroke Dock turned Welsh steel into some of the most innovative and revolutionary ships built for the British (and foreign) admiralties. The cold steel of the *Renown, Duke of Wellington, Hannibal, Drake* and *Repulse* slid in turn down the dock's slipways.[59]

A constant demand for iron and steel also came from the foundries of Wales, which produced specialist machinery for farms, mines and mills. Many of these, such as the Eaglesbush Iron Foundry and Forges of Neath, the Port Talbot Plough Co., Talbot Road, Port Talbot, Hodges and Wright's grandiloquently titled Agricultural Implement Repository in Abergavenny and the Britannia Foundry in Porthmadog, acquired considerable renown for the excellence of their work. Amongst their produce were cultivators, hay presses, turnip drills, swing ploughs, riding ploughs, the New Talbot plough – indeed machines for every conceivable task.[60]

Industry and diversity: copper, tin and transport

> Manufacture is progressing in Llanelly, so much so that scarcely a week passes but that some new branch of business is opened, with additional works in branches of trade already established. On Monday last, Messrs. Bythway and Co. opened a new brewery of large dimensions. Mr Samuel Bevan will soon open a new chemical works, and on Monday last the Burry Tinplate Works was opened with much success and under very honourable auspices.
>
> *Llanelly Guardian*, 4 March 1875

The demands of industry created industrial communities in some remarkable locations. In the 1880s and 1890s twelve companies were prospecting for gold in Meirioneth's mountains.[61] In July 1887, a mini gold rush occurred when the Morgan Gold Mining Company raised £35,000 worth of gold at Gwynfynydd. At Clogau, peak production was reached between 1900–4, when 20,000 ounces were found. One wonders at the poet Eifion Wynn's powers of observation, for at the time when he eulogised Cwm Pennant's perfect peace the Drws-y-coed copper mine was in full production. In Cardiganshire's highlands, lead mining was still active in the 1880s. There were even attempts to mine zinc, although not wholly successfully, so that the Llywernog works closed in 1910. Amongst the placid beauty of Snowdonia, slate was mined extensively in Llanberis, Bethesda, Blaenau Ffestiniog and in smaller endeavours at places such as Abergynolwyn and Corris. At the zenith of production in 1911, over 16,000 men carved a living from the stone.[62] The cavernous quarries – the Penrhyn, Dinorwic, Dorothea and Oakely were major employers. Slate mining and quarrying reached their peak in 1889. The 1890s were particularly hard economically for the quarries and mines and the ports such as Dinorwic, Porthmadog and Aberdyfi, which were dependent upon the export of slates for their well-being. The South African War of the late 1890s and the massive slum clearance schemes in London, Birmingham, Liverpool and Glasgow boosted profits in 1898, but thereafter the industry declined. Industrial relations were as unyielding as the slate. During the 1900–3 strike, the longest trade dispute in British

2 Craftspeople at the Kidwelly Tinplate Works *c*.1910. The tasks which required most dexterity were often undertaken by women and girls.

industrial history, the incompatible views of Anglicised owners clashed with the 'craft culture' of their Welsh workers.[63] This further weakened the industry.

The history of copper manufacturing provides a curious echo of the iron industry's experience.[64] From the end of the eighteenth century until the 1880s, the area between Neath and Llanelli produced about 90 per cent of Britain's copper-smelting capacity but by 1914 the industry, disadvantaged in competition with newer, foreign mills located on deposits of copper ore, had virtually disappeared, leaving behind them a ravaged, lunar landscape. Although the industry, at its productive peak, only employed slightly over 4,000 people, it had a profound impact on towns such as Morriston, Swansea and Llanelli.[65] The copper works operated their own mines to provide coal to smelt the ore and they were instrumental in developing docks at Neath, Llanelli, Swansea and Port Talbot. Out of the copper-smelting industry, too, there developed technical processes and labour skills which made Swansea a major metallurgical centre, with interests not only in copper but also in brass, cobalt, gold, lead, nickel, silver, yellow metal, zinc and, above all, in tin and steel. Thus, the decline of the copper industry was a grievous blow to many towns.

It was the development of the tin and tinplate industry that saved south-west Wales from total economic collapse and social catastrophe. South Wales was close to the Cornish tin ores, it produced suitable coal and limestone, possessed good harbours and had plentiful quantities of running water. There was, too, a labour force with metallurgical skills and local supplies of sulphuric acid (a by-product of copper smelting) which was used for cleaning the tinplate. By 1880, 70 per cent of British tinplate manufacture was undertaken in the Kidwelly–Port Talbot area and Swansea was the business centre of the tinplate trade in the UK.[66] Not to be outdone by its hated rival, the town of Llanelli, home to seventy-one tin plate mills, with typical bombast christened itself 'Tinopolis'.[67] The industry was heavily reliant on exporting its produce, a factor which created profound problems after the protectionist United States of America introduced the McKinly Tariff in 1891 to control imports.[68] Gradually, in the twentieth century, the industry recovered and established new markets in Europe and the Far East. The 1920s and 1930s witnessed considerable integration and amalgamation as companies fought each other to win a share of the market and to remain competitive and profitable. By 1939 some nine companies dominated the industry but, remarkably, twenty-nine continued to trade as independent concerns. Amongst these were a number of companies – Pengelli, Llanelly Association, Bynea, Upper Forest and Llansawel – which were strongly Welsh in management and operation.

The concentration upon heavy exporting industries inevitably led to the growth of seaports. Since the early years of the nineteenth century, Newport and Swansea had both developed as significant ports,[69] yet both were eclipsed in importance by the end of the century by the spectacular growth of Cardiff.[70] Between 1851 and 1911 its population had increased nine-fold, from 20,000 to 182,000, and it exports over fourteen-fold, from 718,000 tons to more than ten million tons. Cardiff was one of the greatest ports in the world. So great was the demand for the industrial produce of south Wales that additional docks were built at Newport, Barry, Penarth, Port Talbot, Swansea, Llanelli and Bury Port. In the north, Caernarfon, Bangor, Porthmadog and Pwllheli expanded significantly to export lead ores and especially slate. Ships were packed so tightly hull to hull that you could walk across from one quay to another and getting a boat out of some ports must have been as hard as getting one into a bottle.

To carry the products of mines and mills, a flotilla of ships was built around the Welsh coast.[71] The great ports of Newport, Swansea and especially Cardiff developed a shipbuilding industry as well as a range of associated trades – ship chandlers, out-fitters, horologists, carpenters, joiners and outfitters. From the nucleus of small companies there developed a few larger-scale shipbuilders, who also developed into significant ship-owning companies. Amongst the largest companies were Evans, Thomas and Radcliffe. Further west, Pembroke Dock also had significant shipbuilding. From the 1870s, the yard specialised in the 'composite ship' of wood planking in iron and steel frames. This was considered suitable for gunboats and other small craft, and indeed these became something of a speciality of the yard, as did royal yachts, five of which were built there. The technological change from sail to steam is shown in photographs of the docks. By the early 1920s, the thickets of masts and sails of the 1870s had been replaced by a blast of chimneys packed in hugger-mugger. Thirty years later, however, the fleets have dwindled to a raggle-taggle collection of tattered craft.

Contrary to the contemporary stereotype that the Welsh did not have an entrepreneurial or speculative bone in their bodies, many people from all walks in society took out shares in shipbuilding and ship-owning companies. Nowhere was this seen more clearly than in north Wales. In January 1874, with perhaps some mock irony, a reporter in *Y Genedl* ventured:

> Bu yma gryn lawer o siarad ambell noson ynghylch Llongau y Chwarelwyr. Wyddoch chi beth, y mae chwarelwyr yr ardaloedd yma yn mynd yn 'ship owners' mawr wrth yr ugeiniau. Fu erioed gymaint o astudio *navigation*. Y mae y bechgyn i gyd, hynny ydi, y 'shipowners', wedi prynu pawb ei fap, ac y maent mor hyddysg

mewn daearyddiaeth ag ydi plant *School Board* Llanrug. Y maent mor adnabyddus â Bombay, Singapore a Valparaíso, ag ydynt â Chwm-y-Glo a Brynrefail.[72]

(There has been much discussion here some evenings about the Ships of the Quarrymen. Do you know what, the quarrymen of this locality are becoming great shipowners by the score. Never was there so much study of navigation. All the young men, that is, the 'shipowners', have bought maps, and they are as well-versed in geography as the pupils of Llanrug Board School. They are as familiar with Bombay, Singapore and Valparaíso as they are with Cwm-y-Glo and Brynrefail).

Between 1875 and 1879, five shipping companies – the North Wales Shipping Co. Ltd, the Arvon Shipping Co. Ltd, the Bethesda Shipping Co. Ltd, the Gwynedd Shipping Co. Ltd and the Eryri Shipping Co. Ltd – were established. Of the 270 investors in the Gwynedd Shipping Company, 149 were quarrymen, as were 49 of the 102 investors in the Eryri Shipping Company. These penny capitalists had the same lust for the bottom line as any captain of industry, for shipping was not a romantic occupation but a continuous voyage for profit.[73]

A number of subsidiary industries developed to serve the needs of the iron, steel and copper industries. The production of non-ferrous metals – copper, lead and zinc in particular – presented additional opportunities for employment. One industry which prospered was the production of chemicals.[74] In 1926, several small west Glamorgan chemical companies merged under the entrepreneurial and managerial genius of Alfred Moritz Mond (1868–1930), to create Imperial Chemical Industries (ICI). Another notable by-product of such interrelated industrial undertakings was the establishment of the Courtaulds artificial fibre factory at Maes-glas, Holywell in north Wales in 1936. Forges and engineering works such as Millbrook Engineering in Morriston, De Berge's boiler-making works at Treforest, and chain and anchor works such as the Vulcan Forge in Swansea, produced specialist products.[75] Tin-stamping and enamelling works and patent fuel manufacturing, such as Mr Warlick's operation in Swansea, were relatively common across Wales. In 1911, there were 5,304 factories in Wales producing a plethora of products. Most of these were small-scale but their number is evidence of at least some diversity in Welsh industrial undertakings.

In the ports of Newport, Cardiff and Swansea and in the northern industrial areas of Flintshire, there was considerable industrial activity. Here were to be found a broad range of industries which had a wide base of clientele and custom. Cardiff, for example, had an extensive range of factories and manufacturers. Many businesses that began on a small domestic scale trade moved on to factory production processes. Poynton shoemakers, established in 1872 in a cottage, expanded into a factory in 1875 and developed into a joint-stock company in 1895. In 1900, proudly relocated to larger premises to house the latest American machinery, Poynton's employed 200 workers who produced 1,500 pairs of shoes a week. The docks were also home to woollen manufacturers, flour producers, wire rope manufacturers, cable and chain producers and two large breweries – Hancocks and Brains. The innovative Wharfedale press, one of several printing companies that used steam printing machines and presses to produce a range of publications and printed material, was also located in the docks. In 1902 the press took delivery of the first Lanston-Monotype typesetter in Britain.[76] Some ports had significant fishing fleets and fish-processing works. Swansea's new 'ice house' produced Arctic quantities of ice to cool the fish before it was moved to English and continental markets. From the 1870s to the 1890s, Swansea was also famous for its oysters, with more than 188 boats dredging the bay for shellfish that were swiftly dispatched to French markets. In defiance of an Act of Parliament which attempted to control stocks, the locals overfished and the trade collapsed so that fewer than twenty-five boats remained in 1891.[77]

Swansea's oyster trade is emblematic of the industrial experience of Wales. Long-term interests were often sacrificed on the altar of short-term profit. Although a variety of industries existed, Wales never developed the diversified industrial base that would have better enabled her to survive economic decline and depression.[78] The late Professor L. J. Williams, who laboured so hard to log the history of industry in Wales, warned that 'industrial' is a term that has to be applied with considerable caution in the Welsh context. Wales was a land of primary production.[79] Woollen manufacture was one of the few industries in Wales, in the sense that it took a home-grown raw material – wool – and turned it into a manufactured product – flannel.[80] In 1911, two occupational groups, agriculture and mines and quarries, collectively employed 44 per cent of the Welsh workforce. In south Wales in particular, the needs and greed of a few industries were allowed to cripple the development of a broader industrial infrastructure. Supplies of capital, labour and raw materials were all monopolised by the industries of coal, copper, iron, steel and tinplate. South Wales, in contrast to the north-east, failed to diversify. In the 1930s, a broader industrial base better enabled Denbighshire and Flintshire to weather the economic storm. The 1930s is the era that is traditionally associated with economic decline and depression and industrial devastation, but the archives of Wales contain voluminous and acrimonious records of bankruptcy reporting proceedings and county court compensation claims from across the period 1870–1945, which reveal that recession and depression were not confined to 'the Devil's decade'.

How black was my valley? The rise and fall of 'King Coal'

> The coal valleys bear the marks, psychological as well as physical, of having been the arena for a scramble by everybody, high and low, for quick money.
>
> *The Times*, 2 April 1927

Awareness of the devastation of the Welsh environment was at its sharpest in the years after 1860. The legal dispute over the effects of the smoke produced by copper and non-ferrous industries, which turned the land around Swansea into a sulphurous wasteland, enveloping the town under carcinogenic, poisonous clouds, continued its tortuous, Dickensian journey through the courts.[81] Yet the ultimate symbol of nature's devastation and despoilation by industry, the much vaunted 'rape of the fair country', was the coal tip. These brooding giants of slurry and slag scarred landscapes around Wales. From the 1860s these black pyramids became such a prominent part of the landscape that one area of south-west Wales became known as 'gwlad y pyramidau' (the land of the pyramids).[82] The pharaohs who erected these pyramids were astute enough not to be buried beneath, or live within sight of them, which was quite an achievement, for between 1870 and 1913 coal tips were dumped around north and south Wales, with the careless abandon of a person on a spree.

Coal mining left its imprint in some highly unlikely places. In the north, by 1913, some twenty coal pits were in production at Bagillt, Chirk, Leeswood, Holywell, Buckley, Mostyn, Gresford, Rhosllanerchrugog and Prestatyn. In all, they employed some 10,224 miners in enterprises which ranged from those of the ragged-trousered entrepreneurs who employed a few dozen employees to mines like Wynnstay, which were sizeable enterprises employing 1,081 underground and 235 surface workers. Perhaps the most remarkably located coal mines in Wales were the collieries near Llangefni on Anglesey, Point of Ayr mine at Prestatyn and Pembrokeshire's Hook colliery, which surprisingly, considering the constant danger of water inundation in most mines, were located beneath the sea. In Carmarthenshire and Pembrokeshire, high quality anthracite coal was mined. In 1900, anthracite production in Wales totalled 2,203,468 tons, which by 1914, had almost doubled to 4,370,239 tons, representing 92.6 per cent of Britain's output of anthracite coal.[83]

These years were a statistician's dream as the insatiable demand for Welsh coal sent every graph of profit and production into a Snowdonian figuration. It was the eastern counties of Glamorgan and Monmouth that saw developments which made them synonymous with coal mining.[84] The statistics for Glamorgan's coal industry are astounding. In 1876, the county produced 11.7 million tons of coal; by 1913, this had risen to 38 million tons. In 1876, the county employed 44,000 miners; by 1914, 157,000 miners burrowed in the county's depths. The valleys of Garw, Ogwr, Merthyr, Cynon, Rhymni, Taff, Ely, Dowlais, Afan, Tawe and Nedd were all the locations of frenzied activity. In 1876, the ports and docks of Glamorgan exported some 5.2 million tons of coal; in 1913, Glamorgan's ports sent out 29.1 million tons of coal around the world. In that year, Cardiff exported 10,278,963 tons of coal. Its coal exchange was the world centre for trade in this highly valuable, essential commodity and it was here, in the 1900s, that the world's most valuable cheque was written, 'one million pounds sterling – only'.[85] Yet in 1913 the efforts of the 'the coal metropolis' were eclipsed by those of its neighbour, Barry, from which 10,875,510 tons of coal were exported.[86]

The two valleys of the Rhondda, the Fach and the Fawr, saw the most intense activity. Amongst the tinsel and trash of Christmas 1855, the first train load of Rhondda coal made its way to the coast. Yet it was not until the 1870s that businessmen with sufficient nerve and money appeared to make a concerted attack on the valley's deep and rich seams. By 1914, there were 53 large collieries in the two valleys, 21 of which employed 1,000 or more miners underground. The main coal owner in the Rhondda Fawr was David Davies, the 'Midas of the Mines'. Born in rural Llandinam, the 'Top Sawyer' rose from the bottom of a saw-pit and became one of the richest people in the world. His Ocean Coal Company owned and operated pits in the Garw and Ogwr valleys, as well as the Rhondda, and in 1890 employed 5,583 men who raised 1,726,480 tons of coal. He also owned railways and the Barry docks.[87]

The reason for the phenomenal growth in the Welsh coal industry was the insatiable appetite for fuel to power 'the age of steam'.[88] The higher quality and smokeless nature of Welsh coal gave it an edge in many markets over lower quality and smokier rivals. The decision of the British Admiralty to choose Welsh coal as its preferred fuel greatly facilitated this position. What was good enough for the most powerful navy in the world proved good enough for its merchantile equivalent. Thus, by the 1870s, there was a constant call for the steam coal produced in many Welsh valleys. Additional demand came from railways, steam engines, ironworks, factories and for domestic fuel. Appropriately, given its name, the Ocean Steam Coal Company Ltd boasted in 1915 that it supplied coal to the English Admiralty, the royal yachts, the Italian

Royal Navy, the Spanish Navy, several rail companies and the ill-fated *Mauretania* and *Lusitania*.[89] To keep the world's navies steaming, Welsh companies such as Cory Brothers established a host of coaling stations around the globe.[90]

The railways both created a demand for and were a consequence of the existence of coal in Wales. Many railways served as essential conduits for coal to be carried from collieries and for miners to be carried to the mines. Their puffing engines and clanking trucks carried coal across the country. By the 1870s an extensive network of railway lines had been established linking collieries to ports. Perhaps the most impressive example was David Davies's railway line, which linked his coal mines in the Rhondda valley with the port of Barry. There were also several 'mineral' lines linking places like Penarth, Llanelli, Swansea and Saundersfoot to local mines.[91] To deal with the incessant streams of coal that flowed down the valleys, the ports of Newport, Cardiff, Penarth, Barry, Port Talbot, Swansea and Llanelli expanded substantially in the years down to 1914. New docks were added as each port sought to increase exports and maximise profits. Cardiff acquired substantial capacity in the West and East Docks, the Roath Basin and the Alexandra Dock. Penarth developed its own dock in 1865, as did Port Talbot in 1898. Swansea, like her eastern rivals, had a geographically correct but unimaginatively titled North Dock and South Dock and a sycophantic Prince of Wales Dock (1904) and King's Dock (1909).

Although the overall trend in the Welsh coal industry in the period 1870–1914 was an upwards trajectory, it is important to remember that there were years of decline, depression and distress in coal mining, as in all industries.[92] The year 1871 was a time of hardship and suffering, when several costly industrial disputes led to a reduction in output. The world trade depressions of the mid 1870s and 1880s deeply affected the coal industry. In the 1880s, the Ogwr and Llyfni valleys, were exceptionally depressed. The closure of the ironworks at the heads of the south Wales valleys heralded hard times for the local collieries, which had previously supplied their coal. In these periods of decline, weaker companies were the prey of the predatory combines, who savagely picked them off. In the 1890s, there were costly and lengthy disputes, especially those of 1893 and 1898, which deeply affected the industry for a generation. In 1904 and 1910, there were further disputes and a decline in output, especially during the long strike which affected the Cambrian Combine, resulting in rioting in Tonypandy.[93] In some localities, the particular problems of a mine, fractured seams of coal and financial shortages, could cause difficulties.A marked feature of the development of coal mining was a substantial increase in the size of companies. In 1873, the old iron companies, which had pioneered the development of mining in order to supply their company's need for fuel, were dominant; pre-eminent among the ten largest companies was the Ebbw Vale Steel, Iron and Coal Co. which raised 1,020,000 tons of coal.[94]

As the insatiable lust for the bottom line intensified, these companies were amalgamated and combined into giant 'combines'. Amongst the biggest in 1914 were the Cambrian Combine, which controlled 7.3 million tons of coal, United National with 2.4 million tons and T. Beynon and Company, which produced 4.8 million tons of coal. In 1914, over 40 per cent of the total output of coal in south Wales was produced by giant capitalistic enterprises, which had tragic implications for industrial relations. Miners believed that mining was a skilled craft, which called for considerable aptitude and ability in order to operate safely. They also considered that management had no sympathy or understanding of their work and treated them as drones or drudges.[95] It was, one wag complained, 'a case of mind over matter – the masters did not mind, and the miners did not matter'. As the companies grew in size, this innate tension between masters and men intensified. Companies controlled and consolidated by shareholders were impersonal and had no human interaction, driven solely by the pressure to produce a profit. Thus there was a widespread feeling that the old bonds of interpersonal loyalty had disappeared. To paraphrase *The Times*, the attitude of the new combines seemed to be 'get in, get rich, get out'.

Another noticeable feature of the coal companies was the fact that, despite the immense profits realised, they did not create significant supplementary industry in their wake.[96] At Ferndale, there were large yards which produced wagons for their own railways and those of other companies. Across south and north Wales, there were many brickworks which used the clay and colliery waste to produce bricks for use in the mine and in local building trades. Emlyn brickworks at Pen-y-groes, the Penlan works at Dunvant and the Cefndy works at Rhyl acquired considerable renown for the quality of their bricks. It was the products of such works that provided the material to house the Welsh in the remarkable transformation of the built environment that took place in the years leading to 1914. Many collieries had plants for the production of coke and patent fuels. But despite these initiatives, most coal companies operated on a simple, single monolithic business model totally geared towards the creation of a profit from selling coal.

In the same way that companies were either unable or unconcerned to diversify, because short-term profit did not require it, they also failed to invest in machinery and more effective methods of raising coal. Throughout the years of King Coal's dominance, coal companies were primarily dependent upon human and animal muscle power. George Elliot, the Powell Duffryn colliery engineer, not the novelist, claimed in 1871 that 'the system of air machines will entirely supersede the use of horses; they are the most handy things that were ever introduced.' It is to be hoped that his engineering skills were better than his powers of prophecy, for the Welsh coal industry in 1914 was still almost wholly dependent on muscle power. The reasons were simple. Machinery was rare, expensive and valuable. Men were plentiful, cheap and expendable. Though a few companies such as Hendreforgan and Llansamlet did innovate, the majority did not. It is a stark indictment of the owners of south Wales collieries that in 1912 they used only 114 coal cutting machines, whereas 148 were working in the much smaller northern coalfield.[97]

In August 1914, as the lights were extinguished all over Europe, few thought that when they were re-lit they would illuminate a very different world for the British coal industry. In *The British Coal Trade*, published in 1915, Stanley Jevons expanded on his father's earlier work, and provided an optimistic assessment of the future for British, and especially Welsh, coal mining.[98] Journalists in the *South Wales Daily News* and the *Western Mail* waxed lyrical as to how the future was black.[99] Yet such boundless optimism ignored weaknesses which were already clearly perceived by pessimists and realists. Coal mining is a transient activity. The resources it utilises are finite. The moment the first coal is raised is the point from which the graph of decline begins its downward trajectory. Mines had raised coal with the set objective of achieving quick profits and with little regard to longer-term strategies. Thus many pits that on paper had substantial reserves were, in practice, finding it difficult to operate. In the years of the Black Gold Rush of 1870–1913, mining operations had been profligate but in the new conditions of the 1920s, lack of investment in equipment and machinery resulted in serious problems in getting coal out of thinner, deeper seams. The supremacy of coal as a source of power was also being challenged. The merchant and military navies of the world were turning to oil as their chosen fuel. In 1913, the British Admiralty had purchased 1,750,000 tons of Welsh coal to power the ships of the line. By 1925, this had declined to 350,000 tons of coal. In industry, manufacturing and several undertakings which burnt coal, improvements in boiler and furnace design meant that less coal was required. In the early 1920s, the establishment of the national grid introduced another powerful competitor; electricity was powered by oil and hydroelectric sources as well as coal and its generation became increasingly more energy-efficient, so that the overall demand for coal from this industry declined.[100]

Most worrying for the coal industry was the international situation. The First World War was a period of intense disruption for the industry. Despite mining's status as a reserved occupation, many miners still flocked to join the colours, creating shortages of labour. Germany's U-boats disrupted the distribution of coal, which was a grievous blow to an export-dependent industry like Welsh coal. Before 1914, more than 80 per cent of the coal was exported to north-western Europe, the western Mediterranean, and South America. The post-war world did little to help the Welsh coal industry. The Peace Treaties of 1919 forced Germany, in reparation for war damage, to transfer the productive Ruhr coalfield to France. Thus, at the stroke of a pen, the treaty's signatories removed France as one of the biggest markets for Welsh coal. In 1925, sterling returned to the gold standard but did so at a gross over-valuation, which gave another grievous blow to an export-dependent industry. Prices were now too high for the market to afford. Between 1927–1930, exports of Welsh coal fell by 23 per cent, and by another 25 per cent between 1927–30 and 1933–8.[101]

The years between 1919 and 1939 were exceptionally difficult ones for the coal industry. The industry's problems were assessed, analysed and articulated in several reports, most notably in the *Sankey Commission Report* (1919), the *Samuel Commission Report* (1926), the Coal Mines Act (1930) and the Coal Act (1938). Despite the eloquence, little was achieved. The deep-set problems of the coal industry proved insoluble. The reports were punctuated by periods of intense industrial dispute and dislocation. There was a strike in 1921, another in 1925 and a 'great lock-out' in 1926. In the 1930s miners continued their protests. Innovative tactics such as 'stay down protests' and 'lock-ins' were adopted, which affected production but reduced the worst effects of strikes on miners' families.[102] In the 1920s and 1930s, the consolidation of companies continued and coal and iron companies grew more integrated. Through mergers and takeovers, Powell Duffryn Associated Collieries became one of the largest industrial undertakings ever seen in Wales,[103] but despite the impressive inventory, at its heart this was still a coal company. As the number of companies decreased, so too did the numbers of people employed. In 1920, at the coal industry's peak, 271,516 miners were employed. By 1924, this had declined to 250,000 and fell further, to 112,337, in 1944.[104]

During the Second World War, King Coal's condition was edging towards the terminal. Although there was a growth in home demand, this was insufficient to compensate for the loss of export markets. Keeping the home fires burning was not enough. Profits fell with France. In every year of the war, there was a decline in output – from 35.3 million tons in 1939 to 26.7 million tons in 1941 and to 21.6 million tons in 1945. Despite the best efforts of Bevin and his boys, the Welsh coal industry was in serious economic difficulty, which many hoped would be resolved by nationalising the industry. Despite the substantial decline in profits, productivity and production, it is important to remember that even in 1945 coal continued to be the largest single occupational category in Wales and the major economic support for several Welsh regions.

2

'Lead us into Temptation': Consumerism, Creativity and Change

Technology makes it possible for people to gain control over everything, except technology.

John Tudor

Envy – 'keeping up with the Joneses': consumerism, fashion and beauty

Yr oedd ar dân am gael mynd i'r siop deganau. Yr oedd yno ddigon o ddewis, gannoedd ohonynt, o bob math o liw, a maint a llun. Daeth dyn bach prysur ati, yn gwisgo sbectol ac yn edrych fel rhyw dderyn bach â thrwyn cam. Eglurodd hithau iddo yn betrus beth oedd arni ei eisiau . . . 'Mae gen i yr unionbeth sydd arnoch chi i eisio', meddai yntau, gan bicio yn fân ac yn fuan i gwr anweledig o'r siop . . . Daeth geiriau Twrgenieff i'w chof: 'Ni ŵyr hapusrwydd am yfory, ac nid oes ganddo ddoe. Mae hapusrwydd yn anghofio'r gorffennol, ac nid yw'n meddwl am y dyfodol. Ni ŵyr ond am y presennol – a hynny nid am ddiwrnod, eithr am foment.'
'Mor wir! Mor wir!' A rhoddodd y gwirionedd hwn foment o hapusrwydd iddi hithau.

(She was on fire to go to the toy shop. There was plenty of choice, hundreds of them, of all types and colours, and size and type. A bespectacled, busy little man looking like a bird with a crooked nose came to serve her. She explained to him what she wanted . . . 'I have exactly what you need', he said, and went swiftly and softly to an obscure part of the shop . . . Turgenev's words came to her mind: 'Happiness does not know tomorrow, and has no yesterday. Happiness forgets the past, and does not consider the future. It only knows the present – and that, not for a day, but for a moment.' 'How true. How true.' And this truth gave her too a moment of happiness.

Kate Roberts, *Prynu Dol a Storïau Eraill* (Denbigh, 1969)

In *Prynu Dol*, Kate Roberts reveals the tensions, temptations and therapeutic power of the act of purchasing. At the end of her lifetime (1891–1985), it was broadly established that Wales had become part of a consumer society.[1] The years 1870–1945 have perhaps the strongest claim to have witnessed a consumer revolution,[2] for in these years both the demand for and the supply of consumer goods increased substantially. Demand grew for three reasons. Firstly, there were more people in Wales who wanted a broader variety of goods. Secondly, those people had more 'disposable' income with which to purchase. Thirdly, there were far more suppliers to meet and create demand.[3]

The history of industrial relations in Wales, the battle for a decent 'living' wage, has been exhaustingly and comprehensively studied. But concentration on the fact that people were fighting for their livelihoods has meant that it has often been forgotten that, from the mid-nineteenth century onwards, the purchasing power of the weekly earnings of most workers actually increased. It is notoriously difficult for historians to trace with any precision wages and earnings across different time periods. However, two surveys conducted by the Ministry of Labour in 1937/8 and 1953/4 provide valuable evidence of consumer expenditure. Care is needed, as the surveys reveal patterns of consumption in two very different, yet complementary economic climates – the 'locust years' of the 1930s and the 'years of austerity' of the early 1950s.[4] Accepting all the flaws and defects embedded in the statistics, it is probable that Welsh households in the 1930s were better off than those of their parents' generation. Certainly by the 1950s, despite the austerity and continued rationing, their capacity to spend was greater. Increasingly, as households became relatively more affluent, their expenditure on 'non-essential' items, such as recreation, increased.

Demographic forces served to further extend and enhance the demand for consumer goods. Coal mining, manufacturing and quarrying areas all over Wales employed larger numbers of young unmarried men who, if not especially wealthy or well off, did have a surplus of money that they could spend. It has been calculated that, whereas the real wages of adults rose by some 25 per cent between 1938 and 1958, those of adolescents increased twice as quickly over the same twenty-year period.[5] The memoirs and reminiscences of young collier boys living at home reveal that they made a financial contribution to the family's costs, but they also retained an element of their wage. Those who lodged with kith and kin did the same after board and lodging were paid for. Oral evidence reveals that, as the twentieth century wore on, boys and girls who worked were able to retain a larger portion of their wage. Comparisons were made constantly with earlier and supposedly less sophisticated times: 'What would our grandmothers have thought of girls, sixteen or eighteen, parading the fair alone, dressed in jockey-caps . . . imitation open jackets and waistcoats and smoking cigars or cigarettes?' wondered one fashion-conscious wanderer in the 1900s. Such concerns resurfaced time and again.[6]

Unlike the concern about spendthrift youth, the growing economic power of the elderly aroused few anxieties. The development of the 'grey consumer'[7] seems a surprising trend, for there remains a tendency to associate old age with frailty, incapacity and poverty. Such associations, were of course, all too painfully real in earlier years, but it is important to realise that, over the period 1870–1945, a combination of demographic and material changes wrought a fundamental and beneficial transformation in the economic circumstances of the elderly. The end of the nineteenth century saw the emergence of the concept of 'retirement' as a new epoch in human life between work and death.[8] Despite the parsimony of its provision, the value of the state pension should not be undervalued. The non-contributory scheme of 1908 paid a maximum of five shillings a week, which approximated to around 20 per cent of a miner's earnings. Within four years of its inception, the non-contributory scheme of 1908 covered 60 per cent of those aged 70 or above; and by the early 1940s it, together with the contributory scheme of 1911, embraced some 84 per cent of the elderly population.[9] 'God bless Lloyd George' proclaimed the placards held by pensioners as they collected their first pensions in Cwmdu, Carmarthenshire, in 1911.

This grizzled group knew that, for them, the dreaded spectre of the workhouse, the abode of abject pauperism, had been exorcised.[10] The redistribution of economic power in favour of the elderly benefitted women more than men, for they lived longer. Women also gradually benefitted from increasing wages and growth in professional and clerical occupations in which they could receive relatively higher wages.

The other fundamental aspect of the 'consumer revolution' was that people's attitude towards consumption changed. The harsh theological prohibitions against purchasing relaxed over the course of the nineteenth century.[11] That one should seek for improvement in this world, as well as the next, was generally accepted by 1900. At the turn of the twentieth century, ministers were better dressed and better housed than the hell-fire prophets of the early nineteenth century, testimony that religion led, not only to respectability, but to earthly reward. They also smelled fresher. Goods now signified grace, not greed; what one wore on the outside reflected what went on in the heart and stains on clothes were stains on the soul. Clothes were a public covenant that one's private world was one of good behaviour and moral uprightness. A cluster of liberal concepts – individualism, cosmopolitanism, scientific rationalism, the empowerment of women – combined in complex ways that fostered greater consumption. In the denominational and secular press, articles confirmed that decorating the home was conceived as a serious, high-minded activity. The ideas provided by literature had implications for the home's form and gave meaning to decorating, which was perceived as benefitting its occupants and society at large.

In essence, there were three essential aspects to the change in attitude towards consumption – manipulation, emulation and amelioration. The first suggests that consumers were manipulated by advertisers and their commercial interests; the second that people were, like Kate Roberts's doll purchaser, satisfying a deep-seated need to emulate their fellows; the third that they were satisfying an even deeper need to improve the material (and other) circumstances in which they found themselves. As one worker, describing life at the end of the First World War explained, 'if you were keeping up with the Joneses, you had a piano and left your front door open so that people could hear'.[12] The whole purpose of the parlour, that Beckettian stage-set, was to be filled with possessions, and the bigger, brighter, brasher and more noticeable they were the better.[13] In the tenements of Cardiff, Wrexham, Bangor and Aberystwyth, bay-windowed parlours confirmed family respectability and refinement. In some communities, this conspicuous consumption became obsessive. The Rhondda valleys, despite high levels of piety and higher levels of poverty, proved too materialistic for the poet Idris Davies (1905–53). He fled to the East End of London where he penned his iconic poem of the 1926 strike, 'The Angry Summer'.

The growth in retailing was notable. Many Welsh towns turned clap-boarded, ramshackle buildings into decorous market halls and developed distinct streets which served as retail centres, such as Stepney Street in Llanelli, Queen's Square in Wrexham, High Street in Bangor, Queen's Street and St Mary's Street in Cardiff.[14] A similar process was at work in the mining towns, where parts of ribboned terraces acquired a commercial character. In Tonypandy, for example, on the night of the infamous riots in 1910, no fewer than sixty-three shops, damaged or destroyed by looters, were packed hugger-mugger in Dunraven Street.[15]

Most shops remained simple branches, dark places lit by oil lamps and candles. Decaying bacon joints hung from the rafters, alongside a conglomeration of books, tin cans and brushes, all in glorious confusion. In many a shop in a potholed backstreet in a county town, problems with cleanliness, mould and mice were endemic. Storing goods was difficult before the development of domestic refrigerators and most customers had to carry their goods home. As a customer opened the door, a bell would ring with a faint ping that summoned the slowly moving wife to service. Cash payments were rare, for the matriarch who presided over the sell-all emporium entered the transactions in laborious copperplate in a large ledger which contained hundreds of accounts for sums down to a penny.

In a town with many shops, the crafty impecunious could spread their credit around. Customers at the shop run by the writer Rhys

Davies's family sometimes put a penny down on a two-and-six-penny jug and were still paying it off five years later.[16] Many shopkeepers relied on their dexterity in mental arithmetic, gambling on who should be given credit and who, and how, to refuse. The 1950 census of distribution reveals that single-shop proprietors controlled 45 per cent of the retail market.[17] Customers relied on the local shop for their regular purchases.

Bigger shops, with a broader range of goods, offered a better lifestyle. General stores sold most things from butter to screws, nails, 'delph' and china. In coastal villages the stores even sold rope, anchors, fishing nets, Wellington boots, tweeds and rashers of Carmarthenshire back bacon, which the shopowner would slice into translucent slivers and women would select as if they were examining gold leaf.[18] Some enterprising shopkeepers, like William Evans of Porth, pioneered doorstep deliveries, when grocer boys would cycle hill and vale on heavy Raleigh bikes that were made even heavier by customers' weekly goods.[19] The development of delivery vans in the 1920s eased their burden and extended their range. Some acquisitive shops took over rival companies and established chains of businesses in towns and villages across Wales. The chain stores, Pegler's, Terry, Spar and Mace, had their origins in Welsh towns and villages.

The arrival of fixed shops did not result in the displacement of itinerant traders, but those who had previously peddled their wares in the countryside moved to more profitable urban areas. They sold perishables as well as clothing, drapery, haberdashery and a bewildering array of goods. Thomas Jones in his evocative *Rhymney Memories* remembered seeing, as a boy in the 1880s, Italians on the streets selling plaster statuettes which they balanced on a board on their heads.[20] These devotional figurines were probably produced by Louis Galleozzi, his wife and five sons, figure-makers, of Picton Street, Merthyr Tydfil.[21] Many Welsh women were brought into the expanding consumer market by the tallymen or 'Scotch drapers'. Several, if not most, of the perambulating tallymen used shady business practices to entice wives on their doorsteps to purchase their wares. This created problems and tensions for both seller and buyer. Some traders used strong-armed tactics to recover debts, while others resorted to the law. The records of the county courts of Wales contain countless examples of tallymen trying to recover goods and debts from their customers. A few husbands, much to the chagrin of moralists, were even imprisoned because of the 'irresponsibility' and 'fecklessness' of their wives in overextending the family budget.

The availability of credit at more preferential rates and on more flexible terms and conditions was a great boost to people's capacity to buy. Many consumers bought on hire purchase terms, the colloquially much-loved 'never-never'.[22] The miner B. L. Coombes and his wife moved into two rented rooms during the First World War. He recalled later, 'I remember how proud I felt when I saw them furnished for the first time, and realised that all that shining new furniture was ours even if most of it still had to be paid for.'[23] One of the pioneers of the new purchasing methods was Sir Pryce Pryce-Jones's Royal Welsh Warehouse, established in 1869 at Newtown. The company established mail-order retailing, and by the mid 1880s served a client base of over 100,000 customers. The business, which remained under Pryce-Jones's personal direction until 1895, expanded rapidly in the late nineteenth century. An impressive new warehouse was opened next to the railway station at Newtown in 1879 and this was extended in 1887, when a printing works was attached which, from 1890 onwards, printed an illustrated catalogue distributed to over 200,000 customers. The company's profits were greatly boosted when it received an order for 60,000 of their Patent Euklisia Rugs, a type of sleeping bag, from the Russian government during the Russo-Turkish war of 1877–8. Sir Pryce Pryce-Jones, in order to secure his interests, was a director of the Welshpool and Llanfair Railway Company. He was also an influential advocate of the parcel post, first introduced in 1883. This proved so important that a branch of the post office was opened inside the warehouse to facilitate rapid dispatch.[24] Technological developments and Pryce's personal ingenuity enabled him to develop a worldwide web of trade from this outpost of rural Wales.

Department stores, those 'gateways to dream worlds', emerged in the later nineteenth century. Amongst the large national and international chains that developed were a number established by Welsh entrepreneurs, revealing that the Welsh did have a flair for business. David Morgan opened his first drapery store in the shadow of Rhymney's Egyptian-styled iron works in 1858. In the 1870s the business prospered under his dedication and diligence and by 1875 he had branches at Pontlottyn and Abertillery. Soon he leased larger premises; despite the general economic depression of the late 1870s, such was David Morgan's optimism that he secured a lease on premises in the Hayes in Cardiff. Although this was a fair distance from the town's developing commercial and retail areas, he was so convinced of the merits of his concern that by 1890 the store had taken over two adjoining public houses, several shops and the Pavilion Hotel. In 1899, David Morgan invested £27,000 in building Morgan's Arcade. This 'Arcadia' of an arcade linked his premises through into St Mary Street and his company had become larger than its older rival, Howells.[25]

In England, Welsh-born retailers were even more successful than their home-based counterparts. In Chester, John Mortimer Green Harris (1864–1939), helped to develop Browns into the 'Harrods of the North'. Lucy Duff Gordon considered the store 'the best store in England'. In 1868, Owen Owen from Cwmrhaeadr near Machynlleth set up a drapery business in London Road, Liverpool, hoping to attract the city's large Welsh population. He concentrated on rapid turnover and low profit margins. So successful was this business philosophy that by 1873 Owen had over 120 employees and a quarter of an acre of floor space. The 1880s saw continued expansion as he purchased neighbouring properties until the business, by 1891, was one of the largest in the north of England.[26] Newcastle Emlyn-born Peter Rhys Jones (1843–1905) was another who made riches from the rags of the draper's trade.[27] After an apprenticeship in a Carmarthen draper's establishment Jones left, in 1868, to seek his fortune in London. Eventually, after several moves, he settled in King's Road. The venture was a remarkable success, reaching a turnover of over £44,000 and a staff of fifty by 1884; both numbers soon doubled.

The Davies Bryan brothers took the lessons of Welsh retailing to the furthest shores of the empire and established the Cambria, the largest store in Egypt's capital, Cairo. By 1898, Davies Bryan and Co. boasted that it was 'the largest British Establishment in Egypt', with branches at Cairo, Alexandria, Port Said and London. They also owned several properties and hotels, including the Continental Savoy, 'the most exotic hotel in the East'.[28] David Edward Lewis (1866–1941), of Llandysul in Cardiganshire, showed that he had his share of the alleged financial acumen of the Cardi and became the most successful draper and shop owner in Australia.

Despite the resilience of small firms and corner shops, retailing underwent a fundamental transformation, and experienced an important 'form of industrial revolution'. Food processing and drink manufacturing also underwent a similar process of development. Again, the Welsh experience is instructive and indicative of general trends. At the tender age of nineteen, William Evans (1864–1934), after a series of jobs in a variety of stores, became the manager of the Porth branch of Pegler's Stores in the Rhondda. In 1888, he branched out on his own and established a grocery store in the town. A bakery was added in 1890, followed by three branch shops at other locations by 1895. In 1897, Evans, an adherent of the temperance movement, experimented in the manufacture of soft drinks following a chance meeting with an Indian 'quack doctor'. The production of soft drinks at Porth, comprising hop bitters, ginger beer and lemonade, commenced in 1900 under the label Welsh Hills Mineral Waters. The works expanded rapidly, especially after assuming the name Corona in 1920. By William's death in 1934, the company ran twenty-seven factories and over fifty depots throughout England and Wales. William Evans's business insight was to ease the customer's ability to purchase by delivering his products to their doorsteps. Another who prospered was the brewery entrepreneur, Samuel Arthur Brain (1850–1903).[29] In 1882 he purchased the Old Brewery in Cardiff, capable of a weekly output of 5,000 barrels of beer. By 1887, he had extended it into the largest brewery in south Wales, utilising state-of-the-art equipment at a cost of £50,000, Brains Brewery sold their beer to their own chain of public houses and over 150 working men's clubs.

It is important to note that the Welsh were not affluent, and that for the greater part of the period they had the lowest portion of surplus income of any part of the United Kingdom. For many communities and trades, depression and decline were frequent experiences. Nevertheless, the fact that people were better off than previous generations did have significant effects on Welsh life. Retailers quickly realised that, although the Welsh might not be rich, there were large numbers of low earners who together could spend a little and so provide high profits. The seaside resorts of Wales saw considerable investment in accommodation, entertainment and public amenities. Penarth, Aberystwyth, Llandudno and Bangor were part of the pier-building mania of the 1870s. On their walkways, what-the-butler-saw machines and mother-of-pearl encrusted peep-boxes showed illuminated scenes of such delights as her ladyship in the bath, the Folies Bergère and King Edward VII opening Parliament. It cost £60,000 to build Rhyl's Winter Gardens. The results were spectacular. By the turn of the century, the Palace at Rhyl boasted a ballroom, extensive roof gardens, forty shops and offices, table-tennis rooms and an imitation Venice featuring 'real Gondolas propelled by real Italians'.[30] Later, Butlins and Pontins established holiday camps along the coast so that Mary Fach, and her husband could, when she thought they could afford it, 'give the kids a treat'. The company's slogan, 'Holidays with pay – holidays with play', captured the imagination of many.[31]

Storekeepers and shopkeepers soon grasped the seasonal demands and needs of their customers. No sooner had the mannequins shed the heavy coats and clothes of winter than they wore lighter summer frocks and fineries. Advertisers, in particular, were aware of the changing seasons and urged consumers to consume. Perhaps the best example was the frenzied commercialisation of Christmas, which took place from the 1860s onwards and accelerated again in the decade or so before 1914 as a result of the cinema. By then, no less than nine films of Dickens's *A Christmas Carol* had been produced and the template for the perfect Christmas was clear. Across Wales, shopkeepers decked their halls with holly and ensured that their stores bulged with seasonal essentials and inessentials. Customers hurried to purchase the perfect present before the shops closed at midnight on the night before the big day. From 1888, Peter Jones's shop in Sloane Square had its Santa's Grotto,[32] from which Father Christmas, the portly patron saint of the season, radiated warmth and bonhomie to entice young and old to spend. From 1870 onwards Lewis's Bon Marché in Liverpool offered a 'snow-filled Christmas fairyland' every year.

Such were the seasonal pressures that the *Draper's Record* urged shoppers to buy early in order to make life easier for shop assistants, but they continued to be amongst the most disadvantaged of Welsh workers. Advent Sunday, Christmas Eve, the First Night of Christmas, Twelfth Night, the dates by which the church signalled and measured the season, were pushed aside by the commercial countdown. The central Christian message was reshaped, reordered and repackaged into a secular festival.[33] Advent was no longer a period of liturgical expectation, but a time for limitless expenditure.

Another unexpected consequence of the consumer revolution was the revelation of the power and position of women within Welsh society. Advertisers soon realised that many household purchasing decisions were taken by women. The advertising of chocolate was 'feminised' in the 1930s, with Black Magic unashamedly targeting upper-class women, whereas milk chocolate Dairy Box was marketed to working-class women. The long-standing association between chocolate and female sexuality, temptation and sensualness was ignored, as the advertisers emphasised the noble housewife nurturing her family with chocolate goodness. Subsequent feminist historians might have derided them, but the advertisements of Lever soap were direct: 'Why does a woman look older sooner than a man?'[34] The reason, naturally, was the burden of the weekly wash, yet even in the 1890s the solution lay close to hand, for 'with Sunlight soap the work is so cut down that a young girl or delicate woman can do a family wash and not get tired'. To many Welsh housewives, Lever's scented soap was clearly more attractive than their mothers' washing solution – a jelly made from sheep's dung. Offering prints of Curnow Vosper's painting *Salem* in an incentivised campaign boosted sales. In the years following the First World War, the manufacturers of consumer durables increasingly targeted the housewife. 'It's so silly to go on wearing myself out', declared the exhausted housemaker in one Hoover advertisement of 1938, for with a vacuum cleaner, 'I can have a maid at 4d a day'. The publishing, beauty, fashion and medical industries soon realised the power of the female pound. Women's magazines and special columns within local newspapers boomed as never before. *Women's Weekly* (1911), *Woman's Own* (1932) and *Woman* (1937) were purchased, read and handed on to friends by a broad range of women.[35]

Soap manufacturers began to advertise their products in new ways; Cuticura soap was a beauty aid, whilst the Welsh wife could have skin as soft and smooth as Barbara Stanwyck's just by using Lux toilet soap. Medical advertisements also became somewhat more refined. In the late nineteenth century, the advertisements of Towles, Pennyroyal and Steel, promised women relief from painful gynaecological disorders and 'blockages'; in the 1930s, medical firms advocated products reputed to offer them 'radiant health in middle age'.[36] 'Institutes of Beauty' sprang up, promising to rejuvenate women who feared they were losing their charms. Women, in short, expended more and more time, effort and money in trying to be different from what they were, so that the ideal of feminine beauty, far from being an inspiration, must have been, at least for some, a source of constant anxiety. Advertisers told them to worry about their complexion, their skin, their teeth, even the size of their busts (too small and too big) and offered them guaranteed solutions. Some companies even went so far as to include in their advertisements endorsements of their products allegedly written by local people.[37]

Another result of the consumer revolution was the feminisation of town and city centres.[38] Department stores were theatrical, therapeutic centres, as much as retail outlets. Shopping meant a day out in town. As well as window-shopping, inspecting and buying goods, a day in town often also entailed lunch or tea. Smaller shop owners complained that larger retailers pandered to the irresponsible, uncontrollable urges of the woman consumer. The stores countered, arguing that they provided a controlled, civilised environment of doormen, lady shop assistants, catering facilities and lavatories. Yet shopping remained somewhat culturally ambivalent. Concerns were often expressed that the woman who shopped was a pleasure seeker, seduced from her domestic responsibilities by her lust for goods and the distractions of urban life. Thus department stores presented themselves as safe and emancipated places for women, providing an acceptable form of femininity and complemented by coffee houses and tea shops, such as Lyons and Kardomah cafes. These places were not the exclusive preserve of the genteel, little-finger raising ladies as they delicately sipped their tea. Ladies who lunched in Swansea's Kardomah cafe in the 1920s and 1930s had to suffer the teasing and taunts barked by Dylan Thomas, Daniel Jones, Vernon Watkins and a remarkable group of artistic 'young dogs'.[39] Wales, by the opening decade of the twentieth century, had a flourishing cafe culture. Cafes offered, in addition to the satisfactions of the belly, an atmosphere of friendship and fellowship, gossip and a certain gaiety and grace of behaviour. Spinsters, bachelors, the lost and the lonely found solace in the ballads of the sad cafe. One woman from the north remembered a cafe that was 'all glitter, gilt and splendour'. In south Wales, from Tenby to Tonypandy, Italian immigrants established cosy cafes. Their service varied from the courteous to the curt, but their cafes provided companionship, comfort and conviviality.[40]

The history of the fashion trade, of frocks and finery, reveals how women's feelings of envy fuelled the rise and fall of industries.[41] One item of clothing, the simple stocking, tells a remarkable tale.[42] In the 1890s silk stockings were the preserve of the rich. At the turn of the century, only members of the elite wore such stockings, most women wore thick homespun or factory-produced stockings. By the 1910s, however, many middle-class women deemed silk stockings to be more desirable and began to emulate the habits of upper-class women. Between 1914 and 1923, the production of silk and 'artificial silk' (made of rayon at Courtauld's factories) increased 417 per cent. Sir John Coldbrook Hanbury-Williams (1892–1965) was responsible for Courtauld's collaboration with Imperial Chemical Industries (ICI) in the development of nylon.[43] In the 1930s, as Hollywood films glamorised and fantasised the sheer, silk-covered legs of movie stars, many Welsh women aspired to silk stockings.

Clothing was another area where women's envy of the fashionable and privileged led to a remarkable series of transformations. Kate Davies revealed in her poignant memoirs, *Hafau fy Mhlentyndod*, that she, like many rural young women, relied on her own and her mother's handiwork and dressmaking skills, wearing only one dress throughout the week and another for Sundays.[44] So too did Kate Roberts in *Te yn y Grug*. When they could they purchased a new skirt or frock from the local outfitters, but compared with those illustrated in the papers and the mail-order catalogues, these appeared old-fashioned and outmoded. Rural cultures fell under the sway of a national and homogenising urban culture as farmers' daughters attempted to dress like the daughters of financiers. Countless dress shops in villages and towns across Wales displayed the 'latest French and Parisian fashions' for women. Many clothes shops in simple Welsh villages assumed fancy French titles. After the First World War, the French emphasis declined as, in F. Scott Fitzgerlad's phrase, 'America now leads in all that is fashionable and fun'.[45] 'American Wales' had a feminine dimension.

Men were also dedicated followers of fashion. By the early twentieth century, the importance of hats as a status symbol had become such that neither men nor women dared show themselves out in public without one, and that of a kind appropriate to the rank to which they aspired. In 1910, a photograph of the striking Cambrian miners reveals that, above the privet hedges of luxuriant moustaches in every style from Fu Manchu to Colonel Blimp, flat caps and bowler hats were all the rage in Tonypandy.[46] Old habits died hard, however; a decade later another photograph shows the town's miners on strike again, but the sartorial collier now preferred the comradeship of the Russian Revolutionary hat. Gaze at the photographs in the Cardiganshire Constabulary's Register of Felons, and one cannot help but be struck by the extensive range of head-gear worn by the county's miscreants.[47] Flat caps, bowler hats, mini bowler hats, top hats, cloth caps, trilbies, boaters and more, all graced these graceless heads. As women abandoned bonnets and the witch's stove pipe hat of the alleged traditional Welsh costume, mountains of feathers, flowers and fruit, largely manufactured in Cardiff sweatshops, adorned their hats.[48]

Makers of boots and clogs, who had secured a regular income in the mid-nineteenth century, found times increasingly hard as the century progressed. Northamptonshire-made factory boots were widely available in Anglesey and the craftsman bootmakers of Llanerch-y-medd disappeared rapidly.[49] In praising Captain Pritchard Rayner, the Tory candidate for the county in 1880, it was said that he provided work for as many as sixty Llanerch-y-medd and Llangefni cobblers, who were on the brink of starvation as a result of the contraction in their industry.[50] In contrast Poynter's, the Cardiff shoemakers, moved from a cottage to a factory equipped with Italian shoemaking equipment and employing more than 200 people in little under a decade. The woollen industry witnessed a substantial and painful restructuring as production transferred from the Llanidloes and Newtown areas to the new factories of the Teifi valley. In the 1870s and 1880s the valley prospered, so that by the 1890s 'hardly a spot on any river bank remains where it would be convenient to place another mill'.[51] The industry flourished during the First World War but woollen manufacturing was overly dependent upon the south Wales mining valleys and, as depression set in there during the 1920s and 1930s, demand declined and mills closed. In 1926 there were 250 mills on Tivyside; by 1947 there were 81.[52]

In the furniture and building trades, fashion also dealt cruelly with Welsh industries. Against much competition, Newborough was described as the most miserable spot on Anglesey. Even at the close of the nineteenth century, it was the abject poverty of the village people that struck travellers. Local womenfolk had supplemented their family income making mats from marram grass in their homes. As the twentieth century dawned, it was increasingly clear that fashion and new materials had ended the demand for their tortuous labours. Elsewhere across Wales, small craftsmen who had produced fine furniture, with a guarantee of several generations, found their businesses declining as stores, especially department stores, sold cheaper mass-produced furniture.[53]

The new consumer society which had emerged by the First World War, with its abundance in clear and tantalising sight of all, broke down traditional ideologies and boundaries. Women proved, through their purchases at small village shop and large town department stores, that they believed what the new generation of advertisers had told them: certain products carried deeper social meanings.

A dress was not merely a dress, it was a symbol and a signal. Social connotations made goods desirable to material girls.[54]

The conquest of time and space

> Things are travelling dreadfully fast just now. New inventions and new scientific discoveries are chasing each other so quickly that to the man in the street they pass like pictures in a panorama, before he has had time to grasp half their significance.
>
> *The Welshman*, 4 March 1910

The confused commentator, writing in the Carmarthenshire newspaper in 1910, could be forgiven this expression of bewilderment, for the author had lived through a period of remarkable innovation and invention which produced a fundamental transformation in daily lives. Amongst the technological developments were the telephone, wireless telegraph, phonograph, x-ray, cinema, bicycle, automobile, vacuum cleaner and airplane. These changes in technology created distinctive new modes of thinking about and experiencing time and space. If our commentator lived another two decades, then she or he would probably have been even more disorientated at the effects of the communications revolution which saw the development of radio, radar and television. Transport between 1870 and 1945 went from tracks and trails to tarmac and vapour trails. Fundamental to several developments was the existence of new ways of generating and distributing power, particularly electricity. It seems that no superlative or hyperbole is too extreme to describe the effects of this novel new power source. The eminent historian of architecture, Rayner Banham, described electrification as 'the greatest environmental revolution in human history since the domestication of fire'.[55]

As with so much in historical studies, it is vital that we remember that change coincided with continuity and that the true effects of inventions and innovations were often only seen over longer periods. The development of the internal combustion engine undoubtedly had a profound impact on the lives of the Welsh people, but older means of transport continued. Ox-carts drawing heavy loads with unbelievable slowness and ill-will were still at work in the age of the automobile. The first speeding ticket was issued in 1910 on what were still sleepy equine streets. Horses were vital in the First World War; despite the introduction of new technologies of destruction such as the tank, the British Army in 1917 had 591,000 horses, 213,000 mules, 47,000 camels and 11,000 oxen. The caravanserai of packhorses, priests and prostitutes following the troops, which would have been familiar to Sir Thomas Picton and the generals of the Napoleonic Wars, still shadowed soldiers during the First World War. The date in which technology developed was, and is, significant, but it takes time for an innovation to be understood and used. Use-centred history is not simply a matter of moving technological time forward, for time was always jumbled up; people worked with old and new things, as miners, for example, used iron hammers and electric drills. Timelines of progress are not as tidy as many historians imagine. Steam power was vital to the 'electric Edwardians'.[56]

On 1 September 1879, the ballroom of the Lord Nelson Hotel in Milford Haven became the first in the UK to be lit by electricity. People debated which was the bigger shock – the innovation, or the fact that the Nelson Hotel had a ballroom. A few, select inhabitants of Cardiff were the first in Wales to receive electricity in their homes when, in the mid-1880s, the town's corporation granted a licence to the Anglo-American Brush Company to supply a direct current to the Hayes. The next development was in Ogmore Vale, where John Williams, a local grocer and draper, introduced a 'novelty' to open a bazaar in 1891.[57] The display was so successful that some influential locals arranged for a supply to be provided from two generating stations in Ogmore Vale and Nantymoel. The 1890s saw similar developments across Wales. Cardiff in 1893, Gorseinon, Newport and Aberystwyth in 1894, Llandrindod in 1897 and Llandudno in 1898 all established companies and generating plants to provide power. The first year of the twentieth century saw the illumination of Bangor, Colwyn Bay, Menai Bridge, Rhyl and Wrexham in the north, Pontypridd and Pontypool in the south. Throughout the period down to the First World War, there was tension between municipal interests that petitioned Parliament for powers to generate and distribute electricity and private companies that argued that it was they who provided the most effective and economic means of generating power. It was not until 1926, with the establishment of a publicly owned Central Electricity Board, that the arguments were finally resolved.[58]

Though electricity was at first treated as a novelty, it was soon appreciated that it had a vital role to play in all areas of people's lives. Coal companies, such as the Ocean, Ferndale, Glamorgan and the Cambrian, had, by 1904, established their own plant to provide them with electricity. These companies and others in south Wales worked by and large against the electricity supply companies that had been established by municipal corporations. However, in the north there appears to have been greater cooperation between private and public enterprise. The North Wales Electricity Bill of 1904 was intended primarily to provide electricity to the Beddgelert and Croesor Railway and a number of narrow-gauge light railways, but it was soon extended to include a supply for domestic use in Caernarfonshire, Merionethshire, Anglesey, most of Denbighshire, and a small area of Flintshire.[59]

Electricity had profound effects on people's lives. Far more so than flickering candlelight or dim gaslight, electric light broke down the barrier between day and night. Natural light was no longer required to work indoors and so began one of the great disasters of the human spirit. Waves of workers came to work in the darkness of a winter's morning and departed in the evening without once seeing the sun. The shops of Wrexham, Bangor, Swansea, Cardiff, Carmarthen and Cardigan soon glowed at night, especially in the weeks before Christmas. Nightlife and the night-time economy were electrified and hotels, bars, cafes and restaurants all beckoned customers with their radiance. Street lighting was also directed towards the defence of the property and safety of the more prosperous and the poor were left to the twilight of poverty, disease and filth. But electricity was also a source of illumination in a broader sense, for it allowed for greater flexibility in its use as a source of power.[60] This resulted in a number of novel solutions to timeless problems. In the home, for example, new inventions were created which eased the burdens on homeworkers. Washing machines became less like medieval instruments of torture and easier to use. In 1905, Walter Griffiths manufactured Griffiths's Improved Vacuum Apparatus for Removing Dust from Carpets. It might have looked like 'a bagpipe attached to a cake box', but Griffiths's new electric cleaner was portable, easy to store and could be used by 'any one person (even the ordinary domestic servant)'. By 1955, a vacuum cleaner was in over 50 per cent of Welsh homes and electric irons were owned by 75 per cent of households by 1939.[61]

The thinly dispersed population of rural Wales made it difficult for electricity companies to invest and return a profit on that investment. Nevertheless, electricity did have a significant impact on Welsh agriculture, especially those farms closest to large centres of population. Thus, by 1941, more than 30 per cent of farms in Glamorgan were connected to some form of public electricity source. At Llanfihangel-yng-Ngwynfa in north Montgomeryshire, a small hydroelectric plant supplied the local mills and farms with electricity.[62] A whole range of farm operations became electrified – food preparation, sheepshearing and woodsawing. Poultry farmers along the north Wales coast and in the vale of Glamorgan could hatch eggs and keep the newly born chicks warm without the need for the suffocating and fire-prone paraffin lamps. Moreover, with reliable artificial illumination and a safe source of heat, egg production became an all-year-round enterprise, providing higher profits in the winter when produce was previously scarce. Electric milking parlours, much promoted by the newly established Milk Marketing Board in the 1930s, enabled farmers to produce liquid milk more swiftly and hygienically.[63]

Transport was dramatically transformed at the end of the nineteenth century.[64] Despite its frightening appearance and bone-cracking ride, the high-wheeled 'penny farthing', arriving in the 1870s, had an immediate success, popularised in a famous, and much-sung Welsh folk song. Henry Stormeys's *Indispensible Bicyclist's Handbook* of 1879 listed some 300 different machines made by about sixty firms. By 1880, there were over 50 cycling clubs in Wales, and knickerbocker-clad men hurtled around the country's lanes with an anxious expression, known as 'bicyclist's face', balancing precariously on the high wheel. Newspaper warnings that cycling would produce 'a hunchbacked and torture-faced future generation' did nothing to deter enthusiasm. As prices fell from £20 for a bicycle in the late 1870s, to nine guineas in the mid 1880s, more and more people could purchase the less fearsome 'safety bicycle'. 'Ladies' also participated in the new craze, especially after the journey became smoother on new pneumatic tyres.[65]

It was in the first decade of the twentieth century that cycling changed from being a largely middle-class pursuit to being a working-class enthusiasm and essential means of transport. Its ever-widening popularity was evident in the 'Clarion' cycling clubs established by early socialists, which assisted members to buy their own bicycle. Cycling was not just a pleasure, since it was essential for many people travelling to work; by the 1930s, more than 40 per cent of Welsh miners travelled more than five miles to work. The value of the new technology was also quickly grasped by local police forces. Across Wales, police constables covered astonishing distances on their bicycles. In 1900, the chief constable of Cardiganshire considered that the bicycle was an 'inestimable boon' to the squad, and a few years later his successor in the post considered it 'of great value to the County'. The bicycle was equally valued by the county's criminals. In 1906 Charles Williams, recently discharged from prison, stole eight bicycles in Cardiganshire but still the long legs of the law caught up with him.[66]

Bicycles created new industries and demands, not just for their manufacture, but also in producing accessories. In the 1900s, the Stepney Spare Wheel Company of Llanelli achieved a significant hold on the international market for bicycle and automobile wheels, with branches across England and Wales, several European countries and Egypt. Cyclists enjoyed innovations in metalworking that gave them stronger, lighter bicycles. By 1907, several specialist cycling shops across Wales were offering bells, brushes, carriers, lamps, polish, pumps, repair outfits, spanners and stands. The career of Tom Norton (1870–1955) of Llandrindod Wells reveals how the entrepreneurial Welsh took advantage of innovations. Starting in 1899 with the first Raleigh bicycle depot in Wales, by the time of the First World War he had opened the ornate art deco Palace of Sport which served as the first Ford agency in Wales and the base for one of the first public motor bus services, from Llandrindod Wells to Newtown. Renamed the Automobile Palace in 1925, Norton's sales impressed no less a person than Henry Ford.[67]

Many innovations and inventions were initially the preserves and playthings of the rich, but with time and mass production they filtered through to benefit greater numbers of people. Such was the story of the automobile in Wales. The Welsh aristocracy gleefully embraced the motor car. In July 1895, Evelyn Ellis, the youngest son of Lord Howard de Walden, together with S. F. Edge, undertook a fifty-six mile journey between Dutchet and Windsor, which took five hours, thirty-two minutes 'exclusive of stoppages'.[68] 'It was', Edge claimed, 'the first ever made by a petroleum motor carriage in this country'.[69] Despite the tortuous journey, the car, a Panhard-Levassor, survived and is today in the Science Museum in South Kensington. In the north, patrician taste in motor cars was impeccable. The marquess of Anglesey's car, a 22 h.p. Mors, was considered one of the most handsome vehicles in Britain – no wonder, its interior fittings were of solid silver and the exterior of silver plate.

Perhaps the best example of the involvement of 'society's cream' with the car was the role of C. S. Rolls, younger son of Lord Llangattock, a Monmouthshire landowner, in the development of the motor industry.[70] In 1902 he set himself up in London, selling 'high-class cars to high-class people'. Ruthlessly exploiting his aristocratic connections, Rolls established a reputation as a salesman and demonstrator. By 1903, he numbered Lord Rosebery, Lord Willoughby d'Eresby and the Duke of Sutherland among his clients. In the following year, his customers included foreign princes, two dukes, two earls, one viscount, seven barons and three baronets.

Initially, Rolls sold foreign cars, but a meeting with the engineer Henry Royce resulted in the establishment of the car manufacturer Rolls-Royce. By 1910 their car, the 'Silver Ghost', was modestly claimed to be 'the best car in the world'. It was a leviathan that handled like a steamship but it was the ultimate status symbol. Rolls was also an ardent balloonist and in 1903 founded the Aero Club to promote the sport. He then turned his attention to aeroplanes. In 1908, he visited Le Mans to study Wilbur Wright's aeroplane, and soon bought one of his machines for his own use. Early in 1910 he set a new record by flying the English Channel both ways in his Wright aeroplane. In July 1910, he took part in a flying tournament in Bournemouth and was killed when his plane crashed following the collapse of a tailplane, thus becoming the first Welsh person to die in an aeroplane accident.

Charles Rolls's passion for speed on ground and air were surpassed by John Godfrey Parry Thomas (1884–1927).[71] With financial support from his mother, Thomas set up his own business producing, with mixed fortune, electrical transmissions for motor cars. Driving a converted Higham special with a Viz Liberty aeroplane engine, fondly christened Babs, he broke the world land speed record in 1925. A year later, at Pendine on 27 and 28 April 1926, Thomas became the first man to break two world speed records during two consecutive days. Sadly, only a few months later, once more attempting to regain and break the record on the same sands at a speed of over 180 mph, he was killed.

The male members of the aristocracy were not the only ones to revel in this world of speed and flight. Mildred Mary Bruce (1895–1990), wife of Victor Austin Bruce (1897–1978), youngest son of Hugh Campbell Bruce, second Baron Aberdare, enjoyed considerable renown as driver and pilot.[72] Mildred, with a trademark string of pearls swinging round her neck, won the *Coupe des Dames* at the Monte Carlo rally, covering 1,700 miles in seventy-two hours. In between her record-breaking motor drives she established, in September 1928, the fastest time for a Dover–Calais channel crossing by motor boat. She was also the first woman in Britain to be fined for speeding, and the first to ride a motorcycle.

The Hon. Mrs Victor Bruce was, like Charles Rolls, also enchanted by flight. Passing a car showroom off London's Pound Street, she saw a Blackburn Bluebird light aircraft for sale at £550. It bore the sign 'Ready To Go Anywhere'; on enquiring if the plane would travel round the world, she was assured by the salesman, 'Of course

. . . easily!' She bought it, learnt to fly in a matter of weeks at Brooklands School of Flying and, in the early hours of 25 September 1930, set off. In the next five months, she proved herself a serious aviator, covering 20,000 miles by air and averaging more than 400 miles a day in forty-seven days of flying. She reached New York on 5 February, via Rangoon, Shanghai, Tokyo and Vancouver. In 1928 she produced *The Woman Owner-Driver*, a response to 'the growing tendency for women to drive and look after their own cars'. She also contributed a series of articles to the *Sketch*, which were later collected in a book, *The Peregrinations of Penelope* (1930). Mildred Bruce was not only an adventurer, she understood the practical and commercial value of aviation. In 1937, she founded Air Despatch Ltd, a company that carried both freight and passengers.

Pioneer aviators were in frenzied activity across Wales at the turn of the twentieth century. Bill Frost of Amroth in Pembrokeshire appears to have a strong case to be regarded as the true father of aviation. It is almost certain that he flew before the Wright brothers.[73] He built, piloted and patented his own machine, which he offered to the War Office. In return he received a curt reply from Mr William St John Broderick, the minister: 'this nation does not intend to adopt aerial navigation as a means of warfare'. On Anglesey, Robert Loraine, Vivian Hewitt and William Ellis Williams were amongst the pioneers in 1909–11. In 1911 Hewitt became the first person to successfully fly across the Irish Sea. In Glamorgan, E. T. Willows built a series of airships – the Alexandra and the Willows I, II and III – which were flown around the country for pleasure and business. In 1910–11, many individuals flew Blériot aircraft, lightweight, insubstantial constructions of wood and cloth held together only by glue and hope. By 1913 plane design and construction had improved substantially and people like Edwin Prosser now flew Caudron biplanes around the country. From 1931, German-designed Fokker F.VIIa machines were the basis for Barnard's Aerial Circus and the new Cardiff to Bristol air service. Two years later, the Western Airways and the Railway Air Services offered services between Cardiff and Plymouth, Teignmouth, Birmingham, Liverpool, Bristol, Southampton and London.[74]

3 Perhaps the first photograph of an aeroplane in flight in south Wales, on 23 January 1911. The magnificent man was Ernest Sutton, the flying machine a Blériot XI at Oxwich Bay. *South Wales Daily News*.

To the majority of Welsh people, the travels and travails of Evelyn Ellis, Mildred Bruce and the marquess of Anglesey were worlds away, but many Welsh people quickly grasped the opportunities and potential offered to them by motor vehicles. Less romantic than the car, commercial vehicles probably made greater inroads and had more importance in the development of transport in Wales. In January 1897, the South Wales Motor Car and Cycle Co. arranged for a Thornycroft van to travel from London to Cardiff.[75] The journey was penitential; when, eventually, the van reached Roath, a large crowd gathered to cheer and chase it into town. Surprisingly, given that it moved so slowly, it somehow managed to run over the foot of the company's secretary, Mr William Duncan. Thus it detoured to the Cardiff Royal Hospital so that the first motor-traffic victim in Welsh history could receive treatment.

The advantages of light commercial vehicles were expounded with zest by Edwin Pratt in his *History of Inland Transport* (1913). He described how 'in the recesses of wild Wales, they are worked as mobile shops travelling from village to village'.[76] Such vehicles extended the reach of relatively small commercial enterprises, such as grocers, drapers and fruiterers, into broader markets. Trucks and tractors get little attention in histories of the automobile, but the steam wagons of Leyland, the lorries of Foden and the early tractors transformed travel and trade in Wales.[77] Improved grass rollers and lawnmowers were responsible for a remarkable transformation in sports such as tennis, football and rugby, which could now be played on even and smoother surfaces. The numbers of such vehicles operating in Wales greatly increased. In 1926, there were some 13,205 trucks and light vehicles in use; by 1948, there were 44,504. The number of cars also increased substantially in these two decades, from 29,291 in 1926 to 87,749 in 1947.[78] Despite economic depression and war, the Welsh became a motoring nation.

For most people, the vehicle which was of greatest assistance in eroding the 'friction of space' was the motor omnibus.[79] From the 1880s, several Welsh towns had horse-drawn trams of the 'knife-board' and 'garden seat' type, which journeyed along rails on fixed routes. These trams were later powered by electricity delivered by overhead cables. Time, better roads and above all, perhaps, the First World War, with the demand it generated for trucks and the experience it gave to drivers, enabled the bus to realise its potential. The national rail strike of 1919 and improvements in the manufacture of buses, such as pneumatic tyres and firmer suspension, were also influential. From the 1920s, two distinct types of operator emerged; municipal authorities and private companies such as Rees and Williams, the South Wales Transport Company, and United Welsh. In some places, the links with the old electric companies were significant, for tramway operations in the Rhondda and elsewhere sought to diversify. Elsewhere, new commercial enterprises flourished where previously there had been no tram, train or trolleybus. The rail companies quickly realised that they could generate more traffic for their trains through providing a bus service linking remote villages to the main line.[80] The Great Western Railway and the London and North Western Railway provided such services. Bus operators fought a savage battle to undercut their rivals' fares and even to steal passengers. In the 1930s there were several reports of buses racing each other from bus stop to bus stop to secure the most passengers. People were terrified as conductors pulled passengers off the bus stop on to their still-moving buses.

Not everyone, however, welcomed the greater mobility of the masses. On a visit to St David's in August 1936, Patrick Abercrombie had the 'madly depressing experience' of finding the ancient town packed with visitors carried there by bus. Seeking solitude two miles away at the saint's grave on the headland, 'the second holiest place in Europe', he was horrified to find it packed with motor cars 'and hundreds of awful people . . . a really appalling menagerie'.[81]

Though the twentieth century is seen as the age of the automobile, rail travel continued to be of considerable importance. Both the London and North Western Rail Company and the much loved Great Western Railway Company (God's Wonderful Railway) greatly extended the number of miles of track in Wales – from 2,894 miles in 1870, to 9,177 in 1921. Above all, the number of passenger journeys increased. In 1871, the GWR and the LNWR had, between them, carried 54,119,271 passengers. By 1921, the number of passenger journeys had risen to 287,442,185 and remained at or around this figure throughout the 1920s and 1930s. In 1909, there were forty-four companies and rail lines in Wales, many of which carried passengers, though a number, such as the Penarth lines and the Corris light railways, were principally mineral and goods lines.[82] The railways gave rise to a number of subsidiary service industries providing food, drink and entertainment to passengers. From the 1870s, W. H. Smith sold books and magazines at more than fifty south Wales rail stations.

Communications technologies saw remarkable developments in the late nineteenth and early twentieth centuries. The telegraph gained in popularity and range from the 1850s. Amongst the most notable of its developers was Sir William Henry Preece (1834–1913) of Caernarfon.[83] Preece appeared to have a natural talent for the new technology and in 1877 he became electrician to the Post Office system and spent the next two decades directing the expansion and improvement of the British telegraph network. Preece also pioneered other technologies. In 1877, during a visit to the American inventor Edison, Preece suggested a method through which the human voice could not only be broadcast, but recorded. As a reward for his ideas, Edison sent Preece the first phonograph to be made. One of its first uses was to record Welsh folk songs, for Preece was the active president of the Welsh Folk Song Society. Preece also pioneered an early method of wireless telegraphy using induced currents and in 1896 he gave an enthusiastic reception to Guglielmo Marconi's new system using Hertzian waves.[84]

Those initial messages sent by Marconi from Sully Island to a recipient on the Welsh mainland gave rise to a number of enthusiastic amateur radio hams across Wales. Amongst the most famous was Artie Moore (1887–1947) of Pontllanfraith, who intercepted the Italian government's declaration of war with Libya in 1911 and the distress call of RMS *Titanic.* The gifted Moore later worked for Marconi and was a pioneer of an early form of sonar. By 1919, the discoveries had given rise to a relatively extensive industry.[85] In north Wales, message reception and relaying stations were established at Tywyn and Waunfawr, employing around forty to fifty people, many of whom were women. These innovations were soon followed by the establishment of a national radio network, which in addition to news and current events provided an extensive range of light entertainment for people. By 1943, more than 75 per cent of the nation's houses had a wireless or, as it became more familiar, a radio set. The establishment of the BBC Welsh region in 1936 was considered by the eminent historian Dr John Davies as one of the first truly significant confirmations of Welsh nationhood.[86] Despite its popularity, the new medium was a mystery to many. In 1941 Iorwerth Peate, visiting an elderly couple on the Epynt moors during the great clearances of people for an army base, noticed that, although hard of hearing, husband and wife were sitting as far as possible away from the radio. Enquiring why, he was told that the radio presenter had been coughing, and they did not wish to catch his cold.[87]

Such dumbfounded reactions to new technology can also be found in the history of the early cinema in Wales. In 1905, at Bangor, audiences were so startled by the image of a fast-moving train coming towards them that many viewers stampeded for the exits. The technology of the early cinema developed rapidly in the opening decade of the twentieth century as new cameras and projectors made production easier and clearer. Edison and several rival companies soon realised that they would make far greater profits in 'kinescope parlours' than they could from their kinetic 'peep-show machines'.[88] These parlours, more affectionately referred to as the cinema, created a better environment in which to view films.[89] In Wales, William Haggar (1851–1925) was a notable pioneer in filming and broadcasting movies. His 'stock company' was his own family (his wife and eight of their eleven children appeared in his films). Haggar's *The Salmon Poachers* (1905) was the world's highest-selling film before the First World War.[90] By 1921, 1,834 people were employed in Welsh theatres, music halls and picture palaces, a figure that increased to 3,011 in 1931. By 1951, around 3,577 were employed exclusively in cinemas.[91] Despite its depiction as the entertainment media of masculine 'American Wales', the backbone of the cinema audience was 'working-class women, housewives and young single girls'. In the 1940s the much maligned women's pictures, costume dramas such as *Madonna of the Seven Moons* (1944) and *The Wicked Lady* (1946), were the main attractions.[92]

The Welsh are often portrayed as being uninventive and unimaginative, but in a number of areas they proved themselves to be innovative and creative. Some, however, pushed the novelty of new media to their creative extremes. An air of mystery, bordering on bathos, still appears to hang over the history of Harry Grindell Matthews (1880–1941) for his experiments in attempting to produce a Death Ray in the 1930s on Clydach mountain. His legacy seems to lie in the realms of science fiction, as the inspiration for Batman's bat signal and the Daleks' death ray, rather than in 'serious' science, but his achievements were notable. He was the first to send a radio message to a plane and the first to establish a radio telephone (linking the Cardiff's *Western Mail* building and Newport's Westgate Hotel). In 1921 he created a 'talking picture'. He used light to record and transmit audio of a short interview with the explorer Ernest Shackleton just before his final fatal journey to Antarctica.[93] Unfortunately his invention went the way of the explorer and was forgotten until, in the 1930s, there were experiments by people such as Charles Francis Jenkins (1867–1934), who produced 'radio-vision', an elemental form of television which, despite the unclear, flickering images, was the basis for the world's first television station, W3XK in Maryland.

Technology and social change

> A'r syber fro o'r Bari i Borth-y-cawl yn gignoeth dan beiriannau rhwth y Diawl.
>
> (The gentle area from Barry to Porthcawl is raw under the Devil's infernal machines.)
>
> Iorwerth C. Peate, 'Cysgod Heb Liw', *Y Genhinen*, 14/3 (Summer 1964)

Taken together, these innovations and inventions created profound transformations in the way people experienced time and space.[94] Until the 1870s there were several instances of local time in Wales, most of which were fixed by astronomical observations of fixed stars. The Chester and Holyhead Railway insisted on setting its clocks by the Craig-y-Don gun, fired daily on the estate at 'noon', precisely sixteen and a half minutes after the hour local time. This was especially annoying to travellers, since the line principally served the Irish Mail, which ran on Greenwich time.[95] Most other railway companies demanded that times be standardised and codified. Eventually, in 1912, an international conference on time fixed the zero meridian.[96] The image of farm workers and 'guides to the fasting girl' waiting at Pencader station in the morning for the arrival of the afternoon train was now symbolic of a life more wasteful than idyllic. In the 1880s, most people leisurely consulted chain watches kept in waistcoat pockets. In the 1900s, many Welsh people feverishly checked the time on their wristwatch.[97] Punctuality and work discipline did not begin in the twentieth century, but it was greatly assisted in the age of the wristwatch.[98] Most works had clocking-in machines which logged a person's exact hours of work. For rich and poor, quite literally now, time was money.

The telegraph, whose development had been greatly enhanced when cables had been laid across the Atlantic in the 1870s, added to this sense of urgency. News now, even in rural Welsh newspapers, was quite literally 'hot off the wires'. Kate Davies remembered that the gathering swallows soon adapted to the village's newly installed telegraph wires, but that it took longer for Pren-gwyn's inhabitants to grasp their importance.[99] Stories unfolded day by day, hour by hour, almost minute by minute. News reporting became fragmentary and immediate. The new telegraphic style of journalism, much to the chagrin of Thomas Gee and others, used shorter sentences, fewer adverbs and simpler grammar. Journalism appeared to have speeded up. The *Western Mail*, the *South Wales Daily News*, the *Cambria Daily Leader* now contained far more daily and local news than previously.[100] The telephone gave the impression that people could quite literally be in two places as once. It also gave an immediacy to decision making that had not previously existed. It made life tense, vivid, alert. There was now no need to wait for answers, they were given at once. J. P. Morgan averted a financial crisis in 1907 when, over the phone, he extended $25 million in credit to several major banks threatened with extensive withdrawals.[101] News reporters around Wales filed reports from the courts over telephones and raced each other to be first with the news. The historian A. J. P. Taylor famously argued that the intensity of the crisis preceding the First World War was the result of the inflexibility of railway timetables, but the inability of diplomats to cope with the new urgency of the telephone was also a factor.[102] In 1892, telephone exchanges were opened in Cardiff, Swansea, Newport, Carmarthen, Holyhead, Bangor and Caernarfon. In 1897 there were 231 telephones in private houses in Swansea. By 1907, the local authority's telephone exchange provided 1,215 lines to subscribers.[103]

The new 'moving pictures' at the cinema, gave the impression of exaggerated speed, so that life appeared faster and frenetic. Cinematic news coverage was greatly accelerated in 1911, when a special express train outfitted with a dark room was used to develop and transport a film of the investiture of the Prince of Wales at Caernarfon at four o'clock in the afternoon, and have it ready for public viewing in London at ten o'clock that night.[104] In 1917, film footage of battles in the First World War caused a sensational reaction in Llanelli when a mother recognised her son as one of the dead. Photography and the cinema altered the experience of war for contemporaries. Even before the eleventh hour of the eleventh day of the eleventh month had tolled, the portraits of these mass media froze the images of those who died like cattle. In the cinema people would experience their dreams, their dreads and their desires in an emotional enlightenment that was created in the moving images of black and white.[105]

Life seemed to be accelerating to unacceptable, unprecedented levels. The bicycle was four or five times faster than walking and pneumatic tyres made the ride more comfortable. 'Everywhere life is rushing insanely like a cavalry charge, and it vanishes cinematographically like trees and silhouettes along a road', complained D. A. Thomas in 1912.[106] In 1903, the *Daily Telegraph* campaigned for a speed limit, at which C. S. Rolls protested: 'Our hereditary instincts are shocked at seeing anything on a road faster than a horse, but as our senses become educated, we shall recognise the fact that speed of itself is not dangerous, but the inability to stop is dangerous'.[107] In 1904, Parliament raised the speed limit for a car from the pace of a man walking in front of the vehicle holding a red flag, to twenty mph and then soon afterwards raised it again to thirty mph.[108]

In all areas of life, electricity speeded up all sorts of machines. In confectionery, G. E. Davies of Bridgend installed, at a cost of £3,000, a new electric powered sugar-boiling room which could produce an immense variety of sweets, including Black Sweets, Broken Scotch, Real Welsh Toffee, Cobbler's Mix, Shoe Leather and My Mother's Packet of Courting Lozenges.[109] In the late 1880s, new rotary printing presses could print more copies of newspapers than had previously been possible. In 1873, the infamous Edward Lloyd, publisher of *Lloyd's News*, the first newspaper to have a circulation of over one million, introduced the first web press. New electric Monotype and Linotype machines cast type in a way that would not change for a century. Compositors could now work far closer to print deadlines to ensure that the news literally was hot off the press. Electricity made houses safer, as people were no longer wholly dependent upon fire for illumination.

The swift, staccato movements of the stars of the early cinema also seemed to amplify the sense that life had accelerated. With creative editing, action could move as fast as it did in William Haggar's or D. W. Griffiths's last-minute rescues. The story could change settings as rapidly as the interval between frames and since, in the early movies, the picture was taken at sixteen frames per second and projected at twenty-four, people seemed to fly across the screen.[110] Bewilderingly, directors seemed to play with time itself; freeze-frames stopped time, whilst flashbacks took one back in time, before the action would resume at helter-skelter pace. The cinema dazzled audiences all around Wales. Luminous, numinous images projected on to a screen through veils of cigarette smoke invaded the public mind like a phantom army. People became voyeurs who could enjoy their greatest desires and dreads. The coming of sound, in the 1920s, one of the swiftest technological revolutions in history, further transformed film. It also transformed the stars. Gareth Hughes had been one of the most popular and highest-paid stars of the silent movies, but audiences were horrified when the drop-dead-gorgeous actor opened his mouth and spoke in a high-pitched, falsetto Llanelli accent. He eventually finished up as a missionary amongst the Paiute Indians. The magic lantern shows of the 1880s and 1890s had been magical but the speaking pictures, like spirits, created irresistible illusions. Audiences across Wales were seduced by synthetic romance and won by sublime love. The comic anarchy of the Marx Brothers, Charlie Chaplin, W. C. Fields and Mae West were infectious. The cinema provided an alternative reality for many people. At street corners all over Wales, people could be found who strutted like Jimmy Cagney, spoke like Humphrey Bogart, vamped like Marlene Dietrich, and even postured like Errol Flynn.[111]

The new technologies had a liberating effect on people's lives. As the price of bicycles fell, usage increased and people could travel further afield. Thus their social circles expanded, and broadened even further for people who could afford cars. Improved mobility increased the choice of marriage partners. Women cyclists, dressed in casual trousers and without the constraints of a corset, travelled around the countryside. No longer did a person who wished to travel over twenty-five miles have to arrange a change of horses. Social groups and Sunday School outings from iron towns and coal- and slate-mining villages ventured far afield to seaside resorts. The 1920s and 1930s were thus a new 'golden age' for some coastal towns, yearning for the pleasures and profits of their late Victorian heydays. One of the legends of Pontyclun was the annual charabanc expedition of the town's 'Jolly Boys Club' from the Windsor Arms. Occasionally, they actually reached their destination. Though the Jolly Boys had the discretion to keep the stories from their tours 'on tour', Dylan Thomas had no such prudence, for he revealed all the antics of his uncle and cronies in the tender short story 'The Outing'.[112]

It was not only the material world which was transformed by technology; the spiritual life of Wales also experienced significant change. In 1905, the embers of the country's religious fires were fanned into 'burning flames' by telegraphs, telephones and newspapers. The frenzied press reports in newspapers seemed to present Evan Roberts as omnipresent. 'Thou canst tell whence he cometh, nor whither he goes – like an express train, full steam ahead' recalled one eye-witness. It was not just the evangelist who travelled; crowds packed trains to attend the chapels at which he was due to speak.[113] Evan Roberts, 'the sky pilot', attracted countless followers in those remarkable years when the Holy Spirit seemed to many to be blazing the earth of Wales in 'the society of the spectacle'.[114] It was perhaps immensely significant and appropriate that Roberts prepared his first 'revival sermon' while travelling on the train from Newcastle Emlyn, where he had seen the devil, to Carmarthen. He tested himself to see if he was ready to preach by addressing his fellow passengers in the carriage. The captive audience discovered that he was ready to speak of salvation, as too did the startled travellers in the station when he alighted to change trains, the commandments in his eyes, Bible under his arm. The Great Welsh Revival quite literally was steam powered.[115]

Telephones were also liberating. Men took liberties in conversations with Marconi operators which they would never dream of taking in person. Couples courted on the telephone; some men even proposed marriage. The telephone reduced privacy with 'party lines', but it also strengthened bonds of comradeship and community.[116] Crime detection, as the Cardiganshire chief constable quickly realised, was greatly enhanced with the use of the telephone. By 1901, the force in this remotest outpost of rural Wales used telegraphs, telephones, typewriters and bicycles in their battle with the county's felons. Criminals also kept up with the times. In that year, local thieves stole a range of expensive electric goods from the newly electrified Frongoch mine, as well as several bicycles.[117]

Yet despite greater liberation for many, a careful reading of the literature, especially the newspaper press, reveals that there was an element of uncertainty and fear for many people in the early twentieth century. The bewildered commentator in the *Welshman* was not an unique voice. Many men, undermined by the greater use of machinery in mill and mine, experienced a crisis of masculinity and feared for their future. At the turn of the nineteenth century, all the mournful jeremiads had an enjoyable time predicting doom. Some even identified devastating new maladies – neurasthenia, neuralgia, nervous dyspepsia, nervous exhaustion, even premature baldness. All were the result of the new, faster, frenetic life. Those most susceptible to the illness were people at the forefront of new technology – telephone operators, drivers, railway workers, typesetters, engineers. Unlike hysteria, which was considered, until 1915, to be a female malady, neurasthenia was overwhelmingly a male problem. The advertisements for a 1903 patent elixir sold by the Rexall company christened the disease 'Americanitis'. Countless press advertisements and brightly painted posters and street-corner metal signs warned that the 1900s were a bad time to be a man. Across Wales, sanitaria, like Allt-y-mynydd in Llanybydder, and mental hospitals were a refuge for people who could no longer keep up.

This sense of exhilaration and then exhaustion can be discerned in the art and literature of the period. Will Evans, Ceri Richards and Graham Sutherland produced spectacular images of blurred dislocation. The Cardiff-born painter and printmaker Merlyn Oliver Evans (1910–73), in his Surrealist and Cubist works, gave visual expression to the dislocation and the broken patterns of space and time. In 1937, Myfanwy Evans organised a symposium, *The Painter's Object*, to promote these works.[118] In literature, the 'super-tramp' W. H. Davies's life was a saga of escape from respectability and responsibility. He wrote perhaps the best-known poem ever published by a Welsh person. In a series of wistful questions, he mused about the quality of life:

> What is this world if full of care
> We have no time to stand and stare.

and concluded

> A poor world this, if full of care
> We have no time to stand and stare.[119]

Prose writers writing in the pastoral tradition also seemed to express a nostalgic yearning for a gentler time. The tension between a speeding present and a slower past generated elegies about the good old days before the rush. *The Captain's Wife*, a novel published by Eiluned Lewis, is set in the years when steamships had finally conquered sail and monopolised ocean travel.[120] Sailing ships were portrayed as majestic and graceful, instead of unreliable and cramped. Speed and frenetic energy appeared to be the characteristic hallmarks of the 1904–5 Religious Revival in which Evan Roberts played such a crucial role. 'Evan Roberts travels quicker than his watch', wrote the Revd Morgan Jones, a Calvinistic Methodist minister from Llwydcoed, 'but the press travels quicker than Evan Roberts.' He added the bitter corrective, 'but shall we suggest that the Supernatural can travel quicker than the press?'[121] Evan Roberts himself put his sense of time's arrow's speed in a poem:

> Time swiftly moves from day to day;
> We see its footprints on our way.
> It rushes with bewildering light,
> And changes all things in its flight;
> But, yet, its movements lag behind
> The aspirations of the mind –
> Fond Memory clips to days gone by,
> But Hope must to the future fly.[122]

Roberts was perhaps a better preacher than he was a poet, yet his experience is characteristic of the neurosis of his age. In late 1905, exhilarated, exhausted, his flame extinguished, he disappears into the spiritual wilderness of England. Will 'Stamp', a part-time undertaker but a full-time wag in Merioneth, remarked when his brother-in-law died unexpectedly that 'even death is in a hurry these days'. William Howells wrote eloquently that:

> power has outgrown its servitude and the unprecedented speed of life has made people irritable, nervous, querulous, unreasonable and afraid. People are born and married, and live and die in the midst of an uproar so frantic that you would think they would go mad of it.[123]

3

'Bonfire of the Vanities': Ambitions, Aspirations and Education

Nid yw golud ond gwaeledd, – nid yw'r byd,
Er ei barch, ond gwagedd:
Dan sêr 'does ond oferedd,
Oes o boen i aros bedd.

(Wealth is but a weakness, – the world,
Despite its pride, is but vanity:
Beneath the stars is only waste,
Ages of pain awaiting the grave.)

William Williams (Gwilym Cyfeiliog), 'I'r Bedd'

Ambitions and aspirations, classes and masses

The difference between England and Wales is that England consists of an upper class, a middle class and a democracy, while Wales is just a democracy.

T. W. H. Crossland, *Taffy Was a Welshman* (1912)

Wales was, and in many aspects still is, portrayed as a land of limited ambition and low aspiration. The usual tale is that a farmer was the son of a farmer, who himself was the son of a farmer, who, in his turn, had been sired by a farmer himself the son of another son of the soil, and so on, with the story traced monotonously back along the branches to the roots of the family's generational tree. Substitute other occupations for farmer, and whether it was a miner, a miller or a milliner, then the same barriers of tradition and lack of opportunity were perceived to operate. In the time-worn phrase of one commentator, 'all jogged along the well-beaten paths of their forefathers'. The poet Albert Evans-Jones (Cynan, 1895–1970) evoked this when he wrote 'unig uchelgais llanc o'r wlad yw torri cŵys fel cŵys ei dad' (the only ambition of a country boy, is to cut a furrow like his father's).[1] For a girl, the options were even bleaker. In the immensely popular novelette *Teulu Bach Nantoer* by L. M. Owen (Moelona), the children discuss their ambitions with their mother. The boy wants to do good like Abraham Lincoln; the girl aspires to be a maid.

Many warned about the dangers of unrestrained ambition. Proverbs, those distillations of peasant and proletarian wisdom, were succinct: 'paid cnecu yn uwch na dy dwll tin' (don't fart higher than your arse hole), 'a elo yn hwch i Rydychen, yn hwch y daw yn ôl' (if you go as a pig to Oxford, as a pig you return) and 'a aned o'r hwch a ymdroes yn y dom' (born of the sow, wallows in the dung).[2] People were warned to watch out, for pride, no matter how little, went before a fall. Ellis Humphrey Evans (Hedd Wyn, 1887–1917) put it simply in one of his epigrams:

> Diddim yw anrhydeddau;
> Nid yw bri yn ddim ond brau.[3]
>
> (Honours are as nothing,
> Celebrity is fleeting).

Theological decrees dictated that one should not aspire to rise above or beyond one's allotted place. One of Caradog Prichard's favourite poems, by the 'supertramp' W. H. Davies, warned against ambition:

> I had ambition, by which sin
> The angels fell,
> I climbed and, step by step, oh Lord,
> Ascended into Hell.[4]

What doctors had to say about ambition from the point of view of health, was even worse. The ambitious man 'becomes pale, his brow grows furrowed, his eyes withdrawn into their sockets, his glance becomes unsteady and worried, his cheekbones become prominent, his temples hollow, and his hair falls out or grows old with time'. If these were the warnings of respectable doctors, then imagine the fears raised by quacks in Welsh newspapers. The only answer was to purchase their advice books, unguents and potions, which were efficacious in every way to alleviate the worst effects of ambition. The mental hospitals housed many unsuccessful ambitious people who believed that they were generals, captains of industry, even God. At the Liverpool National Eisteddfod of 1891, William E. Williams won the competition for the best *awdl* on the subject of *uchelgais* – ambition.[5] Despite a memorable metaphor claiming that persistence was the vehicle one rode along ambition's road to success, Williams's warnings against unchecked and unbridled ambition were as dire as some of the verses. Many of the warnings were issued so that overly ambitious and aspirational people would not upset society's natural order. People should know and remain in their allocated station.

The adversarial and antagonistic model of society, so beloved of the rural radicals of the 1870s, 1880s and 1910s and the Marxists in the twentieth century, placed two rival classes in competition with each other. Above or below ground, the Welsh worker was an oppressed character. These social modellers were excellent at noting polarities – landlord rivalled tenant, coalowner confronted collier, owner battled worker, capital fought labour, and so on, in incompatible social groupings. In Welsh historiography, this view has dominated, for politicians, historians and polemicists have deemed it appropriate to perpetuate this presentation. However, the argument that there was an unbridgeable gulf and an ever-deepening conflict between employers and employees, based on the irreconcilable differences and divisions between capital and labour, misunderstands and misrepresents the economic, organisational and social realities of the workplace. Capital was not monolithic, but divided into a host of areas – industry and finance, goods and services. Despite the establishment of a few large-scale companies, industry in Wales was still based on relatively small-scale operations. In 1911, according to the Factory Inspector's Report, there were 5,304 factories in Wales employing an average of twenty people.[6] William and Beryl Jones, the owners of Alltcafan woollen mill, established in 1885 in a precarious location on the river's bank at Pentre-cwrt, Llandysul, and employing twenty-five people, were probably typical of such capitalists. They owned the means of production which, in the classic Marxian analysis, placed Mr and Mrs Jones in the capitalist class, but they were hardly captains of industry.[7]

Miners and quarrymen, often regarded as the vanguard of working class militancy, also owned some of the means of production. The tools of their trade, the mandrills, hammers, crowbars, shovels and picks, were their own private property. Part of the ritual of a strike or lock-out was enmeshed in the theatre of men bringing their tools out of the pit. The significance of such a residual property stake in their work is not easy to assess. Did it evoke a deeper psychological involvement and pride in their work than was the case for people who only contributed their labour to the workplace?[8]

Capitalism was as much about cooperation and community as it was about conflict and coercion.[9] The troubled and tumultuous years of industrial discontent – 1893, 1898, 1900–3, 1910, 1915, 1921, 1925 and 1926 – stand out against a longer period of relative compromise. This is not to deny the existence of class and group solidarity, of workers fighting passionately and powerfully for their class interests. The six-month strike of miners in 1898 and their nine-month stoppage in 1926 provide ample and eloquent testimony of solidarity and steadfastness. The bitter legacy of the quarrymen's strike, which lasted for an unbelievable three years between 1900 and 1903, was a slate that would never be wiped clean; industrial relations were as unyielding as the slate they sliced. But the rhetoric of working-class unity and solidarity was not always matched by reality. Indeed, the rhetoric often failed to realise reality; the working class was too sectional, too localised and too fragmented. This was clearly shown in the 'Coal Wars' of 1910–11. Workers of the Cambrian Combine and Powell Duffryn found themselves facing their companies alone, having failed to persuade miners in neighbouring valleys to join with them. The miners, disunited, were defeated but the lesson was soon forgotten. In 1926, the miners were abandoned after nine days and the General

Strike became yet another conflict in which they were on their own.[10]

However true the two-class model might have been as a description of the impact of the 'dark Satanic mills' on Manchester society in the 1840s, the development of Wales in the years 1870–1945 followed a more complex path towards a structure which Marx had not foreseen.[11] There was a proliferation of new professions – the battalion of sales people and shop workers, the army of clerks and office workers, male and female, who by trade, status and pay were difficult to place within a class system. Above them in salary, and perhaps status, were those members of 'higher' professions – doctors, lawyers, teachers, administrators – whose numbers, qualifications and incomes were all expanding as the twentieth century progressed. Thus some commentators outlined a tripartite model for society, giving room between the upper, aristocratic level and the workers for another grouping, the middle or middling classes. One commentator claimed that this 'really was a class and it really was in the middle . . . It was separated from the class above and the class below'.[12] However, closer examination suggests that this group also was too big and too varied to be a single class, and was not separated from its alleged superiors and supposed inferiors. Indeed, none of these social groups were distinct monolithic structures. Groups merged and melded into each other according to factors such as income, status, social standing, manners and morals. It was, and is, impossible to allocate a social class to some people – to what social class does a journalist belong? What about the class role of women? And what about those social groups who do not have an occupation?[13]

Decline and fall or adaptation and survival, whatever the fate of a class, its composition and coherence was often in the eye of the beholder. The size of all social groups obviously depends on how they are defined. Whether the boundaries are set by education, wealth, income, environment, upbringing, social networks, or morals and manners, the devils are in the detail.[14] In gathering this detail, it becomes clear that 'class' or social group boundaries were fluid. The upper, middle and working 'classes' were each 'imagined communities'. The divisions between them could not be drawn scientifically or sociologically with any exactitude. As with definitions of national identity, those characteristics which were used to define social classes gave rise to considerable problems. Wealth was, and is, an obvious defining feature but it varied greatly within, let alone between, social groups. Respectability, eagerly claimed as the defining characteristic of their group by both the middle and the working class, was equally problematic.

Such subtleties and differences are lost in the traditional classic social analysis based on the differences between social classes. It might therefore be more instructive to view Welsh society not in terms of classes or masses, but in terms of a complex hierarchy.[15] Photographs taken of Welsh workers by the Liverpool photographer John Thomas, such as those of the post office staff at Llanfair Caereinion in 1885 and Llandovery in the 1890s, or the shoemakers at Trawsfynydd in about 1885, reveal strict orders of hierarchy. The photograph of John Ashton's shop at Carno, Montgomeryshire about 1885 is an even clearer representation of status and hierarchy. John Ashton, the owner, the only person allowed to sit, is in the centre front. His male and female lieutenants stand behind him, in receding order of importance. The further away from the boss people are positioned, then the less authority they have and the unhappier they appear. Furthest away of all are the maid and the outdoor servant – even the dog appears to be higher in rank and affection than these poor souls.[16]

Class issues were pondered by D. Caradog Jones and A. M. Carr-Saunders in their *Survey of the Social Structure of England and Wales*, first published in 1927. 'Do social classes exist?', they asked. 'We hear less than formerly of the "upper", "middle" and "lower" social classes', they reported and their view was that this was right. Despite their best efforts, they failed to recognise an upper class, and as for the middle class, 'it never was anything more than a heterogeneous assemblage of very diverse and non-cohesive elements'. The working class, or what they called the 'wage-earning element', was, they revealed, a divided group. Their conclusion was that social classes were a 'sheer figurement of the imagination . . . and . . . that it was a mistake to speak of class divisions and class distinction today'. When the survey was republished in 1937,

Jones and Carr-Saunders saw no reason to revise their original findings, and so, in conclusion, they repeated their question: 'is it not a misreading of the social structure of this country to dwell on class divisions when, in respect of dress, speech, and use of leisure, all members of the community are obviously coming to resemble one another?'[17]

An important social distinction in Welsh society was the division between 'professional' and 'unprofessional'.[18] All business people were, to a greater or lesser extent, profit-orientated, whilst many professional people were, by definition, insulated from the direct play of market forces, subscribing, as many of them did, to an ethic of 'service'. In some cases, professions proudly asserted their sense of a separate identity, even within the professions. Scientists, for example, such as Dr E. J. Williams, often asserted their superiority. In 1919, aged only sixteen, he told a friend, without apparent boasting, that before he was thirty, he would have a fellowship of the University of Wales, an 1851 exhibition scholarship, a DSc and a fellowship of the Royal Society, all of which he duly achieved.[19] The sense of a 'calling' was clear in his personal history. Gradually, the notion gained ground that those who owed their position to learning were superior to those social classes based upon birth, manual labour and the possession of capital. There were also divisions and tensions in the way people won their livings. Some lived off dividends; a significant but forgotten social group, especially in Cardiff and Newport, were rentiers, many of whom were women. Such people did not 'work', but lived off rental income. Others lived off profits, especially from commerce and business. Yet others, such as surveyors, lived off the fees they charged their clients. At the turn of the twentieth century, an increasing number, including school teachers and a range of officials employed in the growing public sector, drew salaries. Thus the notion grew that such people did not have a job, but a career.

The spread of income within the middle class was enormous. At one extreme there were some individuals who were almost, if not actual, millionaires, such as the Phillips family (bankers), the Guests and the James-Jenkins family (industrialists) and the Brains family (brewers). For a lucky handful of professional men, too, incomes could be high; Alfred Thomas Davies, a successful barrister, was drawing fees worth between £10,000 and £15,000 p.a. and a permanent secretary in the civil service, such as Sir Guildhaume Myrddin-Evans (1894–1964), could earn between £2,000 and £2,500 p.a. Sir Bartle-Frere, who bumbled and blundered into war with the Zulus, earned over £10,000 a year as a diplomat in the 1880s. But most professional men in 1890 received less than £500 p.a. Barristers earned on average £478, GPs £395 and dentists £368, while many clergymen on £206 p.a. had an income lower than that of skilled industrial workers in full employment, such as boiler-makers. Still further down the income scale was the elementary school teacher, on an annual salary of £154. Teachers, like many other members of the much derided lower-middle class, often lived in genteel poverty, aspiring to a middle-class lifestyle without the wherewithal to achieve it. Small shopkeepers and clerks suffered the added disadvantage of job insecurity.[20]

In general, in 1900, no one could really afford a lifestyle that qualified for membership of the middle class without at least an income over the tax threshold of £860 p.a. It was a social expectation that such people should employ at least one domestic assistant. Yet many people quite obviously could not afford such help (certainly not live-in help) and paid little or no income tax, while many privileged manual workers did both. In 1921, in Glamorgan, there were 3,560 men and 29,950 women who derived their livelihood from domestic service of some type.[21] The major difference between the manual workers and those of the lower levels of the middling classes was that the latter had received a more protracted education and did not work with their hands. Thus an important distinction drawn by contemporaries was that between mental and manual labour.

As at its upper level, the frontier between the working and middle classes was poorly defined, with a large and variegated population living in a border area. The derogatory term 'plebeian' was devised to describe the inhabitants of this rather ambiguous social world. Neither middle nor working class, this group was especially prevalent in the urban areas, particularly in Llandudno, Rhyl, Tenby and the new coastal towns. How, in class terms, are we to describe groups such as lodging-house keepers, landladies, publicans, street vendors, and superior domestic servants such as governesses and ladies' companions?[22] Much to the chagrin of landlords, sub-letting was common across Wales. In Cardiff, an estimated 37.4 per cent of people who leased properties took in either a single lodger or entire families in order to supplement their income. In the mining communities in north and south, the practice was even more common, for they had a surplus of single men and a shortage of accommodation. Some beds were even let on a night and day shift basis. In social terms there was probably little difference between both parties to these arrangements, but what effect did this relationship have on their standing and status? Jane Blaker (1869–1947) was a close friend and confidant of the Davies sisters of Gregynog, but was she their equal in class terms?[23] Mr and Mrs Evans, who kept the Atlantic Hotel on the Esplanade in Tenby, are problematic. Were they aspiring working-class people, up on their luck, or despairing middle-class down on theirs?

Work

> Gwerin y graith, bonedd pob gwaith
> A pherthyn i honno wyf fi'
>
> (A scarred people, the aristocracy of work
> Is the group to which I belong)
>
> T. E. Nicholas (Niclas y Glais: 1879–1971),
> *Cerddi Gwerin* (Aberystwyth, 1912)

Work has often been viewed as the cornerstone of Welsh society. It conferred identity, social status and standing to individuals and, most obviously, provided a wage, or at least a reward. Attitudes to work were complex and contradictory, so that it is difficult to identify a homogenous 'work ethic'. Work was both a duty and a drudge, a benefit and blight. Even in the twentieth century, in spite of the best efforts of masters to instil work discipline, many workers were still devotees of St Monday, with a few of the more devout canonising St Tuesday.[24] In his memoirs, David Rees Griffiths

(Amanwy), remembered the excited anticipation of the sleepless night before his first day at work, at ten years of age, at Carmarthenshire's Betws mine in 1892. But 'getting disenchanted' with work was soon part of his and most apprentices' industrial education.[25]

Work was almost a kind of sacrament, for 'useful toil' was a valuable remedy for that notorious mother of all vices, idleness. For many, work was not merely an economic imperative and a moral duty, but an all-absorbing psychological passion. Some followed the coal owner David Davies's example and worked eighteen hours a day. 'Duw fendithier slafdod' ('blessed be drudgery') proclaimed a collection of sermons in 1903.[26] The secular wisdom of proverbs echoed the saintly – 'gloywaf arf, arf gwaith' (the best weapon, work). Poets eulogised both work and workers; 'awdlau moliant' (songs of praise) were sung to many occupations. Gwilym R. Tisley composed perhaps the best such *awdl* to the collier:

> Caner a rhodder iddo glod dibrin
> Y werin a'i caro;
> Nydder y mawl a haeddo
> I arwr glew erwau'r glo.[27]
>
> (Sing and proclaim praise to him
> The hero of the common people;
> Carve deserved praise
> To the brave hero of coal's acres).

Elfed in his 'Rhagorfraint y gweithiwr' sang:

> Nid cardod i ddyn ond gwaith
> Mae Dyn yn rhy fawr i gardod'[28]
>
> (Not charity for man but work,
> Man is too great for charity).

Behind the emphasis on the social, economic and moral imperatives of labour one can discern the rudiments of an altogether more positive view, which instead of representing work as a tiresome means to a desirable end portrayed it as intrinsically satisfying in itself and stressed its potentialities for human happiness and fulfilment. Many authors evoked the 'gangs of prattling females' engaged in haymaking, who chattered incessantly.[29] Washday was another time when women, who usually worked alone, could enjoy company. Again, tongues, allegedly, never stopped wagging. The ritual of the day began with the boiling of water, then the warm waves of bleach would wash over the whites, the Sunday best, then the underwear, some much worn, some, much to the embarrassment of aunts and elder sisters, flimsier and scantier, and finally the sweaty and heavily soiled work clothes.[30] In a sense people's enjoyment of such tasks was fortuitous, for it was in the fair weather of summer that agricultural workers worked their longest hours.

In the period 1870–1945, two notions of time clashed.[31] To the farmer time is work; life is work; work brings subsistence and independence.[32] In the towns, time and work had other meanings: productivity, surplus, profit, comfort, leisure. Internalised rhythms of labour were replaced by learned skills and norms. Gradually more and more farmers grasped the notions of productivity and the use of time and appreciated that subsistence farming, far from being the road to a glorious autonomy, was the essence of futility and self-exploitation.

Work, in most occupations, was expected to fill all the hours of daylight. Even when the Eight Hours Act was passed in 1908, many employers treated the legislation as permissive, so that individuals still spent most of their lives at work.[33] Miners would only see the sun briefly on a Sunday between October and February, for they went to and returned from their dark work in darkness. Thus, for many, it was during the long hours of labour that their individual identity was forged. There were working people who also had reputations as singers, dancers, drinkers, wrestlers, boxers, lovers, preachers, storytellers, but work probably remained the moulding characteristic. Men in particular often looked to their work as their source of identity. Hence the nicknames conferred on individuals – Butcher Beynon, Dai Bread. If men were what they did, women, by contrast, tended to be defined by what their husbands or fathers did – Mrs Dai Bread One, Mrs Dai Bread Two, or Nansi Ferch y Pregethwr Dall.[34] This is why the mass unemployment of the

1920s and 1930s was such a traumatic and tortuous experience for so many people. It not only robbed them of their livelihoods, but also deprived them of a profoundly important part of their personality.[35]

In the early twentieth century, analysts influenced by Mill, Marx and Durkheim, tried to construct a general sociology of work,[36] but their best efforts all floundered against a patchwork of almost infinite variety. Within a single occupation, hours of work, practical techniques, methods of recruitment, physical hazards, and division of labour between the skilled and the unskilled, together with the entire custom, language and philosophy of working life, could vary profoundly. Agricultural labourers, often viewed as a down-trodden, depressed and poverty-stricken class were, in the vicinity of Cardiff, Newport and Swansea, actually an independent and affluent group, confidently conscious of their market value.[37] The role of women in the workplace was often problematic. In the woollen industry and the clerical trades they were often highly skilled workers in their own right, whereas in the dockyards they were usually unskilled appendages to a male labour aristocracy.[38] New employment opportunities for young girls and women were created in the munitions and armaments factories during the First and the Second World Wars at Pembrey, Bridgend, Hirwaun, Mold, Pontypool, Newport and Cardiff. The number of insured female workers in Wales increased by 135 per cent between 1939 and 1945, as opposed to only 30 per cent for the whole of Britain. In 1941, more than 70 per cent of the 28,327 munitions workers at ROF Bridgend were women. In November 1940, Alderman Degwell Thomas warned that south Wales was on the verge of a 'cultural revolution' as young girls, who had once been regarded as a 'liability in the miners' homes', had become the main breadwinners.[39] The most important activity undertaken by women, work in the home, was not even acknowledged as genuine work, although it was the nation's largest single occupation. Moreover, work was not confined to the 'working classes'. Just as attitudes to work varied from class to class, so too did people's viewpoints of class and occupation and the identities they conferred. Yet, despite such differences, the centrality of work as a pillar of social, economic and moral life makes it imperative for us at least to consider how contemporaries grappled with issues of life and labour, skill and status.[40]

The data of occupations recorded every ten years as part of the general census of population provide some indication of how the ambitions of people were satisfied or frustrated. In 1871 the employment profile of Wales was dominated by agriculture. In all, some 111,815 men and 13,541 women gained their living from the land. The figure for women, in particular, was probably greater, for the Herculean labours of wives, daughters and spinster sisters were mostly unpaid and unacknowledged. After agriculture, the occupations that employed most men were mines and quarries (89,656), metals (53,727), building (33,603), conveyance of goods (26,547), food and drink (19,078), dress (18,142), and professional (9,047), domestic (6,133), and commercial (5,427) occupations. In all some 61,274 men were employed in occupations which were simply described as 'other', a reflection of the terminological inexactitude of the census enumerators, the difficulty of categorising employment types and people's uncertainty as to their status. Women, in 1871, found most employment opportunities in domestic occupations (83,896), dress (29,886), food and drink (8,187), professions (3,862), metals and machines (3,134) and 'other' occupations (3,320). As with their sisters who laboured on the land, there were undoubtedly many women who worked in a host of occupations on an unpaid basis. Many shopkeepers, for example, could not survive unless their wives, summoned by a bell, served customers.[41]

The censuses are often mute witnesses to profound social and economic changes. The occupational tables in the 1951 census reveal the devastation that had befallen mining and quarrying. No longer was this the major occupational group for the Welsh. That role was now occupied by metal workers with 112,430 men. Mining and quarrying was in second place employing 110,000 men and 7,345 women. Transport and communication had increased to employ 86,167 men and 5,353 women, indicative of the revolution that had taken place following the invention of the internal combustion engine. Agriculture employed 79,457 men and 10,267 women, whilst other 'heavy industries' such as labouring employed 67,736 men and 17,988 women. Stationary engine-driving and building, both heavily masculine trades, employed respectively 22,472 and 63,098 men. The commercialisation and professionalisation of Welsh society had expanded since the 1920s. The occupational category of services, sport and recreation now employed 67,059 women and 31,960 men, clerical 45,393 women and 36,715 men and sales 60,996 men and 42,219 women, whilst 'professional workers 'accounted for 37,326 men and 30,334 women. Administrators and managers employed 15,691 men but now apparently fewer women. Although the war had ended in 1945, men were still being enlisted for national service and thus in 1951 there were 20,776 men in Wales in the armed forces.

The transformation in Welsh society down to 1951 had been remarkable. It is notoriously difficult to ascribe social categories to occupation, but Wales had shifted from being a nation predominantly employed in physical work to one which was now principally engaged in lighter, perhaps more 'middle-class' activities. Group all the heavy industrial occupational categories together for both men and women, and in 1951 they provided employment for 494,713 individuals (484,268 men and 10,445 women). In contrast, occupations which were not reliant on muscle power, in 1951, gave employment in the same year to 598,171 individuals (349,255 men and 248,916 women). Despite the presentation of Wales as a masculine, working-class nation in which heavy extractive industry was dominant, in actual fact, in 1951, the Welsh were overwhelmingly not engaged in heavy manual labour.[42]

The general patterns of employment in Wales were mirrored in the particular experiences of individual counties. Radnorshire had only 7,045 men and 2,111 women in paid employment in 1871; this decreased to 6,629 men and 1,793 women in 1951. Unsurprisingly, over half of the county's people were employed in agriculture. Most women, in 1951, found employment in 'services, sport and recreation' (including the intriguing group 'personal services'), whilst most of the county's men not employed on the land laboured at building work. The occupational statistics offer sharp commentary on the social and economic devastation of Merioneth. In 1871, two occupational groups were dominant; agriculture provided work for 7,611 men and 769 women, and mining and quarrying gave work to 4,220 men and 14 women. By 1951, agriculture accounted for only 3,493 men and 402 women, whilst mining and quarrying employed only 1,058 men and no women. Between 1871 and 1951, the total numbers employed in Merioneth had fallen from 20,410 men and 6,821 women to 14,347 men and 3,856 women. In Glamorgan, the period 1871–1951 saw the swift rise and fall of mining and quarrying as occupations. Mining still dominated in 1951, with 61,463 men and 17 women employed, but the glory days when it had provided employment for more than 100,000 men had ended. In 1951 there were almost as many sales workers (30,052 men and 20,445 women) in Glamorgan as there were miners. Heavy and extractive industries were no longer dominant. Some 217,289 people still found employment in Glamorgan's traditional occupations, mines, metals and labouring, but 292,872 were now engaged in newer professional and commercial activities.

There had been a substantial organisational change since the 1870s. In the 1860s, most companies, apart from the very largest, employed a solitary clerk to 'double entry book-keep' and copy letters in a ledger which would have been familiar to Bob Cratchit.[43] But by the 1900s, colliery, slate, shipping and iron companies had acquired a white-collar establishment which performed the routine tasks of lower industrial management: record-keeping, calculation of wages, payments, storekeeping, and (from 1912) deduction of contributions for national insurance. They used telegraphs, typewriters and time clocks to monitor production and profit. At the turn of the twentieth century, many areas of expertise that were crucial to business management and advanced production in a global economy, such as accounting, advertising, marketing, surveying, and electrical, mechanical and structural engineering, were added to the establishments of several companies. These white-collar workers were either based in small offices at quarry or pit-head, or in larger buildings in the commercial and managerial centres in Cardiff, Swansea, Barry, Bangor and Wrexham. A hierarchical order operated here as it did elsewhere in Welsh society. In her poignant novel, *Traed Mewn Cyffion* (Feet in Chains), Kate Roberts artfully delineates the gulf separating quarryman Ifan from manager, steward and foreman.[44]

'The Corn is Green' – education, 'the great escape ladder'

> My own experience, extending now over thirty-seven years in Wales, has witnessed a Renaissance period, a time of extraordinary activity, of rapid development and reconstruction. So completely have the mental outlook and social life been transformed, that anyone who had known the Principality before the eighties, and had been cut off from all communication with it ever since, would hardly recognise his surroundings if he returned to it now . . . During this brief period, a great system of secondary schools has been established, and the small and struggling College of 1872 has grown into a National University with four times as many teachers as the original college possessed students.
>
> H. R. Reichel, 'Patriotism, True and False', *Welsh Outlook* (1921), 104–6.

The self-congratulatory epistle of Sir Henry Rudolph Reichel (1856–1931), published in the current affairs magazine *Welsh Outlook*, could have added his own equally remarkable transformation from 'Irish Rudolph' to 'a great Welshman'.[45] His view is typical of the heroic portrayal of the educational development of Wales. The schoolteachers, in their worn, dark suits and academic regalia, appear as the militia of a new age, harbingers of enlightenment and a modern message that reconciled the benighted masses with a new world, superior in well-being and knowledge. As one of the chroniclers of Welsh educational history has noted, 'the development of Welsh education shows that history is no respecter of logic . . . Wales was in the singular position of building its educational system from the top instead of the bottom'.[46] The process was also assisted by the efforts of many people who lived outside Wales. In the 1850s and 1860s, groups of London-based Welshmen had chastised the educational shortcomings of Wales and campaigned for their improvement.[47] In 1846, William Williams, the MP for Coventry, had infamously raised questions in the House of Commons, which led to the notorious Education Report of 1847 – the hated Treason of the Blue Books.[48] Even stranger to relate, the Welsh university movement was initiated by a body of Welsh clergy ministering in England, whilst Reichel himself had directed his reminiscences to the Manchester Welsh Society on St David's Day, 1921.[49]

In a sense this 'top down', 'outside-in' approach is not surprising. Many claimed education was a democratic force enlightening the expanding family of voters. However, the kind of education adopted in Wales, which in principle claimed to be egalitarian, was in practice inegalitarian. The values preached by the teachers were not on the whole values which inspired, or were aspired to, by the Welsh masses.[50] Rather, mass education could be seen as an attempt by the elite to avoid a mass civilisation, and to impose aristocratic values on the people. Education also had a profound influence on social relationships. Examination success and failure separated people, branding some bright, others failures. Education represented an organised onslaught on regional and local eccentricity, in the name of good taste and higher culture. Literary and verbal skills became prized at the expense of physical strength or other talents. Birth or wealth, by themselves, no longer sufficed to ensure consideration. New dividing lines cut across old social barriers. Public examinations and school certificates became a new way of judging people, clashing with the traditional systems. The main beneficiary was probably the new mandarinate, which emerged with a complicated hierarchical organisation and a largely self-recruiting membership. Contemporaries were conscious of this situation. In *Welsh Outlook* in December 1919, J. Tywi Jones complained 'we were simply robbed of our birthright by a foreign system of education and its paid servants . . . our system of education was moulded to help the few favoured ones to get on in the world'.[51] Educating greater numbers also had a profound psychological impact. The grip of old beliefs, superstitions and customs began to wane. In some respects, urban values were imposed over those of the countryside, but though the schools attempted to discredit and undermine certain ways of thinking and behaving, they were not wholly successful in abolishing them.[52]

It is the structures and systems, the bricks and mortar of the buildings, that have, understandably perhaps, featured most prominently in the history of education in Wales.[53] The late nineteenth century saw a remarkable acceleration of the educational development of Wales and the Welsh. From the 1870s onwards, the new Jerusalem would be an educated world. In 1869, there were 509 elementary schools dotted around Wales, 209 of which were provided by the Church of England's National Schools movement; by 1877, following the landmark Education Act of 1870, there were 1,316 elementary schools. This number increased gradually to 1,730 in 1903, and to 1,909 in 1938. A similar pattern of growth is to be seen in the history of secondary education. In the 1860s, though there were a few ancient grammar schools that offered bursaries and scholarships, only a few pupils could take advantage of them. In 1867, for example, there were only 1,110 boys and 140 girls in Wales receiving an education in endorsed grammar schools. In secondary education, the landmark act was the Welsh Intermediate Education Act of 1889, which set up school boards and empowered them to establish secondary schools. By 1906, the number of pupils had risen to 8,412 boys and 8,757 girls, and it rose again to 23,414 boys and 21,971 girls in 1938.[54]

There was also an increase in the number of teachers to instruct and inspire the growing numbers of pupils. In 1871, an estimated 917 teachers worked in the elementary schools of Wales. By 1903, their number had increased to 11,916 and it rose again to 13,685 in 1914. Alongside them, in that fatal year, were 1,014 secondary school teachers. It is noteworthy that teaching was, from 1913, overwhelmingly a feminine occupation. From that year on the number of women schoolteachers always outnumbered their male counterparts.[55]

The years down to 1914 also saw a substantial growth in university education in Wales. In 1872, when the university opened its doors in a gothic extravaganza of a building on the seafront in Aberystwyth, there were only twenty-five in the brave band of brothers – the first university students in Wales. Their ranks swelled gradually; by 1894 there were 903 students in the newly established University of Wales, with its branches at Aberystwyth, Bangor and Cardiff. The number rose again to 1,234 on the eve of war in 1914, and to 1,892 men and 720 women in 1938.[56] The University of Wales, through the constituent colleges and their teacher-training centres, taught and trained the teachers who would serve at all levels of the Welsh educational system. There also developed, within the universities, a professional cadre of people who spent their entire careers within academic life. How some would have coped with life outside their ivory towers is debatable, for academia at least gave them the opportunity to cultivate their eccentricities. The pattern became quickly set for a host of people – stay in university education for as long as possible and then get a permanent post. Many seemed to have enjoyed being students more than studying. Tom Ellis (1859–99), politician and Welsh nationalist, spent ten years of his brief life at Aberystwyth and Oxford. The poet T. H. Parry-Williams (1887–1975) also spent a decade studying in an impressive group of universities that included Aberystwyth, Jesus College, Oxford, Freiburg and the Sorbonne in Paris, before settling back in Aberystwyth. For such people education was not just the key to unlock one's future, it was the future. The universities also provided the educational foundation for a host of people to enter a range of professions.

Systems and schools are valueless without a fundamental social transformation that renders the learning and teaching imparted meaningful and relevant to pupils and parents. The date of the establishment of a school was, and is, significant; but, without more deep-seated changes in society, the schoolroom would remain an island. It was of immense importance that the legislation of 1870, 1889 and 1902 required all children to attend school and to do so free of charge.[57] But the attendant changes in society – better transport, better roads on which children could get to school, altered values and perceptions, changing occupational and employment patterns – meant that what the schools offered was appreciated by Welsh society. It was only when what the schools taught made sense that they became important to those whom they sought to teach. It was only when what the schools said became relevant to recently created needs and demands that people listened to them and, appreciating this relevance, took heed of the rest of what the school had to offer. People went to school not because school was offered or imposed, but because it was useful. The world had to change before this came about.

There were reports of excellent standards in Welsh schools before the 1870s. One hears several reports of village schools that imparted a good fund of knowledge and of countrymen who knew how to read and actually did read. The Cribyn area in Cardiganshire, for example, had a number of schools run by inspirational individuals. The Revd Rees Cribin Jones (1841–1927) received his early education in John Davies's school at the Three Horse Shoes pub, and then established his own school in Newton Nottage. His son, also a minister, Watcyn Samuel Jones (1877–1964), was educated at the Revd David Evans's school at Cribyn (1892–4). But these were perhaps the exceptions.[58] There is no need to revisit the tortuous episode of *Brad y Llyfrau Gleision* (the Treason of the Blue Books) of 1847 to find reports of the abysmal and atrocious conditions that existed in Welsh schools.[59] Government inspectors on both sides of the 1870 divide were eloquent in their condemnation of Welsh schools. Many schools must have been like the one at Betws Gwerful Goch, Denbighshire, which was held by an elderly spinster, who could teach only prayers, and 'the first two rules of arithmetic . . . she had heard of a third but had never learned it'.[60] Inspectors complained that to many pupils letters, words and sentences were formulas and spells. 'No child understands what he reads', complained one inspector at Dolgellau in 1871. In such circumstances Latin was no more difficult, no more incomprehensible, than English. Many a village child 'could rattle along in Latin like a phonograph, without understanding a word of it', and was capable of writing in four different hands, accomplishments most impressive to their illiterate parents.[61] In many classes across Wales, inspectors complained that children 'recited by rote, what they do not understand'. Teaching them must have been like training parrots.[62]

The physical condition of many schools was parlous. In 1890, the master of Esgairdawe school in the parish of Pencarreg complained in his logbook of the dampness of the walls and declared that it was impossible to work in the school during windy weather, as smoke was blown back down the chimney.[63] In 1894, the headmaster of Caeo school noted that 'the school has been exceedingly cold all this winter. The windows ought to be mended as the children are too cold to write'.[64] The pitch-pine-partitioned lavatories were Augean stables of filth. Given such conditions, it is not surprising that the historian, in reading the logbooks of the country's primary schools, encounters a catalogue of sickness and early death. In 1903 the headmaster of Coedmor school recorded that 'it was impossible to go on with the work owing to the children's coughing',[65] the snot running out of them in ropes. The condition of the children was further affected by the adverse conditions which confronted many of them on their long journey to school.

This problem of travelling long distances over bad roads was common to all children in the rural schools of Wales. The words of the master of Penwaun school in Capel Iwan can stand for many: 'The situation of the school is such that during very wet and stormy weather it is impossible for the children to attend.'[66] On Mynydd Hiraethog, on the Berwyn and Aran mountains and Yr Eifl in Llŷn and Penllyn, children were prevented from attending school by rain and storms in October, November and February, whilst snow in December, January and March meant that there were many lonely masters and mistresses in schoolrooms across Wales. The braver pupils, booted and balaclava'd, eventually made it through to cough and chant their times tables, touch their toes and calculate how long it took a slowly dripping tap to fill a bath – though they would never warm themselves in one when they reached home.

The Education Act of 1870 and the establishment of schools across the country did not of themselves create a new attitude towards education.[67] In virtually all rural parishes, it is a fairly accurate generalisation to state that school was, for most pupils, a peripheral and ephemeral experience. Even when the politicians decreed that schooling was compulsory, people in rural and urban society viewed it as secondary to the dictates of economics or the agricultural calendar. In urban areas, the pattern of apprenticeship at an early age, whether to a miner, shopkeeper, chemist or another trade, necessitated that a person sought employment as soon as possible. This is one of the factors which helps to explain the fact that, as the authors of the Aberdare report on intermediate education found to their surprise, only fifteen boys in a population of over 10,000 in Carmarthen town received a grammar school education.[68] The novelists Howard Spring (1889–1965) and Caradog Prichard both left school at twelve years of age, as did the scientist Alfred Russel Wallace, one of the few figures of true genius to be raised in Wales. Between 1870 and 1910 only one person from Cefnarthen undertook the fouteen-mile journey to Llandeilo Grammar School and only a handful went from many villages to Friar's School in Bangor.[69]

In rural areas the elementary school was of secondary importance to the requirements of farming. School attendance was cyclical, following the demands of working the land. In June 1895 the master of Nantcwmrhys noted:

> The attendance for this week again is very low. Several of the scholars are employed in helping their parents to cut turf (which is used as fuel) on the surrounding moors. A country schoolmaster has many difficulties to contend with which the town master knows nothing of.[70]

Two weeks later he added: 'The farmers have commenced mowing and attendance is very low in consequence.'[71] At the end of July he reluctantly declared a holiday for the duration of the hay harvest. The next month was worse. 'Attendance very low today and yesterday owing to the corn harvest, deem it advisable under the circumstances to give a week's holiday.'[72] Following the resumption of school in September, delays in the corn harvest meant that attendance was still low. October saw further disruption, for the potato harvest was a crucial element for the economic survival of cottagers. By April a new agricultural cycle had commenced: 'Several of the children kept at home, the farmers have commenced sowing and harrowing.' In May the children were gathering stones in the fields.[73]

The timing of the harvest varied according to local climatic factors and the organisation of agriculture. In the north, harvests were later and briefer. The fact that a cottager could owe a debt of labour to more than one farm meant that particular children were absent from school for long periods. This made it difficult for school boards to regulate holidays, but it is doubtful whether many board members, themselves being farmers, wished to interfere. The logbook at Cefnarthen noted in August 1882 that since the weather was bad for hay there was a good attendance. Across Wales other elementary schoolmasters recorded the ebb and flow of the agricultural season in their logbooks.[74]

Cultural events could also cut across the schools. In Tonypandy school, on 15 May 1905, the master reported that 'a Gymanfa with the Methodists and a bazaar with the Baptists reduced very materially the attendance on Monday'. Whilst, on 14 July, 'all the children are away in Sunday School outings'.[75] In urban areas the children of the poorest families were needed for childcare, homework and a host of odd jobs.[76] The earnings from child labour in scavenging, working in shops and workshops, even from begging, kept families from the workhouse, and no priority could be greater than that. Thus, the introduction of compulsory full-time education cut across a culture where children were considered to be a useful economic asset and valued for their potential earnings. Schooling was sacrificed for short-term economic expediencies. Education, for all its alleged and acknowledged benefits and value, had to play second fiddle.

Many families could not afford boots, so many children went to school barefoot in all weather. In his reminiscences, a former miner from Hook in Pembrokeshire recalled his fellow pupils as sad, rickety, tubercular children. Dressed in ragged, misfitting clothes, they walked barefoot to school, hair uncombed and laden with lice, unwashed and dirty.[77] Teeth rotten, skin pockmarked by flea bites, they were treated with contempt. The small fires in large schoolrooms were inadequate, particularly on wet days when children, having walked long distances, arrived wringing wet. There was the agony of trying to dry scores of wet garments while children took turns to sit by the fire, their clothes steaming, before going back to their desks. In their memoirs, Picton Davies and Kate Davies remembered overcrowded classrooms, incomprehensible English, leaking roofs, dripping lavatories, and no running water (in some schools water was carried in bowls from the nearest fountain). These conditions, coupled with physical punishment, did not encourage a love of books.[78]

These problems were compounded by the fact that the teaching provided by the school was incomprehensible. The schoolmaster sought to impart knowledge in English whilst the monoglot Welsh children stared open-eyed and closed-mouthed.[79] The master of Rhydcymerau school, on taking up his duties in 1874, 'found the children very backward in everything. Not one was able to speak a word of English.'[80] In the north, the problem was more severe in the monolingual Welsh communities of Merioneth, Caernarfonshire and Anglesey. At Caeo school the arrival of the five Evans children in 1892 added to the problems: '[They] have just arrived from Patagonia. Unable to speak English since their languages in Patagonia were Welsh and Spanish, both of which they speak and write'.[81]

Many schoolteachers adopted the 'Welsh Not' to punish Welsh speakers for the use of the language inside the school grounds. To the torment of his own conscience, the young Beriah Gwynfe Evans, later one of the great champions of the language, punished small children in his classes for using their mother tongue.[82] A passage from the Esgairdawe logbook of 1887 would have been echoed throughout the country: 'Today the teacher informed the scholars that no more Welsh is to be spoken in school hours within the school premises. The Regulation is to come into force on the first of November.'[83] Thus it was that Kate Roberts, herself a teacher, and others saw schools in Denbighshire as 'y peiriant mwrdro' – the machine that murdered the Welsh language.[84]

Other teachers adopted the more practical and prudent approach of using the Welsh language as the medium for learning English. Dan Isaac Davies (1839–87) and others in the Society for the Utilisation of the Welsh Language advocated the greater use of Welsh in classrooms. In 1908 His Majesty's Inspectors endorsed this approach, informing the master and the school board at Llanllawddog that:

> The scheme of work should be drawn up with a view of training the children to an intelligent and accurate observation of their surroundings rather than to aim at mechanical results. To this end, Welsh should be methodically taught and utilised to a greater extent than at present.[85]

But even in this there were difficulties. The observers who noted the reticence, shyness and unresponsiveness of Welsh children in the rural areas of Wales failed to appreciate that many of the concepts which they sought to teach were urban and therefore strange and alien to the children. The children's world was full of the rich and concrete idioms of local speech. In west Wales, a person who wavered was like a 'rhech mewn pot jam' (a fart in a jam jar), a fat boy was like a 'llo yn sugno dwy fuwch' (a calf sucking two cows) and a fat man 'fel pot llaeth cadw' (a pot of kept milk). These and countless other phrases coloured the speech of rural people. In contrast, the new knowledge, the new worlds that the children encountered in the classroom were incomprehensible. The fact that more girls were being schooled and taught English had profound implications for the Welsh language. More mothers could speak English to their children if they chose to do so. Women had perpetuated local speech, but this might now change. In *Free Associations* (1959), Ernest Jones, the biographer of Freud and one of the fathers of British psychoanalysis, remembered his schooling at Llandovery:

> All the masters were from English public schools and they never let us forget their opinion of our native inferiority, from which our only hope of redemption was through cultivating the *Herrenvolk* whose outposts they were.[86]

The logbooks and reports of school inspectors offer valuable and vital insights into the conditions which prevailed in Welsh schools in the years 1870–1945, but alternative views are offered in the reminiscences of individuals, which reveal that their schooldays were a tale of malevolent teachers and miserable children. Many noted the shock to sensibilities when children moved on from the lavender-smelling, motherly women teachers of their infant years to the angry, old, embittered men who taught religion, music and games in the upper years. Children passed from Miss to Miss, season by season, until they reached 'the psychopath in chief – the magenta-nosed headmaster'. The transfer from 'infants' to 'proper school' was often presided over by gorgons, 'hard and thin as driven nails', to whom children took an instant dislike. Belts and straps were used in legendary abandon with vigorous enthusiasm, for corporal punishment was rife in virtually every school and at every level. Like the psychopathic headmaster named Jones who taught Charles Dickens, Welsh schoolmasters never seemed to lose their delight in wielding a cane. 'Preis Scwl', the psychopathic headmaster in Caradog Prichard's semi-biographical *Un Nos Ola Leuad,* was a character from the Brothers Grimm, the kind whose liking for children expresses itself in terms of recipes. Dictionaries were used not for enlightenment, but to thump thick heads. Wynford Vaughan Thomas remembered his Swansea schooling as 'dreadful and dreary', the teachers 'draconian'. His education started after he left school.[87] Each year the rituals of humiliation became more elaborate. To physical cruelty, teachers added psychological torture. Pupils were called to the blackboard, not so much to test their knowledge as to publicly display their ignorance. Teachers became apoplectic when they discovered a notebook covered with the wrong coloured paper. Some hopeless half-wits never lasted a day in these erroneous zones without receiving a beating. Terror ensured that many schoolrooms were quiet – just the sound of thirty or so concentrating children and the scraping of thirty or so pieces of chalk as thirty or so minds went blankly and bleakly through the motions. It was no surprise that on the final bell of the day the class would erupt to freedom.

In their reminiscences, people such as Patrick Hannan, Byron Rogers and Dannie Abse, all of whom were in school in the later part of our period, considered that conditions and the gap between teacher and taught in the secondary and grammar schools were even worse.[88] School was a period of almost universal boredom, when the teachers were people who spoke in other people's sleep. Sport 'was a torture in a cold room, jokingly called "the gym"', with its unscalable ropes and painful medicine balls. Here, the 'sadist in daps' presided over ritual humiliations and sweaty somersaults. At lunch time when a clutch of lunch boxes was opened in synchrony, 'the smell was asphyxiating'. Gwyn Thomas, the broadcaster, novelist and short-story writer, himself a teacher for twenty-two years, was at the top of his form in his recollections of his schooldays. Of his career, he recalled that 'teaching was a profession that holds more opportunities for static misery than most others. Our classrooms reek of dead and wasted talents.'[89] Nevertheless, there were some remarkable success stories. William Meloch Hughes (1860–1926), photographer, minister, adventurer and author, was in the same class in Ysgol Tan Domen, Bala, as Tom Ellis,

O. M. Edwards, J. Puleston Jones, Mihangel ap Iwan, and the ill-fated Llwyd ap Iwan.

Conditions were even worse in the public schools of Wales, like Rydal in Colwyn Bay, Llandovery College and Christ College, Brecon. In these emotional ice-houses, boys were regularly thrashed, bullied, fagged and flogged. This was just by the other boys, the teachers often meted out even worse indignities. Conditions sound more akin to a brutal prisoner-of-war camp than an educational establishment. It was a world of bullies, beatings, battles and bruises in which brains were effeminate. For many children, childhood finished abruptly in the hour they entered these grim places. Griffith Pugh, the physiologist who helped the 1953 team to climb Everest, left the Edenic setting of his family's ancestral home, Rhos-y-Gilwen in Pembrokeshire, for public school in the 1920s. He recalled:

> The great thing about going to a public school is that you know that nothing as bad as that can ever happen to you again . . . It took me forty years to recover from my public school.

His daughter, Harriet Tuckley, would probably dispute the claim that he got over the experience for she recalled a dysfunctional, unemotional, unfeeling parent.[90]

People gradually began to appreciate the possibilities which schools opened up, and recognised that their material interests could be best served by sending their children to school regularly. This profound change took place parish by parish in Wales in the period leading up to the First World War. The recognition of new possibilities and of the school as a key to their expectations was in full evidence by the 1920s. Passing the 'eleven plus' and getting a scholarship to a grammar school was now an event of profound significance for the child and had a glint of a better future. Education, in the 1920s and 1930s, was seen as the 'great escape ladder' from depression and deprivation. Emlyn Williams's auto-biographical play *The Corn is Green* has at its core Miss L. C. Moffat, a strong-willed Welsh schoolteacher working in a depressed coal mining town in north Wales, who inspires one of her charges to flee poverty for the glories of Oxbridge's ivory towers.[91] In 1945, the successful Broadway production of the play was turned into a film starring Bette Davis (herself of Welsh descent) as Miss Moffat, and thus the concept of education as the escape route became firmly embedded in the Welsh national character. The factual model for the fictional Miss Moffat was Grace Cooke, Emlyn Williams's teacher at Holywell. Richard Burton and Stanley Baker were another pair rescued from oblivion by dedicated schoolteachers.

By the First World War there had been a natural evolution, in which the school certificate, significant because of the material advantages it could help secure, became an end in itself. This is why so many individuals in so many families were willing to sacrifice themselves in order that an academically brighter brother, and sometimes sister, could graduate and so gain entry to a higher profession.[92] Not all could be accommodated in Wales. The 1930s saw an exodus of talent from south Wales as teachers sought employment opportunities in the south-east of England.

Schools brought suggestions of alternative values and hierarchies and of commitments to other bodies than the local group. They eased individuals out of the latter's grip and shattered the hold of previously unchallenged cultural and social creeds. The cultural underpinnings of Welsh society, already battered by material changes, were further weakened by shifting values. Manual labour was devalued – or, more often, the natural aversion to its drudgery was reinforced. The elementary schools neglected producers. The school glorified labour as a moral value, but ignored work as an everyday form of culture. The emphasis was placed on learning and passing examinations. The schools inverted the old balance, for now the idle boys and girls were the ones most likely to be pressed into hard physical labour. The successful were now the ones most enterprising with their books. The rewards of work, in twentieth-century Wales, came to those doing what had not previously been considered to be work at all. Book-learning had been condemned as suspect, but now it was seen as vital. Primary education had been accepted, and demanded, as the essential basis of human dignity and equality, the indispensable stepping stone to advancement and social mobility. Education, especially when allied with ambition, was one of the most powerful forces affecting Welsh society. Richard Jones

(Glaslyn) expressed this succinctly in *Cymru* in February 1907 – 'the future of Wales', he predicted, 'is in the ink bottle'.[93]

4

'Ffair Wagedd' – Vanity Fair: People, Class and Hierarchy

Cos din taeog: efe a gach yn dy ddwrn
(Tickle a serf's bottom, he will shit in your fist).

Hen ddihareb (old proverb)

The decline and fall of the Welsh aristocracy?

After a long illness in a London hotel, Miss Clara Thomas departed this life at an opportune moment, for the country was then within a few weeks of the opening of the Great War. The coffin was brought down to Llwyn Madoc, and her funeral took place on a glorious afternoon in mid June, with the birds singing and the falls of the Cammarch murmuring gently in the warm air . . . I spoke to the vicar of Eglwys Oen Duw of ensuing changes that were inevitable. 'Yes, Mr Vaughan, it is all over!' he replied briefly, as he pointed to the valley, to the school, to the church, to the pretty cottages around. Yes, it was, in truth, all over. A long rein of beneficence and practical piety had come to an end; the reign of the Welsh squires . . . was at last finished and done with.

H. M. Vaughan, *The South Wales Squires: a Welsh Picture of Social Life* (London, 1926), pp. 142–3

Herbert Vaughan's *South Wales Squires*, a sort of *Brideshead Revisited* with the occasional fact, is an elegiac and eloquent lament for a lost social class. Vaughan's is the haunting and daunting tale of the transience of human life and the impermanence of worldly dominion. His lachrymose outpourings would not have been out of place in the pages of Ecclesiastes, St Augustine or Gibbon. Miss

Thomas's death is a requiem not just for a woman, but for a class. It is a lament not just for a life, but for a whole way of living. Vaughan charts a move away from an era of confidence and certainty to a time of weakness and woe for the Welsh aristocracy that had taken place in his own lifetime. He portrays a crumbling society, cemented only by a scattering of gilt and glitter. But the aristocracy of and in Wales had, like all social groups, seen considerable change.[1] Country and town houses were bought and sold, demolished and built at will, as architectural fashion changed, and as owners came and went. They were not untouched and unchanged shrines, but places that were lived in. This was not an ancient regime but one in a state of continuous change. It is easy to forget, but vital to remember, that many of the wealthiest families in 1870 traced their riches back no further than a generation or two.

In the 1870s, land was still perceived as conferring the highest level of social status and standing and the Welsh aristocracy, as proud as the Hapsburgs, remained perhaps the most class-conscious social class. The alleged antiquity of the aristocracy was displayed in a range of heraldic symbols.[2] On a host of family crests and emblems, heraldic figures dashed and dodged. In this menagerie of status, the mythical merged with the real as demons, dragons, wyverns, lions and a host of animals, rampant, winged, maned, horned, sharp in tooth and claw, cavorted. Even more prized than a family's crest were the high-flown honorifics of titles conferred by royalty. These designations of social standing, signifying precise degrees of rank, were jealously guarded and zealously gathered by the Welsh gentry. Of the 163 individuals included amongst the great landowners of Wales in 1873, fourteen were baronets, two knights, sixteen lords, six earls, five marquesses and one a duke. In the late 1870s, another four members of the class were raised to baronies, four to lordships, one to an earldom and one to a dukedom. These were the status elite of Wales, acutely conscious of their preferment and prestige, their pride and their panache. The fortunate who reached the rank of knight looked down on common, lowly commoners. The blessed who crossed the next threshold into the peerage considered themselves a cut above the knights.[3] It was one of the great ironies of Welsh history that Lloyd George, the hammer of the Welsh aristocracy, was responsible for the creation of more aristocrats than any of his predecessors. In 1910, he tormented and taxed Welsh landlords, but in 1918–22, in a desperate bid to raise money to assist his political ambitions, he traded honours with reckless abandon.[4]

The *Return of the Owners of Land* (1873) reveals the inequalities within the ranks of the great landowners of Wales.[5] In all, 61 per cent of the land of Wales was held by a mere 672 owners. But within this group, 163 individuals represented an elite within the elite; they owned 1,702,057 acres or 41 per cent of the land of Wales, and luxuriated on a total rental income of £1,910,850.[6] Although this group had an unassailable and unassailed position at the top of the social scale, it was not an unified class but riven with divisions, for even within the elite there were hierarchies. In terms of land owned, the real acreocracy was a select group of twenty people, each of whom owned more than 20,000 acres. At the top was Sir Watkin Williams Wynn of Wynnstay, the proud and privileged owner of 141,909 acres. Lord Cawdor was next, with over 51,538 acres in Wales and a further 50,419 acres in Nairn and Inverness. Next in the ranks of the super-landowners came Lord Penrhyn, holder of 43,974 acres, the earl of Lisburne, possessor of 42,706 acres and Lord Tredegar with 38,750 acres.

Acres might give status, but they did not necessarily confer riches. At a time when land was expected to yield an annual rent of £1 per acre, there was an enormous variation between the profitability of various estates. In 1873, the lands of the marquess of Bute earned over £9 per acre, while those of John Herbert of Llanarth Court, the earl of Jersey and Thomas Charlton-Meyrick of Bush, Pembrokeshire, each yielded more than £5 an acre. In contrast, Thomas Pryce Lloyd of Nannau, the earl of Lisburne, Baroness Willoughby de Eresby and W. T. R. Powell of Nanteos barely achieved in excess of two shillings an acre. Urban and industrial estates were far more profitable than rural and agricultural properties. Thus the wealthiest man in Wales, perhaps the world, was the fabulously endowed marquess of Bute, with an annual rental income of £203,613. Immortalised by Disraeli in his novel *Lothair*, his wealth enabled him to engage in eccentric, mystical, medieval fantasies on a prodigious scale;[7] he had no serious rival. In second place, with a rental of £124,598, was Lord Tredegar and third in this list of the mega-rich was Lord Penrhyn, who enjoyed an annual rental of £63,373. Then came Christopher Rice Mansel Talbot of Margam Castle, with rents yielding £44,175, who narrowly pipped Sir Watkin Williams Wynn, in fifth place with £43,274. There was then a gradual decrease down to the £3,000 per annum rental-income threshold which demarcated the super-rich of Wales.[8]

Generations of some families seemed to have reposed in resplendent splendour on their boundless acres for centuries. So rooted were the Williams Wynn dynasty of Wynnstay and the Philipps family of Picton Castle, that they almost appeared to be a physical part of the landscape. The Rices, Lords Dynevor, traced their lineage, through some creative genealogy, back to Hywel Dda. John Junior jested in *Vanity Fair*, 'it is said that the head of the Price family of Rhiwlas could show a written pedigree tracing his descent back to the original Adam',[9] 'it is said', in this context, being a synonym for unreliable gossip or conjecture, for genealogies were inventive and deceptive. Many families stumbled over the hazards of biology and survived through their female line. To give the impression of continuing through the male line, some dynasties resorted to the substitution or addition of surnames, hence the complexities of Campbell-Davys, Williams-Drummond, Wynn Griffith-Wynne, Battersby-Harford and Gwynne-Holford. These partners in hyphenisation adopted convoluted titles and linguistic gymnastics to strengthen the appearance of tradition. A lineage had to be safeguarded for it was a prerequisite for status.

A fact often forgotten is that a significant portion of the great landowners of Wales were women.[10] There is a somewhat gloomy portrayal of life in the country houses of Wales that contrasts the lives of men and women. While the men were out all day, hunting, shooting and riding, the women stayed behind closed doors sewing, thinking and waiting, listening to the dreary tick, tock of the hallway clock – the metronome of domestic depression. Yet the reality was vastly different, especially for the eleven women who, in their own right and on their own terms, were themselves great landowners. In terms of land owned, the greatest female landowners were

Baroness Willoughby de Eresby (30,688 acres), Sara Kirkby of Maesneuadd in Merioneth (16,023 acres), Clara Thomas of Llwyn Madoc, Breconshire (14,332 acres) – whose death, in 1914, was so eloquently lamented by Herbert M. Vaughan – Anna Maria Eleanor Gwynne-Holford of Buckland, Breconshire (12,728 acres) and Mary Anne Jane Corbett-Winder of Vaynor (6,693 acres). These manic impressive dowagers were highly effective and efficient characters running their own estates, organising the household and fulfilling the role that traditionally was undertaken by men.

There would have been more women amongst the great landowners of Wales had not the rights of ten women passed to their husbands upon marriage in the late 1860s and early 1870s. These included Johanna Isabella Dawkins Pennant, the heiress of Penrhyn and May Dorothea Phillips, heiress of Slebech, whose rights had passed to her exotically titled husband, Baron de Rutzen of Riga. Irrespective of their looks, their income must have been irresistible. Some husbands, however, must have learned the bitter lesson that nobody works so hard for their money as the person who marries it. Much Welsh land had been acquired by calculated courtships. To paraphrase Jane Austen, that astute chronicler of the follies and foibles of the landed elite in the nineteenth century, it was a truth universally acknowledged that a single woman in possession of a good fortune must be in want of a husband. The lineage property of some wives was safeguarded in complex legal agreements. Those who tried to disentangle them found a bewildering and obscure bundle of intersecting and conflicting rights.

'Aristocracy', Robert Lay once remarked, 'is a fair-weather way of life.'[11] In many portrayals of the Olympian, Elysian world in which the privileged and powerful lived, it was the women who were assumed to be most enjoying the good life. Their existence has almost universally been portrayed as being conducted within domestic borders ruled by their petty prides and provincial prejudices. Aristocratic wives were the vacuous and vacant hostesses at balls, soirées and socials who smiled at all, enchanted all.[12] Before the big day, the ladies' dresses would arrive from London or even Paris, in long black cases like coffins. Then there would be a hysterical coming and going of milliners, hairdressers and shoemakers, and exasperated servants would be dispatched after them with desperate notes to the fitters. At the events, orchestral manoeuvres in the half-light and candlelight would be eagerly watched and the slightest hand-kiss would be pregnant with meaning. Girls sent to finishing schools in England would return home to Wales, their accents refined and all traces of the melodic home intonation erased. An aroma of young smooth skin pervaded these events – the girls' bedsheets must have smelt like paradise. Invitations to Lady Penrhyn's soirées were an important barometer of social favour in north Wales. Those ladies overly touched by the local Nonconformist conscience tended to drown any gaiety, and were not asked again. The rites of passage of aristocratic families were marked with lavish rejoicings. In 1873, Edward Davies's twenty-first birthday was celebrated in Llandinam in Montgomeryshire by more than 6,000 guests, 3,400 of whom had been carried in four special trains from the Davies's coal pits in the Rhondda.[13] Menus detailed repasts of mountainous opulence.

The lives of aristocratic women were more complex than the stereotypical images of gilded idleness allow. Margaret Thomas, Amy Dillwyn and many others were successful in business. Leonora Philipps, Lady St Davids (1862–1915), a 'radical of the deepest dye', was a committed feminist. Her pamphlet *An Appeal to Women* (*c*.1891), was an attempt to rouse women to political action. Margaret Haig Thomas, *suo jure* Viscountess Rhondda (1883–1958), tireless campaigner for the women's suffrage movement, took over her father's business empire when he was appointed to government in 1915. In 1919, the *Directory of Directors* listed Visountess Rhondda, as she now was, as the director of thirty-three companies and chairperson of sixteen of them. In 1926 she became the first woman president of the Institute of Directors.[14] The movement for women's suffrage would have been far less effective without the efforts of several titled women.[15] In a host of spheres, they campaigned through press and protest to advance the rights of women.

Gwendoline Elizabeth (Gwen) Davies (1882–1951) and Margaret Sidney (Daisy) Davies (1884–1963) enjoyed lives of untold luxury.[16] They purchased a clutch of French Impressionist paintings, served as patrons of museums and established their own fine press in their home, Gregynog, which became a remarkable cultural centre. Yet their lives held not only the gilt and glamour of the very rich. When the First World War began, the sisters assisted Belgian refugee poets and artists to settle in Wales, and in 1916 they opened a canteen and a field hospital in Troyes for French troops. They saw at first hand that the First World War was not the gentlemanly, chivalric conflict that was so euphorically announced in August 1914, but total war and a total hell. Lady Muriel Paget organised an Anglo-Russian hospital on the eastern front, and her namesake, Lady Leila Paget, went off to nurse the sick in Serbia. Lady Caernarvon nursed in London, whilst many aristocratic ladies turned their mansions into convalescent homes and nursing hospitals for wounded soldiers.[17] At home and abroad titled women undertook a range of horrible tasks and witnessed terrible pain, pointless agony and nightmarish death. The privileged elite toiled long hours at dirty work in the same way that their sisters in lower social groups did.

It was their sumptuous and sensual style of living which goaded the radicals and the land campaigners to castigate the 'idle rich'. In the 1870s and 1880s, the Revd Evan Pan Jones and Thomas Gee campaigned eloquently for tenants and against landlords. In his newspaper, *Baner ac Amserau Cymru*, Gee described the landlords as 'dynion creulon, dihud, afresymol . . . yn sugno'r mêr o esgyrn eu tenantiaid' (cruel, unfeeling, unreasonable and uncaring men . . . devourers of the marrow of their tenants' bones).[18] In the campaigns against the House of Lords in 1910–11, Lloyd George, the consummate master of the political insult, took this tradition of radical protest to new heights in pillorying the aristocracy as 'an idle and parasitic class who toil not, neither do they spin'. 'Oh, those dukes', he once exclaimed with all his sham showmanship, 'how they oppress us.'[19]

The rhetoric was magical and memorable but it needs to be tested objectively against the evidence. Had Lloyd George looked around him, he would have surely realised how indebted he was to several members of the Welsh aristocracy. Henry Duncan McLaren, second Baron Aberconway, was his parliamentary private secretary until 1910, and a member of his wartime government at the Ministry of Munitions.[20] John Wynford Philipps, first Viscount St Davids, established the Lloyd George Fund and helped to set up the National Liberal political fund to provide Lloyd George with independent financial backing. Freddie Guest, scion of the great dynasty of south Wales ironmasters, was another influential aristocrat in Lloyd George's political world. From an early age Guest busied himself with the torment of others. Like so many members of his family, he sought promotion in the peerage and preferment in government. As had his brother Ivor and his cousin Winston Churchill, Guest crossed the floor of the house to advance his own cause. Upon his appointment as the Liberal Coalition chief whip in 1917, he became a significant and sinister political figure. For the next five years, Guest was responsible for raising money for Lloyd George's personal campaign funds. As a result he was closely involved with the sale of honours and probably set up Maundy Gregory in the title-touting business. He was completely cynical about honours and probably knew more embarrassing secrets than any other man in public life. Viscount Gladstone described him as Lloyd George's 'evil genius'. Even his obituarist in *The Times* hinted that Freddie Guest was not a nice man to know and that he had climbed the ladder to success, wrong by wrong.[21]

The aristocrats of Wales were the chameleons of Welsh political life. Naturally many people such as Lord Tredegar, Lord Powis and Richard John Lloyd Price of Rhiwlas were bred-in-the-bone Conservatives, but the Liberal party also had its share of patrician parliamentarians. The Labour party also had members of the elite in people such as Hugh Dalton,[22] the son of the Church of England clergyman and tutor, Canon John Neale Dalton, KCVO, CMG and Catherine Alicia Evans-Thomas (1863–1944), the daughter of a major Welsh landowner. Living in resplendence at The Gnoll, near Neath, Dalton was not obviously destined for a career as a socialist politician. Yet he became one of the best known labour leaders of the interwar and early post-Second World War period and one of the most influential intellectuals in politics of his generation. Despite an aristocratic pedigree, Wogan Philipps, second Baron Milford (1902–93), also found his sympathies veering to the left during the national strike of 1926, a process which accelerated after his experiences in the Spanish Civil War in 1936. He joined the Communist

Party in 1937. When he finally succeeded to the title as second Baron Milford in 1962, he used the occasion of his maiden speech in the House of Lords to argue for its abolition. For three decades, Philipps was the only avowed communist to sit in parliament.[23] His experiences in Spain were in marked contrast to those of Esyllt Priscilla (Pip) Scott-Ellis (1916–83). This 'dove of war', through a little naivety and a lot of love, worked as a nurse for the Fascists at Frentes y Hospitales.[24] Such complexities and subtleties are sometimes lost. Our history is often told in shades of black and white, in which the polar opposites of bad, grasping, greedy, lazy landowners, coalowners and ironmasters, and good, noble, industrious workers clash. Yet real life often deals with more than fifty shades of grey.

For men and women, it became increasingly difficult to maintain landed estates as the nineteenth century closed and the twentieth opened. Agricultural depression, government legislation and radical polemic reduced income and eroded status. In 1894, thirty-five farms of the Gwydir estate were sold by Lord Ancaster, who had come into Sir John Wynn's inheritance through a tortuous descent. The twentieth century opened with one of the greatest transfers of land ever seen in Wales, the liquidation of the Beaufort estate in Monmouthshire, the ancient inheritance of the Herberts of Raglan. This estate, extending over 27,000 acres and including Tintern Abbey, four castles, twenty manors and twenty-six hotels, was sold in 428 lots, only one of which failed to sell. Lords Harlech, Glanusk, Ashburnham, Denbigh and Winchelsea, all of whom were great landowners with greater interests outside Wales, followed Beaufort's example. Between 1900 and 1914, every major landowner with the exceptions of the giants of the south Wales coalfield, Tredegar, Bute, Talbot and Dunraven, sold some land, most of which was bought by the tenants.[25] Desperate for funds after his marriage to the spendthrift Lady Randolph Churchill, George Cornwallis-West mortgaged the Ruthin Castle estate. In 1920, separated from his wife and his money, he finally had to sell.[26] In 1912, Lord Penrhyn disposed of land in Llŷn worth £45,000, the Wynns of Rhug received £40,000 for farms in Merioneth and the duke of Westminster obtained £20,000 for property in Flintshire.[27]

Sales of land continued throughout the war. In 1915, the duke of Beaufort proceeded to dispose of a Breconshire estate and was emulated in Monmouthshire by the marquess of Abergavenny. In 1915 parts of the Kemeys-Tynte estates in Glamorgan and Monmouthshire were put on the market. A year later, Lord Tredegar sold much of his urban land in the Monmouthshire valleys, whilst in 1917 a portion of the Margam estate of the Talbots was sold for £22,000. In 1918, J. Capel Hanbury received £55,000 for a thousand acres of Pontypool Park. Other wartime sales included the Bodelwyddan estate in Denbighshire, the Sunny Hill estate in Cardiganshire, the Aberhafesp estate in Montgomeryshire, and the Hawarden estate of the Gladstones, ironically forced to sell, it was claimed, by punitive Liberal legislation. The end of the war saw no abatement in estate sales.[28] Between 1918 to 1922 every major Welsh landowner placed at least part of their estate on the market.

The histories of many landed families in these years were dreary journeys, a slow funeral procession of the decline of riches. Like sandcastles in an inrushing tide, the fortunes of the Tylers of Mount Gernos, the Lloyds of Bronwydd, the Lisburnes of Crosswood and the Powells of Nanteos were overwhelmed by their accumulated encumbrances. Lands were sold, houses were let, expenses were cut. One of the Powells of Gogerddan, once lords of all they surveyed, became a barman in Shanghai, another a tramp, while a third, allegedly, fled abroad with the proceeds of the Talybont Flower Show.[29] Symbolic of their masters' decline were the gardeners, brushing winter into their smoky fires. Yet, despite what J. A. Vann termed 'the Green Revolution' in the ownership of land, it is important to note that few of the major landowners of Wales had sold everything when the sales boom ended in 1922. In 1873, there were twenty very great estates in Wales, which exceeded 20,000 acres. All were still in existence in 1922.[30]

Contrary to the apocalyptic promises and prophecies of the radical press, the landed gentry proved itself to be a resilient and resourceful group. Despite the lachrymose portraits of the chroniclers of gentry decline and the tales of cobwebbed, crumbling mansions the opening decades of the twentieth century saw investment and expenditure. In and near to Cardiff, as the nineteenth century drew to a close, the marquess of Bute completed his gothic extravaganzas of Cardiff Castle and Castell Coch. In 1913–15, the Arts and Crafts architect C. E. Mallows designed a house and garden at Craig-y-parc, Pentyrch (Glamorgan) for Thomas Evans, whose fortune derived mainly from land and coal. The great exponent of the Italianate architectural style, T. H. Mawson, designed and then extended Dyffryn (Glamorgan) in 1906 for its owner, Reginald Cory. In 1908, the Liberal MP Hudson Ewbanke Kearley, Viscount Davenport, extended an old hunting lodge on Hiraethog Mountain. The new house, Gwylfa Hiraethog, at 496 metres above sea level, was the highest house in Wales, enjoying spectacular views. It was enlarged again in 1913 when Lloyd George spoke from its balcony to a large crowd. At the peak of activity just before the First World War, over 1,400 birds were shot in regular avian holocausts. By 1911, the writer and garden architect, H. Avray Tipping, had completed the rebuilding and restoration of Mathern Palace (Monmouth) and set out three superb gardens. But perhaps the most remarkable initiative was the bizarre and beautiful creation of the 'architect errant', Clough Williams-Ellis, at Portmeirion, which commenced in 1913. The years 1880–1914 have been described as 'the golden age for gardens' in Wales. The industrialist Henry Pochin laid out the superb gardens at Bodnant. At Shirenewton Hall (Monmouth), Charles Liddell, a wealthy shipper in the Far Eastern trade, laid out an ornate Japanese garden. At Brynkinallt, over 90,000 bedding plants a year were prepared in the hot house for the twenty acres of garden.[31]

Great expectations: nobility and mobility

> It is sometimes said that west of Newtown, the spirit of enterprise does not exist.
>
> Editorial in *Welsh Outlook*, February 1917

One of the reasons for their survival was that the aristocracy had never been isolated or islanded on their estates.[32] To survive, they had always diversified into a host of entrepreneurial and employment opportunities beyond estate walls. The church was one avenue traditionally open to the gentry's sons. The house of Dynevor, for example, had given a prudence of vicars to the church. The vicar of Swansea was, until 1920, an uncle of the sixth peer, whilst the fifth Baron Dynevor, who succeeded his cousin in the title and estate, was the son of a dean of Gloucester and himself vicar of Fairfield. When, in advanced years, he eventually succeeded to the title, he is said to have found running the estate a considerable burden. Bishop Lewis of Llandaff was likewise drawn from the squire class, for he owned the estate of Henllan in the parish of Llanddewi Velfrey, Pembrokeshire. Other squire-parsons, or 'squarsons', included Garnons-Williams of Abercamlais (Brecknockshire), Prichard of Dderw (Radnorshire), and Archdeacon William North, rector of Llangoedmor who was, at one time, professor of Latin at St David's College, Lampeter.[33]

The Church of England was not the only ecclesiastical career open to aristocratic siblings. The children of John and Elizabeth Louisa Vaughan, relatives of the Rolls family of Hendre, Monmouth, had a remarkable devotion to the Church of Rome. Four of their daughters became nuns (the fifth was only prevented from doing so by poor health), whilst of their eight sons, six became priests and three bishops – Herbert Alfred Vaughan, cardinal-archbishop of Westminster, Roger William Vaughan, archbishop of Sydney, and John Stephen Vaughan, auxiliary bishop of Salford. Another son, Bernard John Vaughan (1847–1922) was a celebrated Jesuit leader.[34] Whilst aristocratic sons entered the church for a vocation, daughters married into it from piety or desperation. Two of the four daughters of the squire of Nantgwyllt in Radnorshire married clergymen of very different types. Anna, the eldest sister, married the Revd Rhys Jones Lloyd, rector of Troed-yr-aur in Cardiganshire, whilst the youngest was married to the Revd William Williams, vicar of Llandyfaelog, near Brecon.[35]

The army provided another traditional, occasionally less dangerous, career path for sons of the gentry who provided a morbidity of majors. General Sir Charles Warren (1840–1927) combined a military career with a host of diverse interests, as did Field Marshal Lord Grenfell (1841–1925).[36] Grenfell served in South Africa, India, the Sudan, Egypt, Malta and Ireland. He was an Egyptologist of considerable attainment who conducted important excavations at Aswan in his off-duty hours. Grenfell's access to explosives was, sometimes, a considerable advantage to the archaeologist. He was also a talented amateur artist who used his skill well in painting the far-flung places to which he was posted.

The gentry had long been aware of the dangers of its loyalty to the military. Ronald George Elidor Campbell, of the Coldstream Guards, was killed in a skirmish with Zulu warriors near Isandlwana in March 1879. His younger brother, Frederick Campbell must have blessed that assegai, for he inherited the family estates at Golden Grove (Carmarthenshire), Stackpole Court (Pembrokeshire) and Cawdor Castle (Nairn). Such deaths were the tragic exceptions until the years 1914-18 saw a cascade of coronettted corpses. Captain Alan Peel, of the South Wales Borders, was killed in Cameroon on 17 November 1915. Less than a year later, on 3 September 1916, Lieutenant Robert Peel of the 4th Welsh Division died at Ypres. The Philippses and the de Rutzens of Pembrokeshire and the families of the earls of Denbigh and Powis also lost two sons in the Great War. Hardly had the bells fallen silent after welcoming in the new year of 1915 than they tolled at Hawarden, in mourning for William Gladstone, grandson of the former prime minister. Before the year's close, Lord Penrhyn lost his eldest son and two half-brothers and the precociously gifted MP, Lord Ninian Crichton-Stuart, was also dead. For the Llangattock family, wartime deaths quite literally meant the end of their line.[37] Laura Elizabeth McLaren (née Pochin), Lady Aberconway (1854–1933), industrialist, campaigner for women's rights and horticulturalist, lost one of her two sons in 1917. Winifred Coombe Tennant's beloved son Christopher died in the trenches at Ypres in 1917. Distraught and devastated at his death, Winifred sought to reconnect and recover their relationship through a remarkable range of spiritualist activities. Using the nom de plume of Mrs Willet, she worked as a celebrated spirit medium.[38]

For those who were left behind, the 1920s were pervaded by a palpable sense of loss – the empty chairs, the extra elbow room at the dining tables, a sense of ghosts. Lady Philipps could never believe that her son was not coming back and would leave the porch light on so that he could see his way home. The Second World War, as well as the First, blighted the blessed lives of Gwendoline and Margaret Davies, two of the richest women in Welsh history. In 1915, their cousins Edward and Ivor Lloyd Jones were killed at Suvla Bay and in Palestine. In 1944 Gwendoline and Margaret were devastated by the death of their brother, David, and soon afterwards by that of his son, Michael.[39]

Linked together in this way, it is easy to understand how so many have written of a 'lost generation', whose names are recalled and recounted on war memorials and marble tablets on church and chapel walls. On Armistice Day 1918, Alan Lascelles pithily and poignantly commented that 'even when you win a war, you cannot forget that you have lost your generation'.[40] C. F. G. Masterman, politician and historian, lamented what he described as 'the passing of Feudalism' on the fields of Flanders; 'the Feudal system vanished in blood and fire, and the landed classes were consumed.'[41] The aristocracy had fought with the chivalry and bravery of knights of old, but they had been 'slaughtered like cattle' and 'fallen like flies'.

As well as serving in the church and the army, many of the aristocracy were capitalists and commercial potentates of the first rank. By the 1870s, more landowners were more involved with the more profitable exploitation of their estates than ever before. Welsh landowners were active in the development of the commercial, mineral, and industrial resources available to them. This was nothing new;[42] as Britain evolved from the first industrial nation into the workshop of the world, landowners eagerly sought to profit. The new wealth garnered from coal, iron, slate and ground rents financed the giant gothic castles of Cyfarthfa, Clyne, Hensol, Margam and Penrhyn. The great landowners were not only involved with agriculture, but also with minerals and transport. Distinctions between arrivistes and aristocrats were blurred. In north Wales, the promoters and shareholders of both the Ellesmere Canal and the Montgomery Canal included Sir Watkin Williams Wynn, Lord Powis and Lord Clive.[43] In south Wales, it was Lord Bute who decided, in 1825, to finance and construct the Cardiff Docks, a decision which was to have momentous consequences for the region.[44]

These diverse involvements continued at the century's close, in the same way as they had at its commencement. In a famous and oft-quoted remark, Thomas Arnold, headmaster of Rugby, welcomed the steam train as 'heralding the downfall of the aristocracy. I rejoice to see it, and think that feudality is gone forever'. It is hoped that his teaching was of a higher quality than his power of prophecy, for the aristocracy of Wales rapidly went on the rails. The marquesses of Bute backed the Rhymney Railway as a means of bringing their Glamorgan coal to their Cardiff docks. Rival companies they always resisted; they contested and expressed strong opposition to the plans of David Davies to run a railway from the Rhondda to a new port at Barry. They also presented fierce opposition to the efforts of Sir George Elliott (1815–93) to develop the Pontypridd, Caerphilly and Newport railway to carry coal from Aberdare, Merthyr and the Rhondda valleys to Newport.[45] This railway, which greatly enhanced the commercial importance of Newport, where Elliot had promoted the construction of the Alexandra Dock in 1875, was eventually opened in 1893.

The Great Western Railway had a significant number of patricians on its board of directors. Sir Daniel Gooch (1816–89), the Ruabon colliery owner, was chairman in the 1860s and 1870s. Henry Oakley, owner of the Dewstow estate at Caerwent, served with distinction in the 1890s and 1900s. He used some of the dividends to finance the fabulous underground grottoes which stretched for five acres in the gardens. But perhaps the best example of patrician participation in the railways was the involvement of Frederick Archibald Vaughan Campbell, third Earl Cawdor (1847–1911) in the development and operation of the Great Western Railway. In 1890, he became a director and a year later, deputy chairman, and from July 1895 to March 1905, chairman of the company.[46]

The nobility were actively involved in the revolution in road transport. Charles Rolls, the younger son of Lord Llangattock, the Monmouthshire landowner, was one of the founders of the elite motoring company Rolls Royce.[47] Evelyn Ellis, a younger son of the sixth Lord Howard de Walden, made the first motor journey in Britain and continuously campaigned to raise speed limits in order to fulfil the car's potential.[48] The most famous upper-class motorist during the interwar years was Mrs Victor Bruce, who married Lord Aberdare's fourth son in 1926. She was the first woman to ride a motor cycle, the first to be in an accident, and the first to be summoned for speeding. 'Speed', she recalled in her autobiography, 'has always fascinated me since my very first pony bolted. Going slowly always makes me tired.'[49]

Other means of transport also created opportunities for the wealthy and privileged to prosper. Just before the First World War, Sir Samuel Instone (1878–1937) set up Instone and Co. Ltd of Cardiff to trade between Cardiff and Antwerp and London and Antwerp, with coal as the principal cargo. Together with his brothers, he set up the Instone Airlines, which flew from London to Paris in 1919 and eventually evolved in 1924 into Imperial Airways, pioneers of exclusive international vacations.[50]

Carmarthen-born Sir Alfred Lewis Jones (1845–1909) went to sea as a cabin boy with the African Steam Ship Company in 1859. Within only four years he was manager of the firm and in 1878 established his own company as a shipping and insurance broker. In 1879, he took a major part in the Elder Dempster Line Ltd, which ran steamships to west Africa. His dedicated, visionary style, forceful personality and abundant mental and physical energy ensured the success of the company, especially when, through the West Africa Shipping Conference, he created a cartel to control prices. On the strength of this Jones was able to diversify into African coastal boating and river services, hotels, cold storage, victualling, chandlery, cartage, oil mills, plantations, collieries and metal mines, and the Bank of British West Africa. By 1900 he owned the British and African Steam Navigation Company, with a fleet of 101 ships on a variety of routes. When he died, Jones was senior partner in at least twenty companies and chairman of five, president of the Liverpool Chamber of Commerce and of the British Cotton Growing Association.[51]

Traditionally it was for their debts that the aristocracy were most renowned, but a number also made significant fortunes from banking, commerce and the stock exchange, for gentlemen preferred bonds. John Howard Gwyther (1835–1921) of Milford Haven made a substantial contribution to the success of Chartered Bank as manager, managing director and chairman.[52] His detailed knowledge and experience of the Far East in Singapore, India and Shanghai proved invaluable in safeguarding Chartered Bank from the fate of several of its competitors. In the 1870s and 1880s, he argued correctly that gold and then bimetallism should be the basis for the Indian and other Far Eastern currencies. Although Chartered Bank remained his main interest, he also accepted seats on the boards of City Bank, Anglo-Egyptian Bank and Anglo-Californian Bank. Henry Duncan McLaren, second Baron Aberconway (1879–1953), was a director of both the National Provincial Bank and London Assurance. He was also director of English Clays, Lovering Pochin and Co. Ltd, the engineering company John Brown and Co., Bolckow Vaughan, Palmer's Shipbuilding and the Tredegar Iron and Coal Companies. From these companies he drew, in the 1930s, the income to fund the magnificent terraces and wonderful walled garden at the family's estate in Bodnant, north Wales.[53]

The most impressive figure in this portfolio of stockbrokers was John Wynford Philipps, first Viscount St Davids (1860–1938), financier, politician and another member of the Pembrokeshire gentry who prospered in the world of high finance.[54] The Philippses were a remarkable family, almost Sicilian in their use of preferment and power. St Davids's primary interests were in shipping but blossomed into investment trusts. By 1890, he was influential in the Oarium Investment Company, the Government and General Investment Trust Ltd, the Consolidated Trust Ltd, the Trustees Industrial and Investment Company, the Premier Investment Company, the London Investment Company and Barings Bank. He was also a director and chairman of several rail companies operating in Costa Rica and Argentina. St Davids was also active in British Electric, Associated Portland Cement Manufactures Ltd and British Portland Cement Manufacturers Ltd. To help control many of these investments, he arranged for the appointment of other family members, Ivor, Laurence, Richard and Bertram Erasmus Philipps, to their boards. By 1912 St Davids had established a substantial shipping empire known as the Royal Mail Group.

Minerals, not motors or merchandising, made a fortune for many. George William Duff (1848–1904) assumed the surname Assheton-

Smith in 1859, when the Vaynol estate near Bangor in Caernarfonshire, which included Dinorwic slate quarry, was bequeathed to him in his great-aunt Matilda's will.[55] For an inheritance of 36,000 acres of land with an annual rental of £25,000, he was willing to change his name but he retained both his moustache and 'a serious countenance'. The wealth created by the Dinorwic quarry, carved out of the south side of the Elidir mountain at Llanberis, enabled Assheton-Smith to indulge his passions for sailing and horse-racing. An animal lover, he also had a bizarre menagerie of wild animals at his Vaynol estate. He spent money to improve the land and built more than a hundred new farm houses for his tenants.

In the eyes of the magazine *Vanity Fair* and many others, slate was synonymous not with Vaynol, but with Penrhyn.[56] The Penrhyn estate had been active in exploiting slate since 1765 when Richard Pennant, a Liverpool merchant grown rich on the profits of West Indian sugar and slaves, commenced work. Under the leadership of Edward Gordon Douglas-Pennant, Lord Penrhyn (1880–6), the estates increased to more than 45,000 acres of land worth over £65,000 a year, but this was less than half the income produced by the 2,500 men employed at the quarries in Bethesda.[57] In 1886 George Sholto Gordon Douglas-Pennant succeeded to the peerage and to an inheritance which included 41,348 acres of land in Caernarfonshire, and the Penrhyn quarry, which, with 3,000 men, was the largest slate quarry in the world.[58]

Coal was the substance that fuelled the fortunes of many of the Welsh aristocracy. Henry Austin Bruce (1815–95), first Baron Aberdare, used the mineral royalties from the Duffryn (Aberdare) estate to finance a glittering political career which took him to the post of home secretary in Gladstone's first government.[59] Coal provided an even greater fortune to John Patrick Crichton-Stuart, third marquess of Bute (1847–1900).[60] Under his ownership the Cardiff docks (which his father had begun building) were completed, contributing substantially to both the prosperity of the city, and his own. When he died in 1900, Bute left an estate valued at £1,142,246.10s.4d. In spirit and substance, Bute was totally out of place in the nineteenth century. He regretted any time given to his 'irksome and fatiguing' business affairs, instead of his passions for early Christianity, Judaism, Islam and Buddhism, spent a large part of each year in the Mediterranean and the Middle East, and directed that his heart be buried in the Mount of Olives. He twice served as mayor of Cardiff, which he candidly conceded was rather a sham:

> I get on pretty well with my civic government here. My official confidants are nearly all radical dissenters, but we manage in quite a friendly way. They only elected me as a kind of figurehead; and although they are good enough to be glad whenever I take part in details, I am willing to leave these in the hands of people with more expertise than myself.[61]

His business interests he also left to people with more expertise and interest than himself, one of whom was the redoubtable William Thomas Lewis, first Baron Merthyr (1837–1914), the Bute estate's mineral agent and directing spirit and a significant coalowner in his own right. Lewis's stewardship was exercised energetically, shrewdly and conscientiously. The upward trajectory of mineral and urban incomes was quickened both by the proving of viable and valuable new coal seams and by soaring ground rents for residential properties in attractive situations. His personal colliery holdings were concentrated in the firm of Lewis Merthyr Consolidated Collieries, mine owners in the Rhondda and Ogmore valleys. Yet he was no inconspicuous back-room operator, for Lewis had a considerable public profile.[62] With his bald pate and long flowing white beard, Lewis had an uncanny resemblance to Santa Claus. In *A History of the Pioneers of the Welsh Coalfield*, Elizabeth Phillips concluded that 'despite Lord Merthyr's somewhat terrifying presence there was no kinder heart'.[63]

In industrial matters, however, William Lewis was stern, strong and severe. On the waterfront he defeated the dockers in 1891 with contemptuous ease.[64] He was 'unscrupulous' in his dealings with the Taff Vale Railway workers.[65] In the 1898 coal strike he refused to negotiate, even with the government-appointed conciliator. At the end of the strike, as the miners met to accept humiliating defeat, Lewis sent a telegram emphasising that he would accept no variation from the dictated terms; this provoked a question from the floor: 'Oddi wrth bwy mae hwnna, Mabon? Oddi wrth yr Hollalluog?' (Who's that from, Mabon? From the Almighty?), and the response, 'Yn agos iawn' (Very near it).[66]

If anyone was closer to the Almighty than Lewis, it was his successor as the employers' representative, Sir Evan Williams (1871–1959) a coalowner from Pontarddulais, Carmarthenshire.[67] His small, slight frame belied a steely constitution. Williams was elected chairman of the Monmouth and South Wales Coal Owners Association in 1913, was president of its crucial conciliation board from 1919 to 1944, and president of the Mining Association of Great Britain from 1919 to 1944. His message was concise and consistent – no interference by anyone, miners or government in the coal owners' right to manage the coal industry. His tenacity in the protracted presentation of this view could undermine even the most powerful. In the dying days of the 1926 stoppage, Churchill threatened government action if the owners did not provide an element of settling disputes by national action, whilst Williams argued for district agreements. After a heated argument (the typescript of which runs to fifty-six foolscap sheets), Churchill gave way.[68]

Coal also created fortunes for many who rose into the ranks of the powerful and privileged. David Davies (1818–90) was the archetypical hero of the Smilesean self-help philosophy so beloved of the late Victorians and Edwardians.[69] The original 'self-made man' who, Disraeli cruelly mocked, 'worshipped his own creator', Davies expanded his commercial and industrial empire into ironworks, railway companies and docks as well as coal mines and was the first Wales-raised, Welsh-speaking millionaire. The industrial empire he created proved to be a millstone around the neck of his son Edward, who died young in 1898.[70] His grandson, David Davies, first Baron Davies (1880–1944), proved to be of the same ilk as his namesake. From the outset, he was a multi-millionaire.[71]

David Alfred Thomas, first Viscount Rhondda (1856–1918) was the fifteenth of the seventeen children of Rachel and Samuel Thomas, a Merthyr Tydfil shopkeeper turned coal entrepreneur.[72] Upon his father's death in 1879, Thomas inherited the estate as the eldest surviving child. His career was spent almost equally between enlarging and extending his business empire and politics. By 1906 he controlled a dozen colliery undertakings with an output of 52 million tons, together with their sales agencies, and was chairman of a further sixteen companies. In 1915, he eventually received the political recognition he had craved for so long, when he was appointed president of the Local Government Board and later, in 1917, Food Controller. In recognition of his success he was created Baron (1916) and then Viscount Rhondda (1918). In 1915, Thomas and his daughter, Margaret Haig Thomas Mackworth, who took over his industrial interests upon his political appointment, survived the sinking of the *Lusitania.*

Thomas's move from the industrial to the political world presented the opportunity for his protégés Henry Seymour Berry (1877–1928), later Baron Buckland of Bwlch, and Sir David Richard Llewellyn, first baronet (1879–1940), to flourish.[73] The Berry brothers had serious disadvantages to overcome. They were from a non-aristocratic family and the unfashionable industrial town of Merthyr Tydfil; even worse, they were Welsh. But it is probably a record of sorts that not only Seymour, but his two brothers William Ewart Berry (1879–1954) and Gomer Berry (1883–1968) (later Viscount Camrose and Viscount Kemsley, respectively) attained peerages.[74] Together with David Llewellyn, a coalowner in his own right, Seymour Berry began a series of avaricious acquisitions which saw them control more than sixty companies, including Guest, Keen and Nettlefold. In 1935, their companies eventually fused with the Powell Duffryn Steam Coal Company into a consortium which controlled over ninety pits, produced more than 20 million tons of coal, and employed more than 37,000 people.

Swansea's proud claim to be 'the metallurgical centre of the world' was made possible by the energy and enterprise of a remarkable group of industrialists.[75] In the early nineteenth century, John Vivian laid the foundations of a copper and non-ferrous metal business, but it was his eldest son Sir Henry Hussey Vivian, first Baron Swansea (1821–94), who fulfilled its potential.[76] Through the distillation of the smoke into chemical by-products, most notably sulphuric acid, Vivian was to establish the foundations of Swansea's chemical industry and play a significant role in the development of the tinplate industry.[77] Amongst the most influential of the amalgamation of metallurgists was the 'meditative, urbane' Sir John Jones Jenkins, Lord Glantawe (1835–1915), who soon acquired a well-deserved reputation as 'Swansea's optimist'.[78] The son of humble parents, he went to work at the Upper Forest Tinplate Works in 1850 at the age of fifteen and, by the time he was twenty-three, was manager. He played a key role in securing Landore as the site for the Siemens steelworks. In addition to his tinplate businesses he also had interests in the Swansea Docks and Harbour Trust and in local railways. His business philosophy was underlined by Bossuet's maxim: 'God does not always refuse when he delays. He loves perseverance and grants it everything.'

One who appeared to have everything was Elizabeth Amy Dillwyn (1875–1935),[79] daughter of Lewis Llewelyn Dillwyn (1844–92) industrialist and politician of Swansea, granddaughter of Lewis Weston Dillwyn, owner of the famous Cambrian Pottery and great-granddaughter of William Dillwyn, the American Quaker abolitionist. Yet her life was tinged with tragedy. In 1894, on the eve of their wedding, her fiancé, Llywelyn Thomas of Llwynmadog, died of smallpox. Her beloved brother Harry, possessor of a 'Rabelaisian thirst', died drunk and dissipated at the young age of forty-six. When her father, Lewis, the widely respected leader of the Welsh radicals in Parliament, died suddenly in 1892 she found that he had left a crippling burden of debt. With dedication and determination Amy took on the onerous commitment, turned the ailing companies around and sold them, in 1904, at a very substantial profit to Metallgesellschaft of Frankfurt.

By 1902, Amy Dillwyn's fame as a hard-headed businesswoman, capable of holding her own with the shrewdest of her male rivals in the intensely masculine and competitive industrial world, had won her widespread recognition. The *Pall Mall Gazette* considered her 'one of the most remarkable women in Great Britain'. Small, neat, bespectacled Amy became a national celebrity. She campaigned vigorously for women's rights, state education and medical services and was one of the first women to stand for election to a borough council after the passing of the Qualification of Women

Act in 1907. Like Sybil Haig Thomas, another successful woman in a man's boardroom world, Amy 'the grand old lady of Swansea', was a heavy smoker of cigars and a devotee of the gaming tables at Monte Carlo.

People and professions: the middling people

> Gentility will be the ruin of the Welsh, as it has been of many things.
>
> George Borrow, *Wild Wales* (1862)

At some indeterminate point, the upper class merged into another group that shared many of their characteristics. They often received the same public school education and the values which it imparted, and were interlinked by marriage. The prejudice within landed society against trade and industry, as we have seen, was substantially eroded over the course of the nineteenth century. Some families who derived their income from land may, as Herbert Vaughan suggested, have continued their snobbery against the detested nouveau riche who earned their wealth from coal, copper or iron, but most never let their principles stand in the way of their prosperity.[80] Many business people were attracted by the aristocratic way of life, weekending at country houses, participating in field sports and even buying landed estates. On their new estates some of Wales's large employers consumed increasingly conspicuously, displaying the paraphernalia of matching horses, carriages and liveried servants, then later turning their stables into garages for their Rolls Royces and Daimlers. Such 'gentrification', it has been argued by Martin J. Weiner in *English Culture and the Decline of the Industrial Spirit, 1850–1980*, 'led to a haemorrhaging of talent' from business life, so contributing to the nation's economic decline.[81] But a weekend in the countryside would surely not make hard-headed men neglect their business interests, and indeed much business was conducted on the sporting and hunting fields of Wales.

It was a myth that became accepted as a fact in the nineteenth century that the Welsh were not entrepreneurial.[82] As usual, such prejudice ignores the actual situation. Both at home and abroad a number of Welsh people seized every opportunity to prove that they were enterprising and talented entrepreneurs. James Coster Edwards (1828–96) of Trefnant, Denbighshire, left school at ten or eleven years of age to serve an apprenticeship to a draper and then established himself as a shopkeeper.[83] About 1860, his father bought a coal mine and Edwards used the waste clay from around the coal seams to make common bricks and earthenware in a yard where he employed a man and two boys. He became the first to exploit fully the value of the Ruabon marls and so helped to initiate the recovery of the economy of north-east Wales from the long recession caused by the decline of the iron industry. When Edwards died in 1896, the firm employed a thousand men in four large factories. Edwards soon bought himself into the world of landed gentility, acquiring Trevor Hall in Llangollen and the adjacent West Tower estate.

Welsh talent, like Welsh capital, was exported to assist the development of other countries. Lewis Thomas (1832–1913), of Llanfihangel Genau'r Glyn, Talybont, Cardiganshire, seized his opportunities as a colliery owner in Australia.[84] Sir William Price (1865–1938), of Llanwrtyd Wells, Breconshire, escaped from his lowly origins to the riches of London's milk trade.[85] A superb communicator, perhaps Price's greatest contribution was the re-organisation of the milk supply to London and the south-east of England, for which he was knighted in 1922.

Welsh speakers also revealed a flair for business. Robert Davies (1816–1905) of Llangefni, Anglesey, expanded his father's store into timber export and imports, an iron foundry, shipping and shipbuilding.[86] During his lifetime, Davies was popularly credited with having donated over half-a-million pounds to local religious causes. The fledgling university college in Bangor also benefited greatly from his largesse and amongst the most eccentric of his almsgivings was the weekly distribution of twelve pounds of flour to between seventy and a hundred people, who personally collected this dole from his home, Bodlondeb, every Tuesday. Another Welsh speaker and a 'penny capitalist' of the first rank was Thomas Gee (1815–1898) of Denbigh.[87] In 1837, he modestly wrote to his parents

4 The staff and owner of John Ashton's shop in Carno, Montgomeryshire, about 1885. A clear representation of power and prestige in the hierarchy of a rural enterprise. John Thomas Collection, National Library of Wales.

that 'it is my wish to employ my talent (which I know is but very small) to the Glory of God'. Yet it was not in the ministry that he made his fortune, but as a 'publisher, wholesaler, printer, binder, newspaper proprietor, stationer and retail book seller'. In addition, he had interests in mining and slate-quarrying, the Ruthin Soda Water Company (of which he was the director), and both the Vale of Clwyd Railway and the North Denbighshire Building Society (of which he was the first president in 1866). Through his great newspaper *Baner ac Amserau Cymru*, Gee 'was one of the pioneers of Welsh liberty', which obviously made sound business sense.

Entry into the professions was seen as the most obvious manifestation of a person's class position. This was clearly shown in the local editions of *Who's Who* which were published by several Welsh towns in the early twentieth century.[88] The years between 1870–1945 saw a significant broadening of the professions in Wales. Doctors, in particular, became a larger and more respected group. In the early nineteenth century, the 'anterliwt' performers jested that all doctors were quacks who turned up to present their bill just before their patient's demise. By the twentieth century, the literary and theatrical presentation of medics was more respectful. A. J. Cronin's 1934 novel, *The Citadel*, made into a film in 1938 by King Vidor, is perhaps the most famous example. Despite the improbable casting of that 'quintessential English gentleman', Robert Donat, as a Scottish doctor working in a Welsh coal-mining valley, the film superbly conveys the medical profession's decency and dedication.[89] A real life model for Cronin's fictional hero was Alexander Tudor Hart, who worked as a doctor in the Rhondda and other south Wales valleys. The social deprivation experienced by his patients was captured in a series of poignant and powerful photographs taken by his wife, Edith Tudor Hart (1908–73).[90]

The careers of Welsh doctors covered a broad range of experience. Sir John Williams (1840–1926) was born into the austere background, the son of the tenant of a Welsh upland farm in Gwynfe, Carmarthenshire. Yet, despite the immense disadvantages and hardships, John Williams rose to become the pre-eminent 'surgical gynaecologist' of Victorian and Edwardian times. Amongst the more prominent of his patients was Queen Victoria. Williams attended the births of both the future King Edward VII and Princess Beatrice. His reward was a baronetcy in October 1894 and a KCVO in 1902.[91]

In contrast to Sir John Williams, William Price (1800–93) had perhaps the most bizarre career of any character in nineteenth century Wales.[92] Apprenticed to a physician in Nantgarw, Price managed to qualify at St Bartholomew's Hospital, London, in the remarkably short time of a little over a year. Involved with the Chartists in 1839, Price had to flee to France for a period after the 'uprising failed'. Thereafter, he was a watched, if not a marked man. When he dressed, for he was a pioneer of naturism, it was in a famously bizarre 'druidic' costume of green one-piece jumpsuit and fox-skin headdress. He grew his hair long, his beard longer. He lived, gossips complained, 'in sin' with a succession of young girls. Price claimed they were 'housekeepers', a claim weakened when one of them bore him a son in 1884. Price named the boy Iesu Grist Price (Jesus Christ Price). Despite his claims that the child was the new messiah, Iesu died in 1884. Price cremated the body on a pyre at Cae'r-lan Fields hilltop above Llantrisant. Subsequently tried in Cardiff at the winter assizes of 1884, he was found not guilty, in a landmark decision that legalised cremation in Britain. Price was an excellent doctor and charged according to the ability of his patients to pay – the poor had his services free. Yet, despite his undoubted abilities, his legend remains that of an eccentric loner. *The Dictionary of Welsh Biography* simply describes him as 'dyn od' (an odd man).

The majority of Welsh medics subscribed to the legacy of John Williams.[93] However, the most famous, or infamous, Welsh doctor in our period appears to have been firmly in the Price mould. Like Price, Ernest Jones (1879–1958) qualified at a precocious age, decorated with gold medals and academic plaudits. He found his métier not in mainstream medicine but in the new science of psychoanalysis, 'the talking cure' pioneered by Sigmund Freud.[94] Jones proved himself at ease in the dark world of the sexual psyche. On numerous occasions there were official expressions of concern at his methods and practices. He flitted from post to post until, at the age of fifty-two, he was appointed leader of the International Psychoanalytic Association. 'I've always had a hell of a superego', he once modestly noted. Through Jones, Freud's ideas and concepts reached a wide audience – thousands who have never read the master's work are familiar with the Oedipus and other Freudian concepts.

Lawyers never achieved the popularity enjoyed by medics.[95] *Y Ffraethebydd*, a compendium of jokes by D. L. Jones (Cynalaw) published in and around 1889, continued the traditional presentation of the solicitor as grasping and greedy.[96] By the turn of the twentieth century, however, the standing of solicitors compared favourably with that of the despised attorney of earlier decades, thanks mainly to improved professional training and higher educational standards, especially the Law Society's campaign to eradicate 'unethical' practices. Lawyers, less convincingly perhaps than doctors, also tried to present themselves as the selfless servants of the people, working for the common good. Following the Second Reform Act of 1867 and the Liberal party's domination of Welsh politics from the 1870s onwards it seemed almost axiomatic that a Welsh MP should have had a legal training.[97] Despite increasing salaries for members of parliament, many still required the buttress of a professional income to support them. Sir John Herbert Lewis (1858–1933), who did so much to establish so many national institutions, was only one of an eloquence of people to combine law and politics.[98] Some, however, argued that a lawyer was simply the larval stage of the detested politician.

Useful toil: labouring lives

> I have seen little besides pain, sorrow, darkness and trouble. We are wearing out a miserable existence, anxiously looking for something we may never attain.
>
> Jane, in a letter in the *Flintshire Observer*, 5 December 1862, quoted in Alan Conway, *The Welsh in America: Letters from the Immigrants* (Minnesota, 1961), p. 318

Working-class society was also complex, with a whole range of characteristics that both defined and divided people. The manual working class, which comprised a significant section of the labour force, lived in very disparate circumstances. Despite mounting threats to their traditional privileges, engineers who had served an apprenticeship earned almost double the wages of labourers who worked alongside them, and were highly conscious of their superiority in terms of status and responsibility. Railway workers jealously guarded their positions, even against fellow workers. The Amalgamated Society of Railway Servants refused to adopt an 'all-grades movement', whilst engine drivers, in order to protect their interests, split away into their own union. The divisions between them were bitterly seen in the 1911 rail strike, which for a time paralysed south Wales and led to rioting in Llanelli.[99] The daughter of a skilled tinworker, who grew up in Port Talbot, considered that hers was a 'middle-class' family, as against her neighbours, the 'ordinary people', who were lower-class.[100] They lived in the same terraced street.

Subcontractors were an important group, especially in the mines and quarries. The 'fargen' (the agreement) was a key aspect of working in the slate quarries of north Wales.[101] Foremen, supervisors and checkweighmen in the mines also had complex social identities. They were from the manual working class by origin, but had risen by ability and luck into managerial ranks. In the docklands of Wales, at places as diverse as Cardiff, Newport, Pembroke Dock and Bangor, stevedores and lightermen, the most skilled workers in their trade, enjoyed higher incomes and esteem than ordinary labourers. The concept of a 'labour aristocracy' was developed to describe the class of workers cut off from the wider working class by skill, higher wages, and commitment to respectability. But this concept is also problematic in a number of ways. This group was a relatively small one within the wider working class, and indistinguishable from those who described themselves as members of the 'respectable' working class. Dock workers who unloaded crates emblazoned with strange alphabets, however skilled, could all be undercut by non-union, casual and female labour.[102]

Labour hierarchies took many forms. In coal mining and iron-working, stratification was based on age and strength rather than skill and thus almost every man had an opportunity to earn higher wages at some point in his career. 'Skill' was also a highly problematic concept, prone to innumerable definitions. In coal mining, even the most highly paid workers were 'unskilled' in the sense that they had neither served an apprenticeship nor studied at trade school. However, their work required a high level of experience and expertise, derived from years of work, making it difficult for employers to replace them with 'blacklegs' in the event of a strike.

Miners are traditionally viewed as an unified group; it is as if all individuality had been obliterated by the coal dust which uniformly covered the workers.[103] But they too were hierarchical in structure and organisation. Of the underground workers, the most important and highest-paid group were the colliers, who arduously laboured in atrocious conditions, often on their backs or bellies, for one-third of Welsh coal seams were under three feet in height. Colliers were men of immense physical power, who usually served a five-year 'apprenticeship' as a 'collier boy' alongside a father, brother or other family member. The boys cleared the rubbish, gathered the coal cut by the collier and loaded it into trams. But colliers were not the only workers underground. Lower in status and wages were rippers, roadmen, hitchers, timbermen, ostlers, oilers, fitters, masons, cogcutters, airwaymen, shacklers and spragmen, watchmen, lamplockers and lampmen. The mine could not function without the skills and expertise of a host of trades. Repairers, for example, were highly skilled and experienced older men, whilst hauliers were renowned for their agility.

A significant group of workers, usually around one-fifth of a colliery's work force, never went underground. These were the 'surface' workers. They included lorrymen, blacksmiths, oilers, greasers, rubbishmen, sawyers and pit carpenters. As mechanisation and electrification increased in the twentieth century, new groups of workers – engineers, engine drivers and grids of electricians – joined the ranks of surface workers. Many of the older and injured miners, who could no longer cope with the work of the collier, were employed as labourers in the even more physically demanding and unpleasant work of the coal-screening plants. Again, some trades above ground were especially highly skilled. Banksmen, for example, looked after the fans, ropes, chains and cables and ensured the safe operation of the cage that lowered the men down into and up from the mine shaft. Every morning when he woke, every collier hoped that the banksman had not quarrelled with the wife before work and did not have a hangover. Amongst the ranks of the surface workers were a group who are sometimes treated as if they were the fifth column of the class war – the enemy within. These were office staff, whose numbers varied, but who undertook administrative, financial, clerical, secretarial or marketing functions which were essential to the pit's success or failure. These were the balances of accountants and the audits of bookkeepers whose skills were essential for survival and success.

It is a fact, often forgotten but essential to remember, that women continued to work in Welsh collieries until well into the twentieth century. Physically impressive women, as A. J. Mumby excitedly confided to his diary in the 1870s, continued to work illegally underground as colliers. The female hauliers at Abergorci colliery in the 1880s proudly posed for a photograph. Bonnetted and besmirched with grime, they stare confidently at the viewer. The mother of painter Nicholas Evans, who produced powerful images of Welsh miners, was a pit girl in the early twentieth century. Many more women worked in colliery screens and washeries. Others scavenged and scoured the waste tips in search of discarded coal. In a series of paintings, T. H. Thomas captured the heroic stature and statuesque beauty of these 'tip girls'.[104] Women also worked at the heavier tasks in the copper industry as 'copar ladies'.

Industrial disputes, such as those that split the coalfields of north and south Wales asunder in 1893, 1898, 1910–11 and 1926 and the 1900–3 slate-mining dispute could plunge people from relative comfort into penury. Payments from miners' unions were supplemented by a host of charitable and public sources. In the Rhondda in 1910–11, chapels and sports and social clubs swiftly set up soup kitchens to feed strikers and especially their children. The Penygraig Constitutional Club, the Penygraig Conservative Club, the White Hart and other public houses all gave free meals on a daily basis to a number of children. The Welsh Rugby Union donated £20 to the Rhondda Children's Distress Fund. The harsh winter of 1910–11 had strikers' families scouring the slag tips for discarded coal. Everywhere schools, supported by emergency powers granted to the Local Education Authorities, granted free school meals to hosts of schoolchildren. As one eyewitness recalled, 'there were many a family that were half-starved, but for the soup kitchens. Mention any school and it had a soup kitchen.' Privation prevailed, but whilst people were undoubtedly hungry, they were not dying of starvation as their forefathers had done a century earlier at times of great social discontent.[105]

Domestic servants, those strange creatures who so often lived on the happiness and hopes of others, are difficult to incorporate into a class.[106] They were a part of, but apart from the lives of the aristocracy and the middling classes, whilst by salary they were amongst the lower sections of the working classes. Many were 'maids of all work', who laboured in lonely servitude that was little short of slavery. But in many respects servants were the embodiment of the worst aspects of the petty snobbery that underlay

Welsh society. In larger households, the servants' internal organisation mirrored other social hierarchies. Indeed, the hierarchy below stairs was infinitely more complex than anything going on above. Even the servants had servants. At the top of the pile were 'the upper ten', consisting of the steward, who managed the house, the butler, the wine butler and valet (the gentleman's gentleman), the housekeeper, cook, groom of the chambers and the lady's maid whose job it was to dress, undress, re-dress and undress her ladyship. The upper ten were not expected to wear livery like their inferiors, but to dress as faded versions of their employers. At the lower end were 'the lowers'.[107] Their numbers would vary. On some Welsh estates there would have been as many as thirty or more, including scullery maids, footmen, grooms, housemaids, chambermaids and laundry maids. There was little or no social interaction between the upper and lower servants, who ate different food in separate rooms, where they sat in strict hierarchical order. Sneers of butlers would rarely socialise with their inferiors.

Possession of a talent and the luck and wherewithal, the guts and the gumption, to realise it was the way to escape at least some of the stereotypes and structures of one's social position. The performing arts, in art, music and the theatre gave many an opportunity to escape poverty. The singer Dorothy Squires (1915–98), popular singer and serial litigant, was born on 25 March 1915 in a travelling van at Bridge Shop field, Pontyberem, Carmarthenshire. Opportunity knocked with one appearance on BBC radio in 1936, and fame followed.[108] One of the chief musical figures in nineteenth-century Wales was the great choral conductor, Griffith Rhys Jones, Caradog (1834–97). Caradog exhibited a precocious musical talent as a violinist, winning renown as 'the Paganini of Wales'. Yet, it was as a choral conductor that he won fame and perhaps fortune. In 1872, the 450-strong Welsh Choral Union – Côr Mawr Caradog – won the Thousand Guinea Challenge Cup under his baton. The ecstasy generated in Wales by this achievement became frenzied a year later when the choir repeated the victory after being challenged by the Paris Prize Choir. The success of Caradog's last choir standing served to cement the idea that musicianship was an important element in the cultural and national identity of Wales.

Caradog's career off stage was more flamboyant than on it. Initially a blacksmith, for a while he kept the Treorchy Hotel; in 1875, he retired and was listed in the census as 'a gentleman of independent means'. Most of his money was made in the brewing industry – he was a founding director of the Rhondda Valley Brewing Company. The company acquired a whole host of brewing and bottling companies, as well as properties, particularly public houses. The deft manipulation of funds and other interests (the companies were regularly wound up and instantly reconstituted under new names, so as to maximise profits) allowed Caradog to leave an estate valued at more than £38,000 in 1897. The Paganini of Wales proved himself adept at fiddling the books.[109]

The Powell family of High Street, St Asaph, Flintshire, had a brother, brother, sister and sister musical act that enabled them to offset some of the poverty of their upbringing by a widowed dressmaker.[110] As the Harlequinaders, they shot to fame in 1913 when their song 'Queen of Summer' achieved celebrity status. But true success followed in August 1915, when Felix wrote the music to 'Pack up your troubles in your old kit bag', one of the iconic songs of the twentieth century. Yet the family's troubles were never so neatly packed away. George, a Christian Scientist and priest, resorted to touring the country in a caravan, selling alternative medicines. Felix ran a public house, then was a musical impresario in Peacehaven, where he committed suicide in 1942 with a service revolver.

Art was the escape route for Sir William Goscombe John (1860–1952), sculptor and medallist, and the painters, Augustus and Gwen John and J. D. Innes. Mary Grace Agnes Adams (1898–1984), television producer and programme director, was raised in dire poverty in Penarth by her mother after her father died of consumption in 1910. Gareth Hughes, Ivor Emmanuel, Ivor Novello, Richard Burton, Stanley Baker, Glyn and Donald Houston, Emlyn Williams, Meredith Edwards, Rachel Roberts and several others found fortune and fame in the footlights and the cinema.

Equally adept at acting, others sought careers amongst the convertings of preachers with the Nonconformists and the prudences of Anglican vicars. As Welsh religion became more respectable and refined in the mid-nineteenth century, a whole host of people saw a secure future in the ministry. William Evans (1869–1948), John Hughes (Glanystwyth; 1842–1902) and Euros Bowen (1904–88) are only a few of the legion who served in dark suit and dog collar. The ministry was often the best way people could rise out of peasantry or poverty. At Bala, Bangor, Brecon and Carmarthen, denominational seminaries provided training for aspiring ministers. For many families it was a real struggle to get their son through the training and, justifiably, those who succeeded took on new airs and graces. The designation of BA, or BD after a son's and sometimes after a daughter's name was almost a magical incantation. Henry Jones, later professor of moral theology at Glasgow, remembered how, as a boy, he had lain in wait to see a BA walk past.[111] Lewis Probert (1837–1908), was one of the great developers of the Congregationalist movement in Wales. As with so many of his fellow ministers, Probert moved every two or three years, in a peripatetic journey of salvation across Wales. The 'class' and social position of these people is highly problematical. Their origin was often lowly, but their professional 'calling' was at best meritorious, at worst pretentious.[112] Often they lived in a tied house – 'y mans' – with servants and all the trappings of the upper social classes.

Nonconformist ministers were exceptionally successful in propelling their sons, and a few daughters, to positions of social influence and prestige. Thomas Gee ensured that all nine of his children, girls and boys, received an excellent education both in Wales and, unusually for a Welsh radical, in the public schools of England. Thomas Jones (1819–82), the famed 'Jones Treforris', had a varied career as a commercial traveller, collier, checkweighman and flannel manufacturer before he entered the ministry of the Calvinistic Methodists in Llanelli.[113] He had three remarkable sons. The eldest was Sir David Brynmor Jones (1852–1921), QC, Master in Lunacy, MP and co-author of *The Welsh People* (1900).[114] The second son was John Viriamu Jones (1856–1901), a professor of physics, a university administrator and the first principal of the University College of South Wales at Cardiff. The third son was Leifchild Stratten Jones (Leif Jones), later Baron Rhayader (1862–1939), a temperance advocate and MP.[115]

Although they did not all enter the ministry themselves, the sons and daughters of the clergy created a new intelligentsia, similar to the Russian *popovichi*. They carried on, in secularised form, the clergy's belief that it alone represented both moral integrity and true Welshness, the values of the 'gwerin' who were not corrupted by sin as the nobles and the merchants were. Secularising the notion of individual salvation and of a future messianic redemption of humanity, they refused to separate the political from the personal, instead insisting that the struggle for change in the sociopolitical order be accompanied by tireless efforts at moral and spiritual self-improvement. In newspapers like *Y Genedl Gymreig* and magazines such as *Welsh Outlook*, the secular sons of the holy fathers penned countless articles imbued with a sense of their own saintly mission in a society where elites were corrupted by sin and estranged from the sacred traditions of Wales. Only they, they felt, aspired to a life of godliness, service to the people and devotion to the true national essence of Wales.[116]

That 'a woman's work is never done' has become a hackneyed cliché, but the oral evidence gathered by the Welsh Museum of Life in the 1970s reveals that there was considerable truth in the statement.[117] It was only through the Sisyphean efforts of Welsh women that families could be regarded as 'respectable'. A dirty doorstep, unwashed and unkempt children, an unstarched shirt for the husband on a Saturday night or Sunday morning, failure to conform to the street's habit of displaying all washing promptly at 10 a.m. every Monday and a host of other petty infringements could all lead to a fall from grace. Although a number of devices were introduced to ease domestic burdens, women were crushed under the relentless pressures of homeworking. The rare spare minutes of the day were spent knitting, darning or mending. Every day in the mining valleys and the quarrying towns, gaggles of women had fires to light, clothes to clean and dry, endless meals to prepare for ever-hungry children and returning workers, while the daily battle against the all pervading coal dirt and slate dust meant constant cleaning, polishing and scrubbing. Gas and electricity were late arrivals in many Welsh towns and villages. In Mrs Eirona Richards's home in Morriston, Glamorgan, her father installed his own supply of electricity in 1949. In Tre'r-ddôl, Powys, a supply did not arrive until 1957. In Llanbedr, Gwynedd, locals had to wait until 1961.[118] Thus the women of these and countless other villages had no recourse to labour-saving machines. One of the daily chores for Margaret Bridgman, Llangynwyd, in 1915, and Mary Jane Lewis, of Llangennith on the Gower, in 1924, was the backbreaking work of carrying water from a distant well and a communal pump.

There were curious and subtle distinctions between women who provided cleaning and washing services for others. Marged Ifans, who lived in a tiny cottage at Llanrwst, Anglesey, had to keep the back door open, be it summer or winter, to accommodate the wash tub in the confined space of her kitchen. She would provide this service for her regular customers for nine pence per dozen garments, irrespective of size. By being able to cope with it within the walls of her own domain, however, she qualified for a higher social standing and status than Marged Jones, who had to abandon her home for the day and brazenly wash undergarments outside.[119] Jane Jones, the wife of a low-paid slate-quarry worker in Betws Garmon, Caernarfonshire, bought a house for her family for £100 in 1902 with the income she earned washing for local households.[120]

In rural Wales there were also considerable differentials in wealth and prestige between individuals. The 'gwerinwr' (peasant) was idealised in countless poems as the backbone of rural society. 'Y werin' were the defenders of the language and morality and custodians of everything that was good in Wales. Yet the reality was vastly different. There was considerable tension in rural Wales between social groups. Status and standing were further confused by the varieties of payment methods. A single harvesting group had a mix of regular wages, casual pay, payment in kind, even debts of honour. Only a few were paid in cash. No wonder so many sought to augment their income through poaching. This was a world held together as much by tension as by pastoral sleepiness.[121] This unwashed Brueghel peasantry battled with a severe rural economy in which even dung was a supremely valuable commodity. It was used for fires and building and was even believed to possess medicinal qualities. The innate conservatism of farmers stemmed from their desperate desire to cling on to their own plot of soil. People in rural Wales, as the figures for emigration show, were perhaps the most insecure part of the nation.[122] The jubilant crowds who greeted the tenants when they purchased their farms in the great estates' land sales in the twentieth century reveal the local relief that ownership secured continuity.[123] Yet, the farmer as owner found it increasingly difficult to retain his farm as the realities of economics brought cruel lessons. Farm size varied enormously, as did income, status and standing. Many farmers were in debt to the tax collector, the banks, the shopkeepers and a host of others. The farmer saw the bailiff at his heels whenever inclement weather threatened crops. Daniel Parry Jones's reminiscences of his *Welsh Country Upbringing* is an eloquent evocation of the farmer's fears of debt.[124]

Thus the farmers' role as the ballast which kept Wales stable is questionable. They were often in a state of turmoil and internal rivalry. Their conflicts were no less important because they did not fit simply into a clash of capitalist against worker and because their aim in seeking land was seldom to rise into a higher social class. The conflicts were all the more intense because their society was collapsing. Between 1814–1914 Welsh agriculture appears to have been in a constant state of crisis. Migration to the towns undercut rural society in cruel ways, taking away the more industrious and inventive members of the community. Those who were left appeared to be deserted, not liberated. Rural depopulation was a neurotic worry instead of a sign of increasing opportunity. For example, in many areas around Carmarthenshire's anthracite mines and Caernarfonshire's slate quarries, there were farmers who owned twenty to thirty acres of land who were also colliers and quarrymen, an odd hybrid type of industrial labour force.[125] For most of the week they toiled underneath the land they tilled at night and on weekends. Friction often arose between them and their colleagues who had no contact with the land, because they, growing a lot of food themselves, could afford to work for less.

At the turn of the twentieth century, wage differentials may have contracted slightly.[126] The working classes merged into each other as the numbers and fortunes of the skilled, the semi-skilled and the unskilled varied, making it very difficult to clarify the relationship between these groups. As Charles Booth and then Seebohm Rowntree showed, the working classes comprised a bewildering variety. Like the debates that raged over the rise and fall of the gentry and the causes of the industrial revolution, historians have expended considerable energy in analysing wage rates. In Wales these varied enormously. Overall, over the period 1870–1945, it is probable that the wage rates indicated a slight increase, but as with all statistics, particular experiences of profound importance are hidden in generalities. In the mines for example, wages rose over the years 1870–1914, apart from the years of great industrial discontent in 1893 and 1898. A key period was the First World War. In 1914 miners in north Wales earned 5s. 10d a week, whilst those in the south earned 6s. 9d a week. By 1918 their wages had risen to 11s. 1¼d in north Wales and 14s. a week in south Wales. Miners wages seem to have peaked, in 1921, at 16s. 10½d in the north and 21s. 6½d in the south. Thereafter they fell catastrophically to below the weekly rates of the 1900s. In contrast, those who stayed to work on the land saw their wages rise between 1870 and 1945. There was a marked differential in agricultural wages between Welsh counties, with the highest wages (27s. a week in 1917) being paid in Glamorgan. Of industrial workers, the boilermen of Cardiff's docklands appeared to be the best paid, earning 45s. a week in 1898, whilst the city's lithographic printers earned 75s. 6d in 1924 and only a shilling less in 1939. Thus it is difficult to see the working class as homogenous; the variations within it were considerable and it was changing all the time.[127]

Bleak expectations: poverty and pauperism

> He knew what he wanted: nothing. And he went after it with both hands tied behind his back. No man could have moved with less fuss on to the outermost and desolate rim of existence . . . He learned the whole map of human gullibility, the thousand ways of wheedling a dime from the friendlier matron. He could coax a meal from a brick

wall if the mortar were soft enough. Regular work he dodged as if it were bubonic.

Gwyn Thomas on W. H. Davies, the 'Super Tramp', in *A Welsh Eye* (London, 1964), p. 91

According to Gwyn Thomas, W. H. Davies rivalled a lion as one of life's laziest life forms. Compared with him a sloth was a dynamo. Davies existed, for a period, at the lower end of the social spectrum, where the 'respectable' merged into the 'rough' working class and then into a lower subsection of society. Several families learnt that there was but a note's width between poverty and pauperism. Sir William James Thomas (1867–1975), orphaned at an early age, was eventually cared for by his grandparents. He later became a major coalowner and one of the greatest of all Welsh philanthropists. Mary Jane Evans, née Francis (Llaethferch, 1888–1922), the much loved elocutionist, eisteddfod reciter and preacher and her family endured years of hardship. They scratched a living from the milk they got from a few cows; on her way to school Mary Jane sold the milk, hence her nom de plume, Llaethferch. Energised by the 1904–5 religious revival, she began to preach and entered a training academy in Carmarthen. In order to pay her fees, the family sold their only possessions, the cows. Richard Jones (1848–1915), an itinerant bookseller of Machynlleth and Cemaes, and William Owen (Gwilym Meudwy, 1841–1902), a tramping poet, spent their lives on the edges of poverty against a backdrop of sorrow.[128] The death of seven-month-old Edith Annie Eley of starvation in December 1899 had all the seasonal pathos of Dickens's fiction. Sadly, this was real life. The scenes of desperation and dissipation described in the *Western Mail* on 12 January 1902 are truly tragic. Edith never knew it, but her people were classed as pariahs, a sub-class, 'the people of the abyss' who caused profound concern to moralists. Biblical dictate might have decreed that the 'poor were always with us', Oscar Wilde might have considered that they could only afford self-denial, but contemporaries were never slow to criticise and condemn.

Poverty was providential. The sick and crippled, the old and orphaned, the widowed and deserted, the victims of epidemics and casualties of war were poor through no fault of their own, and their

5 Despite his disability, 'Harri Bach' of Bodedern, Anglesey, had to struggle to survive or otherwise starve. The work of such carriers was a vital aspect of rural Wales (*c*.1875). John Thomas Collection, National Library of Wales.

plight warranted at least a minimalist benevolence. They were 'the deserving poor', a description reflective of moral values and redolent of individual tragedies. In direct contrast were 'the undeserving poor'; people who were drunk, dissipated and derelict. Pauperism stemmed from laziness, fraud and associated moral degeneracies and it called for correction and chastisement, not charity. The types of assistance given reflected the nature of the pauper; the deserving had 'outdoor relief', the 'undeserving' suffered 'indoor relief'. In 1871, at one of the peaks for the poor law system, 82,474 people were dependent upon outdoor, whilst 84,770 were in receipt of indoor relief.[129]

'Indoor relief' was the rather innocuous description of the dreaded and despised workhouse. Here were confined society's moral refuse – those people who were mad, bad and dangerous to know. Many children were raised in these institutions across Wales. Some attempts were made to provide specialist care. Roman Catholic girls with a physical or mental disability were sent to Nazareth House in Cardiff. The Cambrian Institution in Swansea cared for deaf and dumb children, such as the foundling child found in the town and appropriately named Moses. But more went to the workhouses. In Cardiganshire, in the 1870s there were more than 1,000 children resident in the county's workhouses.[130] Across Wales, a total of 27,251 children were confined in workhouses in 1871. Matrons and masters dispensed strict discipline. Alfred and Mary Roskilly's tenure as workhouse master and mistress were infamous for the beatings they gave to girls. But some matrons and masters must surely have offered at least a little compassion and comfort to their charges. Even so, a childhood amongst the pimps and prostitutes, the damaged and the deranged, must have been fearful. It was no wonder that the most famous children of Welsh workhouses – Henry Morton Stanley and Winifred Wagner – were such flawed characters.[131] Stanley described St Asaph workhouse as 'a house of torture'. Those who rebelled against the workhouse were sent to the even harsher and darker world of the 'training' ships, such as the *Clio* in the Menai Straits or the *Havannah* in Cardiff. On the *Havannah*, the former boatswain William Jayne evoked loyalty from the boys and admiration from the female visitors when he stripped off to reveal his tattooed body.

The old and the frail and those people who had no families or had outlived them also passed their last, sad days within workhouse walls. The one-eyed Abel Jones (Bardd Crwst; 1830–1901), 'the prince of Welsh ballad-singers', died in the Llanrwst workhouse in June 1901.[132] Edwin and Agnes, the celebrated Llangefni tinkers, who were photographed by John Thomas in 1885, wandered in and out of several workhouses across north Wales, as did Gwen y Potiau of Llandrillo-yn-Edeirnion, who posed for the same photographer in 1875. Not all people used emotive and emotionally charged terms to describe the poor. Merfyn Lloyd Turner (1915–91), the great penal reformer, was imprisoned for three months' hard labour in 1940 for his stand as a conscientious objector to war.[133] He never forgot this experience 'of how prison disregarded the man – I felt as if all the world had abandoned me'. Thereafter, he was involved in practical social work to aid the reclamation of prisoners to society in Tiger Bay, Cardiff, and later with the poor in London. But Turner was an exception. Most people were condemnatory of the very poor.[134]

Charitable giving was one of the methods adopted to alleviate the poor's suffering. Some people were remarkably generous. The *Western Mail* reported on 12 March 1913 that Godfrey Charles Morgan, Viscount Tredegar, donated over £40,000 a year to charities across south Wales. John Cory (1828–1910) and Richard Cory (1830–1914), shipowners and coalowners, gave substantial sums every year to chapels, churches, bands of hope, and Dr Barnardo's homes. Whatever form the charity took, the recipients were often meant to acknowledge their shame at being dependent on others. In the early 1870s, the late 1890s, the 1920s and the 1930s severe economic depression and recession increased the tensions. Stanley Baker (1928–76), the screen actor, was raised in great poverty after his father was unable to work, having lost a leg in 1917 in an accident in a coal mine. The experience of living on and at other people's tender mercies forged the actor's hard-edged character.[135]

Disabled sailors and soldiers, gypsies, tinkers and all classes of mendicants were found in every town, village and hamlet. Largely unprotected by the poor law, organised charity or the police, neglected and abandoned children could be found everywhere and anywhere. Their lives poisoned by poverty, they suffered the overcrowding, abuse and brutality of the low lodging-house. Old and young alike, they dressed in old clothes, usually in several layers as they had no safe storage place and needed warmth. Old coats, trousers and shirts represented the former emblems of a higher class which over the years were slowly passed down through the ranks of society, getting progressively more threadbare as they descended. Along Cardiff's Bute Street, Newport's Corporation Road, Bangor's Lôn Glan Môr and Ffordd Garth Uchaf, Caernarfon's Mill Lane and Swansea's ironically named Salubrious Way (it was anything but) were the ragged places where the ravaged people went. Here were poor houses in which were gathered together the waifs, the strays, the halt, the lame, the blind, the aged, the feeble and infirm, the flotsam and jetsam of economic failure. In these dark areas the lower classes had their bars, shebeens, drinking clubs and dance halls, places offensive to sensibility, not known for their bridge tournaments. Violent and vengeful drunks from under the tables would dispense their alcoholic wisdom from the morning's earliest hours in dank and dark pubs smelling of beer and vomit. These people, never entirely sober, unattached to any group, were always alone, often lonely. Slowly moving on legs that were a delta of varicose veins and seeing the world through a drinker's eyes, they had their own itineraries that involved an easy sociability, banality, indeed everything but work. For work was the curse of these drinking classes. In these abodes of poverty, the very poor sought companionship, company, even compassion. This was the world of the very low, of washerwomen who never washed, workers who never worked, and labourers who never laboured. With their pungent stench of sweat, wet wool, stale urine and excrement, a blind man could smell his way to these fetid abodes. Here were the characters in a crowd scene by Hieronymus Bosch come to life. A world of woebegone people and places.

At its lowest levels, the working class melded and merged into a darker underworld.[136] This is where people with temporary homes were transferred into people with no fixed abode; the polymorphous, migratory people of the open road. Despite the best efforts of local police to keep them moving, tramps – begging, sitting, standing, lying down, or collapsed in a heap – were legion across Wales. They relieved themselves in the streets and slept under the stars. Mingled with the social fear and resentment of vagrants was a fascination with the romance of the road. Welsh newspapers sent their 'social explorers' into the casual wards to discover the ways and wiles of the tramping fraternity. 'Amateur Casual', of the *Carmarthen Journal*, discovered the 'gager' and 'griddler', the 'grubbers', the 'moucher' and the 'door thumper'. 'Amateur Casual' of the *Llanelly Mercury*, discovered the 'Mushfakir', the 'Welsh Prophet', the 'man with the Bible' and the 'tramp schoolmistress'.[137] They told the tales of the old man with the false hump and detachable club foot, the mimic epileptic and the girl with eyes scarred to suggest blindness. 'Idle beggar' was a contradiction in terms; many individuals were inventive, resourceful, ambitious and hugely hard-working. The poet Dewi Emrys in *Rhigymau'r Ffordd Fawr* (1926) and W. H. Davies, in *Beggars* (1909), *Time Traveller: A Tramp's Opera* (1922) and *The Autobiography of a Super-Tramp* (1908) revealed the fraught interrelationships and interweavings of this netherworld.[138]

Tramps developed a host of ruses to elicit charity from the tender-hearted. Bold letters on boards hung from their necks told heart-rending tales of heartbreak and hard luck: the pianist or violinist deprived of his arm, and thus his livelihood in an accident; the celebrated tenor, Eos, whose voice was ruined in a shipwreck whilst carrying out a rescue, or some other selfless act of heroism. It all depended on the imagination of the person doing the writing. However, the illiteracy of the very poor was often a serious problem. A reporter in the *Carmarthen Weekly Reporter* complained, in 1907, that begging in Carmarthen was of an 'epidemic character', and described a 'typical scene' on the town's bridge:

> A man was looking about him and taking stock of the passers-by whilst he bore on his manly chest a board which stated that he had lost his sight in a colliery explosion! Feeling convinced there must be a mistake I asked the man how he was able to see so well after a total loss of sight in a colliery explosion. He could not read evidently and he asked in an agitated state what the board said. On it being read to him, he said, 'Here's a pretty mess. I've taken out some other chap's board. I'm really deaf and dumb.'[139]

Street children or 'urchins', as they were picturesquely referred to in the press, often acted in little packs of enterprise and cunning, often cold, always hungry. Women tramps were trained to beg or feign a nervous complaint, unless, by luck, they actually suffered from one – the constant trembling of a limb, the face, even the whole body in spasmodic convulsions. Chapels and churches, especially in the poorer parts of towns, were often fruitful places for beggars, for piety was deemed to be a soft touch or easy target. The fixed itineraries of supplication frequently included a church or a chapel. The beggars knew that on Sunday evenings, eye contact counted. Tatterdemalion, barefooted women would stop dead in front of congregation members as they left the service, staring at them with frantic insistence, holding out a trembling hand,[140] or launching into a tirade of insults and innuendo which could only be silenced by silver.

After the First World War the numbers of mutilated beggars increased. The glib slogan 'Homes fit for heroes' meant little to heroes without homes. The limbless wandered the streets. For a period in 1918–20 in Cardiff, a legless beggar, mounted on a board like a piece of ghastly taxidermy, gleaned a living from the shoppers around the Hayes. Another, a recycling rag-picker with half his face missing, looked as if he had been clumsily guillotined. He had no nose, no lips, no chin, and clamped in his teeth, which were perpetually exposed, was the bruised plug of his tongue. In 1904 Sir Marteine Lloyd revealed the panic, persecution and paranoia that were characteristic of the public utterances of the rich when confronted by the very poor. He complained to the *Carmarthen Weekly Reporter* that more than 6,000 tramps were passing through the country. 'On going to the fox hounds', he stated, '[he] saw seven in 200 yards, horrible-looking fellows that it would be a pity for any lady to meet on the road'.[141]

Sensitivities apart, the actual numbers of vagrants present the historian with problems, for the same individual could be counted several times in any monthly or annual figures because many moved from workhouse to workhouse across the country. Thus the figures for vagrants in workhouses must be treated with caution.[142] For example, in Carmarthenshire in the year ending 31 March 1913 there had been 3,239 vagrants at Carmarthen, 5,000 at Llandeilo, 8,021 at Llanelli, 2,033 at Narberth, 2,999 at Newcastle Emlyn and 3,385 at Llandovery.[143] This restless, rootless army of the very poor was hounded and harried across Wales. What is certain is that contemporaries were acutely conscious of the presence of vagrants. In 1903, the *Carmarthen Weekly Reporter* complained of 'a plague of tramps in the town of Carmarthen', which was 'as bad as the ten plagues of Egypt rolled into one' and advocated a 'campaign of terror against them'.[144] In 1905 the town was described as the 'Mecca' for tramps, and a 'plague of tramps' was reported as having descended upon Llandeilo.[145] In many towns in north Wales, the casual wards were packed within a half-hour of opening, and police had to turn people away every evening. At Bangor and Caernarfon in 1906 vagrants, desperate to escape the terrible weather, committed obvious thefts and even broke police station windows so that they could be arrested and get shelter in the cells. In Kate Roberts's *Te yn y Grug*, the children, Begw and Winni Ffinni

Hadog, are warned before they set off for their tea in the heather to beware of tramps.

Whilst beggars expected charity from the better off simply because of actual or claimed ill-luck, a whole host of others resorted to a life as street entertainers. They included buskers, musicians, vocalists, solo artists, organ grinders, and Italian 'music by the handle' players. Technological advances also benefitted the poorest. By 1895, the old barrel organ and hurdy-gurdy had given way to the piano organ on wheels and Panharmonicons. Street-corner singers and players were often tone-deaf amateurs, whose wailing was the next best thing to begging, or blackmail – 'pay up or I'll sing again'. In the 1920s the craze for 'nigger minstrels', brought the Ethiopian Serenaders, faces made up with lampblack and varnish, on to the streets of Llandudno; shady characters, even before the make-up. Amongst the street entertainers were slack-rope walkers, tight-rope walkers, acrobats, conjurers, even a Frenchman with a performing parrot, and the ever-present never-thriving of jugglers; easy turns, hard lives; bleak expectations. Street puppeteers with Punch at the forefront attracted crowds, but did not make much of a living. 'All Punches die in the workhouse', one told the Board of Guardians at Penrhyndeudraeth (Caernarfonshire) in May 1900.[146] The perambulating performers of Atkins and Wombell's menageries trundled around Wales with their cast of grotesques – giants, dwarfs, 'Malays', the Wild Indian woman, the bearded lady, a mermaid, even a cannibal chief. The voluptuous Ellen Chapman (1830–99), the glamorous lion tamer, performed her famous, or infamous, serpentine dance for the last time in the lion's den in Lord George Sanger's Circus at Merthyr Tydfil in 1895.

These people whose lives were blighted by bad luck and worse judgement merged imperceptibly into the criminal underworld which existed across Wales. Poverty's house, like the Lord's, had many mansions. This world of desperation and the desperate was also organised into a hierarchy. At the head were forgers and the fixers who used their guts and gumption to scam their way to a living. At the lower levels were those muscle-bound masters of mayhem for money and the dissipated petty thieves who stole to fund their thirst or their dependency on alcohol, opium or heroin.

This was a fatalistic world which resented do-gooders and God-botherers and established its own standards and codes of morality and behaviour.[147]

Street life, and life on the streets, had a motley liveliness, a *tableau vivant* that lent vigour and vitality to folk tales and ballads. At the bottom, morally, were the raunchy dives and brothels that lined the waterfronts of Wales at Newport, Cardiff, Swansea, Llanelli, Bangor, Caernarfon and Holyhead. Some were drinking dens devoted to oblivion, but other desires could usually also be accommodated on the premises – in gambling rooms, cockpits, or ersatz seraglios complete with women in costumes more mawkish than sensual. These were the workshops and sweatshops of commercial sex, brothels geared to satiate the lusts of sailors and labourers. The madams, entrepreneurs of sex, charged the girls – the appropriate term, as many of the whores were between ten and fifteen years of age – weekly board and took half their income. They were models of race relations, for they served men of all classes, colours and creeds – all the men needed was money. Given their interest in productivity, the madams insisted on a high volume, high turnover strategy. Some Stakhanovites of sex could service up to sixty men in a good weekend. Their motto was simple – get it up, get it in, get it out, get on to the next one.

5

Hiraeth and Heartbreak – Wales and the World: Curiosity, Boldness and Zest

Y llanciau a'r llancesau glân
Oedd gynt yn gân i gyd
A aeth hyd bedair ffordd o'r fan
I bedwar ban y byd.

(The happy lads and lasses
Once so full of glee
Followed four roads from this lee
To the four corners of the globe)

Sarnicol (Thomas Jacob Thomas), 'Ar Ben y Lôn'

River out of Eden: migration and emigration

Derfydd aur a derfydd arian,
Derfydd melfed, derfydd sidan,
Derfydd pob dilledyn helaeth
Ond er hyn, ni dderfydd hiraeth.

(Gold and silver both corrode,
As does silk and so too satin,
All expensive materials erode
But heartache will endure).

Traddodiadol (Traditional)

Hiraeth, an amalgam of heartache and heartbreak, is the lachrymose and lugubrious undertone of much modern Welsh history; a leaden-hearted yearning for, and by, those displaced, enduring beyond other sentiments. T. Gwynn Jones, in his elegiac poem to 'Tir na n'Og', noted that 'cyfaredd cof yw hiraeth', for hiraeth was not transient, but permanent.[1] Balladeers and folk-song writers tapped a rich vein of sentiment with several variants of songs for the heavy-hearted on topics like 'Hiraeth' and 'Ffarwel'.[2] Hymnists penned mournful dirges about weary travellers lost in strange lands amongst strangers. As the great traveller, T. H. Parry-Williams once said, 'marw ychydig, yw gadael' (to go away is to die a little).[3] But for many Welsh people, staying put was no option, for to stay was more likely to threaten lives; leaving was the price people paid for survival. For generations the poor left the ancient litany of rural life in seasonal tramping migrations. The eternal pressure of need, the endless search for a bit of cash to make ends meet, to pay an outstanding debt, to buy a horse, a cow, or a tempting plot of land, to re-roof a house or build one, drove poor men and women out of their native 'bro', to work as carters, herdsmen, harvesters, thatchers and domestics. For generations, people went away from home because that was the only way to keep the home going. Emigration and exile, the journey to and from home, are the very heartbeat of Welsh culture.[4]

Seasonal migrations, such as those celebrated peregrinations of the drovers and 'merched y gerddi', were a traditional part of rural life.[5] Much rural migration was to rural areas, according to a well-established circuit in which deprived men and women visited almost equally deprived areas. They sowed, reaped, harvested or sheared according to the annual timings of different districts. Gradually, from the middle of the nineteenth century, many of these migrants became emigrants. Those agents of modernisation – railways, newspapers, the postal service and the school – played a crucial part. Railways eased the pressure of a population too numerous for the land to feed. The railway line was a magnet attracting the loose filings of humanity.[6] The postal service and newspapers also made communications easier. Letters, with their stories of wonder and wondering, published in newspapers and carried by the postman, suggested the possibility of leaving to those who had not yet taken the plunge.[7] The towns of Wales and England were portrayed as enchanted places. Here people worked fewer hours, for higher pay, enjoyed greater leisure and took pleasure in a more convivial social atmosphere. In contrast, rural Wales was disenchanted. Life there was dull and drab, a remorseless drudge interrupted only by a weekly prayer meeting or a seasonal fair. The emigrants served as the carriers of modernisation. They sent home parcels containing cash, all sorts of curious sweets, fabrics and novelty goods. The return of the native for holidays, or retirement, brought new ideas, notions and the fashions of the towns into the countryside. They were the first to use dishes at the table, to show off a bicycle, to paint their house, to install lighting, to wear silk stockings, they could even speak English, albeit falteringly.[8] A native of Ffair Rhos in Cardiganshire recalled a typical conversation:

> We're fools to stay in a place like this. In Treorchy there's electric light. Just put your finger on the switch and the place lights up . . . Turn on the tap in the scullery and there's plenty of water . . . There are pavements to walk on . . . The street lamps are on all night. There are plenty of picture-houses for somebody to have some fun. If you haven't any dinner ready you just send the children round to the Bracchi shop for fish and chips. On Saturday there are cheap trips to Cardiff. Oh yes, we're mugs to hang around here.[9]

Almost every Welsh town that grew in population did so primarily as a result of local migration. Of the 6,060 people who moved, in the 1880s, into Blaina, 3,556 came from elsewhere in Monmouthshire and 420 and 349 from the neighbouring counties of Breconshire and Glamorgan respectively. Only 1,428 moved into the bleak mining community from outside Wales. The return of 79 of the latter group of people was unsurprising, for they were monoglot Welsh speakers.[10] The surprise, perhaps, was that they had lasted so long in exile. In the 1880s Cardiff, hailed as 'the metropolis', 'the Chicago of Wales', attracted 929 Irish, 5,320 people from England and 671 people from 38 countries around the world, including 8 individuals who were quite literally at sea in the Welsh port, for these pelagic beings had been born on the oceans. But the largest single group of the 17,110 inhabitants aged two years and over who moved into Cardiff in 1881–91, were from Glamorgan (8,053 people) and adjacent Welsh counties.[11] To imagine Wales in the late Victorian period is to imagine a journey.

Down to the First World War, poverty and the lack of opportunity prised people from the pastoral parishes that were, perhaps, paradises only in poetry. People were dug into their tired soil as deeply as their crops, but powerful outside forces dislodged them. In ebbs and flows tied to the fortunes of industries, people moved out of rural and into urban Wales or even further afield. But in the 1920s and 1930s this pattern fell apart with frightening speed. The collapse of coal mining and other heavy industries as a result of the dislocation caused by the inability to adapt to peace, and the great depression in the world economy in the 1930s brought hard times.[12] People were plunged into a world in which neither the present nor the future seemed to hold much prospect of a job, let alone career advancement or social mobility. In the economic apocalypse of the 1930s, mine and mill gates swung shut, furnaces cooled. One of the most perceptive historians of the twentieth century noted that the depression 'was the worst peacetime crisis to afflict humanity since the Black Death. More, it was the economic equivalent of Armageddon.'[13] To escape the calamitous conditions, 268,707 people left Wales between 1921 and 1931 and a further 181,464 moved out between 1931 and 1951.

Thus the emigrants' tale of farewell as they set off, back view as ever, down the yellow brick road in their search for freedom or fortune was, and is, a frequent and familiar part of Welsh history. At several scenes of farewell, there was a traditional, tragic group. The male members, especially the uncles and brothers, stand awkwardly at the fringes. They stare at the floor, take deep drags on their cigarettes, for they are just a few seconds away from a tearful breakdown that will destroy forever the macho image they have spent a lifetime cultivating. In the centre are the swollen-eyed, sobbing matrons with dripping handkerchiefs, there to support the main actor, the woman in black: mother. Throughout the years between 1870 and 1945, the scene was often enacted at street corner and railway station: the weeping family watching as the emigrant walked away or boarded stagecoach or steam train, then sadly, madly, waving at a receding handkerchief-holding-hand until it finally disappeared.[14]

This was the old, sad tale of entire families being broken up and distributed to the four corners of the earth. In later life those occasions when families traditionally gathered, marriages, christenings, coming-of-age ceremonies and funerals, provided opportunities for people to ponder the way brothers and sisters had lost contact with each other. Walter Haydn Davies, from Bedlinog, remembered how

> as the years went by, and as the anniversaries of the dead children came and went, my mother would say sadly, 'David William would be so and so today' and 'little Philip lying far away in Alabama would be so many years old'. I wonder what they would have been had they lived?

Of Philip, who died in the USA, he wrote that 'the loss of this child broke my mother's heart'. Neither the years nor the distance could heal her hurt.[15]

In 1881, William and Mary Evans and their ten children gathered for a family photograph outside their tiny cottage on the outskirts of Llandeilo. How they all fitted into its damp, dark confines was a mystery. In the children's faces you can perceive a burning desire to go, to move, to get under way, to escape to any place away from here. Thirty years later, two of the survivors returned for the youngest child's funeral. They believed that three others were still alive. Jack was either in London, or somewhere in south Wales. Or was he? His mother always asked for him, especially before her death. Hanna was in London. She sent a telegram. Then a letter. William, they thought, was still alive. He left for love; he had met someone – the usual story. They never found him, but they always looked. Those present remembered youth. They remembered loneliness. They remembered pure sadness. They noted the transience of their life and their family's lives and pondered how they had moved so quickly into the past. How they had gone so swiftly from homestead to hiraeth?

Travel separated and it could also reunite families, but even when families were reunited the pains of hiraeth were not always softened. They simply changed focus. On 14 September 1945, the newspaper *Y Cymro* printed one of the most poignant of all of Geoff Charles's photographs. It shows the frail, elderly couple, Carneddog and his wife, Catrin, as they are leaving their farmstead, Carneddi, Nanmor in the mountains of Eryri to go to live with their son's family in Hinckley, Leicestershire. The sense of displacement is accentuated by the topography; in the photograph the frail couple are in the left foreground gazing over the rugged ridges rolling away across the distance. *Y Cymro's* headline-writer hit gold with the caption 'Rwy'n edrych dros y bryniau pell' (I stare across the far hills), evoking William Williams Pantycelyn's lament for an absent presence. In a letter to his friend, Bob Owen, Croesor, the hyperactive bibliophile Carneddog outlined his feelings of loss:

> a digon o wireless. Clywais di yn aml. Clywais di am bethau hynafol a phwysig o'th lyfrgell . . . Clywaf lawer o Gymraeg ar y Radio. Mae'r canu penillion yn fendigedig, nes yr wylaf . . . go symol wyf. Rhaid tewi yrwan. Daw'r 'angau du' heibio i mi yn fuan .[16]
>
> (and a lot of the wireless. I heard you often. I heard you about ancient and important things from your library . . . I hear a lot of Welsh on the Radio. The singing of verses is wonderful, so that I cry . . . I'm quite simple. I must fall quiet now. The 'black death' will come by for me soon).

Gwalia Deserta: the Welsh in England

> Yes, there is a tension, an emotional tension, a tension between contrasting qualities and instincts. But yes, there is a Welshman hidden in many an Englishman, a Wales hidden in England. That is the enigma.
>
> Enoch Powell, quoted in Roger Thomas,
> *The Welsh Quotation Book* (London, 1994), p. 70

The adventure and romance, the bathos and the pathos of the salt-water tales of the Welsh diaspora around the world have captured the imagination, but the majority of emigrants went off, not to Philadelphia in the morning but, like Hanna Evans, to England.

Many Welsh people realised that the potential and opportunities for advancement were significantly better east of Eden in England.[17]

The professions in England had long attracted ambitious Welsh people. The law, for example, was a magnet for many, often from very humble origins, who scaled the heights of the legal profession. Elwyn Jones, Baron Elwyn-Jones (1909–89), son of a Llanelli tinplate worker, rose to become Lord Chancellor. During the Second World War, he attended many court martials and inquiries into Nazi brutalities. This resulted in his inclusion in the prosecution team at the Nuremberg War Crime trials in 1945.[18] John Roland Phillips (1844–87) of Cilgerran, lawyer and antiquary, received no formal education but entered a solicitor's office in Cardigan at twelve years of age.[19] In 1867, he moved to London and was called to the Bar on 10 June 1870. Phillips combined legal work with his antiquarian interests, publishing *A History of Cilgerran* (1867) and *Memoirs of the Civil War in Wales and the Marches* (1874), and several other titles. John Lloyd (1833–1915) was another who combined his antiquarian interests with a career at the Bar and in local government. This rural radical in the metropolis used his legal and antiquarian skills to champion the rights and liberties of the common people against the incursions of privilege, effectively opposing the seizure of common lands by large metropolitan corporations and landlords.[20]

The list of the Welsh who prospered in the legal profession in England is not endless, but it is very long. Amongst the plethora who made a success for themselves in London legal circles were Sir Frederick Albert Bosanquet (1837–1923), Sir Samuel Thomas Evans (1859–1918), Sir Roland Lomax Bowdler Vaughan Williams (1838–1916), Sir John Herbert Lewis (1858–1933), Clement Edward Davies (1884–1962), Sir Wilfrid Hubert Poyer Lewis (1881–1950), John Gwyn Jeffreys (1809–85) and John Humphreys Parry (1816–80).

Many people combined a career in the law with politics. Sir John Herbert Lewis, one of the four who refused the Liberal whip in the 'Welsh Revolt' of 1894, was a county councillor and MP for Flintshire, a junior minister in several governments, and head of a glamorous legal practice in London.[21] Others, such as Aneurin Bevan (1897–1960), James Griffiths (1890–1975) or Sir William

Jenkins (1871–1944), were less versatile or more dedicated to a cause and concentrated their energies on their political careers as members of parliament. In contrast, James Purdon Lewes Thomas (1903–60), might have been considered to be without political ambition, having stood as a Tory candidate in the rock-solid Labour constituency of Llanelli, but he was that relatively rare beast – a successful Welsh Conservative. Born at Cae-glas, Llandeilo, Thomas was MP for Hereford from 1933 until his elevation to the peerage as Viscount Cilcennin in 1955 and one of the most loyal and trustworthy members of the Conservative administrations of the 1930s and 1950s.[22]

Closely allied to the political world, many people sought their livelihood in the civil service. Sir Perry Emerson Watkins (1871–1946), son of a Llanfyllin, Montgomeryshire, auctioneer, valuer and estate agent, made a successful career for himself in the newly established departments of education, national insurance, health and trade.[23] Despite the claims of some that the Welsh, especially in the years of Lloyd George's political domination, were clannish and nepotistic, Watkins and several others suffered greatly at the hands of John Rowland, another Welsh civil servant. Watkins's advancement was severely curtailed on several occasions by this vengeful rival, whose devious machinations would have captured the admiration of the Capulets and Montagues.

A near contemporary of Watkins's was Thomas Jones (1870–1955). This 'pocket dynamo', affectionately known as 'T.J.', was cabinet secretary from December 1916 to 1930. In this post he served four very different prime ministers in the unique capacity 'of a fluid person moving among people who mattered and keeping the PM on the right path'.[24] He used his extensive contacts within the labour movement to serve as a go-between in industrial unrest, especially in the coalfields. Perhaps Jones's greatest influence was on Irish affairs, where he used his personal knowledge to participate actively in formal and informal negotiations which ultimately led to the Anglo-Irish peace treaty of 1921 and the creation of the Irish Free State. As secretary to the British delegation in the negotiations between October and December 1921, he conversed in Welsh with Lloyd George both to maintain secrecy and to impress Sinn Fein.[25]

The Welsh involvement with English industry, commerce and business, as we have seen above, was active and extensive. In retail, Owen Owen, Peter Rees Jones, Sir William Price and several others were innovative. In the slate, coal and iron industries, George Sholto Gordon Douglas-Pennant, second Baron Penrhryn (1836–1907), John Crichton-Stuart, fourth marquess of Bute (1881–1947), David Davies (1880–1944), first Baron Davies, Margaret Haig Thomas, *suo jure* Viscountess Rhondda (1883–1958) and many others represented their interests in the London-based world of business and finance.[26] In publishing, Sir William Emrys Williams (1896–1977), who never spoke a word of English until he was eight years of age, was one of the founders of the highly successful Penguin books. Thus the Welsh, despite being portrayed as uninventive, were, when circumstances allowed, enterprising and entrepreneurial.

Newer, non-traditional industries also provided opportunities for the ambitious London-based Welsh. Miles Webster Thomas (1897–1980), Baron Thomas of Ruabon, Denbighshire, was raised in genteel poverty by his widowed mother. In 1913, following night classes, he became an engineer with Bellis and Morcan Ltd of Birmingham. In the 1920s and 1930s he worked in the motor and aviation industries becoming director of several companies. In 1941, he became a member of the advisory panel on tank production and chaired the British tank engine mission to the USA in 1942, by which time his income had reached over £20,000 a year. In the 1950s, Thomas was influential in creating the British Overseas Airways Corporation (BOAC), one of the world's greatest airlines and the first to use jet aircraft. Thomas went on to become chairman of the US Monsanto Chemical Company and held board positions with Sun Life, *The Sunday Times*, Carbon Electric Holdings Ltd and Britannia Airways.[27]

Journalism, at many levels, was also a career that the Welsh in England eagerly embraced. There was usually a scoop of Welsh journalists scribbling their trade in most English newspapers. The novelist Eiluned Lewis was a journalist from 1931 to 1936 with the *Daily News* and later a caustic drama critic for *The Sunday Times*. The infamous short-story writer Caradoc Evans (1878–1945) was a journalist with the *Daily Mirror* (1917–23) and then editor of *T.P.'s Weekly* (1923–9). The poet and novelist, Caradog Prichard (1904–80) wrote for the *News Chronicle,* then the *Daily Telegraph,* during a guilt-ridden exile from Wales. James Edmund Vincent (1857–1909) of Bethesda, Caernarfonshire, was the principal descriptive writer for *The Times* and later editor of *Country Life.*[28] John Cowburn Bevan (1910–94) was editor of the *London Evening News,* the *Manchester Guardian* and the *Daily Herald.*

At higher levels within London journalism, the Welsh were exceptionally influential. Henry Lascelles Carr, the London- and Cardiff-based owner and editor of the *Western Mail* and the *News of the World,* appointed his son editor of both papers. In 1925, with equal Borgian nepotism, Lloyd George appointed his son, Gwilym Lloyd George, first Viscount Tenby (1894–1967), as the managing director of United Newspapers. Sir Trevor Maldwyn Evans (1902–81) of Abertridwr entered journalism after he lost his work as an electrician during the 1921 miners' strike. After periods with the *Daily Despatch* and the *Daily Mail,* Evans joined the *Daily Express* in 1930, becoming one of a renowned editorial team – the 1933 club.[29] Frank Humphrey Owen (1905–79), son of the innkeeper of the Black Swan, near Hereford, followed a similar path to edit Beaverbrook's *Evening Standard,*[30] then Rothermere's *Daily Mail.*

The Welsh brought a family dimension into the world of journalism. Percival Thomas James Cudlipp (1905–62) served on several south Wales newspapers before moving, in 1925, to become a drama critic and humorous columnist on the staff of the *Sunday News.* He later edited the *Daily Herald* and the *New Scientist.* His brother, Hubert Kinsman Cudlipp, Baron Cudlipp (1913–98) had a similar apprenticeship before moving to edit the *Manchester Evening Chronicle,* the *Daily Mirror, Sunday Chronicle* and *Daily Telegraph.*[31] Perhaps the most remarkable Welsh journalistic family was that trinity, the Berry brothers from Merthyr Tydfil. Together, Henry Seymour Berry, Baron Buckland (1877–1928), William Ewart Berry, first Viscount Camrose (1879–1954) and James Gomer Berry, first Viscount Kemsley (1883–1968) created a newspaper empire that included over thirty regional newspapers, the *Daily Telegraph* and the *Sunday Times,* as well as the more downmarket *Daily Sketch.*[32]

The identity adopted and articulated by Welsh people beyond Wales in England was complex and contradictory. Many, chameleon-like, merged into their new environment with remarkable ease. The pressures of work, a new life and a different environment were too powerful for the home identity to survive. Often the ability to speak Welsh was the first item to be jettisoned. It was this tendency that was so savagely caricatured and criticised in the figure of 'Dic Siôn Dafydd' – the Welshman who had turned his back on everything Welsh within a few seconds of crossing the border.[33] These were people of Welsh extraction who had had most of their Welshness extracted. For them, the great advantage of travelling was that they could recast their lives in patterns that they would not dare, or dream of, at home. Better to be someone else somewhere else. Emigrants need to grow a memory and grow it fast in order to convert the uncanny into the homely and achieve a stable footing in their new land.

Many Welsh people, perhaps the majority, transplanted their identities, their cultural pursuits and pastimes into their new environment. Welsh chapels, schools and cultural societies, such as the Gwyneddigion, the Cymreigeiddion, the Gymdeithas Gymraeg, and the Cymmrodorion, were established in London, Liverpool, Bristol, Newcastle, Manchester, on Tyneside and in several other places in England where there were sufficient numbers of Welsh settlers. The Welsh Presbyterian chapels such as those on Charing Cross Road, London, and Toxteth Road, Liverpool, were corners of foreign fields that, spiritually, were forever Wales. Sadly, many people learned that these religious and cultural pursuits did not offer them a return to their roots, for that was lost in the foreign country of the past and the pains of hiraeth were perhaps heightened for many Welsh exiles by such activities. Contemporary commentators at home had little sympathy for their plight. W. J. Gruffydd characteristically thundered in an editorial in *Y Llenor* in the spring of 1931, 'digon hawdd caru Cymru, chi sydd yn bell ohoni yn gwneud ffortiwn yn Lloegr' (it is easy to love Wales, you who are far away from it making a fortune in England).[34]

Welsh people were mostly employed in the heavier industries in England, but several also entered newer occupations and professions.

Many worked in the servant-keeping areas of west London, close to the rail link to south Wales at Paddington. The Welsh made up a large proportion of London dairymen and milkmaids. One of the most poignant symbols of this diaspora were the coffins sent home by train to be buried by the few surviving members of the family in Llanddewi Brefi and other villages across south-west and mid Wales. They were 'famous among London drapers' and laid down a rich seam of London gold smelters – 'handsome, portly and jovial', as Charles Dickens saw them in the late 1850s.[35] During the years of intense economic depression in Wales in the 1930s, many followed the example of poet Idris Davies and taught in schools across the south-east of England. Other youths, according to the historian C. L. Mowat, were 'uprooted from south Wales to become waiters in London'.[36] The Welsh insisted that they were devout and decent. However, the 'worst kind of Welsh' – 'the pimps and whores, cardsharps, confidence tricksters, counterfeiters, pickpockets, abortionists, charlatans, fortune-tellers, false prophets, beggars with sham disabilities, illegal distillers, tax officials, thieves, prodigal sons and dissolute daughters', also left Wales for England's and especially London's gold-paved streets.[37]

Traditionally, the Welsh were believed to have settled convivially into their new homes in England. Supposedly, they loved, and in return were loved, by their neighbours. But the reactions of the English natives to the Welsh incomers varied from a warm welcome to words of warning. In all, some 90,000 Welsh people were resident in Liverpool in the 1890s, at least 90,000 lived in London and the south-east of England, and around 20,000 to 30,000 had moved to Tyneside. At Oxford in the 1930s there was a substantial influx of Welsh people into the rapidly developing motor industry. Their influence, through their 'well developed trade-union traditions', was allegedly prominent during the 1934 pressed steel strike.[38] One interesting sidelight which is revealed by the strike is that the Welsh presence in Oxford was far from welcome.[39] Indeed, the Welsh, supposedly in the vanguard of trade unionism and class solidarity at home were, in the context of London and the south-east of England, considered to be blacklegs, strike-breakers, 'scab labour'. In the building trades, especially in London and the English

Midlands, former Welsh miners were employed at wages substantially below recommended trade union rates. Thus the Welsh were demonised. The communist agitator Wal Hannington reported that 'in some London localities where large numbers of south Wales workers have settled, rivalry has expressed itself in street fights between groups of young men'.[40] Arthur Exell, who moved to Oxford in 1928 remembered:

> The Oxford people didn't want the Welsh, because the Welsh were undercutting the English. When the Florence Park housing estate was being built in 1933–4 it was built by Welshmen brought here by the developer . . . Those men worked for a shilling an hour. When I went to live on the estate the hatred against the Welsh was terrible.[41]

Thus, contrary to the views of some historians, there was real antagonism against the Welsh in England that did rise to the level of violence.[42] Throughout England, as the poisoned pen of the anonymous author of *The Perfidious Welshman* showed, there was considerable hatred of the Welsh. This was particularly acute against Lloyd George and his acolytes.[43] There were complaints that the London Welsh, with their own cultural, religious and social institutions, were 'clannish'. At the turn of the twentieth century, Sir Herbert and Lady Lewis created a convivial atmosphere for a 'Celtic circle of friends' in the metropolis, which helped incomers such as the precociously talented Morfydd Llwyn Owen to settle.[44] But Arthur Tysilio Johnson and many others saw such environments not as cosy centres of gentility, but as sinister coteries.

Wandering Stars

> O'i wynfa aeth yr ynfyd
> I wlad bell i weld y byd
>
> (From his heaven the idiot went
> To a far country to see the world).
>
> Morus Cyfanedd (Morris Jones; 1895–1982),
> 'Epigramau', *Morus Cyfanedd* (Llandybïe, 1978)

Despite the work and opportunities created within her borders by industrialisation and commercialisation, many of the people of Wales were wandering stars. The journey into England was adventure enough for some but others, in their search for fulfilment, followed Sarnicol's 'llanciau a llancesau glân' (happy lads and lasses) to the four corners of the globe. One of the great conundrums of modern Welsh history is why the country was a land of both emigration and immigration. Like Scotland, but unlike Ireland, Wales was both a destination and a place for departure. In attempting an answer it is important to note that different people had different social, cultural, economic and vocational aspirations , not all of which could be satisfied within Welsh borders. Thus, at different times, different groups of people within Welsh society set out to achieve their ambitions abroad.[45]

People would simply pack up as much of their lives in Wales as could fit in a suitcase and leave. Like pelagic birds whose migratory itinerary is embedded in their genes, the Welsh followed their dreams. Restlessness told them that it was fatal to be at rest. Wales could not cater for or contain their personal, cultural, economic and spiritual ambitions and aspirations. Several yearned for the better life they thought that they could realise somewhere, anywhere over the rainbow. The traditional arrangement was for men to travel alone until they had settled. Once embedded, they would write home for wives and children to join them. Receipt of the letter from her loved one, inviting her to join him in the happy-ever-after must have been one of the most exciting things to happen to a young girl. This was often the eagerly awaited and much anticipated climax, when all the saving for the big day was, at long, long last, at an end. Finally she could bring out the contents of her bottom drawer – the linen, the crystal and crockery that she had saved bit by bit, piece by precious piece, for years. How on earth would she get it all safely to her new home?

The high hopes of the embarking emigrants were soon dashed when they arrived in their new home. Jane from Wrexham, in a series of remarkable letters published in the *Flintshire Observer*, recalled how she had travelled to America through storms at sea, across hundreds of miles of inhospitable country, all with her young daughter in her arms. For months, she had lain awake at night, in the ship's berth and then in the rocking wagon, dreaming of when the travelling would eventually stop, of when they would reach their new lives. 'And', she wrote, 'this was it. A frontier outpost of shacks and huts, dishevelled, dusty, dirty'.[46] The disappointment was palpable. Other Ishmaelian reports from the diaspora indicate equally poignant and painful human dramas. It is little surprise to read the tragic tales of those who, unhappy and lonely in Wales, were unhappier and lonelier in their new homes. At Grand Central Station, many Welsh women quite literally sat down and wept – trapped outside their own history, unable to retrace their steps because their footprints had been swept away. W. J. Gruffydd left Llanddeiniol for an 'exile' in Cardiff. A constant yearning for a lost arcadia underlies much of his work – 'alltud yw pob dyn wedi'r deugain mlwydd, ac â chlust hiraethus yr alltud y gwrendy ar ymadroddion ei febyd' (every man beyond forty is an exile, and it is with the heartbroken ear of the exile that he listens to tales of his youth).[47] For others the experience of a longer journey was even more heartbreaking. David John Davies and Finwen Davies emigrated with their four children to Canada, after he obtained a job as a lumberjack in British Columbia in 1930. When Finwen gave birth to twins all alone in a snowbound cabin, her mind became unsettled. The family had no choice but to return to Wales. Finwen was confined to the St David's Lunatic Asylum in Carmarthen, where she remained for the rest of her life. With or without her, David John could not cope with the six children. The two eldest, Mair and Eirlys, were sent to help their aunt and grandmother, whilst the four youngest were put in a home for illegitimate children in Lampeter called the First Workhouse. The family's dreams of a brave new world had been shattered.[48]

Many emigrants endured the corrosive and erosive effects of loneliness. Gwilym Mynech, in his poem of 1876, 'Cwyn hen lanc o Kansas' (The complaint of a bachelor from Kansas), repented of his love's labour lost:

Gwrthodais lawer menyw lân
Ar fryniau glân Meirionnydd
O'u hachos heddiw rwyf yn brudd
A'm calon sydd mewn tramgwydd.[49]

(I refused many a comely maid
On Meirionnydd's lush hills
Because of this, today I'm sad
And my heart is heavy.)

Given the traumas people encountered on their journeys, it must have been a relief to some women if their loved ones never honoured their promise to write to summon them to their new home. Indeed some men actively used emigration as a means of escape. In July 1878, the Glamorganshire assizes heard the tragic tale of the death of two-year-old Alice Vincent of Neath. Her father had absconded to California. Her mother, distraught, spent the pittance she received in parish relief on a life of dissipation and dissolution. Amongst the dirt and squalor, Alice starved to death, and her mother Mary was imprisoned for the child's manslaughter. Whilst awaiting trial, Mary gave birth to twins, one of whom died.[50] In July 1880, Robert Smith of Garndiffaith took his three sons to Abergavenny, on the pretext of saying farewell to a friend who was emigrating. At the train station, he sent the youngest son, a cripple, home to tell his mother that his brothers and father were bound for America on the *Germanic*. She informed the Pontypool Poor Law authorities, who sent officers to intercept them. Robert was later imprisoned for a month's hard labour with costs for abandoning his family.[51]

Traditionally, economic distress and depression at home are seen as the forces which pushed people into emigration. Agriculture, coal, iron and slate suffered greatly in the 1870s. Perhaps the major economic crisis point before the 1930s was 1875, when serious lockouts and strikes devastated the Welsh coal and iron industries. 'Famine fever' was said to have gripped south Wales.[52] One newspaper report lamented that 'the phantom of hunger and starvation was creeping through the Welsh valleys . . . babies are crying in vain for food'.[53] However, these particular scenes of depression coincided with a major economic downturn in both America and

Canada. Thus neither country, traditionally popular destinations for the Welsh, was attractive for emigrants at this time and the number who emigrated in the early 1870s was amongst the lowest in the nineteenth century.[54]

The general improvement in the world economy in the late 1870s and the 1880s served to draw more people out of Wales. From 1879 the Welsh slate industry entered a period of deep stagnation, causing the Quarrymen's Union to encourage emigration. By 1883, the tinplate industry, adversely affected by a downturn in the American economy and over-production at home, entered a period of crisis. Many people in the Swansea area were on the brink of famine. Meanwhile granite workers found themselves unemployed, as did lead workers from 1884. Agriculture, always a parsimonious master, was in severe depression from 1874 until the mid 1880s. Poor harvests, low prices and American competition were responsible for the fact that agriculture, according to the 1882 Royal Commission, was at best 'a hopeless struggle'.[55] The *Cambrian News* suggested that 'the only way for farmers to save themselves is to sell out while they still have some capital left, and betake themselves to Canada, Australia or New Zealand'.[56] From the late 1870s, Queensland and New South Wales in Australia and New Zealand became significant centres for emigration from England and Wales.[57] In 1887 some 792 people moved to Bilbao in the Basque region of northern Spain to work in the area's iron industries. Here the dampness of the oceanic climate proved convivial to the Welsh and they quickly established male voice choirs and, in one suburb of Portugalete, a Nonconformist chapel called Bethel. By the First World War there were 2,839 people of Welsh origin living in the area.

Local shipping companies made fortunes. The South Wales Atlantic Steamship Company, trading out of Cardiff, was only one of several enterprises which sought to profit from the emigrants. Bristol-based companies, such as the Great Western Steamship Company, established local agents across south Wales, as did Liverpool shipping companies in the north.[58] Within the ranks of the travellers could be found examples of all human kind, hordes of people decrepit enough to take the magic out of the word 'emigration' – the long-out-of-work, the illiterate, the chronically drunk. Their costs were often paid by Welsh poor law authorities, who considered that it was better to pay for them to go abroad than to suffer and support them at home. As one traveller wrote upon embarkation for his 'new life in the new world . . . never, probably, since Peter the Hermit preached the Crusade has such a motley group of people been collected together'.[59]

Though the traditional tale is that the emigrants' journeys were trails of tears made necessary by poverty, not all who journeyed were paupers or poverty-stricken. Ellen Joyce (1832–1924), of the Dynevor family who owned extensive estates in Carmarthenshire and Glamorgan, was an active proponent of women's emigration, establishing several emigration societies during her long life. She believed that emigration both benefited the women themselves and boosted the Christianisation of the British Empire. Her intention was to send the best of British womanhood overseas so that the colonies should have the advantage of their civilising powers and their potential as mothers of an imperial race. America, Canada, Australia and New Zealand all had, at different times, shortages of particular skills. Thus governments enlisted the services of advertisers to entice those who possessed the desired aptitudes and abilities across the sea with a whole range of inducements. In 1877, Australia and New Zealand offered free passages to female domestic servants, agricultural labourers, general servants, cooks, housemaids, nurses and dairymaids. Even so, the journey was still penitential. To compensate for the horrors of the trip, the London Line boasted that its clipper *Young Australia* carried not only an experienced surgeon, but also a 'cow, a piano, and a distilling apparatus for ensuring a plentiful supply of fresh water'.[60] The Allen Line assured travellers that it supplied stewardesses in steerage.[61] Despite the hardships of the journey, Welsh people were attracted to Australia, especially during and after the Gold Rush to Western Australia in 1893. Even more people followed Lewis Thomas to mine the black gold of the coal-mining margins of the Hunter Valley in New South Wales and Blackstone in Queensland. Here they worked as miners or ran shops such as the Gwalia Co-op Store and gave Australia its most remarkable cultural product – the eisteddfod.

The American Dream

> Onid yw ambell un wedi meddwl a phryderu mwy ynghylch ei fynediad posibl i'r America nag am ei fynediad sicr i dragwyddoldeb?
>
> (Have not a few spent more time wondering and worrying about their possible journey to America than their certain journey to eternity?)
>
> Daniel Owen, *Hunangofiant Rhys Lewis Gweinidog Bethel* (Wrexham, 1888) p. 71

America, however, had little need of financial inducements; the Pied Piper flutings of the American Dream were sufficient to entice people across the sea. In March 1870, the north Wales town of Bethesda, according to *Baner ac Amserau Cymru*, was stunned once more by 'ysbryd ymfudiaeth' (the spirit of emigration). Almost everyone, it seemed, was talking about emigration to America; several had left recently and many were intending to do so soon.[62] As one newspaper correspondent noted: 'yr ydym yn deall fod rhai llythyrau pur addawol wedi dyfod drosodd rai o'r dyddiau diwethaf' (we understand that some very promising letters have come over in the last few days). Receipt of such letters from America was a notable event 'and its contents were soon relayed throughout the parish', recorded the historian of Llanegryn parish in Meirionnydd in 1948.[63]

Letters from America attracted many affluent people to travel. This was especially the case in the 1870s, when only the relatively rich were able to make the journey. In 1873 a Cardiff auctioneer working with London and Liverpool agents was advertising land at two to five pounds per acre in a new colony being formed in Minnesota.[64] In 1876, the American Land Company in London was still promoting the state with land available at between three and four pounds per acre. [65] The 1880s saw the opening up of the north-western states of the United States of America. The price of land was set by the railroad companies. In 1881 the North Pacific Railroad advertised that people could make new homes on the wheat and grazing lands of Minnesota, Dakota, Montana and Washington. Others emphasised that Texas was the best place for the land- hungry Welsh.[66] In 1878, Dr W. Kingsbury, a Texas land, emigration and railroad agent in London, and John Anthony of Aberdare floated the idea of a Welsh colony in Texas. Their promotional propaganda suggested that this Texan Elysium could be an 'asylum for the unemployed, unions can buy land for their members; whilst those with capital can acquire land rich with mineral wealth'.[67]

These were years of unregulated advertising, when copyrighters were free to exalt their prospects in the language of magic and miracles. The railway companies engaged prose poets and fanciful artists to represent the American prairie as a new Arcadia. In countless shop windows across depressed rural Wales, posters showed rich soil peeling away from the plough's blade turning into a stream of gold coins, each stamped with the figure of liberty or freedom. The railroad brochures hymned the climate of Montana – it was temperate, invigorating, medicinal, which was news to those who had been there and experienced the drought, the winters of -40 degrees, and the area's biblical hail, lightning and thunder. The Welsh-American Land and Emigration Company was equally creative and inventive in promoting the virtues of Kansas. John Jones, the land agent, advertised land in Arvonia explaining that in 'Kansas . . . heat is not very extreme and . . . the mosquitoes do not bite frequently'. Such prose drew a remarkable group of entrepreneurial Welsh farmers to the Flint hills of Kansas, where ranches and homesteads named Arvonia, Powys, Gwynedd and Dyfed were echoes of home.[68] Here indeed was a great irony of Welsh history. 'Y werin', the farmers, the nation's mainstay, were migrating in a solid mass to America. They were meant to stand solid, starkly implacable, like a dry-stone wall in a windstorm. But, bags packed, the country's spiritual and cultural backbone was leaving, whereas the sailors, the rootless, the restless, stateless sailors, came home, eventually.

Despite the false claims the people still went, for reality did not undermine the ideal until it was too late. One settler wrote home to his brother and sister in Wales on 11 April 1870:

> The Welsh have brought very poor land from the land sharks. Those who have lived here ten years look more like Indians than Welshmen. They have not been able in ten years to save enough money to build a house of any kind. They live in holes in the ground, something like the potato-catches that you see in Wales . . . There is land in every state which is not worth having even if you got it for nothing . . . I understand that oppressed Welshmen are being invited here but it would be better for them to vote for the Tories of Wales, of England and of Llanrwst and suffer the consequences than come here . . . It is a poor, yes, a very poor place here, especially the further west you go.[69]

Many Welsh people learnt the bitter lesson that the United States of the Gilded Age suffered a form of crony capitalism in which corrupt private and public vultures exploited the naive. As Jane of Wrexham wrote so eloquently, disappointment, loneliness, depression and horribly memorable suicide were the realities of an American nightmare. The poignant letter of one unidentified writer in *Y Drych* in 1887 provides a hint of one person's loneliness and isolation:

> Eisiau Gwraig – dymunaf agor gohebiaeth â merch ieuanc neu wraig weddw ieuanc; dim gwrthwynebiad fod ganddi un plentyn ieuanc. Rhaid iddi fod o gymeriad da ac yn proffesu crefydd. Y bwriad yw gwneud dau yn un i gario mlaen ffarm yn y Gorllewin, a gwneyd cartref yn gysur. Dim twyll na chwareu. [*sic*]
>
> (Wife wanted – I wish to commence correspondence with a young woman or a young widow; no objections should she have one young child. Must be of good character and profess religion. The intention is to make two into one in order to run a farm in the West, and to make home comfortable. No trickery or playfulness).[70]

Despite the hardship and heartache of some, others prospered.[71] George Price, whose father had emigrated from Wern Goch farm, close to Cwm Hir Abbey near Rhayader, farmed more than 30,000 acres on the slopes of the Black Hills in Dakota. Amongst the people he sold horses to were Wild Bill Hickok, Buffalo Bill and Calamity Jane. Charles Samuel Thomas left the Berwyn mountains to breed and sell cattle and sheep in Denver, Cheyenne and Fort Laramie. He and his brother, with the help of the US army and the Texas Rangers, drove herds of more than 20,000 sheep and 10,000 cattle to market.[72] Townspeople gave them the contemptuous soubriquet of 'cow-boys' but profited from their lavish spending. The Thomas brothers fought in the Range Wars of the 1890s against characters such as the trigger-happy and ill-tempered Billy the Kid. On his journey from Presteigne to Kansas, the swoopingly moustachioed Thomas Arthur Radnor had one constant companion, a Hereford bull named Radnor. Together they changed cattle rearing in America. Their adventures were the basis for the western entitled *The Rare Breed*, which starred James Stewart.[73]

The Welsh also streamed into America to work in mines and in iron, steel and tinplate mills. Primarily they went to places like Scranton, Lackawanna, Wilkes Barre and Chicago.[74] Their expertise enabled a number to rise to positions of prominence and ownership within these industries. The Welsh were not only miners, but managers and masters. In the forefront of such men were the slate tycoon John F. Roberts of York County, Pennsylvania, and F. R. Phillips, who formed the Welsh-American Tinplate Company with a capital of over a million dollars. This created considerable tension among other nationalities. During the great strike in the Scranton coalfield in 1871, an Irish writer using the pseudonym 'A Doomed Labourer' penned a scathing letter in the *Scranton Republican*, in which he condemned the Welsh, not only in Scranton but in Wales, for their treatment of the Irish and other nationalities:

> The Welsh say that the mines are theirs by inheritance . . . that they should force the companies into compliance with their terms, starve the Irish, English and Scotch out of the coalfields and that then the coast was clear for them to do as they have done in Wales – to hunt down Irishmen as they have done from Aberdare to Mountain Ash . . . They grow rich on other men's toil . . . get more pianos, more harmonicums, and hundreds of other things that we hard-toiling Irish cannot enjoy. We cannot afford to dress our wives in silks and satins. Now is the time for the English, Irish, Dutch and Scottish who have never got anything but drudgery from the Welsh foremen.[75]

In a bitter fight between Irish strike-breakers and Welsh pickets, two Welshmen, Benjamin Davies and Daniel Jones, were shot. The racial tensions continued for a considerable period after the miners were forced to return to work.

Many merchants and milliners who sold the 'silks and satins' to Scranton's miners were themselves Welsh. Some had risen from itinerant traders and peddlers to become shopkeepers, grocers, butchers and bakers. A little capital, shrewdly invested, enabled many Welsh people to venture into business. The *Webb's Scranton Directory* of 1870 recorded a wide range of shops and services run by Welsh people. Two decades later, these nascent penny capitalists were joined, according to *Williams's City Directory*, by Welsh restaurants, barbers, booksellers, dressmakers, druggists, cigar and tobacco shops, a plumber, a carpet weaver, a photographer, several confectioners, sheet music and musical goods sellers, and even a Welsh elocutionist, Sarah J. Jones ('Shwd mae nawr fuwch frown?'). Thomas D. Thomas of Blaina, Monmouthshire, despite being crippled in an accident in the area's Pleasant mine in 1867, carried their mail, presumably slowly, around town. R. J. Edwards and John Davies served in the police, while the lawyers H. M. Edwards, William T. Lewis and George Maxey kept people from their long arms. As at home, Welsh teachers enthusiastically inflicted corporal punishment on Scranton's children – Principal J. T. Jones was even censored in the local press for his over-eagerness to use the cane. Whatever the profession, the Welsh were sure to be represented.[76]

When America introduced the McKinley Tariff in 1893, it decimated the tinplate industry of south-west Wales.[77] Many Welsh entrepreneurs soon realised that they could produce tinplate more cheaply in America. Whole communities were uprooted and transplanted across the Atlantic. Pentre Estyll chapel, which was located across the road from Cwmfelin Tinplate Works in Swansea, lost 229 of its 500 members between 1895 and 1898.[78] Many Welsh people also followed the various gold rushes to California, the Yukon or wherever the lure of a quick and easy buck took them. Women journeyed as well. Ann Ellis (1840–1934) of Dolgellau established a number of lodging houses in Kansas City and Abilene, thanks to the patronage and friendship of Wyatt Earp, Wild Bill

Hickok and Bat Masterson. In the Yukon Gold Rush of the late 1890s, Welsh women revelled in the freer environment and ran bars, laundries and sawmills, made and sold fabrics and comforted tired prospectors with their home-made hot-water bottles. Other girls, like the danseuse Miss Millie, provided bodily warmth through their work as prostitutes and high-kicking, dazzling, dance-hall girls. For in addition to the piety and praise of their pitch-pine chapels, the Welsh brought to many settlements a Sodom-and-Gomorrah style of plush velvet, gilt and crystal chandeliers in the disreputable culture of the dance hall, the saloon, the whorehouse-hotel, and the player piano parlour.[79] Many such characters lived on the edge of town and of the law, doing brisk business with outlaw cattle rustlers and stagecoach robbers. Where Welsh farming communities in America were founded on abstemious virtue and steadfast labour, the mining towns were founded not just on labour, but on luck. The lives of many such characters were not so much those of history as of legend. With considerable resentment, tee-totallers and moralists amongst the Welsh emigrants to America, such as Dewi Emlyn Davies of Ohio, warned that

> it is best for the emigrant to be a total abstainer; it is better for those who cannot live without intoxicating liquor to stay in Wales. Many a grave in America is filled by the corpse of a drunken Welshman and we do not want any more. Let the worshipper of intoxication stay at home rather than come here to shorten his life with the fiery and poisonous liquor of this country.[80]

The Welsh were not only consumers of powerful spirits, they also created them. One of the most famous was Jack Daniels. One of thirteen children, Jack went to work at ten years of age for Dan Call, a minister who distilled whiskey. When Dan realised that his calling did not suit his profession, he converted to temperance. He transferred his business to the young Jack, who quickly established his distillery as a major industrial undertaking. A fit of pique, not drink, proved to be Jack Daniel's undoing. While trying to open his safe, he forgot the combination, lost his temper, kicked the safe and broke his big toe. Soon blood poisoning and gangrene set in and Jack died in 1911.[81] It was this tippling tradition which so upset an anonymous author in the Welsh-American newspaper, *Y Drych*, in 1870:

> Ar Main Street mae yna Gymry yn cadw bar bron bob yn ail dŷ. Os ydych . . . am grogshops Cymreig, whisky holes, gin mills, rum cellars ac ati, ewch i Lackawanna Avenue, Main Street a Hyde Park. Yno fe welwch feibion a merched, wŷr a gwragedd, yn hanner meddw'n feunyddiol, yn chwarae'n wirion, yn loetran ac yn canu'n Gymraeg fel y maent yn codi cywilydd hyd yn oed ar y Gwyddelod hanner-gwaraidd. Os ydych am ddiffyg parch ar Ddydd yr Arglwydd, os ydych eisiau clywed iaith uffern . . . o gegau Cymreig, ewch am hanner awr ar hyd strydoedd ac i'r salŵns Cymreig yn Hyde Park.[82] (On Main Street, there are Welsh people keeping bars in almost every other house. If you want Welsh grogshops, whisky holes, gin mills, rum cellars and so forth, go to Lackawanna Avenue, Main Street and Hyde Park . . . if you want to hear Hell's language . . . from Welsh lips, go for a half hour stroll on the Welsh streets, and to the Welsh saloons in Hyde Park).

Welsh migration to America reached its peak in 1900, when the Welsh stock in America was officially determined by the United States Bureau of Census as 267,160, of whom 93,744 were immigrants and 173,416 the children of Welsh immigrants. Thereafter those of Welsh stock in the USA declined to 248,947 in 1910 and to 230,380 in 1920, when the number of Welsh immigrants was noted as 67,066. The Welsh were scattered in almost every state of the union, but they were particularly numerous in areas of heavy industry, especially coal mining and iron, steel and tinplate manufacturing centres. Thus the three states of Pennsylvania (100,143), Ohio (33,971) and New York (20,456) contained over one third of the Welsh stock in America.[83]

Great expectations were also placed by the Welsh on several American cities. Despite the lack of a metropolitan tradition at home, the Welsh were drawn to the cities. These were Platonists who still believed America to be an ideal, a land of magic that could overcome and, perhaps, even eliminate fate. The Welsh people in Utah were concentrated chiefly in Salt Lake City (2,205), the result of the siren calls of the Mormon faith in south Wales. In 1900, having survived the gruelling sea voyage, 4,436 Welsh people saw no reason to travel any further and settled in New York, whilst 5,037 ventured a little further west to pursue their dream in Chicago. Amongst the most intrepid and dogged of these travellers were the forty-one who settled in Alaska and the twenty-one who moved to Hawaii.[84]

The motives that drove the Welsh emigrants up the ships' gang-planks were as numerous as the individuals who trod them. A remarkable number had been enticed across the sea by the Mormons. In 1866, *The Cambrian* newspaper reported that 5,000 people from Merthyr Tydfil had gone either 'to leave their whitened bones on the track, or live in wretchedness in the land of Mormon'.[85] Charismatic converts, such as Dan Jones, who could 'talk the parrot off a pirate', persuaded thousands to follow him across the Atlantic. During hard times locally in south Wales, Mormons were good with alms and advice. They told wonderful stories of Jehovah and Jesus and promised a better world in their shimmering city across the sea.[86] Other travellers went for other reasons. John William Morris, Baron Morris of Borth-y-Gest (1896–1979), made the journey to America in 1920 to take up a Joseph Hodges Choate fellowship at Harvard University. Rhys Gwesyn Jones (1826–1901) left the wide expanses of his mountainous home at Abergwesyn to take up the ministry of Welsh chapels in New York and California,[87] whilst Ellis Pierce (Ellis o'r Nant, 1841–1912), bookseller and author of historical romances, fled to Utica to escape the litigation cases brought by people who were enraged by his scurrilous, libellous portrayals of them.[88] John Cowper Powys (1872–1963) spent large parts of each year between 1909 and 1934 on American lecture tours. An enthralling, enchanting and theatrical lecturer, Powys could draw American audiences of more than 2,000 to listen to a lecture on literature.[89]

The self-congratulatory epistles of the American-Welsh, or the Welsh in America, continued in the twentieth century. With a distinct lack of modesty or a grasp of social realities, William Allen White wrote in his newspaper, the *Emporia Gazette*, in 1911:

> The Welsh people of this community have lived here for over a generation. They have been the best single strain of blood in our Emporia life. They have Americanized, but have retained their strong qualities of thrift, of honesty, of industry, of deep moral qualities. Also they are the basis of the best artistic feeling in the community. More than the Americans of several generations, these newer Americans have the sense that money is not all of life, that there is something better than hard cash, and they have given Emporia much of its best tone, its steady-going homely purpose and its wholesome details. The Welsh people in Emporia and vicinity probably number several thousand souls; yet there are no Welsh paupers, no Welsh criminals, no Welsh loafers, no Welsh snobs; they are the salt of the earth, and Emporia is a better, cleaner, kindlier town because it is the home of these people.[90]

In 1872, *Y Drych* published an article that echoed the *Emporia Gazette's* claims:

> though they rush to make themselves notable American citizens, they do not allow this to interfere with their Welsh nationality . . . It is the maintenance of their nationality which makes the Welsh the most respectable citizens, the bravest soldiers and the best Christians in the United States. Before politics, the Welshman thinks of his chapel, his bible and his eisteddfod.[91]

The Welsh had certainly created a remarkable cultural and social heritage across the United States. Henry Blackwell (1851–1928), bookbinder and bookseller, migrated to New York in September 1877.[92] He soon took a prominent part in Welsh-American life. He was a life member of the St David's Society of the State of New York, a life member of the Welsh Society of Philadelphia, a member of the committee formed in 1890 to found a chair of Celtic at Marietta College and secretary of the eisteddfod held in New York in February 1886. His bibliography of Welsh books published in the United States listed more than a thousand items.

Despite the Edenic portrayals of *Y Drych*, recreating 'Yr Hen Wlad' – the Old Country in the New proved difficult. Even if a person could retain many of the core moral values of Welshness, it proved increasingly difficult for the Welsh to retain their language. As the nineteenth century turned into the twentieth, the Welsh language increasingly retreated from the everyday lives of Welsh emigrants, despite the sterling efforts of people like Henry Blackwell. Welsh newspapers increasingly published articles in English or switched completely to that language. Chapel services underwent a similar process. People found it hard to sing the Lord's song in a strange land. The repertoires of Welsh choirs and choral societies also increasingly adopted English. So too did that remarkably Welsh cultural competitive event, the eisteddfod. A writer in *Y Drych*, which was itself forced to publish more material in English, sadly noted, 'English is breaking in everywhere these days, especially in this country. There is not a Welsh family in the county where English cannot be heard in the house'.[93]

The men and women who left Wales in pursuit of their American dream were loyal not only to the land of their birth, but increasingly so to the land of their adoption. This was clearly shown in the United States census of 1920 and 1930, when 73 per cent of Welsh immigrants had become citizens of the United States. The average for all countries whose people took on formal citizenship was only 47 per cent. It is perhaps highly significant that the Welsh head the list.[94] It was this reality which persuaded people like Samuel Roberts and Michael D. Jones of Bala to look elsewhere to found a settlement in which Welsh could be the community's language.

It is impossible to give a full account of the contribution the Welsh made to life in America. In industry, commerce, finance, administration, advertising and in so many different walks of American life, Welsh people and people of Welsh descent could be found. The diversity of this contribution can be captured if we pause to consider the lives of only a few individuals. Griffith J. Griffith (1850–1919), the industrialist and philanthropist, made a fortune in America from newspapers, land speculation and publishing. Griffiths donated 3,015 acres of land to the city of Los Angeles which became Griffith Park and he bequeathed money to build the city's Greek Theatre (1929) and the Griffith Observatory (1935). His legacy, however, was marred by the fact that he was a secret drunk and subject to paranoid delusions. On 3 September 1903, in the presidential suite of the Arcadia Hotel, he shot his wife as she knelt on the floor before him. Incredibly she survived, went to court and obtained a divorce within the record time of four and a half minutes.[95]

One who had more success with firearms was Llewelyn Morris Humphreys (1899-1965), alias the Camel, the Hump or Murray Humphreys, whose family hailed from Carno in Powys. He was the organising power behind Al Capone's criminal empire. So well regarded were his mental faculties amongst the criminal underworld that he also acquired the nicknames 'Mr Einstein', 'The Brainy Hood', and 'Mr Money Bags'. Humphreys was the organiser of the St Valantine's Day Massacre, when he had Capone's main rivals brutally slaughtered in a hail of machine-gun fire. His cruel philosophy of life was neatly summed up in the terse statement: 'any time you become weak, you might as well die'. When his time for death arrived, an American newspaper quipped, 'Humphreys died of unnatural causes – a heart attack'.[96]

Finding it difficult to make a living in south Wales and then in London, Avis Townes Hope, a music hall comedienne and singer, and her stonemason husband left for America in 1911 with their seven sons. After an unpromising start when he appeared as the third act behind a set of Siamese twins and a trained seal, Bob Hope became one of America's most famous comedians, played golf with five serving presidents, and received a world record of fifty-four honorary degrees.[97] Welsh-speaking John Lewis (d.1881) of Jefferson County found a different kind of celebrity. He was the shortest dwarf ever, reputedly a foot shorter than the celebrated Tom Thumb; Lewis weighed a little over a stone and toured America with Barnum's circus. Tennessee Williams (1911–83) made his fame and fortune behind rather than in front of the curtains as one of the most successful dramatists in American history. He won the Pulitzer Prize for *A Streetcar Named Desire* in 1948, and again for *Cat on a Hot Tin Roof* in 1955. Most of his plays are drawn from his direct experience of a dysfunctional family. His father Cornelius was a hard-drinking travelling salesman – friends never described him as an alcoholic, 'for no alcoholic could drink as much as Cornelius did'. His mother, Edwina, was a borderline hysteric. His sister

Rose, a slim beauty of a girl, was institutionalised several times for schizophrenia. Tennessee himself was effeminate and a guilt-wracked homosexual. Over them all towered the dark psychological shadow of his Welsh-speaking maternal grandfather, the local Episcopsal priest. This was not so much a family as a freak show.[98]

Undoubtedly such characters are at the opposite extreme from the traditional portrayal of the Welsh in America, but their experiences serve to show that the reality was more diverse and wide-ranging than the image of the American Welsh as pious and priestly suggests.

East of Eden: the Pacific Welsh

> Wyllt hiraeth y pellterau.
>
> (The wild heartache of distant lands).
>
> T. Gwynn Jones (1871–1949), 'Gwlad y Bryniau'

The ebb and flow of powerful economic currents drew Welsh people in their slipstream into mines, mills and a variety of works across the world – a whole nation shimmering upstream like elvers. One such remarkable exodus followed the industrialist John Hughes (*c*.1816–89) to Russia. Hughes had signed a deal with the Russian government in 1869 to set up the New Russia Company Ltd, with a capital of £300,000, to establish the Russian iron industry. The site Hughes chose for the factory lay on the open steppe, far from the ports. Hughes and 200 hand-picked men from south Wales left for the frozen wastes in an epic of survival. All the equipment they needed to build the ironworks had to be hauled by bullocks across the steppe from Taganrog on the Sea of Azov. Despite the intense hardships of their first winter and a cholera epidemic, they managed to get the ironworks in full production by 24 April 1871. Amongst the hundreds who went to work for Hughes was Gwen, the mother of the journalist Gareth Jones, who was murdered by rebels in Mongolia in the 1930s. Gwen was a tutor for the Hughes family in the 1890s.

Down to 1917, the iron works continued to employ Welsh people in senior managerial positions. The factory was known as Hughes's Ironworks, a testament to the forceful personality of its founder. Further testimony was the fact that the settlement which coalesced around the works also took his name, Hughesovka (Yuzovka). Later it was named Stalino after a greater tyrant, and then renamed Donetsk. When the Russian Revolution erupted in 1917, Hughes's works had a registered capital of £2.25 millon.[99]

Another who prospered from Russian trade was Greville Maynard Wynne (1919–90) of Ystradmynach. During and immediately after the Second World War, Wynne established and ran a prosperous business as a consulting engineer in Russia and Eastern Europe. A chance encounter with Oleg Penkovsky, a Russian spy, led Wynne to work for the CIA and MI6 as a go-between. Some of the material he traded was of world importance, for it enabled the Americans to force down the Russians in the Cuban Missile Crisis of 1962. Arrested by the Russians and imprisoned for a year, he was eventually traded for a Russian agent who had been arrested in London. His adventures are recounted in Wynne's fanciful, semi-autobiographical *The Man from Moscow* (1967) and *The Man from Odessa* (1981).[100]

Russia was also one of the obsessions of the barrister and novelist Sir Elias Wynne Cemlyn-Jones (1888–1966), who travelled more than 7,000 miles across the country in 1929–31. In a novel based on his experiences, *Red Rainbow*, he sought to warn people of the danger presented to the world by communism. Cemlyn-Jones was remarkably well travelled, having undertaken a 'world tour' in 1910–11 with his aunt. These journeys took him to the United States of America, Canada, China, Korea, Japan and several other countries in the Far East.[101] The specialist in gold and silver plate and a professor of fine art in Yale, Edward Alfred Jones (1871–1943), travelled the world in pursuit of his interests, spending a considerable period in Russia and the Pacific rim. The result of his research work there was published in *The Old Silver Plate of the Emperor of Russia* (1909).

'Draw, draw yn Tseina a thiroedd Siapan' was a refrain often sung in Sunday Schools across Wales. Despite this, only a few intrepid souls ventured that far east. Elizabeth Phillips Hughes (1851–1925), the Carmarthen-born pioneer of women's education, held a chair in Tokyo University just before the First World War. Mary Myfanwy Wood (1882–1967) was a missionary in Japan and in China between 1908 and 1951.[102] The much-hyphenated Admiral Algernon Walker-Heneage-Vivian (1871–1952) worked on the China seas for more than a decade before being transferred to 'Hell' – Gallipoli.[103] Anna Leonowens (1831–1915) of Caernarfon, travelled extensively in China and Japan before being appointed tutor to the wives and children of the King of Siam, experiences she chronicled in *The English Governess at the Siamese Court* (1870). She later travelled across Europe to Russia and on to Canada, where she eventually settled. Edith Picton-Turbervill (1872–1960), tireless campaigner for the rights of women, spent two years (1936–8) in Malaya, investigating child slavery.[104] Sally, daughter of Wogan Philipps, died of poliomyelitis in Indonesia; her husband, the poet, P. J. Kavanagh, composed the poem 'A Perfect Stranger' (1966) in her memory.

For no apparent reason, the antiquarian Thomas Pryce (1833–1904) left school and emigrated to Java, where he spent twenty-eight years. Fitzroy Richard Somerset, fourth Baron Raglan (1885–1964), soldier, anthropologist and author, was ADC to the Governor of Hong Kong (1912–13). Gilbert Wooding Robinson (1888–1950), a world authority on soils, spent considerable time researching in Australia, New Zealand and the Pacific Islands. So too did Alfred Russel Wallace, whilst the brothers John Wynford Philipps, first Viscount St Davids, and Owen Cosby Philipps, Baron Kylsant, had extensive business and shipping interests in Japan and the Pacific.

But such individuals were rare lone birds of passage; no flocks of Welsh people followed in their trails. People from Wales who went to the Pacific were far more likely to go in significant numbers to Australia and New Zealand, where the language was familiar, the landscape slightly less daunting and communities of 'corresponding cultures' had already been established.

'I wlad sydd well i fyw': Patagonia

You may be of the opinion that it is not possible to be happy here.

Anonymous Welsh colonist in a letter to his wife, quoted in Chris Moss, *Patagonia: a Cultural History* (Oxford, 2008), p. 130

The desire to achieve a livelihood was not the only motive that drove the emigrants up ships' gangplanks and gangways. Some sought to establish new homelands in which the Welsh language would be free of the 'pernicious' influence of the English language. The urge to establish linguistic and ethnic predominance for Welsh as the community's main language led to some bizarre and eccentric endeavours. Several small settlements were established in central and south America. John Jones of Blaenannerch (1807–75) and Dafydd and Rachel Jones emigrated to one such sylvan idyll, a veritable Welsh Shangri-La near Rio Grande. Many of their descendants, such as Dafydd Rhys Jones (1877–1946), later a teacher in Ceredigion and Patagonia, were trilingual, fluent in Portuguese, Spanish and Welsh. David Stephen Davies (1841–98), a minister and temperance campaigner, established an emigration agency in Wales and then in America in the 1870s, gathering groups of hopefuls to seek new lives in America, Brazil and then Patagonia. The settlers were to transplant the linguistic *Pura Wallia* in the Americas. Davies must have been a most unlucky organiser. His settlements failed, and two of his ships – the *Lucerne* and the *Electric Spark* – sank. When the latter was lost, rumours were rife, both in Wales and in America, that Davies was dead. He had the unsettling and upsetting experience of reading his own obituary and gatecrashing his own memorial service. What he read and heard was not encouraging.[105]

Of all the tales of the Welsh diaspora, the story that still resonates and captures most imaginations is the heroic and heartbreaking tale of the establishment of the Welsh community in Patagonia – Y Wladfa. Patagonia possessed the ultimate in topographical mystique, for like Tartary and Christendom, it did not seem to be pinned down by boundaries.[106] This exodus in search of a promised land had the biblical resonances so beloved by the Welsh. The recruitment work of people such as the Liverpool printer and biographer Lewis Jones was vital. Equally important was the money of the Oxford-educated landowner, Sir Thomas Duncombe Love Jones-Parry. Through their efforts, land was obtained in Patagonia, a group of settlers gathered and set sail. The storm-tossed ship, the *Mimosa*, eventually reached land on 28 July 1865 in New Bay, Patagonia.

The subsequent history of Y Wladfa is one of remarkable endurance and endeavour. The settlers were grossly unprepared and only survived the first winters thanks to the generosity of the Indians.[107] The land they reached was poor and unfertile. Water was either absent in the seasons of drought, or present in such profusion in the wet years that crops and houses were washed away. Severe floods in 1899, 1900 and 1901 had Welsh ministers evoking Noah, whilst the more practical Welsh Patagonian Committee in Wales began to view the settlement in Chubut as a potentially dreadful humanitarian crisis. Lewis Jones (1836–1904), one of the founders of Y Wladfa, was devastated when the floods of 1899 destroyed all that he and his friends had worked so hard for over thirty-five years to create. It was said that when he died in 1904, it was of a broken heart.[108]

Between 1874–6, 500 newcomers from Wales and a further twenty-seven emigrants from New York joined the settlement in Patagonia. Numbers were boosted again in 1880–1 and 1885–6 when the *Vista* brought 465 people. Amongst the travellers was William Meloch Hughes (1860–1926), inventor, author and photographer, who, from 1881, spent over forty years in Patagonia, working as a schoolteacher and minister. In 1926 he returned to Wales, where his *Ar Lannau'r Camwy* (1927) was published posthumously. Aged only sixteen, the orphaned Jonathan Ceredig Davies (1859–1932) emigrated to Patagonia and lived there for over two decades before moving on to Australia, France and Spain. His works *Patagonia: a Description of the Country* (Treorchy, 1892), and *Adventures in the Land of Giants: a Patagonian Tale* (Lampeter, 1892) did much to publicise the settlement. The last great emigration was that of the *Orita*, in November 1911, when 120 people arrived. Some people were born on the way to the New World. Ellen Jones gave birth to a daughter, Eluned, on board the ship *Myfanwy* in the Bay of Biscay in 1870 on the journey to Patagonia. The girl was given the surname Morgan, from the Welsh 'môr ganwyd' (sea-born). And what a birth it was, amongst the seasick and the hardtack. Eluned's cradle was the rolling ship that shivered and shook in the Atlantic.[109]

Farming in the community improved to such an extent that the settlers were awarded gold medals at international expositions in Paris and Chicago. Chapels were built. Newspapers, such as *Y Drafod, Seren Patagonia* and *Ein Beirniad,* were published. New townships like Trevelin (1875), Cwm Hyfryd (1885) and Esquel (1906) were established. Despite everyone and everything, these communities survived a fragile life on the periphery, on the very edge of the world. In many of the heroic tales of this diaspora, such as Abraham Matthews's *Hanes y Wladfa Gymreig yn Patagonia* (1894) and *Y Wladfa Gymreig yn Ne Amerig* (1898), exile was the route to achieve the greater glory and destiny of a chosen people. The Welsh clung to their identity and language in Patagonia with the determination of molluscs. In 1882–3, Richard Jones Berwyn (1836–1917) and others were imprisoned for their protests against the Argentine government, which was threatening Welsh rights.[110]

One of the great ironies of the tale is that the Welsh who moved to Patagonia, to escape the oppression of the English, themselves persecuted local Indians. The local tribe, the Tehuelche, who became extinct soon after the 'Glanfa' (the arrival), were the doomed doppelgängers of the Welsh. The Welsh 'settlers' displaced the 'wanderers', those people who had actually lived on the land for thousands of years.[111]

Tragedy seems always to have tinged and touched the tale of the Welsh in Patagonia. One of the saddest aspects, perhaps, is that many of the people who emigrated there had to return to Wales, or sought another new start elsewhere. Travelling towards and away from borrowed and broken dreams, Welsh people were pushed and pulled around the world. At least 150 of those who had gone to Patagonia moved to Australia between 1910 and 1916. Migrating as groups, they formed two 'Welsh settlements' in the Murrumbidgee area of New South Wales and Moora Miling in

Western Australia. Yet their trails of tears did not end there. Drought, depression and infertile land forced them to move again to Collie, Perth, northern Victoria and further afield, but they never found their promised land. Amongst them was Morgan Jones. Morgan left Pontypridd in 1875 at the age of fourteen to live in Patagonia. Thirty-nine years later he arrived in Australia with seven of his children to make yet another new start.[112] Many other people left with Morgan; a photograph taken aboard the ship *Rotorua* in July 1915 shows the Rowlands, Oliver and Thomas families, with two Spanish friends. The assembled group stares expectantly, excitedly, yet with a visible sense of anxious trepidation at the camera. Perhaps they had cause to be nervous about the adventure they had embarked upon, as only one of them, John Rowlands, could speak English.[113]

Estimates vary but either two fifths or one third of all emigrants from Wales in the years 1870–1945 returned home. The return of the native, however, as Daniel Owen showed in his novel *Gwen Thomas*, was at best bittersweet; most often it was bewildering, for home was no longer the same, it was in the past. These pilgrims on their return journey to paradise learnt that you cannot go home again because home has ceased to exist except in the filigrees of memory. The familiar names reassured but it was no homecoming, for although all looked the same, in actual fact all was different – it was the shock of the old. Some added to the sense of displacement by naming themselves and their homes after their place of temporary sojourn, as did the insomniac farmer Utah Watkins of Salt Lake Farm in Dylan Thomas's *Under Milk Wood*.[114]

'To boldly go': adventure and adventurers

Mynd y mae i roi ei droed,
Ar le na welodd dyn erioed.

(He's gone to place his foot,
On a place humans have never seen).

John Ceiriog Hughes (1832–7), 'Llongau Madog', in
Y Bardd a'r Cerddor, gyda hen ystraeon amdanynt (1865)

The call of the wild, the awareness of an urgent demand in the blood drew many Welsh people to wander and explore, but one of the saddest aspects of Welsh history is that adventurers, explorers and the doers-of-daring-deeds are often ignored. Historians have shied away from those wandering stars, the *Boys Own Adventure Book* heroes and larger-than-life heroines who strived, sought, found and never yielded. Those who sailed, steamed and boldly walked – for these really were the walking classes – where no one had gone before and achieved heroic feats are left out of our history. If their tales are considered at all, then they are often treated as stories of epic endeavours that have little relevance to Welsh life. Incorporating such tales and stories, however tall, into the mainstream has the merit of restoring at least some of the light and shade of the world we have lost. Welsh history also had an eclectic mix of adventurers, drifters, soldiers and sailors, the old, the bold and the brave. Their exploits should be considered alongside the achievements of the more sedentary, stay-at-home Welsh. One aspect to remember is that Welsh people of relatively simple origins and means were intrepid explorers. The Welsh settlers in Patagonia, for example, traversed vast distances of the 'wilderness' in search of new lands to farm and minerals to exploit. Their world view, framed by their biblical readings, created a portrait of a brutal, hostile environment which they would seek to tame. Thus, their ventures into the interior were termed 'Hirlam Uffernol' (Hellish Journey), 'Hirlam Ffyrnig' (Fierce Journey) and 'Hirdaith Edwyn' (Edwyn's Long Journey) to 'Hafan yr Aur' (Gorge of Gold) through 'Bannau Beiddio' (Daring Peaks).[115]

Two Welshmen with ruined reputations stand at the forefront of African exploration. John Petherick (1813–82) worked with John Hanning Speke trying to discover the true source of the Nile in the early 1860s and made significant discoveries in the company of his remarkable wife Katherine in the Bahr el Ghazal. Yet charges that he was involved in human trafficking and slavery continue to stain his reputation.[116] The nineteenth century's greatest explorer and adventurer was Welsh. Henry Morton Stanley (1841–1904) endured a childhood in St Asaph workhouse that could have served as a more extreme plot for Dickens's *Hard Times*. A brilliant but flawed personality, a cauldron of contradictions – tough yet neurotic, religious yet brutal, Stanley, like Hamlet, was a study in isolation. Starved of affection, he left Wales in search of the American Dream. After a period of rootless travel, he hedged his bets and fought on both sides during the Civil War before getting a job, at the age of twenty-seven, as a self-financed reporter with the *New York Herald*. In 1869, his publisher, James Gordon Bennett, gave him an assignment to find David Livingstone, the saintly explorer who was supposedly lost somewhere in Central Africa, searching for the source of the Nile. Out of Africa came Stanley's fame and fortune.[117]

Arriving in Zanzibar in 1871, Stanley had no moral scruples in taking advice from Arab slave-traders on how to organise his expedition.[118] He even accepted one of them, Ngaliema, as his blood brother. Within only eighty-four days, he and his entourage had covered the 843 kilometres to Kwihara, near Tabora. Livingstone was duly 'discovered' in 1871. Three years later, Stanley returned to Africa. By 1877 he had circumnavigated Lake Victoria, the world's second-largest freshwater lake, proving Speke's supposition that Ripon Falls were its only northerly outflow. He then circumnavigated Lake Tanganyika, finally proving that it did not feed the Nile. Between 1879 and 1884, Stanley returned to the region to establish twenty-two river stations along the Congo for King Leopold of Belgium. He even built long stretches of roadway and a railroad, which earned him the nickname Bula Matari, the Smasher of Rocks. Three years later he led the expedition to relieve Emin Pasha, who was under threat from the Mahdi in Sudan's beleaguered Equatoria province. Stanley navigated the Aruwimi river, traversed the unexplored Itwi forest and eventually brought Emin Pasha back, but not before half of his expedition had perished.

Despite his undoubted achievements, contemporary reaction to Stanley was almost universally hostile. The mandarins of the Royal Geographical Society were outraged that a brash American journalist had succeeded where their brave members had failed. Sir Henry Rawlinson, in his first presidential address to the society, sneeringly stated that 'if there has been any discovery and relief, it is Dr Livingstone who has discovered and relieved Stanley'.

When it was revealed that the American interloper was actually John Rowlands, a 'workhouse bastard' from north Wales, then their spite was virulent. Historians have been even harsher. Outraged at the unreliability of his jungle books, historians have portrayed Stanley as a fantasist incapable of telling truth from fiction, a masochistic homosexual who took pleasure in the hardships of African travel, even a sadistic racist. To many, his involvement with King Leopold of Belgium's murderous campaigns in the Congo actually put the darkness in the heart of Africa.[119]

Contemporaries, especially in Wales, were more sympathetic. Stanley, who was only just over five feet in height even in his marching boots and pith helmet, had a constant fear of people and intimacy. People, especially crowded together, unnerved and unsettled him. His discovery of Livingstone was almost ruined due to the crowds who greeted him. Of another occasion he recalled:

> As I moved through the crowd, I felt hands touch my coat, then, getting bolder, they rubbed me on the back, stroked my hair, and finally thumped me hard, until I felt that the honours were getting so weighty I should die if they continued long.[120]

This was a description, not of an unruly African mob, but of the reaction of the audience who had packed into a hall in Caernarfon to hear Stanley lecture on his adventures. The audience clearly worshipped the local boy made good, the adventurer who had achieved so much against all odds; and this local boy, through his adventures, recounted in hair-raising detail in a series of best-selling books, really had made good, for in the 1890s fortune shone on Stanley with the force of the African sun at midday.[121]

To many Welsh people, the magic of the far away was too tempting to resist. Margaret Jones, 'Y Gymraes o Ganaan' (the Welshwoman from Canaan), was one such intrepid traveller who became famous for her travels. In a photograph taken in John Thomas's Cambrian Gallery in Liverpool, Margaret proudly poses in full burka, confirmation of her internationalism and her depth of feeling and respect for the cultures she visited and studied. She travelled widely from Morocco through to Palestine. The letters she sent home to her family from Palestine were published in *Llythyrau Cymraes o Wlad Canaan* (1869). Her experiences in Morocco were retold in the later, larger volume, *Morocco a'r Hyn a Welais Yno* (1883). Margaret eventually settled in Australia and married a farmer named Josey; she died in 1902 – 'Ymlaen mae Canaan'.[122] Also captured by John Thomas's camera was W. O. Thomas, the intrepid traveller and author of *Dwywaith o amgylch y byd* (Utica, 1882). The volume recounts his five-year odyssey across Europe, Asia, Africa, America and Australia. Thomas seems to have had an incredible knack for discovering representatives of the Welsh diaspora in the remotest places.[123]

Exploration societies enabled other individuals to travel to a variety of places around the world. The artist and poet Ernest David Bell (1915–59), worked for the Egypt Exploration Society in the Sudan at Sesebi and Amarah between 1936 and 1938. Despite contracting encephalitis lethargica (sleeping sickness) in the worldwide epidemic, Bell published collections of poems on his experiences, as well as the innovative *The Artist in Wales* (1957). Gwladys Perrie Williams (1889–1944), who graduated with a DLitt from the University of Paris in 1917, also gave years of devoted service to the Egypt Exploration Society. Between her travels, she managed to serve as an external examiner for several education boards and published the influential report on *Welsh Education in Sunlight and Shadow* (1918).

Work, more than wanderlust, took Gwladys Williams's husband, Sir Rhys Hopkin Morris (1888–1956) to several overseas countries.[124] During his period as an MP for Cardiganshire (1923–2) he served on the parliamentary commission to Africa (1928) and was a member of the inquiry into the riots in Palestine (1929). In 1946 he served on the Commission for Indian Independence and he and the commission's leader, the Wrexham MP Robert Richards (1884–1954), won the respect of the Indian leaders Gandhi and Jinnah. Robert Richards later recounted his travels in India in a series of articles in *Yr Eurgrawn* in 1951. Gareth Richard Vaughan Jones (1905–35), a precociously talented journalist, reported on famines in the Ukraine and Russia (1933) and the plight of the people of Italy's Pontine Marshes. In 1934, as a reporter for the *Western Mail*, he set off on a world tour. After a series of hair-raising experiences in China, he was murdered by a group of pirates and kidnappers in central Mongolia on 12 August 1935.[125]

The tradition of a 'world tour', which had been such a marked feature of the gentry in the eighteenth century, was a notable aspect of the nouveau riche Welsh in the late nineteenth century. Sir John Herbert Lewis (1858–1933) was brought up in Mostyn Quay in an affluent commercial family with strong connections with shipping. From childhood, his life was enriched by frequent visits to the Mediterranean and the Middle East for the winter months. In 1884–5 he travelled across the United States, Japan, China and India. Lewis was probably the most widely travelled member of parliament of his generation.[126] Sir Willmott Harsant Lewis (1877–1950), like his namesake Herbert, was raised in considerable luxury as the son of a Cardiff coal-shipper. Willmott Lewis enjoyed a superb education at Heidelberg and the Sorbonne. After a brief period as an actor, this 'brilliant irresponsible, and adventurous young man' went across Europe to Africa, and travelled extensively in Japan and China. He then became editor of the *North China Daily News*. Working as a correspondent for the *New York Herald*, he was in China during the Boxer uprising and in Korea during the Russo-Japanese war. After a brief period in San Francisco, he returned to Asia to edit the *Manila Times* from 1911 to 1917. Here, he made important contacts among the Americans who then controlled the Philippines. At the request of one of those contacts, General Pershing, he went to France and handled American propaganda in Europe. He also attended the peace conference as a representative of the *New York Tribune*. For his services in France he was made a Chevalier of the Légion d'Honneur. From the 1920s to the mid 1950s, he was the American correspondent for *The Times*. His letters from America were highly influential and are credited with initiating the special Anglo-American relationship. Tall and handsome, Lewis was much admired in America, a fact he attributed to his origins: 'I am not English but a Celt'.[127]

In addition to the nouveau riche, Wales had many aristocratic adventurers who took the tradition of the world tour to new extremes. Windham Thomas Wyndham-Quin (1841–1926), fourth earl of Dunraven and second Baron Kenry, owner of over 39,756 acres in Glamorgan in 1883, enjoyed a life of almost unbelievable luxury. In 1867 he served with General Sir Robert Napier, brother of Glamorganshire's Chief Constable of Police, in the Abysinian campaign. There he shared a tent with H. M. Stanley, who was at that time a reporter with the *New York Herald* and even, Wyndham-Quin claimed, wrote Stanley's press reports for him. He then travelled around Europe and America, adventures he recounted in books such as *The Great Divide: Travels in the Upper Yellowstone* (1876). After spending over a year (1884–5) travelling around the world, the temperance campaigner John Herbert Roberts, Baron Clwyd of Abergele (1863–1955), recounted his adventures in *A World Tour*. The Welsh version of his travels, *Ymweliad â Bryniau Kasia* (1888) ran to a second edition and he also published an article, 'Tro yn yr Aifft', in *Y Traethodydd* in 1896.

A host of other people from less privileged backgrounds were also inveterate travellers. Vincent Llewellyn Griffiths (1902–84) went to teach in a small rural school in Gorakhpur, India, in 1924. From there, in 1926, he made an adventurous trip into Tibet, walking with a cook-companion for 200 miles on the 'forbidden' Lhasa road. Later, in 1934, he went to the Sudan where he set up that nation's Institute of Education.[128] David Glyn Bowen (1933–2000), a 'multi-denominational minister', also travelled widely in the east and on one occasion discussed metaphysics with the Dalai Lama.

Cultural pursuits also carried the Welsh around the world. The eisteddfod, that remarkably plebeian festival, was in reality an international phenomenon, for eisteddfodau were organised in many countries. In 1897 a large eisteddfod, to which shiploads of Welsh people travelled, was held to support the Chicago World Fair. Madame Hughes-Thomas took her famous ladies choir to America, Canada, South Africa and across Europe. Her husband, Edward Thomas (Cochfarf; 1853–1912), followed in their slipstream as the choir's lucky chaperone.[129] John Thomas (1867–1938), a Calvinistic minister from Llandybïe, won the chair competition at the San Francisco eisteddfod in 1915. Despite the war in Europe, the artist Frederick Charles Richards (1878–1932) travelled to Florence, Venice and Rome. When based in Egypt in the late 1920s and early

1930s, he travelled widely in the Near East; these experiences are chronicled in *A Persian Journey*. Religious leaders were exhorted to cast their bread upon the waters and so a number of evangelicals had extensive opportunities to travel. In the years before the First World War, the Jesuit missionary Bernard John Vaughan (1847–1922) was much in demand due to his skill in repartee and as a raconteur, and undertook preaching tours to Rome, Ireland, Canada, the United States, Japan, China and South Africa. So powerful was the sermon he delivered impromptu at Cannes on Mary Magdalene, 'The woman that was a sinner', that it had a profound influence on one of his listeners, the Prince of Wales, and a highly unlikely close friendship developed between them.

Arnold Henry Savage Landor (1865–1924), an artist with Swansea antecedents, also travelled widely in Italy and France. In 1888 he set off around the world, financing himself by painting portraits of distinguished people he met along the way. In Japan his adventures among the aboriginal Ainu people were recounted in the enigmatically titled *Alone with the Hairy Ainu* (1893) and *Corea or Chosen, the Land of the Morning Calm* (1895). His book *In the Forbidden Land* (1898) recounts his capture and torture in Tibet. In 1899, he climbed Mount Lunysa in Nepal and in 1900 he joined the allied march on Peking during the Boxer uprising. Between 1903–11 his exploits edge towards the incredible. He traversed the deserts of Persia and Baluchistan by camel, crossed central Africa at its widest point (described in *Across Widest Africa*, 1907), and explored the Mato Grosso of Brazil, where his men mutinied and made two attempts on his life. Starving and stricken, he eventually arrived back in 'civilisation'. Upon recovery, Landor promptly put pen to paper to recount his epic adventures in the switchback narrative of *Across Unknown South America* (1913). In the Philippines he visited head-hunters in Luzon and discovered the white-skinned Mansaka people in Mindanao, experiences recounted in *The Gems of the East* (1904). During the First World War, he toured the western front and submitted designs to improve airships, armoured cars, automobiles and a host of other devices. Given his life of high adventure, the title of his autobiography was almost an understatement: *Everywhere: the Memoirs of an Explorer* (1924).[130]

Llwyd ap Iwan, son of Michael D. Jones of Bala, one of the founders of the Welsh settlement in Patagonia, was an active explorer across much of Chile and Argentina. His sketch map of the northern and central regions of Patagonia (1901), preserved in the Royal Geographical Society's vaults, was the result of a journey of more than 3,000 kilometres on horseback, investigating the potential for establishing a colony beside the Lago Colhué Huapi. In December 1909, Ap Iwan's travels ended, when he was shot, many still claim, by Butch Cassidy and the Sundance Kid.[131]

Perhaps the greatest Welsh traveller was Norman Lewis (1908–2003). 'Bizarre' might capture something of the eccentricity of his upbringing by spiritualist parents, partly in Enfield, partly in Carmarthen. Lewis had three older brothers, all of whom died 'fairly mysteriously' one by one in their teens. When he was eleven years of age, his parents sent him away to Carmarthen to live with three aunts. 'One had an epileptic fit every day, one would weep all the time and the other would laugh. They were very, very ignorant people imbued with a savage form of religion.'[132] Presiding over them was Lewis's grandfather, who despite being a chapel deacon still managed to make a fortune selling damaged goods and even kept a French mistress in this cosy citadel of Nonconformist Wales. After service in the Second World War, recalled in *Naples' 44*, 'one of the greatest of all travel books', Lewis, travelled several times around the world. In works such as *A Dragon Apparent* (1951), *The Honoured Society* (1964), *Semara* (1949), and *An Empire of the East* (1993), Lewis provided a sceptical and acerbic view of the world. He clearly relished the outlandish, the grotesque and the laughable, and recorded them all with cool surety, his viewpoint honed by his early experiences in Carmarthen.[133]

A strong sympathy with the plight of indigenous people and their mistreatment by modern society also underpins the career of the social anthropologist Sir Edward Evan Evans-Pritchard (1902–73).[134] His parents were both Welsh speakers, his father a Church of England clergyman from Caernarfon and his mother, Dorothea, from a Liverpool Welsh family. Evans-Pritchard never lost the values and sentiments of his upbringing and also maintained a strong attraction to the unconventional, the Bohemian and even the raffish. As a student at Oxford he was a member of the ultra-privileged artistic coterie, the Hypocrites Club. In the 1920s, Evans-Pritchard pioneered the study of so-called primitive peoples, undertaking extensive field research conducted through the native language. Evans-Pritchard's first book, *Witchcraft, Oracles and Magic among the Azande* (1937), was a brilliant analysis of Zande mystical beliefs and practices, which implicitly raised general questions of the relationship between faith and reasoning. The work reveals two traits which were to characterise his career: the development of general ideas through detailed ethnography rather than by abstract argument, and unusual insight into the intellectual and moral coherence of apparently disparate social phenomena. Evans-Pritchard never allowed sociological analysis to deprive the reader of a vivid and sympathetic impression of the people themselves. People who held to their own customs and beliefs in the face of powerful foreign influences had his sympathy, he explained, 'because I am a Celt'.[135]

Service in other academic disciplines and general interest took many Welsh people around the world. The palaeontologist Dorothea Minola Alice Bate (1878–1951) of Carmarthen, had very little formal education. 'My education', she once remarked, 'was only briefly interrupted by school.' Her work on fossils, published regularly from 1901 in the *Geological Magazine*, took her to Cyprus, Crete, the Balearic Islands, Corsica, Sardinia, Malta, Palestine and China. One of her most enduring works is the results of her excavations at Mount Carmel: *The Stone Age of Mount Carmel: Palaeontology, the Fossil Fauna of the Wady el-Mughara Caves*. The pioneer of the new field of archaeozoology, she took charge, aged sixty-nine, of the National History Museum's zoological branch.[136] Laura Elizabeth McLaren (née Pochin), Lady Aberconway (1834–1933), socialite and tireless campaigner for women's rights, was also a notable horticulturalist. After she inherited the Bodnant estate above the river Conwy from her grandfather in 1895, she scoured the world in search of new plants for the gardens. Her obituarist in *The Times* described her as one of the foremost horticulturists in Europe.[137]

Perhaps the greatest collector of plants and scientific material was the indefatigable and indomitable Alfred Russel Wallace (1823–1913). Rather surprisingly, Wallace commenced his fieldwork in the industrial environment of Neath in the 1840s. In the early 1850s he travelled widely in the Amazon and the Rio Negro. Most of his time was spent studying the area's ornithology, entomology, physical geography, primatology, botany and ichthyology. His fascination was directed at two particular problems: how geography influenced species distribution boundaries and the way in which the adoptive sites of many populations seemed more attuned to ecological station than to closeness of affinity with other forms. Although most of his notes and samples were destroyed in a fire at sea aboard his brig, Wallace still managed to publish his findings in the ethnobotanical survey, *Palm Trees of the Amazon* (1853) and in *A Narrative of Travels on the Amazon and Rio Negro* (1853). He then, with the aid of a grant from the Royal Geographical Society, undertook eight years' field work in the Malay archipelago. His efforts, drawing on perhaps seventy separate expeditions, reaped the astonishing harvest of 126,500 natural history specimens, including more than 200 new species of birds and well over 1,000 new insects. His adventures trying to capture specimens of the bird of paradise, his pursuit of the orang-utan and his other experiences are recaptured in the superbly readable *The Malay Archipelago* (1869). Reading the book today you can still feel his scientific curiosity shining through like sunshine.[138]

A paper presented to the Linnean Society in 1859 included Wallace's delineation of the abrupt zoogeographical discontinuity between the oriental and Australian faunal realms that now bears his name: Wallace's Line. Convalescing in the Moluccas in February 1858, Wallace arrived at the notion of natural selection. The debate as to whether Wallace or Darwin should be regarded as the true father of the concept of natural selection of species continues. Suffice it to say that the treatment he received from the Victorian scientific establishment was less than gentlemanly. A sage and a seer, a scientist of considerable genius, Wallace made signal and significant contributions to a host of subjects – zoology, ethnozoology, botany, physical geography, physical anthropology and a host of others.[139]

Particular careers also provided a wealth of opportunities for Welsh people to travel. Thomas Ifor Rees (1890–1977) of Bow Street, Cardiganshire, was a British diplomat in France, Venezuela, Nicaragua, Spain, Mexico, Italy and Peru; in 1847 he was the first British ambassador to be appointed to Bolivia. His books, *Sajama, Illimani* and *In and Around the Valley of Mexico*, show his superb photographic talents, but also his deep fellowship and friendship with common people. His translation of Omar Khayyám's *Rubáiyát* was the first Welsh book to be published in Mexico. While in Nicaragua he worked alongside Edmund Owen Rees, who had left Carmarthenshire for Central America forty years previously. To maintain confidentiality and secrecy, the Welsh-speaking namesakes arranged 'ein bod yn defnyddio'r Gymraeg ymhob telegram cyfrinachol, gan y teimlwn yn lled hyderus na cheid neb yn swyddfeydd teligraff Nicaragua yn ddigon hyddysg i fedru dehongli y negeseuon hynny' (we arranged to use Welsh for each confidential telegram, as we felt confident that no one in the Nicaraguan telegraph offices would be able to interpret those messages).[140]

'The worst journey in the world': explorers and exploration

> Whether the result be victory or defeat, the third attempt to conquer Everest will mean like the two before it an inspiring display of the resolution and endurance and indifference to discomfort and danger that, all through the ages and to the utmost ends of the earth, have made the people of these islands, above all a race of pioneers. When General Bruce says that the great adventure of Everest has now become almost a pilgrimage, he touches upon a profound truth.
>
> *The Times*, 28 January 1924

Sport was another endeavour which enabled the Welsh to travel the world. The bonds of the 'British West' were strengthened by sporting endeavours. In a real sense, in an age of playing-field imperialism the British Empire on occasion resembled an enormous sports complex. The professionalisation of football, rugby and cricket and the establishment of tours by international sporting teams provided countless numbers of individuals with the opportunity to play for or to support their teams around the world. The legendary Welsh victory over the touring New Zealand All Blacks in Cardiff in 1905 was followed by a bruising and brutal tour to the islands. The victory resonates with the force of legend in Welsh sporting history; the defeat is forgotten.[141] Oddly, defeat was more important than victory in a number of sports, for the role of gallant losers soon became a feature of the Welsh character. Big-game hunting was also highly popular, as the huntsmen of Wales turned their sights from the avian holocausts of the Welsh moors to the game of the African plains and the bison of the American prairies.

Perhaps the sport that provided Welsh travellers with the greatest opportunities for adventures and challenges was mountain climbing. Local crags and cliffs in north Wales provided a superb training environment for many who went on to tackle further, higher climbs. Mary Williams (1873–1942), one of the first women to climb in the Alps, was a member of both the Alpine Club and the Climbers' Club. She climbed alongside her husband, William Jones Williams (1863–1949), and others such as Owen Glynne Jones and Roderick Williams.[142] Emmeline Lewis Lloyd (1827–1913) of Nantgwyllt, Caernarfonshire, another pioneer of Alpine climbing, was one of the first women to conquer Mont Blanc on 22 September 1871. With her sister, Isabella, she climbed the peaks of Aiguille du Moire and Monte Viso near Chamonix and nearly conquered the Matterhorn.[143]

'Because it was there' and was named after a Welshman, it was perhaps inevitable that Everest should have a considerable appeal to Welsh mountaineers.[144] One of the most remarkable of this redoubtable breed was Brigadier-General Charles Granville Bruce (1866–1939), the youngest of the fourteen children of Henry Bruce, first Baron Aberdare.[145] Charles Bruce was a fine athlete and a champion wrestler.[146] He had perpetual good humour, enthusiasm and a love of alcohol, coupled with competence and shrewdness. In India he soon became fluent in Nepali and introduced hill-running to his Gurkha regiment. In the summer of 1887 he went for the first time to the Alps, where his climbing style and ambition earned him the nickname 'MMM', for Mad Mountain Maniac. Martin Conway, a fellow climber, described Bruce's energy as 'that of a steam engine plus a goods train'. It was said by some that he had slept with the wife of every enlisted man in the force. To keep fit, Bruce regularly ran up and down the flanks of the Khyber Pass, carrying his orderly on his back. As a middle-aged colonel he could wrestle six of his men at once. To his friends he was known as 'Bruiser Bruce'; the men of the regiment called him simply Bhalu, the Bear, or Burra Sahib – the Big Sahib. Bruce was a rare spirit. His charm and charisma bridged the gap between Sahib and Sherpa. In 1891 he took his champion runner Pabir Thapa to Zermatt in Switzerland to learn ice-climbing. On their way there, the two stayed at Aberdare, where Thapa and Bruce enjoyed 'running down' poachers. Despite his poor English and non-existent Welsh, Thapa proved very popular with the locals. He disappeared for the last three days of his visit and was discovered by Bruce on a drinking spree with coal miners in Tonypandy.

Charles Bruce's climbing experience was impressive. He spent ten seasons in the European Alps and participated in the earliest climbing expedition to the Himalayas. In 1892, with a group of Gurkha soldiers, he accompanied Conway on his exploration of the Balforo region of the Karakorum, visiting Muztagh Tower, Broad Peak and K2. They climbed to 22,600 feet on Kabru, a peak just south of Kangchenjunga.

In 1892 he was with Francis Younghusband on a mission to the Hindu Kush, and together they laid the groundwork for future Everest expeditions.[147] In 1895 he climbed Nanga Parbat and in 1907 his team climbed Trisul, a 23,600 foot peak revered by the Hindus as the trident of Shiva, the god of destruction and procreation. For more than two decades this would be the highest mountain ever climbed. In 1914, Bruce went to Gallipoli, in command of the 107 Battalion of the 6th Ghurkha Rifles. After two months in the front line he was 'cut down with machine-gun fire that nearly severed both his legs'. Advised by the medical board to retire to a quiet life and to be especially careful never to walk strenuously uphill, Bruce responded with typical aplomb. He led the second British expedition to Everest in 1922 and the third in 1924. George Bernard Shaw gave a flippant description of Bruce's team when he described a photograph of the mountaineers looking like a 'Connemara picnic surprised by a snowstorm'.[148] But these plucky men were not bumbling amateurs; Bruce's obsession with Everest dwarfed Captain Ahab's pursuit of the great white whale. The 1924 group might well have seen the first successful ascent of the mountain by George Mallory and Andrew Irvine. Certainly, during this expedition, Charles Bruce's nephew, Geoffrey Bruce, used oxygen to set a new height record of 27,300 feet on Everest via the North Col.[149]

Charles Bruce was universally respected by his fellow climbers, and much loved by his men, whom he insisted on calling porters rather than coolies. Unlike his fellow climbers, Bruce seemed to have been little concerned with locals who measured all distances in cups of tea. His military background was to be seen in his writings. 'Strategies' were developed, he and his men 'laid siege', 'fought', 'triumphed', 'battled' and then 'conquered' the mountains. Mallory and Irvine were 'killed in the final assault'.[150] Those 'besieging' the mountain did not lack for nourishment, for amongst their supplies were '60 tins of quail in foie gras and 48 bottles of champagne, Mountebello 1915'.

Bruce's expeditions to Everest were in many respects the last hurrah of a remarkable generation. Already forged by public school, university, army, empire, and a strong hint of homoeroticism, they were further seared in the terrible fires of the First World War. Of the twenty-six white climbers on the Everest campaign in 1924, twenty had been through the worst of the War, and six, like Bruce, had been badly wounded. After the angel of death had fluttered so close, the Himalayas represented one last attempt to assert their masculinity. 'They had seen so much of death', wrote Wade Davis in *Into the Silence,* 'that life mattered less than the moments of being alive'.[151] Everest was the latest attempt by the British to assert their dominance over the world. 'Foreigners' had won the race to the poles, and, as Bruce noted, 'they were damned if they were going to be bested again'. Everest was a sentinel in the sky, a destination of hope and redemption, a symbol of continuity in a world gone mad. The 1924 expedition was 1914 revisited, and similarly tinged with tragedy in which death took its toll from the young and the best.[152]

Harold William Tilman (1889–1977/9?) of Barmouth was another who climbed on Everest in the 1920s and 1930s. After distinguished service in the First World War, Tilman scaled the twin peaks of Kilimanjaro (Kibo and Mawenzi) and Mount Kenya, and then in 1934 and 1935 took part in reconnaissance expeditions to Mount Everest. In 1936, he climbed Nanda Devi, which at 25,646 feet was the highest peak hitherto climbed. Tilman's service in the Second World War was heroic, with periods in India, Iraq, the West African desert and France, where he took part in the evacuation of Dunkirk. His adventurous spirit continued after the war. He sailed single-handedly from Barmouth to Patagonia, circumnavigated the Patagonia ice cap and South America, and then Greenland and Svalbard. He disappeared in 1977 when his ship, a converted tug, was lost. He was officially pronounced dead in 1979.[153]

Wynn Harris and Griffith Cresswell Evans Pugh both made significant contributions to the success of the 1953 expedition to Everest. Pugh, a noted physiologist, was an expert in high-altitude respiration and advised on acclimatisation, respiration, nutrition and the thermal properties of clothing. His discoveries appeared in several articles in medical journals and a film, *Physiology on Mount Everest* (1954).[154] His research was instrumental in the successful ascent of Edmund Hillary and Tenzing Norgay. Alongside him on that expedition was Sir Robert Charles Evans (1918–95), a surgeon and later principal of the University College of North Wales, Bangor. Together with Tom Bourdillon, Evans made the first ascent of the south summit of Mount Everest on 20 May 1953. Faulty oxygen equipment and lack of time prevented them reaching the main summit, which Hillary and Tenzing climbed a few days later. His book, *Eye on Everest* (1955), was an astute analysis, sometimes mocking the neo-imperial aspects of the 1953 Everest expedition, a viewpoint which was later amplified in *Coronation Everest, 1953*, the work of the young *Times* reporter who accompanied them, James (later Jan) Morris.[155]

High latitudes, rather than altitudes were the draw for some brave souls. The North and the South Poles were in many senses the final frontiers at the opening of the twentieth century and the scenes of a frenzied dash to be the first to reach the globe's extremities. Antarctica was perhaps the ultimate symbol of the heroic age of exploration before the First World War, or simply imperialism gone mad. Unlike the Arctic, Antarctica had no human settlement, so the explorers who bravely endured 'the worst journey in the world' modestly busied themselves naming glaciers, peninsulas and mountains after themselves. In this the Welsh were no exception.

Two contrasting characters dominate the history of British Antarctic exploration – Scott and Shackleton.[156] Both in their respective ways were heroic and flawed men. Scott, famously, was pipped to the Pole by Roald Amundsen, perishing with his men on the tortuous return journey. Shackleton, despite enduring horrific sufferings, brought back all his men alive. In the expeditions of both, the Welsh had a significant role. Scott's ship, the *Terra Nova*, set off from Cardiff in 1910 and was heavily financed by the city's coal and shipping magnates.[157] With him on his fateful last journey was Edgar Evans of Rhossili, Gower. Evans had experienced the privations and agonies of Antarctic exploration on Scott's 1903 expedition to the high plateau of Victoria Land. During this trip his strength, joviality and nobility of character so impressed Scott that he chose him again for the 1910 expedition, and despite Evans's fondness for drink selected him as one of the elite four to make the final fatal assault on the pole.[158] Even in death, Scott's charisma drew the crowds. When his ship, the *Terra Nova*, made her return journey to Cardiff in 1913, crowds of more than 60,000, carried on special trains from all over south Wales, were drawn by death's magnet to witness the macabre spectacle. Amongst the Welsh, the Evanses appear to have almost a monopoly on cold weather exploration, for Commander Teddy Evans and Captain Edward Evans both journeyed to the Antarctic.[159]

Amongst Shackleton's colleagues was Perce Blackborow (1894–1949) from Newport, who had stowed away on the ship, the *Endurance,* in Buenos Aires, unaware that it was bound not for Britain but for the South Pole. The ship became trapped in pack ice in January 1915 and remained stuck fast until October, when the ice closed in and crushed it. Shackleton and his men then camped on the ice until April 1916, when the floe broke up and they were forced to sail more than 1,000 miles in three lifeboats to Elephant Island. One boat then sailed on to South Georgia. Unbelievably, no one died. Blackborow lost all the toes on his left foot from frostbite at Elephant Island, but returned home in time to serve in the naval convoys of the First World War.[160]

A similar experience to Blackborow's was that of Huw Williams, a farmer's son from Anglesey. Bored with farming, Williams one day threw down his pitchfork and announced to his startled father that he wanted to replace agriculture with adventure. In 1912, as Scott's expedition headed for the furthest point south, Williams joined the expedition of Vilhjalmur Stefansson to the Arctic. Disaster struck as their ship, the *Karluk*, became trapped in pack ice, which then proceeded to crack around them as the terrified crew listened to the ship's prolonged death throes for four months. Eventually the *Karluk* was lost. The sailors had to survive several months of near starvation, during which they had to walk hundreds of miles from the pack ice to solid ground. During this epic journey, Williams fell through the ice and struggled on through conditions of -40 to -50 degrees Celsius, even enduring the amputation of his hand using tin-cutting shears without anaesthetic or antiseptic. His experiences and endurance take us into the strangest and most alien of all landscapes, that of the Edwardian male mind.[161]

Less famous but more successful as an Antarctic explorer than Scott or Shackleton was Sir Tannatt William Edgeworth David (1858–1934) of St Fagans, Cardiff. David emigrated to Australia in 1881 and worked in Sydney University as a geologist. In 1896 and 1897 he went to Funafuti, a Pacific atoll, to examine the formation of coral atolls and published the well-received account *Funafuti, or Three Months on a Coral Island*. In mid 1907 he joined the *Nimrod* expedition to Antarctica. His courtesy, consideration for others and sense of humour and honour made him an ideal explorer. Amongst his notable achievements were leading the first ascent of Mount Erebus, the only active volcano in Antarctica, and, on 16 January 1909, the arrival at the South Magnetic Pole, possession of which he claimed for the British crown.[162]

As Joseph Conrad's novels showed, sailors who endured sea voyages of pathos and peril were well acquainted with adventure.[163] Many seamen, hardened to winds and weather, made ideal members of several expeditionary forces, as the careers of Edgar Evans,

Captain Edward Evans and Commander Teddy Evans confirmed. A life on the ocean wave also had about it an air of romance and an aura of freedom absent from other trades. Novels such as *Ynys y Trysor* (1925), *Atgofion Hen Forwr* (1926), *Capten* (1928) and *Mêt y Mona* by Robert Lloyd Jones (1878–1959) showed how strong the association was between sailors and adventure. The poet Simon Bartholomeus Jones (1894–1964) also captured the heroic nautical linage in his poem 'Rownd yr Horn', which won the crown at the Wrexham National Eisteddfod in 1933. Fiction, as usual, had roots in fact, as W. H. S. Jones, in his splendid book *The Cape Horn Breed*, revealed. A spirit of heroism hovered about those who went down to the sea in ships, which was not diminished by the hard realities of the penny-and-halfpenny-pinching economics of making a profit from seafaring. It seemed to be more than just a job. Rather, it was a calling to adventure in which a person's 'inner soul was touched'. This was particularly true in the years before sail yielded to steam, a process that for many Welsh crews lasted until the First World War.

Sailing ships were undeniably beautiful in their elegant and well-ordered complexity. Crews had to undertake Herculean labours in horrendous conditions. Climbing the rigging against the force of winds off Beaufort's scale, frostbitten, fighting off deep-in-the-bone tiredness and so drenched and wet that skin often peeled off were constant hazards. The Cape Horn route had a particular relevance for Welsh sailors, a place of terror where men and a few women, such as the 'Cape Horner' Annie Mendus-Thomas, were proven. Others followed the southerly winds, not in pursuit of copper but to gather nitrates from the west coast of South America to enrich the agricultural lands of Wales. Many did so in the service of the Nitrate King, J. T. North the wheeler-dealer, who had previously speculated in the Welsh coalfields. Deep in the pages of Joseph Conrad you will encounter characters like North, who gave no consideration to the atrocious conditions which faced his sailors and ships as a result of his unscrupulous behaviour.[164] In 1907, after seventy-seven days trying to round Cape Horn, the Welsh ship the *Denbigh Castle* ran off to the east, arriving like a ghost ship in Freemantle, 223 days out and presumed long lost, her crew a group of dead men walking. It was no surprise that

6 'The Kid': Owen Rhoscomyl in his cowboy years, *c.*1880–4.

Swansea copper ships, carrying coal to Chile and copper ore home, acquired a reputation for hardness. In Aberaeron, Aberarth and Aberystwyth, the odd confluence of tradition and family expectations turned out ship captains by the score.[165] They often endured hard times, when sailor's lives were hanging by a thread.

Some individuals deliberately sought to foster amongst their fellow men and women a spirit of bravery that could be enhanced by adventure and exploration. One such character was Arthur Owen Vaughan (1863–1919), alias Robert Scourfield Mills, alias Owen Rhoscomyl, alias Owen Vaughan. His early life was a boys' own adventure, working in America as a cowboy and then as a prospector in the mining camps. Between 1887 and 1890 this Rider Haggard hero was in the Royal Dragoons. He served with Rimington's Guides and Damant's Horse in the Boer War, rising to the rank of captain in Howard's Canadian Scouts. Rhoscomyl delighted in the crude camaraderie of the cowboy camp and the mercenary hideouts, collecting several nicknames during his remarkable career including the Kid, Roving Rob, Panther Killer, the Night Hawk, Steel Ribs and Old Fireproof.

His love of pageant, spectacle and the spectacular was evidenced in the National Pageant of Wales, which he organised in 1909. Here the great and the good of south Wales donned suits of armour and re-enacted heroic episodes from medieval Welsh history. This love of the stirring tales from the Welsh long-ago was also prominent in his historical writings, such as the adrenaline-charged and sensationally titled *Flame-bearers of Welsh History* (1911). Owen believed that the heroic acts of old would inspire and instruct twentieth-century Wales. He understood the empire itself in medieval terms as an inherently multinational entity, a collection of diverse peoples striving to serve a monarch who belonged equally to them all. This belief underpinned the investiture ceremony he helped to create at Caernarfon in 1911. Although the Welsh people were few in number, Rhoscomyl believed that Wales was destined to play a special place in the world as a 'breeding place for leaders'.[166]

One who shared Rhoscomyl's love of adventure was Henry Roger Ashwell Pocock (1865–1941), the Tenby-born adventurer and writer.[167] The self-styled 'lone-wolf adventurer', raised by his father on the training ship the *Wellesley*, Pocock was spectacularly unsuccessful in a series of jobs. He was the quintessential warrior archetype, lusting for deeds of glory and heroism, enduring incredible hardships for trivial gains. In November 1884, he enlisted at Winnipeg in the North-West Mounted Police and in 1885 he served during the north-west uprising in Manitoba. His feet were frostbitten and his right toes amputated and in 1886 he was honourably discharged with a pension. He then travelled in the Canadian wilds and worked as an Anglican missionary among the Gaetkshians in the Skeena Valley, British Columbia. Contrary to his claims in his sensational memoirs, he was not invited to train as a missionary but asked to leave, as the church authorities were concerned that his interest in Indian women was more than pastoral. In 1898 he was in the Klondyke during the gold rush and was rumoured to have killed a companion. Determined to 'set a record in horsemanship, or die in the attempt', from June 1899 to January 1900 he rode 3,600 miles from Canada to Mexico, meeting several outlaws along the way. He then travelled to South Africa, where he fought against the Boers in Butler's Scouts.

Pocock's greatest achievement was to establish, with a little help from his friends and adventurers like Owen Rhoscomyl, the Legion of Frontiersmen. The legion was one of the varied responses to a crisis in British masculinity which arose after the Boer War. The awareness that the inept and physically imperfect British troops, who had struggled against the robust Boers were about to be challenged by the more powerful Germans, created panic in the press. The legion was intended to be a patriotic, imperialist, a-political, volunteer, part-time, armed, informal, auxiliary force in Britain, the empire and elsewhere. Men hardened 'in the wild countries at sea or in war' would be trained for home and imperial defence.[168] Amongst them was Owen Rhoscomyl, who despite his devotion to Wales was an active patriot of the British Empire. By 1908, there were about 3,500 members of the legion in Britain, all dressed in the statutory uniform of stetson, neckerchief, loose shirt, breeches, boots, gunbelt and revolver (in 1908 anyone, even a child, could legally buy and own a revolver and ammunition). However, Pocock's increasingly erratic and eccentric behaviour led to his

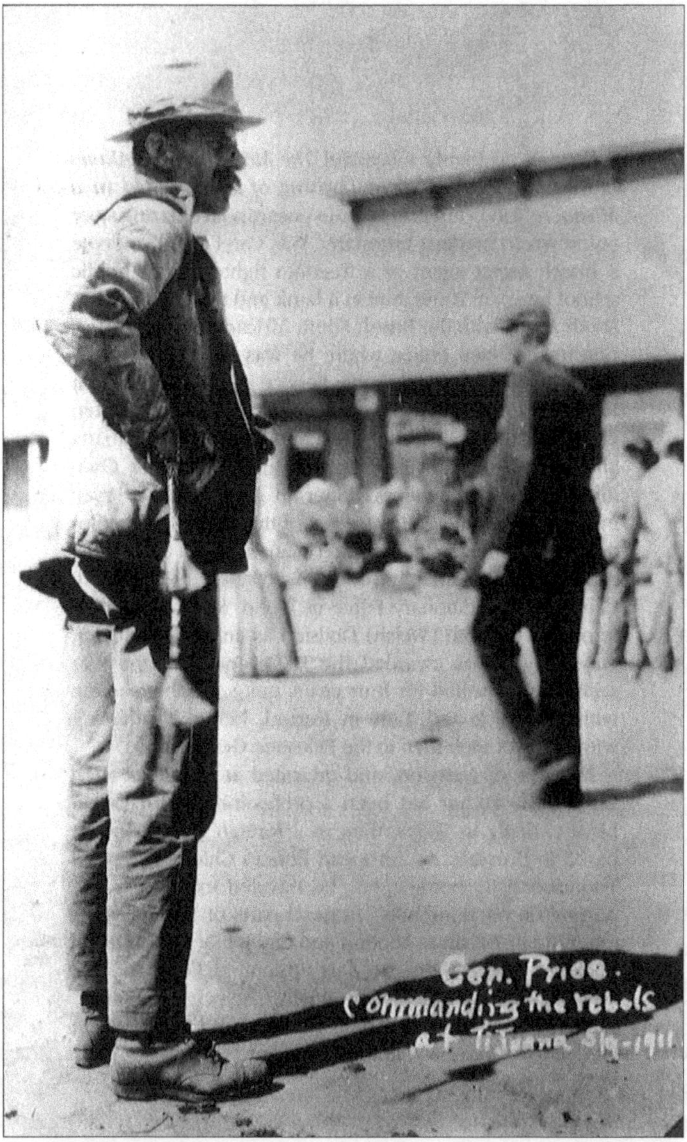
Gen. Price.
Commanding the rebels
at Tijuana 5/9-1911

7 The original Welsh action hero, Caryl ap Rhys Pryce. Public-school educated, son of the Welsh Raj, soldier and policeman in Africa and leader of the socialist revolution in Mexico in 1911.

being expelled from his own legion. Without him it prospered and had 17,500 members ready to fight in 1914, equipped, as H. G. Wells quipped, not for a war in Europe but for Arizona in 1890.[169] Pocock eventually managed to enlist in the army, and served for seven months on the Ypres salient, an experience he considered to be 'the greatest adventure in a varied life'.[170]

Another who rode tall in the saddle in the pantheon of Welsh heroes was Caryl ap Rhys Pryce. A direct descendant, or so he claimed, of the Welsh freedom fighter Owain Glyndŵr, Pryce fought in both the Matabele Rebellion and the Second Boer War. During the Magonista Revolution in Mexico in 1911, Pryce served as an intelligence officer for the British, seeking to counteract US influence in Central America. Upon the death of Stanley Williams, Pryce took over as leader of the foreign legion involved in the rebellion. After a battle with government troops, his forces took control of Tijuana. He later fought with distinction in the First World War, being awarded the Distinguished Service Order, for his bravery in single-handedly destroying an enemy machine-gun nest. He also served as an intelligence agent in the Irish War of Independence (1919–21) and later commanded the infamous Black and Tan detachment in Palestine. Ever ready to blur the line between fact and fiction, he eventually finished up as a film star in the silent movie era in Hollywood, once playing himself in *The Colonel's Escape*, a film based on the Magonista Revolution.[171]

Brave in blood and bone, these women of action and action men, adventurers and explorers, do provide some valuable insights into Welsh society. Some Welsh heroes had an innate sympathy for the world's indigenous peoples, as Norman Lewis and E. E. Evans-Pritchard so eloquently showed. Like the knights in their medieval tales and Arthurian legends, the Welsh heroes were noble, stoic, heroic, resilient, understated, unyielding, unfearful and intrepid. In his *Flame Bearers of Welsh History* (1905), Owen Rhoscomyl, no mean hero himself, presented Welsh history as a chain of valiant fighters and princes with whom he personally identified. But his motivation was not 'mooning' after the 'picturesque in the past', but rather a desire to provide practical help in the problems most pressing in the Wales of his day.[172] In an obituary piece, Lord Howard de Walden explained Rhoscomyl's essential character:

> To him it seemed so obvious that the race which bred the heroes of the past should be at home today in every function; that the glories were the same for his race however gained, with harp or pen, on the football field or in the prize ring . . . he had truly the one desire to show his fellows that they were members of no mean people and that the glamour of the past was not only an inheritance to be prized, but the very quality at the heart of present success.[173]

'Swift of foot', 'high spirited', their adventures while crossing burning deserts, mountainous seas, ice-cold waters and craggy mountains reveal the characteristics that the Welsh cherished in their heroes and heroines. Such enthusiasm was clearly in evidence in 1909 at the Abertridwr Hall at Senghennydd, which 'rang with cheers', as did several other halls across south Wales, during a lecture tour in which Sir Ernest Shackleton explained the trials and terrors of exploring Antarctica.[174] For the Welsh clearly appreciated their heroes. The talented historian Howell T. Evans, author of *A History of England and Wales, from the Earliest Times to 1485*, made his case for the commemoration of heroes:

> Heroes are a national asset. The masses are born, live, die, and are no more. Heroes live on; and it is they who are thrown into the scales which estimate the moral and intellectual worth of people.[175]

Never aggressive, arrogant or antagonistic, their innate bravery revealed that, in extremis, there was a warrior at the heart of the Welsh. Neither were the Welsh afraid of, nor averse to, the exploitation of native people. Their tales of derring-do 'should', as one commentator noted in the *Western Mail* at the time of the investiture in 1911, 'be a mark to all the world that Wales is a special country in the Empire . . . a land to which the Empire may look for help and strength in their hour of temptation and in the day of danger. Cymru am byth.'[176]

6

'The Blood never Dried' – the Welsh in Empire: Envy, Greed and Zeal

Go back Wasambywe (Swahili) you are bad!
Wasambywe are bad, bad, bad! The river is deep,
Wasambywe . . . You have not wings, Wasambywe.
Go back, Wasambywe

One of the Wenya boatmen addressing Stanley's expedition on the river Congo, 19 November 1876, quoted in Thomas Pakenham, *The Scramble for Africa*

The Welshman's burden: the Welsh and empire

There is no portion of the United Kingdom which is prouder of the British Empire than Wales.

Herbert Roberts, MP, House of Commons, 1898

'Paham na fydd yr haul byth yn machlud ar yr ymerodraeth Brydeinig?' (Why will the sun never set on the British Empire?) was the remarkable question posed by *Trysorfa'r Plant* in 1881. The answer? 'Oherwydd na fydd Duw yn ymddiried i Sais yn y tywyllwch' (Because God will never trust the English in the dark).[1] It is difficult to decide with hindsight how common such sceptical voices were but it is certain that they were not unique. In 1929 the short-story writer D. J. Williams prophetically wrote, 'y mae Cymru'n hŷn na'r ymerodraeth Brydeinig, a bydd byw'n hir ar ei hôl hefyd' (Wales is older than the British Empire, and will also live long after it).[2] Waldo Williams was another who lamented that Britannia ruled the waves at Heaven's command, warning in 'Y Tŵr a'r Graig':

Gostwng a fydd ar gastell,
A daw cwymp ciwdodau caeth
A hydref ymerodraeth.

(Castles will crumble,
Conquerors will fall
And autumn for empires).

Edmund Hope Verney (1838–1910), whose wife, Lady Verney (1844–1930), did so much to promote higher education in Wales, wrote a scathing tract against imperial expansion, *Four Years of Protest in the Transvaal* (1881). Bertrand Russell was consistently scathing in his view of empire, describing it as 'a cesspool for British moral refuse'.[3]

Others, however, took a different view of the empire. Despite the claims of many that the Welsh were the first victims of British, or English, imperialism, they were also eloquent exponents of imperialism and colonialism. The Welsh were oppressed and oppressors, colonised and colonists; those sinned against sinned against others. In the dramatic and traumatic history of empire, the Welsh were victims and victimisers. They too fought the brutal battles for country, commerce, cross and class.

The empire had an insidious but far-reaching impact on the lives of the Welsh people, which could be seen in all aspects of life.[4] Cigarette packets, playing cards, soap wrappers and newspapers all carried the icons and images of empire.[5] The packaging of commodities like tea, coffee, cocoa and chocolate was emblazoned with imperial imagery. In the Nonconformist chapel vestry where, as a child, the novelist Eiluned Lewis attended choir practice, she remembered that 'there hangs a brown map . . . of the mission-field in the Khasia Hills of India'.[6] If she looked closely at the geography laid out on the walls, then she would have realised that from Everest, the highest place on earth, to Cape Evans, one of the coldest, several places were named after Welsh people.[7] This was the cartography of command and control. Providing familiar names for faraway places was the conqueror's traditional prerogative, in an attempt to domesticate the exotic. But the trend had a parallel at home, for local places were often named after far-flung outposts. How many twenty-first-century inhabitants of Hopkinstown in the Rhondda Valley know that Tel el-Kebir Street was named in memory of the Egyptian battle of 1882? The sections of Universal Colliery, Senghennydd, which were devastated by the worst mining disaster in British history when 439 men lost their lives on 14 October 1913, were named Ladysmith, Pretoria, Mafeking and Kimberley.[8]

The pageants and parades of empire were celebrated with much pomp and more pretension even in the remotest outposts of rural Wales. In 1902 and 1910, most of the buildings in Market Square, Llanfair Caereinion flew Union Jacks to mark the coronation, whilst the grandiloquently named cafe, the Bon Marché, offered slap-up celebratory teas. The entire population of Llanfair, Llangadfan and Meifod, children, women, men and howling dogs, were out in unison on 24 May each year from 1905 onwards to celebrate Empire Day and the 'wonders of our worldwide Empire'.[9] Such regular ritual and occasional spectacle served to keep the empire in the public mind. The inhabitants of Penrhyndeudraeth displayed their thespian talents, as well as their imperialistic traits, when they appeared in the dramatic works *Britannia* and *Britain Awake: an Empire Pageant Play*, penned by the village's very own dramatist, Alice Helena Alexandra Williams (1863–1957) of Castell Deudraeth.[10] Thomas Michael Jones or Thomas Michaeliones (1880–1960), that unusual combination of priest and gold-mine owner in Caernarfonshire, was also deeply patriotic, for he composed a series of poems to the Union Jack, which were set to music and appropriately published by the Empire Music Publishers.[11]

The sculptor and artist W. Goscombe John (1860–1952), a loyal Welshman, was a tireless illustrator of the British imperial ideal. From bronze and marble he forged and carved a national ideology of successful leaders, historical triumphs and iconic military moments. John's work gave immortality to the notion of heroic masculinity. In Cape Town, Calcutta, Cairo, Lucknow, Surabaya, Nairobi, Nagpur, Montreal, Washington and several English and Welsh towns, his statues of emperors, proconsuls and victorious generals still stand, mute witnesses to vanished splendours.[12] The artist, journalist and cartoonist David John Davies (1870–?), served as a freelance artist with the regiment Roberts' Horse during the

Boer War. His writings and paintings lauded British heroism. Davies's most famous painting, 'African Sunset', was shown at the 1924 Empire Exhibition at Wembley.[13] Schools, with their emphasis on *mens sana in corpore sano*, a healthy mind in a healthy body, considered that they were creating a band of brothers, combining in trust and loyalty to organise a new world order in the days of the Pax Britannica.[14] Appropriate reading material for fledgling heroes was provided in the high adrenaline-rush of the adventure tales in the *Boys' Own Paper*, *The Girls' Own Paper* and *Boys of the Empire*. Stories such as 'How to be Strong' and 'Where the lion's cubs are trained' stirred youthful passions.[15]

The penny press and its 'new journalism' fostered the 'new imperialism' of the late nineteenth century.[16] More highbrow material was also produced by Welsh scholars to inspire and instruct the nation's youth on valorous deeds of empire. The University College of Wales, Aberystwyth had a department of empire and colonial history from 1915 to 1946. Sir Charles Prestwood Lucas (1853–1931) of Crickhowell, after a period in the Colonial Office, took up a fellowship in All Saints College, Oxford, writing and lecturing on the British Empire. His major contribution was the multi-volumed series, *A Historical Geography of the British Colonies*.[17]

Travelling panoramas, dioramas and cosmoramas, featuring imperialistic spectacles such as the battle of Omdurman, criss-crossed the country. The superiority of the British imperial identity was a theme frequently broadcast by the BBC, especially in the 1930s. Programmes such as *The Four Feathers*, *Life Among the Native Tribes*, *Africa: the Dark Continent* and the alarmingly titled *Africa Shrieks* relayed tales of heroism, courage and perseverance, together with the 'governing genius' of the British, into Welsh hearths and homes.[18] Audiences packed into the Plazas, Palladiums and Odeons of Wales to watch the swashbucklingly epic films on inspirational themes such as *Lives of a Bengal Lancer* (1935), *Clive of India* (1935) and *The Sun Never Sets*, *Gunga Din* and *Stanley and Livingstone* (all 1939).[19] So entrenched did the empire become in the fabric of life that C. L. R. James could write in 1950 that 'it is now an organic part of the thought process of the nation and to disgorge it requires a herculean effort.'[20]

The empire, whether acquired in a 'fit of absence of mind' or the result of a 'sleepwalker's gatherings', certainly provided the Welsh with a wealth of opportunities to travel.[21] Perhaps the social group to profit most from the worldwide empire were mariners, for the sea lanes and trade winds were to the British Empire what a straight road had been to the Romans. Some Welsh people worked in those outposts of empire which were actually in Europe, places such as Gibraltar, Malta and Cyprus. These were vital stepping stones for the passage of goods to and from India, but their garrisons also allowed the Royal Navy to dominate the Mediterranean.[22] It is a fact not often acknowledged that the Mediterranean had a vital role in the British Empire and was crucial to its global ambitions. Possessions such as Gibraltar, Cyprus and Malta mattered not just because they guarded vital routes, but as ports and harbours that allowed the Royal Navy to control the approaches to southern Europe, North Africa and the Levant. British rule in those outposts of 'the Middle Sea' were the usual contradictory mix of enlightenment and exploitation. Schools, academies and hospitals were established along with naval and military bases. During the Second World War, Cyprus and Malta became static 'aircraft carriers' for the British.[23]

A number of Welsh people enjoyed profitable careers in these imperial outposts. Sir Evan Davies Jones (1854–1949) of Fishguard spent periods working as a civil engineer at the ports of Gibraltar, Singapore and Suez and the Aswan Dam.[24] The Cory brothers of Cardiff, coalowners, shippers and shipowners, established several fuelling stations in the 'Middle Sea', especially after the opening of the Suez Canal in 1869.[25] Sir George Elliot (1845–93), one of the owners of the Powell Duffryn Steam Coal Company, developed railroads across North Africa and led the official investigation when Cyprus was transferred from Turkey to Britain in 1878.[26] The grimmer side of Britain's Mediterranean empire was shown in the occupation of Egypt in 1882. Provoked by fears that nationalists would seize the Suez Canal and refuse to honour Egypt's crippling debt repayments, the British response was cruel and bloody.[27] Soldiers such as Sir William Heneage Wynne-Finch (1893–1961) and Fitzroy Richard Somerset (1885–1964), fourth Baron

Raglan, engaged in brutalities that saw the deaths of thousands of Egyptians.[28]

The sheer extent of the vast and varied imperium meant that people could find themselves in all manner of place from the familiar to the fabulous, for this was a transoceanic empire. In the windswept Falkland Islands, the James family farmed sheep on hillside pastures reminiscent of their home in Merioneth (though perhaps it rained less). In the early 1870s others harvested guano on the Penguin Islands off Namibia's Skeleton Coast. Many Welsh emigrants found communities with fellow subjects in Australia, New Zealand, South Africa and Canada in what could be regarded as 'the British West'.[29] Some enjoyed a paradisal sojourn in the West Indian islands of Trinidad and Tobago, Barbados, Jamaica, the Leeward and the Windward Islands. Half-time was called on the international career of the superlative Welsh rugby full back, Arthur Gould, in 1890 when work took him to the West Indies.[30] The ship owner, Sir Alfred Lewis Jones (1845–1909) rescued some of the damage his reputation suffered for his involvement with the horrors of the Congo under King Leopold of Belgium through his work in saving the trade of the West Indies.[31] Sir Daniel Morris (1844–1933), the botanist, spent substantial periods of time collecting samples and seeds in Ceylon and Jamaica and was responsible for reviving the ailing cotton and sugar crops in the West Indies.

Other Welsh people were part of the more traditional portrayal of the empire, in the invading forces which fought and conquered in 'small wars', ostensibly for a native people's own good. Thus many Welsh people found themselves ruling and routemarching in forlorn outposts in Africa and Asia. This was the aggressive gunpowder and gattling-gun empire rather than one of laissez-faire and liberty. General Sir Hugh Rowlands (1828–1909), the first Welsh person to win a Victoria Cross, was a firm stalwart of the empire's militaristic traditions. He saw the world, for he served in Greece, Malta, Turkey, the West Indies, Ireland, South Africa, West Africa, Canada and India.[32] His final command was as head of the armed forces in Scotland. Sir Hugh's proudest moment was when his only son, Hugh Barron Rowlands, became a major in the King's African Rifles; his greatest sadness was his son's death in Somaliland in

1903. Ornate, ornamental, imperial awards decorated many a proud Welsh breast and tender ego. Both Sir Evan Davies Jones (1859–1949), Baron Pentower of Fishguard and Sir William Heneage Wynne-Finch (1893–1961) were proud holders of the Order of the Nile. The much-decorated Sir Walter Henry Cowan (1871–1956) was awarded the Africa General Service Medal three times, with clasps for the campaigns in Benin and Mwele.

'Rwy'n gweld o bell': religion and imperialism

> O bob ymffrost, ymffrost crefyddol yw'r gwrthunaf.
> (Of all bombast, religious bombast is the most revolting)
>
> Robert Ambrose Jones, *Y Faner*, 20 December 1882

As the nineteenth turned into the twentieth century, a complicated interrelationship developed between Christian evangelisation in Africa, America and Asia and the emergence in Wales of a new narrative of modernity that was enshrined in the concept of progress. To many authors, imperialism was an honourable pursuit, based on the laudable motive of civilising the barbarian. In contrast to the Roman Empire – which was enmeshed in vulgarity, venality and violence – the British Empire was valorous, victorious and virtuous. The claim was often made that Britain's empire was won as the result of virtue, not vice.[33]

In essence, three ideological strands were deeply intertwined in the fabric of the Welsh involvement in empire. The first was the wish to be associated with the higher ideals of one of mankind's most civilised races, the British, who had a 'sacred trust' to civilise and manage the property of their colonial subjects. Lands and resources would be best looked after by the British until 'the child races' or 'infant races' were capable of looking after them for themselves – and the longer that process took, the better it would be for the British. The second thread in the imperial tapestry was the practical extension of evangelism, it being Britain's duty to convert subject peoples to Christianity. The third ideological component was linked to growing support for the principle of basic human rights for all peoples. This concept emerged in the nineteenth century but gained support in the twentieth due to the influence of two groups which are traditionally seen as opposed to each other – trade unions and merchants. Trade unionists emphasised the rights of all workers; notable examples of Welsh origin were Thomas Jessie Jones and David Ivon Jones, who championed the rights of workers in the USA and in South Africa. Merchants argued that free trade was the most effective generator of human rights, as 'commerce would ensure the fundamental human right of freedom from suffering'.[34]

Other factors in the creation of the empire, such as greed, God-lust or glory, were downplayed, diminished and even denied. Emrys ap Iwan, in trenchant and sophisticated articles in *Baner ac Amserau Cymru* at the close of the nineteenth century, was a sharp critic of Welsh subscription to concepts of modernisation and Christianity and of their subservience to a British, and especially to an 'English', empire. But his was something of a rare voice wailing in the wilderness.[35] Even the spiritual world was not exempt from the crude social Darwinism of the survival of the fittest and the doctrine of progress. Watcyn Wyn gave rousing confirmation to Christianity's civilising mission in 'Rwy'n gweld o bell' (1895). This was more of a war song than a hymn:

Rwy'n gweld o bell y dydd yn dod,
Bydd pob cyfandir is y rhod
Yn eiddo Iesu mawr;
A holl ynysoedd maith y môr
Yn cyd-ddyrchafu mawl yr Iôr,
Dros wyneb daear lawr!

(I see from afar the day's coming,
When every continent under the sun
Will belong to Jesus;
And the myriad islands of the seas
Will celebrate and praise God,
Across the entire world!)[36]

William Nantlais Williams (1874–1959) complained that 'draw, draw yn China a thiroedd Japan, India a glannau Ceylon, Brazil a Pheriw' (across, across in China and the lands of Japan, India and the shores of Ceylon, Brazil and Peru), 'miloedd ar filoedd sy'n galw o hyd / Am oleuni'r Ne' (thousands upon thousands are constantly calling for the light of Heaven).[37] Indeed it is perhaps in their musical tradition that the Welsh missionaries had one of their most potent weapons. The hymn tune 'Aberystwyth', written by Joseph Parry as an eulogy to the town where he was unhappily a professor of music, acquired immense popularity in Africa.[38] It was translated into Xhosa, Zulu, Sesotho and Afrikaans. 'Aberystwyth' became the somewhat incongruous, unlikely, national anthem for Namibia, Tanzania, Zimbabwe and Zambia. Almost as soon as it was adopted by the Welsh as their national anthem, 'Hen Wlad Fy Nhadau' became the anthem of the Khasi people in northern India. Pianos and harmoniums provided the essential accompaniment to the conversion of native peoples around the world.[39] In jungle clearings in Asia and Africa, the tinkling notes of the piano confirmed that the new religion was superior to the old.[40] The kindly and humorous Daniel Owen Jones (1880–1951), during his period as a missionary in Madagascar between 1900–27, composed many hymns in Malagasi which transposed theology into song.[41]

Missionaries have almost universally been lionised and idolised in Welsh historiography.[42] Like St Paul, these devoted men and women would labour through all the stations of the cross, so that the heathens would be 'shown a still more excellent way'. 'In the name of God, go!' to convert and conquer souls was the motivation for many individuals. Denominational rivalry extended from the home front into the missionary field. Saving any soul was good, but saving them for Baptists, Methodists or Independents was special. Daniel John Davies (1885–1970) took great pride in the fact that six young men became missionaries during his period as minister at Capel Als, Llanelli.[43] Timothy Richard (1845–1919), of Ffaldybrenin in Carmarthenshire, was even more enthusiastic. He did heroic work in China, especially during the horrific famine of 1876–9.[44] But his ambitious plans for the social and economic, as well as the spiritual, reform of China, presented too much of a challenge to the innately cautious and conservative Baptist Missionary Society. Thus, eventually, he left the society to edit a Chinese daily newspaper, the *Shibaoi* (the Times).[45]

Griffith John (1831–1912), an intrepid traveller, undertook extensive missionary expeditions into the interior of China, which sometimes stretched to distances of 3,000 miles or more. He was credited with a Mandarin translation of the New Testament, the Psalms and Proverbs, as well as a Wenli New Testament, published in 1885. Although he was critical of the opium trade organised by British government agencies, John was not, on occasion, averse to calling upon their gunboats for protection. He was especially partisan in his response to the 'Christian' or Taiping uprising.[46] John actively and aggressively sought financial recompense for missionaries whose properties were damaged or destroyed in the uprising. He was convinced that China's problems were directly attributable to the ineptitude and self-serving intransigence of its leaders, and that the Chinese masses all yearned for British rule and freedom from what he perceived as the tyranny of their own rulers. In a remarkable career of over sixty years, John remained convinced that the British Empire provided the best solution to China's problems. He played a notable role in the scramble for China by European powers in the late nineteenth century.[47]

William Evans (1869–1948), missionary and minister in Madagascar, worked from a similar wellspring of ideas and inspiration. He spent twenty-eight years translating the Biblical Dictionary into Malagasi and published a translation of the Welsh translation of *Taith y Pererin* (*Pilgrim's Progress*) which some regarded as a great improvement on the original.[48] John Charles Jones (1904–56), small and frail of frame, had a serene spirituality and strength of faith and vision. Before he became bishop of Bangor in 1949, the first to undertake the ceremony in Welsh, Jones had served as a missionary in the Bishop Tucker Memorial College, Mukono, Uganda from 1934 to 1945. He had prepared well for the work, for his previous post before taking up his duties in Uganda was as a curate in Aberystwyth, with special responsibility for students. The charismatic Jones was that relatively rare figure – a Welsh-speaking Anglican missionary.[49]

The missionary was often an exotic figure in an even more exotic land.[50] They were people of undoubted integrity and steadfast earnestness of purpose. Their deep-seated loneliness, which comes through in their letters and diaries, was only somewhat alleviated by their fathomless faith. Despite their courage in proclaiming the Lord's song in a strange land, their behaviour and beliefs were incongruous and alien intrusions that were not always successfully adapted or integrated. Daniel Owen Jones had responsibility for more than seventy churches in the area around Lake Alaotra, Madagascar, in the 1920s. To help him travel across the vast distances, the women of the Welsh Congregational chapels in Swansea raised funds to buy Daniel a motor boat. Good intentions and best efforts do not always result in a practical outcome. Although there was water in profusion, the tightly knotted foliage of the mangrove rendered the motor boat redundant.[51]

Given the cliché that a woman's place was in the home, it is surprising to learn that the majority of Welsh missionaries were female. In 1924, for example, of fifty-six Welsh missionaries in the field in India, thirty-six (66 per cent) were women, twenty-one of whom were unmarried.[52] Jane Helen Rowlands (1891–1955), Helen o Fôn, inspired by her brother, William, a minister with the English Presbyterians amongst the Australian Aboriginals and the inventor of the now forgotten Leeds Memory Method, entered the missionary service in 1915. Helen did remarkable work with the two most disadvantaged groups in India, the untouchables and women. She learned Bengali, preached in the language and also taught at several schools and colleges. The redoubtable Helen spent a sabbatical period in Paris in 1930, where she gained an MA and a DLitt from the University of the Sorbonne. She then returned to Assam to educate and evangelise.[53] Susannah Jane Rankin (1897–1989), was the first woman to gain the degree of DD from the University of Wales in 1925. In 1931, disenchanted with her pastorate in Llanfyllin, she became a missionary amongst the headhunters in Papua New Guinea. For twenty-six years Susannah, together with her husband, the Revd Robert Rankin, established churches for the Congregationalists in the remotest mountain districts, turning the natives from skull hunting and cannibalism. A gifted linguist,

Susannah translated several Welsh and English Christian works and sections of the Bible into the native languages.[54]

Susannah's story is one of the most remarkable of all Welsh missionary epics. All missionaries faced considerable challenges in their deployment. They had to find ways not only of transporting themselves and their families to their chosen location and of retaining links with their society's organiser. They also had to establish networks of support so that they could ensure a regular supply of clothes, medicines and civilised comforts such as coffee, sugar and tea, as well as tools and essential equipment to make their presence effective and a stock of bibles to rescue the natives from the Prince of Darkness. They ran not just a chapel, but a complete centre of cultural conquest, including schools, hospitals, houses for the converted and invariably a printing press. But in Susannah's case, the problems of supply and support were infinitely greater over the great distances, dense jungle and disjointed topography of Papua New Guinea.

The dangers which missionaries faced were considerable. Gwenfron Moss (1898–1991), worked as a chemist and a missionary in India and China. She braved a period of considerable danger when the Communists began to purge Christian missionaries from whole areas of China in 1947.[55] Mary Myfanwy Wood (1882–1967) was another who encountered and endured considerable dangers in China. Between 1908–21 she worked hard to enhance the role of Chinese women in the missions. Her knowledge of China was keenly sought by a number of countries during the Second World War. She was eventually forced to leave China in 1951, when several of her friends and colleagues were shot by Communist forces.[56] Mary Rees went to Tientsin in China in 1888, to help her brother Frederick Roberts (1862–94), a medical missionary, run his hospital. Upon his death, Mary took over its management.[57]

The motives of such medical missions were not purely altruistic. In order to retain a welcome the missionary had to offer more than spiritual benefits – perhaps the least desired of her or his gifts. Their medical skills were a major attraction of many missions.[58] This is why people like John Thomas Jones (1889–1952) of Llanegwad, Carmarthenshire, a missionary amongst the Mandritsara in the land of Tsimihety in the north of Madagascar, undertook a basic medical training before leaving Britain.[59] The history of Dr Griffith's work at Mawphlang in Khasia, India, makes explicit the usefulness of the medical mission in the task of evangelisation: 'Giving medicine to the Khasis and making them better not only won their respect and goodwill, and opened a path to them, it also shook their faith in demonism, and tended to make them think favourably of Christianity.'[60]

Despite their undoubted and undeniable heroism, Welsh missionaries appear to have undertaken a complicated and contradictory role in the development of relationships between the British and native peoples around the world. In some areas the relationship between Christianity and colonialism was more formalised. Merac Thomas (1816–92), of Llanbadarn Fawr, Cardiganshire, worked for the Colonial and Continental Church Society from 1851, and became one of the first bishops in New South Wales in 1863.[61]

Altruism had unintended consequences, often of an unfortunate nature. The missionaries' Christian work was often the crest of a wave that brought coercion and conquest in its wake. This, perhaps, explains why missionary societies concentrated their efforts in those lands which were not wholly under British dominance – countries like China, Madagascar and the Congo. Both Lewis Thomas (1859–1929), a missionary and educationalist, and David Christopher Davies (1878–1958) worked in the Congo at the turn of the twentieth century. Their work in many parts of the country, but especially in the area around Leopoldville, seriously affected the interests of the Belgians. At the initiative of Alfred Tully of Cardiff, the Livingstone Inland Mission was formed in the Congo in 1878; he also helped to establish branches in Peru and Argentina in the 1880s.

Madagascar, in particular, shows how an active missionary presence could serve to foster British interests in areas that were controlled by other countries. Strategically located in the Indian Ocean, the island was ruled by Queens Ranavalona I, II and III for most of the nineteenth century until it was eventually annexed by the French in 1896. Under both systems of government, Welsh missionaries were exceptionally active. William Evans (1869–1948),

Daniel Owen Jones (1880–1951) and John Thomas Jones (1889–1952) all served the Congregationalists as missionaries on the island. Their presence was a continued source of anxiety and annoyance to the French. The tensions simmered into open warfare in 1940–1, when British troops including that most unlikely of soldiers, the Welsh scholar Thomas Jones (1910–72), fought in Madagascar against Vichy government forces.[62]

The role of Welsh missionaries gives rise to one of the supreme and greatest ironies of Welsh history. Ignorant of or deliberately ignoring their own nation's experiences, the missionaries used the oppressor's language to emphasise the superiority of white religion and culture. They taught natives that they must abandon their own gods, and with them the myths, songs, dances and rituals central to their culture and identity, and embrace the faith of those who were bringing them not to eternal life, but to the verge of annihilation. Welsh missionaries were often the representatives not only of Christianity, but of capitalism, for their activities eased and greased the onset of exploitation. Missionaries emphasised the millennial end of time and the fear of hellfire to people who had only ever known eternity. Under their influence, tribes learned to work for things and needs they had never had before – clothes, matches, salt, sugar. They learnt the gospel of money and the market. 'Gifts' to indigenous tribes forced them deeper into debt. Religion and the rise of capitalism were inextricably linked in several countries across the world. It was a great paradox that the Bible was both the west's greatest inspiration and its most infamous tool of oppression.

'If this is your land, where are your stories?': settlers and natives

Peidiwch a bod ofn yr Indiaid bois.

(Don't be afraid of the Indians boys).

Thomas Davies, Custer County, Colorado

The Welsh relationship with native peoples around the world was complex, contradictory and confusing. Undoubtedly, much good was done by people who believed genuinely in advancing the rights of native peoples. In the United States of America, Thomas Jesse Jones (1873–1950), did a remarkable amount of work for the education of Afro-Americans and the peoples of Africa. He was instrumental in the Commission for Racial Co-operation in 1919 and organised two educational commissions to Africa. Jones was influential in the establishment of educational institutions in the 1920s in Kenya, Uganda, Tanganyika, Liberia and amongst the Navajo Indians in the United States.[63] Wild Bill Williams and Robert Owen Pugh of Dolgellau lived happily with tribes of American Indians. Respecting their rights and traditions, Pugh took the name Istachtonka (Big Eyes), and even fought alongside the Indians in the Battle of Little Big Horn against General Custer.[64] Joseph Jenkins Roberts, president of Liberia (1872–6), was the son of a Welsh planter who was given his freedom by his father. The banker Gwilym Cleaton Jones (1875–1961) of Llanrug in Caernarfonshire served as honorary treasurer of the Cape Western Regional Committee of the South African Institute of Race Relations.[65] Bowen Rees (1857–1929) of Ystalyfera worked as a missionary in South Africa in the twentieth century's opening decades. He laboured hard to defend the Ndebele people against the British South Africa Company, which was intent on stealing their land. Rees was also active in the Aborigine Protection Society.[66]

Such altruism, respect and toleration were not always in evidence in the dealings of the Welsh with native peoples around the world. Welsh farmers in South America hunted local Indians for reward money, which led to the extinction of some tribes. One ex-rancher reputedly had a full set of saddle gear and harnesses made from the skin of Indians he had shot. [67] In June 1880 the Independent denomination's best-selling weekly magazine for children, *Trysorfa'r Plant*, published, amongst the usual stories glorying in the deaths of pious children, a serialisation of a sensational novel recounting the adventures of Albert Maywood in America.[68] The thrill-a-minute tale contains many instances of Maywood's dexterity in using his grotesquely titled gun, his 'Killnigger', to shoot native American Indians. Forty years later Professor W. J. Gruffydd could still recall, in *Hen Atgofion*, the excitement engendered in him as a boy by these tales of derring-do and death.[69] Real life was equally brutal. Lewis Jones, David Davies, William Williams and Lieutenant John Roberts, fought a series of battles against the Sioux.[70] In a letter home, Thomas Davies of Custer County Colorado expressed no concern at the displacement of the Indians from their lands:

> Mae deddf wedi i phasio'n mynnu bod yr Utes yn gadael y reservation; dyma'r lle gorau yn y dalaith, mae'n llawn o fwynau! Am le i gael trefedigaeth Cymreig, hogia! Dowch yma pan fydd yr Indiaid wedi gadael![71]
>
> (An act has been passed insisting that the Utes leave the reservation; this is the best place in the state, it is full of minerals! What a place to have a Welsh settlement, lads! Come here when the Indians have gone!).

Times of heightened crisis intensified the resentment the Welsh felt towards other peoples. In July 1895 Ieuan Ddu of Provo City, Utah, stressed that, although the Welsh were perfectly entitled to be a part of 'the genedl fawr Americanaidd' (great American nation) it would be 'futile and foolish to argue that all the tribes and nations of our Republic should melt into each other. Would it be appropriate for Gomer's race to mix with the black Negro and the red Indian, or the Bloody Dago?'[72]

The conclusion is almost inescapable: here were the Welsh, 'Gomer's race', choosing to do unto others what had already been done unto them in their own history. Conquered, colonised and thoroughly humiliated themselves, the Welsh helped to inflict the same fate on other nations around the world. Many of them eagerly embraced the arrogant concept enshrined in Palmerston's application of the claim *civis Romanus sum* to British subjects . The Welsh provided ample evidence that one of the hallmarks of colonialism is that the poorest, least powerful citizens of an occupying nation can wield enormous power in an occupied territory. The cheery banner of that profound contradiction in terms, 'liberal imperialism', justified the use of force to conquer first, to civilise later. There was a sanctimonious self-righteousness implanted in British imperialism of the late Victorian period which wrapped a cloak of virtue, benevolence and altruism around the injustice and inhumanity of the system. The empire was often portrayed as the trustee of liberty and freedom. This was especially so when the work of the Christian missionaries were added to the white man's burden to civilise the natives. Joseph Conrad, writing in 1902, in a Cardiff buoyant with the profits of coal that powered the empire's steamships, pointed to the deeper truth: 'the conquest of the earth, which mostly means the taking away of it from those who have a different complexion or slightly flatter noses than ourselves, is not a pretty thing when you look into it.'[73]

Native peoples around the world, as the stories in *Y Cenhadwr, Trysorfa'r Plant* and *Yr Eurgrawn* showed, were regarded at best as wayward children. The moral issues of the displacement of native inhabitants from their homelands by Welsh colonists, or the more morally sanitised term 'settlers', in America, Australia, Canada and Patagonia received little attention. William Griffith (1853–1918), the mining engineer, prospected for gold and diamonds in South and Central Africa. A friend of Cecil Rhodes and Dr Jameson, Griffith obtained properties for the British South Africa Chartered Company. His adventures were recounted in graphic, almost sensationalist prose in *Anturiaethau Cymro yn Affrica* (1894 and 1895), but he showed no moral concerns over the displacement of native peoples. In a letter to his fellow Welshmen from 'y Cyfandir Tywyll' (the Dark Continent) in 1895, he wrote:

> Os dangosem mewn unrhyw fodd fod arnom ofn y dyn du byddai yn amhosibl byw gydag ef . . . Rhaid cael y llaw uchaf arno beth bynnag fo'r gost . . . Bu raid i mi roi cosfa go sownd i ambell un.
>
> (If we show in any way that we fear the black man it will be impossible to live with him . . . We have to retain the upper hand over him whatever the cost . . . I had to give a good hiding to a few.)[74]

His near namesake, Sir Samuel Walker Griffith (1845–1920) of Merthyr Tydfil, became one of the most influential judges in Australia and worked hard for the preservation of 'white' Australia, as exemplified by the Queensland Defence Act of 1884. His strong advocacy secured the annexation of New Guinea. He was also influential in the confederation issue in 1901, when the Australian parliament expelled Pacific Islanders and prevented 'non-whites' from entering the country to settle.[75] Phillip Salisbury (d.1906) took race hatred to a new extreme, first as a soldier in the Serbian army, and afterwards as a soldier in the service of the Belgians in the Congo.

Welsh Christians, Marxists and global free-marketers could all justify their diverse actions by reference to a one-word ideology – progress. Even for missionaries, the pursuit of the material rewards of earthly empires proved stronger than the future rewards of celestial paradises. The Welsh often ventured bravely into what was described as *terra nullius*, a place where there was nobody or, if peopled, then the nomads were regarded as nobodies. According to this logic, as Thomas Davies of Colorado noted so bluntly, native peoples did not have any visible means of support, no property, no farms, no written history, no faith, no legal systems, no get-up-and-go. Thus they were forced to do just that – get up and go.

Such issues are clear if we consider the remarkable career of Henry Morton Stanley, the nineteenth century's greatest explorer.[76] He, undoubtedly, was the most controversial figure in the long involvement of the Welsh in Africa. Stanley was a well-balanced character, for he had chips on both shoulders. Before his expeditions, maps of Africa may as well have been marked like fringes of the Mappa Mundi – 'here be unicorns', 'here be dragons'. Stanley's 'discovery' of Livingstone and the source of the Nile, and his exploration of the Congo and Central Africa rank with the greatest geographical achievements. Stanley defied cannibals and cataracts, snakes and starvation in his odysseys. Unlike the saintly Livingstone, whom he idolised as a lost father figure, Stanley was convinced that the world required mastery as well as charity.[77] In books like *The Congo and the Founding of its Free State*, he explained how he turned exploration into a species of warfare. Even Richard Burton, himself no angel, disapproved of Stanley's methods. 'He shoots negroes as if they were monkeys', Burton complained.[78]

Above all else, perhaps, Stanley was the bridge between the golden age of exploration and the iron age of exploitation.[79] His exploration of Africa's physical geography led to a new political cartography of the continent. Following the Berlin Conference of 1884–5, European powers drew bold lines on the map and to mark their ownership and coloured the areas so enclosed – red (Britain), purple (France), brown (Germany), green (Portugal) or yellow (Belgium).[80] Without regard to race, language, topography or nature, the powers drew new countries into existence, in ways which would not be tolerated in Europe. Stanley, in effect, set in train the 'Scramble for Africa', which characterised the European conquest of the continent in the final quarter of the nineteenth century. European powers haggled over pieces of the continent that they could neither pronounce nor locate on a map. Together with his paymaster, King Leopold of the Belgians, Stanley helped build what became the most bloodthirsty colonial enclave in history, the grotesquely named Congo Free State, a 'vampire growth, intended to suck the country dry'.[81] It was here that Joseph Conrad set his great novella, *Heart of Darkness*.[82] Roger Casement considered Stanley 'one of the most unscrupulous villains the West has excreted on the continent of Africa'.[83] Stanley was acutely conscious of the commercial value of colonialism. As he told the Manchester Chamber of Commerce:

> There are forty millions of people beyond the gateway of the Congo, and the cotton spinners of Manchester are waiting to clothe them. Birmingham foundries are gleaming with the red metal that will presently be made into ironwork for them, and the trinkets that shall adorn those dusky bosoms, and the ministers of Christ are zealous to bring them, the poor benighted heathen, into the Christian fold.

This was the civilisation process instituted by the unholy trinity of commerce, chauvinism and the cross, and imposed by means of baubles, brandy, breech-loaders and the Bible.

'The day of the scorpions': the Welsh and the Raj

> We left Deolalie on the evening of the following day and the old soldier wished us the best of luck. As the years rolled on, I came to agree with him as to how the natives should be treated, and I still

agree with him that what is won by the sword must be kept by the sword.

Frank Richards, *Old Soldier Sahib* (Eastbourne, n.d.), pp. 79–80

India in particular, the jewel in the imperial crown, provided a wealth of career options to Welsh people who failed to satisfy their ambitions at home.[84] It was little surprise that Sir Herbert Winthorp Young (1885–1950) of Wrexham, army officer and administrator, should have a varied career in India, for the family had an almost nepotistic control of the country. They established an impressive imperial network of interlinked and interlocking administrative, civil service and legal interests. Winthorp Young's father and maternal grandfather were both lieutenant-governors of the Punjab. His brothers included Gerard Mackworth-Young (1884–1965) a senior civil servant in India and an eminent archaeologist, and Sir Mark Aitchison Young (1886–1974), a much-travelled colonial governor. Winthorp Young's major achievements, however, came in Iraq, where he won the admiration of T. E. Lawrence.[85] John Conway Rees (1870–1932) had a remarkable claim to fame. He won three rugby caps for the Welsh rugby XV in each game of a triple crown, one of the few ever to do so, but he also spent three decades as a teacher in India.[86] Sir Roger Thomas (1856–1960) of Clunderwen, Pembrokeshire, after graduating in history from Aberystwyth, spent periods in Egypt, Sudan, Mexico and the United States of America. In 1927, he went to work for the British Cotton Growing Association in Khanewal in the Punjab.[87] Thomas was representative of the people who were transforming the workshop of the world into the globe's warehouse. He became agricultural minister in the Sind government and advised European governments on the position of India and Pakistan. His work, published in *Planning for Agriculture in India* (1944) and *Drainage and Reclamation of Irrigated Lands in Pakistan* (1956), laid the basis for the agricultural development of both countries. Griffith Evans (1835–1935) of Towyn, the great microscopist and bacteriologist, served as veterinary officer with the cavalry in the Punjab. His research on and discovery of a cure for the mysterious disease known as 'surra' was recognised when the bacillus which causes it was named 'Trypanosoma Evansi'.[88]

Medicine in India also greatly benefited from the presence of the Welsh. John William Watson Stephens (1865–1946), the great parasitologist, of Ferryside, Carmarthenshire, worked in the late 1890s at Muktesar in the Himalayas. Here he developed treatments for snake bites and malaria which were put to great use locally and especially during the First World War. Hugh Gordon Roberts (1885–1961) mixed the career of surgeon and missionary and spent long periods between 1913 and 1945 in the Khasian hills, establishing hospitals there and in Assam.[89] Sir William Rice Edwards (1862–1923) of Caerleon, the eminent surgeon and soldier, was director-general of the Indian Medical Service (1918–23).[90]

To the empire coloured red on the map, city banks added an imperium glued together by debt and defended by gold. The worlds of banking and commerce provided opportunities for the enterprising and entrepreneurial Welsh, for the empire was often as much about financial power as firepower. John Howard Gwyther (1835–1921) of Milford Haven became chairman of the Chartered Bank and his advice and guidance steered it through the calamitous banking collapse of the mid 1890s. His genius enabled the Far Eastern banks to embrace bimetalism as the basis for several currencies in order to survive. Another who emphasised the advantages of bimetalism was Samuel Smith (1836–1906), millionaire politician and philanthropist and MP for Flintshire from 1886 to 1905. After a visit to India in 1886, Smith was probably more active in defending the Indian people than his own constituents. He did, however, occasionally despair of the Indians saying, 'whatever is done for the people, nothing is done by the people'.[91] Henry Neville Gladstone, Baron Gladstone of Hawarden (1852–1935) and Sir Ivor Philipps (1861–1940) were scions of Welsh aristocratic families who made fortunes for themselves as bankers in India.[92] Such people, who were representative of the resilience of 'gentlemahly capitalism', were, as the nineteenth century closed, increasingly supplemented by the professional middle class as 'the dominant social force in British imperialism'.[93]

The Indian legal system had an eloquence of Welsh lawyers. At the pinnacle, in the early twentieth century, was Sir Lawrence Hugh Jenkins (1857–1928), KCIE, Chief Justice of Bengal. Jenkins delivered several astute verdicts in a number of high-profile conspiracy and bombing cases in 1915. These cases required considerable adroitness, for they were politically highly charged and controversial. But his main interest seems to have been the Freemasons, for whom he served as the grandmaster for Bombay and Bengal.[94] Thomas Peter Ellis (1873–1936), who later wrote a magisterial study of *Welsh Tribal Law and Custom in the Middle Ages* (1926), also had a distinguished career in the Indian legal system, eventually becoming legal remembrancer (attorney-general) to the Punjab government in 1917. Ellis drafted the ordinances for the guidance of the civil and military authorities when martial law was imposed in India after the massacre at Amritsar on 13 April 1919. He had an extraordinary range as an author, for in addition to his historical works he produced detailed tomes on *Punjab Custom* (1918), *The Law of Pre-Emption in the Punjab* (1918) and *Welsh Fairy Tales*.[95]

Welsh lawyers undertook a vital role in the enhancement of the empire, that of supplanting local customs and legal systems with the rule of law as it had developed in Britain. The process by which the Welsh laws of Hywel Dda were supplanted by English common law was re-enacted by Welsh barristers and solicitors in India. Amongst the most damaging acts they introduced was the Criminal Tribes Act (1871), a terrible piece of legislation which criminalised people just by virtue of their birth. The importance of the rule of law in controlling India was clearly set out in an article by Sir Bartle Frere, 'On the laws affecting the relations between civilised and savage life, as bearing on the dealings of colonists and aborigines'. Needless to say colonial needs took precedence over native rights.[96]

Sir William Milbourne James (1807–81) of Merthyr Tydfil advised on equity procedure whilst a judge in India. His experiences were chronicled in the posthumously published *The British in India* (1882).[97] John Allsebrook Simon, Viscount Simon of Stackpole Elidor (1873–1954), chaired the Statutory Commission on India between 1927–30 and later became Lord Chancellor.[98] Sir Evan and Sir Owain Jenkins, as befitted the sons of Sir John Lewis Jenkins (1857–1912), also reached the pinnacle of the Indian Legal

Service. Sir John, more than any other person, was responsible for the transference of the capital from Calcutta to Delhi.[99] The barrister Edward Owen (1853–1943) spent forty years diligently working from the India Office in London, with the occasional trip to the subcontinent. His main energies, however, were devoted to his arduous antiquarian work enshrined in the four volumes of the *Catalogue of the Manuscripts Relating to Wales in the British Museum*.[100]

Cultural pursuits also provided the Welsh with a passage to India. The actor and director Lewis Casson (1875–1969) of Ffestiniog went on four tours of dramatic productions to India, as well as to South Africa and Australia. In India, he and his wife, Sibyl Thorndike, celebrated the jubilee of their wedding with a production of *Eighty in the Shade*.[101] The painter John Griffiths (1837–1918) became head of the Bombay School of Art and created many paintings of Indian scenes.[102] Griffiths was responsible for the design and decoration of the new buildings in Bombay. His main contribution was the preservation of the cave paintings at Ajanta. The pianist Idris Lewis (1889–1952), later the first musical director of the BBC in Wales, went on a recital tour to India in 1911–12.[103] Cultures crossed continents. Sir Mortimer Wheeler (1890–1976), formerly director of the National Museum of Wales and serving as a brigadier during the invasion of Italy in 1941, was transferred not to another army posting but to the Archaeological Survey of India. With his irrepressible, Terry-Thomas-style moustache, Wheeler's characteristic exuberance and enthusiasm reinvigorated the moribund institution. Wheeler's work, especially the journal *Ancient India* which he established, served to provide the emergent nation in 1947 with a 'useable past'. Even so, the transfer of Wheeler from army duties to archaeological digging at a time of serious national insecurity is one of the more perplexing decisions of the war.[104]

The study of native cultures was a notable trait of several administrators in India. In some respects this can be seen as a noble attempt to reveal the cultural richness of local tradition. Yet it was also a form of cultural supremacy in which authors sought to rule by the pen. The torrents of learning gathered in censuses, gazettes, magazines, books and lithographic reports indicated another reality. India, for example, was in these works revealed as a mass of incompatible fragments, divided by race, language, caste, occupation and religion. Divided, that is, until the British arrived. Up until then, India had been just a 'geographical expression' – a fate familiar to many Welsh people.[105] It was only unified by the myth manufactured by the British.[106] George Howells (1871–1955), principal of the Baptist Missionary Society's college in Serampore, played a vital role in establishing the institution's supply of literature and texts. Such publications not only assisted the college's spiritual work, but they also helped to emphasise the cultural, linguistic, racial and theological superiority of its message.[107] Dilys Grace Edmunds (1879–1926) played a similar role in the service of the Calvinistic Methodists and as a teacher in Karimganj.

Technical superiority was also vital to the empire. The manufacturing and mechanical trades in the subcontinent had a clutch of Welsh engineers, such as the Aberystwyth-born duo David Edward Evans and Dan Roberts, respectively chief engineers for Bengal and Narayangang in 1911. David Evans had previously been commissioned into the Royal Indian Marine, and had seen active service in the Burma War of 1886–7, which resulted in the final annexation of that country. David Evans became chief engineer to the Royal Indian Marine and a founder member of the Indian Institution of Mechanical Engineers in 1910. Evans was the proud owner of the first motor car in Calcutta and only the second in the whole of India. W. C. Wordsworth, the managing editor of the great Indian newspaper, *The Statesman*, also had family connections with Aberystwyth.[108]

The careers of Welsh lawyers, administrators, clerks, engineers, barristers and bureaucrats are useful reminders of one of the deeper realities of empire. It was not a continuous process of conquest and massacre, of brave boys on burning decks, but a slow, mundane bureaucratic drudge.[109]

'Emerald Peacocks': imperial identity and the experiences of empire

Who is it climbs the summit of the road?
Only the beggar bumming his dark load.
Who was it cried to see the falling star?
Only the landless soldier lost in war.

And did a thousand years go by in vain?
And does another thousand start again?

Alun Lewis, 'The Maharatta Ghats', in Meic Stephens (ed.), *Poetry 1900–2000* (Cardigan, 2007), p. 184

Alun Lewis's questions indicate one of the truths of the experience of empire. Behind the grand word and the great facade stood a mass of individuals, a network of lobbies and loyalties and a mountain of hopes.[110] There was no single, simple empire but global networks of power and dominance, commerce, government, communication and faith, which interlocked the peoples of Britain and native peoples around the world. The empire was a gallimaufry of experiences, a welter of contradictions. In certain places, at certain times, it was a modernising creative force; elsewhere, and at other times, it was rigidly hierarchical, negative and atavistic.[111]

The empire was a multifaceted conglomeration and thus the identities presented by Welsh Orientalists were complex. Some postured as English, others paraded a British identity, but an element were clearly proud of the Welsh dimension to their lives. Categories of imperial communities were difficult to identify with any precision.[112] Subscribing to empire did not exclude other ties and identities and could reinforce them. For many Welsh people, empire was not only a vast field of emigration and opportunity but it also supplied a collective focus of loyalty less overwhelmingly English than the three unions with England out of which the United Kingdom had been made.[113] In a number of ways, Welsh people saw opportunities for advancement in the empire.[114] The trade of Wales, especially that of the coalfields, benefited. The country was proudly portrayed as the source of the fuel that powered the empire and Welsh businessmen took an active part in trade, especially in Africa and India, whilst the missionaries of Wales were committed to converting the heathen and her soldiers devoted to conquering him. This had a dual effect. It provided a reminder – though no reminder was really needed, for the columns of newspapers like the *Western Mail* and periodicals like *Wales* and *Welsh Outlook* provided frequent eulogies of empire – that Wales without empire would have been a poor relation of England. And it provided a huge reinforcement to Welsh self-belief; her role in the empire gave confidence to some that Wales could survive as a distinct national community, with distinctive traditions and her own path to modernity.[115] In countless cartoons scattered in the yellowing pages of fading newspapers, Dame Wales is portrayed as the perfect partner for John Bull.

In 1892 Gwilym Tawe, in an article on 'Nationalisms: their uses and abuses', clearly expressed the view 'that we have not been so much conquered as allied to England . . . While we are Welshmen in heart, speech, and behaviour, we need not to cease to be Britons in the imperial sense.' The Swansea-born journalist John Arthur Sandbrook (1876–1942) wrote some of the most graphic and vivid reports from the Boer War for the *Western Mail*. In 1910 he was appointed editor of *The Englishman*, a Calcutta newspaper. In India, he noted that it was difficult to differentiate between Welsh, English, British, Eurasian and native.[116] It is fascinating to note that the Raj, the pre-eminent symbol of English ascendancy, status and snobbery was, in many places, represented by people who were Welsh, Nonconformist and Welsh-speaking. Particularly problematic was the category 'poor white', those drudges of empire, the dockers, drifters, drunks and prostitutes whose lowly status and unpredictable behaviour consistently threatened to tarnish 'white prestige'. A Methodist missionary in Fiji lamented that so many vulnerable native men were 'always in Suva picking up ideas from loafing low-class whites . . . the pernicious examples of a degenerate civilisation'.[117] The experiences of the soldier Frank Richards in India seem to indicate that interracial sex was less the exception than the rule, for 'poor whites' were everywhere; the social distance between them and their supposed inferiors was only intermittently maintained.[118] What effect this merging and melding of peoples had on class or race or status is difficult to interpret.[119]

To celebrate their national origins, emigrants established Welsh societies across all outposts of the empire. The St David's Day celebrations in South Africa in 1898 were 'emphatically a loyal display of cultural solidarity'. On the big day:

> Mr James Lewis, once of Porth, now landlord of the Park Hotel near the railway station, stretched 'Croesawer Cymry' above his entrance, Mr David E. Jones, late of Glynarthen, had 'Cymru am Byth' across his Arcade Bar, while Mr Goodman, a good man from Pontypridd, bade welcome in the Guildhall to all his countrymen with the words, 'Cymry, dewch at y Cymro'.[120]

On such occasions, the antics of the Welsh in foreign parts descended into pure slapstick – a cross between *Carry On Up the Khyber* and a Shakespearian tragedy. In 1898, Cymdeithas Gwladol y Cymry yn yr India, of which 'none but the Welsh people are eligible for membership', was established. At their annual St David's Day dinner, the band accompanying the mastication must have played all night to give enough time for them to consume an impressive repast that included: 'Caviare and anchovies, Welsh broth, fish, mutton cutlets, quail, roast turkey and ham, roast game, leeks, cabinet glacé pudding, Welsh rarebit and Neapolitan creams'. The toast list reveals where their loyalties lay: 'Ein Frenhines ac Ymherodres' (Our Queen and Empress), 'Tywysog Cymru' (the Prince of Wales), 'Gwyl Dewi Sant' (St David's Day), all proposed by the president, and finally, before they fell in a drunken stupor, 'Y wlad a'm magodd' ('The country which raised me'), proposed by the Hon. Justice Jenkins.[121]

On 31 July 1909, Cymdeithas Cymry Bengal held its inaugural meeting in Peliti's, one of the social centres of Edwardian Calcutta. Both Cymdeithas Gwladol y Cymry and Cymdeithas Cymry Bengal held soirées and concerts where the audience were often a blubbering mass, reduced to tears both by the quality of the singing and the topic of the songs. The Welsh person in a foreign land could not withstand the saccharine lachrymosity of tear-jerkers such as 'Braint, Braint', 'Taffy', 'Gwlad y Delyn', 'Cymro Dewr', 'Cartref', the incomprehensible 'Hob y Deri Dando' and the horribly sentimental 'Sassiwn yn'Nghymru'. In misty-eyed hiraeth, they idealised the land that had made emigrants of them.

One notable thing is that many men of empire seem to have been genuinely happy men who, like Sir Lawrence Hugh Jenkins and Thomas Peter Ellis, sat in their offices dispensing justice to 'backward' peoples, decreeing imprisonment here, a fine there, in the absolute knowledge that the Raj was right.[122] Real happiness often emanates from the pages of the missionary journals, such as *Y Cenhadwr*, with their bright-eyed conviction of Christian opportunity. A less imperialistic figure than the pacifist poet Thomas Gwynn Jones (1871–1949), it is hard to imagine, yet he spent an idyllic period in Egypt in 1905, recuperating from illness and working as a freelance author. His writings seem oddly at variance with those of his later career, in which he expressed concerns at the empire's baneful influence.[123]

Many of the emigrants, however, must have hated the places to which their jobs and responsibilities had taken them. Irrespective of the climate or weather, Welsh people continued to dress in the numerous layers and heavy fashions of a home winter and their stifling, inhibiting Britishness. The empire's effects on families were particularly poignant.[124] Silent headstones around the world record a catalogue of early deaths. At Simla in India, four horizontal stones record the deaths in 1865 of the Daniel family's four children under four years of age. For families to survive their imperial years, girls and boys were sent back 'home' to boarding schools, where they saw out their youth as discarded children of the empire, waiting for the precious sea-mail letters that told of their lost lives abroad. George Woosung Wade (1858–1941), minister and author, was born in Shanghai and sent to school in Monmouth, whilst Sir George Lewis Barstow (1874–1966), civil servant and president of University College Swansea, was born in India but educated in Builth.[125] Griffith Pugh, the physiologist on the successful Everest expedition of 1953, was sent from India to Rhos y Gilwen in Pembrokeshire at the start of the First World War.[126]

Considerable distances thus separated families, but they were united by rumour and gossip carried on the trade winds between settlements. The women of the empire often powered such stories. Sent out in the 'fishing fleets' of women who went trawling for husbands in India, their major purpose was to make a marriage.[127] These paragons of virtue were amongst the saddest figures in the empire's sorry saga. With some notable exceptions, they lacked both essential work and an independent role. They were deterred from learning local languages by their alleged impropriety. They were fed lurid tales of coloured lust. They found themselves in an alien, sometimes hostile and often incomprehensible world. They wore flannel underwear because they thought it absorbed sweat more efficiently.[128] Those who broke out of this mould were relatively rare free spirits. The experiences of Mary Eliza Isabella May Frere (1845–1911), a writer on Indian folklore, and Edith Picton-Turbervill (1872–1960), the tireless social worker amongst the very poorest of India, Malaya and Hong Kong, were truly remarkable. They were laudable successors to the tradition of intuitive and intelligent interpretation of native culture established by the remarkable Fanny Parkes, a Welsh travel writer who lived in India in the 1820s and put her experiences into *Wanderings of a Pilgrim in Search of the Picturesque, during Four and Twenty Years in the East, with Revelations of Life in the Zenana* (London, 1850).[129]

Like many human endeavours, the empire was not wholly bad or good, and not uniformly vicious or vindictive. There were several examples of 'servants of Empire' who did remarkable work for the good of peoples around the world. As that astute critic of the empire, Robert Ambrose Jones (Emrys ap Iwan; 1851–1906), wrote: 'Gall blodau teg darddu o domen ffiaidd' (sweet flowers can flower even on a foul dung heap).[130] Thomas Jerman Jones, a missionary for twenty years with the Calvinistic Methodists in the Khasi Hills in India, served with bravery and distinction at Shillong during the cholera epidemic of 1875. The National Museum in Cardiff has over twenty examples of the Albert and Empire Gallantry Medals that were awarded to Welsh people for altruistic and heroic acts. During the outbreak of bubonic plague at Canton in January 1894, at Hong Kong later in the same year, at the Messina earthquake in 1908 and during the Quetta (Baluchistan) earthquake on 31 May 1935, Welsh people showed exceptional valour and self-sacrifice. On the waterfront of Hong Kong in 1894, when 40,000 lives were lost in a horrific plague, Welsh soldiers drove the mortuary carts and the death cars and undertook the dreaded fumigation duties.[131]

As with most imperial situations, the Welsh in Africa undertook a contradictory role. William Griffith, of Felinheli near Caernarfon, was one of Cecil Rhodes's Pioneer Column, which was busy, in 1898, stealing land in Mashonaland and Matabeleland. Howell Arthur Gwynne (1865–1950) of Swansea was editor of several right-wing newspapers in the 1920s and 1930s. His views were probably more extreme than those of his readers. His experiences in South Africa during the Boer War, when he organised Reuters' coverage of the action, gave him his lifelong obsession and cause – the furtherance of the empire. So far as he was concerned, no part of it was to be relinquished or allowed more responsibility for governing itself.[132] But several Welsh people diligently worked in the best interests of the people of Africa. David Ivon Jones (1883–1924) emigrated to South Africa in 1910, where he joined five of his eight siblings. A communist of conviction and conscience, Jones was one of the first whites in South Africa to champion equal rights for black South Africans. Jones's campaign for equal rights for all nations resulted in his imprisonment.[133] The philanthropist John David Rheinallt Jones (1884–1953) helped to establish the University of Witwatersrand in Johannesburg, the South African Institute of Race Relations, the journal *Race Relations* and the monthly newsletter *Race Relations News*.[134]

'The making of history': the Welsh and the Colonial Office

> In March 1950 I had entered upon my work as Colonial Secretary with trepidation. I felt like a traveller entering a strange world. Twenty months later I was to leave with the deepest regret. I was beginning to find my way in this new world and to understand the hopes and aspirations as well as the fears of the people who dwelt

> in it. One had the feeling of being in at the making of history. The revolution which, within a decade, was to transform the British Empire into a Commonwealth was already gathering momentum.
>
> James Griffiths, *Pages from Memory* (London, 1969), p. 119

The Welsh were not simply the chaff of empire blown hither and thither by the winds of the world. In a number of areas they devised and dictated the policies which developed the empire and colonies. Over the period 1870–1947 the British Empire underwent a remarkable transformation. Colonial conquest and coercion gave way to decolonisation and independence, as the unstructured, undefined dominions gave way to a commonwealth. At times of war, especially the Second World War, the reality of the Britannic vision was clear. Despite the myth, Britain did not stand alone in 1940, but was supported by partners in a commonwealth of nations. The Welsh played a notable part in this transformation. The particular careers of a few Welsh politicians enable one to trace the general transformation.[135]

The career of Lord Lloyd as high commissioner in Egypt seemed to represent the worst caricature of the empire and its rulers. With his cocked hat, ceremonial orders and ribbons, and Rolls-Royce, he behaved with supercilious proconsular pomp in laying down the law.[136] Henry Howard Molyneux Herbert, fourth earl of Carnarvon (1831–90), twice served as colonial secretary in Tory administrations in the 1860s and 1870s. His policy was neatly expressed in the slogan 'conciliation is better than coercion'. Perhaps his worst mistake was to send Sir Bartle Frere of Clydach to be governor of Cape Colony and high commissioner for South Africa in March 1874, which shattered his plans for peace.[137] Sir Samuel Walker Griffith (1845–1920) of Merthyr Tydfil, a leading judge in Australia, was the most eloquent exponent of empire unity at the Empire Conference in London in 1887. In 1891, as chairman of the Sydney convention for the federation of the Australian colonies, he drafted the constitution which was later enacted as law by the British parliament.[138] William George Arthur Ormsby-Gore, fourth Baron Harlech (1885–1964), served as a parliamentary under-secretary at the Colonial Office between 1922 and 1929. In 1926 he visited West Africa, and in 1928 Ceylon, Malaya and Java. In 1929 he served for two years as colonial secretary, a post for which he was well suited, as he had travelled almost the entire length and breadth of the empire. George Henry Hall, Viscount Hall of Cynon Valley (1891–1965), also served as a parliamentary undersecretary of state for the colonies in the 1940s, as did Sir Edward John Williams (1890–1963).[139]

Those within the Labour political fold also served within the Colonial Office with equal ability. The inimitable James Henry Thomas ('Jimmy' or 'Jim'; 1874–1949), born the illegitimate son of Elizabeth Thomas, a domestic servant of Newport, served as colonial secretary and dominions secretary in the 1920s and 1930s. A delight to the cartoonists with his pudgy figure and chubby face, Thomas's manner generated countless humorous stories. Complaining to F. E. Smith, Lord Birkenhead, after a hard night's drinking, 'Ooh Fred, I've got an 'ell of an 'eadache', he is said to have prompted Birkenhead to reply, 'Try a couple of aspirates'. Thomas had, to say the least, a chequered political career, forever blighted by his and his government's inability to conquer unemployment in the 1930s. But he had some success to his credit, particularly the solution of the Irish boundary problem. One who clashed with his views in the Colonial Office was Sir Hubert Winthorp Young of Wrexham, who spent periods as envoy extraordinary and minister plenipotentiary in Baghdad, and as governor respectively of Nyasaland (1932–4), Northern Rhodesia (1934–8) and Trinidad and Tobago (1938–42). Young's views, in particular on the creation of Arab states and a new British Central Africa, proved to be highly controversial.[140]

Perhaps the most gifted Welsh holder of the post of colonial secretary was James Griffiths (1890–1975). A colliery blacksmith's son and himself a former miner of Ammanford, Griffiths had a truly Sisyphean approach to the post, for he was in office at the time of the strategic transformation of the empire into the commonwealth. Within only nineteen months from his appointment in 1950 he prepared twelve new constitutions, which were promptly adopted in emerging colonial countries, including Kenya, Nigeria and Singapore.[141] Despite his deep socialist principles and genuine sympathy with indigenous peoples, Griffiths was prepared to use force against left-wing insurgents in Malaya and other countries. His period of office as colonial secretary was not without embarrassment. He oversaw the crackbrained plan to pour more than £36 million into producing eggs in Gambia for British housewives still suffering food rationing. The flora and climate, uncongenial to the human British settlers, were hostile to chickens, whilst the predatory local fauna could not believe their luck. The scheme foundered amidst allegations of corruption, incompetence and embezzlement. James Griffiths had to announce details of the scheme's failure to the House of Commons, which seemed oddly unconcerned at the loss of the funding, but profoundly concerned at the fate of the few surviving chickens. The debate degenerated into a level of farce which, even in House of Commons terms, was unedifying. It cost George Morgan, first Baron Trefgarne of Cleddau (formerly George Morgan Garro-Jones; 1894–1960), his post as the chairman of the Colonial Development Corporation in 1950.[142]

Remarkably, the link between the oldest British colony and the colonial office continued. The next Welsh holder of the post of secretary of state for commonwealth affairs was Herbert William Bowden, Baron Aylestone (1905–94), the eldest of the eleven children of a Cardiff baker. Political principles were not, perhaps, Bowden's strongest feature, for when he was appointed, the Queen remarked 'how delighted she was that that kind of non-political man was in the job'.[143] Eirene Lloyd White, Baroness White (1909–99), was an under-secretary of state in the Colonial Office in Harold Wilson's Labour government from 1964, thus completing a remarkable Welsh stranglehold on the Colonial Office.[144]

Soldiers of the Widow: some 'small, sad wars of empire'

> Y mae pob ymerodraeth a adeiladwyd trwy gelwydd, a thwyll, a thrais, yn sicr o ymchwalu yn fuan neu yn hwyr. Y mae hi, wrth ymehangu, yn lluosogi'r gelynion sydd yn barod i ddial eu cam arni.

(Every empire built on lies, and deceit, and violence, is certain to collapse sooner or later. Through expansion, an empire increases the number of enemies who will wish to revenge their injustices.)

Robert Ambrose Jones (Emrys ap Iwan: 1821–1906),
'Cydymffurfio â'r byd'

In churches in Caernarfon, Brecon and Wrexham, torn and tattered regimental battle honours recall imperial wars. Open the door swiftly in St Peter's church, Pentre, and the draught sends a flutter through the flag of Field Marshal Lord Grenfell of Kilvey, captured at the battle of Toski (Egypt). These frail and fragile relics are meant to invoke the heroic last-ditch stand on foreign shores of the brave, battered and invariably outnumbered British soldier. Such icons were not uncharacteristic emblems for there is a stain of scarlet running throughout the empire's history. Violence was perennial, as local resistance and revolt was answered with repression. Much of the violence occurred not in battle but in skirmishes, raids, reprisals and police actions – a relentless, continuous, low-austerity warfare that appeared never-ending. In many respects the British bought imperial power with blood, some of it their own. If the sun never set on the empire, then neither did the blood dry on it.

Despite the constant haemorrhaging of lives and the fatuous declarations of newspaper reports that the 'fallen shall live forever', the small wars of empire in which British soldiers matched barbarian in brutality are now forgotten.[145] In a sense this is not surprising, for in Victoria's reign alone the empire was enmeshed in 246 armed conflicts or wars. Even allowing for her longevity, that indicates a predilection towards pugnacity that surely negates claims of the British being a peaceful people. Sir Charles Warren (1840–1927) of Bangor, army officer, police commissioner and archaeologist, was seriously wounded during the Transkei War of 1877–8; the battle was forgotten almost before his wounds healed.[146] The war against Zanzibar has acquired a strange character, part farce, part brooding Conradian fable of darkness, in which three modern British cruisers fired shells at a forlorn coast. It lasted for just thirty-eight minutes, although some pedants insist it lasted longer. They time the war at forty-five minutes – from just after 9 a.m. to a little before 10 a.m.

on 27 August 1896. Yet that was enough time for around 500 people to die, amongst them able seaman David Jones. The celebrity status of being killed in the shortest war on record was probably no consolation to David's kith and kin.[147]

Another conflict that appears to have acquired posthumous pathos is the War of the Golden Stool, or the Yaa Asantewaa War, or the Third Ashanti Expedition, or the Ashanti Uprising. This certainly lasted longer, from March to September 1900. This war between the British imperial government of the Gold Coast (later Ghana) and the Empire of Ashanti, a powerful semi-autonomous African state, was the last conflict in Africa in which the commander of one of the opposing armies was a woman, the queen mother of Ejisu. Despite their technological advantages, 200 Welsh troops were amongst those who were ignominiously besieged in Kumasi.[148] Two years earlier and further along the coast, Lionel Wilmot Brabazon Rees was one of several who fought in the Hut Tax War of 1898 in Sierra Leone. One of the many victims of the brutal encounter was the Reverend W. J. Humphrey. It was rumoured that he was so unpopular that he was killed by his own supporters who fondly used to say 'Here comes that bastard now'.[149]

Such wars became a part of the everyday British experience. Despite their farcical nature, they were none the less bloody ventures into the killing fields. They were both exhilarating and deeply tragic for those who never learned to ask the reason why. One such unfortunate was Norman Biggs (1870–1908), the Welsh rugby international whose speed clinched victory against Scotland and the first ever Triple Crown for Wales. Biggs, a captain in the Glamorgan Yeomanry, survived the Boer War, but was killed by a poison arrow in a 'native ambush' whilst serving in the Nigerian police, aged thirty-seven years.[150] Another adventurer of empire was Sir Walter Henry Cowan (1871–1956) who, after a period on the East India station, served as a captain and commander of a series of riverboats and battle-cruisers, the *Redbreast, Sultan* and *Boxer*, along the west coast of Africa. His experiences are factual examples of Conrad's fictional representations of conquest in darkest Africa. Cowan also took part in the shameful battle of Omdurman (1898).[151]

The armed services, from the mid-nineteenth century onwards, provided a wealth of opportunities for the Welsh to travel to interesting places, meet interesting people and shoot them. The army was the most unpredictable of travel agents, and had a broader range of destinations than the emerging merchants of sun, sea and sand. Welsh soldiers were sent around the world to 'butcher and bolt'. Sir Lloyd William Mathews (1850–1901) joined the navy at thirteen years of age. His first battle was in the Anglo-Ashanti War of 1873–4. He was afterwards stationed in East Africa for the suppression of the slave trade but was seconded from the navy in order to form an European-style army for Sultan Bargash of Zanzibar. Mathews's army numbered more than 7,000 troops and was used to suppress the slave trade and rebellions against the Zanzibar government.[152]

To ensure that Britannia ruled the waves, her soldiers travelled the world. Francis Wallace Grenfell (1841–1925), first Baron Grenfell, served in South Africa, fighting against the 'warlike' Galeka tribe. He probably felt at home, for he fought in the oddly Welsh-sounding, Gwili-Gwili Mountains. Grenfell then served in Egypt, the Sudan and India, and later as governor of Malta (1899) and commander-in-chief in Ireland.[153] Sir James Hills-Johnes (1833–1919) of Dolaucothi, Carmarthenshire, fought in the Indian 'Mutiny' (1857–8), winning the Victoria Cross, the Abyssininan campaign (1867–8), the Lushai campaign (1871–2) and the Afghan War (1878–80), before being made military governor of Kabul. The much-named Llewellyn Isaac Gethin Morgan-Owen (1879–1960) was the military administrator in India in the 1920s; without his administrative and financial skills, British forces in India would not have been able to move. But Morgan-Owen was not merely a pen-pusher; he was mentioned no fewer than five times in despatches during the taking of Baghdad in 1917. Thomas Wynford Rees (1898–1959) survived active service in two world wars. A fluent Welsh speaker, 'Dagger', or the 'Pocket Napoleon', learned many Indian dialects and was widely reported to be one of the bravest of all Welsh soldiers. The medals that weighed down his chest were ample evidence that 'Dagger' had managed to survive in some very scary places. Fear would have been frightened of Rees.[154]

During the Second World War, despite the propaganda which portrayed an united empire, Britain was obliged to use more troops to sustain its internal control of India in the face of militant nationalists than were deployed against the Japanese.[155] British colonists were at their most violent when acting in reprisal; the humiliation of rebellion demanded a response that was nothing less than overwhelming. Welsh papers like the *South Wales Daily News* and the *Western Mail* often articulated the spirit of revenge. Irrespective of where the battle was joined, the enemy was vilified, emasculated, insulted. Afghanistan and China were 'medieval', 'uncivilised'. Fighters from Asia to Australia to Africa were 'cowardly', 'underhand', 'devious', 'cowards', 'sly', whereas the British troops were invariably 'noble', 'brave', 'valorous', 'courageous' and 'decent'. Frank Richards catalogued the casual brutalities and beatings meted out to native peoples in India and Burma in *Old Soldier Sahib*. Rorke's Drift, Omdurman, Lhasa and Amristrar are sorry sagas in which women, children and unarmed men confronted men who were heavily armed.[156]

It is important to remember that not all soldiers were trigger-happy morons. Many were cultured and civilised. They learnt native languages and appreciated local archaeology, cultures and customs. The Welsh scholar and academic Stephen Joseph Williams (1896–1992) spent four years from 1914 with the 11th Gurkha Rifles in northern India. Perhaps the most sensitive analysis of the soldier's role in empire, and especially in India, is given in the works of Alun Lewis (1915–44).[157] Lewis never recovered from the shock of his exposure to the land and its people – the unimaginable scale of it, 'the nihilist persistence of the sun'. Despite holding strong pacifist beliefs, Lewis, a history graduate, enlisted with the South Wales Borderers in 1940. In his collection of poems, *Raider's Dawn* (1941), in his short stories in *The Last Inception* (1942) and in his letters to his wife, published as *Letters from India* (1948), Lewis offered a highly nuanced, subtle and sensitive portrait of the Welsh soldier. Fighting against the Japanese near Chittagong (Bangladesh), Lewis died mysteriously of wounds caused by his own gun.

The most detailed examination of the Welsh soldier's life came not from the highly educated, like Alun Lewis, but from a more rambunctious character. Frank Richards left south Wales because of the intimidation he received from trade union leaders during the coal strike of 1898. In his memoirs, *Old Soldier Sahib,* he revealed what life in India was like for a 'foot soldier of death'. Frank had the hard-faced cynicism of the long-term soldier. His greatest ambition was to avoid action. Life might have been boring in camp, but he was safe from bullets there. It was tedious, but at least it was not terrifying. Frank was not a coward; he was canny. It was better killing time than being killed. In his memoirs, he proudly recalled tales of fighting (usually against other British troops) and fornication with overly friendly and enthusiastic native girls; within his copy of the King's Regulations there was usually some neatly folded pornography of an anthropological nature. He and his colleagues were obsessed with the usual military occupations – drinking, gambling and whoring. The 'irrepressibly randy' Frank was the epitome of Bernard Shaw's 'old soldier', carrying as much food with him as ammunition. Undependable in daily life, Frank was a rock in a crisis, when things mattered. As he reported how he 'rose to be a private', he expressed no reservations or doubts about the justice of the cause he was in India and then Burma to defend.[158]

In 1886, intent on obtaining detail for the blank on the map that was northern Asia, Francis Younghusband, escorted by General Charles Bruce and a small party of the 5th Gurkhas, ventured through the Karakoram.[159] Bruce had created a unique military unit, the Frontier Scouts, a prototypic counterinsurgency force that specialised in infiltration, ambush and assassination. The Gurkhas excelled as guerrilla fighters and Bruce trained them to be mountain soldiers prepared to take the fight aggressively to the enemies of the Raj – the Wazirs, Orakzais, Afridis and a host of frontier tribes whose villages were to be razed, elders killed and younger men and women cowed into submission. Bruce and his forces had been hardened by the stresses and strains of the battles of the Great Game along the North-West Frontier. Encounters such as those in the Black Mountains – Hazara (1891), Miranzai (1891), Chitral (1893), Waziristan (1894–5), Tirah (1897–8) – were not trivial conflicts. In the Afghan border campaigns of 1897, hundreds were killed, scores of villages put to the torch, and prisoners on both sides slaughtered without mercy. 'Severity always' was the motto of the Frontier Scouts, 'justice when possible'.[160]

In 1904, in one of the empire's most shameful episodes, a number of Welsh soldiers stormed into Lhasa with Francis Younghusband's troops. In this futile, fatal act of the Great Game, 'the last stronghold of romance was breached, the curtain to the forbidden lifted'.[161] Tibetans were terrified when they saw the moustachioed troops and traumatised by the wheeled carriages, which seemed to them to be propelled by magic, for they had never seen a wheel. Then, as if these apocalyptic spectres were not enough, the maxim guns fired. As one Tibetan eyewitness recalled, 'the sound of firing continued for the length of time it would take six successive cups of hot tea to cool'.[162] It was another Omdurman; a massacre; an effortless, senseless, colonial victory.[163] The Tibetans simply turned away and, as if impervious to the bullets that cut them down, began to move north towards Lhasa. 'It was an awful sight', wrote one officer, 'and I hope I shall never again have to shoot down men who are walking away.'[164] Henry Savage Landor, infamous for his own graphic exploits in Tibet, wrote of the 'battle' at Guru as 'the butchering of thousands of helpless and defenceless natives in a manner most repulsive to any man who is a man'.[165]

One of the most fascinating Welsh figures of empire, was Sir Henry Bartle Frere (1815–84) of Clydach. Able, energetic, cultured and puncticillious to the tips of his exquisitely groomed moustache, Frere had distinguished himself in India. He was one of the British leaders who brutally suppressed native peoples following the 'Mutiny' or uprising of 1858. A gifted linguist, he acquired several languages. En route from India to Africa, Frere soon learned 'enough Arabic to scold his way across Egypt'. He took a sternly paternalistic line in dealing 'with barbarous folk'. Frere's proconsular pomp took 'ornamentalism' and the ceremonialism of his office to new extremes. With his cocked hat, his ceremonial sword at his side and his gold-fringed gown, this caped crusader was the very embodiment of 'fine dignity'. As governor in Bombay, Frere had acquired a sublime faith in his own ability and judgement, a faith that was to be severely tested when he was transferred to the post of high commissioner in South Africa.[166]

As British high commissioner in Cape Town, one of Frere's first acts was to issue an ultimatum demanding the disarmament of the warlike Zulu tribes.[167] When discussions failed, he sent out a slow-moving army troop of about 18,000 white-hatted, red-coated soldiers from Pietermaritzburg. Wheels creaked, sjamboks cracked and the band played 'I'm leaving thee in Sorrow, Annie', the tune that had sent the Confederates off to fight in the American Civil War. The troops trundled into disaster under the command of the inept General Lord Chelmsford, whom most of his troops considered unfit to be even a colonel. Frere was inept but Chelmsford took incompetence to depths unchartered even by the British military. He deemed it too time-consuming to form a laager every evening, and even divided his central column. With half his command, he slowly pursued war parties of the fleet-footed Zulus over the high plateau, a landscape of grass, bush and boulder, broken by kloofs (ravines) and kopjes (hills). The rest of his men Chelmsford left in an exposed camp beneath a sphinx-shaped crag called Isandlwana.

Here, on 22 January 1879, twenty thousand Zulu warriors who had hidden throughout the cold, dewy night in a nearby valley, sustained only by a hallucinogenic snuff, launched their main attack. Enraged, determined to protect their land, kraals and cattle, they swept forward, a dark wave breaking over the grey-green veldt. At a distance, said one Welsh trooper, the Zulu impi was 'black as hell and thick as grass'.[168] The inevitability and totality of the massacre makes one's flesh creep.[169] The images of small units of redcoats surrounded by howling masses of Zulus conjure the anxiety of nightmare. The Zulus, far taller, stronger and faster than their British enemies, drove forward hissing like so many mambas, drumming assegais against black and white shields. Muskets fired wildly; sabres slashed in the sunshine. Far more deadly were the volleys of the Martini-Henrys, their heavy, soft-nosed 45 calibre bullets 'cutting roads' through the ranks of the charging throng. The Zulus adopted their traditional taurine tactic; bearing the brunt of the punishment on the chest of their impi, while flinging out two 'horns' to envelop the enemy.[170]

As British ammunition was exhausted, the battle disintegrated and degenerated into scattered hand-to-hand fighting, bayonets against iklwas – razor-sharp blades, so named in imitation of the sucking sound they made when pulled from human flesh. Particularly harrowing was the plight of the bandsmen, who had nothing but a conductor's baton or their instruments to protect themselves. A prophetic sense of Armageddon settled on the battlefield, as a partial eclipse of the sun brought darkness at noon. The Zulus 'washed their spears' in the blood of more than seven hundred Europeans and nearly five hundred Africans, disembowelling their bodies to release spirits which would otherwise have haunted the killers.[171] The Welsh also perpetuated atrocities. Edwin Valentine Lewis, the son of a Neath Abbey veterinary surgeon, was one of a troop of riders chasing Zulus after the 'ceasefire' had been sounded. He recalled on 1 May 1879 in a letter to a 'lady friend' that 'they (the Zulus) had got away clear with the exception of three that we caught, who had been wounded, trying to make for the bush. We cut off their heads, the three of them, and let them lay'. One wonders whether the lady friend was impressed.[172]

The 'butcher's bill' was extortionate. The Zulus had killed 1,349 soldiers (fifty-two of them officers) and non-combatants. At least 1,500 Zulus were also killed, in a Phyrric victory. After the battle, Frere, with breathtaking insensitivity, declared, 'I'm awfully cut up'. His opponent, the Zulu King Cetshwayo, was slightly more eloquent, saying that 'an assegai has been thrust into the belly of the nation'. The British Prime Minister, Disraeli, censored Frere and called him back home in disgrace. Newspapers such as the *Western Mail*, the *Cambria Daily Leader* and especially *Baner ac Amserau Cymru* expressed horror at the worst disaster inflicted on a British army by 'savages' since the retreat from Kabul in 1842.[173]

Since so many Welsh soldiers of the South Wales Borderers and the 21st and 24th and other regiments were present, local newspapers in Wales provided several eyewitness accounts. Indeed, one of the first letters to appear in print from the Zulu War was published in the *South Wales Daily Telegram* on 8 March 1879.[174] It was an English translation of a letter written originally in Welsh by Thomas Evans to his wife in Tonypandy. The letters sent home reveal that Welsh troops possessed a remarkable degree of literacy and literary flair in both languages. These letters offer a poignant window into the tragedy and pity of war. Henry Moses of Pontypool listed several of his friends, all local boys, who had been killed and concluded:

> I know what soldiering is now. We have marched 200 miles and haven't had a night's sleep this month. We are in fear every night, and have to fight the Zulus, who came on us and killed 800 of our men. I wish I was back in England [*sic*] again . . . It's sad times here . . . Dear father, and sisters, and brothers, goodbye. We may never meet again. I repent the day that I took the shilling.[175]

But not all the Welsh were on the British side. The *Argus*, a French ship sailing out of Cardiff, was rumoured to have carried 800 guns and 50,000 pounds of trace gunpowder to Cetshwayo and his Zulu warriors.

The British partially vindicated themselves a few hours later at Rorke's Drift, though the eleven Victoria Crosses won in its defence were awarded not just for valour, but for vainglory.[176] Indeed, the defence was not as effective as is imagined; in order to kill some 650 Zulus, the defenders fired more than 200,000 rounds of ammunition. Ironically, this famously desperate fight enabled the British to portray themselves in their favourite role, that of brave underdog and it soon became a sort of imperial Thermopylae. At Rorke's Drift, the British undertook a heroic last-ditch stand in a small trading station. Unlike the open ground of Isandlwana, the confines of the mission settlement made a stern defence possible.[177] The heroism of some was truly remarkable, often the latest act in a long series of heroic deeds. William Fox Leet, who won the Victoria Cross for saving his men, had previously fought in the Crimean War and the Sepoy Rebellion of 1857 in India.

Legend has it that, at Rorke's Drift, the savage hissing and demonic drumming of the Zulus were countered by the Welsh battle song, 'Rhyfelgyrch Gwŷr Harlech' (The War Song of the Men of Harlech).[178] For decades afterwards the rhetoric of martial heroism outweighed the reality of military incompetence. In 1905, the popular monthly *Royal Magazine* announced a series of articles, called *Survivors' Tales of Great Events*. The series would cover 'the greatest deeds of British valour in times of war and disaster, both on land and sea, during the last fifty or sixty years'.[179] Amongst the first features to appear was the eyewitness account of Private Henry Hook of Monmouth, who survived the battle at Rorke's Drift. Hook was awarded the Victoria Cross for his gallantry in defending wounded colleagues, despite being 'scalped' by an assegai himself. Hook's life seems to confirm F. Scott Fitzgerald's pronouncement: 'show me a hero and I will write you a tragedy'. He arrived home to discover that his wife, believing him dead, had 'run away' with another man. He married again in 1897 and died of pulmonary tuberculosis in 1905. For others, the ferocity of the fighting never relented. Private Robert Jones of Clytha, Raglan, was awarded a Victoria Cross for his bravery in the hospital at Rorke's Drift. Ever after he had recurring nightmares of the savage hand-to-hand fighting until he ended the torment with a shotgun on 6 September 1898. Although he was buried in consecrated ground in the cemetery at Peterchurch, his coffin was forced to enter the churchyard over a wall, and his headstone faces away from all other tombs, starkly signifying the shame of his suicide.[180]

The Zulu War had a lasting impact on several towns in Wales. Monmouth, Pontypool and Abergavenny lost many of their soldiers. Brecon, being the base camp for the South Wales Borderers, was exceptionally badly affected. The Zulu War, more than any other conflict, even the First World War, was the one which wreaked the deepest devastation on the town. It was from this point that the Zulu warrior captured the psyche and the imagination of the Welsh. Within only a few weeks of the massacre, in a remarkable example of bad taste and worse timing, several Zulu shows toured Wales and even visited the traumatised town of Brecon. Incredibly, as local balladmongers lamented the losses, the wheels of another circus with a speciality act of 'Burnt Cork Zulus' rolled into the still grieving town. Indeed, no carnival in south Wales for the next half century was complete without a group of men in makeshift grass skirts blacked up as ferocious Zulu warriors.

The wars against the Zulu in 1879 set the tone for much of the Welsh contribution to Britain's involvement in Africa. A few incidents such as Isandlwana and Rorke's Drift were allowed to balloon into heroic status. The Sudan was another complicated episode which was similarly distorted into a few simple, iconic incidents. Hearts beat just as fast in 1883 as they had in 1879, when the 11,000-strong Hicks Pasha column was defeated at Shaykan, Sudan by the Mahdi – God's Expected One. General Gordon's tragic last stand led to the fall of Gladstone's government. Amongst those who fought to save Gordon were forty-two-year-old Major David F. Taffy Lewis of the Cheshire Regiment and a battalion of Egyptian and Sudanese troops. Pioneer Jones, the company carpenter, a six-foot giant, fought using the axe he had brought with him. A Baggara poked at him with a spear. Jones dodged and brought his blade down with a tree-felling blow that cleft the warrior's head in two. Jones was the epitome of the Victorian soldier – gung-ho, brave, big, beefy, perhaps not too bright.[181] Another who fought at Sudan, having also fought in the Zulu War, where he won the Victoria Cross, was Evan Jones (1859–1931) of Ebbw Vale. In all, Evan Jones spent forty-three years at war; he fought in South Africa, North Africa and Burma and went on to the trenches of the First World War. In a photograph taken in about 1917, Jones, a pocket battleship of a man, stares intimidatingly at the camera. He was just over five foot in height, and roughly the same in width from dorsal to pectoral – the Napoleonic complex incarnate. A short man whose fuse was shorter still, the indestructible Jones did everything at full power and full volume.[182]

The Boer War has also been compressed into a few iconic episodes.[183] As so often in military history, incompetence was ignored and victory was conjured from defeat. The relief of Mafeking and then of Ladysmith were greeted with ecstatic rejoicing across Wales. Newspaper vendors from Cardiff to Caernarfon, from Pembroke to Prestatyn, proclaimed the proud news. The improvement in transport, telegrams and telegraph technology meant that communication was rapid and immediate despite the enormous distances. The Welsh people waited with baited breath for the next exciting instalment.[184] Letters from Welsh troops or the experiences of eyewitnesses to great events were printed at extensive length in every Welsh newspaper. Despite Lloyd George's opposition to the Boer War, the majority of Welsh people adopted a pro-war stance. Beriah Gwynfe Evans (1848–1917), a reporter with *Y Genedl Gymreig*, *The North Wales Observer* and the *Liverpool Daily Post*, was one of several who supported the imperial cause. Foremost amongst those calling for British action was Samuel Evans of Tredegar, a key figure in the Transvaal Chamber of Mines, who was heavily involved in Uitlander policies for reform. He kept the minutes of the Uitlander Committee in Welsh to protect them from the prying eyes of Kruger's policemen. A close collaborator in this strategy was the British vice-consul, J. Emrys Evans.[185]

Stealth rather than aggression was the operating principle for some. H. A. Bruce, later ennobled as Lord Aberdare, was perhaps the slickest imperial operator, for he succeeded in gaining substantial areas of Africa for the British without ever leaving his desk. In his role as the governor of the Royal Niger Company from July 1886, Aberdare ensured that Britain, rather than France or Germany, took responsibility for large parts of west and central Africa. Liberalism and the extension of the rule of law were mentioned but the company's real motive was economic. British merchants wanted to obtain palm oil and other products in exchange for cotton goods, guns and rum.[186] Despite his professed Liberalism, Bruce too, when required, was willing to unleash the dogs of war. Alfred Jones seemed to have learnt the lessons of Aberdare's example that commerce was better than conflict. A major owner of several Liverpool-based shipping companies, Jones was actively and substantially involved in the West African trade. Sir Glyn Smallwood Jones (1908–92) enjoyed careers as cadet, district officer, commissioner and governor across South Africa. However, his Calvinistic Methodist upbringing did not prevent 'Jonas', as he was affectionately known, from brutally suppressing several riots in the copper mines.[187] Profit could not be sacrificed for principles. Brutality was never far beneath the surface of the empire.

Glyn Jones's career spanned the decline of the British Empire, the fading of glory, the trumpets sounding the Last Post as the flags were hauled down again and again and again. A crisis of confidence appears to have beset the empire after the First World War.[188] In a sense this was inevitable, as four of the great land-based polyethnic empires – the Ottoman, the German, the Russian and the Austro-Hungarian – had come to an abrupt end in 1918. Billy Hughes, the Welsh-born Australian premier, was not alone in the 1920s and early 1930s in considering that 'the splendid glow which the British Empire cast on the earth reflected not its noon-day greatness, but the fading hues of sunset'.[189] The effect of the retaliation and retribution enacted by the British in 1916 and 1921 against the Irish, and in 1919 against the Indians at Amritsar, resulted in a crisis of confidence.[190] Moral authority seemed to have moved from the 'victor' to the victims. In the 1920s, the empire seemed to be characterised not by the arrogance of the late nineteenth century, but by a perpetual state of anxiety. The anonymous author in *Trysorfa'r Plant* of 1881 would have been perhaps surprised, but probably pleased, for dusk was settling on the eternally sunlit empire. The Second World War showed just how prescient Hughes's comment had been. In the Far East, for example, the inept British were outgunned, outfought, outmanoeuvred and out-thought by the dynamism of the Japanese. Compared with their modern planes, the RAF's menagerie of Buffalos, Wildebeests and Walruses proved to be as acrobatic as their names suggested. In 1941, during the Japanese invasion of Malaya, Admiral Sir Tom Phillips (Tom Thumb), against sage advice sailed his battleship, *HMS Prince of Wales*, without air cover;[191] it was soon attacked by the Japanese. With his ship damaged beyond salvation, Phillips took the only option available to him. He sent for his best hat and went down with his ship. Phillips has the distinction, probably unwanted, of being the highest-ranking Allied officer killed in battle during the war. If one particular act can serve as a symbol of general demise, then Phillips's slow descent into the depths carries a deep symbolism of empire's sad decline.

7

'Ha! Ha! among the Trumpets' – a Century of Warfare: Cowardice, Courage and Hatred

They bury deep in England;
They bury light in France.
I would be buried where my bones
Would shiver to a fairy's dance.

Hywel Davies, 'Dead Man's Joy' in Alan Llwyd (ed.), *Out of the Fires of Hell: Welsh Experiences of the Great War 1914–18 in prose and verse* (Llandysul, 2008), p. 212

'Gwaedd y bechgyn': Wales and the Welsh fight to end war

Mae Prydain yn galw
Ei rhengoedd ynghyd.
'I'r gâd, ddewr Frythoniaid',
Yw'r fanllef o hyd;
Tra gwaed fel afonydd,
A'r hollfyd yn syn,
Pwy droa yn llwfrddyn
Ar adeg fel hyn?

(Britain calls
All her troops together.
'To war, brave Britons',
Is the constant cry;
Whilst blood like rivers,
And the world is in shock,
Who will turn cowardly
At this time?

Eliacim Evans, 'Y Rhyfel' (The War), quoted in Alan Llwyd and Elwyn Edwards (eds), *Gwaedd y Bechgyn, Blodeugerdd Barddas o Gerddi'r Rhyfel Mawr, 1914–1918* (Llandybïe, 1989), p. 29

8 'Welcome, 1915. May It Be His To Sound The "Cease Fire". 'The Great War 1914–1915'? Sadly, the optimism of the *South Wales Daily Post* in January 1915 proved to be very premature.

In August 1914 the world realised that the Dark Continent was not Conradian Africa, but barbaric, brutal, bloodthirsty Europe. The two shots fired by the Bosnian Serb Gavrilo Princip outside Moritz Schiller's cafe in Sarajevo on 28 June 1914 killed Archduke Franz Ferdinand of Austria and reverberated around the world. The tubercular 19-year-old committed probably the most successful act of terrorism in world history. By 4 August, Britain, France and Russia, enmeshed in a series of alliances, treaties and *ententes cordiales* designed to ensure peace, had slithered into war with Germany and Austria-Hungary. The colonies, dominions and protectorates for control of which these powers had scrambled in the Americas, Africa, Asia and Australia ensured that this contagion infected the entire globe.[1] In mid August 1914 the 2nd Battalion South Wales Borderers landed not in Europe, but at Lao Shaw Bay, China, for operations against the German territory of Tsingtao.[2]

The historiography of the Great War, as it was known until 1939, when it became the First World War, has created several layers of fable, illusion and myth. Like the wreck of the cruiser *Monmouth*, which was sunk by the Germans off the coast of Chile in 1914, there are so many encrustations that it is difficult now to see the original shape and significance of some of the events.

The war seems to have generated a range of complexities and contradictions.[3] It was a 'futile war'; it was an 'essential war'. Many parts of Wales, traditionally considered to be a stronghold of pacifism, greeted the war with enthusiasm and euphoria. It would be a brief war that would finish by Christmas 1914. It lasted so long because the leaders were 'butchers and bunglers', the soldiers 'lions led by donkeys'. The war saw heroism and honour. It saw heinous crimes and horror. It saw cowardice and avarice, tragedy and triumph. But in the 'heat of hell' many, given the choice, chose dishonour before death. In retrospect it appears a very literary war, with soldiers of the Royal Welsh Fusiliers producing more than their fair share of great poetry and war prose.[4] But probably more people played football in the Christmas truce of 1914 than joined the dead poets society.[5] Above all, it was the war to end all wars. To some, like Paul Mainwaring Jones of Llanelli, it was 'a great adventure – the best of times', to others it was the worst of times.[6]

It was 'God's great crusade', but it was also the time when God was 'ar drau ar orwel pell' (ebbing on a far horizon).[7]

Hindsight clouds so much of our views of the Great War; we seem never able to forget that we know what happened next. We know that apocalypse was then, but in August 1914 people had no conception that apocalypse was now.[8] It is a truism of military strategy that upon entering a new conflict, the armed forces are ready to fight the previous war. It cannot be otherwise, for strategists are planners, not prophets. Even so, the fact that any rational person should have volunteered for war in August 1914 is remarkable. The fact that thousands from Wales did so, to defend 'King and Empire', is uncontestable. What has been contested is the significance of the actual numbers involved. Almost as soon as the guns fell silent and the gas and smoke dissipated at 11 a.m. on 11 November 1918, a statistical war took place to measure the actual level of Welsh involvement in, and commitment to, the war. Some claim that, between August 1914 and 1918, a total of 272,924 Welsh men enlisted in the services. Others contend that the figure should be more than 280,000, to include those who enlisted in the navy.[9] Accepting the latter figure, Nicholson and Williamson state, in *Wales: its Part in the War*, that based on the 1911 census, 13.82 per cent of the people of Wales volunteered. This placed Wales ahead of England (13.30 per cent), Scotland (13.02 per cent) and Ireland (3.87 per cent).[10] However, the figure used for the population of Wales, 2,032,024 did not include Monmouthshire and thus it should be amended to 2,420,958. On this basis the War Office estimated that 10.96 per cent of the people of Wales volunteered as compared with 11.57 per cent of the English, 11.50 per cent of the Scots, and 3.07 per cent of the Irish.[11] Perhaps a more appropriate measure is to calculate the number of volunteers as a percentage of the adult male population, those people most likely to go to war. In 1914 there were in Wales 1,268,284 males over twenty-one years of age, giving a figure of 21.52 per cent for the male population who fought, which compared with 24.02 per cent in England, 23.71 per cent in Scotland and 6.14 per cent in Ireland.[12] Since the dogs of war were leashed in 1918, these statistics have been the foundations for some to argue that Wales was a bellicose and belligerent society that worshipped the gods of war, and others to emphasise the opposite view that pacifism and peace were the true characteristics of the Welsh.[13]

The response to the call to arms varied. A newspaper report of a meeting chaired by the lord lieutenant of Montgomeryshire in Welshpool in early 1915 was sensationally headed 'Farmer's Sons in Hiding!' The lord lieutenant indicated the he knew that 'when recruiters had been around, the men had run up into the hills and hidden themselves.' Lord Kenyon, experiencing difficulties in raising the 2nd Welsh Horse at Newtown, also complained that the 'farming class' was reluctant to enlist. At the Oswestry Tribunal, a Mr Brotherton, a farmer of Gobowen, declared that his two sons would 'never go under military orders . . . if a soldier puts his hands on you resist him to the death.'[14]

War enthusiasm often crossed class, gender and social lines. Bertrand Russell, the great crusader for peace, watched with dismay the 'cheering crowds . . . and discovered to my horror that average men and women were delighted with the prospect of war'.[15] Miners appear to have been especially keen to escape the confines of their workplace. Of the 230,000 miners at work in Wales in 1914, 115,000 had enlisted by June 1915. Some mining villages were almost empty of young men. The Powell Duffryn Steam Coal Company saw 800 men enlist, eighty of whom did not return. For one rare occasion in the history of Welsh mining, men and management were united.[16] Major John McMurtrie, manager of the Penallta Colliery, was killed at the battle for Mametz Wood.[17] At Abercynon, 1,500 miners enlisted, 1,200 of whom were employed at the local Dowlais-Cardiff Colliery; 143 of them were killed.[18] In the north, the manager of the Rhosydd slate quarry in Ffestiniog formed a small unit of quarrymen to serve in the army. C. H. Derbyshire, the owner of the Penmaenmawr Quarry, formed a 'quarry battallion' of stone-workers from Penmaenmawr, Llanfairfechan and Trefor.[19] When the Cardiff Railway Company offered its employees job security, dependants' allowances and pensions if they joined up, the response was so huge that they had to withdraw the offer.[20] Despite the spirited stand of a number of trade-union leaders against the war, one profound characteristic of the workers was their loyalty to

Wales and to Britain, and their willingness to make the ultimate sacrifice. Patriotism was stronger than class solidarity or socialist commitment. The miners' strike of 15 July 1915 was a pay dispute, a traditional protest within well-established industrial relationships, not a mutiny or a revolution.[21] The gun-wielding Charles Butt Stanton (1873–1946), a member of the fiercely patriotic Socialist Nationalist Defence Committee, avoided active service himself, a fact which did not stop him from urging others to go to fight. Stanton was victorious in two virulent election campaigns in Merthyr Tydfil in 1915 and 1918 against the pacifists James Winstone and the Revd T. E. Nicholas.[22]

Some former miners had remarkable careers in the military. David Watts Morgan (1867–1933), the miners' trade union leader from Neath, and his two sons enlisted on 4 August 1914 as privates in the 10th (Service) Battalion of the Welsh Regiment (1st Rhondda).[23] Morgan was commissioned in October and, by April 1915, was a lieutenant in the 17th (Service) Battalion of the Welsh Regiment (1st Glamorgan). By early 1916 he had been promoted to the rank of captain. He played a leading part in recruiting campaigns both in the Rhondda and in north Wales, where his fluency in the Welsh language was particularly valuable. He is said to have recruited 15,000 Welsh miners for military service, for which a committee of leading Rhondda figures presented him with a cheque for one hundred guineas in March 1915, and the *Western Mail*, somewhat prematurely, termed him 'The Organiser of Victory'. Unlike many who urged others to fight but ensured that they themselves kept clear of the front, Morgan himself went on active service in France. He was mentioned in despatches on three occasions, and was awarded the Distinguished Service Order (DSO) early in 1918 for his exploits with the 'pick and shovel' brigade at Cambrai in November 1917. After the armistice, he commanded a demobilising unit, was promoted to lieutenant-colonel and made a CBE. Thus David Watts Morgan, MP, DSO, JP, CBE, OBE, who for so long had avoided a nickname, acquired the sobriquet 'Dai Alphabet'.

The recruiting missions of Dai Watts Morgan, the Revd John Williams (Brynsiencyn) and Sir Owen Thomas (1858–1923) produced millenarian celebratory scenes. Indeed, for a period in late

1914 and early 1915, there was a sense across Wales of an imminent religious revival. At these gatherings, green sprigs bounced on the kepis of the soldiers, roses garlanded the guns, housewives and girls gave kisses freely and gifts grudgingly whilst the band invariably played the 'Radetzky March', the march that is more polka than march. A final goodbye, a last blown kiss and quick slow, quick slow, the new warriors pounded and panted past the crowds on their journey to destiny. Grace Williams, a rare figure in Welsh history– she was a Welsh composer, even rarer she was a woman Welsh composer – recalled that her earliest musical influence was the sound of a military band in 1914.[24]

Recruiting had a shady side and a distinctly sleazy one. Early in the war, recruiters were paid a minimum of 2s. 6d for each man enlisted. It was not unknown for recruiters to prey on the inebriated in public houses.[25] In *From Khaki to Cloth* (1948), Major Morgan Watkin-Williams recalled that one woman in the crowd as he left for France christened the departure platform at Cardiff railway station 'the valley of the shadow of death', but he noticed 'little fear but much frolic and friendship'.[26] The silver bands of Llanddeiniolen, Bethesda and many villages were busy in late 1914. In several towns and hamlets laughter mingled with the music in an alfresco dance festive with sun and the crowds sported happy masks as the young went off to war, content, if slightly off key.[27] When the euphoria subsided, how many of them must have asked themselves the stark and simple question – why? Why did so many go so willingly to war?

In reality there were probably 280,000 reasons why 280,000 Welsh men decided to volunteer and conscript to fight.[28] Attraction to war, like that of moths to a flame, was a peculiarly masculine characteristic woven into the marrow of the sex. But men also went because they were deferential, desperate, drunk, destitute, deluded or disenchanted. The recruitment techniques were good – the poster of Kitchener and his finger, partly accusatory, partly elective, was iconic.[29] There was female pressure – join up, become a hero, impress the girl and let her kiss you before she waves you goodbye. There was peer-group pressure – at street corner and pithead, one could not allow a friend to claim the glory. There was a herd instinct, in which several from the same village and town enlisted together, giving rise to the much-loved 'Pals battalions', like the Swansea Pals, the Carmarthen Pals and the Newport 'bantam battalion', the 12th Service Battalion (3rd Gwent) of the South Wales Borderers.[30] The practice of Pals battalions was rapidly reconsidered when the battles began and whole villages faced calamitous casualties.[31] There was naivety, there was optimism that in only a short time everyone would be marching together up the Unter den Linden in Berlin. There was even, according to the Gowerton psychoanalyst Ernest Jones, a suicide instinct amongst the young.[32] There was the economic imperative because, for some, the army's pay, living conditions and food were far better than what they suffered at home. Oliver Powell of Tredegar recalled quite simply that, 'Oh yes, a great patriot I was, bloody glad to get out of the pit. I thought we could have a good time, have a good adventure, it was supposed to be over by Christmas of 1914, what a joke.'[33] There was the impulse for adventure, the once-in-a-lifetime chance to enact deeds of valour.

Many Welsh youths were in accord with the spirit of Sir Henry Newbolt's poem, 'Vitaï Lampada' (Torch of Life). This cumbersome epic is set on a remote battlefield at an unspecified location abroad. Above the tumult, the voice of a youth rallies the ranks with the cry, 'Play up! Play up! and play the game!'[34] This naive nobility of spirit was not confined to the English public schools.[34] In August 1914, eighty students at University College of Wales, Aberystwyth enlisted and another ninety joined them later in the year.[35] At least 554 students of the University College of North Wales, Bangor, served in the war, ninety-four of whom were killed. Morgan Watkin-Williams was one of several who eagerly joined the 21st (Public Schools) Battalion of the Royal Welsh Fusiliers. Lieutenant-Colonel Richard James Walter Carden of the 16th Battalion of the Royal Welsh Fusiliers was last seen during the battle for Mametz Wood leading his men into battle with just a stick. Captain Harold Thorne Edwards displayed equal bravery but slightly more battle sense on 8 May 1915 at the Second Battle of Ypres, for in addition to his stick he had a service revolver. A painting by Fred Roe, in the Newport Museum and Art Gallery, shows the heroic Edwards,

9 The Swansea 'Pals' Battalion with their mascot, Tawe. The initial belief that collecting men from the same area into battalions known as the 'Pals Battalions' would aid recruitment was disabused, when the fighting began and a single area or town was confronted with catastrophic casualties. Source: Bernard Lewis, *Swansea Pals: a History of the 14th (Service) Battalion the Welsh Regiment in the Great War* (Barnsley, 2004).

heavily outnumbered, refusing to surrender and firing into the ranks of the advancing Germans.[36] Paul Mainwaring Jones (1896–1917), whose father Henry edited the *South Wales Daily News*, was a brilliant student. In July 1916, he wrote that he was 'longing to be in the thick of the fighting'. His letters, published posthumously in 1918 as *War Letters of a Public-school Boy*, reveal the Homeric face of war: masculine camaraderie, loyalty, honour, chivalry, patriotism, sportsmanship and leadership.[37] Many of these boys had been raised on the muscular and macho tales of the story and comic books for boys, in which the brave, lantern-jawed hero defeated the beastly German. Some were the products of the Boys Brigade, military training groups and Boy Scouts, which made a natural link between militarism and masculinity.[38]

The role of chapel and church leaders in persuading people to enlist cannot be underestimated, and neither can the impact of the war on organised religion in Wales.[39] The consciences of many gentle souls were torn asunder in August 1914. The Revd Joseph Jones of Brecon and the Revd Dr Puleston Jones of Pwllheli were eloquent opponents of the war.[40] The great poet T. Gwynn Jones, who later described himself as a 'pacifist with the emphasis on the fist', stormed, family in tow, out of Bethel Baptist chapel in Aberystwyth, after a particularly war-crazed sermon.[41] In contrast, many other religious leaders and elders had no qualms in declaring that 'war is a great crusade', 'killing is a Christian duty, is indeed divine service'.[42] As a vital part of Britain, Wales, it was claimed, was engaged in 'a war for purity, for freedom, for international honour and the principles of Christianity . . . everyone who dies in it is a martyr'.[43] 'Gwnaed Uffern yn yr Almaen' (Hell was made in Germany) claimed the Revd Peter Price.[44] Brigadier Owen Thomas, owner of the fiercest moustache west of Kaiser Wilhelm, worked tirelessly in recruitment work and emphasised that there was no conflict between religion and the crusade against the Germans.[45] From his descriptions, recruits could be forgiven for getting the impression that they were joining a Band of Hope outing, not a military regiment off to war. Remarkably, Owen Thomas continued to work for the war despite the fact that his three sons were killed in action. Timothy Rees (1874–1939), later Bishop of Llandaff, won the Military Cross for his work as an army chaplain.[46] In the darker days of the war, some people even prayed, 'give us each day our enemy dead'.

That enemy, dead and alive, was vilified and demonised in the press and from pulpit and public platform; Germany represented evil.[47] A cabal of Welsh academics, writers and leaders argued that the ideological architect of German policies was Nietzsche.[48] In an article in *Y Geninen* in January 1915, Professor Miall Edwards, discussing, 'Athroniaeth yr Almaen a'r argyfwng presennol' (German philosophy and the present crisis), equated Nietzsche's notions of the will to power and superman with the Kaiser's intolerant, instable notions.[49] German actions certainly made it easy for people to hate them. When they fire-bombed the beautiful city of Louvain in 1914 and burnt the university library's priceless collections, O. M. Edwards, W. Llewelyn Williams and many other writers were outraged.[50] The sinking of the *Lusitania* in May 1915, the execution of nurse Edith Cavell and the bombing raids of the Zeppelins were further confirmation of German perfidy.[51] *Y Brython* and *Y Dinesydd Cymreig* waxed eloquent about 'barbareiddwch yr Almaen' (Germany's barbarism); Germans were 'anianol, diafolaidd a chythreulig' (inhuman, devilish and fiendish).[52] T. Gwernogle Evans even penned an 'englyn' to the Zeppelin:

> Cythraul yw'r Zeplin scathrog – o Army
> Y German llofruddiog;
> Gwyrth y crank, ac wrth crog
> Ystryw Uffern wastraffog.[53]
>
> (The bedraggled Zeppelin – from
> Germany's murderous army
> Is a miracle of deviousness
> From a destroying, wasteful hell).

Put simply, the Germans were devilish murderers. Other writers in the Welsh denominational press entered a darker world and warned that 'unspecified vices of the Cities of the Plains', and 'pechodau a gredid a gladdwyd yn Sodom a Lesbia' (sins that were believed buried in Sodom and Lesbia) were rampant in Germany. Compared with this propaganda the reasoned voices and rational arguments of the pacifists were powerless, at least until well on in the war.[54] Bertrand Russell, highly sympathetic to peace, noted after one meeting of the Union of Democratic Control that 'when they plotted how to end the war they seemed like eight fleas talking of building a pyramid'.[55]

In the hysteria that greeted the outbreak of war, it was easy for people to believe all sorts of strange stories. O. M. Edwards, writing in *Cymru*, had it on 'good authority' from one who had seen the Belgian refugees that the Germans had mutilated children by cutting off their hands.[56] At Conwy, two men were arrested after a local claimed to have overheard them describing a plot to blow up the steel bridge spanning the Menai Straits.[57] It was said that, at Fishguard, two 'well-dressed Germans' (so obviously they stood out from the locals), were detained after their bags were found to contain bombs and wire cutters.[58] German spies were here, they were there, they were everywhere in this climate of paranoia. Even the Russians had arrived. The *South Wales Echo* quoted an engineer named Champion, who vouched for the fact that he had sailed with the Russians from Archangel and tried to give veracity to his report with the verisimilitude of statistics, claiming that he travelled with the one hundred and ninety-second trainload to pass through York.[59] Thereafter, the Russians' route to France became even more circuitous, for they were next reported, by a Revd Clark, at Cardiff.

'All quiet on the Western Front': some experiences of war

This Dai adjusts his slipping shoulder-straps, wraps close
his misfit outsize greatcoat – he articulates his English
with an alien care. My fathers were with the Black Prinse of Wales
at the passion of
the blind Bohemian king.
They served in these fields,
it is in the histories that you can read it, Corporal – boys
Gower, they were – it is writ down – yes.
Wot about Methuselum, Taffy?
I was with Abel when his brother found him,
under the green tree.
I built a shit-house for Artaxerxes.
I was a spear in Balin's hand
that made waste King Pellam's land.

David Jones, *In Parenthesis* (1937)

So much has been written that it is now almost impossible to say something new about the war. Summarise it all and it is quite a simple tale. For those who went to fight in France, war was 'uffern' – hell.[60] The horrors that faced soldiers by 1915 made those conditions described in pre-war hellfire sermons appear tame, for this was the Book of Revelation, rewritten by H. G. Wells. The four horsemen of the Apocalypse had dismounted to drive swifter, infernal machines powered by internal combustion. As the war wore grindingly on, real life presented images of such horror that those of the scriptures seemed tamed. The Bible's central image of suffering, a crucified man with a spear in his side, seemed somehow lessened alongside the thousands of men trapped in the barbed wire with their intestines hanging and dripping out. 'Rhuddai frain rhag rhyfel wŷr' – it was a good time for the ravens, red with soldiers' blood.[61]

The Western Front was a gut-wrenching, bone-chilling, soul-destroying shambles.[62] On the battlefields blood gushed out of people, holes gaped, eyes burst, skulls were torn off, headless torsos jigged for a few minutes in a grotesque *dance macabre.* The stench of carrion, cordite and excrement was intolerable. Fragments of human beings and horses were everywhere. Death was ubiquitous and arbitrary. There were fire showers, burning debris raining from the sky, wreaking destruction whenever and wherever it landed. Bullets whistled everywhere and suddenly, with just a whizz of a warning, a whole area would be pulverised by an explosion. Cynddelw Williams remembered that one soldier from Flintshire just disappeared. Tom Davies, Tymawr, and David Lloyd, Esgairgarn, Llanddewi Brefi were simply vaporised; nothing survived, not even their boots.[63] Single words in the war memoirs convey volumes – blood, guts, cold, slaughter, noise, water, mud, gas, barbed wire, shrapnel, stench, putrification, fleas, mice, rats, hunger, agony, devastation, death. The Welsh-language writers echoed the English; the war was 'y Moloch uffyrnol' (hellish Moloch), 'yr uffern aflan' (filthy hell), or a 'cigfa' (bloodbath).[64] Siegfried Sassoon recalled that 'floating on the surface of a flooded trench was the mask of a human face which had detached itself from the skull'.[65] Another soldier noted almost offhandedly, 'part of our trench went through a cemetery. We cleared out the contents of the family vaults and used them to shelter ourselves from artillery fire: hits from heavy shells could hurl the coffins and semi-rotted corpses high into the air'.[66]

Equipment was often scarce. The 16th Welsh (Cardiff City) Battalion had no rifles until October 1915 and no large guns until the following April.[67] Their cavalry, the outriders of the Apocalypse, had no horses. Poorly trained soldiers were sent into horrific conditions. On 7 July 1916, in the early stages of the battle of the Somme, the Welsh division were sent in to clear the great slab of Mametz Wood, jutting down from Longueval Ridge.[68] The sun dappled brightly and blindingly through the full summer foliage, creating a frightening and disorienting environment. Captain Llewelyn Wyn Griffith remembered scenes of carnage and confusion:

> Limbs and mutilated trunks, here and there a detached head, forming splashes of red against the green leaves, and, as in advertisement of the horror of our way of life and death, and of our crucifixion of youth, one tree held in its branches a leg, with its torn flesh hanging down over a spray of leaf.[69]

This literally was a band of brothers. Lance-Corporal Henry Hartridge went to the assistance of his older brother, Corporal Tom Hartridge, who was lying mortally wounded during the battle for Mametz Wood. Whilst giving his brother water, Henry was also shot and they are reported as dying in each other's arms. The brothers Henry John Morgan and Charles Morgan of Cardiff were also killed at Mametz. Llewelyn Wyn Griffiths's brother Watcyn, a private soldier in the same Royal Welsh Fusilier battalion (unthinkable in the old army), was killed. 'I had not even buried him', lamented Griffith as he left 'this charnel place', 'nor was his grave ever found'.[70] 'O brother, where art thou?' Watcyn was a victim of the efficiency of modern weapons of war that pulverised or liquidated bodies. The missing became a ghostly legion. After a month on the Somme in September 1916, the dead still lay where they had fallen – swollen, black, swarming with maggots, shrivelled, bones brilliantly white in a mess of slime, some even built into the fortifications. Many soldiers were less than sensitive and looted corpses of boots, jackets, watches, gold teeth, anything that would be of value to the living; waste not, want not, let the dead bury the dead.

In such conditions it is remarkable that people were willing to fight. As with the question of why people enlisted, a plethora of reasons can help to explain the more testing question of why they fought. Peer pressure, the fear of not letting one's friends, one's unit, one's company, one's lineage or one's home and family down, were powerful factors. The words of Private W. Williams, Cilan, as he was carried away injured on a stretcher at Ypres, are pathetic and poignant, 'Deydwch wrth mam mod i wedi gwneyd fy ngoreu', (tell mam that I did my best).[71] Despite the horrors, for some men the clothing, shelter, tobacco, food and alcohol were better than they had at home. Alcohol in particular was very important. David Jones and Robert Graves noted that the rum ration was sacrosanct. The poet Cynan, in 'Mab y Bwthyn', recalled, 'Ond O! am fynd o'r gwaed a'r twrw / I'r angof sy'n y gasgen gwrw'[72] (But O! to escape the blood and bluster / for the oblivion of the beer barrel). When alcohol was unavailable, unaffordable or undrinkable, then morale would plummet.

Revenge was a great motivator. Men fought to avenge the honour or good name of their fallen comrades. From early 1915, when the trench system had become embedded between Switzerland and the North Sea, men knew which German troops were opposite them and were acutely aware of who had killed whom. Thus it was that Robert Graves, Frank Richards and others often ignored the opportunity to take prisoners and simply shot German soldiers.[73] At the Somme the 9th Welsh were motivated by a desire to even the score after their calamitous losses at Loos. Quite simply and quite worryingly, some men just enjoyed killing. The air ace Ira Jones had no qualms or concerns about 'killing Huns'.[74] War was a great adventure and men found thrills and enjoyment in the joy of it. Some took risks that appear reckless. The attitude is enshrined in a song which was very popular with Welsh troops – 'The bells of hell go ting-a-ling-a-ling for you but not for me'. Some had to be forced to fight at pistol point by their own officers. Deserters were often shot by their own unit and the condemned men would scream, shout, weep and plead for life.[75] Some inflicted wounds on themselves so that they would be spared. There was even a trade in gonococcal pus, which soldiers bought and smeared over their genitals in the hope of a long stay in hospital. The more desperate even smeared it into their eyes, resulting in permanent blindness. From the comfort of his study, the Revd J. Vyrnwy Morgan wrote about the psychology of the soldier. His greatest insight was the importance of humour to the troops for 'it sustains and vitalises, it brings exhiliration'.[76]

One vital aspect to remember is that the troops were not at the front for extensive periods. On average, seven to ten days was the timespan of a soldier's front-line duty – another seven days were spent in reserve and a further seven days at rest.[77] This is why the tour of duty of the 21st Royal Welsh Fusiliers at Cordonnerie near Fromelle from 22 October to 14 November 1914 was so remarked upon. Discipline was often maintained at pistol point. Ernest Thurtle (1884–1954), later a Labour politician, the son of a Griffithstown, Pontypool, shopowner and seamstress, was horrified by the cruelty of the military punishment casually inflicted at Cambrai. He later spearheaded a campaign to abolish the death penalty for offences such as desertion and cowardice and published two books on the issue, *Military Discipline and Democracy* (1920) and *Shootings at Dawn* (1922).[78]

A lot of time was spent behind the lines. Here, some of the pain of what was seen in battle could be relieved, bodies and souls could be repaired and the soldier could enjoy a variety of sports and, judging by the photographs in the archives of the Royal Welsh Fusiliers, suffer some of the worst female impersonators ever seen.[79] Behind the lines, boredom was the enemy – the endless periods of sitting, waiting and listening while time passed, slowly. Writing letters home was one technique to reduce tension and boredom. Letters, of course, also cemented familial bonds of loyalty and love. Wilfred Owen, having censored his men's mail, thought that 'the Daddy's letters are specially touching', and it may indeed have been the case that some were more affectionate to their children in writing than they would have been in the flesh.[80]

As the war wore wearily on, increasing efforts were made to counter such disenchantment, both on the fighting fronts and on the home front. Technology was soon utilised.[81] The American film director of Welsh descent, D. W. Griffith, was brought to Britain in 1917 to make war films to rekindle popular enthusiasm for the war amongst a public growing increasingly disenchanted. Neither *The Great Love* or *The Heart of the World* are amongst Griffith's best work, but they probably were the most popular.[82] The latter, which includes a scene in which the vulnerable Lilian Gish is nearly raped by a vicious German officer, combined everything calculated to please a wartime audience: action, romance, a hated villain, a hint of sex and a happy ending.

Recruitment campaigns brought together some strange combinations of characters as bunking partners, for the social problems of the home society were replicated in the army.[83] Lurking amidst the decent, salt-of-the-earth types essential to all social success were the deviant ones – thieves, villains, cowards and cheats. The brave and gentle chaplain Cynddelw Williams was distressed to find that his unit consisted mostly of 'tramps', who were drunk, lousy, unshaven, seedy, smelly, and given to 'smoking, spitting, quarrelling, making water all over the room . . . hiccupping and vomiting'. The first funeral at which Cynddelw officiated on the Ypres salient, was that of a Welsh soldier who had been shot by a fellow soldier who was drunk on methylated spirits.[84] The soldiers' attitudes on a host of topics were, at best, controversial. Naturally they showed little regard for the hated 'Hun', the 'Boche', 'Fritz', 'Jerry', 'Kraut', but they also, as David Jones recalled, detested the lower-paid French soldiers, 'the Frogs' and despised the higher-paid American soldiers who fought alongside them.[85] Jones, however, reserved his strongest resentment for the 'rosary-wallahs of Pembroke Dock'. The Royal Welsh Fusiliers had a longstanding vendetta against a Scottish battalion, which dated back to a brutal inter-regimental football match. Frank Richards often expressed his hatred of 'both types of Scots – the trousered and the bare-arsed type' and took every opportunity to fight them.[86]

Welsh soldiers' favourite word was 'fuck', used, as Harold Davies recalled, as a noun, an adverb, a verb and an adjective and often, for greater effect, even in the middle of words.[87] Frank Richards believed that 'one in ten soldiers were twisted somewhere inside'.[88] A recruiter in Anglesey estimated that the original height requirement of 5 feet 6 inches (1.68 metres) barred up to 70 per cent of the island's volunteers.[89] Even with this restriction, the condition of those accepted did not fill one with confidence that they were the pride of humanity. Standards undoubtedly slipped with the protracted nature of the war.[90] The poet R. Williams Parry was refused a commission in 1915 because of his poor eyesight, but accepted as 'A1' in 1916.[91] Thus more doctors and dentists were called into war service to ensure that the soldiers were healthy and fighting fit to die for their country. Welfare was determined by the needs of warfare.

The expertise of Welsh miners was vital in creating the trench system which by early 1915 effectively locked the Western Front into a state of siege warfare, a stalemate war of attrition in which the defensive forces (usually the Germans) had the advantage.[92] The tunneller's war inevitably was one of darkness, but it also had the protracted and profound fear that one could be buried alive. Far underground these troglodytic warriors often clashed in brutal hand-to-hand combat with their German foes. The miners also played a notable part in one of the most innovative attempts to break the stalemate. In 1916, troops entrenched opposite the Messines ridge, a natural stronghold south-west of Ypres in western Flanders joked that the only way to take the ridge was to tunnel underneath and blow it up.[93] By 7 June 1917, the tunnelling work had been completed and 455 tonnes of ammonal explosive had been set in twenty-two mines under the ridge. The skills of geologists and miners was vital in creating 8,000-metre-long channels through a layer of blue clay.[94] For a week before the charges were set, British forces bombed the ridge, forcing the German defenders to shelter deep underground. At 2.50 a.m. the guns fell silent. The Germans, expecting an infantry attack, resurfaced. At 3.00 a.m., the plungers for the chargers were thrown. Then nothing. For a few seconds there was silence. Then everything. In the war's most frequently used cliché, 'all hell was let loose'. The force of the blast was heard in Westminster, allegedly waking the prime minister. In all, 10,000 German troops were killed. Sadly, typically, British forces failed to take full advantage of the chaos in German ranks.

The contribution of the cavalry to the war has been much misunderstood.[95] Inevitably and obviously historians have pointed out that horses were of little value in trench warfare, where the land had been broken into deep, muddy craters and barbed wire was scattered everywhere. Even the tank struggled in this environment, where a little mud was won at great cost. However, in the glorious summer of 1914, and well into the autumn, the war on the Western Front was one of considerable movement, in which the horse was supreme. At its conclusion, as British and Dominions forces at last broke through, the cavalry recaptured at least some of its long lost elan. As the career of Sir James Frederick Noel Birch

10 Two war horses and heroes from Swansea. King and Bob, two greys working for Hancock's Brewery, 'joined up' in the euphoria of August 1914 and survived, winning the 1914–15 Star Ribbons, the Victory Ribbon and the General Service Ribbon. They worked until 1929. *South Wales Daily News*.

(1865–1939) of Llanrhaeadr, near Denbigh, shows, the army was indebted to the horse for its survival. The author of *Modern Riding* (1909) and *Modern Riding and Horse Education* (1912), Birch taught the army that with the artillery and the heavy guns the horse still had a valuable and vital role to play.[96] Two such valiant quadrupeds were King and Bob, greys working for Hancock's West End Brewery in Swansea. They 'joined up' in the rush in August 1914, and hauled guns for the Royal Artillery in France. The warhorses returned to civilian work in 1919, pulling beer for Hancock's Brewery along Swansea's streets. From that time on, until they retired in 1929, they clopped along the streets proudly wearing the Star Ribbon, the Victory Ribbon and the General Service Ribbon.[97]

Amongst the carnage and chaos of war, some events stand out for their silence and serenity. The Christmas truce of 1914, which involved the Royal Welsh Fusiliers and the opposing German troops, was one such occasion.[98] Christmas morning opened the soldiers' present of peace. As dawn broke on a cold but sun-filled day, Vivian de Sola Pinto's Royal Welsh Fusiliers hoisted a board above their trench reading 'Merry Christmas'. Fraternisation, friendliness, football and the exchange of gifts, especially of beer, cigarettes and wine, marked the day. A sergeant greeted his opposite in the German ranks with the words, 'On behalf of the king and the Royal Welsh Fusiliers, I present you with this Christmas pudding'.[99] Some, like Frank Richards, felt that the German's reciprocal gift of a barrel of 'flat, weak' beer was an insult.[100] Many complained that an even greater injustice had been perpetrated when the Germans were deemed to have won the football match 3–2.[101] Both sides had advanced further during the four hours of a Christmas frolic than they had during four months of fighting. At the end, a pistol shot rang out to mark the resumption of killing as usual, as the plaintiff notes of 'Silent Night' lingered in the air of no-man's-land.

It seems appropriate that at the close of 1914, the year of Dylan Thomas's birth, the Welsh were already thanking their maker that they were a musical nation. Two of the world's and the war's iconic songs were written by Welsh people; Ivor Novello wrote the anthem for doomed youth, 'Keep the home fires burning', and George Henry Powell wrote the words and his brother Felix the music for 'Pack up your troubles in your old kit-bag'. There is a heart-stopping account of a Welsh battalion moving up in the dark singing 'Aberystwyth', a battle cry as much as a hymn, until the voices were lost in the sound of shellfire.[102] The Welsh Guards choir came second in the male voice competition at the Welsh National Eisteddfod in 1918, but its finest hour had probably come earlier, as the regiment's historian, an eyewitness, remembered:

> The really effective singing did not come from the choir standing in a body on a rough platform, but from the heart of the battalion when going into battle or after the fight. 'In the sweet bye and bye, we shall meet on the beautiful shore,' after the engagement at Gouzeaucourt when the shattered battalion was withdrawn to a wood behind the village, brought a hush over the camp. The singers

were hidden amongst the trees in the moonlight and the air was frosty and still. This was not a concert, but a message, a song of hope and faith.[103]

The Revd Harold Davies was struck by the paradox in the behaviour of a Welsh battery he visited:

The most foul-mouthed lot that I have struck since I came to France. Yet after nauseating me for an hour this afternoon with their 'poisoned gas' they suddenly began to sign hymns with real feeling and piety. There is some real religion deep down in the hearts of these lads – one cannot call them godless because no sooner has one come to this conclusion than some spark of the Divine flashes out of them. The difficulty is to seize it and kindle a real fire within them.[104]

During the Great War of 1914–18, the judgement that, irrespective of where it was being fought, war was hell, was continuously voiced. The ill-fated and ill-considered Gallipoli campaign added a whole new series of agonies to the soldiers' plight, especially for the two hundred or more South Wales Borderers who died.[105] Disease, dehydration, diarrhoea, dysentery, sunburn, heat, dust, sand, thirst, ants and flies were the infernal irritants that troubled troops. Life was lived at a basic, elemental level. Everything was exposed to shellfire, even the latrines. The men sat on a pole over a deep hole, 'like sparrows on a perch', as a Sergeant Laurence noted.[106] Once, he recalled, a shell burst over a latrine:

In the scatter that followed, none waited to even pull their trousers up. The roar of laughter that went up would have been heard for miles. It's only these little humorous happenings that keep things going here.

Lieutenant Vivian de Sola Pinto of the Royal Welsh Fusiliers remembered sights at Gallipoli to which 'Goya at his most macabre might have done justice'.[107] All deaths in war are tragic, but those caused by a direct hit on the latrine a few hours later must surely have been amongst the most undignified.

Those captured by the Turks understandably feared that a fate worse than death awaited them for their captors had a reputation for savage brutality.[108] In 1916, at Kut in Mesopotamia, a force of 20,000 British troops was surrounded and forced to surrender in perhaps the most ignominious defeat since Yorktown in 1781. Less than half survived the war and returned home. They were beaten, driven through the desert by bayonet and the bastinado, deprived of food and water and force-marched in the searing heat. Stragglers were raped or murdered. A legion of skeletal scarecrows, they eventually reached a camp.[109] One of the very few who escaped the ordeal was Elias Henry Jones (1883–1942) of Aberystwyth, a soldier in the Indian army. Between February 1917 and October 1918 Jones, together with the Australian C. W. Hill, sought to dupe the Turks into releasing them from the infamous Yozgad prison. Initially, they attempted to terrify their captors into thinking that they were spirit mediums, adept in calling up spirits via an Ouija board. Despite some success with the more credulous Turks, this ruse failed, and so they acted as if insane and even, to convince the guards, faked suicide by hanging. Eventually this ploy succeeded in getting them repatriated to Britain. Ironically they arrived home only a few days before their fellow prisoners were freed. The remarkable stranger-than-real-life tale was told in Jones's sensational war memoirs, *The Road to En-dor* (1919).[110]

The Welsh soldiers who fought with Allenby's troops in the east could quite literally claim that they had survived Armageddon, for they had fought at Megiddo, its actual biblical location. The Welsh troops who marched into Jerusalem were the first to do so since the Crusaders. Newspapers across Wales proclaimed the glad tidings and Frank Brangwyn proudly painted a scene of orderly troops marching through the narrow streets. But the celebrations coincided with the feast of Hanukkah, which commemorates the rededication of the Temple in Jerusalem at the time of the Maccabee Revolt, and deeply offended Muslims.[111]

The biblical atmosphere was an appropriate backcloth for the mission of T. E. Lawrence, 'Lawrence of Arabia', who strutted in robed and daggered drag, leading the Arabs in revolt against their Turkish rulers.[112] The significance of the 'Revolt in the Desert' has probably been inflated because of the magic and charisma of Lawrence.[113] Compared with other campaigns against the Ottoman Empire, such as Gallipoli, this was little more than a sideshow, a desert storm in a teacup. But for 'one glorious, dashing year', 1917, 'El Aurens' and his 5,000 men captured imaginations as they attacked columns, disrupted supply routes and repeatedly blew up the Hejaz railway connecting Damascus to Mecca, tying up large numbers of demoralised Turkish troops trying to protect it. Lawrence pioneered a form of guerrilla warfare that later inspired Orde Wingate, the Long Range Desert Group and the SAS. Lawrence also devised ingenious schemes to destabilise Turkish authority. Magicians were trained by him to convince superstitious tribesmen that they were ascetic marabouts, holy men with supernatural powers, who could prophesy the future. Their prophecies were simple – anyone who served the Turks would suffer the wrath of Allah. In the end, the Greater Arabia which Lawrence and his men fought for never materialised, but he was influential in the establishment of modern Iraq, Jordan and Lebanon. His influence is still controversial, indeed somewhat mysterious. Some of his mystique, his inner tension and tragedy, is captured in Augustus John's remarkable pen-and-ink sketch made in Paris in 1919. To some Lawrence was a charlatan, a poseur, to others 'a man of hope and glory', a hero in life and legend.[114] Lord Tweedsmuir, better known as John Buchan, a dour Scot little given to gushing, recalled, 'I could have followed Lawrence over the edge of the world. The only man of genius I have ever known'.[115]

One who followed 'the man of genius' to the perimeter, if not over the edge, was Sir Herbert Winthorp Young (1885–1950), the Wrexham-born army officer and administrator. Young had met and impressed Lawrence in 1913 at Carchemish. At Lawrence's request, Young was transferred to the Hejaz operation in March 1918 as general staff officer, grade 2 (GS02). Young organised the force which destroyed the railway behind the Turkish army. For his role he was mentioned in despatches and received the DSO (in 1919) and the order of Al Nahdha. Even more rare, Young was praised in Lawrence's *Seven Pillars of Wisdom*, as 'energetic, strong-willed, a regular of exceptional quality . . . rising as ever to any occasion.'

Further south in Africa, Captain E. H. Edwards and his troops fought a 'hit-and-run' war with an elusive enemy which was barely glimpsed in broad expanses of uninhabited land.[116] Deaths from battles and bullets, shells or shrapnel, were relatively rare. Death, here, was a stealthier enemy, wreaking devastation with blackwater fever, dysentery, jigger fleas and guinea worms.[117]

The maritime war combined many of the most brutal aspects of modern technological warfare with one of the most dangerous and unpredictable of battlefields – the world's oceans. There is a terrifying aspect to the deaths of many Welsh sailors in shipwrecks, whose bodies lie deep beneath the waves with all the broken metal. It was a fact universally acknowledged that down to 1914, Britannia ruled the waves.[118] The race before the war to build the gargantuan warship, the dreadnought, was widely believed to have been won by Britain.[119] In reality, those who expected a modern Trafalgar were disappointed in 1914–18.[120] There was only one major naval battle, that fought between the Royal Navy's Grand Fleet and the Imperial German Navy's High Seas Fleet at Jutland in the North Sea from 31 May to 1 June 1916.[121] The Royal Navy had the advantage as they had captured and cracked the German Navy's signalling system. At Jutland all the latest technological developments and the most impressive military hardware clashed. Battle cruisers, airplanes, torpedo boats, zeppelins all fought in a brutal encounter that resulted in the death of 6,094 British and 2,551 German troops and sailors. Despite the greater losses for the British, Jutland inflicted more damage on German shipping, with the result that the Grand Fleet never went to sea again in any significant numbers. Amongst the leaders of the British fleet at Jutland was Vice-Admiral Sir Hugh Evan-Thomas (1862–1928) of landlocked Beulah, Powys, where his family owned the Llwynmadoc estate.[122] Stoker Thomas Picton of Pentre in the Rhondda was another. Picton, the lightweight boxing champion of the navy in 1917, was mentioned in despatches when his ship, HMS *Gloucester*, was torpedoed and he volunteered to go back and relieve the ship's boilers. He spent six hours in the freezing Baltic for his pains.[123]

Thereafter, the war at sea took the form of episodic battles between a few scattered ships or attacks on shipping by German U-boats.

Troopships were particular targets for the U-boat. Soldiers, who probably envisioned that they were destined for a different form of glory, tasted a sailor's fate. Germany's declaration of unrestricted U-boat warfare against all 'legitimate' targets was greeted with typical outrage from the Welsh press. This became hysterical after the sinking of the American ship, the *Lusitania*, on the morning of 6 May 1915, some 750 miles west of Ireland.[124] The issue of whether or not the ship, which did carry materials from America for the Allied war effort, was a legitimate target is still controversial. The ballad *Suddiad y Lusitania gan y Germaniaid* reveals the extent of outrage felt in Wales at the act of 'infamy', which resulted in the drowning of 1,201 passengers.[125] Amongst the survivors were D. A. Thomas, later Lord Rhondda, the government's food controller and his daughter Margaret Haig Thomas. In her remarkable autobiography, *This was my World* (1933), she recalled the fateful trip.[126] Rescued after hours naked in the freezing water, she later reflected that the shipwreck had altered her opinion of herself. Having survived the ordeal and faced death close up, she no longer feared anything. The *Britannic*, the sister ship of the ill-fated *Titanic*, hit a mine on 21 November 1916 and sank in thirty minutes. Third Officer David Lewis of the White Star Line, was less fortunate than Lady Rhondda. He was torn to pieces by the propeller when the lifeboat he had charge of was lowered too quickly.

Various forms of subterfuge were utilised to assist British shipping against the depredations of the German U-boats.[127] Convoy systems developed and special ships were created which were disguised as ordinary ships in order to entice U-boats to the surface and then attack them. It was aboard such a ship, the HMS *Pargust*, that William Williams from Anglesey was awarded the Victoria Cross for his gallantry.[128] Unusually, the entire crew was nominated, and a ballot resulted in the award of the VC to Williams. The moral issues of the deception involved in disguising powerful ships of war as pathetic naval specimens that seemed ideal targets troubled some. The popular author Alfred Noyes (1880–1958), based in Aberystwyth, who is still remembered for the poem 'The Highwayman', was severely censured in 1916 when working for the Ministry of Information for writing a book criticising the devious methods used to entice enemy submarines. Much of what Noyes wrote was public knowledge, but he was still deemed to have betrayed trust.[129]

One who was familiar with the darker arts of submarine warfare was Sir Max Kennedy Horton (1883–1951) of the Maelog Lake Hotel, Anglesey.[130] At only twenty years of age, Horton was given charge of *A1*, a submarine of 200 tons used for experimental work. On the outbreak of war in 1914, he was in command of *E9*, a new ocean-going submarine which he took into the fortified harbour of Heligoland. There he sank the cruiser *Hela*, the first enemy warship to be destroyed by a British submarine. In October, Horton took *E9* into the dangerous waters of the Baltic, where he sank two destroyers, torpedoed a large German cruiser and disrupted the Swedish iron ore supplies to Germany. For his role in this he was awarded the order of St Vladimir with swords, the order of St Anne with swords and diamonds and the order of St George by Russia, made a chevalier of the Légion d'Honneur of France, and given a bar to his DSO. 'A gambler', 'a bit of a pirate', Horton had the wisdom to know that 'in submarines, there is no margin for mistakes, you are either alive or dead'. After the war, in 1920, he resurfaced in the Baltic, this time in charge of a submarine flotilla with the delicate task of assisting the Baltic states against Bolshevik aggression. He served again during the Abyssinian crisis, the Spanish Civil War and in the Second World War, became commander-in-chief of the western approaches.

Aerial warfare came into its own during the First World War.[131] One of the great founders of the Royal Flying Corps, the forerunner of the Royal Air Force, was Sir William Sefton Brancker (1877–1930), son of a Denbighshire family.[132] Having first flown in India in 1911, Brancker was soon convinced of the advantages of airpower for both offensive and defensive warfare. Despite the opposition of many, he cut through War Office 'red tape' to establish a strong aerial presence in support of the armies in France. By March 1916 he was head of air organisation in the War Office. A clash of personalities, however, between the charming, dapper, monocled Brancker and the dour General Sir William Robert Robertson resulted in his temporary demotion and transfer to Egypt.[133] Another who suffered from the political infighting which blighted most military organisations was the air force officer Violet Blanche Douglas-Pennant (1869–1945), daughter of the north Walian slate-mining family.[134] After philanthropic work with disabled children, she led both the Women's Royal Naval Service and the Women's Legion. She thus appeared to be the natural choice when the position of commandant of the Women's Royal Air Force (WRAF) became vacant. Despite her reforms and improvements to the service, justified complaints about inefficiencies and unjust allegations about WRAF immorality continued, leading to Douglas-Pennant's dismissal on 18 August 1918. A storm of protest ensued. The case became a cause célèbre – somewhat exaggeratedly known as 'the British Dreyfus case'. The officer who dismissed her was Sir William Sefton Brancker.

The war in the air had an echo of the heroic chivalry of medieval knights that was not present to the same extent in the other theatres of war.[135] This is certainly the theme of the career of Cecil Lewis (1898–1997). A 'stringy beanpole of a boy', Lewis joined the Royal Flying Corps in 1915 at seventeen by lying about his age; after just eighty minutes of in-air instruction, he flew and fought with 56 Squadron. He recalled his experiences in the remarkable book *Sagittarius Rising*.[136] Another enchanted by the 'romance of the air' was Raymond Collishaw (1893–1976), scion of a Wrexham family.[137] He commenced flying with the Royal Naval Air Service in 1915. Despite the slower, more inefficient planes he flew, Collishaw succeeded in shooting down several German planes. Perhaps he never achieved the sixty or so he claimed in his memoirs, *Air Command: a Fighter Pilot's Story* (1973), but he certainly destroyed twenty-seven enemy aircraft. Remarkably, although the life expectancy for a pilot was reputedly just twenty-seven minutes, Collishaw survived the war, fought against the Bolsheviks in 1919–20, in Iraq (1920–3) and in Egypt during the Second World War.

Unlike Collishaw, there was little doubt about the numbers shot down by James Ira Thomas Jones (1886–1960) as an air ace.[138] Standing at five feet, four inches, the diminutive Jones was a larger than life character. One brush of a feather and he would go off like a landmine. Ira faced several disadvantages – he was born illegitimate, he stammered and had, or soon acquired, a drink problem. But once he learnt how to fly a plane, Ira Jones became one of the leading 'air aces of the war'. Problematically for a pilot, he never mastered the art of landing. On one occasion, chasing two German planes, he shot the highest so that it fell on to the other. When he saw the plane crash in flames, he 'gloried over the roasting of the departing Huns'.[139] When he and his colleagues recovered one body, they placed it in a hangar, dressed it in pyjamas and a dinner jacket and toasted it in champagne. Such macabre humour was relatively common amongst those who lived so close to death. Ira's memoirs, *An Air Fighter's Scrapbook*, *King of the Air Fighters* and *Tiger Squadron*, show little of the false heroism or chivalry displayed in the films of Errol Flynn or David Niven or the Biggles stories of W. E. Johns.[140] With thirty-seven 'kills', this remarkable man in his flying machine had no Arthurian concept of war as a chivalrous quest for glory in the aerial jousts of the cloud-strewn skies. He utilised every stratagem to kill Germans:

> My habit of attacking Huns dangling from their parachutes led to many arguments in the mess. Some officers, of the Eton and Sandhurst type, thought I was 'unsportsmanlike' to do it. Never having been to a public school, I was unhampered by such considerations of form. I just pointed out there was a bloody war on, and that I intended to avenge my pals.[141]

Disappointed when the armistice was signed, Ira went to Russia and fought against the Bolsheviks. On one occasion, having exhausted his supplies of bombs, he dropped vodka and whiskey bottles on the Bolshevik forces. Ira even fought in the Second World War, taking off to attack a Junkers 88 over Swansea armed with only a Very pistol.

The experiences of other Welsh air aces appear to be a mix of the idyllic nobility of Cecil Lewis and the hard-nosed pragmatism of Ira Jones. Gwilym Lewis, the youngest pilot in 32 Squadron, longed to fight the 'Hun planes', but when the fighting began he was scared to death. 'You have no idea', he wrote, in a letter home, 'how scared I am when I go for those brutes.' Yet he found dogfights 'wildly exciting'. Of Lionel Rees, his squadron commander and fellow Welshman, he wrote: 'Everyone knows that the major is mad. He is never happier than when attacking Huns. I wouldn't be surprised if he comes home with a VC.'[142] Another who found the experience terrifying was the actor Mervyn Johns, who candidly admitted: 'I don't think there was a single moment when I was not scared to death'. The faith of many carried them through, but others sought fortification from spirits of a non-spiritual kind. Major F. J. Powell, MC, when commanding an SE6 squadron in 1917, thought the centre of his squadron was the bar. It was not something he discouraged. He always carried, when airborne, a small flask filled with rum. At altitude in winter his moustache would get frozen into a block of ice; 'a dip of alcohol had an immediate and glorious effect'.[143]

As the expertise of the geologists involved in tunnelling to lay the mines beneath Messines ridge indicate, the contribution of Welsh scientists was a vital aspect of the war effort.[144] Technology has always been an important part of warfare – long bows at Agincourt, rifles in the Crimea – but the technological advances during the First World War were astounding. Though the war would ultimately be decided by men, it was very much a war of machines. Soldiers went to war by steam trains and returned by oil-powered vehicles. Sir Lewis Thomas Casson (1875–1969), later an actor and theatre director, became a major in the Royal Engineers and was awarded the Military Cross for his work.[145] He was also the inspiration in the Chemical Warfare Committee that developed a range of poisons. Though his war experiences may have provided useful background for his role as an actor with the ghoulish Grand Guignol theatre in the 1920s, they seared his conscience and he forever regretted his role in creating and releasing poison gas. Sir Frederick Brundrett (1894–1974) of Ebbw Vale served in the Royal Naval Volunteer Reserve, joining the wireless branch in 1916. After demobilisation in 1919, he joined the scientific staff of the Admiralty, helped to establish the Royal Naval Signal School and became one of the chief scientific advisers in the Royal Naval Scientific Service.[146] Sir Frederick Noel Birch (1865–1939), of Llanrhaeadr, Denbighshire, was an innovative inventor of equipment for the field artillery, particularly the self-propelled gun which appeared in two forms, both becoming known as 'Birch' guns.[147] Many British soldiers had cause to thank Sir Rhys Rhys-Williams (1865–1955), for his ingenuity. Rhys-Williams invented a device which prevented bombs from exploding accidentally whilst they were being transported to the battlefield. He received several mentions in dispatches, the DSO and the prize of the Guild of St Vladimir by the Russian government for his work with the Welsh Guards.[148]

The palaeobotanist Hugh Hamshaw Thomas (1885–1962) of Wrexham, later nominated as one of the world's top twenty biologists, served as an officer in charge of aerial photography.[149] Working for the Royal Flying Corps, his work greatly aided the success of the campaign of Sir E. H. H. Allenby. Twice mentioned in despatches, Thomas was awarded the Order of the Nile, and appointed MBE.[150] The telecommunications engineer Sir Albert George Lee (1879–1967), son of a Conwy, Carnarfonshire, Post Office engineer, was commissioned in the Royal Engineer Signals Service, becoming officer in charge of the general headquarters signals area. Lee received the MC and continued his military service throughout the subsequent years of peace as lieutenant-colonel, Royal Corps of Signals (supplementary reserve). Throughout the 1920s his interest was the use of radiotelephony and radiotelegraphy for international communication. When the Second World War broke out, Lee became director of communications, research and development at the Air Ministry, and in 1944 was appointed senior telecommunications officer in the Ministry of Supply.[151] Elsewhere, industrialists, bankers and businessmen used their leadership, organisational, financial and administrative skills to further the war effort. Sir John Coldbrook Hanbury-Williams (1892–1965), scion of the owners of a Pontypool ironworks, was one such industrialist who used his skills with the 10th Royal Hussars.[152]

Brains rather than brawn also characterised the contribution of the cartoonists to the war, [153] several of whom served in a battle of witticisms. Leslie Gilbert Illingworth (1902–79), the cartoonist and illustrator from Barry, drew the famous *Punch* cartoon, 'Do I know if the Rooshuns has really come through England?' that appeared in the paper on 23 September 1914. Illingworth took newspaper cartoons to a new level of excellence during the Second World War, with some visceral images.[154] Herbert Samuel Thomas (1883–1966) drew the even more famous cartoon 'Arf a mo, Kaiser!', featuring a grinning Tommy lighting a pipe before engaging the enemy. Described as 'the funniest picture of the war' by the *Daily Mail*, it was sketched, supposedly in ten minutes for the *Weekly Dispatch* and published on 11 November 1914, as part of the paper's tobacco-for-troops fund, for which it raised more than £250,000. Thomas also served as a private in the Artists Rifles (1916–18) and from March 1918 was official artist for the government's war bonds campaign, producing Britain's largest poster, a 75-foot-long, 30-foot-high oil painting of Sir Francis Drake facing the Spanish Armada, which covered the front of the National Gallery in 1918.[155]

'Keep the home fires burning': the war at home

Keep the home fires burning
While your hearts are yearning
Though your lads are far away
They dream of home.
There's a silver lining
Through the dark clouds shining,
Turn the dark clouds inside out
'Til the boys come home.

Ivor Novello,'Keep the home fires burning'
(London, 1914)

The fact that so many men were away at war and the continued demand for the products of the key industries of coal, iron, steel and chemicals and of agriculture provided several opportunities for women to enter paid employment. Home fires were kept burning because women dutifully kept furnaces stoked. New employment opportunities were created in retail, administration, marketing and in transport – both as drivers and conductors. Women had always helped on the land, garnering and gathering harvests, milking cows and in countless thankless tasks, but now tasks previously the preserve of men were undertaken by women. Mrs J. C. Teare of Four Mile Bridge, Anglesey, worked as a 'striker' for her father in their smithy, preparing iron to shoe horses.[156] Others handled equipment which had previously been guarded by men as their exclusive prerogative with the zeal of the medieval guilds. The Women's War Agricultural Committees were established in 1915, both to encourage women to work on farms, but even more challengingly to persuade some misogynist farmers that women could do the work. Training centres were established at Margam Park, on the Plymouth estate at St Fagans, and at Madryn and Lleweni Hall in north Wales. In 1917, the Women's Land Army Service Corps and the Women's Land Army were established to further extend the involvement of women in agriculture. In 1918, Margaret Haig Thomas, later Lady Rhondda, became the chief recruiting officer for women in Britain. The rancorous dispute over the dismissal of Violet Douglas-Pennant from command of the WRAF, which involved Lady Rhondda, reveals that everything did not run smoothly for working women.[157] There were often complaints about the character, morality and industriousness of the land girls. Lady Mather Jackson of the Ladies Committee of the Monmouthshire War Agricultural Committee was in frequent correspondence with Miss Talbot of Port Talbot, head of the Food Production Department of the Board of Agriculture, about the several and serious failings of the 'Women's Land Army'.[158]

In the munitions industries many factories, such as those in Pembrey in Carmarthenshire or Queensferry in the north, were major employers of women, with more than 10,000 employed in dangerous conditions producing TNT and high powered munitions.[159] These women were jocularly referred to as the 'canaries' because of the discolouration of the skin brought on by TNT poisoning. Working women found themselves in an unenvious position. If they neglected their homes in order to be good workers, they were cursed by society for being poor mothers. Yet if they took time off work to look after their family, they were criticised for being unreliable and unpatriotic workers.[160]

Women also worked within the armed services.[161] The establishment of the Women's Army Auxiliary Corps in 1917 was one of the most revolutionary measures in the war, for it was the first time that women were enlisted into uniform. In the *Welsh Outlook*

11 Nurse Mary Jane Hughes (1887–1986) and some of her patients, all of whom were from Llanelli. Being cared for by a Welsh-speaker must have eased some of the hurt and hiraeth of these wounded soldiers. Source: Joyce Mollet, *With a Camera in my Pocket: the Life and Times of a First World War Nurse* (Baddeley, 2005).

of July 1917, Margaret Haig Mackworth argued that this was the iconic moment for the women of Wales, their equivalent of the 'Your Country Needs You' posters. Large recruitment meetings were held across the country, with exceptional turnouts reported at Bangor, Caernarfon and at Cardiff.[162] The women were aviators, engineers and mechanics within the army, air force and navy. They worked within the telecommunications and ammunitions industries as signallers, telegraphers and technicians. They instructed troops on the use of new equipment such as gas masks, guns, signalling equipment and aircraft and on countless new devices. Close to the fighting alongside the front lines at France and Gallipoli, women served as medical officers, nurses and ambulance drivers. Here, in conditions of almost unimaginable trauma, several women, such as Mary Jane Hughes of Llanelli, compassionately tended to the wounded, the mutilated, the dying and the dead.[163] They saw in graphic detail that flesh, blood and bone were powerless against the fiendish machinery of modern military technology.

Much has been written about the value of the prose and poetry produced by male combatants, but the creative works of women also offer a profound insight into the emotional and psychological impact of war. Kate Roberts wrote to come to terms with the loss of her brother in the war. The scene in her novel *Traed mewn Cyffion* (Feet in Chains), when the postman delivers a telegram in English to a monolingual Welsh mother to inform her of her son's death speaks profoundly of alienation, loss and injustice. Some of the most poignant and soul-searching descriptions of the effect of war are to be found in the diaries of Winifred Coombe Tennant, the suffragist, spiritualist and confidant of Lloyd George. When her son Christopher was killed by a shell, she wrote:

> Thank God he never suffered, never knew he was wounded or dying, had no pang about me. He had won his Dark Tower and has woken up to find himself in the heaven where he would be . . . I am deeply thankful. If I had known that he was going to give his life during the war I would have chosen for him such a death as this, and on his first entering into active warfare. God bless you dear son – it is well with you, and I am calm and loving and desiring to be a tower of strength to you as you are to me. Margaret Verrall's words, written

> the day A. W. [Verrall] died come to me: 'The long companionship here is broken and the deeper intimacy begun.'[164]

A little later she wrote,

> 19 September – loneliness. I reach out to him with such passionate yearning. How good when I, too, can pass on to their world. I read Fred's 'On a spring morning at sea'. Fred, Fred, take care of my boy – sometimes the hunger for his bodily presence is like a huge ache in my heart.'[165]

Many grieving mothers must have felt such emotion, few put it into such poignant words.

Then, after so long in the bustle and bedlam of battle, on the eleventh hour of the eleventh day of the eleventh month of 1918, the guns fell silent. A silence crept around the world before the bells rang out to signal peace. It was a day of joy and sorrow. But the war was not all over for many. Several people had to live with the loss of limbs or senses.[166] David Morgan Williams (1909–97), the miner and poet, recalled that his father was so shell-shocked that he cowered in the corner for the rest of his life. At fourteen years of age David, the eldest of twelve children, had to become the breadwinner. He worked for the next twenty-four years underground at Penllwyngwynt colliery, including eighteen years on night shifts.[167] Robert Graves was mentally unprepared for peace. His overwrought nerves were forever at war. Sudden noises, like a backfiring car, triggered a Pavlovian reaction in which he flung himself face first to the floor. The telephone terrified him, thunder was traumatic. Shells burst above his bed as he slept. For him and for many compatriots, it was difficult to adapt to home. Despite all that had happened in the war, Graves could never accept that the sheep and goats still grazed on the hillsides above Harlech and the women still bustled about their business, as they had done since time immemorial. It seemed impossible that they had lived through the same period of time, that the same dates had passed over them.[168] Graves, and many of his generation, could not get over the war; it was both a gigantic upheaval and an astonishing adventure in his life, an unparalleled episode in which he had found himself and felt that his work had been meaningful and useful. Despite the horrors, he and his generation seemed to have been happy at war. Family members often referred to the fact that, although they survived the fighting, Dai or John or Will, forever furtive and frightened, never really returned from the war. These were men with shattered minds and broken spirits. The men 'whose minds the dead have ravished', as Wilfred Owen so poignantly observed. For David Jones, the war was quite literally *In Parenthesis*. Ivor Gurney died in 1937 in a mental hospital, where he had continued to write 'war poetry', convinced that the war was still going on.[169]

Some families had endured perpetual fear for the four years of war, as those who stayed at home worried about their sons, siblings and lovers at war. The Raikes family of Treberfedd near Llangorse must have suffered many sleepless nights, for five of their six sons were at war. All five were awarded the DSO; all five returned home. Some villages had similar good fortune, for they were 'thankful villages' which did not experience a single death in combat in 1914–18. Llanfihangel-y-Creuddyn in Cardiganshire, Colwinston in the Vale of Glamorgan and Herbrandston in Pembrokeshire do not have war memorials for the fallen of the Great War, for none of their sons who fought 'fell'.[170] But as the countless silent statues of sentinel soldiers around Wales testify, other villages were less fortunate. Particularly unfortunate was the Lowry family from Llandyfaelog. They had three sons who served in the war, all of whom lost their lives. Captain Auriol Lowry, who was awarded both the MC and the DSO, and Cyril Lowry died in northern France, while William Lowry died at Gallipoli.

Every man's death is diminishing, but there is a particular sadness about those unfortunates who died on the last day of the war – the last men falling. Edwin George Ellison had enlisted in August 1914; he died on 11 November 1918. He started fighting in Mons and died in Mons four years later. John Lloyd (1873–1918), a miner from Eglwyscumin in Carmarthenshire, also died that day fighting with the 1st Canadian Pioneers. Vivian de Sola Pinto remarked that 'the war produced as much grim farce as nobility' and referenced it when his fellow officer was killed by a shell at 10 a.m. on

11 November 1918 while squatting in a latrine. Able Seaman Richard Morgan of Devauden, Monmouthshire, is claimed to be the last man to die during the fighting, for he expired aboard HMS *Garland* almost as the bells tolled for peace. It is, almost certainly, a claim to fame to which he did not aspire. [171]

Of all the piteous experiences of the war, it is hard to imagine a sadder experience than that of Mrs Susan Owen. The war had officially been over for an hour when a War Office messenger delivered a telegram, informing her of her son Wilfred's death a week earlier on the Sambre. As he wrote in one of his greatest poems, 'My subject is war, and the pity of war. The poetry is in the pity.'[172]

The Hall of Mirrors: the illusion of peace 1919–39

> The hand that signed the treaty bred a fever,
> And famine grew, and locusts came;
> Great is the hand that holds dominion over
> Many by a scribbled Name.
>
> Dylan Thomas, 'The Hand that Signed the Paper'

Wilfred Owen never lived to discover that the true pity was in the peace. So many of the ideals that people had fought to defend in the Great War were revealed in peacetime to have been craven images. This was 'the war to end all wars'; time would reveal that it was the first act in the world's bloodiest century – a modern Thirty Years War. People fought for 'homes fit for heroes'; time would reveal that few heroes had habitable homes in the 1920s. They fought for a new world order of conciliation not confrontation in international relations, controlled by the League of Nations. But when the United States refused to support it, the League, despite the best efforts of people like Lord Davies of Llandinam, was ineffectual. They fought for the right of 'the little five foot nations' like Belgium against the 'bullying six foot two nations'. But in the Paris peace negotiations of 1919 self-determination, much to the disgust of former soldiers such as Saunders Lewis and Lewis Valentine, did not extend to Wales.[173]

Contemporaries often lamented that if only more attention had been paid to the voices of small nations like Wales, then the world would have been a far better place. Though newspapers and subsequent authors and commentators made much of the fact that many Welsh men carried influence at the highest levels of world affairs in 1919, it is debatable how much benefit was derived from their activities. The problems created by the break-up of the great dynastic empires that had ruled central, eastern and south-eastern Europe for centuries – the Romanovs, Habsburgs, Hohenzollerns and Ottomans – were far beyond their powers of solution.

At the Paris Peace Conference of 1919, Welsh people figured prominently. 'Easily the most picturesque personality', Frances Stevenson recalled, was Augustus John, who was there as one of the official artists. John 'held court in Paris'. In the spring of 1919, Paris was the vortex of the social and political world, and at its centre was this son of a Pembrokeshire solicitor. All red carpets led to him. Kings and maharajas, dukes, generals and judges posed for him, the prime ministers of Britain, France, Canada and New Zealand submitted to his brush, whilst Lawrence of Arabia waited patiently in the queue. From dusk to dawn he enthralled the *beau monde*.[174] In some ways, the Paris Peace Conference was the finest hour for north Wales. Three of its sons – Lloyd George, William Hughes and T. E. Lawrence – featured prominently, writing new countries into being by lamplight . But they were no Absaloms, for despite their best efforts, they did not father peace.[175]

In 1919, Lloyd George, prime minister of Britain since 1915, was at the pinnacle of his fame and power, as yet untarnished by the falsity of his claims regarding 'homes fit for heroes' or his later sale of honours. He was 'the man who won the war'. Babies born in 1919 could thank Lloyd George that theirs would be a blessed generation, free from the spectre of war that had blighted earlier generations. The economist and member of the British delegation, John Maynard Keynes, who created many of the myths about the peace conference, wove a special one for Lloyd George. 'How can I convey to the reader, he pondered, 'any just impression of this extraordinary figure of our time, this goat-footed bard, this half-human visitor to our age from the hag-ridden magic and enchanted woods of Celtic antiquity.'[176]

Lloyd George was anything but a Celtic relic. A great orator who embraced his audience in inspiring and intimate speeches, Lloyd George was a consummate politician who understood that politics was the art of the possible. In office, he soon became a superb, if unconventional, administrator. Yet despite his undoubted strengths, Lloyd George had some very serious failings which undermined his reputation. To many, his realistic pragmatism appeared unscrupulous and unprincipled. The American president Woodrow Wilson, Myopic of his own but sharp-eyed on the failings of others, believed that Lloyd George 'had no principles whatever of his own . . . he reacted according to the advice of the last person who had talked to him . . . expediency was his guiding star'.[177] Lloyd George was unwilling to listen to advisers, especially those from government departments, preferring the advice of friends, who like himself were often self-made men. On occasion his knowledge was shockingly lacking. 'Who are the Slovaks?' he asked in 1916, 'I can't seem to place them.' His geography was equally sketchy. In 1919, when Turkish forces were retreating from the Mediterranean, he talked dramatically of their flight towards Mecca.

Lloyd George's proposal to make Danzig a free city, with a corridor to the sea for Poland, divided Germany and became one of the most contentious of the clauses of the peace treaties. The 1917 Balfour Declaration, influenced by Lloyd George, ultimately helped to give legitimacy to the creation of the state of Israel but also led to the dispossesion of Palestinians. To Lloyd George the Jews were a 'small people' like the Welsh, a perspective and policy based partly on his belief that the Bible was a history book. When General Allenby commenced his military campaign in the Holy Land, Lloyd George presented him with a *Historical Atlas of the Bible*, which he insisted would be more useful than any reconnaissance maps prepared by British military intelligence, a force he considered an oxymoron. Lloyd George's bibliocentric policy proved disastrous for the British Empire, not least because another Llŷn 'ego-maniac', Lawrence of Arabia, was at the same time promising Palestine to Sherif Hussein. To break the power of the crumbling Ottoman

Empire in the Middle East, Lloyd George's government promised the Promised Land not once but several times. In a meeting in Downing Street in December 1915, Lloyd George and the French leaders agreed to divide the Middle East between themselves, with a line on the map running from the 'r' in Acre to the last 'k' in Kirkuk marking the division, irrespective of actual topography, peoples or places.[178] He distrusted the Turks as 'carpet salesmen' who indulged in 'unnatural sexual practices' and seemed overly keen to be the statesman who would serve the last rites to the Ottoman Empire, Europe's notorious 'sick man'. In 1918, Lloyd George's encouraged the Greeks to attack Izmir and Smyrna, enabling them to slaughter their way across Anatolia.[179] Lloyd George's imperial largesse towards selected 'small peoples' 'opened a Pandora's box, whose demons are still at large' in the twenty-first century. His and the other leaders' solution to the German problem in Europe in 1919 sowed dragon's teeth which would be savagely harvested in the 1930s.

In reality Lloyd George entered the 1919 Paris Peace Conference holding the strongest cards of any European leader, only to see them frittered away in discussions with the intransient Clemenceau, the idealistic Wilson and the intolerant and intolerable dominion premiers. Perhaps his greatest weakness was one of his most endearing qualities – his indifference to social conventions. In Paris he stayed, not in one of the hotels of the official British delegation, but in a luxurious flat in the Rue Nitot which had been lent to him by a rich Englishwoman.[180] With him was his youngest daughter and favourite child, Megan, and his secretary and long-time mistress, Frances Stevenson. Frances was allegedly Megan's chaperone, but many suggested that, perhaps 'it was the other way around'.[181] Lloyd George's behaviour ensured that he was never free from such snide innuendo. Tickets for the official ceremony to sign the peace treaty in the Hall of Mirros at Versailles were at a premium, with only twenty available for each country. Yet Lloyd George allowed the glamorous red-haired writer Elinor Glyn, herself of Welsh origin, to charm him into allowing her to attend as a 'reporter'. 'Would you like to sin with Elinor Glyn on a tiger skin, or would you prefer to err with her on some other fur' ran a popular contemporary jingle. It is idle to speculate; Lloyd George probably had. His personal affairs frequently intruded into his public life. Lloyd George's actions seem always to have been poised between the immortal and the immoral.[182]

Perhaps the most colourful character at the Peace Conference was the hyperactive 'scrawny dyspeptic' William Hughes, the Australian premier.[183] His parents were William Hughes, a London carpenter of north Welsh stock and Jane Morris, daughter of a Montgomeryshire farming family. Following their deaths, Hughes was raised in abject poverty by an aunt in Llandudno. Having worked as a pupil teacher, he emigrated to Queensland in 1884. A string of casual jobs on the docks and a role as an extra in *Henry V* were followed by his active involvement in the growing labour movement, entry to parliament, ministerial office and eventually, in 1915, the premiership. A veteran of the rough and tumble of Australian politics, his despotic will, acerbic wit and Machiavellian guile enabled him to survive and thrive. Hughes made Australia's policies in Paris virtually single handed. He was cantankerous, idiosyncratic and deaf, both literally and figuratively, to arguments he did not want to hear – he very theatrically turned off his hearing aid whenever an opponent voiced contrary opinions. Living on nothing but fingernails, tea, toast and tomato sauce, Hughes looked like a 'wizened gnome'. To a portrait painter who told him that he would try to do him justice, Hughes replied, 'I don't want justice, I want mercy.' But the spirit of a warrior animated that flimsy frame.[184]

Like Lloyd George, whom he resembled in many ways, Hughes sacrificed his radical principles on the altar of the war god. He suppressed dissenters, imposed censorship, introduced conscription and promoted xenophobia. At the peace conference, Hughes actively and aggressively pushed the case for Australia to receive reparations from Germany in the Pacific. One of his main achievements was obtaining an Australian mandate over German New Guinea, though when President Woodrow Wilson asked him whether the natives would have access to missionaries, Hughes assured him that they would 'because as it was these poor devils do not get half enough to eat'. Wilson thereafter considered Hughes a 'pestiferous varmint'.[185] This view was shared by Lloyd George who had promised lands to Japan, causing frequent quarrels with Hughes over the division of spoils in the Far East. On one remarkable occasion, the work of the peace conference was halted as the two prime ministers verbally abused each other in Welsh. Following what must have been the biggest challenge to the peace conference's translators, Lloyd George declared that he would not be 'bullied by a damned little Welshman' – a sentiment that must have been familiar to many of his own opponents. Hughes was equally abrasive about the League of Nations. Supported by Sir William Massey, the New Zealand premier, he actively quashed the Japanese proposal to include a clause enshrining racial equality in the League's covenant. Hughes ranted, 'sooner than agree to it, I would rather walk into the Seine or the Folies-Bergères with my clothes off'.[186] The Japanese were understandably aggrieved. They went to Paris as one of the 'victors', but left as if they were amongst the vanquished. This 'slap in the face' festered into a poisonous sore. Resentment fostered revenge; in 1946 Emperor Hirohito cited it as a prime cause of the Second World War.[187]

A more exotic figure at the peace conference, was the fair-haired, blue-eyed T. E. Lawrence, later to acquire legendary status as Lawrence of Arabia.[188] Despite the strength of his attachment to Arabia, Lawrence had been born, on 16 April 1888, at Tremadoc in north Wales, where his father, Thomas, had fled with his mistress (Lawrence's mother), to escape the wrath of his wife – 'the Holy Viper'. A man of many and exceptional talents, who succeeded as soldier, scholar and scribe, Lawrence was, in Lloyd George's words, 'a most elusive and unassessable personality'. Even today, after several biographies and an epic, multi-Oscar-winning film, his mystique remains. He continues to be an enigma – the 'man of masks', 'the Sodomonic Saint', 'a modern Hamlet with a pinch of Puck', the riddle of the sands. Immensely charming, Lawrence could also be devastatingly rude. When his neighbour at a dinner during the peace conference said nervously, 'I'm afraid my conversation doesn't interest you much', he replied, 'It doesn't interest me at all'.[189]

Lawrence had a fervent belief that 'the freedom of the Arab race' was his personal gift to bestow as he wished. Elie Kedourie has argued, in *The Chatham House Version*, that the dismantling of the Ottoman Empire was one of the worst decisions made at Versailles in 1919.[190] Lawrence's sentimentalisation of Ibn Saud led him to stand aside while the former's 'Arab gentlemen' massacred 3,000 Turkish prisoners at the capture of Damascus in 1918. Even worse, Lawrence's self-important empire-rigging led him to impose King Faisal, a Sunni, on mainly Shi'ite Iraq. The lines in the sand drawn by Lawrence proved problematic. Six thousand British soldiers died realising this arbitrary redrawing of the map of the Middle East. Lawrence shaped his own legend in art as well as by action, in the huge, complex, richly textured saga of the Arab Revolt, *The Seven Pillars of Wisdom* (1926).[191] This Arabian Nights fable is a modernist classic, with more in common with Pound's *Cantos* or David Jones's *In Parenthesis* than with standard war memoirs. Rather than a traditional history, this is interpretive mythology. It is a monument to a monumental ego which eulogises the Arab campaign as an imperial epic, glittering with oriental romance set amid the gloom of Armageddon. One of the few truths included in the book was Lawrence's admission of 'being trapped in a lie'.[192]

8

'Once more unto the breach' – Wales and the Welsh go to War, Again: Fear, Terror and Tragedy

'The morbid age?': Wales in the twenties and thirties

> The first source of anxiety in all individuals is the working of the death instinct and the impulse towards death . . . The crisis of civilization was particular to the post-war generation which bears within it a much heavier burden of guilt due to the war and its aftermath. The consequences of trying to fly from this intolerable burden have assumed desperate, panicky and always irrational forms.
>
> Ernest Jones, extracts from his lecture, 'Morbid Anxiety', quoted in Richard Overy, *The Morbid Age: Britain and the Crisis of Civilization, 1919–39* (London, 2010), pp. 130, 164, 165

'Being trapped in a lie' was a common feeling in the 1920s and 1930s, for the 'greatest pity' was that the peace which came was fragile. The guns were never silenced; there was no farewell to arms in 1919.[1] These were the years that the Aberystwyth historian, E. H. Carr, christened 'the twenty years' crisis'.[2] This was the *vicennium* of Europe's civil wars – Russia, Ireland, Italy, Hungary, Austria, Germany, Finland and Spain followed each other into intercernine conflicts. Conflict was an universal part of the human condition and these battles, far from being mad or irrational, were fought on principles of order and organisation. Between 1919 and 1939, peace was as elusive as fairy dust.[3]

British troops were in battle before the ink was even dry on the peace treaty. Just as he casually handed over Palestine (then 90 per cent Arab) to the Zionist movement, Lloyd George encouraged his friend Eleftherios Venizelos, the Prime Minister of Greece, to annex chunks of Anatolia. Under the protection of British troops, the Greeks attacked Turkish forces in Smyrna and then pushed inland to attack Mustafa Kemal Ataturk's new Turkish Republican Army. Lloyd George dismissed Ataturk as a 'carpet seller in a bazaar . . . given to unnatural sexual intercourse'. His policy proved to be a disaster, for Ataturk was more than a match for the chaotic Greeks. Lloyd George's dogged support of the Greeks was one of the most divisive of several issues which ended his coalition government.[4] Lloyd George's policy was a disaster both personally and politically and created suffering on an almost unimaginable scale; it produced one of the most horrific humanitarian disasters of the early twentieth century. The Turks wreaked their revenge in 1921 for earlier Greek atrocities, when an estimated two million people were killed in a wrathful vengeance that the Old Testament would find it hard to rival.[5]

Simultaneously with their involvement in Anatolia, British troops were also embroiled in fighting in Ireland, Afghanistan and Iraq between 1919 and 1922. In Ireland, many units of the infamous 'Black and Tans' were led by Welsh officers, such as the adventurer and mercenary Caryl ap Rhys Pryce.[6] These soldiers of fortune showed little spirit of comradeship with their fellow Celts. The Russian Revolution, a threat to the rich, an example to the poor, provided ample opportunities for Welsh people to fight on both sides. Those on the political left, enraptured by the socialist, communist ideals of Lenin and Trotsky, fought alongside the Bolsheviks. To others, the ten days that shook the world presaged terror, not utopia.[7] The air ace Ira Jones, who had thoroughly enjoyed the First World War, continued his heroic exploits in aerial sorties against the Bolsheviks above the frozen steppes.[8] Major John Fitzwilliams and Duncan Fitzwilliams of Cilgwyn, Cardiganshire, were organisers of the White troops in a number of clandestine missions against the Bolsheviks, whilst Sir Max Kennedy Horton used his experience in submarines to counter Bolshevik aggression in the seas around the Baltic States.

It is difficult to ignore the dictates of hindsight and to regard the 1920s and 1930s as the post-war period, rather than the pre-war years. There seems to be a doomed chronology in the 1920s and 1930s that led inexorably to disaster. Dylan Thomas gave voice to this feeling of uncertainty and impending catastrophe when he wrote, in 1934, that 'artists, as far as I can gather, have set out, however unconsciously, to prove one of two things: either, that they are mad in a sane world, or that they are sane in a mad world'.[9] Whether the drift to war could have been halted is frequently debated. One of the great counterfactual events of the 1930s, the outcome of which could have been vastly different for world history, took place in August 1931. John Scott-Ellis, son of Lord Howard de Walden of Chirk Castle, was driving down the Brienner Strasse in Munich in a little Fiat. A gentleman in his early forties with a small square moustache stepped out into the road without looking where he was going and Scott-Ellis ran him over. Relatively unharmed, the pedestrian apologised, shook the driver's hand, and went on his way. A friend in the car then told Scott-Ellis he had just knocked down 'a politician . . . who talks a lot. His name is Adolf Hitler'. Every if, of course, is futile, after time's tide has turned. But it is hard not to refrain from guessing how it would have been, had Scott-Ellis driven a little faster. As he himself pondered years later, 'for a few seconds, perhaps, I held the history of Europe in my rather clumsy hands'.[10]

In many respects, the first salvos of the Second World War were fired long before 3 September 1939, when Britain reluctantly, inevitably, eventually declared war on Germany. Japan's invasion of Manchuria in 1931, Italy's invasion of Abyssinia in 1935, Germany's remilitarisation of the Rhineland or the Anschluss with Austria of 1936, the beginning of Franco's war against the Spanish Republic in 1936, or Japan's assault on China on 7 July 1937, are equally appropriate dates for the commencement of the Second World War. During these upheavals Wales and the Welsh provided refuge and support for a number of victims. Amongst the more exotic exiles was Emperor Haile Selassie of Ethiopia. After Italy invaded his country, he spent periods between 1936 and 1939 as a guest of the missionary Rees Howells (1879–1950) at his bible college at Glynderwen House, Blackpill, near Swansea.[11]

Of these revolts and rebellions, the one which probably had the greatest salience and significance for Wales and the Welsh was the Spanish Civil War. This battle between monarchists and republicans, between fascists and communists, between 'infidel Catholics' and 'Christians', is often portrayed as the dress rehearsal for the Second World War. It marked the point when it became increasingly difficult for many people to tolerate the British government's policy of non-intervention and neutrality. It was the moment, for many, when the iron entered the soul, the end of innocence.[12]

Spain represented the closest thing since the Thirty Years' War, to an all-out ideological campaign. To many, the Spanish fascist Franco was the sinister puppet of the forces of evil. Hitler, Mussolini and the fascist leaders in Europe gave him money, munitions, machinery and men. Their victory in Spain would presage decades of moral darkness. To others, Franco represented a brave attempt to stave off the forces of communism and safeguard Europe against further revolution. Behind the republic – if you were against it – you could see the bloodcurdling faces which had so alarmed Burke when he reflected upon the French Revolution 140 years earlier, figures such as the lovely Dolores la Sardinera, a great orator and Stalinist, said to have cut a priest's throat with her own teeth. Behind these figures was an even more sinister puppet-master, Stalin. 'Marxism, with its Mohammadan utopias, with the truth of its dictatorial iron and with the pitiless lusts of its sadistic magnates was a new Saracen invasion', claimed the ultra-Catholic fascist Onésimo Redondo.[13]

The prolific novelist Eric Robert Russell Linklater (1899–1974) found the Spanish imbrogolio a dispiriting experience, for whichever side one chose, there was evil. He became 'emotionally disabled', finding it impossible to support either side wholeheartedly. His fictional response took the form of *The Impregnable Woman* (1938), a loose adaptation of the *Lysistrata* of Aristophanes, inspired by angry revulsion against the prospect of the war's renewal.[14]

In Welsh historiography, the Spanish Civil War, that most photogenic of conflicts, has achieved an almost epic significance. It was 'the Dragon's dearest cause', a heroic saga of mythical significance. But, as with the Russian Revolution, Welsh attitudes towards the Spanish bloodbath were more complex. In all, somewhere between 148 and 200 Welshmen went to join the International Brigades in Spain to fight against the fascists. In the battle at Albacete, no fewer than seventy Welshmen fought with the Republicans. Deeply committed individuals like the novelist Lewis Jones campaigned actively for volunteers to fight in Spain. Morgan Havard, Thomas William Poynter, Thomas Picton, Henry Stratton and Alun Menai Williams all fought against the fascists in spite of the government's policy of 'active non-intervention'.[15] The person responsible for the non-intervention policy was Ivor Miles Windsor-Clive, earl of Plymouth, a major figure in south Wales, owner of a splendid home at St Fagans and an impressive collection of business interests.

Lord Plymouth's efforts were in vain, for Welsh people could be found fighting for both sides. That fascinating character Wogan Philipps, despite being from a strongly right-wing family, drove an ambulance for the Republicans. In company with the poet Stephen Spender, Philipps drove a lorry with supplies to Barcelona. On 20 August 1936, the *North Wales Observer* carried a report of the exploits of a Spanish air ace who had been brought up in Wales.[16] Flight Commander Alvaro Matamoros was the grandson of a lady from Abergele and a former pupil of the celebrated Friars School in Bangor. Matamoros, on some of his bombing raids, might well have dropped explosives on some other ex-pupils of Friars. Undoubtedly the Welsh person who saw most action in the Spanish Civil War was Frank Thomas, the son of a wholesaler from Rhiwbina, Cardiff, who served as a rifleman in the 6th Bandera of the Spanish Foreign Legion for the Nationalist cause. A convinced fascist, he fought in most of the major battles around Madrid. He saw appallingly brutal behaviour on both sides, hated the Falangists but considered the brutality of the Republicans to be even worse. He went on to have a 'good Second World War', being wounded at Tobruk. Despite all his fighting, he died of old age. In many respects, Spain was simply the overture, in which the principal themes of the grander opera to follow were rehearsed.[17]

The winter years of the 1930s, that 'low, dishonest decade', saw a deep pessimism pervade all areas of life like a cold shadow.[18] Uncharacteristically, the eisteddfod organisers for 1939 set an appropriate theme for the 'pryddest' competition – 'Terfysgoedd Daear' (Earthly Storms). Typically, they failed to award the prize to the greatest poem ever submitted to the eisteddfod, Caradog

Prichard's darkly prophetic work forewarning that tempests were gathering around Europe and that many might feel an urge to escape earthly storms through suicide. As Prichard remembered later in *Afal Drwg Adda*, the mid 1930s were 'dyddiau o bryder ac ofn, a'r cymylau'n casglu i daenu drosom y fagddu fawr a ddwg yr Ail Ryfel Byd yn fwgwd dros fywyd pob un ohonom' (these were days of worry and fear, the clouds gathering to bring the great darkness that ushered the Second World War into all our lives).[19] After her tour of Europe in the mid 1930s, Winifred Coombe Tennant recalled that when she encountered fascism in Italy and Germany, she experienced a chilling 'in my bones, I knew I disliked that creed'. The Communism of Russia was no better: 'Holy Russia has been destroyed and a savage rule of hatred and fear replaces it . . . it was a world from which all human values and all spiritual values have been removed and a mechanical maniacal tyranny of violence and slavery set up.'[20]

Alun Lewis, before his self-inflicted death in 1943, recalled that in the late thirties, 'the world reverberated destruction'. In a letter to Richard Mills on 30 May 1939, he wrote, 'I have a deep sort of fatalist feeling that I'll go. Partly because I want to experience life in as many phases as I'm capable of. But . . . I'm not going to kill. Be killed perhaps, instead?'[21] At Laugharne Castle, Richard Hughes wrote his novel *In Hazard* (1938), based on the true story of a hurricane in the Caribbean, in which the storm is a symbol of the world war about to begin. Ambrose Bebb (1894–1955) captured some of the fear and foreboding so characteristic of the two weeks before war began in his journal of his trip to Brittany, appropriately titled *Dydd-lyfr Pythefnos, neu y Ddawns Angau* (1939) (Journal of Two Weeks, or Death's Dance).[22] This sense of encroaching doom and disaster is why, for many, the relief at the news from Munich in 1938 was physical and visible in the faces of passersby; they could sleep undisturbed for at least one night. Despite the obloquy subsequently attached to it, the policy of appeasing Germany had considerable support in Wales. The maxim if at first you don't capitulate, fly, fly again was considered not shameful, but sensible.

The Nobel Laureate and Aberystwyth scientist Frederick Soddy (1877–1956), in his writings for the Le Play Society, gave eloquent expression to the profound fear and pessimistic foreboding that increasingly characterised Welsh literature and media.[23] Soddy, with Sir Ernest Rutherford, had discovered that radioactivity is a phenomenon accompanying the spontaneous transformation of radioactive elements into different kinds of matter. Their discovery that matter was not indestructible would soon be severely tried. The surrealist painters, Ceri Richards and Graham Sutherland, in a series of brooding works painted in 1938–9, captured the gathering storm and gave visible expression to the general sense of foreboding. In this eternal gloom, this darkness at noon, misapprehensions gathered like wraiths. Newsreel footage gave the dangers a terrifying immediacy. The news presentations on cinema screens across Wales showed images of a frightening enemy – a Blitzkrieg of rolling tanks, screaming Stukas and invincible goose-stepping storm troopers. In the black and white of print, several authors captured the colour beyond the monochrome media. Fear intensified, as from late 1939 Britain faced a triumvirate of evil in Hitler's Germany, Mussolini's Italy and Stalin's Russia. The latter's alliance with Hitler caused some communists to distance themselves from the British fight against the Nazis. Graffiti in coalmines and steelworks spoke against the 'imperialist war' and the 'capitalist war'. Aneurin Bevan, a standard-bearer of the left, hedged his bets by calling for a struggle on two fronts: against Hitler and against British capitalism.[24]

'Wish me luck as you wave me goodbye'

> 'Twice in one generation is pretty stiff!' we said on the morning of September 3rd 1939, when we knew we were at war with Hitler. Now again, as twenty-five years before, German hands had pulled the levers that had launched the Death Ship.
>
> Hugh Dalton, *Hitler's War: Before and After* (London, 1940), p. 9

The disputes and debates which still mark the causes, course and consequences of the Great War rarely appear in the historiography of the Second World War. In contrast to the First World War, which is often portrayed as a 'Futile' war, the Second World War was presented as the 'Just War'. This was moral combat. Real life, however, was more complicated and contradictory. People's views of the war between 1939 and 1945 varied considerably. The difficulties experienced by conscientious objectors, spivs running illegal rackets on the black market, farmers and tradespeople operating outside the laws on rationing and those people who contravened moral and sexual codes and countless others, all indicate that elevated ideals of behaviour were not always observed or obeyed.[25] Moreover, an individual could be exemplary in one area, but 'problematic' in another sphere. For example, many women were criticised for their sexual immorality, but still played a full and active role in the war as conscripted industrial workers.[26] The contrast between brave soldiers, sailors and flyers and conscientious objectors was also not straightforward. Airmen with their 'stylish', well-cut uniforms appeared the embodiment of heroic masculinity, but many were tortured by fear, whilst as Wynford Vaughan Thomas showed, many of those who undertook the bombing raids on German cities were wracked with guilt for fighting an immoral war.[27] In contrast, conscientious objectors who served as ambulance officers, or as air-raid wardens during the bombing of Cardiff and Swansea, acquitted themselves with true heroism.

Dissenting voices who opposed the war are almost silenced in the historiography of the Second World War, but people like Waldo Williams, Iorwerth Peate and Gwynfor Evans, the nationalist, Christian pacifist and secretary of the Peace Pledge Union, were steadfast in opposing the war. Plaid Cymru urged a neutral stance. S. O. Davies, the Labour MP for Merthyr Tydfil, and members of the Independent Labour Party opposed war, as did John Hooper Harvey, a member of the Imperial Fascist League. Jehovah's Witnesses such as Iris Cooze, and the saintly George Maitland Lloyd Davies were pacifists of profound conviction. For their opposition, T. E. Nicholas (Niclas y Glais) and his son Islwyn of Aberystwyth were the victims of a witch-hunt organised by a vengeful chief constable determined to have them imprisoned. Three young nationalists in the seafront town were actually imprisoned for turning their backs and walking away from the singing of 'God Save the King' at the end of a summer concert show on the promenade.[28]

In the early part of the war, a logic stranger than that of the Red Queen in *Alice in Wonderland* made it hard to differentiate friend and foe. Soviet oil fuelled the Luftwaffe planes above Swansea. When France fell, the troops of the Vichy regime fought fiercely against the British in Syria in 1941, and in Madagascar and briefly in north Africa the following year.[29] The Cardiff writer, Roald Dahl, who flew a Hurricane in that campaign, wrote later: 'I for one have never forgiven the Vichy French for the unnecessary slaughter they caused.'[30] More Frenchmen carried arms for Vichy security forces or the Germans than ever fought for the resistance or the Allied armies.[31]

The sense of panic is epitomised in the fact that late August and September 1939 witnessed the greatest rush to get married that Wales had ever experienced. Winding queues outside Welsh banks were also symptomatic of people's fear. It is easy to forget that the past was once the future and to expose failures in foresight with the benefit of hindsight. No war in history has been more widely foreseen, yet to some it still came as a shock. As hostilities commenced, historians gifted with hindsight showed lack of foresight. The inimitable Gwyn A. Williams was more concerned with a personal problem acquired in the Urdd camp in Llangrannog: 'I had VD! . . . I never slept all night . . . How was I going to tell mam? Tell her that I had VD . . . But in the morning, a Friday, Hitler did indeed march into Poland . . . and I forgot about my VD.'[32] According to Richard Cobb, the young historian Alun Davies was so engrossed in his work on the French Revolution in the Paris archives that he failed to notice the gathering storm and was caught up in the contemporary conflict. Cobb also related the story of 'the finest Germanist in Wales', who went, aged fifteen to visit a pen pal in Cottbus, Germany, in August 1939. Arriving in Dresden in early September, he found that the British consul-general had already left – a habit of British consuls in times of international crisis. He saw out the war working in a local paper mill.[33] The artist Gwen John fled Paris as the Germans advanced in 1914 but, despite this experience, she still left it too late to escape in 1939. She died in

Dieppe, where, unrecognised, she was buried in an unmarked grave.[34]

Even more so than the First, the Second World War was to be a total war that impacted on all areas of life. Thus it is perhaps no surprise that the great poetry of this conflict was written to celebrate and commemorate not the fighting on fronts around the world, but the home front. Dylan Thomas's 'A refusal to mourn the death by fire of a child in London' and 'Ceremony after a fire raid' and Alun Llywelyn-Williams's 'Ar Ymweliad' show how 'death's dark angel' cast a shadow on Welsh hearths. Waldo Williams in his elegiac poem, 'Y Tangnefeddwyr' (The Peacemakers), contrasts the tender innocence of his parents with the terror and tragedy of flaming, fire-bombed Swansea. This war took its unknown victims from all sections of the population – young and old, men, women and children.

One of the great contradictions of the Second World War is that it saw both the globalisation and the domestication of conflict. The war, total and global as it was, killed more civilian men, women and children than soldiers, sailors and airmen. The Blitz, in particular, brutally brought the realities of industrialised warfare home to the Welsh.[35] Cardiff, Newport and Swansea, with their industrial and manufacturing complexes and ports, were obvious targets. In July, August and September 1940, January and February 1941, June and July 1942, and May 1943, each suffered heavily from the German airforce's bombing raids.[36]

Suddenly, on 17 May 1940, at close of day, German bombers appeared in the skies above Wales. They came back the next night, and then the next. One moonlit night in Cardiff 'it seemed as if the end of the world had come'. The raids on Cardiff on the night of 17–18 May 1943 were believed to have been in retaliation for the famous Dambusters' raid, for its leader Guy Gibson had strong links to the city and neighbouring Penarth. One of the worst nights was the ten-hour onslaught that started at 6.37 p.m. on 2 January 1941 and lasted to 4.50 a.m. on 3 January. It was a night of terror and lamentation. In all some 111 German bombers – the droning Dorniers, Junkers and screaming Messerschmidts dropped 115 tons of high explosive. A total of 165 people were killed in the raid and 168 suffered serious injuries. Some 95 homes were totally destroyed and 233 were so badly damaged they had to be demolished, whilst a further 426 homes were rendered uninhabitable. The stands at Cardiff Arms Park and parts of Llandaff Cathedral were also badly damaged. Jim Davies, who later saw action as a soldier in Korea, Malaysia and Oman, had his worst experience of the war on the last air raid in Cardiff in the early hours of 18 May 1943. His three cousins, aged between four and fourteen, and his aunt were sitting just yards from him in the cellar and were all killed as their house, 28 Frederick Street, was destroyed by a high-explosive bomb. Miraculously, Jim was physically unharmed.[37]

Swansea's worst ordeal came over the three nights of 19, 20 and 21 February 1941. Light snow fell as a prelude to heavy bombs. A total of 227 people died during those 72 hours – 122 men, 68 women and 37 children under the age of 16. A further 254 people were seriously injured and 137 slightly injured. The town centre, including the market, was wiped off the map. The area from Castle Street to the corner of Union Street and Oxford Street was laid waste. Homes, chapels, churches, schools, pubs, nursing hospitals, all were destroyed or heavily damaged. Contemporary reports tell how, by the third day, a Friday, the whole town appeared to be on fire. Amongst the saddest incidents was the death of Constance Camden, aged thirty-seven, her daughters Constance (eleven) and Judith (five) and son Wallace (fifteen), all of whom were killed when a bomb fell on their home at 16 Mayhill Road. The news was broken to Constance's husband, who was serving in the Royal Army Medical Corps. One inhabitant who survived the devastation bravely but boldly described Swansea's experience as 'Bombed, Battered and Blitzed, but not Beaten'.[38] People had vanished to the obituary pages. The painter Will Evans, in a series of remarkable works, captured death in the town's streets. Graham Sutherland (1903–80) also revealed some of the human suffering in a series of evocative paintings of war-ravaged Swansea.[39] But perhaps the most evocative imagery was provided by the seaside city's most famous poet, who was traumatised by the loss of his childhood Swansea. Dylan Thomas's war poems have a deep sense of moral outrage, especially for the death of children or the newly born:

A child of a few hours
With its kneading mouth
Charred on the black breast of the grave
The mother dug, and its arms full of fires.[40]

Thomas's rich lyricism was his counterweight to the dreary khaki which pervaded life. The violent compassion of his poems is one of his responses to the obligatory wartime hate of the enemy that so depressed him.

The largest fire in Britain since the Great Fire of London in 1666 occurred at Pembroke on 19 August 1940, when a lone German bomber dived out of a clear sky at 3.15 p.m. A single bomb hit an oil storage tank which exploded, sparking fires that resulted in the destruction of another eight tanks, setting over 12,000 tons of oil on fire. Smoke billowed thousands of feet into the air. In all, more than 600 people had to fight the inferno that raged for three weeks.[41] The reactions were, according to the reports of Mass Observation and some press reporters, mixed and incongruous. The imminent destruction of the Blitz and the arbitrary judgement of bombs created fear, intensified lusts, produced a fragile jollity on the edge of hysteria. Expectations of life, like everything else, were rationed. Some citizens were hysterical. Some were consumed with an overwhelming anxiety. Sensitive souls such as the artist Augustus John and the author Ambrose Bebb were wracked with depression and a sense of dark foreboding throughout the Second World War. David Richard Davies (1889–1958) saw all vestiges of left-leaning idealism crushed by the rapid succession of Spanish Civil War and Second World War, and attempted to commit suicide by drowning at Southerndown on the south Wales coast. A vision of his mother, reading from the popular catechism *Rhodd Mam*, rescued him and turned his attention to religion.[42] Others drowned their worries in stronger fluids. It was reported that Hugh Dalton, the Neath-born minister of economic warfare, 'has a strong head, drinks hard and has a particular liking for brandy'.[43]

Some were angry, and stubbornly determined to continue their ordinary lives even in the face of extraordinary difficulties. Some tried to be jovial and perky, apparently unphased by the presence of death. What is certain is that the mass panic and social collapse, 'the Bedlam' foreseen by Bertrand Russell in his pamphlet *Which Way to Peace*, did not take place.[44] People were calm and controlled, not catatonic and chaotic, despite the chaos. One who walked through Swansea's streets soon after a raid recalled that 'the air felt singed, I was breathing ashes . . . The air itself, as we walked, smelt of burning.' Another recalled, 'in imagination one smelt brimstone'.[45] There were open spaces where streets had been.

In a sense, given the strategic importance of these cities, such devastation and damage was perhaps to be expected. Less fortunate were those areas that had little strategic, military or industrial importance. They were just unfortunate. On 29 April 1941, German bombers overshot Cardiff during a raid, and, as was common, unloaded their bombs before flying back to France. Half a mile in any direction would have meant the death of only a few sheep. Instead, fourteen high-explosive and parachute mines landed on the small village of Cwmparc in the Rhondda. In all twenty people were killed, including six children, four of whom had recently been evacuated to the village for their safety. As one eye-witness recalled:

> one of my schoolfriends was found dead in an armchair with her baby . . . and she was pregnant with another one . . . we heard the following morning about thc bomb near the cemetery, and I was afraid that my mother had been blown out of her grave'.[46]

Wrexham suffered on 28 August and 1 September 1940, when bombers overshot Liverpool and jettisoned their payloads. One wonders at the navigational skills of some German pilots, for on the night of 20 September 1940 a bomber dropped bombs on Llanarth, Mydroilyn and New Cross in Cardiganshire. Tenby had a similar experience on 21 October 1941, when a lone, lost raider dropped four bombs on the seaside town. A direct hit on St Roman's in the town's Queen's Parade killed the owner, 76-year-old Mrs Haydn Thomas. A more unlikely Welsh war victim it is hard to imagine. Yet Mrs Thomas was emblematic of a conflict in which three-quarters of all those who perished were unarmed victims rather than armed and active participants in the struggle. Civilians could fare worse than combatants, confirmation of Trotsky's dictat that 'you may not be interested in war, but war is interested in you.' The dramatist and humourist Gwyn Thomas remembered the fear engendered across Wales by air raids:

> Personal memories were the most bearable reaction to theories of what might have happened during the ghastly September of 1940. One remembers phases of moonlight so lovely and made lovelier by the thought that shortly we might be running out of moon. We all waited for the church bells that would ring to tell us the Germans were here.[47]

A Mass Observation reporter, near Newport on 10 September 1939, was informed that 500 Germans had landed nearby, 499 of whom were shot in three seconds. The last was said to have escaped. The visceral fears of an imminent invasion gave rise to a paranoid fear that spies, the enemy within, were actively undermining the country. Elias Henry Jones, who had in the previous war undertaken a heroic escape from the Turks, was convinced that a group of Welsh nationalists, especially Professor J. E. Daniel, was plotting with the Germans. Rumours were rife that Raymond Davies Hughes was the scriptwriter for the detested broadcasts of Lord Haw Haw.[48] In Bethesda, north Wales, the novelist John Cowper Powys began to pen his great novel *Porius: a romance of the Dark Ages*. Although it is set in ancient times, when the Roman Empire was crumbling as the Germanic tribes clamoured at the gates, whilst Arthur stood alone for Britain, *Porius* is really a parable for Dunkirk and 1940.[49] The air raids gave rise to one of the most evocative and poignant symbols of the war, the Mickey Mouse gas mask. More bizarrely, it was rumoured that air raid wardens in Pembrokeshire had problems enforcing the blackout because of the ambulant, premonitory flickering lights of corpse candles.[50]

Allowing the ghostly lights to shine might have been more beneficial, for the number of pedestrians injured on the darkened streets of late 1939 were double those of 1938. Many others were injured fumbling around in the dark. Alongside the air raid wardens another harassed group, the Home Guard, entered popular legend.

Charged with home defence should Hitler's troops arrive, this collection of good-natured and well-intentioned people was often either very young or of such advanced age they were often asleep on duty, resembling the soldiers in the battle in the woods in *Alice Through the Looking-Glass*.

Some places, despite their importance as industrial or manufacturing centres or ports, escaped unscathed. Ebbw Vale, the centre for extensive steel production, was listed in a book of Welsh targets issued to German pilots, but was relatively undamaged. Caerphilly was bombed once, but the only victims were seven sheep killed by a bomb that landed at Rudry on 27 July 1940. Local legends developed to explain the survival of some towns. Caradoc Evans related the story of Mary Tycanol, who insisted that Hitler had been to college at Aberystwyth, and so gave orders not to bomb the place.[51] Carmarthen was not bombed on account of the mist which arose out of the river, which meant that the Luftwaffe could not find it, though they were searching all the time. With death such an arbitrary predator, these explanations appeared as credible as any other. The experience of the Blitz, according to the Gorseinon psychoanalyst Ernest Jones in 'Psychology and War Conditions', unified and strengthened the British. The brutality and 'the apparently irresistible form of the Blitzkreig when we saw the Germans marching at will into France and we realised their invincibility' meant that 'the country was seized with a united determination . . . a sense of unity . . . a conviction that there was something we could believe in and trust namely each other'. The war also, according to Jones, made people feel better. The pessimism of the late 1930s was now dispersed. The war confirmed 'how much easier it is for the human mind to tolerate external danger than internal dangers'.[52]

'Run, Rabbit, Run': the war at home

> The factory canteen . . . was a happy place to go into. It was a club, a concert hall, a debating society as well as a place to eat . . . Especially when women were employed, these breaks for tea were a great feature of the working day, life was strenuous, life was earnest, but there was also drama and excitement, a heightened sense of living

> in those wartime factories. The men and women in them were earning their living. But they were doing a great deal more than that and were very conscious that they were. This was their way of fighting Hitler. They were answering back in the one way they knew.
>
> Jennie Lee, *This Grand Journey: A Volume of Autobiography, 1904–45* (London, 1963), pp. 200–1; quoted in Mari A. Williams, *A Forgotten Army: Female Munitions Workers of South Wales* (Cardiff, 2002), p. 71

To provide the munitions and materials required by the leviathan of conflict, much of the economy and the land of Wales was turned over to the war effort. On Anglesey three air force training bases were established at Bodorgan, Mona and Valley. The construction of the bases gave a much needed boost to the local building industry and to the island's economy, which had suffered greatly since the 1930s. At Pwllheli, between 1939 and 1940, Billy Butlin developed a camp for the navy, which he purchased after the war and developed as a holiday centre. It was an appropriate symbol of the austere 1950s, for despite the change in function, as local wags pointed out, the facilities and food were the same. At Aberystwyth, more than 1,200 RAF officers were in training. Local hotels, such as the Queen's, the Belle Vue Royal and the Lion Royal, received a much needed injection of income. Tregaron, unlikely as it now seems, given the town's landlocked nature, was a base for the Royal Marines. A series of photographs taken in 1941 shows the marines on the town's square preparing for manoeuvres, in front of the disapproving statue of the Apostle of Peace, Henry Richard. As the protests engendered by Saunders Lewis, Lewis Valentine and D. J. Williams in 1936 against an RAF bombing base showed, these developments had profound cultural, social and linguistic implications. The War Office appropriated three-quarters of the Stackpole Estate in Pembrokeshire to create the 6,000-acre Castlemartin bombing range. Despite Lord Cawdor's vocal protests, scores of families were evicted. Stackpole Court itself was requisitioned to house military personnel, many of whom stole the lead off its roof, so that the building soon fell victim to both dry and wet rot and had to be abandoned.

Most evocative of all, perhaps, was the great clearance of the Epynt moors, the embodiment of all that was serenely pastoral, one of the loneliest and loveliest regions in Wales. Epynt was a timeless place, where the present seemed to merge into the paths of pre-history, where travel was still, in 1939, confined to horses, with the women riding side-saddle. In all more than 400 men, women and children had to leave Epynt's fifty-four farms and smallholdings to make way for an artillery range. In that green and pleasant land a people's dream died. These were strange, sad days for the locals and theirs became lost, forgotten lands. The scholar Iorwerth Peate, on a visit to collect material for the National Folk Museum in St Fagans, Cardiff, was simply told to return there as soon as possible, for 'mae'n ddiwedd y byd yma' – 'it is the end of the world here'.[53]

Prisoner of war camps were established in several places around Wales. Hitler's deputy Rudolph Hess was rumoured to be buried in Abergavenny; he was imprisoned there, which some cruel people suggested amounted to much the same thing. Enemy prisoners are usually portrayed as relatively indolent because, unlike their British counterparts who were forever concocting and conducting ingenious escape plans, they seemed content to see out the war in relative safety in Wales. Italian prisoners at Henllan, Cardiganshire, were allowed to work on local farms, under informal arrangements and without pay, much to the delight of parsimonious farmers. A frisson of excitement and fear, however, swept across Wales, when on the night of 10–11 March, 1945, sixty-seven German prisoners escaped from the Island Farm, Camp 198, near Bridgend. One prisoner almost reached an English channel port; all were recaptured. Some had blackened their faces, hoping to be mistaken for miners, one man with a thick German accent hopefully explained his behaviour to a policeman at midnight: 'I'm only a poor Welsh miner out looking for my children.' Three boarded a bus near Neath and raised suspicions because they did not talk. The other passengers, being Welsh and unused to silence, spoke with the driver, who then did a quick detour and stopped the bus outside a local police station. But for seven traumatic days, local people across a large swathe of south Wales lived in fear that the enemy was loose in their midst.[54]

The state soon intruded into all areas of people's private lives. Not only were men conscripted into the services and essential industries, so too, from 1941, were women. This was a measure that was beyond anything introduced by other combatants, even autocratic Japan, Germany or Russia. The armaments industries in particular gave new employment opportunities to Welsh women.[55] At Mold and Rhydymwyn in the north, Bridgend, Hirwaun and Pontypool in the south, women were an essential part of the workforce of the Royal Ordnance Factories (ROF). At the peak of production there were probably around 30,000 to 35,000 women employed in ROF centres. By August 1941, women formed more than 70 per cent of the 28,327 munitions workers employed at Bridgend ROF. The work was at best unpleasant; at worst, it was extremely dangerous.[56] The Bridgend ROF, a filling factory which produced detonators and fuses for mortar bombs, was known to many as 'the Suicide Club'. Whilst hundreds of Welsh combat casualties lost limbs, thousands of workers at home became amputees as a result of industrial accidents. Many lost their lives in explosions in the munitions factories. Women were also employed in agriculture, accountancy, medicine and the manufacture of steel and other metals, in positions that had previously been masculine preserves. New stock characters soon entered the cast list of Welsh society – uniformed, power-crazed women tram-conductors, or the receptionist, cinematically smoking on the job, whilst the pre-war rogue, now a filmic 'spiv', would disappear conspiratorially down hotel corridors.[57]

A person's patriotic duty extended even as far as diet. Shortages of food soon forced people into miracles of improvisation. A visitor to Dylan Thomas's wartime flat recalls 'being served a particularly curious starling pie'.[58] Only a month after the war commenced, the Ministry of Agriculture launched a campaign to increase home-food production. The slogan for the organisation that ran the campaign, 'Dig for Victory', was coined by Michael Foot, later MP for Ebbw Vale and it was intended to give impetus to both food production and propaganda. Civilians could help both themselves and the war effort by patriotically digging up lawns, flowerbeds, playing fields and parks and ships facing the deadly U-boat onslaughts could carry materials other than food. Allotments appeared on Welsh railway sidings and the fringes of towns. There was even a

Dig for Victory anthem ('Dig! Dig! Dig! And your muscles will grow big') and films with cartoon characters, such as Potato Pete and Doctor Carrot, to instruct and inspire people. Garden pests were regarded as enemy agents. The humble house sparrow was identified as 'Hitler's feathered friend' and the rabbit vilified as 'Herr Rabbit: Fifth Columnist'. Dig for Victory transformed many lives by reconnecting people with the natural world from which, since the industrialisation of Wales, they had been increasingly estranged. The campaign also brought health benefits. Infant mortality, 'that most sensitive barometer of a nation's health', actually fell between 1941 to 1944, by which time it was the lowest ever recorded.[59]

Welsh Warriors

> I put my hand on a shrivelled body and felt the flesh hardened into carbon . . . Nothing had prepared me for the smells of war, above all that of roasted flesh. It was very unnerving for a young lad.
>
> Corporal Iolo Lewis, a wireless operator in one of Montgomery's Sherman tanks during the battle of the Scheldt, quoted in Max Hastings, *Armageddon: the Battle for Germany 1944–45* (London, 2004), p. 167

The war gave an opportunity for professional Welsh soldiers and sailors to exhibit and exercise the skills they had spent a lifetime acquiring. Many welcomed the career opportunities Hitler provided. Those who survived and gathered competence gained promotions in months that in peacetime would have taken years. Edmund Frank Davies (1900–51), the son of the bandmaster of the 4th Queens Hussars in India, had an action-packed career. His 'independence, intolerance, robustness, keen sense of humour and a kind of disciplined bolshevism' earned him the nickname 'Trotsky'. He served in Ireland and Palestine in the 1920s and 1930s. At the outbreak of war he was a chemical warfare officer in France and was later evacuated from Dunkirk. In 1943 Davies was 'asked to volunteer' to lead a Special Operations Executive (SOE) mission into the occupied Balkans. Grievously wounded, he was captured by a group of Albanian quislings, and after a 'rough interrogation' by the Gestapo, was transferred to the 'unpleasant' Mauthausen concentration camp and then to Colditz.[60]

War, of course, was an unavoidable occupational hazard for Welsh soldiers, but even so some seem to have been involved in a remarkable series of conflicts. Llewellyn Isaac Gethin Morgan-Owen (1879–1960) of Llandinam, after a period with the Caernarfonshire militia, served in South Africa with the 24th South Wales Borderers until 1902 and then in Nigeria. During the First World War he fought in Gallipoli at the battle of Sari Bair and organised the evacuation of Suvla. He then fought in Mesopotamia, where he was five times mentioned in despatches while taking part in the capture of Baghdad. Thereafter he went to India and Pakistan and then, between 1931–44, he was a colonel with the South Wales Borderers. How he survived is almost inexplicable.[61] Lewis Pugh Evans (1881–1962) of Gelli Angharad, Aberystwyth, was another who fought in a remarkable series of conflicts, from the Boer War to the First and Second World Wars, with a host of smaller skirmishes in between. He was the first, perhaps the only, Welsh soldier to be awarded the DSO twice and the Victoria Cross for his courage and valour. General John Vaughan (1841–1956) had a martial spirit which he claimed he had inherited from his ancestors, the Welsh princes of the early Middle Ages. He fought in Mashonaland, the Sudan, the Boer War, and the First and Second World Wars. Twice awarded the DSO he also received the Légion d'Honneur.[62] Though the son of a minister of religion from Barry, Thomas Wynford Rees, also known as 'the Docker', 'Dai', 'Pete' or 'Napoleon', fought in a series of battles. His greatest contribution came as General Slim's Welsh general in the Burma campaign. Always leading from the front, he acquired the respect and affection of his men and his commanders.[63]

Welshmen without military training were also influential and successful. Owen Lloyd George, later the third Earl Lloyd-George of Dwyfor, was commissioned into the Welsh Guards in 1942 and fought with the third battalion of the regiment in Italy. For him, as for many of his contemporaries, the war was the defining experience of his life. Norman Lewis, the great travel writer, was also involved in the Italian campaign, which he chronicled in *Naples '44*.

With his characteristic wryness, bordering on sarcasm, he noted: 'it was characteristic of this adventure that the intelligence corps sergeant with whom I joined forces, a PhD in Hellenic Studies, should be fluent in the Greek of the time of Pericles, but spoke no German'. Lewis also recorded the part-time prostitutes he and his colleagues encountered – 'they might have been selling fish, except that this place lacked the excitement of a fish market' – and the savage rape of Italian women by Allied troops.[64] Caradog Prichard (1904–80), the journalist, poet and novelist, recalled his almost surreal war experiences in *'Rwyf innau'n Filwr Bychan*.[65] Sir Tasker Watkins (1918–2007) became the most decorated war hero in Welsh history following the D-Day landings in France and his role in liberating the Dutch city of 's-Hertogenbosch. He recalled:

> I'd seen more killing and death in twenty-four hours – indeed been part of that terrible process – than is right for anybody. From that point onwards I have tried to take a more caring view of my fellow human beings, and that, of course, always includes your opponent, whether it be in war, sport, or just life generally.[66]

Others suffered a bone-chilling sense of fear throughout each conflict. Soldiers vomited, they urinated in their pants, in the most terrifying moments they lost control of their bowels. As John Ellis observed, 'stereotypes of "manliness" and "guts" can readily accommodate the fact that a man's stomach or heart might betray his nervousness, but they make less allowance for shitting his pants or wetting himself.' Captain David Elliott of the Welsh Guards found himself 'terribly depressed' on returning to barracks after a weekend leave:

> There is nothing so utterly boring, so utterly narrow and so utterly petty as regimental soldiering which lacks the accompaniment of a state of battle . . . Certainly in this battalion there is no charity, no loving kindness, no loyalty . . . Among the officers, if not the men, there are many problem children.[67]

Ifan Gruffydd, 'y Gŵr o Baradwys', spent four years in the horrors of Mons, Arras, Béthune and the Somme.[68] He grew to hate war, especially as it had been caused by the 'imperial pretensions and ambitions of the English'. Feeling this hatred, he lived to watch four of his five sons serve in the Second World War. The Newport-born banker, Bickham Aldred Cowan Sweet-Escott (1907–81) left the chairmanship of Courtaulds to lead section D of the Secret Intelligence Service, later the SOE. He organised sabotage activities in the Balkans, Egypt, France and Greece. In *Baker Street Irregular* he provides an entertaining account of the dangerous work undertaken by the SOE.[69]

The Special Operations Executive had been established under the guidance of Hugh Dalton, with a broad brief for clandestine escapades across Europe and North Africa; deception and deceit became an important aspect of the SOE's work.[70] Major Buckley, scion of the Llanelli brewing family, led a group of tradesmen, craftsmen, artists and magicians in North Africa on operations involving camouflage and the application of magic and illusion on the battlefield. Amongst their most innovative achievements were the concealment of whole towns and the introduction to aircraft pilots of a heat-resistant cream used by circus fire-eaters.[71] Some Welsh people also revelled in the underground world of espionage. One of the most successful of British espionage agents in the war was the Welsh inventor Arthur Graham Owens. Described by his 'handlers' in 1935 as 'an underfed Cardiff type', Owens succeeded in duping the Germans into believing that he was an extreme nationalist intent on achieving revenge for the indignities that the English establishment had inflicted on him and his family. There was also a Welsh involvement in the most successful military deception of the war, Operation Mincemeat. The body of a penniless, alcoholic vagrant named Glyndwr Michael from Aberbargoed was given false papers and official documents and cast into the sea off the coast of neutral Spain. The documents strongly indicated that the Allies would invade Europe through Greece and Sardinia, not Sicily. The Spanish government 'lent' the documents to Germany, who, convinced of their authenticity, diverted significant forces from Italy and Russia to counter the nonexistent threat.[72]

'The Wizard War': the battle of wits

> Words cannot express the combined brilliance of the Bletchley Park World. Perhaps if all its personnel had been kept together after the war to consider the problems of world peace and universal prosperity, they might have cracked those problems too.
>
> Gwen Watkins, a code-breaker at Bletchley Park, *Western Mail*, 14 July 2006

Ingenuity, innovation and intelligence were vital aspects of the war. Far from consisting of the inefficient bunglings of unimaginative amateurs – the usual way in which the British war effort is portrayed – there were ingenious solutions to problems in several spheres.[73] The crisis of war created the conditions for genius to flourish and the skills of a diverse group of people were brought into play. Sir John Coldbrook Hanbury-Williams (1892–1965) of Pontypool, the industrialist and director of Courtaulds and the Bank of England, was influential in the deliberations and initiations of the Ministry of Economic Warfare from 1942 to 1945. The work of Sir George Stapledon (1882–1960) was essential in extending the capacity of British uplands to support grasslands and produce food at higher altitudes. Sir Reginald Smith, the minister of agriculture, claimed that without the achievements of Stapledon Britain would have starved and been incapable of mounting any military challenge.[74]

Scientific endeavour proved an essential aspect of the British war effort.[75] Amongst the most vital was the work of the government's communications headquarters at Bletchley Park.[76] Here Gwen Watkins and her poet husband Vernon Watkins, as well as a host of other linguists, code-breakers and crossword and puzzle experts, worked on the encryption of German ciphers and codes. Roy Jenkins, later a British statesman, decrypted German signals. He and his colleagues knew the importance and urgency of their work, but contrary to the impression given in films about Bletchley, they were told nothing about the impact of their contributions.[77] However, they were aware that they were engaged in a crucial battle of wits. Another person with Swansea links who worked at

Bletchley was Charles Eryl Wynn-Williams (1903–79), one of a brilliant nucleus of physicists recruited to work on radio direction finding (radar). His mastery of valves and circuits and his connections with government and industrial researchers soon drew him into the development of code-breaking machines. He and a team of Post Office engineers made fundamental contributions to the development of machines for deciphering Enigma messages and to the Heath Robinson cryptoanalytic device, forerunner of the Colossus decoding machine. This equipment proved vital to the war effort by breaking German signals and formed the basis for the development of modern digital electronics and computing.[78]

Welsh scientists made notable contributions to the development of new technologies and weapons in both the air and the sea wars. Ezer Griffiths (1888–1962), the Aberdare physicist, worked on such problems as the vapour trails made by aircraft and the cooling of armoured fighting vehicles for crew comfort. Douglas McKie (1896–1967) made similar contributions through his studies of extreme heat and cold. The Wrexham-born metallurgist Norman Percy Allen (1903–72) was instrumental in devising new gas turbine engines for planes. The alloys he invented made the Whittle engine a practical reality, and even today remain the standard blading material for many aircraft and land-based gas turbine installations throughout the world.[79] Reginald Cockcroft Sutcliffe (1904–91), the meteorologist, also from Wrexham, was instrumental in predicting the weather and likely cloud cover for the battles in France and later the bombing raids on Germany. He was one of the last soldiers to escape via the sea through Marseilles and Gibraltar when France fell in 1940. His book, *Meteorology for Aviation* (1939), was the standard work for Royal Air Force flight crews.[80] A third son of Wrexham, Hugh Hamshaw Thomas (1885–1962), later a well known palaeobotanist, served as a wing commander in charge of photographic interpretation.[81] Sir Granville Beynon (1914–96), the physicist, assisted the RAF with work on the refinement of radar.[82] Albert G. Lee (1879–1967) of Conwy, the telecommunications engineer, made similar contributions to radio and radar communications.[83] The young scientific intelligence officer R. V. Jones played a crucial role by identifying German navigational beams and showing the way to jam them.[84] Sir Frederick Brundrett (1894–1974) of Ebbw Vale made significant contributions to research on underwater communications with submarines.[85]

Perhaps the most significant contributions by a Welsh theoretical scientist during the Second World War were made by Evan James Williams (1903–45), of Cwmsychbant, Cardiganshire. A precociously gifted scientist and an inveterate practical joker, Williams joined the Royal Aircraft Establishment at Farnborough to develop new physical methods of detecting submerged U-boats from the air. He was then promoted to the operational research section at Coastal Command, where his task was to improve the methods of finding and sinking U-boats. His ingenuity resulted in considerable improvements in both. In 1941, Williams became director of operational research at Coastal Command. There he was particularly concerned with such questions as the size of convoys, which he successfully made larger, and the concerted offensive against U-boats in the Bay of Biscay on passages to and from their shore bases. The anti-submarine campaign in 1943 was, its historian claims, 'waged under closer scientific control than any other campaign in the history of the British armed forces'. It gave rise to the term 'slide-rule strategy' and Williams was one of its foremost creators. In 1944, Williams learned that he had cancer. After an operation in January 1945 he nevertheless visited Washington to discuss with the Americans tactics for the Far Eastern War.[86]

Intellectual skills were essential in a broad range of endeavours. The writer Eric Robert Russell Linklater (1899–1974) from Penarth moved from the command of Fortress Orkney to the directorate of public relations in the War Office, where he wrote pamphlets on a wide range of war-related topics.[87] In 1944–5 he was transferred to Italy, which provided the basis for his novel *Private Angelo* (1946), a searing exposé of both the follies and the nobility of war. Not everyone appreciated Linklater's or his colleagues' efforts in wartime propaganda. Aneurin Bevan, the acerbic critic of the war effort, complained in 1940 that 'the impression is now universal that if the Germans do not manage to bomb us to death the Ministry of Information will bore us to death'.[88]

A highly unlikely author of propaganda films was the poet and pacifist Dylan Thomas. Thomas had stated, at the start of the war, that 'I do not intend to waste my little body (though it's little no longer, I'm like a walrus) for the mysterious ends of others'. In films such as *These are the Men*, Thomas set out the challenges facing Britain. Perhaps his most remarkable film was, *A Soldier Comes Home*, in which he tackles the difficulty of readjusting when Daddy, haunted by war, tries to fit back in with family life after four years away.[89] Most effective of all, in propaganda and morale building, was the work of Welsh cartoonists. Leslie Gilbert Illingworth (1902–1979), in a series of visceral cartoons in the *Daily Mail*, gave a graphic account of the ebb and flow of British forces in the war.[90] His duotone, black-and-white drawings set out the clearest expositions of the threat posed to the forces of light by the powers of darkness. Herbert Samuel Thomas (1883–1966) of Newport did the same in a series of brilliant cartoons for the *Evening Standard*. A few, deft brush strokes and the danger presented to decency by the forces of evil were boldly outlined. Such images were worth thousands of words. [91]

'These are the men': Dunkirk and other disasters

> A dear old French lady came waddling to the outer fringe of the mines wanting to come through. I shouted at her to stop. Then holding her hands, I brought her through the minefield in a nerve-racking 'pas de deux'. She was quite oblivious of the risk.
>
> Lance-Sergeant George Griffin, Welsh Guards, quoted in Hugh Sebag-Montefiore, *Dunkirk: Fight to the Last Man* (London, 2006), p. 178

The early years of the war seemed to confirm the worst fears of the pessimists of the 'morbid age years' of the 1930s.[92] Despite the propaganda, the spirit of the years 1939–41 was that of defeat. Like a slowly dispersing marsh gas it meandered, loitering in pockets here and there, bitter, clinging, a sickening presence. All the vaunted citadels of British power, seemed now, like Miss Haversham's wedding cake, to be crumbling in defeat and cobwebs.[93] The lack of success in Europe was overshadowed by the abysmal incompetence of the campaign in the Far East. The BBC and the Ministry of Information created an illusion about the power of the empire in the East. They vilified the Japanese as 'bandy-legged dwarfs too myopic to shoot straight', who flew planes made from bamboo shoots and rice paper and sailed in sampans and junks. But the reality was that the Japanese out-fought, out-thought, out-manoeuvred and out-foxed the British. Within swift succession, Singapore collapsed, Malaysia fell, and Burma was overrun. The much vaunted power of the Royal Navy was exposed as the *Prince of Wales* and the *Repulse* were both sunk.[94] Force Z's commander, Admiral Sir Tom Phillips, was a diminutive and pugnacious sailor whom Winston Churchill nicknamed 'the Cocksparrow'. Arrogantly assuming that his armoured leviathans were more than a match for 'mechanical Japanese harpies', Phillips's lack of seamanship and inexperience were cruelly exposed on 10 December 1941. Defenceless, he went down with his ship, taking over eight hundred seamen with him.

In terms of the profligate bloodshed and brutality of the Second World War, the battles and other events that so obsessed the Welsh hardly register. Seven of the war's bloodiest battles were fought between German and Soviet forces. In Hitler's campaign against Russia, at least 1,582,000 soldiers and countless civilians died. In contrast, 4,650 died at Alamein. Britain's civilian losses amounted to 0.1 per cent of the population, whereas the figures for Poland and Byelorussia were respectively 18 per cent and 25 per cent. The British military death toll was 144,000 (of whom some 14,000 were Welsh). The Russians lost at least 11 million combatants, perhaps 10 per cent of them shot by the NKVD to encourage the others to fight. Germany lost 3.5 million soldiers. The fact that, statistically, the sufferings of some were less terrible than those of others was meaningless to those concerned. An important truth about the war, as about all human affairs, is that people can interpret great events only in the context of their own circumstances. Thus some events were allowed to gather an iconic importance and even defeats acquired a heroic, victorious aspect. A special spirit of resilience and resistance was claimed to have characterised the Blitz. But perhaps the best example of how defeat and disaster were conjured into victory was Dunkirk.

The story of the 'little ships' that sailed to the French port of Dunkirk to evacuate troops trapped by the swift German advance has been much told on screen and paper. Rose Marie (Ray) Howard-Jones, one of the few female war artists, captured the scenes of heroic escape in her characteristic mixed media. Amongst the ships was the *Galloping Gertie*, a pleasure steamer, whose more usual task was ferrying holidaying families around the Bristol Channel from Barry to Ilfracombe, Tenby and Bath.[95] *Gertie* rescued some 3,000 troops from the beach at Dunkirk. But the heroic actions were not confined to sea; the crucial battles took place outside Dunkirk. On 24 May 1940, the German panzer divisions which had bludgeoned their way through France halted briefly at the canal line south of Dunkirk. On 27 May, they advanced again, intending to encircle and capture half a million Allied soldiers. They would have succeeded, had it not been for the British battalions ordered to stand in their path. Their job was to shield the corridor down which the rest of the army was retreating to Dunkirk. Amongst them were the Welsh Guards, who had been ordered to fight to the last man and the last bullet – a terrifying suicide mission.

After the order was issued, Lieutenant Christopher Furness prepared his men for battle. Twenty-eight-year-old 'Dickie' Furness was perhaps one of the most popular men in the regiment, and probably one of the richest. The son of a viscount, he was the heir to a vast fortune that in 1940 was valued at £1 million.[96] He was also very well connected; his stepmother, Thelma Furness, had been the lover of the Prince of Wales. He had obviously inherited her interests. In 1935 he had been asked to leave the Welsh Guards after he had been caught in flagrante with another officer's wife. But if he did not always give his fellow officers the respect that was their due, he certainly had the common touch with his men, and that may explain why, after war was declared, the Welsh Guards welcomed him back. On 24 May 1940, after twenty four hours of almost non-stop, hand-to-hand fighting, Furness was killed. Thanks to the counter-attacks which he led, the battalion's transport escaped before it could be shot up by German guns. As a belated tribute to his courageous stand, Furness was rewarded with a posthumous Victoria Cross in 1946.

Amongst those fighting to the bitter end was 19-year-old Lieutenant Rhidian Llewellyn of 2 Company, Welsh Guards, who was awarded the Military Cross for his conspicuous bravery. Llewellyn resolved many moral quandries that day. In one instance he and one other soldier were surrounded by a large number of Germans. The Germans, rather than shoot Llewellyn and a fellow Welsh Guardsman, promptly surrendered. Llewellyn however ignored this and decided to open fire with his Bren gun, killing and wounding as many Germans as was necessary to persuade the others to leave their way clear.[97] The bravery of the Welsh Guards and other defenders enabled more than 330,000 soldiers to be evacuated from France in the last week of May and the first week of June 1940. Much attention was, and has been, given to the heroism of the troops, but Dunkirk was a side issue which drew attention away from the stark fact that the Germans had achieved their main objective: France had fallen.[98]

It is the heroism and the horrors of conflict that characterise most war stories and history books. But war also gave rise to passages of tedium and periods of unbearable boredom. There were dramas of cowardice, where soldiers actively avoided military glory. Amongst the slaughter and the mayhem, survivors recounted tales of surreal events which at their best revealed the deeply comic and cynical attitudes of the troops; at their worst, they degenerated into sadism. Landing in Sicily, Norman Lewis encountered an astonishing vision of 'unearthly enchantment'. Washed by the glow of a late sunset, the three great temples of Paestrum stood in clear view. In the immediate foreground lay a pair of dead cows, their feet in the air – 'cattle with rigor mortis framing classical columns'. In his characteristic, elegant shorthand, Lewis calibrated the extremes between the absurd and the sublime. In the pacing and narrative of *Naples '44*, he established a subtle hum of dissonance, his terse language and mordant wit occasionally fired up by blistering fury. After the initial débacle of the landings, Lewis felt that 'history must be left to dress up this part of the action of Salerno with what dignity it can'. His own enduring impression was of 'ineptitude and cowardice', a contagion from the top. But the complete lack of forward planning allowed Sergeant Lewis and his section to spend much of those weeks on Italian soil 'lotus-eating' at Paestum. The apocalyptic nature of Easter 1944 was given an appropriate background when, on 19 March 1944, Vesuvius erupted: 'the most majestic and terrible sight I have ever expected to see', wrote Lewis. The 'slow, grey snowfall' continued for weeks.[99]

The author and broadcaster Wynford Vaughan Thomas (1908–87) became a war correspondent after reporting on the Blitz for the BBC. He was the first reporter to fly in a Lancaster bomber on a night raid on Berlin (1943). The bomb run, which he brilliantly described as the aircraft was caught by the German searchlights and dodged the flak, gave listeners a vivid picture of the gruelling perils RAF crews endured. Like Norman Lewis, Vaughan Thomas landed on the Anzio beachhead from where he recorded memorable dispatches and later covered the liberation of Rome. The most gruelling of his war experiences was the liberation of Belsen concentration camp. He described a 'living hell' and was outraged by the assault on human dignity he found there. But Vaughan Thomas also experienced something of the bacchanalian nature of war. He also 'liberated' the vineyards of Burgundy, remarking typically, 'We had three marvellous days in a cellar and I emerged with the Croix du Guerre! Oh, what a campaign – it was known after by the troops as the "champagne campaign" although we were liberating Chateauneuf du Pape and Tavel and Burgundy.'[100] The miner and novelist Ron Berry, based in Africa for much of the war, recalled: 'Daytimes we randied in brothels. Main aims, booze, fuck, return aboard before dark . . . plenty of sideways-faces Good Soldier Schweiks at various removes.'[101]

Another son of Swansea who was present at the invasion of Sicily and the Italian mainland, as well as the North African campaign, was Sir Harry Donald Secombe (1921–2001). From the very onset, his war was one of absurdity, comedy and the surreal. On his way to call-up he rode in a friend's car, standing up in it to give an impersonation of Hitler, with a black comb as the moustache. Considered to represent too much of a danger to friend rather than to foe, Secombe was transferred from the artillery into the entertainments section in North Africa.[102] Here he met Spike Milligan and one of the great comedy partnerships began. Milligan's memoirs of the closing phase of the war, *Where Have All the Bullets Gone?*, describe in detail the blunderings of the anarchic duo, especially those of 'the singer and lunatic, a little myopic blubber of fat from Wales'. After a frustrating tussle with two prostitutes in Florence, Milligan recalled that:

> We depart virgo intacto, trousers bursting with revolving testicles and dying erections. We retrace our steps to the hotel. We are lost. 'Fancy', says Secombe. 'Who in the Mumbles would dream that I was lost in Florence?' I tell him I gave up: who in Mumbles would know he was lost in Florence? A tart hovers by. Lily Marlene? She knows the way to the hotel. Do we want a shag? It is only fifty lire after ten, she'll do us both for forty. Sorry dear, we're training for the priesthood. OK. We can find our own fucking way back. Finally we did. 'Home at last', says Secombe, 'and forty lire to the good![103]

The background of the anarchic action and adventures of soldiers like Secombe is the weirdness and anguish of men permanently on the verge of violent death. Secombe yoked the hilarious and the horrific in a vision of hell played for laughs. It is important not to overstate the case, but Secombe's and Milligan's antics pointed to a deeper truth about the war. The war was so serious it was ridiculous. It was indescribably cruel and insane. Despite all its horrors, the First World War still had about it an air of Victorian social, moral and ethical values and, especially in its early years, a hint of a heroic crusade. The madness of the Second descended to new depths of horrors – the unsurrendering Japanese soldiers, suicides and *kamikazes*, public hangings of civilians, gassings of innocent people and its horrendous, appropriate conclusion in atomic radiation.

The Real Cruel Sea: the war at sea

> It was not long before the end came for *Sikh* as she heeled over to starboard and finally sank. We were left feeling alone in the world,

> shocked, afraid, yet still struggling to survive. It is a solemn, heart-breaking experience to see the ship you have loved going to the bottom.
>
> The survivors now gathered together in small groups . . . some cry – usually the result of shock, not weakness; some curse with a long tirade of abuse against everyone else; some laugh and try to crack jokes – 'Where's that bloody taxi I ordered?' – or the most standard naval joke, 'If only mother could see me now she'd buy me out'. And some just give way to despair and slide away into the depths.
>
> Chief Engine Room Artificer Trevor Lewis, quoted in Max Arthur, *Lost Voices of the Royal Navy* (London, 2005), pp. 398–9

In one sphere of warfare, there could ultimately be only one victor, for humanity would always be vulnerable to the cruel sea.[104] Sailors everywhere battled against giant waves that could bend four-inch armour plating. They were perpetually wet and cold, shivering in uninsulated cabins or sweltering in the heat of summer. But those mariners on merchant and Royal Navy ships on the Arctic runs had to endure further dangers. Ice greatly added to the weight of a ship and affected stability, so that she might collapse or overturn. With hammers and crowbars, sailors had to hack great lumps of ice off guns and deck metal, taking care not to touch it and become entrapped. In the perpetual darkness of the Arctic winter the sun never rose, whilst in summer it never set, making them clear targets for the enemy submarines who constantly hunted and harried them. The cold and wet were ever present, icy winds often beat faces deep red and frostbite was a real fear. Greater dangers lay within the ships. British dockers gained a deplorable reputation for carelessness in cargo storage and loads often shifted or broke loose. On the one side the men had the sea, on the other sorrow.

The death toll was heavy, Newport lost 654 seamen, Cardiff lost more than 100 ships and, it was estimated, more than 1,000 sailors, Barry lost more than 360 men, 14 of whom were under eighteen years of age. Per capita, more men from Barry died at sea than from anywhere else in Britain. A report in the *Barry and District News* on 2 July 1943 described the seaside town as 'the Port that craves adventure', claiming that 'there are few streets in the town and dock area which have not lost men at sea as a result of enemy action'. Welsh losses were further increased by the convoys which gathered at Milford Haven for the longest and most important battle of war, the Battle of the Atlantic.[105]

The sea was often the scene of horrific panic. Desperate sailors were hoisted or hurled themselves screaming over the side, as ship after ship went down, alarm bells sounding, claxons ringing. Snowflake rockets illuminated the scenes at night, as their yellow brilliance lit up the wild water of this sea of death. Huge waves would crash in and over as boats were lost in a flurry of bubbles. Then nothing, not even bubbles. The sea was often so cold that there would only be a few minutes for a person to survive in the water. Three or four minutes between waving and rescue, between a smile and fixed-for-ever, rigor-mortis grin. Some had to resort to violence against their fellow sailors to survive. Captain Clement Stott, the Welsh accountant, captain of the ill-fated *Lancastria*, found himself being pulled under the surface by a man who was holding onto his feet: 'I realised I had to get rid of him quick, or we'd both drown . . . I kicked hard and struggled free of him. Sticking to heavy army boots had paid off already.'

The lists of those ships and crews that were lost are a long litany. Many learnt the harsh lesson that any ship could be a minesweeper once. In the early hours of a cold December night in 1941, the British dreadnought the *Neptune* was sunk by mines off the coast of Libya. All 836 men were lost, thirty-five of whom were from Wales. Like the loss of the *Lancastria*, the news was suppressed for over fifty years.[106] In October 1940, the Cardiff tramp *Ruperra* was torpedoed by the German U-boat U-46. Captain D. T. Davies, twenty-nine crew members and a naval gunner were lost with her. Carrying steel scrap and aircraft, she sank quickly. Only seven men were saved by the merchantman *Induna*, which gallantly stopped amidst the mayhem. Captain J. M. R. Davies's *Baron Blythwood* sank even more swiftly, going down in only thirty-three seconds. Consult the lists of those drowned and you find a legion of captains, first mates and chief officers named Ellis, Jones, Griffiths, Davies or Williams who were lost in horrific circumstances. Captain H. Griffiths's ship, the *King Gruffydd*, sank with equal speed and heavier loss of life. In addition to iron ore and 500 tons of tobacco, she carried 493 tons of high explosives, a fact which accounts for the sheer panic amongst the hands as they tried to escape. Some were remarkably fortunate, Trevor Davies of Cardiff survived three sinkings. If some sailors had an albatross around their necks, Trevor Davies must have had a flock. Many Wrens, such as the radio mechanic Beryl Jones of west Wales, also survived shipwrecks and the horrors of the open sea.[107]

Those who survived the torpedoes and the ship's sinking often took to open long boats where they endured horrific privations. When Captain W. E. Williams's *Upwey Grange* was sunk, three groups took to the lifeboats. After three days, one of the boats reached the coast of Ireland, the sailors aboard having suffered greatly. The German auxiliary cruiser *Widder* sank the Newport ship the *Anglo-Saxon* 810 miles west of the Canary Islands on the night of 21 August 1940, then machine-gunned most of the survivors in the water. Chief Officer C. B. Denny and six men managed to get into a 'jolly boat'.[108] A badly wounded man, L. H. Pilcher, who apologised for the stench of his gangrenous foot, died on 27 August. F. G. Penny, also wounded, later quietly slipped into the sea. Denny and the third engineer committed suicide by stepping over the side. They held each other as they sank beneath the waves. They had given their vests and shirts to the survivors, but kept their trousers on 'for fear of mermaids'. A day later, another Newport man, an assistant chef named Morgan, declared that he was 'going down the road for a drink' and stepped over the side.[109]

The two remaining sailors, Robert Tapscott and Roy Widdicombe, together contemplated suicide several times. They survived by drinking rainwater and eating floating seaweed and some crabs attached to it. On 27 October they glimpsed a glittering beach at Eleuthera in the Bahamas, after a passage of 2,275 miles. They had lost more than six stone in weight. When they landed, they were ragged skeletons of men 'with sunken eyes and erupted flesh'. They were sent back to Wales by different routes. Roy Widdicombe was on the liner *Siamese Prince*, which was torpedoed off the coast of Scotland on 3 February 1941. There were no survivors. Tapscott came back to Cardiff, but he never recovered from his ordeal. He gave evidence in the post-war trial of the *Widder's* captain for war crimes. He died in the gas-filled sitting room of a house in Grangetown in September 1963.[110] Many other sailors failed to survive in the vulnerable lifeboats or the ironically named 'jolly-boats'. In 1942, a Welsh ship discovered one such vessel, whose crew of eight were bleached corpses, held together only by their life-jackets and a cord that seemed to hold them in a grisly embrace. The collective noun was problematic. Was this a school of skeletons? A corpse? A body?

The importance of the Royal Navy and its merchant equivalent cannot be underestimated: not only did it play a vital role at Dunkirk and on D-Day in the blockade of Germany, but its victory in the Battle of the Atlantic kept open the crucial supply lines between Britain and North America. Given Wales's seafaring tradition it is no surprise that many Welsh people made a significant contribution to the naval war.[111] The novelist Charles Langbridge Morgan 'Meander' (1894–1958) served in the navy in both world wars. Algernon Walker-Heneage-Vivian (1871–1952), a descendant of the Swansea copper magnates, also served in both wars. By the second conflict he looked what he was, an ancient mariner who had already given of his best. Philip Esmonde Phillips (1888–1960) was another called back into service in 1939 after retirement, serving in Milford Haven and then Trinidad as a vice admiral. Most notable of all, perhaps, was John Tubby Linton of Newport. He took command of the *Turbulent* in late 1941 and by 1943 he and his crew had sunk thirty-one enemy ships. They survived 250 depth charges until fate, inevitably, intruded and the ship was lost in the Tyrrhenian Sea. His ever-changing nicknames chronicled his journey of destruction: 'Seven Ships Linton' (for the seven ships he sank in March 1941), or 'Linton the Train Wrecker' (for his role in attacking the trains and railway line on the Italian Calabrian coast).

'Their finest hour': the war in the air

Rhyfel nid erbyd heddiw mo'r diamddiffyn dlawd;
o'r awyr bell daw'r difrod dirybydd yn hyrddiau
o ddur a thân mwy deifiol na ffrewyll Duw dialedd.

(Today war does not spare the defenceless poor;
from the skies without any warning come storms
of iron and fire more fierce and hellish than a vengeful God's).

Alun Llywelyn-Williams, 'Ar Ymweliad', in Thomas Parry (ed.), *The Oxford Book of Welsh Verse* (Oxford, 1998), p. 519

The potential power of aerial warfare, shown in the First World War, was taken to a new dimension during the Second. As Alun Llywelyn-Williams noted in his poem 'Ar Ymweliad', death and destruction could descend without warning from a clear sky. The morality of war, often the justification for retaliation for the enemy's misdeeds, is complex. The one area in which Britain seemed to have crossed into moral turpitude was the aerial bombing of German cities. One who seriously pondered the morality of such action was Sydney Osborne Bufton (1908–93), an air force officer and businessman of Llandrindod Wells.[112] Having served in the flying corps in Egypt and Iraq before the war, he was evacuated from Nantes just as the Panzers rolled in on 17 June 1940. From 1943 he became director of bomber operations at the Air Ministry. Here Churchill's 'little Air Commander' initiated a series of improvements – the provision of emergency airfields, radar navigation and target-finding aids, and the establishment of a Pathfinder force. In 1944 Bufton advocated attacks on precision targets such as oil supplies and the ball-bearing industry rather than area bombing of German cities. Bufton's more sensitive and strategic approach led to several disputes with the commander-in-chief, Sir Arthur 'Bomber' Harris, the author of the policy of indiscriminately bombing German cities.[113]

Despite its glamorous portrayal by Hollywood, aerial warfare was often mundane, boring and monotonous. In a series of letters to his family, published as *Letters from Iraq (1942–1945)*, Glyn Anthony, of the mining village of Tumble, revealed that an aviator's life consisted of a constant battle against boredom and drudgery. 'Life is pretty monotonous, work from early morning till one o'clock, a stinky, sweaty, inactive afternoon, a boring evening and then to bed', he wrote on 3 June 1943.[114] Closer to the traditional mythology attached to the RAF were the experiences of Roald Dahl, a Spitfighter pilot for most of the war. His one constant companion was fear. Dahl recalled that 'fear whispered at you at odd moments during the day'.[115] The experiences of Sir Frederick Ernest Rosier (1915–98) of Wrexham are also closer to the Homeric face of war. Rosier was the first to fly a plane from an aircraft carrier, the HMS *Furious,* reaching Malta to lead the island's aerial defence. In 1944, he became group captain operations at 84 Group. Comprising twenty-nine squadrons, mainly Spitfires, Typhoons and Mustangs, the group was associated with the First Canadian Army during the 1944–5 campaigns. Modest, kindly and humorous, Rosier was one of the 'RAF's greatest fighter men'.[116] One who was even more successful in terms of fighting was Wing Commander Douglas Alfred Oxby, DSO, DFC, DFM and Bar, of Canton, Cardiff. Between 1942 and 1945, Oxby fought in most of the significant aerial battles of the war, achieving the highest number of enemy 'kills' of any British pilot.[117] Equally brave, but less fortunate was Lewis Reginald Isaac of Llanelli. He was killed on his first mission as part of the Battle of Britain on 5 August 1940.[118]

The special range of skills required in the airforce, coupled, perhaps, with the romance of the uniform and the open sky, drew people of academic and cultured backgrounds. William Lionel Desmond Ravenhill (1919–95) of Carmarthen, the geographer and historian of cartography, served in the RAF in Malta, Italy, Yugoslavia and Egypt.[119] Despite never speaking a word of English until he was seven years old, Sir Huw Pyrs Wheldon (1916–86), the television broadcaster, joined the airborne forces of the Royal Welsh Fusiliers.[120] John Casson (1909–99), the theatre producer and later a management consultant, trained as a fighter pilot in the 1930s, taking part in operations against Chinese pirates. In 1940 he was shot down in Norway and then spent five years as a prisoner of war. In two prison camps, Dulag Luft and Stalag Luft III, he worked as a clandestine code master, passing messages in cipher via the prisoners' mail to MI9 in London, the department of military intelligence dealing with prisoners of war, escapees and evaders. In the latter camp he helped to mount what became known as the 'Great Escape', after which fifty of those recaptured were shot on Hitler's orders. He produced plays in the camp's theatre and studied German, Russian and philosophy.[121] The actor and documentary film-maker Kenneth Griffith of Tenby was eventually, after several attempts, accepted into the RAF in 1941. His superiors' reluctance to admit him were understandable, for Griffith carried a copy of Hitler's *Mein Kampf* with him throughout the war, because he 'wanted to understand fully what the war was about', an early illustration of his indifference to other people's possible view of him.[122]

Hell on earth: prisoners of war

> All that could be heard now was the weary steps we took, the jangle of the tins, the laboured breathing and occasionally a half-suppressed groan. Men were now suffering in silence, each with their own particular aches and pains. Each with their own thoughts and each so terribly exhausted. I only knew that my whole body seemed to be on fire. My head, like a drum, seemed to be rolling about uncontrollably. My eyes seemed raw and were kept open with the utmost difficulty. My shoulders were skinned raw from the chafing shoulder straps of my pack, which was worsened by the loss of flesh. Each day brought an increase in the protrusion of my bones, the gnawing pain in my stomach, my knees ready to give way at every step and my feet like lumps of raw beef.
>
> Idris 'Taffy' Barwick on his experiences of the forced march out of Changi, quoted in Brian MacArthur, *Surviving the Sword: Prisoners of the Japanese 1942–45* (London, 2005), p. 117

It is the historian's task to go back, sympathetically, into the minds of former generations, but there are areas of their thought where we cannot penetrate except to record without comprehension, areas opaque to our understanding, where sympathy dies. One such area is the brutality, humiliation and inhumanity inflicted on prisoners of war by the Japanese. John Hutchin, a 20-year-old from Newport, was sent behind enemy lines to serve with the famous Chindits, a special forces unit, in the Burmese jungle. He recalled, 'our casualties were so heavy that they dropped us lime because the stench was too bad. A full battalion is 1,001 men. Only 80 of us marched out.'[123] Gwyn Martin of Aberystwyth, John Escott of Cardiff and many more worked in the construction of Burma's infamous 'Death Railway'.[124] Here 17,000 Allied prisoners of war died at the hands of the Japanese as a result of disease, deliberate starvation and torture. Food was meagre and monotonous; always rice; never enough. Occasionally, however the prisoners' 'animal hunger' was satiated with a mixed diet of 'lizards, iguanas, snails, frogs, dogs, even vultures'.[125] One prisoner remembered the treat for Christmas dinner 1941; 'three kittens, gently fried'. Beds were sticks of bamboo, bedding non existent. Any slight infringement of the rules bought ruthless punishment, including periods of two to four weeks in the 'Ice Box', a wooden cubicle five feet high and two feet six inches square, in which it was impossible to lie down. Idris 'Taffy' Barwick recalled that some 'practically walked to the cremation pyre. They stopped eating, laid down and refused to live.' Death was an escape.[126]

Some men forgave their tormentors, but others found it harder to accept the inhumanity and the brutalities inflicted on them. Wilf Wooller (1912–97), one of the greatest ever Welsh all-round sporting talents, was a prisoner of the Japanese from 1942 to 1945. On his way to the Changi camps he 'saw the severed heads of uncooperative Chinese and Malay civilians' and street corner gallows. Wooller realised that 'the nightmare has only just begun'. In an interview on the publication of his biography in 1995, he revealed that the mental wounds were still raw and unhealed. 'The Japanese', he said, 'will never be my friends.'[127] Jack Edwards of Penarth, a tough and hot-headed sergeant major, was horrified at the treatment given to his fellow soldiers by the guards, who had quickly earned themselves the nicknames 'the Beast' and 'the Madman'. Jack's two autobiographies reveal that the years had not softened his resentment; uncompromisingly, they are entitled simply *Banzai you Bastards* and *Drop Dead Jap Bastards*.[128]

The Germans also acquired an unenviable reputation for the brutal way they treated prisoners of war. Eddie Gurmin of Tredegar, spent the winter of 1941–2, the coldest on record, in Stalag III E. In April 1942, fifty-two men escaped from a tunnel under his bed. He was then transferred to Stalag Luft III, the camp made famous by the film *The Great Escape* and then to Stalag 357. Not involved in the escape, Gurmin recalled that 'to keep ourselves entertained, we built a theatre and we would hold shows and concerts. We men held an Eisteddfod to show people what it was like.' One would have thought that they had received enough punishment.[129] More closely involved in the Great Escape was Flight Lieutenant Ken Rees of Anglesey.[130] Rees, the last man to enter the tunnel, was recaptured when German soldiers discovered the plot on 24 March 1944. He was then returned to the camp near Sagan, and spent two weeks in solitary confinement. Guy Griffiths (1915–99) of Pembroke Dock was also confined in Stalag Luft III, having been shot down after only eleven days of warfare. A forger and printer of official documents, his exploits in supplying intelligence to the British intelligence service MI9 were remarkable.[131] The previous year, 1943, had been a notable one for great escapes. One of the most famous, audacious and completely successful escapes was made from Stalag-Luft III's East Compound. Three men hidden in a vaulting horse near the camp's perimeter fence dug a tunnel, whilst their fellow prisoners vaulted over the horse. Then on 29 October the three quietly slipped away and made their way to Sweden. Eric Williams later wrote an account of the venture, *The Wooden Horse*.[132]

The camps were the centres not only for suffering and sorrow but also for entertainment and enlightenment.[133] Variety shows with not-too-subtle hints at the officers were frequent, and concerts and parties were common in virtually every camp in the Far East and in Europe. There was also an almost insatiable search for knowledge. Those men who had expertise in particular areas taught and trained others. At Laurens van der Post's Java camp, the programme of drama, music, arts and crafts and literature were organised 'by a remarkable scholar of French, a sensitive Welshman of great quality and imagination called Gunner Rees, MA[134] . . . For the men imprisonment was transformed from an arid waste of time and life into one of the most meaningful experiences they had ever known.' Some men were even prepared for Bachelor and Master of Arts degrees. Religious leaders were often inspirational figures in the camps. Padre Alfred Webb, a Presbyterian Welshman, created a pulpit from which he bravely condemned the Japanese as 'the incarnation of evil'. Aware that the men had no paper for cigarettes, he allowed them to use pages from his Bible, but only if they read them first. 'Thus as they chain-smoked their way through the Bible men got to know sections they had never read before – Micah, Nahum, Habakkuk, Zephaniah'.[135]

In Europe, similar cultural activities were organised within camps. In Stalag IV B near Mühlberg in Germany, between July 1943 and December 1944, William John Pitt of Treharris (1920–88) edited a Welsh newspaper entitled the *Cymro*.[136] Under the banner title, 'Cymru am byth', the newspaper discussed issues of importance to the prisoners, such as the camp's rugby and football matches, as well as articles on 'Welsh Culture in South Africa'. There was also a regular Welsh-language page and a poet's corner. The authors were part of the camp's Cymric Club. The articles of special interest to the Welsh, on topics such as Emlyn Williams and Stanley Baker, the boxer Charlie Bundy, and Welsh legends of Gelert and Arthur, were signal attempts to maintain a national identity in the harshest environment. The Christmas issue of 1943 added a heavy irony with a special feature, 'Around the shops', advising fellow prisoners on the best place to buy presents. The Second World War had the capacity to foster both a stronger feeling of British identity and an intensification of one's Welshness. Prisoners of war in Thailand held a weekly meeting of the Welsh society:

> In the heart of Thailand jungle there rose the voices of the choir of dying men, the old songs of Wales. Slowly they sang them, 'Land of My Fathers' and the hymns Welsh miners sing. Men who would never again see the valleys and towns of Wales, men almost too exhausted to speak, took up the refrain. And some died singing.[137]

Not all camps were such centres of enlightenment.[138] Each had a 'King Rat', who lived by his wits, marshalling a team of thieves, racketeers, and black marketeers, mostly at the expense of their fellow prisoners, on the Darwinian principle of the survival of the most vulgar. Most harmful of all, however, was the receipt of a perfumed letter from home, informing the unfortunate recipient that his sweetheart was no longer true. After the arrival of such a letter, one man, a friend recalled, 'crumpled psychologically, pined and died of a broken heart'. An even more poignant story is of the Welsh soldier who received a letter from his girlfriend telling him that she had decided to marry his father. She added insult to injury by signing the letter 'mother'.

All the experiences of Welsh prisoners of war reveal varying degrees of agonies, but few match the depths of human depravity witnessed by Charlie Evans of Presteigne.[139] A Royal Welsh Fusiliers soldier captured at Dunkirk, he was imprisoned in Auschwitz. When captured he was thirteen stone and fit. He returned as little more than a five stone, emaciated skeleton. Although wounded in his shoulder he was forced to work in a mine and was a regular witness to the overpowering stench of rotting and burning corpses. When the camp was liberated by the Red Army, he had to find his own way home and took part in a long march to freedom that proved to be another trial of endurance. Others also witnessed the atrocities. Ron Jones of Penarth played in goal for the Welsh football team that was established in Auschwitz in 1944.[140] Aware of the horrors being perpetrated in the camp, he also recalled the stench of burning flesh and his fear that he and his colleagues would be sent to the gas chambers. In 1945, as the Russians swarmed into Germany, Ron Jones and his fellow prisoners were force marched through the Carpathian Mountains to Regensburg in Austria. Only 250 or so out of several thousand survived the death march.

The Revd Leslie Hardman of Glynneath, was a Jewish chaplain with the British army at the liberation of Bergen-Belsen in April 1945.[141] The son of Polish and Russian immigrants, his birth had come less than two years after a series of attacks on Jews in south Wales. So ferocious were the attacks that many Orthodox Jewish families were driven out of the valleys in which they had settled as refugees from Tsarist persecution. Hardman recalled entering the camp: 'at Belsen towards me came the remnants of a holocaust – a staggering mass of blackened skin and bones – the dead walked'. The horrors of Belsen, the only death-camp liberated by British forces, were also witnessed by the politician and writer Lord Elwyn-Jones and the broadcaster Wynford Vaughan Thomas. The senior medical officer, Brigadier Hugh Llewellyn Glyn Hughes was given the unenviable task of cleaning the camp. In all more than 30,000 bodies were moved. Glyn Hughes also set up a hospital, named in his honour, to treat victims of typhus and the other diseases that ravaged the survivors. He told the Reuters news agency that he saw evidence of cannibalism in the camp. 'There were dead bodies with no flesh on them and the liver, kidneys and heart removed.'[142] His response, on occasion, was a scream that only Munch could have painted.

The end of the war in August 1945 brought the same mixture of elation and sorrow as had prevailed in 1918. But for some the war's end also brought surprise. In March 1942, the family of Gordon Meredith Evans of Llanddewi Brefi, Cardiganshire, was informed that he had been lost when the Japanese had sunk the HMS *Exeter* in the Sea of Java. To commemorate Evans a memorial service was held in Bethesda chapel. His grandmother refused to believe that he was dead. Every night she would 'crasu' (warm) his clothes in readiness for Gordon's return. Shortly after the war against Japan ended on 11 August 1945, the startling news arrived in the village that Gordon had spent over three years in a Japanese prisoner of war camp and was on his way home. Those who had penned epitaphs now prepared praise poems. Gordon returned to a world that appeared timeless but was in reality transformed.[143] Victory in Europe, VE Day, marked the end of the nightmare of war, and the beginning of a bad dream as an 'iron curtain' descended over Europe. Victory over Japan, VJ Day, following on from the dropping of the atomic bombs on Hiroshima and Nagasaki in August 1945, inaugurated a new dimension of horror. The Second World War ended threatening an even more obscene third, which not only renewed the concept of illimitable deaths, but also made cosmic destruction feasible. Belial's hand continued to guide modern history.[144]

L'Heure Bleue (The Blue Hour): a brief conclusion

L'Heure Blue is an indefinable period of transit from daylight, to twilight, to darkness, or from night, to dawn, to day, when the world is often suffused with a blue light. It is also the name of a famous perfume by Guerlain that is as evocatively melancholic as its name suggests. The Welsh author Jean Rhys, in her first novel *Quartet*, used the perfume as the bitter-sweet metaphor for the last weeks, days and hours of a doomed relationship. Rhys chronicled the cessation of intimacy, but she traced implicitly the death of old Europe as it slithered into the crucible of war. It is, perhaps, an appropriate title for a conclusion, for we too now move towards a new period of consideration and contemplation, towards, if we are fortunate, a dawn not a dusk.

This study has so far examined the social systems and structures which operated within Welsh society in the years 1870–1945. We have considered the demographic, economic and industrial forces which transformed Wales in those years. Attention has been paid to how people attempted to conquer space and time, how they fought in or fled from the fears of war, how some attempted to profit from empire. We have followed the Welsh on their journeys of adventure and escape, along their roads to perdition or paradise, despair or destiny.

We have already encountered a large number of people from all social levels and walks of life who have been dislodged from obscurity. We have been privileged to hear some of their voices, to discover their anxieties and ambitions, their worries and woes. In the related volume, *Sex, Sects and Society*, we shall attempt to escape further from the demographer's tables and the statistician's graphs and try to give an interpretation of the experiential meaning behind the bare bones of statistical and systematic description and generalisation. It is a tale of resilience and resistance, of a remarkable people and their complex and contradictory responses to their ever-changing world. We will consider their fears and their phobias, their beliefs, their concerns and their conundrums. We will encounter many, many individuals, each of whom has something interesting to say on the condition of the nation. In an age of profound transformation and transience, when many vestiges of the ancient world were finally cast aside, individuals surrounded themselves with a range of defence mechanisms. Law and punishment, piety and religion, morality and prudery, medicine and education are amongst those which are most frequently studied. But one of the most powerful defensive mechanisms was humour. The historian can learn a lot from the court jester of old. Above all, one of the jester's greatest gifts or follies was to blurt out bravely some truths which readers might not wish to hear. It is to be hoped that the portrait of Wales which emerges, warts and all, is significantly different from the traditional.

The material studied in *Sex, Sects and Society* includes the following:

Introduction

'Secret Sins': love and lust in Wales
Laughter in the dark: humour

1 Where, when, what was Wales and who were the Welsh?: Contentment, disappointment and embarrassment

'Gwlad, Gwlad: Wales! Wales!'
'Yr hen ffordd Gymreig o fyw' – rural idylls
Prometheus unbound – urban and industrial Wales
The valley, the city, the village – different viewpoints, differing perspectives
Weird Wales – alternative identities
'Cry the beloved country' – national character and identity

Notes

Introduction: Private Lives, the Individual and Society

1 For Sarah Jacob, see John Cule, *Wreath on the Crown: the Story of Sarah Jacob* (Llandysul, 1976); R. Fowler, *A Complete History of the Welsh Fasting Girl* (London, 1871) and *The Welsh Fasting Girl* (Carmarthen, 1907); J. G. Wilkinson, *The Case of the Welsh Fasting Girl* (London, 1870); S. Busby, *A Wonderful Little Girl: the Story of Sarah Jacob, the Welsh Fasting Girl* (London, 2003); H. Roberts, *Y Ferch Ryfeddol, neu Hanes Sarah Jacob Llethr-neuadd* (Carmarthen, 1869); James Burns, *The Cases of the Welsh Fasting Girl and her Father: on the Possibility of Long Continued Abstinence from Food* (undated report, University of London). One eye-witness reported that 'her complexion was clear; her cheeks ruddy. Her countenance was very sweet. Her head was encircled with a garland of many colours, and a narrow streamer of yellow ribbons flowed down each side of her face', *British Medical Journal*, 9 December 1869; a picture of the idealised, idolised child appears in the *Illustrated Police News*, 1 January 1870. I am grateful to Richard Ireland for these two references.

2 *The Welshman*, 19 February 1869. Richard W. Ireland, 'Sanctity, superstition and the death of Sarah Jacob', in A. Messon and C. Stebbings (eds), *Making Legal History: Approaches and Methodologies* (Cambridge, 2012), pp. 284–302. On the Revd Evan Jones, see David R. Gorman, 'From Teifi to Nevern: the Life and Times of Reverend Evan Jones', *Ceredigion*, XV11/1 (2013), 68–102.

3 Marina Warner, *Phantasmagoria: Spirit Visions, Metaphors and Media into the Twenty-first Century* (Oxford, 2006) p. 67; Joan Jacobs Brumberg, *Fasting Girls: the Emergence of Anorexia Nervosa as a Modern Disease* (Cambridge, 1988), pp. 64–73.

4 These events are part of the remarkable story of Joseph Leycester Lyne (1837–1908), the Church of England monk and preacher who established

a monastery at Capel-y-ffin in the Black Mountains and built Llanthony Abbey. His eccentric, esoteric High Church, Judaic mysticism created an atmosphere ideally suited for miracles and marvels. See A. Calder-Marshall, *The Enthusiast* (London, 1962); R. Kollar, 'Dr Pusey and Fr Ignatius of Llanthony', *Journal of Welsh Religious History*, 2 (1985); 27–40; and B. Palmer, *Reverend Rebels; Five Victorian Clerics and their Fight against Authority* (London, 1993). Despite the fervent hopes of many local people, especially hoteliers, the remarkable visions witnessed at Llanthony never attracted the hoards of visitors who descended on Lourdes. Appropriately for a person so besotted and obsessed with High Church and Catholic ceremonialism, a lock of Father Ignatius's hair is preserved in the Abergavenny museum. Ironically, Ignatius's settlement at Capel-y-ffin became notorious in the 1920s and 1930s as the centre for the group of eccentrics and eroticists who gathered around the sculptor Eric Gill.

5 In the 1970s, when he was editing the diaries of the redoubtable Thomas Jenkins of Llandeilo (1826–70), D. C. Jenkins recalled conversations in his youth with an elderly aunt about the influence of her remarkable father, who had been born in 1774. His immediate family, Jenkins boasted, was 'older than the USA'. Three lives linked three centuries.

6 One of his best short stories on women's position in society is 'The Dress', in Rhys Davies, *Collected Stories* (Cardiff, 1998).

7 Rush Rhees was the great-great-grandson of Morgan John Rhys, a Baptist minister and radical pamphleteer who emigrated to America in 1794 in search of ideological freedom. Rhees, disenchanted with the religious fundamentalism and conservatism of America, reversed the journey in 1924. See the biographical sketch by D. Z. Phillips in Rush Rhees, *On Religion and Philosophy*, ed. D. Z. Phillips and M. von der Ruhr (London, 1997).

8 Carmarthen Record Office, Felons Register, Acc. 4,916, case no 1357. The case is also reported in the *Carmarthen Journal* (15 July 1870) but there is no additional detail.

9 Gwyn A. Williams, *Delegate for Africa: David Ivon Jones 1883–1924* (London, 1995).

10 W. S. Chalmers, *Max Horton and the Western Approaches* (London, 1954) and *The Battle of the Atlantic: the Official Account of the Fight against the U-boats 1939–1945* (London, 1946).

11 Alan Owen, 'Letters from the War: Part 8', *Carmarthenshire Life*, 124 (2008). The brothers reached the conclusion that their presence in Russia was not needed: 'They do not need us here. They're killing each other well enough without us.' See also R. Jackson, *At War with the Bolsheviks: the Allied Interventions into Russia 1917–1920* (London, 1946).

12 Robert Stradling, *Wales and the Spanish Civil War* (Cardiff, 2004), pp. 46, 111–13, 143.

13 On Mary Kelly, see Phillip Sugden, *The Complete History of Jack the Ripper* (London, 2000). As if more suspects were needed, the relationship between Mary Kelly and Sir John Williams, eminent surgeon and royal gynaecologist, has given rise to two theories as to the identity of Jack the Ripper. The first interpretation is that Sir John was the killer; see Tony Williams and Humphrey Price, *Uncle Jack: the True Identity of Jack the Ripper* (London, 2005). This view was further pressed when a locket containing a photograph of Sir John was found by one of Mary Kelly's descendants; see Antonia Alexander, *The Fifth Victim* (London, 2013). The second interpretation is that the murders were not the work of Sir John Williams, but undertaken by his wife Lizzie; see John Morris, *Jack the Ripper: the Hand of a Woman* (Bridgend, 2012).

14 Ludovic Kennedy, *10 Rillington Place* (London, 1971) and F. Tennyson Jesse (ed.), *Trials of Timothy Evans and John Reginal Halliday Christie*. There is also a famous film, *10 Rillington Place*, in which Richard Attenborough plays the part of the sinister John Christie and John Hurt the inept and innocent Timothy Evans.

15 The execution of Ruth Ellis caused such a sensation that hers became a real cause célèbre of the 1950s which eventually hastened the abolition of the death penalty. See R. Hancock, *Ruth Ellis: the Last Woman to be Hanged* (London, 1983). Her daughter, Georgie Ellis, has left a poignant memoir, *Ruth Ellis: My Mother* (London, 1996).

16 On people's lack of awareness of what was about to happen to them, see Claudio Magrio, *Danube* (London, 1990), pp. 40–1.

17 Several of Lloyd George's speeches are available in the Welsh Film and Screen Archive. Watch some and you will probably get the feeling that he is not speaking to his listeners – he was actually speaking to us, to posterity. On the attempts of Lloyd George and Churchill to control the future, see David Reynolds, *In Command of History* (London, 2005), pp. 24, 51, 214, 496, 497. Published between 1933 and 1938, Lloyd George's six volumes on the war and the two on the peace appear to be the work of an 'old man in a hurry'. But the volumes had been originally commissioned by the Merthyr Tydfil-born newspaper magnate William Berry (later Lord Camrose) for £90,000 in 1919. Their publication was delayed due to the rumpus in the early 1920s over Lloyd George's sale of honours and his general profiteering.

18 For a discussion of the history of emotions, see Peter N. Stearns and Jan Lewis (eds), *An Emotional History of the United States* (New York, NY, 1998); Stuart Walton, *Humanity: an Emotional History* (London,

2004); and Cas Wouters, 'Etiquette Books and Emotions Management', *Journal of Social History*, 29 (1995), 107–24, 325–40.

19 Peter N. Stearns, 'Girls, Boys and Emotions: Redefinitions and Historical Change', *Journal of American History* (June 1993), 36–74.

20 Paul Hyams, 'What did Henry III of England think in bed and in French about kingship and anger', in Barbara H. Rosenwein (ed.), *Anger's Past: the Social Uses of an Emotion in the Middle Ages* (New York, 1998).

21 For emotions and the First World War, see Joanna Bourke, *Dismembering the Male: Men's Bodies, Britain and the Great War* (Chicago, IL, 1996).

22 Barbara H. Rosenwein, 'Worrying about Emotions in History', *American Historical Review*, 107/3 (June 2002), 1–27; Rom Harré (ed.), *The Social Construction of Emotions* (Oxford, 1986).

23 Edward Shorter, *The Making of the Modern Family* (London, 1977) makes such claims. For a more balanced study, see Julie Marie Strange, *Death, Grief and Mourning in Britain, 1870–1914* (Cambridge, 2005).

24 On these themes see Russell Davies, *Hope and Heartbreak: a Social History of Wales and the Welsh, 1776–1871* (Cardiff, 2005). On Eiluned Lewis, see Katie Gramich, 'Introduction' to *The Captain's Wife* (Dinas Powys, 2008).

25 Deirdre Beddoe, *Out of the Shadows: a History of Women in Twentieth-century Wales* (Cardiff, 2000), pp. 4–5.

26 Alan Burge, 'The Co-operative Movement in South Wales and its History: a Task Worthy of the most Sincere Devotion and Application', *Welsh History Review*, 23/4 (2007), 67.

27 On Winifred Wagner, see Brigitte Hamann, *Winifred Wagner: a Life at the Heart of Hitler's Bayreuth* (London, 2005) and on William Ewart Berry, see Lord Hartwell, *William Camrose: Giant of Fleet Street* (London, 1992). On the tendency to continue the hero worship of the left, see Raphael Samuel, *The Lost World of British Communism* (London, 2006); Kevin Morgan et al., *Communists and British Society 1920–91* (London, 2006) and *Bolshevism and the British Life: Part 1, Labour, Legends and Russian Gold* (London, 2006). In 1933, the horrors of Stalin's agricultural policies which led to the mass starvation of millions – the Holodomor in the Ukraine – were bravely exposed by Gareth Jones in a series of high-profile newspaper articles. See Margaret Siriol Colley, *Gareth Jones: a Manchukuo Incident* (Newark, 2002) and *www.garethjones.org/overview/contents.htm* (last viewed 21 April 2009). As late as 1952 the Welsh branch of the National Union of Mineworkers sent a delegation to Moscow in the name of 'international socialism and solidarity'. On the general hero worship of the left, see Robert Conquest, *The Dragons*

of Expectation: Reality and Delusion in the Course of History (London, 2007) and Margaret Macmillan, *The Uses and Abuses of History* (London, 2009).

28 Patrick Hannan, *The Welsh Illusion* (Bridgend, 2004), p. 41.

29 On Howell Arthur Gwynne, see *www.oxforddnb.com* (last accessed 21 July 2011).

30 The flu killed more than 9,000 people in Wales in about four months. An estimated 20,000 Welsh people died over four years of war. On the 1918 flu epidemic, see Richard Collier, *The Plague of the Spanish Lady* (London, 1974); Gina Kolta, *Flu: The Story of the Great Influenza Pandemic of 1918 and the Search for the Virus that Caused it* (London, 2001); David Killingray and Howard Phillip, *The Spanish Flu Pandemic of 1918–19: New Perspectives* (London, 2001); Mark Honigsbaum, *Living with Enza: the Forgotten Story of Britain and the Great Flu Pandemic of 1918* (London, 2008). The statistics are drawn from the tables in *Supplement to the 81st Annual Report of the Registrar General. Report on Mortality from Influenza in England and Wales during the Epidemic 1918–19.* A useful discussion on which and why certain topics receive historical attention is given in Piers Brendon, *The Decline and Fall of the British Empire, 1781–1987* (London, 2007) and *The Dark Valley: a Panorama of the 1930s* (London, 2001).

31 J. D. Fuge and R. Oliver, *The Cambridge History of Africa* (Cambridge, 1974–86) p. 101; K. Ballhatchet, *Race, Sex and Class under the Raj* (London, 1980); P. D. Curtis, *Disease and Empire* (Cambridge, 1991).

32 For the song's composition, see Gwyn Griffiths, *Gwlad fy Nhadau: Ieuan, Iago, eu Hoes a'u Hamserau* (Cardiff, 2006).

33 For the artistic tradition of Wales and a discussion of each of these painters and paintings, see Peter Lord, *Imaging the Nation* (Cardiff, 2000).

34 Sue Roe, *Gwen John: A Life* (London, 2002), p. 210.

35 Virginia Nicholson, *Singled Out: How Two Million Women Survived Without Men after the First World War* (London, 2007), pp. 1–3, 28, 44, 101.

36 Gwyn A. Williams, *When was Wales?: a History of the Welsh* (London, 1985), pp. 261–4; Beddoe, *Out of the Shadows*, p. 92 has a photograph of Ceridwen Brown and her fellow marchers.

37 Gareth Miles has mischievously made a number of insinuations about the nature of the relationships between Evan Roberts and his lady followers in his highly entertaining novel *Y Proffwyd a'r Ddwy Jezebel* (Talybont, 2007).

38 The Institute of Historical Research's exhibition on lone mothers, 'Sinners, Scroungers and Saints' (27 October 2007–29 March 2008),

offered many perceptive insights into the complexities of the conceptualisation of women.

1 The Structures of Everyday Life

1 The historian of modern Wales is deeply indebted to the late Professor L. J. Williams who diligently and dedicatedly collected a treasury of statistics on all aspects of Welsh life. These are published in L. J. Williams, *Digest of Welsh Historical Statistics*, 1 (Cardiff, 1985). Pages 1–88 contain information on the Welsh population.

2 Williams, *Digest of Welsh Historical Statistics*, 1, p. 12.

3 Williams, *Digest of Welsh Historical Statistics*, 1, p. 24.

4 Williams, *Digest of Welsh Historical Statistics*, 1, p. 17.

5 For Aberystwyth, see W. J. Lewis, *Born on a Perilous Rock* (Aberystwyth, 1980) and Ieuan Gwynedd Jones (ed.), *Aberystwyth 1277–1977* (Llandysul, 1977).

6 Williams, *Digest of Welsh Historical Statistics*, 1, pp. 43–4.

7 Williams, *Digest of Welsh Historical Statistics*, 1, pp. 43–4.

8 Williams, *Digest of Welsh Historical Statistics*, 1, pp. 43–4.

9 Williams, *Digest of Welsh Historical Statistics*, 1, pp. 25–6. See also D. J. Davies, 'The condition of the agricultural population of England and Wales 1870–1928 in relation to . . . migration . . . age and sex selection (unpublished PhD thesis, University of Wales, Aberystwyth, 1931).

10 Williams, *Digest of Welsh Historical Statistics*, 1.

11 Williams, *Digest of Welsh Historical Statistics*, 1, pp. 26–40. See also M. Anderson, 'The Social Position of Spinsters in mid-Victorian Britain', *Journal of Family History*, 9 (1984) and 'Marriage Patterns in Victorian Britain: an Analysis Based on Registration District Data for England and Wales', *Journal of Family History* (1976); S .K. Kent, *Making Peace: The Reconstruction of Gender in Interwar Britain* (Princeton, 1993).

12 R. Woods, *The Demography of Victorian England and* Wales (Cambridge, 2000). See also M. J. Daunton, *Wealth and Welfare: an Economic and Social History of Britain, 1851–1951* (Oxford, 2007), pp. 323–48.

13 See Williams, *When was Wales: a History of the Welsh* (London, 1985), pp. 220–52, and more especially Brinley Thomas, 'Wales and the Atlantic economy', in *The Welsh Economy: Studies in Expansion* (Cardiff, 1962), 114–29.

14 T. Rowland Hughes, 'Yr Hen Fyd' in *Cân neu ddwy* (Denbigh, 1948), p. 33.

15 Williams, *Digest of Welsh Historical Statistics*, 1, p. 76.

16 W. O. Thomas, *Dwywaith o amgylch y Byd: Hanes Teithiau yn Ewrop, Asia, Affrica, America ac Australasia* (Utica, 1882).

17 The University of Wales Centre for Advanced Welsh and Celtic Studies has completed a magisterial and mammoth study of the Welsh language. See in particular Gwenfair Parry and Mari A. Williams, *Miliwn o Gymry Cymraeg! Yr iaith Gymraeg a Chyfrifiad 1891* (Cardiff, 1999) and Dot Jones, *Statistical Evidence relating to the Welsh Language 1801–1911* (Cardiff, 1998).

18 Williams, *Digest of Welsh Historical Statistics*, 1, p. 79.

19 Geraint H. Jenkins (ed.), *Iaith Carreg fy Aelwyd: Iaith a Chymuned yn y Bedwaredd Ganrif ar Bymtheg* (Cardiff, 1998), *passim*.

20 Williams, *Digest of Welsh Historical Statistics*, 1, pp. 217–40.

21 Rhys Davies, *Print of a Hare's Foot* (London, 1961), pp. 3–4.

22 Daunton, *Wealth and Welfare*, pp. 31–75; E. J. T. Collins, *The Agrarian History of England and Wales, VII, 1850–1914* (Cambridge, 2000).

23 John Davies, 'The End of the Great Estates and the Rise of Freehold Farming in Wales', *Welsh History Review*, 7/2 (1974), 186–212; *Royal Commission on Land in Wales and Monmouthshire, Report* (1896); David Howell, *Land and People in Nineteenth-Century Wales* (London, 1978). Financial tensions were especially tight in lower social groups. Kate Roberts, in her memoir *Y Lôn Wen* (Dinbych, 1960), recounted the sorry tale of a household whose inmates were forced to sell their only cow to pay the rent they owed to a Nonconformist minister.

24 See for example C. O'Grada, 'Agricultural decline, 1860–1914', in R. Floud and D. McClosky (eds), *The Economic History of Britain since 1700: 1860–1939*, 2 (Cambridge, 1981), pp. 117–39; Françoise de Rome, 'The Second Agricultural Revolution, 1815–80', *Economic History Review*, 21 (1968), 300–30; *Royal Commission on Agriculture 1897, Final Report* (C. 8540 (2nd series) 1898), p. 156.

25 David Howell, 'The Impact of the Railways on the Agricultural Development of Wales', *Welsh History Review*, 7 (1974–5), 40–62, and 'Rural Society in Nineteenth-century Carmarthenshire', *Carmarthenshire Antiquarian*, XIII (1977), 49; see also Nicholas Faith, *The World the Railways Made* (London, 1990).

26 David A. Pretty, 'Caethion y tir: gwrthryfel y gweithwyr fferm yng Nghymru', in Geraint H. Jenkins (ed.), *Cof Cenedl VII* (Llandysul, 1992), pp. 133–66, and *The Rural Revolt that Failed: Farm Workers' Trade Unions in Wales, 1889–1950* (Cardiff, 1989).

27 W. J. Rees, 'Inequalities: Caradoc Evans and D. J. Williams', *Planet*, 81 (1990), 69–80; Dafydd Jenkins, *D. J. Williams* (Cardiff, 1973).

28 For D. J. Williams's views of life and literature, see his *Yn Chwech ar Hugain Oed* (Llandysul, 1965).

29 John Harris has worked hard to reclaim Caradoc Evans's reputation; see his 'Preface' in *Fury Never Leaves Us: a Miscellany of Caradoc Evans*

(Bridgend, 1985). An equally, perhaps even more revealing study would be to compare the work of Caradoc Evans with those of one of his fellow pupils at Rhydlewis, Elizabeth Mary Jones, 'Moelona' (1877–1953). Her works, especially *Rhamant y Rhos* (Llandysul, 1918) and the long popular saga *Teulu Bach Nantoer* (Llandysul, 1913), give a gentler, more tender portrait of this remarkable rural community.

30 Rees, 'Inequalities: Caradoc Evans and D. J. Williams', 76.

31 David Jenkins *The Agricultural Community in South-west Wales at the Turn of the Twentieth century* (Cardiff, 1971).

32 *Royal Commission on Land in Wales and Monmouthshire, Evidence,* vols 1 and 2 (London, 1894), vols 3 and 4 (1895); *Report and Appendices,* vol. 5 (1896). The evidence given at Llansawel is in vol. 3, pp. 181–254; that given at Newcastle Emlyn in vol. 3, 440–515; J. W. Jasper, 'A study of changes in farm size that have taken place in Carmarthenshire since the end of the nineteenth century' (unpublished MSc thesis, University of Wales, Aberystwyth, 1959).

33 Harris, *Fury Never Leaves Us*, p. 13.

34 For an impression of the hardship of rural life, see W. A. Armstrong, *Farmworkers: a Social and Economic History, 1780–1980* (London, 1988); J. Hammond and B. Hammond, *The Village Labourer* (London, 1911) is dated but still valuable.

35 John Davies and G. E. Mingay, 'Agriculture in an industrial environment', in A. H. John and Glanmor Williams (eds), *Glamorgan County History, Vol. 5: Industrial Glamorgan 1700–1970* (Cardiff, 1980), pp. 277–310; Elfyn Scourfield, *Ceffylau Dur: Hen Beiriannau Amaethyddol* (Llanrwst, 1996), p. 24.

36 Daunton, *Wealth and Welfare*, p. 58.

37 A. Offer, *The First World War: An Agrarian Interpretation* (Oxford, 1989), pp. 355–67.

38 P. E. Dewey, *British Agriculture in the First World War* (London, 1989) and 'Agricultural Labour Supply in England and Wales during the First World War', *Economic History Review*, 28 (1975), 202–41.

39 On D. A. Thomas, see M. H. Thomas et al., *D. A. Thomas, Viscount Rhondda* (London, 1921).

40 R. S. Thomas, *Collected Poems, 1945–1990* (London, 1993); Richard J. Moore-Colyer, 'Back to the Land – Rural Wales between the Wars', *Planet*, 175 (2006), 73–81.

41 J. A. Venn, *The Foundations of Agricultural Economics* (London, 1933), p. 100, quoted in John Davies, 'The End of the Great Estates', 193.

42 Davies, 'The End of the Great Estates'.

43 Davies, 'The End of the Great Estates', 211. The poem reads:

Rhy ddrud, ddywedsoch, am bedwar cant
Tyddyn fy ngeni a chartref fy mhlant.
Nid prynu yr oeddwn 'rhen fur a'i do
Na'r tipyn daear o'i amgylch o.
Rhy ddrud, ddywedsoch, am bedwar cant
Tyddyn fy ngeni a chartref fy mhlant.

Four hundred, you say, is more than the worth
Of the home of my children, the farm of my birth.
It wasn't the roof and the walls I was buying
Or the piece of land around them lying.
Four hundred, you say, is more than the worth
Of the home of my children, the farm of my birth.

44 Richard J. Moore-Colyer, *Man's Proper Study: a History of Agricultural Science Education in Aberystwyth 1878–1978* (Llandysul, 1982).

45 A. W. Ashby and I. L. Evans, *The Agriculture of Wales and Monmouthshire* (Cardiff, 1944).

46 D. Gwenallt Jones, 'Rhydcymerau', in *Eples* (Llandysul, 1951), p. 21.

47 Ashby and Evans, *The Agriculture of Wales and Monmouthshire.*

48 Richard J. Moore-Colyer, 'The County War Agricultural Executive Committees: the Welsh Experience', *Welsh History Review*, 22/3 (2005), 558–87.

49 Thomas, *Collected Poems, 1945–1990*; Daunton, *Wealth and Welfare*, p. 67.

50 See, for example, Joel Mokyr, 'The second industrial revolution, 1870–1914', in *The Lever of Riches* (London, 1990). See also David Landes, *The Unbound Prometheus: Technical Change and Industrial Development in Western Europe from 1750 to the Present* (New York, NY, 2003).

51 Robert Protheroe-Jones, *Welsh Steel* (Cardiff, 1995).

52 Protheroe-Jones, *Welsh Steel.*

53 Quoted in J. Morris, 'Coal and steel', in A. J. Roderick, *Wales through the Ages*, vol. 2 (Llandybïe, 1960), p. 181.

54 William Troughton, *Industries of Wales* (Stroud, 1997), p. 80.

55 Williams, *When Was Wales?*, p. 151.

56 Troughton, *Industries of Wales.*

57 Daunton, *Wealth and Welfare.*

58 Robert K. Massie, *Dreadnought: Britain, Germany and the Coming of the Great War* (London, 1992), p. 210.

59 Pembroke Dock, however, never developed the expertise to build the larger monster ships of war. In the 1900s, when Admiral Fisher, obsessed with his ambition to create a New Model Navy, scrapped the gunboat concept, the yard at Pembroke Dock entered a period of decline and relied on the occasional commission to build light cruisers

and submarines. The last ship built there, the Royal Fleet Auxiliary oiler *Oleander*, was launched in 1922 and the yard closed in 1926.

60 Scourfield, *Ceffylau Dur, passim.*

61 D. Morgan Rees, *The Metalliferous Mines of Wales* (Cardiff, 1972). See also T. A. Morrison, 'Goldmining in western Merioneth', *Journal of the Merioneth Historical and Record Society* (1973, 1974), 140–87.

62 Jean Lindsay, *A History of the North Wales Slate Industry* (Newton Abbot, 1974).

63 R. Merfyn Jones, *The North Wales Quarrymen, 1874–1922* (Cardiff, 1981), pp. 210–66.

64 Ronald Rees, *King Copper: South Wales and the Copper Trade, 1584–1895* (Cardiff, 2000).

65 Glanmor Williams (ed.), *Swansea: an Illustrated History* (Swansea, 1990).

66 W. E. Minchinton, *The British Tinplate Industry* (Oxford, 1957).

67 In 1936 the town's official guide was grandiloquently entitled *Llanelly: Port, Industrial Centre, Tinopolis, and Scene of the National Eisteddfodau of 1895, 1903 and 1930 – Floreat Llanelly.*

68 For the effects of the tinplate depression on south-west Wales, see Russell Davies, *Secret Sins: Sex, Violence and Society in Carmarthenshire* (Cardiff, 1995), pp. 53–4.

69 For Newport, see James W. Dawson, *Commerce and Customs: a History of the Ports of Newport and Caerleon* (Newport, 1932).

70 M. J. Daunton, *Coal Metropolis: Cardiff 1870–1914* (Leicester, 1977).

71 There is an extensive literature on the ports of Wales; see, for example, Lewis Lloyd, *Real Little Seaport: the Port of Aberdyfi and its People, 1565–1920* (Harlech, 1996), *Whatever Freights May Offer: the Maritime Community of Abermaw/Barmouth, 1565–1920* (Caernarfon, 1993), *Pwllheli: the Port and Mart of Llŷn* (Llanfair, 1991) and *The Port of Caernarfon, 1793–1900* (Harlech, 1989); J. Geraint Jenkins, *Llangrannog – Etifeddiaeth Pentref Glan Môr* (Llangrannog, 1998), *Maritime Heritage: the Ships and Seamen of Southern Cardiganshire* (Llandysul, 1982) and *Traddodiad y Môr* (Llanrwst, 2004). See also Robin Craig, 'The Ports and Shipping, c.1750–1914', in A. H. John and Glanmor Williams (eds), *Glamorgan County History, Vol. 5*, 465–519. On shipbuilding, see J. Geraint Jenkins, *Evan Thomas Radcliffe: a Cardiff Shipowning Company* (Cardiff, 1982) and David Jeffrey Morgan, 'Boom and Slump – Shipworking at Cardiff 1919–1921', *Cymru a'r Môr: Maritime Wales*, 12 (1989), 126–51; David Jenkins, *Jenkins Brothers of Cardiff – A Ceredigion Family's Shipping Ventures* (Cardiff, 1985).

72 Quoted in David Jenkins, 'Llongau y Chwarelwyr: Investments by Caernarfonshire Slate Quarrymen in Local Shipping Companies in the late Nineteenth Century', *Welsh History Review*, 22/1 (2004), 80.

73 Jenkins, 'Llongau y Chwarelwyr', 80. The great chronicler of the Welsh seafaring tradition was Aled Eames. See, for example, his *Morwyr Môn* (Caernarfon, 1982) and *Ventures in Sail* (Caernarfon and Denbigh, 1987).

74 W. J. Reader, *Imperial Chemical Industries, a History: Vol. I, The Fore-runners, 1870–1926* (London, 1970) and *Vol. II, The First Quarter-Century, 1926–52* (London, 1975).

75 John and Williams (eds), *Glamorgan County History,* vol. 5.

76 Colin Baber, 'The subsidiary industries, 1760–1914', in John and Williams (eds), *Glamorgan County History,* vol. 5, pp. 211–76.

77 On the Swansea fisheries, see research carried out at the Univesity College of Wales, Aberystwyth by Lily Newton in 1943 (Aberystwyth University TD425.R.6) and J. Geraint Jenkins, *Nets and Coracles* (Newton Abbot, 1974).

78 Williams, *Digest of Welsh Historical Statistics,* 1, p. 34.

79 These arguments are eloquently presented in John Williams, *Was Wales Industrialised? Essays in Modern Welsh history* (Llandysul, 1995), especially pp. 14–36 and 37–57.

80 J. Geraint Jenkins, *The Welsh Woollen Industry* (Cardiff, 1969).

81 On the copper pollution, see Rees, *King Copper,* pp. 92–5.

82 For 'gwlad y pyramidau', see Aneurin Talfan Davies, *Crwydro Sir Gâr* (Llandybïe, 1970).

83 On mining in south-west Wales, see Rees, *The Black Mystery: Coal-mining in South-west Wales* (Talybont, 2008). See also, Ieuan Llwyd Griffiths, 'The anthracite coalfield of South Wales' (unpublished PhD thesis, London School of Economics, 1959) and Thomas Hughes Griffiths, 'The development of the south Wales anthracite coal area with special reference to industrial and labour organisation' (unpublished MA thesis, University of Wales, 1922).

84 J. H. Morris and L. J. Williams, *The South Wales Coal Industry* (Cardiff, 1958); M. W. Kirby, *The British Coalmining Industry* (London, 1977).

85 Quoted in Jan Morris, *The Matter of Wales: Epic Views of a Small Country* (London, 1984), p. 75.

86 On Barry, see Donald Moore (ed.), *Barry: the Centenary Book* (Barry, 1984).

87 On David Davies, see Ivor Thomas, *Top Sawyer: a Biography of David Davies Llandinam* (Carmarthen, 1988); H. Williams, *Davies the Ocean: Railway King and Coal Tycoon* (Cardiff, 1991).

88 T. Boyns, 'Growth in the coal industry: the cases of Powell Duffryn and the Ocean Coal Company, 1864–1913, in Colin Baber and L. J. Williams (eds), *Modern South Wales: Essays in Economic history* (Cardiff, 1986), pp. 153–70.

89 *Ocean Coal Company Annual Report* (Barry, 1915).

90 On John Cory, see *Western Mail*, 31 July 1875; see also Sarah Palmer, *Seeing the Sea: the Maritime Dimension in History* (London, 2000).

91 See David Egan, *Coal Society: a History of the South Wales Mining Valleys 1840–1980* (Llandysul, 1987), pp. 13–26.

92 Williams, *Digest of Welsh Historical Statistics*, 1, pp. 293–7.

93 Dai Smith, 'Tonypandy: Definitions of a Community', *Past and Present*, 87 (1980), 158–84.

94 Thereafter, in descending order, were the Blaenavon Iron and Steel Company (915,613 tons), the Powell Duffryn Coal Company (857,000 tons), the Dowlais Iron Company (800,000 tons), the Tredegar Coal and Iron Company (564,608 tons), David Davies and Company (500,000 tons), the Glamorgan Coal Company (500,000 tons), David Davies and Sons (485,000 tons), the Rhymni Iron Company (400,000 tons) and the Aberdare Iron Company (454,000 tons).

95 Ness Edwards, *History of the South Wales Miners' Federation* (Cardiff, 1938); E. W. Evans, *The Miners of South Wales* (Cardiff, 1961).

96 See, for example, the arguments presented by J. B. Elliott, 'The Development of Secondary Industry in the Ebbw Valley, 1850–1914: a Study of the Welsh Industrial Tragedy', *Welsh History Review*, 21/1 (2002), 48–74.

97 Williams, *Digest of Welsh Historical Statistics*, 1, p. 336.

98 Stanley Jevons, *The British Coal Trade* (London, 1915).

99 Optimism could give rise to arrogance, as in the editor's assertion in *Welsh Outlook* in April 1931: 'where there is civilization, there is Welsh coal'.

100 Daunton, *Coal Metropolis*, pp. 221, 230.

101 Williams, *Digest of Welsh Historical Statistics*, 1.

102 Hywel Francis and Dai Smith, *The Fed: a History of the South Wales Miners in the Twentieth Century* (London, 1980).

103 In the 1920s Guest, Keen and Nettleford Co. owned mining interests which included the Barry, Rhondda and Llewellyn groups of collieries. In 1930, it acquired David Davies and Sons (which owned, amongst others, the Welsh Navigation Co.) and the Consolidated Cambrian Ltd. Its great rival, Baldwin's Ltd, pursued a similar path until it joined with GKN in 1930 to form the Welsh Associated Collieries Co. A similar pattern was experienced in the anthracite coalfield as the increasingly predatory Richard Thomas and Co. took over smaller enterprises. Perhaps the ultimate combination came in 1935 when Powell Duffryn and the Welsh Associated Collieries Co. merged, creating Powell Duffryn Associated Collieries – one of the largest industrial undertakings

ever seen in Wales. Its portfolio was certainly impressive: it had a capacity of 25 million tons of coal and an actual output of 11.5 million tons per annum, employed 42,000 people, owned 33,000 railway coal wagons, controlled and owned coal-selling and distribution agencies (inland and export), plant for the recovery of by-products and gas manufacture, electrical power stations, steamships, wagon construction and repair works, houses and cottages, brickworks, pipeworks, machine and boiler works, plant for the manufacture of patent fuels, as well as interests in other coalfields.

104 Williams, *Digest of Welsh Historical Statistics*, 1.

2 *'Lead us into Temptation'*

1 On Kate Roberts, see Derec Llwyd Morgan, *Kate Roberts* (Cardiff, 1974).

2 Despite the consensus, the history of consumption, consumerism and the consumer revolution is controversial. As Paul Johnson noted, 'putting a date to the consumer revolution has become a competitive business'. Some date it to the seventeenth century, others, with equal plausibility, press the claims of the eighteenth, whilst some historians see it as a consequence of economic change in the late nineteenth. The claims of the decades between 1919 and 1939, even the austere 1940s, have been pressed by others. Like the causes, the consequences are also a source of controversy. Those on the political left lament that 'life based on the private ownership of commodities is individualised and isolated', resulting in the erosion of community life, the loss of class identification and political consciousness. Those on the right, argue that free markets enable individuals to engage in their most powerful act, that of exercising personal choice in the art and act of purchasing. P. Johnson, *Twentieth-century Britain: Economic, Social and Cultural Change* (London, 1994).

3 There is a valuable discussion of consumers and consumerism in Peter Miskell, *A Social History of the Cinema in Wales, 1918–1951: Pulpits, Coal Pits and Fleapits* (Cardiff, 2006), pp. 17–21.

4 The Ministry of Labour's *Report of an Enquiry into Household Expenditure in 1953–4* (London, HMSO, 1954).

5 On general wage rates in Wales, see William J. Hausman and Barry T. Hirsch, 'Wages, Leisure and Productivity in South Wales Coal Mining, 1874–1914: an Economic Approach', *Llafur*, 3 (1982), 58–66; L. J. Williams, *Digest of Welsh Historical Statistics* (Cardiff, 1985); see also M. Flinn, 'Trends in Real Wages', *Economic History Review*, 27

(1974), 399–404, and A. H. Hasley, *British Social Trends since 1900: a Guide to the Changing Social Structure of Britain* (London, 1988).

6 Quoted in B. Osgerby 'Well, It's Saturday Night an' I Just Got Paid': Youth, Consumerism and Hegemony in Post-War Britain', *Contemporary Record*, 6/2 (1992), 294.

7 L. Hannah, *Inventing Retirement: the Development of Occupational Pensions in Britain* (Cambridge, 1986).

8 Hannah, *Inventing Retirement.*

9 G. R. Searle, *A New England: Peace and War, 1886–1918* (Oxford, 2004), pp. 367–8.

10 Quoted in Russell Davies, *Secret Sins: Sex, Violence and Society in Carmarthenshire, 1870–1920* (Cardiff, 1995), p. 57.

11 See, for example, W. Hamish Fraser, *The Coming of the Mass Market, 1850–1914* (London, 1981), pp. ix–1.

12 P. Johnson, *Twentieth-century Britain*, p. 77.

13 The importance of the parlour was stressed by several witnesses in interviews with the staff of St Fagan's Welsh Folk Museum in the 1970s and the National Library's 'Age of Austerity' project in the 1990s and 2000s.

14 Russell Davies, *Hope and Heartbreak: a Social History of Wales and the Welsh, 1776–1871* (Cardiff, 2005), p. 72.

15 Legend insists that the only shop not to be damaged in the riots was the chemist's shop owned by the celebrated Welsh rugby international Willie Llewelyn. A fine wing three-quarter, Llewelyn scored the winning try against the 1905 All Blacks.

16 For the history of a south Wales shop, see S. Minwel Tibbott and Beth Thomas, *The Gwalia: the Story of a Valleys Shop* (Cardiff, 1991) and Rhys Davies, *Print of a Hare's Foot* (Bridgend, 1998).

17 Fraser, *The Coming of the Mass Market*, p. 114; P. Mathias, *Retailing Revolution* (London, 1967); J. B. Jeffreys, *Retail Trading in Britain 1850–1950* (Cambridge, 1954); and J. Benson and G. Shaw (eds), *The Evolution of Retail Systems, c.1800–1914* (Leicester, 1992).

18 Despite the fact that the abuse of paying workers in tokens which could only be redeemed for exorbitantly priced goods at company or truck shops had been outlawed, such practices had a surprising longevity. It was in such a venture, the Rhymney Iron Company's shop, that the young Thomas Jones, who later became secretary to the British Cabinet in the 1920s and 1930s, was raised in the 1870s; see Thomas Jones, *Rhymney Memories* (Llandysul, 1938).

19 See O. V. Jones, *William Evans, 1864–1934* (London, 1982) and his entry in Arthur Mee's *Who's Who in Wales* (Cardiff, 1921).

[20] Jones, *Rhymney Memories*, p. 5.

[21] Colin Hughes, *Lime, Lemon and Sarsaparilla: the Italian Community in South Wales, 1881–1945* (Bridgend, 2003) p. 27.

[22] Mathias, *Retailing Revolution.*

[23] B. L. Coombes, *These Poor Hands: the Autobiography of a Miner Working in South Wales* (London, 1939), p. 91.

[24] *Montgomeryshire County Times*, 17 and 24 January 1920.

[25] Brian Lee, *David Morgan: the Family Store, 1879–2005* (Cardiff, 2005). 'If the weft of David Morgan's character was honesty, then its warp was frugality.' Amongst his favourite sayings were, 'A pin saved is money made' and 'You'll never be rich if you cut string'. He saw to it that his staff practised what he preached. Every piece of paper, every bit of string, every pin that came into the shops had to be saved for further, future use. Any unnecessary use of artificial light had to be avoided. To guard against the evil of waste, he was ever vigilant and even used a large stick to punish profligate workers. Those who listened, prospered. When he died, Morgan rewarded nine of his loyal employees with substantial bequests in his will. His moral scruples did not prevent him from selling beer, but it could only be delivered to his premises under the cover of darkness.

[26] A. Aldburgham, *Shops and Shopping, 1800–1914; Where, and in What Manner the Well-dressed Englishwoman Bought her Clothes* (London, 1964); D. W. Davies, *Owen Owen: Victorian Draper* (London, 1984). A model employer, Owen built hostels for his staff (many of whom were from Wales), was one of the first big shopkeepers to introduce a weekly half-holiday for his employees, and set up the Owen Owen Trust in 1900 to help retired members of staff. He also invested his profits in other enterprises, such as North American railways, his brother's and his brother-in-law's drapery businesses in London, and Evans and Owen Ltd of Bath. In 1891, he opened a London branch and thereafter became a major property developer in London. A close rival in Liverpool was David Lewis, who established the shops that evolved into the John Lewis Partnership.

[27] By 1893, Peter Jones's glass-gleaming, gas-hissing store had diversified into household linens, books, shoes, ladies' underclothing, clothing and millinery, bedding and carpets, china, glass and electroplated silverware, and a gentlemen's tailoring establishment. By 1900, the shop was successfully floated as a public company. Peter Jones, 'one of the great self-made retailing giants of his time', was also a humane employer, an early supporter of the early-closing movement, and the first London store to provide seating for female shop assistants; see

Oxford Dictionary of National Biography (*http://www.oxforddnb*, accessed 30 August 2007).

[28] Joseph and his brothers learned the secrets of retail at Enoch Lewis's Siop y Cei in Holywell:

> Paradwys i fachgen bach ar ddiwrnod o aeaf fyddai crwydro ymysg y sachau o flawd, y brethyn a'r esgidiau, a phob math o gelfi fferm a thaclau llong. Gellid prynu unrhywbeth yno, o nodwydd i angor, ac o raff i raw. Gwrandawai ar y morwyr yn traethu hanes y gwledydd pell, a'i gyfaill Hugh Parry, brawd John Parry a phrif gynorthwywr ei dad, yn ymddiddan yn ffraeth â gwragedd y glowyr neu yn siarad yn wybodys â'r ffermwyr.

Sian Wyn Jones, *O Gamddwr i Gairo: Hanes y Brodyr Davies Bryan (1857–1935)* (Wrexham, 2005). Joseph Davies later went on to study at the university college in Aberystwyth and, in a remarkable photograph taken in 1884–5, he stares through frosted blue sunglasses at the viewer. In business, however, he was remarkably clear sighted; *The Times*, 2 March 1935.

[29] For William Evans, see Jones, *William Evans*; for Samuel Brain, see S. A. Brain and Co., *100 Years of Brewing, 1882–1982* (London, 1982).

[30] J. K. Walton, *The English Seaside Resort: a Social History 1750–1914* (Leicester, 1983), p. 176.

[31] J. Walvin, *Beside the Seaside* (London, 1978); Anthony Hern, *The Seaside Holiday: the history of the English Seaside Resort* (London, 1967); John K. Walton, *Wonderlands by the Waves: a History of Seaside Resorts* (Preston, 1992). A valuable addition to the academic studies of seaside resorts is John Hassan, *The Seaside, Health and the Environment in England and Wales since 1800* (Aldershot, 2003).

[32] Judith Flanders, *Consuming Passions: Leisure and Pleasure in Victorian Britain* (London, 2006), p. 491.

[33] There is a growing literature on the commercialisation of Christmas. See Mark Connelly, *Christmas: a Social History* (London, 1999); Paul Davies, *The Lives and Times of Ebenezer Scrooge* (Yale, 1990); J. M. Golby, *The Making of the Modern Christmas* (Sutton, 2000); J. Miles and John Hadfield, *The Twelve Days of Christmas* (London, 1961).

[34] Lori Anne Loeb, *Consuming Angels: Advertising and Victorian Women* (New York, NY, 1994); see also Thomas Richards, *The Commodity Culture of Victorian England: Advertising and Spectacle* (Stanford, 1990) and T. R. Nevett, *Advertising in Britain: A History* (London, 1982).

[35] Cynthia L. White, *Women's Magazines, 1893–1968* (London, 1970).

[36] Such advertisements litter Welsh newspapers, for advertisers soon realised that the press enabled them to enter the land behind the door-knocker.

37 This tactic of getting local people to endorse products, many of which were spurious at best, harmful at worst, was widespread in Welsh newspapers by the 1890s; see Nevett, *Advertising in Britain*, p. 70.

38 E. D. Rappaport, *Shopping for Pleasure: Women in the Making of London's West End* (New Jersey, 2000). See also Dorothy Davis, *A History of Shopping* (London, 1966) and Phillippe Perrot, *Fashioning the Bourgeoisie: a History of Clothing in the Nineteenth Century*, trans. Richard Bienvenu (Princeton, 2000).

39 Dylan Thomas, *Portrait of the Artist as a Young Dog* (London, 1940) and Daniel Jones, *My Friend Dylan Thomas* (London, 1977).

40 Hughes, *Lime, Lemon and Sarsaparilla, passim.*

41 Christopher J. Berry, *The Idea of Luxury: a Conceptual and Historical Investigation* (Cambridge, 1994). See also Susan J. Matt, 'Frocks, finery and feelings: rural and urban women's envy, 1890–1930', in Peter N. Stearns and Jan Lewis (eds), *An Emotional History of the United States* (London, 1998), pp. 377–95.

42 Christopher Breward, *The Culture of Fashion* (Manchester, 1995).

43 Quoted in Benson and Shaw (eds), *The Evolution of Retail Systems*, p. 191. Sir John Coldbrook Hanbury-Williams owned a large estate and iron works at Pontypool and was chairman of Courtaulds.

44 Kate Davies, *Hafau fy Mhlentyndod ym Mhentref Pren-gwyn* (Llandysul, 1970).

45 Benson and Shaw (eds.), *The Evolution of Retail Systems*, p. 146.

46 Cyril Batstone, *Old Rhondda in Photographs* (Cowbridge, 1974).

47 Cardiganshire Constabulary's register of miscreants, NLW MS 232 3B.

48 National Museums and Galleries of Wales, *Hanes Merched Cymru – Welsh Women's History, 1900–1918* (Cardiff, n.d.). In a remarkable photograph taken in 1905 in the windswept school at Dylife, Powys, Miss Catherine Ellis sits in a classroom contemplating her future. The new teacher was a statuesque sophisticate wearing all the latest fashions, from feet encased in leather lace-up boots, to fingers covered in white silk gloves, to a head crowned with a straw boater.

49 NLW photographs in the John Thomas collection. See also C. Stevens, 'Welsh Costume: the Survival of Tradition or National Icon?', in *Folk Life*, 1976, 56–70.

50 J. Geraint Jenkins, *The Welsh Woollen Industry* (Cardiff, 1969), p. 57.

51 Jenkins, *The Welsh Woollen Industry*, p. 57.

52 Jenkins, *The Welsh Woollen Industry*, p. 57.

53 Asa Briggs, *Victorian Things* (London, 1988); Deborah Cohen, *Household Gods: the British and their Possessions* (London, 2006). Contrary to contemporary opinion, there was many a man about the house in late

Victorian and Edwardian Wales. See, for example, Jane Hamlett, *Material Relations: Middle-class Families and Domestic Interiors in England, 1850–1910* (Manchester, 2010) and Judith Neiswander, *The Cosmopolitan Interior: Liberalism and the British House 1870–1914* (London, 2009).

54 Kirsta Lysak, 'Goblin markets: Victorian Women Shoppers at Liberty's Oriental Bazaar', *Nineteenth-Century Contexts*, 27/2 (2005), 139–65. On the symbolism of the dress in a Welsh context, see Elena Puw Morgan, *Y Wisg Sidan* (Denbigh, 1939). It was not only women who were status- and fashion-conscious – men were also easily influenced; see Penelope Byrde, *The Male Image: Men's Fashion in Britain, 1300–1900* (London, 1979) and Christopher Breward, *The Hidden Consumer: Masculinities, Fashion and City Life, 1860–1914* (Manchester, 1999).

55 Rayner Banham, *The Architecture of the Well-tempered Environment* (London, 1969), p. 64.

56 On the themes of continuity and change and the reluctance to take up technology, see David Edgerton, *The Shock of the Old: Technology and Global History since 1900* (London, 2008).

57 R. H. Morgan, 'The Development of the Electricity Supply Industry in Wales to 1919', *Welsh History Review*, 11 (1982/3), 317–19; Tom Evans, 'Electricity Comes to Aberystwyth', *Ceredigion*, 4 (2000), 73–80.

58 Morgan, 'The Development of the Electricity Supply Industry in Wales to 1919', 327.

59 Morgan, 'The Development of the Electricity Supply Industry in Wales to 1919', 329.

60 See Stephen Kern, *The Culture of Time and Space: 1880–1918* (London, 2003), pp. 114–15, 185.

61 Nancy F. Koehn, *Brand New: How Entrepreneurs Earned Consumers' Trust from Wedgwood to Dell* (Boston, MA, 2001), p. 21.

62 For the effects of electrification on other parts of Wales see, for example, D. W. Thomas, 'Historical Notes on Hydroelectricity in North Wales', *Caernarvonshire Historical Transactions*, 50 (1989), 80–93; D. Slyfield, 'Dolgellau and its Electricity Supply, 1935', *Journal of the Merionethshire Historical and Records Society*, 12 (1994–7); D. Pugh, 'Electricity in Newtown', *Newtonian*, 15 (2003), 92–121; W. H. Jones, *Light and Power on Farms: a Study of the Users of Electricity in South Wales* (Aberystwyth, 1932); and R. J. Moore-Colyer, 'Lighting the Landscape: Rural Electrification in Wales', *Welsh History Review*, 23, 4 (2007), 72–92.

63 A. D. Rees, *Lfe in a Welsh Countryside* (Cardiff, 1975), p. 48.

64 Michael Freeman and Derek H. Aldcroft, *Transport in Victorian Britain* (Manchester, 1988).

65 David Rubinstein, 'Cycling in the 1890s', *Victorian Studies*, 21/1 (1977), 47–71.

66 Richard Ireland, 'Caught on Camera: Cardiganshire Criminal Portraits in Context', *Ceredigion*, XV/2 (2006), 22–3.

67 Alun Roberts, *Discovering Welsh Graves* (Cardiff, 2002), pp. 103–4.

68 Quoted in Peter Thorold, *The Motoring Age: the Automobile and Britain, 1896–1939* (London, 2003), p. 5.

69 Thorold, *The Motoring Age*, p. 31.

70 David Cannadine, *Aspects of Aristocracy* (London, 1994), pp. 65–6; I. Lloyd, *Rolls-Royce: the Years of Pleasure* (London, 1978); Roberts, *Discovering Welsh Graves*, pp. 78–9.

71 See H. Tours, *Parry Thomas: Designer-Driver* (London, 1959) and M. Berresford, *Parry Thomas and Pendine* (Cardiff, 1985). During the First World War, Parry Thomas advised the government on the design of aero engines and tank design. In the early 1920s, he worked with the Leyland Corporation on producing a luxury car – the Leyland Eight, costing an extravagant £2,500. Only fourteen were ever produced, two of them for the maharaja of Patiala, and one for Michael Collins in Ireland, where it took a bullet through the windscreen.

72 V. Bruce, *Nine Lives Plus: Record-breaking on Land, Sea and in the Air, an Autobiographical Account* (London, 1977); see also Virginia Scharff, *Taking the Wheel: Women and the Coming of the Motor Age* (New York, NY, 1991) and Georgine Clarsen, *Eat my Dust: Early Women Motorists* (Baltimore, MD, 2008).

73 Roscoe Howells, *A Pembrokeshire Pioneer: Bill Frost of Saundersfoot, the First Man to Fly* (Pwllheli, 2007). Other pioneers of aviation in Wales include Ernest Thompson Willows (1886–1926), the Cardiff airship designer, who built, amongst several ships, the *City of Cardiff* – see A. McKinty, *The Father of British Airships* (London, 1972); Gustave Hamel of Llandrindod Wells; the James brothers of Clunderwen; the Abergavenny-based inventor W. H. Jones, who built his own hydroplanes; Sir Arthur Whitten Brown (1886–1948) of Vickers, Swansea, where the Vimy bomber was built; and Sidney Pickles of Llanelli. There are several fascinating photographs on the *Casglu'r Tlysau / Gathering the Jewels* website.

74 Robert C. Thursby, *Glamorgan Aviation: Eheda* (Stroud, 2002), *passim*. On aviation in Anglesey, see Roy Sloan, 'Anglesey's First Aviators', *Anglesey Antiquarian Society and Field Club Transactions* (1996), 77–96.

75 National Musuems and Galleries Wales, *Calendar* (Cardiff, 1997), p. 4.

76 Quoted in Thorold, *The Motoring Age*, p. 164.

77 T. Barker (ed.), *The Economic and Social Effects of the Spread of Motor Vehicles* (London, 1987).

78 Williams, *Digest of Welsh Historical Statistics*, 2, p. 45.

79 T. Moline, *Mobility and the Small Town, 1900–30* (Chicago, IL, 1971); see also Russell Davies, 'The Importance of Motor Omnibus Passenger Services in South-west Wales as illustrated by the 1935 Bus Strike', *Carmarthenshire Antiquary*, 2 (1984), 87–92.

80 Stewart Williams (ed.), *Vintage Buses and Trams in South Wales* (Barry, 1975); D. S. M. Barrie, *A Regional History of the Railways of Great Britain: XII, South Wales* (privately printed, 1984).

81 Quoted in Thorold, *The Motoring Age*, p. 199.

82 Williams, *Digest of Welsh Historical Statistics*.

83 E. C. Baker, *Sir William Preece F.R.S., Victorian Engineer Extraordinary* (London, 1976). Other Welsh developers of the telegraph and telephone include Sir Albert George Lee (1879–1967) of Conwy.

84 Wyn Thomas 'Y Ffonograff a Byd Cerddoriaeth Draddodiadol yng Nghymru', *Canu Gwerin*, 29 (2006), 49.

85 Hari Williams, *Marconi and his Wireless Stations in Wales* (Llanrwst, 1999).

86 John Davies, *Broadcasting and the BBC in Wales* (Cardiff, 1994). The figures for the ownership of radios are given in M. J. Daunton, *Wealth and Welfare: an Economic and Social History of Britain 1851–1951* (Oxford, 2007), p. 431.

87 Iorwerth Peate, *Rhwng Dau Fyd: Darn o Hunangofiant* (Denbigh, 1976). See also Herbert Hughes, *An Uprooted Community: A History of Epynt* (Llandysul, 1998).

88 David Berry, *Wales and Cinema: the First Hundred Years* (Cardiff, 1994), pp. 45–50.

89 Berry, *Wales and Cinema*, pp. 45–50.

90 Peter Yorke, *William Haggar, Fairground Film Maker: Biography of a Pioneer of the Cinema* (Bedlinog, 2007).

91 Miskell, *A Social History of the Cinema in Wales, 1918–1951*, pp. 56–75.

92 Miskell, *A Social History of the Cinema in Wales, 1918–1951*, pp. 56–75.

93 On Grindell Matthews, see Andrew Dulley, 'Intrigue and Invention: the Curious Tale of Harry Grindell Matthews and his Terrifying Ray of Death', *Minerva: Transactions of the Royal Institution of South Wales*, 14 (2006), 61–8.

94 Stephen Kern, *The Culture of Time and Space*. See also Philipp Blom, *The Vertigo Years: Change and Culture in the West, 1900–1914* (London, 2008).

95 On the Chester railway line, see Nicholas Faith, *The World the Railways Made* (London, 1990), p. 71. See also Dan Falk, *In Search of Time: Journeys along a Curious Dimension* (London, 2008), p. 46.

96 Kern, *The Culture of Time and Space*.

97 David Landes, *Revolution in Time: Clocks and the Making of the Modern World* (London, 1984).

98 E. P. Thompson, 'Time, Work-discipline and Industrial Capitalism', *Past and Present*, 38, (1967), 75–90.

99 Davies, *Hafau fy Mhlentyndod*, p. 53; see also Tom Standage, *The Victorian Internet: the Remarkable Story of the Telegraph* (London, 1999), which provides some information on another Welsh telegraph innovator, David Edward Hughes (1829?/31–1900).

100 For the way the press speeded up, see Joel H. Wiener, *The Americanization of the British Press: Speed in the Age of Transatlantic Journalism* (London, 2012).

101 John Brooks, *Telephone: the First Hundred Years* (New York, NY, 1975), p. 115; Edwin G. Burrows and Mike Wallace, *Gotham: a History of New York City to 1898* (Oxford, 1999), p. 1235.

102 A. J. P. Taylor, *The Origins of the First World War* (Harmondsworth, 1975).

103 Williams, *Digest of Welsh Historical Statistics*, vol. 1, p. 111.

104 Quoted in Kern, *The Culture of Time and Space*, p. 18.

105 For an enthusiastic history of the social impact of cinema, see David Thomson, *The Big Screen: the Story of the Movies and What They Did to Us* (London, 2012); see also Vanessa Tomlinson, Simon Popple and Patrick Russell (eds), *The Lost World of Mitchell and Kenyon: Edwardian Britain on Film* (London, 2012).

106 M. H. Thomas et al., *D. A. Thomas, Viscount Rhondda* (London, 1921).

107 C. S. Rolls, quoted in William Plowden, *The Motor Car and Politics* (London, 1971), p. 47.

108 Kern, *The Culture of Time and Space*, especially the chapter on 'speed'.

109 I. M. Pincombe, 'The 'Free' Sugar Generation: the Emergence and Development of the Confectionery Industry in Nineteenth-century South Wales', *Welsh History Review*, 22/3 (2005), 529; see also Briggs, *Victorian Things*.

110 Roman Krznaric, *The Wonderbox: Curious Histories of How to Live* (London, 2012), p. 162.

111 Krznaric, *The Wonderbox*, p. 162.

112 Dylan Thomas, *The Outing* (London, 1971).

113 D. M. Phillips, *Evan Roberts: the Great Welsh Revivalist and his Work* (London, 1906), p. 420.

114 Phillips, *Evan Roberts*, p. 16.

115 Phillips, *Evan Roberts*, p. 519; *Western Mail*, 17 December 1904.

116 Arthur Mee, 'The Pleasure Telephone', *Strand Magazine*, 16 (1898), 34. For a perceptive study on similar themes, see C. Keep, 'The

Cultural Work of the Type-Writer Girl', *Victorian Studies*, 40 (1996–7), 418–28.

117 Ireland, 'Caught on camera'.

118 On Merlyn Evans, see *Catalogue of an Exhibition of Paintings, Drawings and Etchings held at the Whitehcapel Gallery, London, October to November 1956* (London, 1956); and *The Political Paintings of Merlyn Evans, 1930–50* (catalogue, Tate Gallery, 1985). On Myfanwy Evans, see Welsh Committee of the Arts Council of Great Britain, *British Art and the Modern Movement, 1930–40* (Cardiff, 1962), p. 11.

119 This lament for a harassed world is deeply ironic when we remember W. H. Davies's career as a 'supertramp'.

120 Eiluned Lewis, *The Captain's Wife* (Dinas Powys, 2003).

121 There is an excellent study of the links between Evan Roberts, speed, technology and the revival in Edward J. Gitre, 'The 1904–05 Welsh Revival: Modernization, Technologies, and Techniques of the self', *Church History*, 73/4 (December, 2004), 792–827.

122 Gitre, 'The 1904–05 Welsh Revival', 792–827.

123 William Howells, *Through the Eye of the Needle* (New York, NY, 1907), pp. 10–11.

3 *'Bonfire of the Vanities'*

1 Quoted in D. J. V. Jones, *Rebecca's Children* (Oxford, 1989), p. 17. Cynan, 'Mab y bwthyn', *Cerddi Cynan: y Casgliad Cyflawn* (Llandysul, 1987).

2 For proverbs, see H. H. Vaughan, *Welsh Proverbs with English Translations* (London, 1889); T. R. Roberts, *The Proverbs of Wales: a Selection of Welsh Proverbs with English Translations* (London, 1909); Rees Jones, quoted in E. G. Millward, *Cenedl o Bobl Ddewrion: Agweddau ar Lenyddiaeth Oes Victoria* (Llandysul, 1991), p. 70.

3 For Ellis Humphrey Evans, see Alan Llwyd, *Gwae fi fy Myw: Cofiant Hedd Wyn* (Llandybïe, 1991).

4 Menna Baines, *Yng Ngolau'r Lleuad: Ffaith a Dychymyg yng Ngwaith Caradog Prichard* (Llandysul, 2005); J. Hughes, *Byd a Bywyd Caradog Prichard, 1904–80: Bywgraffiad Darluniadol* (Swansea, 2005); quoted in Alan Llwyd, *Rhyfel a Gwrthryfel: Brwydr Moderniaeth a Beirdd Modern* (Llandybïe, 2003), p. 211; *Western Mail*, 12 January 1877.

5 *Cyfansoddiadau Buddugol Eisteddfod Genedlaethol Lerpwl*, 1891.

6 John Williams, *Was Wales Industrialised? Essays in Modern Welsh history* (Llandysul, 1995), p. 26.

7 J. Geraint Jenkins, *The Welsh Woollen Industry* (Cardiff, 1969), p. 388.

8 Williams, *Was Wales Industrialised?*, p. 28. For various views of miners, both of the traditional 'long march of labour school' and the more perceptive, see: Ruth Davies, 'Rural Prophets? William Ferris Hay, Noah Ablett and the Debate over Working-class Political Action in the south Wales coalfield, 1910–1914', *Llafur*, 7 (1998–9), 89–100, and John McIlroy and Alan Campbell, 'The Heresy of Arthur Horner', *Llafur*, 8 (2001), 105–18. (Horner's ghost-written memoir, *Incorrigible Rebel* (London, 1960), is unfortunately unreliable and unrevealing.) David Egan, 'The Unofficial Reform Committee and *The Miner's Next Step*, *Llafur*, 2 (1978), 18–32; Richard Lewis, 'The South Wales Miners and the Ruskin College Strike of 1909', *Llafur*, 2 (1976), 57–73; Mike Lieven, 'A "New History" of the south Wales Coalfield?', *Llafur*, 8 (2002), 89–106, and Julie Light, 'Manufacturing the Past – the Representation of Mining Communities in History, Literature and Heritage . . . Fantasies of a World that never Was?', *Llafur*, 8 (2000), 21. For a very perceptive view of the working class, see Joe England, 'Working-class Culture and the Labour Movement in South Wales Reconsidered', *Llafur*, 8 (2002), 117–30; Chris Williams, *Democratic Rhondda: Politics and Society, 1885–1951* (Cardiff, 1996) and *Capitalism, Community and Conflict: the South Wales Coalfield 1898–1947* (Cardiff, 1998). One interesting development in coalfield history appears to be an obsession with comparative studies. South Wales, it seems, has parallels with West Virginia, the Ruhr, and several other places across the world. See, for example, Roger Fagge, *Power, Culture and Conflict in the Coalfields: West Virginia and South Wales, 1900–1922* (Manchester, 1996); M. J. Daunton, 'Miner's Homes: South Wales and the Great Northern Coalfield, 1880–1914', *International Review of Social History*, 25 (1980), 143–75; Stefan Berger and Neil Evans, 'The face of King Coal in the Ruhr and South Wales: different historiographical traditions and their impact on comparative history', in Stefan Berger, Andy Croll and Norman LaPorte (eds), *Towards a Comparative History of Coalfield Societies* (London, 2003); Keith Davies, 'Roughneck in the Rhondda: Some Ideological Connections between the United States and the South Wales Coalfield, 1900–1914', *Llafur*, 6 (1995), 80–92; Stefan Berger, 'Working Class Culture and the Labour Movement in the South Wales and the Ruhr Coalfields, 1850–1920: a Comparison', *Llafur*, 8 (2001), 5–40.

9 On these themes, see David Cannadine, *Class in Britain* (London, 1998) and D. Smith, *Conflict and Compromise: Class Formation in English Society, 1830–1914: a Comparative Study of Birmingham and Sheffield* (London, 1982).

10 R. Merfyn Jones, *The North Wales Quarrymen* (Cardiff, 1985), pp. 210–66; Jean Lindsay, *The Great Strike: a History of the Penrhyn Quarry Dispute of 1900–1903* (London, 1987); Charles Sheridan Jones, *What I saw at Bethesda* (London, 1903). Guilt that his father was perhaps one of the 'bradwyr' (traitors) was one of several components in the mental torture chamber of Caradog Prichard; see Menna Baines, *Yng Ngolau'r Lleuad* (Llandysul, 2005). On 1926, see Margaret Morris, *The General Strike* (Harmondsworth, 1976) and Christopher Farnam, *May 1926: the General Strike: Britain's Aborted Revolution?* (St Albans, 1974). The strike in Wales is discussed in E. W. Edwards, 'The Pontypridd Area', in Morris, *The General Strike*, pp. 411–25, and a special anniversary issue of *Llafur* (1976) has interesting items. See also Alun Birge, 'The 1926 General Strike in Cardiff, *Llafur*, 6 (1992), 42–61. On strikes, see Deian Hopkin, 'Essays in Methodology: Strikes in Wales 1888–1958, a Case for Computing', *Llafur*, 5 (1987), 81–90.

11 F. Parkin, *Marxism and Class Theory: a Bourgeois Critique* (New York, NY, 1979). Marx's writings are replete with vague references to the 'middle classes', 'middle bourgeoisie', 'intermediate strata' and the like, where growth was inexplicable within the limits of his theory. For a discussion, see Ricardo López and Barbara Weinstein (eds), *The Making of the Middle Class: Towards a Transnational History* (Durham, NC, 2012).

12 A. A. Jackson, *The Middle Classes, 1900–1950* (Nairn, 1991), p. 11; G. Marshall et al., *Social Class in Modern Britain* (London, 1988), p. 110; W. G. Runciman, 'How Many Classes are there in Contemporary British Society?', *Sociology*, xxix (1990), 377–96.

13 A. J. Mayer, 'The Lower Middle Class as a Historical Problem', *Journal of Modern History*, xlvii (1975), 409–31; G. Crossick (ed.), *The Lower Middle Class in Britain, 1870–1914* (London, 1977) and 'Metaphor of the Middle: the Discovery of the Petite Bourgeoisie, 1880–1914', *Transactions of the Royal Historical Society*, sixth series, iv (1994), 251–79. On some attempted definitions of class, see R. S. Neale, *Class in English History* (Oxford, 1981) and P. Joyce (ed.), *Class* (Oxford, 1995).

14 Cannadine, *Class in Britain.* In reality people's imagined communities were immensely complex and contradictory. Individuals fitted into a criss-cross of hierarchies, occupying a different place in each and they could live simultaneously within a three-class (upper, middle and working) and a two-class ('bourgeoisie' and 'proletariat' or 'us' and 'them') system. See P. N. Furbank, *Unholy Pleasure: the Idea of Social Class* (Oxford, 1985) and D. Lockwood, 'Sources of Variation in Working-Class Images of Society', *Sociological Review*, xiv (1966), 249–67.

15 The concept of the rise and fall of various social groups is one that has entertained and enthralled historians of all eras. Historians of the sixteenth century, for example, vigorously debated whether the gentry were ascending or descending; see, for example, R. H. Tawney, 'The Rise of the Gentry, 1558–1640', *Economic History Review*, xi (1941), 1–38. The opposing view in this academic tempest in a teapot was ably put by Christopher Hill in *The Century of Revolution, 1603–1714* (London, 1961). Those historians studying the Industrial Revolution and its aftermath have merrily made and remade classes. E. P. Thompson, in his iconic *The Making of the English Working Class* (Harmondsworth, 1968), was the trendsetter for the emergence of the working class in the period around the 1830s. Others, with equal plausibility, saw these years as the making of the middle classes; see, for example, Asa Briggs, *The Age of Improvement, 1753–1846* and 'Middle-Class Consciousness in English Politics, 1780–1846', *Past and Present*, 9 (1956), 65–74; P. Earle, *The Making of the English Middle Class: Business, Society and Family Life in London* (London, 1989); F. M. L. Thompson, *The Rise of Respectable Society: a Social History of Victorian Britain, 1830–1900* (London, 1988). For an useful discussion of the rival views, see T. Koditschek, 'A Tale of Two Thompsons', *Radical History Review*, 56 (1993), 68–84. Looking at the debates, many of which were exceptionally bitter, from the perspective of the twenty-first century, there are a number of obvious questions. If the gentry had declined in the sixteenth century, how then were they so powerful in 1832 at the time of the Great Reform Act? If the working classes had been so effectively 'made' in the 1830s, then why (and how) did they need to be 'remade' in the last quarter of the nineteenth and the opening decade of the twentieth century? As for the class between them – the middle class – it appears to have been rising perpetually, but to have achieved very little.

16 Iwan Meical Jones, *Hen Ffordd Gymreig o Fyw: A Welsh Way of Life: Ffotograffau John Thomas Photographs* (Aberystwyth, 2008), pp. 28, 133.

17 D. Caradog Jones and A. M. Carr-Saunders, A *Survey of the Social Structure of England and Wales* (London, 1937), p. 67.

18 Thompson, *The Rise of Respectable Society*, p. 355.

19 J. Tysul Jones, *Yr Athro Evan Jones Williams BSc, FRS, 1903–1945* (Llandysul, 1970).

20 G. R. Searle, *A New England?: Peace and War, 1886–1918* (Oxford) 2005; see also Lawrence Jones, *The Middle Class: a History* (London, 2008); M. J. Daunton, *Wealth and Welfare: an Economic and Social History of Britain, 1851–1951* (Oxford, 2007), p. 425.

[21] L. J. Williams, *Digest of Welsh Historical Statistics*, 1 (Cardiff, 1985), p. 113.

[22] G. Crossick, 'From Gentlemen to Residuum: Languages of Social Description in Victorian Britain', in P. Corfield (ed.), *Language, History and Class* (Oxford, 1991), p. 171.

[23] Oliver Fairclough, *Cyfoeth, Celf a Chydwybod* (Cardiff, 2007), p. 42.

[24] W. R. Lambert, *Drink and Sobriety in Wales, c.1820–c.1895* (Cardiff, 1983), pp. 27–37.

[25] On Amanwy, see Huw Walters, 'David Rees Griffiths (Amanwy), 1882–1953', *Carmarthenshire Antiquarian*, 35 (1999), 89–102.

[26] Thomas Parry Evans, *Fy Mhregeth Gyntaf* (Carmarthen, n.d.).

[27] Gwilym R. Tilsley, 'Moliant i'r glöwr', in *Y Glöwr a Cherddi Eraill* (Llandysul, 1958).

[28] Quoted in J. M. Edwards, 'Rhai sylwadau ar farddoniaeth ddiweddar', in J. E. Caerwyn Williams (ed.), *Ysgrifau Beirniadol* (Denbigh, 1974), p. 256.

[29] J. Geraint Jenkins, *Life and Tradition in Rural Wales* (London, 1976); see also Nicola Verdon, *Rural Women Workers in Nineteenth-Century England* (Woodbridge, 2006) and 'The Employment of Women and Children in Agriculture: a Reassessment of Agricultural Gangs in Nineteenth-Century Norfolk', *Agricultural History Review*, 49 (2001), 41–55.

[30] S. Minwell Tibbott, 'Going Electric: the Changing Face of the Rural Kitchen in Wales', *Folk Life*, 28 (1989), 63–74.

[31] See, for example, the comments made by Eugene Weber in *Peasants into Frenchmen: the Modernisation of Rural France 1870–1914* (London, 1976), pp. 221–31.

[32] David Jenkins, *The Agricultural Community in South-West Wales at the Turn of the Twentieth Century* (Cardiff, 1971), pp. 140–57.

[33] R. Hay, 'Employers and Social Policy in Britain: the Evolution of Welfare Legislation, 1905–14', *Social History*, 2 (1977), 435–55.

[34] These, of course, are characters in Dylan Thomas's fictional evocation of a Welsh coastal village, Llareggub, in *Under Milk Wood* (London, 1954). *Nansi: Merch y Pregethwr Dall* is a novel by Watcyn Wyn.

[35] On the experience of unemployment, see the Pilgrim Trust, *Men Without Work* (Cambridge, 1938); Charles Webster, 'Healthy or hungry thirties', *History Workshop Journal*, 13 (1982), 121–41.

[36] R. McKibbin, *The Ideologies of Class: Social Relations in Britain, 1880–1980* (Oxford, 1990); P. Calvert, *The Concept of Class: An Historical Introduction* (London, 1982) provides a useful introduction to the views of several authors on the operation of class within society; see also M. W. Flinn and T. C. Smout (eds), *Essays in Social History* (Oxford, 1979).

[37] John Davies and G. Mingay, 'Agriculture in an industrial environment', in Arthur H. John and Glanmor Williams (eds), *Glamorgan County*

History, V: Industrial Glamorgan 1750–1900 (Cardiff, 1980), p. 304. See also Richard Collyer, 'Conditions of Employment amongst the Farm Labour Force in Nineteenth-Century Wales', *Llafur*, 3 (1982), 33–42; see also A. Hawkins, *Reshaping Rural England: a Social History, 1850–1925* (London, 1991).

38 Eric Hopkins, *A Social History of the English Working Class, c.1815–1945* (London, 1979). On Welsh women at work, see Dot Jones, 'Counting the cost of coal: women's lives in the Rhondda, 1881–1911', in A. V. John (ed.), *Our Mother's Land: Chapters in Welsh Women's History, 1830–1939* (Cardiff, 1991), pp. 109–33, and 'Serfdom and Slavery: Women's Work in Wales, 1900–1930', in D. R. Hopkin and G. S. Kealey (eds), *Class, Community and the Labour Movement in Wales and Canada, 1850–1930* (Aberystwyth, 1989), pp. 119–34; and L. J. Williams and Dot Jones, 'Women at work in the nineteenth century', *Llafur*, 3/3 (1983), 20–9. On the particular experiences of Welsh women in the munitions factories, see Mari A. Williams *'Where is Mrs Jones Going?' Women and the Second World War in South Wales* (Aberystwyth, 1995), pp. 2–7.

39 Mari A. Williams, *A Forgotten Army: the Female Munitions Workers of South Wales, 1939–1945* (Cardiff, 2002), 29.

40 On the early evolution of attitudes to work, see Keith Thomas, *The Ends of Life: Roads to Fulfilment in Early Modern England* (Oxford, 2009), pp. 107–10.

41 The majority of the statistics are taken from Williams, *Digest of Welsh Historical Statistics*, 1, pp. 89–162.

42 Williams, *Digest of Welsh Historical Statistics*, vol. 1.

43 Harold Perkin, *The Rise of Professional Society: England since 1880* (London, 1989), pp. 71–7.

44 Kate Roberts, *Traed mewn Cyffion* (Denbigh, 1936); and J. Melling, 'Non-Commissioned Officers: British Employers and their Supervising Workers, 1880–1920', *Social History*, 5 (1980), 187–210.

45 J. E. Lloyd (ed.), *Sir Henry Reichel: a Memorial Volume* (Bangor, 1934).

46 Leslie Wynne Evans, *Studies in Welsh Education: Welsh Educational Structure and Administration, 1880–1925* (Cardiff, 1974), p. 7.

47 Perhaps the most devoted and inspirational London-based figure was Sir Hugh Owen (1804–81), the tireless campaigner for Welsh education; see B. L. Davies, *Hugh Owen, 1801–1884* (Cardiff, 1977). Another London man who was influential in promoting Welsh education (especially the passage of the 1889 Welsh Intermediate Education Act) was the Conservative MP George Thomas Kenyon (1840–1908).

48 Prys Morgan (ed.), *Brad y Llyfrau Gleision: Ysgrifau ar Hanes Cymru* (Llandysul, 1991).

[49] Geraint H. Jenkins, *The University of Wales: an Illustrated History* (Cardiff, 1993); J. Gwynn Williams, *The University of Wales, 1839–1939* (Cardiff, 1997).

[50] Gareth Elwyn Jones, *Secondary Education in Wales* (Cardiff, 1984); *The Education of a Nation* (Cardiff, 1997); and *Controls and Conflicts in Welsh Secondary Education, 1889–1944* (Cardiff, 1982).

[51] *Welsh Outlook*, December 1919.

[52] For a discussion on these themes see Weber, *Peasants into Frenchmen*, pp. 303–39.

[53] There are several hundred 'official' histories of Welsh schools, so it is difficult to select just a few, but the majority consider the formalities of the school's operational systems rather than their social context.

[54] Williams, *Digest of Welsh Historical Statistics*, 2, pp. 212–22.

[55] Williams, *Digest of Welsh Historical Statistics*, 2, pp. 212–22.

[56] Williams, *Digest of Welsh Historical Statistics*, 2, pp. 212–22.

[57] Searle, *A New England?*, pp. 329–34; Evans, *Studies in Welsh Education*, pp. 117–82.

[58] W. S. Jones, *Helyntion Hen Bregethwr a'i Gyfoedion* (Llandysul, 1940).

[59] Morgan (ed.), *Brad y Llyfrau Gleision*; Peter Ellis Jones 'The Established Church and Elementary Education in Victorian Merioneth: a Case Study of Llansanffraid Glyndyfrdwy / Carrog National School' (3 parts), *Merioneth*, 198 (1997–9); Gerallt D. Nash, *Victorian School-days in Wales* (Cardiff, 1991); W. Gareth Evans, 'Intermediate Education in Carmarthenshire, 1889–1914 (unpublished MA thesis, Aberystwyth University, 1980); idem 'The Aberdare Report and Cardiganshire: an assessment of education conditions and attitudes in 1885', *Ceredigion* IX (1982), 193–226; D. W. Thomas, 'Astudiaeth o dystiolaeth cofiannau i gyflwr addysg yng Ngheredigion yn y bedwaredd ganrif ar bymtheg' (unpublished MA thesis, University of Wales, Aberystwyth, 1967); and Griffith G. Davies, 'Addysg Elfennol yn Sir Aberteifi, 1870–1902', *Ceredigion*, IV (1963), 352–73.

[60] Jones, *The Education of a Nation*, pp. 119–30.

[61] Pyrs Gruffudd, 'The Countryside as Educator: Schools, Rurality and Citizenship in Inter-war Wales', *Journal of Historical Geography*, 22/4 (1996), 412–23.

[62] Gruffudd, 'The Countryside as Educator', 412–23.

[63] Carmarthenshire Records Office Carmarthen (CROC), Esgairdawe School logbook, entries from 31 March 1890 and 11 November 1891. The toilets sound horrific (31 March 1891).

[64] CROC, Caeo School logbook, 7 January 1894.

[65] CROC, Coedmor School logbook, 12 February 1903.

[66] CROC, Penwaun School Education Book, C84/1, 12 November 1897. A school's location was vital. Nantcwmrhys school in Cynwyl Elfed was particularly badly situated. In 1890 the master asked the local council to

> fix a suitable footpath for the children of the south western division of the parish. Hitherto they have to travel over marshy soil, covered with stagnant water augmented in winter times by heavy rain, so that the nominal pathways become almost impassable. The parents in consequence naturally feel reluctant to send their children to school because they know that their feet would be wet before they reached halfway and to remain in such conditions for several hours would be detrimental to their health.

On 1 August 1890, such were the conditions following a rainstorm that not a single pupil turned up for school. The master had complained since 1881 of the dangerous state of the footbridge which crossed the stream. In October 1907 the bridge was washed away in a storm, thereby isolating the school. In 1908, in desperation, the master decided to remake the path himself. Yet the reasons for non-attendance at school were not confined to the vagaries of the weather.

[67] Russell Davies, *Secret Sins: Sex, Violence and Society in Carmarthenshire, 1870–1920* (Cardiff, 1995), pp. 79–88; Robert Gielden, *Education in Provincial France, 1800–1914* (Oxford, 1983).

[68] *Report of the Committee Appointed to Inquire into the Condition of Intermediate and Higher Education in Wales, 1881* (C. 3047 (2nd series, 1881), p. lvi). The commentator said that 'the grammar school at Carmarthen has buildings so objectional in arrangement and situation that, in the opinion of some of those interested in the school, the scanty attendance of 15 boys in a population of 10,000 may be sufficiently be accounted for on this ground alone'.

[69] Muriel B. Evans, 'The community and social change in the parish of Trelech a'r Bettws during the nineteenth century (unpublished MA thesis, University of Wales, Aberystwyth 1980), p. 80.

[70] CROC, Nantcwmrhys Education Book, 14 June 1895.

[71] CROC, Nantcwmrhys Education Book, 21 June 1895.

[72] CROC, Nantcwmrhys Education Book, 23 August 1895.

[73] CROC, Nantcwmrhys Education Book, 20 May 1908; J. A. Davies, *Education in a Welsh Rural County 1870–1973* (Cardiff, 1973); Rhys Davies, *Cefnarthen: y Comin, y Capel a'r Ysgol* (Swansea, 1983).

[74] Davies, *Secret Sins*, pp. 81–4.

[75] Quoted in Gwyn Evans and David Maddox, *The Tonypandy Riots, 1910–11* (Plymouth, 2010), p. 14.

76 Evans, *Education in Industrial Wales: 1700–1900* (Cardiff, 1971); J. R. Webster, 'The place of secondary education in Welsh society, 1800–1918 (unpublished PhD thesis, University of Wales Swansea, 1959); Peter Stead, 'Schools and Society in Glamorgan before 1914', *Morgannwg*, xix (1975), 47; E. Hillary Griffiths, 'The Development of Elementary and Secondary Education in Llanelli, 1847–1947' (unpublished MSc thesis, University of Wales, Aberystwyth, 1971); J. S. Hart, *Elementary Schooling and the Working Classes 1860–1918* (London, 1979); P. Horn, *The Victorian and Edwardian Schoolchild* (Amberley, 1989); Michael Savage, *The Remaking of the British Working Class, 1840–1940* (London, 1994), p. 101; and Paul Thompson, *The Edwardians: the Remaking of British Society* (London, 1992), pp. 117–20.

77 *Reminiscences of a Hook Miner* (Pembroke, n.d.), p. 21.

78 Kate Davies, *Hafau fy Mhlentyndod ym Mhentref Pren-gwyn* (Llandysul, 1970); Picton Davies, *Atgofion Dyn Papur Newydd* (Liverpool, 1962).

79 Davies, *Secret Sins*, pp. 79–84.

80 CROC, Rhydcymerau Education Book, 158/1, 27–30 January 1874.

81 CROC, Caeo Education Book, 557, 19–23 September 1892.

82 Beriah Gwynfe Evans informed the Cross Commission that: 'At Gwynfe I never permitted a word of Welsh to be spoken under any circumstances inside the schoolroom or even in the playground. I am, to this date, ashamed to own that I, as a schoolmaster, did what was at one time a universal custom, and caned my boys for using in my hearing their mother tongue . . . I shall regret it to my dying day'. Quoted in W. Gareth Evans, 'Intermediate education in Carmarthenshire, 1889–1914' (unpublished MA thesis, University of Wales, Aberystwyth), p. 49.

83 CROC, Esgairdawe Education Book, 78/1, 10 October 1887.

84 Kate Roberts, *Traed Mewn Cyffion* (Aberystwyth, 1936), p. 77.

85 CROC, Llanllawddog Education Book, 100, HMI Report, 1908.

86 Ernest Jones, *Free Associations* (London, 1959), p. 35.

87 Wynford Vaughan Thomas, *Trust to Talk* (London, 1980), pp. 2–7.

88 See, for example, Byron Rogers, *Me: the Authorised Biography* (London, 2009), pp. 90–126; Dannie Abse, *Ash on a Young Man's Sleeve* (Cardigan, 2006 edn), pp. 21–37.

89 Gwyn Thomas, *A Welsh Eye* (London, 1957), p. 58. On changes in Welsh society, see J. Geraint Jenkins, 'Technological Improvement and Social Change in South Cardiganshire', *Agricultural History Review*, XIII (1965), 94; for perceptive views of the social effects of technological change, see Gareth W. Williams, 'The Disenchantment of the World: Innovation, Crisis and Change in Cardiganshire, *c.*1880–1910', *Ceredigion*, IX, 4

(1983), 7–24, and David H. Morgan, *Harvesters and Harvesting, 1840–1900* (London, 1982).

90 Harriet Tuckley, *Everest, the First Ascent: the Untold Story of Griffith Pugh, the Man Who Made it Possible* (London, 2013), p. 317.

91 On Emlyn Williams, see Russell S. Stephens, *Emlyn Williams: the Making of a Dramatist* (Bridgend, 2000).

92 This was, for example, the experience of the writer Gwyn Thomas, who was raised by an elder sister.

93 *Cymru*, February 1907.

4 *'Ffair Wagedd' – Vanity Fair*

1 F. M. L. Thompson, *English Landed Society in the Nineteenth Century* (London, 1963); A. Lambert, *Unquiet Souls: The Indian Summer of the British Aristocracy* (London, 1984). On the aristocracy, see David Cannadine, *The Decline and Fall of the British Aristocracy* (London, 1990); M. L. Bush, *The English Aristocracy: a Comparative Synthesis* (London, 1984); and J. V. Beckitt, *The Aristocracy in England, 1600–1914* (London, 1986). Unfortunately, there is no comparable work in the Welsh context. Anyone interested in the topic has to survey the collected works of Francis Jones, who diligently recorded the decline of the Welsh gentry. See, for example, his *Historical Carmarthenshire Houses and their Families* (Llandybïe, 1987). There is also much of value in John Davies, 'The End of the Great Estates and the Rise of Freehold Farming in Wales', *Welsh History Review*, 7/2 (1974), 186–212, and in Richard Moore-Colyer's work, for example 'The Gentry and the County in Nineteenth-century Cardiganshire, *Welsh History Review*, 10 (1980–1), 497–535, and 'The Pryse Family of Gogerddan and the Decline of a Great Estate, 1800–1960', *Welsh History Review*, 9 (1978–9), 407–31. Evocative of the decline is T. Lloyd, *The Lost Houses of Wales* (London, 1986).

2 The great chronicler of Welsh heraldry and hierarchy was Francis Jones, Wales Herald Extraordinary; see also J. E. Griffith, *Pedigrees of Anglesey and Caernarvonshire Families* (privately printed, Horncastle, 1914); T. Nicholas, *Annals and Antiquities of the Counties and County Families of Wales*, 2 vols (London, 1872). Trollope's fictional Archbishop Grantly uttered an undoubted truth with his remark, 'Land gives so much more than rent. It gives position and influence and political power, to say nothing about the game'; quoted in Lawrence Stone and J. C. Fautier Stone, *An Open Elite? England 1540–1880* (London, 1984), p. 71.

3 See Russell Davies, *Hope and Heartbreak: a Social History of Wales and the Welsh, 1776–1871* (Cardiff, 2005), p. 93; see also Ernest Gaskell, *South Wales Leaders; Social and Political* (London, 1905) and J. Austin Jenkins and W. T. Pike (eds), *South Wales and Monmouthshire at the Opening of the Twentieth century: Contemporary Biographies* (Brighton, 1907).

4 On Lloyd George's sale of honours, see D. M. Creiger, 'Lloyd George's lucre: the national liberal fund', in *Chiefs without Indians* (London, 1982).

5 Donald Spring (ed.), *The Great Landowners of Great Britain and Ireland* (London, 1971 edn); see also John Bateman, *The Great Landowners of Great Britain and Ireland* (London, 1876).

6 B. L. James, 'The "Great Landowners" of Wales', *National Library of Wales Journal*, 14 (1965–6), 301–19.

7 John Davies, *Cardiff and the Marquesses of Bute* (Cardiff, 1981).

8 James, 'The "Great Landowners" of Wales'.

9 David Dykes, *Wales in Vanity Fair: a Show of Cartoons by 'Ape', Spy and other Artists of Welsh Personalities of the Victorian Age* (Cardiff, 1993), p. 33. For an excellent discussion of tradition and change amongst the gentry, see Philip Jenkins 'The creation of an "Ancient Gentry": Glamorgan 1760–1940', *Welsh History Review*, 12/1 (1984), 29–49.

10 Davies, *Hope and Heartbreak*, p. 94.

11 David Cannadine, *The Pleasures of the Past* (London, 1990), p. 97.

12 The leading study of these country home idylls, the revisitation of Celtic Bridesheads, is still Mark Girouard, *The Victorian Country House* (London, 1971); also useful is F. M. L. Thompson, *English Landed Society in the Nineteenth Century* (London, 1975).

13 I. Thomas, *Top Sawyer: A Biography of David Davies of Llandinam* (London, 1938), p. 70.

14 On Margaret Thomas, see M. H. Mackworth, Viscountess Rhondda, *This was my World* (London, 1933); S. M. Eoff, *Viscountess Rhondda: Equalitarian Feminist* (London, 1991); Angela V. John, *Turning the Tide: the life of Lady Rhondda* (Cardigan, 2013).

15 Ryland Wallace, *The Women's Suffrage Movement in Wales, 1866–1928* (Cardiff, 2009); see also Deirdre Beddoe, *Out of the Shadows: A History of Women in Twentieth-Century Wales* (Cardiff, 2000), pp. 41–6; and Ursula Masson, 'Votes for Women: the Campaign in Swansea', *Minerva: Transactions of the Royal Institute of South Wales I* (1993), 34–9; Angela John, '"Run Like Blazes": the Suffragettes and Welshness', *Llafur*, 6 (1994), 29–43.

16 E. White, *The Ladies of Gregynog* (Cardiff, 1985); Oliver Fairclough (ed.), *Cyfoeth, Celf a Chydwybod: Llafur Cariad Chwiorydd Gregynog* (Cardiff, 2007).

[17] Cannadine, *The Decline and Fall of the British Aristocracy*, p. 76.

[18] On the radical tradition, see K. O. Morgan, *Wales in British Politics, 1868–1922* (Cardiff, 1963); Elwyn Lewis Jones, *Gwaedu Gwerin* (Denbigh, 1983); I. Wyn Jones, *Y Llinyn Arian: Agweddau o Fywyd a Chyfnod Thomas Gee, 1815–1898* (Denbigh, 1998); Emyr Price, *Thomas Gee* (Bangor, 1977).

[19] Quoted in David Cannadine, *Aspects of Aristocracy: Grandeur and Decline in Modern Britain* (London, 1994).

[20] K. O. Morgan, 'Lloyd George's stage army: the Coalition Liberals, 1918–22', in A. J. P. Taylor (ed.), *Lloyd George: Twelve Essays* (London, 1971), pp. 225–54. One who seemed to enter fully into the cynical nature of the sale of honours was the Cardiff steamship tycoon William James Tatem (1868–1942). He gave a cheque for £50,000 to the treasurer of Lloyd George's political fund and signed it 'Glanely'. Provided he got his title, then the treasurer could cash his cheque.

[21] M. E. Montgomery, *Gilded Prostitution: Status, Money and Transatlantic Marriages, 1870–1914* (London, 1989); G. R. Searle, *Corruption in British Politics, 1895–1930* (London, 1987).

[22] Ben Pimlott, *Hugh Dalton* (London, 1985).

[23] On Wogan Philipps, see T. Milford and G. Evans (eds), *The Art of Wogan Philipps, Lord Milford* (London, 1995) and P. J. Kavanagh, *The Perfect Stranger* (London, 1966).

[24] P. Preston, *Doves of War: Four Women of Spain* (London, 2002) and Baron Howard de Walden, *Earls Have Peacocks* (London, 1992).

[25] John Davies, 'The End of the Great Estates', 190, and 'The Landed Families of Breconshire', *Brycheiniog*, 36 (2004), 69–82.

[26] Cannadine, *Aspects of Aristocracy*, p. 46.

[27] Davies, 'The End of the Great Estates'.

[28] Davies, 'The End of the Great Estates'. Henry Neville Gladstone, Baron Gladstone of Hawarden (1852–1935), was thus forced to make his living from banking and finance.

[29] On the decline and fall of the Pryse family, see Richard Colyer, 'The Pryse family of Gogerddan and the Decline of a Great Estate,' *Welsh History Review*, 9 (1978–9), 407–31, and 'A Landed Estate in Decline: Nanteos 1800–1930', *Ceredigion*, 9 (1980), 58–77. Even more evocative of lost grandeur is Gerald Morgan (ed.), *Nanteos: a Welsh House and its Families* (Llandysul, 2001). See also P. Smith, *Houses of the Welsh Countryside* (London, 1975).

[30] Davies, 'The End of the Great Estates'.

[31] On the investments in gardens, see H. T. Milliken, *Road to Bodnant: the Story behind the Famous North Wales Garden* (London, 1975); D. M. Robinson and D. Williams, *The Historic Gardens of Wales* (London, 1992); and Elizabeth Whittle, *The Historic Gardens of Wales* (London, 1992).

32 See, for example, Cannadine, *The Decline and Fall of the British Aristocracy*, pp. 445–99.

33 Vaughan, *South Wales Squires, passim.*

34 C. C. Martindale, *Bernard Vaughan* (London, 1923).

35 Vaughan, *South Wales Squires.*

36 Vaughan, *South Wales Squires*. As the title of his barony would suggest, he kept his links with Swansea (his father was Pasco St Leger Grenfell, a copperworks owner) and served as president of the Royal Institution of South Wales from 1904–6. Grenfell presented a number of Egyptian antiquities to its museum, including the mummy of the priest Tem-Hor.

37 Cannadine, *The Decline and Fall of the British Aristocracy, passim*; R. Pound, *The Lost Generation* (London, 1964); David Cannadine, 'War and death: grief and mourning in modern Britain', in J. Whaley (ed.), *Mirrors of Mortality* (London, 1981).

38 Peter Lord, *Winifred Coombe Tennant: a Life through Art* (Aberystwyth, 2007), pp. 10–39.

39 Fairclough, *Cyfoeth, Celf a Chydwybod*, p. 71.

40 D. Hart Davies (ed.), *Letters and Journals of Sir Alan Lascelles, 1887–1920* (London, 1987), p. 28.

41 C. F. G. Masterman, *England after the War* (London, 1922), pp. 27–47.

42 W. D. Rubinstein, *Elites and the Wealthy in Modern British History* (Brighton, 1987).

43 Cannadine, *Aspects of Aristocracy*, p. 35.

44 Davies, *Cardiff and the Marquesses of Bute.*

45 Dykes, *Wales in Vanity Fair.*

46 F. Booker, *The Great Western Railway: a New History* (London, 1977).

47 I. Lloyd, *Rolls Royce: the Growth of a Firm* (London, 1978), pp. 8–14, 22–36.

48 P. King, *Knights of the Air* (London, 1989), pp. 39–40.

49 Hon. Mrs Victor Bruce, *Nine Thousand Miles in Eight Weeks* (London, 1927), *passim*, and *Nine Lives Plus* (London, 1977), p. 13.

50 In 1921, Instone and Co. Ltd went public with a nominal capital of £500,000. At this time Samuel Instone was also chairman of the Askern Coal and Iron Company Ltd and of Bedwas Navigation Colliery Company. The combination of his modern ideas, introduction of machinery, and other cost-saving ideas, and his opposition to the South Wales Miners Federation (popularly referred to as 'The Fed') and support of the rival South Wales Industrial Union, resulted in a conflict that lasted over a decade and damaged his reputation. Instone was labelled 'one of the bloodsucking rich'.

51 P. N. Davies, *Sir Alfred Jones: Shipping Entrepreneur Par Excellence* (London, 1978) and A. H. Milne, *Sir Alfred Lewis Jones, KCMG* (London, 1914). Alfred Jones not only revived the fortunes of British West Africa but also assisted the recovery of the economy of the Canary Islands. Calling there on business, he found the local economy devastated as the old staple export crop, cochineal, had been replaced by aniline dyes. He assisted the islanders in growing bananas, tomatoes and other crops. To provide a ready market, Jones introduced the banana to the British people, initially giving them for free to costermongers to sell. From this commenced his contribution to the revitalising of the Jamaican economy, as the colonial secretary, Joseph Chamberlain, asked him to organise a similar initiative to help the islanders. Jones's most enduring act of philanthropy was his foundation, in 1898, of the Liverpool School of Tropical Medicine. Alfred Jones was not without his critics. He paid his loyal workers scandalously low wages and E. D. Morel commented scathingly that Jones never condemned the role Leopold II of Belgium played in the Congo. Yet his vices were matched by virtues. These were shown in 1906, when he survived an earthquake in Jamaica (his hotel quite literally collapsed around him) and Jones was the main organiser and founder of the relief effort. At his death in 1909, more than £325,000 was distributed to charitable causes and to provide education for the people of West Africa.

52 C. Mackenzie, *Realms of Silver: One Hundred Years of Banking in the East* (London, 1954).

53 Milliken, *The Road to Bodnant*.

54 E. Green and M. Moss, *A Business of National Importance: the Royal Mail Shipping Groups, 1902–1937* (London, 1982) and P. N. Davies, 'Business Success and the Role of Chance: the Extraordinary Philipps Brothers', *Business History*, 23 (1981), 208–32. Apart from Viscount St Davids, three of his brothers and one of his sisters achieved distinction – Major-General Sir Ivor Philipps; Owen Cosby Philipps, Baron Kylsant; Laurence Richard Philipps, Baron Milford; and Elsbeth Philipps, assistant director of milk at the Ministry of Food during the First World War. After the war the trusts expanded further into the Old Broad Street Group, financing companies such as Ilford Ltd, Schweppes Ltd, and Court Line Ltd. A very public dispute with his brother Owen, caused by the latter's attempt to heal an ancient family feud with his cousin, Sir Henry Erasmus Philipps of Picton Castle, and his conversion from the Liberal to the Conservative party, was damaging to his business interests. The Royal Mail Group collapsed in 1931. The Court Line was liquidated in 1929 and the Buenos Aires and Pacific Railway

had to be restructured in 1932, whilst British Portland Cement Manufacturers faced severe competition.

55 J. Lindsay, *A History of the North Wales Slate Industry* (London, 1974). In June 1887, Assheton-Smith paid the men's fares to London for the Queen's Jubilee, and on his marriage in June 1888 he remitted six months of his tenants' rent and paid the fares and expenses of a day trip to Liverpool or Manchester for all his employees. Wages were raised by 5 per cent in 1895, and in May 1902 when the Prince of Wales stayed at the Vaynol estate for his installation as chancellor of the University of Wales, the quarrymen were given a day's holiday plus payments of 6s.

56 Dykes, *Wales in Vanity Fair*.

57 R. Merfyn Jones, *The North Wales Quarrymen* (Cardiff, 1985).

58 Lindsay, *A History of the North Wales Slate Industry*, p. 23.

59 J. V. Morgan (ed.), *Welsh Political and Educational Leaders in the Victorian Era* (London, 1908); H. M. Thomas, 'Duffryn Aberdare', *Morgannwg*, 21 (1977), 9–41; I. G. Jones, *Explorations and Explanations* (Llandysul, 1981), pp. 193–214. Bruce took over the Duffryn estate from his father, which proved to be a momentous decision for him. Up to this point, he complained to a friend in 1843, his life had been aimless and he felt himself to be 'a useless member of society'. Under his leadership and stewardship, the estate flourished. Mineral royalties rose steadily to reach £1,800 per annum by 1852, but subsequent expansion in the market for steam coal, a resource in which the estate was particularly rich, sent income soaring. By 1860, mineral royalties from Duffryn Aberdare were worth £12,000 a year. Bruce's consequence grew with the fortunes of the estate. He made significant contributions to the expansion of education, especially primary provision (he, not Forster, was the architect of the 1870 Education Act) and higher education in Wales.

60 Davies, *Cardiff and the Marquesses of Bute* and 'Aristocratic town makers and the coal metropolis, the marquesses of Bute and Cardiff, *c.*1776–1947', in David Cannadine (ed.), *Patricians, Power and Politics in Nineteenth-century Towns* (London, 1982), pp 242–80. For his broad interests, see J. M. Crook, *William Burges and the Victorian Dream* (London, 1981) and 'Patron extraordinary: John, marquess of Bute', in P. Howell (ed.), *Victorian South Wales* (Cardiff, 1970), pp. 115–41. Bute used his great fortune to travel, study and publish, especially on early Catholicism. His conversion to the Roman Catholic faith on 8 December 1868 caused a sensation and is believed to have inspired the plot of Disraeli's novel, *Lothair*. Bute's mediaevalism and Catholicism found aesthetic expression in the architectural wonders of Cardiff Castle and Castell Coch, where his collaboration with the architect William Burges created two

masterpieces of the High Victorian Gothic style. Bute was also active in funding investigations of psychic phenomena and spiritualism and he even published a book on an alleged haunting. He was also actively involved in the support of universities, especially Glasgow and St Andrews.

61 Quoted in Cannadine, *The Decline and Fall of the British Aristocracy*, pp. 565–6.

62 Serving on several royal commissions (accidents in mines 1879–81; mining royalties 1890–1; coal dust in mines 1891–4; labour 1891–4; coal supplies 1901–5; trade disputes 1903–6; and shipping 1906–7). He chaired and served on several public bodies and was president of the Mining Association of Great Britain (1860) and the Iron and Steel Institute (1910) and chairman of the South Wales Coalowner's Association for eighteen years. He was knighted in 1885, received a baronetcy in 1896, was elevated to the peerage as Baron Merthyr of Senghennydd in 1911 and was created a KCVO in 1912.

63 E. Phillips, *A History of the Pioneers of the Welsh Coalfield* (Cardiff, 1925), p. 117.

64 M. J. Daunton, *Coal Metropolis: Cardiff 1870–1914* (Leicester, 1977).

65 *South Wales Daily News*, 17 February 1891.

66 *South Wales Daily News*, 1 September 1898.

67 *Who's Who in Wales* (Cardiff, 1937); C. L. Mowat, *Britain Between the Wars, 1918–1940* (London, 1955).

68 T. Jones, *Whitehall Diary*, ed. K. Middlemas (London, 1969), p. 2.

69 Thomas, *Top Sawyer*.

70 G. J. Jones, *Wales and the Quest for Peace* (Cardiff, 1969); *Who's Who in Wales*.

71 K. O. Morgan, *Modern Wales: Politics, Places and People* (Cardiff, 1995), p. 117.

72 M. H. Thomas et al., *D. A. Thomas, Viscount Rhondda* (London, 1921), and M. H. Mackworth, Viscountess Rhondda, *This was my World* (London, 1933); see also K. O. Morgan, 'D. A. Thomas: the Industrialist as Politician', in Stewart Williams (ed.), *Glamorgan Historian*, 3 (1966), 33–51.

73 On Henry Seymour Berry, see *Western Mail*, 24 May 1928; on David Llewellyn, see *Western Mail*, 16 December 1940.

74 Wealth at death is a particularly crude method of calculating a person's value. This is, however, what W. D. Rubinstein did in his path-breaking study of the very wealthy, *Men of Property: the Very Wealthy in Britain since the Industrial Revolution* (London, 1981). However, a very obvious note of caution is that the most astute, especially after the imposition

of death duties, would have disposed of and dispersed their assets before their death. Whatever the criteria, the Berry brothers seem to have done remarkably well. Henry Seymour Berry, Baron Buckland of Bwlch, left £1,116,447 14s. 9d in 1929, William Ewart Berry, first Viscount Camrose, left £1,480,685 12s. 9d in 1954, whilst Gomer, first Viscount Kemsley, left £310,866 in 1968. Perhaps a greater mark of value was the fact that crowds, thousands strong, lined the routes of their funeral cortèges in south Wales.

75 For the development of Swansea, see Stephen Hughes, *Copperopolis: Landscapes of the Early Industrial Period in Swansea* (Aberystwyth, 2000).

76 S. Vivian, *The Story of the Vivians* (Swansea, 1989); R. A. Griffiths, *Singleton Abbey and the Vivians of Swansea* (Swansea, 1988).

77 Vivian's heart was in Swansea and its commercial development. Amongst the projects which he led was the expansion of harbour facilities, the development of the Rhondda and Swansea Bay railway, and the endowment of schools. Yet Vivian's history was not one of unimpeded success. He was also familiar with failure and financial uncertainty. In his final years his company entered on hard times and the collapse of the family's mining venture in Sudbury, Canada, almost led to bankruptcy. It was fitting that on his elevation to the peerage on 9 June 1893 he took the title Baron Swansea, the town that, according to Leslie Ward in *Vanity Fair*, had accorded him the same honour that Rome bestowed on Julius Caesar, of having a statue of himself erected whilst he was still alive.

78 Dykes, *Wales in Vanity Fair*, p. 79.

79 David Painting, *Amy Dillwyn* (Cardiff, 1987).

80 G. W. Roderick, 'South Wales Industrialists and the Theory of Gentrification', *Transactions of the Honourable Society of Cymmrodorion* (1987), 65–83, 78–9.

81 Martin J. Weiner, *English Culture and the Decline of the Industrial Spirit, 1850–1980* (London, 1005). For a criticism of the effects of the process of gentrification, see F. M. L. Thompson, *Gentrification and the Enterprise Culture: Britain 1780–1980* (Oxford, 2001).

82 As with so many other negative aspects, this myth became deeply embedded following the outrageous comments contained in the infamous Education Reports of 1847.

83 C. Lerry, 'The Industries of Denbighshire: Part 3: More Recent Developments', *Transactions of the Denbighshire Historical Society*, 8 (1959), 95–113.

84 *Australian Dictionary of National Biography*: *http:www.adb.online.anu.edu.au/biogs/A060279b* (accessed 1 December 2009).

85 *The Times*, 18 April 1938.

86 J. Jones, *Atgofion am Mr Robert Davies, Bodlondeb* (Caernarfon, 1906). Upon his death he left an estate valued at £425,501 3s. 6d.

87 T. Gwynn Jones, *Cofiant Thomas Gee* (Denbigh, 1913).

88 Harold Perkin, *The Rise of Professional Society: England since 1880* (London, 1989). See, for example, Alfred S. Williams and R. F. Kewer-Williams, *Who's Who in Llanelly and District* (Llanelli, 1910).

89 A. J. Cronin, *The Citadel* (London, 1934).

90 A. Digby, *Making a Medical Living: Doctors and Patients in the English Market for Medicine, 1720–1911* (Cambridge, 1994), pp. 15, 142–5.

91 Ruth Evans, *Sir John Williams 1840–1926* (Cardiff, 1952); Emyr Wyn Jones, 'Sir John Williams: his background and achievement', in John Cule (ed.), *Wales and Medicine: an Historical Survey* (London, 1975). An intriguing but unconvincing attempt to portray Sir John Williams as Jack the Ripper is provided in Tony Williams and Humphrey Price, *Uncle Jack: the True Identity of Jack the Ripper* (London, 2005).

92 John Cule, 'The Eccentric Dr William Price of Llantrisant, 1800–93', *Morgannwg*, 7 (1963), 98–120, and B. Davies, 'Empire and identity: the "case" of Doctor William Price', in D. Smith (ed.), *A People and a Proletariat: Essays in the history of Wales, 1780–1980* (London, 1980).

93 On the medical profession, see Digby, *Making a Medical Living.*

94 Brenda Maddox, *Freud's Wizard: the Enigma of Ernest Jones* (London, 2008).

95 On the legal profession, see J. Garrard and V. Parrott, 'Craft, professional and middle-class identities: solicitors and gas engineers, *c.*1850–1914', in A. Kidd and D. Nicholls (eds), *The Making of the British Middle Class?* (Stroud, 1998), pp. 148–68.

96 D. L. Jones (Cynalaw), *Y Ffraethebydd* (Denbigh, *c.*1889).

97 K. O. Morgan, *Wales in British Politics, 1868–1922* (Cardiff, 1970).

98 See W. H. Jones and Ben Bowen Thomas, 'Sir John Herbert Lewis: Centenary Tribute', *Journal of the Flintshire Historical Society*, 18 (1960), 131–41, 142–55.

99 D. Hopkin, 'The Llanelli Riots 1911', *Welsh History Review*, 11 (1983), 488–515; Robert Griffiths, *Streic! Streic! Streic!* (Llandysul, 1986).

100 Paul Thompson, *The Edwardians: the Remaking of British Society* (London, 1992), pp. 139–48.

101 Jones, *The North Wales Quarrymen*; J. Melling, '"Non-Commissioned Officers:" British Employers and their Supervisory Workers, 1870–1920', *Social History*, 5 (1980), 197.

102 P. J. Leng, G. W. and A. Hesketh, *The Welsh Dockers* (Ormskirk, 1981).

103 Hywel Francis and Dai Smith, *The Fed: a History of the South Wales Miners in the Twentieth Century* (London, 1980); J. Campbell, *Aneurin*

Bevan and the Mirage of British Socialism (New York, NY, 1987). The coal produced was not homogeneous for Wales, unlike the rest of Britain, contained the whole range of coal – anthracite, bituminous and steam coal. Steam coal dominated, but each coal type faced different markets and hence miners working the different types of coal could not be assumed to be ready for action over wages at exactly the same time and to exactly the same extent. Thus, 1925, not 1921 or 1926, was *the* climacteric year in the anthracite coal field.

104 Peter Lord, *The Visual Culture of Wales: Industrial Society* (Cardiff), pp. 153, 155–8; David Egan, *Coal Society: a History of the South Wales Mining Valleys 1840–1980* (Llandysul, 1987).

105 Gwyn Evans and David Maddox, *The Tonypandy Riots 1910–11* (Plymouth, 2010), *passim*.

106 H. C. Long, *The Edwardian House: The Middle Class House in Britain, 1880–1914* (London, 1993); M. Girouard, *The Victorian Country House*; Judith Flanders, *The Victorian House: Domestic Life from Childbirth to Deathbed* (London, 2004); Trevor May, *The Victorian Domestic Servant* (London, 2007); and H. Long, *The Edwardian House: the Middle-Class House in Britain, 1880–1914* (Manchester, 1993). For women servants in Wales, see Ann Williams, 'Women's Employment in Nineteenth-century Anglesey', *Llafur*, 6 (1993), 39–43.

107 William Evans's reward for his faithful service to the Cawdor estate was the gift of his own house in Bridge Street, Llandeilo.

108 *The Guardian*, 15 April 1998.

109 W. R. Protheroe, *Griffith Rhys Jones (Caradog)* (Cardiff, 1911); Gareth Williams, *'Valleys of Song': Music and Society in Wales, 1840–1914* (Cardiff, 1998), pp. 40–53.

110 C. Nevin, 'Suicide with a smile', *The Independent*, 10 September 2000.

111 Gwyn A. Williams, *When Was Wales?: A History of the Welsh* (London, 1985), p. 176.

112 F. M. L. Thompson, *Gentrification and the Enterprise Culture: Britain, 1780–1980* (Oxford, 2001).

113 A. H. Jones (ed.), *Lyric Thoughts of the late Thomas Jones, the Poet Preacher* (Swansea, 1886); *The Cambrian*, 30 June 1888.

114 The volume was based on Brynmor Jones's work in gathering evidence for the Land Commission in 1893–6.

115 K. V. Jones, *Life of John Viriamu Jones* (Cardiff, 1915); G. B. Wilson, *Leif Jones, Lord Rhayader* (London, 1948).

116 Laurie Manchester, *Holy Fathers, Secular Sons: Clergy, Intelligentsia, and the Modern Self in Revolutionary Russia* (Chicago, IL, 2008).

117 See, for example, some of the evidence gathered in S. Minwell Tibbott and Beth Thomas, *O'r Gwaith i'r Gwely: Cadw Tŷ 1890–1960: A Woman's Work: Housework 1890–1960* (Cardiff, 1994).

[118] Tibbott and Thomas, *O'r Gwaith i'r Gwely*, p. 39.

[119] S. Minwell Tibbott, 'Laundering in the Welsh Home', *Folk Life*, 19 (1981), 54–5. See also Elizabeth Roberts, *Women's Place, An Oral History of Working Class Women, 1890–1940* (Oxford, 1996).

[120] Tibbott, 'Laundering in the Welsh Home', 55.

[121] See above, chapters 1 and 3.

[122] See above, chapters 1 and 3.

[123] Davies, 'The End of the Great Estates', 210–11. For a study of farm organisation and structure, see David Jenkins, 'Trefn Ffarm a Llafur Gwlad', *Ceredigion*, 4, (1962), 244–53.

[124] Daniel Parry-Jones, *Welsh County Upbringing* (London, 1948).

[125] A. W. Ashby and I. L. Evans, *The Agriculture of Wales* (Cardiff, 1944), pp. 96–7, 190–1 (I am grateful to Dr Dafydd Roberts for this reference). See also Edgar Thomas, *The Economics of Small Holdings: a Study Based on a Survey of Small Scale Farming in Carmarthenshire* (Cambridge, 1927) and Spencer Thomas, 'The Agricultural Labour Force in some South-west Carmarthenshire Parishes', *Welsh History Review*, 3 (1966), 63–73.

[126] C. Feinstein, 'What Really Happened to Real Wages? Trends in Wages, Prices, and Productivity in the United Kingdom, 1880–1913', *Economic History Review*, 43 (1990), 329–551; G. Routh, *Occupation and Pay in Great Britain, 1906–79* (London, 1980); D. A. Mackenzie, *Statistics in Britain, 1867–1900* (Basingstoke, 1988); L. J. Williams, *Digest of Welsh Historical Statistics*, 1 (Cardiff, 1985), pp. 167–84.

[127] Feinstein, 'What Really Happened to Real Wages?', 329–551.

[128] Museum of Welsh Life, St Fagan's, MSS 1755/36–37.

[129] There is a rich variety and volume of material on poverty. See, for example, *Royal Commission on the Poor Laws and Relief of Distress, 5 vols, 1881* (volume 5 has material on south Wales. Throughout, the report uses concise terminology to describe the poor.) Keith Laybourn, *The Evolution of British Social Policy and the Welfare State* (Keele, 1995); John Scott, *Poverty and Wealth: Citizenship, Deprivation and Privilege* (Harlow, 1994); Anne Digby, *The Poor Law in Nineteenth-century England and Wales* (London, 1982); Karel Williams, *From Pauperism to Poverty* (London, 1981); Rachel Vorspan, 'Vagrancy and the New Poor Law in Victorian and Edwardian England', *English Historical Review*, 92, (1977), 59–81; M. Rose, *The Relief of Poverty 1834–1914* (London, 1982). There is also a wealth of regional studies of poverty and pauperism in Wales. See, for example, Tydfil Jones, *Poor Relief in Merthyr Tydfil Union in Victorian Times* (Cardiff, 1992); Alun Eirug Davies, 'Poverty and its treatment in Cardiganshire' (unpublished MA thesis, University of Wales, Aberystwyth, 1968).

[130] Alun Eurig Davies, 'Some Aspects of the Operation of the Old Poor Law in Cardiganshire', *Ceredigion*, 6 (1968), 321–42; L. J. Williams, *Digest of Welsh Historical Statistics*, 2, p. 170.

[131] Frank McLynn, *Stanley: Dark Genius of African Exploration* (London, 2004); Alan Gallop, *Mr Stanley, I Presume?* (Sutton, 2004). Another illegitimate boy who rose to greatness was James Henry 'Jimmy' Thomas (1874–1949), the cabinet minister disgraced in the 1930s for leaking the budget. Thomas, as lord privy seal, had the task of conquering unemployment in the Labour and then the National government in the early 1930s. Though he was regarded as having 'the adaptability of a jack of all trades and the versatility of a one-man band', he proved incapable of grasping the scope of the problem. Indeed, as one wag commented, Thomas 'preferred drinking to thinking'. An observer claimed that he had consumed nine gallons of champagne in 150 days. Piers Brendon, *The Dark Valley: A Panorama of the 1930s* (London, 2002), pp. 152–4. For the operation of a few workhouses in Wales, see J. H. Thomas and W. E. Wilkins, *The Bridgend-Cowbridge Union Workhouse and Guardians* (Cowbridge, 1995); David Llewelyn Jones, *Walcott a'r Wyrcws: Tlodi yng Ngogledd Cymru yn Hanner Cyntaf y Bedwaredd Ganrif ar Bymtheg* (Aberystwyth, 1977); A. H. Dodd, 'The Old Poor Law in North Wales', *Archaeologia Cambrensis*, 6 (1926), 111–33; Alun C. Davies, 'The Old Poor Law in an Industrialising Parish, Aberdare', *Welsh History Review*, 8 (1977), 270–89; Christopher Draper, *Paupers, Bastards and Lunatics: the Story of Conwy Workhouse* (Llanrwst, 2005); see also M. A. Crowther, *The Workhouse System: the History of an English Social Institution, 1834–1929* (London, 1981).

[132] *Cymru*, 28, (1927), 41.

[133] T. Cook (ed.), *Practical Compassion: Merfyn Turner, 1915–1991* (London, 1999).

[134] For an example of his civilised, compassionate style, see Merfyn Turner, *Forgotten Men* (London, 1960).

[135] Gwenno Ffrancon, *Cyfaredd y Cysgodion: Delweddau Cymru a'i Phobl ar Ffilm, 1935–1951* (Cardiff, 2003), pp. 43–63; Studs Terkel, *Hard Times, an Oral History of the Great Depression* (Harmondsworth, 1985) and Hilda Jennings, *Brynmawr: a Study of a Distressed Area* (London, 1934); A. Storey, *Stanley Baker: Portrait of an Actor* (London, 1977).

[136] Davies, *Hope and Heartbreak*, pp. 111–12.

[137] P. Keating, *Into Unknown England 1866–1943: Selections from the Social Explorers* (Glasgow, 1976); *Carmarthen Journal*, 26 August 1890; *Llanelly Mercury*, 22 June 1911; *The Welshman*, 10 February 1905; *Carmarthen Weekly Reporter*, 3 January 1908 and 5 August 1904.

[138] Dewi Emrys, *Rhigymau'r Ffordd Fawr* (Swansea, 1926). On Dewi Emrys's life as a tramp, see Eluned Phillips, *Dewi Emrys* (Llandysul, 1971) and T. Llew Jones, *Dewi Emrys* (Barddas, 1981). For the 'Supertramp', see Lawrence Normand, *W. H. Davies* (Bridgend, 2003).

[139] *Carmarthen Weekly Reporter*, 5 April 1907. The paper also reported the case of a 'third man who was even more aggressive. He had only one leg, but he could get about faster on it than most people can do on two. He held his cap in the way of wayfarers and, if he saw anybody trying to dodge him by going on the other side of the road, he promptly hopped over into their way and presented his cap in front of them'.

[140] Mary Higgs, *Where Shall She Sleep* (London, 1910); Pat Thane, 'Women and the Poor Law in Victorian and Edwardian England', *History Workshop Journal*, 6 (1978), 31.

[141] *Carmarthen Weekly Reporter*, 19 February 1904.

[142] Colin Bundy and Dermot Healy, 'Aspects of Urban Poverty', *Oral History*, 6 (1978), 79–98. See also *Returns on Poor Law Relief. Paupers Relieved in a Year and Periods of Relief* (Cd. 250), (London, 1908).

[143] *The Welshman*, 20 June 1913.

[144] *Carmarthen Weekly Reporter*, 23 October 1903.

[145] For Llandeilo, see *South Wales Press*, 22 May 1905; for Carmarthen, see *Carmarthen Weekly Reporter*, 14 April and 14 July 1905.

[146] *Y Genedl Cymreig*, 8 May 1900. The guardians, at the same meeting, complained about an alledgedly blind beggar who always ran away when the guardians or the police appeared.

[147] Davies, *Hope and Heartbreak*. For the fear of the 'underclass', see Louis Chevalier, *Labouring Classes and Dangerous Classes in Paris during the First Half of the Nineteenth Century* (London, 1973) and Gareth Steadman Jones, *Outcast London* (London, 1985).

5 *Hiraeth and Heartbreak*

[1] The Swiss *mal du Suisse* or *Schweizerheimweh* are perhaps the closest to capturing the same mixture of pain, poignancy and pleasure as are encountered in hiraeth. 'Nostalgia' and 'homesickness' certainly do not convey the complexities of meaning encapsulated in the word. For an excellent historical study, see Susan J. Matt, *Homesickness: an American History* (Oxford, 2011); T. Gwynn Jones, 'Tir na n'Og', in *Detholiad o Ganiadau* (Gregynog, 1926).

[2] One of the most popular, a song that still endures, was 'Cartref' by Richard Davies (Mynyddog). See E. G. Millward, *Ceinion y Gân* (Llandysul, 1983), p. 5.

3 T. H. ParryWilliams, *Pensynnu* (Llandysul, 1966), p. 89.

4 On the general experience of emigration and migration, see Eric Richards, *Britannia's Children: Emigration from England, Scotland, Wales and Ireland since 1600* (London, 2004); Carl Bridge and Kent Fedorowich, *The British World: Diaspora, Culture and Identity* (London, 2003); Dudley Baines, *Migration in a Mature Economy: Emigration and Internal Migration in England and Wales, 1861–1900* (Cambridge, 1985); Denis O'Hearn, *The Atlantic Economy: Britain, the US and Ireland* (Manchester, 2001); and James Belich, *Replenishing the Earth: the Settler Revolution and the Rise of the Anglo-World, 1783–1939* (Oxford, 2009). On the Welsh context, the best recent treatment is William D. Jones, *Wales in America: Scranton and the Welsh, 1860–1920* (Cardiff, 1993) and Anne Kelly Knowles, 'Immigrant Trajectories through the Rural-Industrial Transition in Wales and the United States', *Annals of the Association of American Geographers*, 85/2 (June, 1995), 246–66. Despite the criticism the book received upon publication there is still some useful material in Michael Hechter, *Internal Colonialism: the Celtic Fringe in British National Development* (Berkeley, California, 1975). Also valuable are two works by Brinley Thomas, *The Industrial Revolution and the Atlantic Economy* (London, 1993) and *International Migration and Economic Development* (Paris, 1961). See also Phillip N. Jones, *Mines, Migrants and Residence in the South Wales Steamcoal Valleys: the Ogmore and Garw Valleys in 1881* (Hull, 1987).

5 On the journeys of 'Merched y Gerddi' to harvest the orchards of England, see J. Williams-Davies, '"Merched y Gerddi", a Seasonal Migration of Female Labour from Rural Wales', *Folk Life*, 15 (1977), 12–26, and the *Royal Commission on Women and Children in Agriculture*, p. 1870, appendix 1, p. 40. See also M. I. Williams, 'Seasonal Migrations of Cardiganshire Harvest Gangs to the Vale of Glamorgan in the Nineteenth Century', *Ceredigion*, 3 (1957), 156–60.

6 D. S. M. Barrie, *A Regional History of the Railways of Great Britain: South Wales* (Nairn, 1994) and Peter E. Baughan, *A Regional History of the Railways of Great Britain: North and Mid Wales* (Nairn, 1991). For social change linked to the railways, see Nicholas Faith, *The World the Railways Made* (New York, NY, 1990).

7 On the impact of the letters home, see David Fitzpatrick, '"An ocean of consolations"; letters and Irish immigration to Australia', in Eric Richards, *Visible Immigrants* (Canberra, 1989), pp. 41–93, and R. Arnold, *The Farthest Promised Land* (Washington, 1981), pp. 68–77. For the impact of letters through the newspapers, see Robert Tyler, 'Y Wasg Gymraeg yn Nhrefedigaeth Awstralia', *Llafur*, 10/1 (2008), 21–31. For the links with technological development, see Allan R. Pred, 'Urban Systems

Development and the Long-distance Flow of Information through pre-electronic US newspapers', *Economic Geography*, 47 (1971), 498–524; Daniel R. Headrick, *When Information Came of Age – Technologies of Knowledge in the Age of Reason and Revolution, 1700–1850* (Oxford, 2000) and *The Tentacles of Progress: Technology Transfer in the Age of Imperialism, 1850–1940* (New York, NY, 1988); David M. Henkin, *The Postal Age: the Emergence of Modern Communications in the Nineteenth Century* (Chicago, 2006); Yrjö Kaukiainen, 'Shrinking the World: Improvements in the Speed of Information Transmission, *c.*1820–1870', *European Review of Economic History*, 5 (2001), 20.

8 On the themes in general, see Eugen Weber, *Peasants into Frenchmen: the Modernization of Rural France, 1870–1914* (London, 1977), pp. 278–302, and Jack Larkin, *The Reshaping of Everyday Life, 1790–1840* (New York, NY, 1988). For the contrasts between rural and urban societies in a Welsh context, see Gareth Williams, 'The Disenchantment of the World: Innovation, Crisis and Change in Cardiganshrie, *c.*1880–1910', *Ceredigion*, 9/4 (1983), 303–21.

9 William Jones Edwards, *Ar Lethrau Ffair Rhos* (Aberystwyth, 1959), pp. 10–11.

10 L. J. Williams, *Digest of Welsh Historical Statistics*, 1 (Cardiff, 1985), pp. 68–72.

11 Williams, *Digest of Welsh Historical Statistics*, 1, pp. 68–72.

12 There is a comprehensive literature on the interwar trade slump and economic depression and their effects on employment and migration patterns. On the general history, John Stevenson and Chris Cook, *The Slump: Society and Politics during the Depression* (London, 1977) is still useful, as is C. L. Mowat's comprehensive survey *Britain Between the Wars, 1918–40* (London, 1968); a more modern treatment is given in Amity Shlaes, *The Forgotten Man: a New History of the Great Depression* (London, 2007). For the Welsh context, see Brinley Thomas, *The Welsh Economy* (Cardiff, 1962); Trevor Herbert and Gareth Elwyn Jones (eds), *Wales Between the Wars* (Cardiff, 1988); and Dai Smith and Gareth Elwyn Jones (eds), *The People of Wales* (Llandysul, 1999), pp. 179–206.

13 Piers Brendon, *The Dark Valley: a Panorama of the 1930s* (London, 2000), p. 590.

14 For a literary portrayal of the effect of emigration on a family, see T. Rowland Hughes, *William Jones* (Denbigh, 1944).

15 W. H. Davies, *Ups and Downs* (Swansea, 1975), pp. 115–19.

16 Bleddyn Owen Huws, 'Y ddau Garneddi: Golwg ar rai o Lythyrau Olaf Carneddog', *Llên Cymru*, 24 (2001), 150, 153–4. I am very grateful to Dr Huws for a copy of the article and for the references. Though they were taken into the warm embrace of a loving family, there was

great sadness for the ancient couple in learning that none of their granddaughters spoke Welsh, and that their country values and nationalism were in marked contrast with their son's urban ways and socialism. On Carneddog, see also E. Namora Williams, *Carneddog a'i Deulu* (Denbigh, 1985). On the photograph, see Ioan Roberts, *Cymru Geoff Charles* (Talybont, 2003) and the article by William Troughton, 'Geoff Charles', *Friends of the Library / Cyfaill y Llyfrgell* (Winter, 2003) National Library of Wales, *www.llgc.org.uk/fileadmin/documents/pdf/cyfaillgaeaf03.pdf* (accessed 29 January 2015).

17 On the Welsh communities in England, see Emrys Jones, *The Welsh in London* (Cardiff, 2001); H. G. Reed, *Middlesborough and its Jubilee: a History of the Iron and Steel Industries with Biographies of the Pioneers* (Middlesborough, 1881); David Ward 'Culture, Politics and Assimilation: the Welsh on Teeside, *c.*1850–1940', *Welsh History Review*, 17 (1995), 550–70; R. Merfyn Jones, 'The Liverpool Welsh', in R. Merfyn Jones and D. Ben Rees, *The Liverpool Welsh and their Religion* (Liverpool, 1984), pp. 20–43; John Belcham (ed.), *Liverpool 800* (Liverpool, 2008), pp. 344–51.

18 Elwyn Jones, *In My Time* (London, 1983).

19 *Bye-Gones Relating to Wales and the Border Counties*, 8 June 1887.

20 In his final years, spent back at home in Breconshire, Lloyd's knowledge of the county's farms and common lands, published in *Historical Memoranda of Breconshire* (1903 and 1904) and *The Great Forest of Breconshire* (1904), enabled him to save 600 acres of the Buckland estate from enclosure.

21 B. Bowen Thomas, 'Sir John Herbert Lewis: a Centenary Tribute', *Journal of the Flintshire Historical Society*, 18 (1960), 131–41; Kenneth O. Morgan, 'Lloyd George's Flintshire Loyalist: the Political Achievement of John Herbert Lewis, *Journal of the Flintshire Historical Society*, 36 (2003), 114–35.

22 *The Times*, 14 July 1960.

23 P. Watkins, *A Welshman Remembers* (London, 1944).

24 T. Jones, *Whitehall Diary*, 3 vols, ed. Keith Middlemass (London, 1969), 1, p. 15.

25 E. L. Ellis, *T. J. : a life of Dr Thomas Jones* (Cardiff, 1992), and R. Griffiths, *Fellow Travellers of the Right: British Enthusiasts for Nazi Germany, 1933–9* (Oxford, 1983).

26 Viscountess Rhondda was on the board of thirty-five companies, sixteen of which she chaired. See Viscountess Rhondda (Margaret Haig Thomas Mackworth), *This was my World* (London, 1933); see also the excellent biography by Angela V. John, *Time and Tide: a Life of Lady Rhondda* (Cardigan, 2013).

[27] *www.oxforddnb.com/view/articleHL/48340* (accessed 1 January 2014).

[28] *The Times*, 11 June 1981. James Vincent's father, James Crawley Vincent (1827–67), was vicar of Llanbeblig in Caernarfon, where his devoted service during the cholera epidemic of 1867 led to his death. Nevertheless, James and his brothers reached positions of influence – Sir Hugh Corbet Vincent (1862–1931) as a solicitor in Bangor, and Sir William Henry Hoare Vincent (1866–1941) in the Indian Civil Service.

[29] A. C. H. Smith, *Paper voices: the Popular Press and Social Change, 1935–65* (London, 1975).

[30] A. J. P. Taylor, *Beaverbrook* (Harmondsworth, 1972).

[31] H. Cudlipp, *Walking on the Water* (London, 1976) and *The Prerogative of the Harlot* (London, 1980).

[32] S. E. Koss, *The Rise and Fall of the Political Press in Britain* (London, 1984); Lord Hartwell, *William Camrose: Giant of Fleet Street* (London, 1992): and D. Hart-Davies, *The House the Berrys Built: Inside the Telegraph, 1928–1986* (London, 1990).

[33] On 'Dic Sôn Dafydd', see the ballad by Jac Glan-y-Gors (1766–1821), *www.gtj.org.uk/en/small/item/GTJ18696//page1* (accessed 3 August 2010).

[34] W. J. Gruffydd in *Y Llenor*, Gwanwyn (spring) 1931.

[35] On the Welsh in London, see Jones, *The Welsh in London*.

[36] Mowat, *Britain between the Wars*, p. 111.

[37] Jones, *The Welsh in London*, p. 71.

[38] Jonathan Zeitlin, 'The Emergence of Shop Steward Organisation and Job Control in the British Car Industry: a Review Essay', *History Workshop Journal*, 10 (1980), 121–31.

[39] See, in particular, Dave Lyddon, 'Trade Union Traditions: the Oxford Welsh and the 1934 Pressed Steel Strike', *Llafur*, 6 (1993), 106–14. The 'traditional' view was put by Peter John in 'The Oxford Welsh in the 1930s: a Study in Class, Community and Political Influence', *Llafur*, 5 (1991).

[40] Wal Hannington, *The Problem of the Distressed Areas* (London, 1933), pp. 124–7.

[41] Arthur Exell, 'Morris Motors in the 1930s. Part II. Politics and Trade Unions', *History Workshop Journal*, 7 (1979), 46.

[42] Neil Evans, for example, has argued that there was little tension between the English and Welsh settlers; see his 'Immigrants and Minorities in Wales, 1840–1940: a Comparative Perspective', *Llafur*, 5 (1991), 21. A contrasting view that shows the lack of welcome which the Welsh experienced in England is given in Nick Mansfield, 'The Persistence of Anti-Welshness in the Marches', *Llafur*, 11/2 (2011), 116–25.

[43] *The Perfidious Welshman* (London, 1910) was a scurrilous, libellous assault on the London Welsh by Arthur Tysilio Johnson (Draig Glas). A later satire on the ever over-sensitive London Welsh was made by Caradoc Evans in his play *Taffy* (London, 1925).

[44] Rhian Davies, *Eneth Ddisglair Annwyl: Never so Pure a Sight* (Cardiff, 1994).

[45] An excellent recent discussion of similar themes is T. M. Devine, *To The Ends of the Earth: Scotland's Global Diaspora* (London, 2011); see also David Fitzpatrick, 'Irish Emigration in the later Nineteenth Century', *Irish Historical Studies*, 22 (1980–1), 126–43. For the Welsh context, see W. Ross Jordan, 'The Welsh Diaspora', *Llafur*, 6/2 (1993), 50–74.

[46] Alan Conway (ed.), *The Welsh in America: Letters from the Immigrants* (Cardiff, 1961), p. 318. For an interesting range of literary autobiographical sources outlining the experiences of Welsh people from around the world, see Gwyneth Tyson Roberts (ed.), *Even the Rain is Different* (Dinas Powys, 2005).

[47] W. J. Gruffydd, beirniadaeth cystadleuaeth y goron, *Beirniadaethau Eisteddfod Genedlaethol 1926* (Abertawe, 1926). Gruffydd's *Hen Atgofion* is a sentimentalised view of his separation from his northern home, its values, culture and virtues in the 'exile' of Cardiff. His poems are also infused with this sense of loss:

> Ychydig o'r hen wylo yn y glaw
> Ychydig lwch yn Llanfihangel draw.
> (A little of the old weeping in the rain
> A little dust in far Llanfihangel)
>
> 'Cefn Mabli', *Y Llenor*, 9/1 (Gwanwyn, 1930)

[48] Personal knowledge.

[49] Quoted in Eirug Davies, *Gwladychu'r Cymry yn yr American West* (Llanrwst, 2003), p. 65.

[50] *South Wales Daily News*, 7 August 1875.

[51] *South Wales Daily News*, 30 July 1880.

[52] *Monmouthshire Merlin*, 15 and 29 January, 5 March 1875.

[53] Quoted in W. Ross Johnston, 'The Welsh Diaspora', 51; *Merthyr Telegraph*, 4 January1878.

[54] W. Ross Johnston, 'The Welsh Diaspora', 51.

[55] Reports of Assistant Commissioner Doyle on Wales [C.3375 – III], BPP, 15 (1882).

[56] *Cambrian News*, 2 January 1885.

[57] On the Welsh emigration to Australia, see Lewis Lloyd, *Australians from Wales* (Penygroes, 1988); Bill Jones, 'Representations of Australia in mid Nineteenth-century Welsh Emigrant Literature: 'Gwlad yr Aur'

and 'Awstralia a'r Cloddfeydd', *Welsh History Review*, 23/2 (2006), 51–74, and '"Cymry "Gwlad yr Aur": Ymfudwyr Cymreig yn Ballarat, Awstralia, yn ail hanner y Bedwaredd Ganrif ar Bymtheg', *Llafur*, 8/2 (2001), 41–62.

58 See, for example, Lewis Lloyd, 'The Australian Connection: Four Welsh Shipping Losses, 1890–1910', *Cymru a'r Môr / Maritime Wales*, 8 (1996), 54–61.

59 Religious and charitable societies and organisations were also active in organising and paying for certain groups to emigrate. In the 1880s, the Society for the Promotion of Christian Knowledge had an emigration committee; in 1883 its organising secretary took a party of 300 to Canada. During 1881–2 John James Jones took about 1,500 emigrants to Canada on behalf of the Samaritan Society. In 1879, given mass redundancies in the slate industry, the North Wales Quarrymen's Union voted money for miners to emigrate; special allowances were made to those who went west of Chicago, or to Australia, New Zealand or South America. See W. Ross Johnson, 'The Welsh Diaspora', 67–9.

60 *Monmouthshire Merlin*, 25 August 1871.

61 *Western Mail*, 18 April 1874; 16 May 1874.

62 Jones, *Wales in America*, p. 49.

63 Jones, *Wales in America*, p. 49.

64 *Western Mail*, 21 February 1873.

65 *South Wales Daily News*, 3 January 1876.

66 *The Cambrian*, 17 June 1881.

67 Quoted in W. Ross Johnston, 'The Welsh Diaspora', 63.

68 Joseph V. Hickey, 'Welsh Cattlemen of the Kansas Flint Hills: Social and Ideological Dimensions of Cattle Entrepreneurship', *Agricultural History*, 63/4 (1989), 56–71.

69 Alan Conway (ed.), *The Welsh in America: Letters from the Immigrants* (Minneapolis, 1961), pp. 129–30.

70 Aled Jones and William D. Jones, '*Y Drych* and American Welsh identities, 1851–1951', *North American Journal of Welsh Studies*, 1/1 (2001), 51.

71 Jones and Jones, '*Y Drych* and American Welsh identities, 1851–1951', 183.

72 Dafydd Meirion, *Cymry Gwyllt y Gorllewin* (Talybont, 2002), pp. 41–3.

73 Meirion, *Cymry Gwyllt y Gorllewin*, p. 50.

74 This story of Welsh emigration to industrial and urban America has been well told in William D. Jones, *Wales in America: Scranton and the Welsh, 1860–1920* (Cardiff, 1993). Also useful is David Williams, 'The Contribution of Wales to the Development of the United States', *National Library of Wales Journal*, 2/3 and 2/4 (1941–2), 97–108, and Glanmor Williams, *Cymru ac America / Wales and America* (Cardiff, 1946).

[75] Jones, *Wales and America*, pp. 65–6.
[76] Jones, *Wales and America*, *passim*.
[77] W. E. Minchinton, *The British Tinplate Industry* (Oxford, 1957), p. 38.
[78] Minchinton, *The British Tinplate Industry*, p. 38.
[79] Meirion, *Cymry Gwyllt y Gorllewin*; Eirug Davies, *Gwladychu'r Cymry yn yr American West* and *Y Cymry ac Aur Colorado* (Llanrwst, 2001).
[80] Conway, *The Welsh in America*, p. 198.
[81] P. Krass, *Blood and Whiskey: the Life and Times of Jack Daniels* (New York, 2004).
[82] Meirion, *Cymry Gwyllt y Gorllewin*, p. 10.
[83] Edward George Hartman, *Americans from Wales* (New York, NY, 1978), *passim*.
[84] Hartman, *Americans from Wales*, *passim*.
[85] *The Cambrian*, 6 April 1866.
[86] See Russell Davies, *Hope and Heartbreak: a Social History of Wales and the Welsh, 1776–1870* (Cardiff, 2005), pp. 122–3.
[87] *Cofiant Rhys Gwesyn Jones* (Utica, 1902).
[88] *Baner ac Amserau Cymru*, 7 August 1912.
[89] D. Langridge, *John Cowper Powys: a Record of Achievement* (London, 1966), p. 71; J. C. Powys, *Autobiography* (London, 1968).
[90] Quoted in Davies, *Gwladychu'r Cymru yn yr American West*, p. 73.
[91] Aled Jones and Bill Jones, *Welsh Reflections: Y Drych and America* (Llandysul, 2001), pp. 55–76.
[92] *Who's Who in Wales* (Cardiff, 1921).
[93] Jones and Jones, *Welsh Reflections*, pp. 56–7.
[94] This is stated in Williams, 'The Contribution of Wales to the Development of the United States', p. 108.
[95] *The Times*, 7 September 1903.
[96] John Morgan, *'No Gangster More Bold': Murray Humphreys, the Welsh Political Genius who Corrupted America* (London, 1985); Seymour M. Hersh, *The Dark Side of Camelot* (New York, NY, 1997); and Chuck Giancana and Michael Corbitt, *Double Cross: The Explosive Inside Story of the Mobster who Controlled America* (New York, NY, 1992).
[97] He also changed his name from Les Hope to Bob Hope, to avoid critics who simply changed the order to describe his act; *www.bobhope.com/BobBio.htm* (accessed 21 January 2013).
[98] Donald Spoto, *The Kindness of Strangers: the Life of Tennessee Williams* (Cambridge, MA, 1997). On his drinking, see Olivia Laing, *The Trip to Echo Spring: Why Writers Drink* (London, 2013), pp. 15–60.

99 Roderick Heather, *The Iron Tsar: the Life and Times of John Hughes* (London, 2010); Colin Thomas, *Dreaming a City: From Wales to Ukraine – the story of Hughesovka Stalino Dometsk* (Cardiff, 2009); S. Edwards, *Hughesovka: a Welsh Enterprise in Imperial Russia* (London, 1992); and E. G. Bowen, *John Hughes (Yuzovka): 1841–1889* (Cardiff, 1978).

100 G. Wynne, *The Man from Moscow* (London, 1967). See also J. L. Schechter and P. S. Deriabin, *The Spy who Saved theWorld* (London, 1992); one senses a hint or irony in the title.

101 *Who's Who in Wales* (Cardif, 1937).

102 E. Lewis Evans, *Cymru a'r Gymdeithas Genhadol* (Denbigh, 1945), *passim.*

103 Ralph A. Griffiths, *Clyne Castle, Swansea: a History of the Building and its Owners* (Swansea, 1977), *passim.*

104 Edith Picton-Turbervill, *Life is Good: an Autobiography* (London, 1939).

105 On David Stephen Davies, see R. Bryn Williams, *Cymry Patagonia* (Aberystwyth, 1942), *passim.*

106 The two 'Bibles' of Welsh Patagonian history are Abraham Matthews, *Hanes y Wladfa Gymreig yn Patagonia* (1894) and Lewis Jones, *Y Wladfa Gymreig yn Ne America* (1898). The venture is later retold as a heroic tale in R. Bryn Williams, *Y Wladfa* (Cardiff, 1967). The very layout of the book has an almost mythic or folkloric structure – 'Y Fintai Cyntaf', 'Glanio', 'Argyfwng', 'Eldorado', etc.

107 For the harsher, less heroic, story of the Welsh in Patagonia, see Geraint D. Owen, *Crisis in Chubut* (Llandybïe, 1977). See also Glyn Williams, *The Desert and the Dream: A Study of Welsh Colonization in Chubut 1865–1915* (Cardiff, 1975).

108 Williams, *Cymry Patagonia*, pp. 20–31, 43–6.

109 Dafydd Ifans, *Tyred Drosodd* (Bridgend, 1977) and *Eluned Morgan: Bywgraffiad a Detholiad* (Llandysul, 1948); W. R. P. George, *Cyfaill Hoff: Detholiad o Lythyrau Eluned Morgan* (Llandysul, 1972).

110 Williams, *Cymry Patagonia.*

111 On issues of race and ethnicity and their associated tensions, see Glyn Williams, *The Welsh in Patagonia: the State and the Ethnic Community* (Cardiff, 1991).

112 See the superbly detailed study by Michele Langfield and Peta Roberts, *Welsh Patagonians: the Australian Connection* (Darlinghurst, 2005), pp. 154–60.

113 The photograph of the Rowlands, Oliver and Thomas families with two Spaniards is reproduced in Langfield and Roberts, *Welsh Patagonians*, p. 186.

114 Dylan Thomas, *Under Milk Wood: the Definitive Edition*, ed. Walford Davies and Ralph Maud (London, 1995).

[115] For details of the explorations of Welsh settlers in South America, journeys which were encouraged by the Argentinians as it strengthened their claims to Patagonia against Chile, see Glyn Williams, 'Welsh Contributions to Exploration in Patagonia', *Geographical Journal*, 135/2 (1969), 213–27.

[116] John Petherick, *Travels in Central Africa and Explorations of the Western Nile Tributaries* (London, 1869); for a modern biography, see John Humphries, *Search for the Nile's Source: the Ruined Reputation of John Petherick, Nineteenth-century Welsh Explorer* (Cardiff, 2013).

[117] Richard Hall, *Stanley: an Adventurer Explored* (London, 1974) and Alan Gallop, *Mr Stanley, I Presume?* (London, 2004). The best biography, however, is Frank McLynn, *Stanley: Dark Genius of African Exploration* (London, 2004).

[118] Thomas Pakenham, *The Scramble for Africa 1876–1912* (London, 1991), pp. 26–7, 29–33, 187. For scathing criticisms of Stanley's reputation, see Felix Driver, 'Henry Morton Stanley and his Critics: Geography, Exploration and Empire', *Past and Present*, 133 (1991), 134–66.

[119] Adam Hochschild, *King Leopold's Ghost: A Story of Greed, Terror and Heroism in Colonial Africa* (London, 1998) offers a scathing condemnation of Stanley's involvement in Africa. Also insightful into Stanley's dark heart is Daniel Liebowitz and Charlie Pearson, *The Last Expedition: Stanley's Fatal Journey through the Congo* (London, 2005). Posterity has not been kind to Stanley. His request to be buried in Westminster Abbey was refused and when in 2010 a statue was erected in his honour in St Asaph, a storm of protest ensued. Nevertheless, persistence characterised Stanley in death just as it had in life, for the statue stands in Denbigh today.

[120] McLynn, *Stanley: Dark Genius of African Exploration*, p. 319.

[121] Stanley had a remarkably prolific pen, writing one of his major books of over 500,000 words in only eighty-five days. His works such as *Through the Dark Continent*, 2 vols (London, 1878) and *Tales from Africa* (1893, reprinted 1985) still repay reading.

[122] For a new study, see Eirian Jones, *Y Gymraes o Ganaan: Anturiaethau Margaret Jones ar Bum Cyfandir* (Talybont, 2011). The photograph of Margaret is item JTH03326 in the National Library's collection of photographs and can be seen on the *Casglu'r Tlysau / Gathering the Jewels* website.

[123] In the photograph by John Thomas, W. O. Thomas stares wistfully away into the distance as if a victim of wanderlust. See *Casglu'r Tlysau / Gathering the Jewels* website, item number JTH03491.

[124] Thomas John Evans, *Sir Rhys Hopkin Morris, MBE, QC, MP, LLD, the Man and his Character* (Llandysul, 1958) and John Emanuel and D. Ben Rees, *Syr Rhys Hopkin Morris* (Cardiff, 1980).

[125] Margaret Siriol Colley, *Gareth Jones: a Manchukuo Incident* (private printing, Barry, 1993). A website dedicated to Gareth Jones's memory is available at *www.garethjones.org*. A plaque commemorating his bravery and services to the people of the Ukraine during the Holodomor was unveiled in the Quad, Old College, Aberystwyth, in 2006.

[126] Kenneth O. Morgan, 'Lloyd George's Flintshire Loyalist: the Political Achievement of John Herbert Lewis', *Flintshire Historical Society Journal*, 36 (2003), 114–35.

[127] I. McDonald, *The History of The Times* (London, 1984), p. 5.

[128] *The Times*, 7 August 1984.

[129] The story of the Chicago Cymmrodorion's eisteddfod during the World's Columbian Exposition of 1893 has been well told in Hywel Teifi Edwards, *Eisteddfod Ffair y Byd: Chicago 1893* (Llandysul, 1990).

[130] Arnold Henry Savage Landor, *Everywhere: the Memoirs of an Explorer* (London, 1924).

[131] *Geographical*, June 2005.

[132] Norman Lewis, *Jackdaw Cake* (London, 1985), p. 5.

[133] The life of Norman Lewis has been exhaustively told in Julian Evans, *Semi-invisible Man: the Life of Norman Lewis* (London, 2008).

[134] Dafydd Jenkins, *Evans-Pritchard* (Llandysul, 1980).

[135] Mary Douglas, *Edward Evans-Pritchard* (Harmondsworth, 1981), p. 210.

[136] *The Times*, 23 January 1951.

[137] H. T. Milliken, *Road to Bodnant: the Story behind the Famous North Wales Garden* (Caernarfon, 1975); *The Times*, 12 January 1933.

[138] The book is typical of the Victorian penchant for long explanatory book titles: Alfred Russel Wallace, *The Malay Archipelago: the Land of the Orang-utang and the Bird of Paradise: a Narrative of Travel, with Studies of Man and Nature* (London, 1877).

[139] On Wallace, see H. Clements, *Alfred Russel Wallace: Biologist and Social Reformer* (London, 1983); Ross A. Slotten, *The Heretic in Darwin's Court: the Life of Alfred Russel Wallace* (London, 2004); and R. E. Hughes, 'Alfred Russel Wallace: Some Notes of the Welsh Connection', *British Journal for the History of Science*, 22 (1989), 401–18. The year 2013, the centenary of his birth, saw many exhibitions of note at, for example, the Swansea Museum, the National Museum of Wales in Cardiff and in London's Natural History Museum; there were also a number of television programmes. Thus, at least some recognition has been given to this gifted Welsh scientist and sage. On the Victorian craze for collecting samples of insects and plants, see John F. McDiarmid Clark, *Bugs and the Victorians* (London, 2010).

140 Quoted in Leusa Fflur Llewelyn, 'T. Ifor Rees ac ysgrifennu taith yn y Gymraeg' (unpublished MPhil thesis, Aberystwyth University, 2010), p. 49. See also Diana Michelle Luft, 'T. Ifor Rees: a Welsh diplomat in Latin America', in Ryan Prout and T. G. Altenberg (eds), *Seeing in Spanish: from Don Quixote to Daddy Yankee – 22 essays in Hispanic Visual Cultures* (Newcastle, 2011), pp. 300–10. See also *http://s4c.co.uk/pethe/llyfrau-taith-t-ifor-rees/* (accessed 21 January 2013) for a few photographs by and of T. Ifor Rees.

141 The story of the historic but sadly still rare rugby victory in 1905 is superbly told with edge-of-your-seat excitement in the chapter entitled 'Life, Death and the Afternoon', in Gareth Williams and Dai Smith, *Fields of Praise: a History of the Welsh Rugby Union* (Cardiff, 1980), pp. 145–70.

142 *Alpine Journal*, 57, November 1950; *Yr Aelwyd*, October 1949. One of the thirty-one founding members of the Alpine Club was David John Llewelyn (1826–1916), who was also one of the most successful of the early climbers in the Alps. See *Alpine Journal*, 30, 324–30. For Owen Glynne Jones (1867–99), see the chapter on him in Claire Eliane Engel, *They Came to the Hills* (London, 1952) and Ioan Bowen Rees, *Galwad y Mynydd: Chwe Dringwr Enwog* (Llandybïe, 1961) and *Mynyddoedd, Ysgrifau a Cherddi* (Llandysul, 1975). Llewelyn and the founders of the Alpine Club had been inspired and influenced by the climbing of John Clough Williams-Ellis (1833–1913), the scholar, poet and clergyman. Williams-Ellis was one of the first Welshmen to climb several of the highest peaks in the Alps. See J. Ball (ed.), *Peaks, Passes and Glaciers: a Series of Excursions by the Alpine Club* (London, 1959).

143 H. M. Vaughan, *The South Wales Squires: a Welsh Picture of Social Life* (London, 1926), ch. 14; Nea Morin, *A Woman's Reach: Mountaineering Memoirs* (London, 1968).

144 J. R. Smith, *Everest: the Man and the Mountain* (London, 1999).

145 Charles Bruce wrote of his upbringing and early days as a soldier in *Himalayan Wanderer* (London, 1934). For some of the colour of this larger-than-life character, see Michael Underhill, 'A Gurkha in Wales', *Country Life*, 2 February 1984. He features prominently in Wade Davis, *Into the Silence: the Great War, Mallory and the Conquest of Everest* (London, 2011), pp. 71–9, 132–5, 369–79, 398–408, 489–92. See also the report on the 1924 Everest expedition in the *Geographical Journal*, 63/6 (June 1924), 525–7. Bruce's first-hand account, 'The Organisation and Start of the Expedition', appears in the *Alpine Journal*, 36/229 (November, 1924), 241–4. There is also a lot of fascinating detail in P. H. Hansen, 'The Dancing Llamas of Everest: Cinema, Orientalism and Anglo-Tibetan relations in the 1920s', *American Historical Review*,

101 (1996), 712–47. Bruce's adventures in the mountains on military campaigns and while mountaineering can be found in his *Twenty Years in the Himalaya* (London, 1910).

146 Sporting endeavours were a family trait. His oldest brother, Clarence Napier (later the third Baron Aberdare, 1885–1957), was the British rackets champion in 1922 and 1931, the British tennis champion in 1932, Canadian tennis champion in 1928 and 1930, the USA tennis champion in 1930, real tennis champion of the US in 1930 and of England in 1932 and 1938; he also won several tennis doubles championships and played first-class cricket for Middlesex.

147 On Younghusband's mission, see Patrick French, *Younghusband: the Last Great Imperial Adventurer* (London, 1994); for the invasions, see Charles Allen, *Duel in the Snow: the Race for Lhasa* (London, 1982).

148 Davis, *Into the Silence*, pp. 181–2.

149 On Geoffrey Bruce, see Davis, *Into the Silence*, pp. 377–9, 387, 393, 523–5. He gave his first-hand account of the expedition in 1924 in 'The Journey through Tibet and the Establishment of the High Camps', *Alpine Journal*, 36/229 (November 1924), 251–60.

150 See Charles Bruce's typically militaristically titled volume, *The Assault on Everest, 1922* (New York, NY, 1923).

151 Davis, *Into the Silence*, p. 556.

152 On the theme of the obsession with death that pervades the late 1910s and early 1920s, see Joanna Bourke, *Dismembering the Male: Men's Bodies, Britain and the Great War* (Chicago, IL, 1996). One of her core arguments is that after the war the anonymity of death in the trenches and the endless images of scarred and broken bodies came to symbolise the emasculation of a nation. The 'honour' and 'sacrifice' of the Everest expeditions gave an opportunity to recover some past glories. For a fascinating discussion, see Peter Boyers, *Imperial Ascent: Mountaineering, Masculinity and Empire* (Boulder, CO, 2003).

153 J. R. L. Anderson, *High Mountains and Cold Seas: a biography of H. W. Tilman* (London, 1980) and T. Madge, *The Last Hero, Bill Tilman: a Biography of the Explorer* (London, 1995).

154 *Alpine Journal*, 100 (1995). Harriet Tuckey, Pugh's daughter, has produced a highly intelligent and honest portrait of her tortured relationship with her father in *Everest, The First Ascent: the Untold Story of Griffith Pugh, the Man who Made it Possible* (London, 2013). Pugh was a deeply driven, committed individual who devoted his life to improving the physiological development of humans. His difficult personality made it easy for others to claim the credit for his innovations. Without his emphasis upon oxygen, hygiene and hydration it is unlikely that the 1953 expedition would have succeeded. It appears

scandalous that so many people in the mountaineering community should ignore his contribution. The 2003 BBC film *Race for Everest*, specially commissioned to mark the fiftieth anniversary, made no reference to Pugh.

155 James Morris (later Jan Morris), *Coronation Everest* (London, 1953); *Alpine Journal*, 99 (1994), 334–41; Charles Evans, *Eye on Everest* (London, 1955) and *On Climbing* (London, 1956).

156 On Scott, see the surprisingly good biography by Ranulph Fiennes, *Captain Scott* (London, 2004); Stephen Gwyn, *Captain Scott* (London, 1924); Richard Huntford, *Scott and Amundsen* (London, 1979); and David Crane, *Scott of the Antarctic: a Life of Courage and Tragedy in the Extreme South* (London, 2005). On Shackleton, see Roland Huntford, *Shackleton* (London, 1986).

157 There was a major exhibition at the National Waterfront Museum in Swansea from July to October 2010 outlining the links between Wales and Scott's expedition; see *www.museumwales.ac.uk/en/whatson/?event_id=4424* (accessed 23 July 2010). See also *Western Mail*, 15 June 2010. For more detail on the Welsh links, see Anthony M. Johnson, *Scott of the Antarctic and Cardiff* (Cardiff, 1984). Money (*c.*£5,000) was provided by the city's Coal Exchange and coal, patent fuel and fitting at the docks were provided free to the expedition, though the ship-fitters, in the light of the constant leakages the *Terra Nova* suffered, would have been wise to refrain from boasting about their contribution.

158 On Edgar Evans, see C. G. Gregor, *Swansea's Antarctic Explorer: Edgar Evans, 1876–1912*, and Isobel Williams, *Captain Scott's Invaluable Assistant: Edgar Evans* (Stroud, 2012). In the last stages of the journey to the Pole, even Evans's usually strong resolve had begun to break and as the sledges collapsed and the men fell repeatedly, he uttered his strongest malediction: 'May the curse of the seven blind beggars of Egypt be upon you'.

159 For their experiences, see Edward Evans, *South with Scott* (London, 1952) and *The Antarctic Challenged* (London, 1955).

160 Lennard Bickel, *Shackleton's Forgotten Men* (London, 2000).

161 See F. A. Worsley, *Shackleton's Boat Journey* (London, 1940), and Peter King (ed.), Ernest Shackleton, *South: the Story of Shackleton's Last Expedition 1914–17* (London, 1999). The volume was dedicated by Shackleton to 'my comrades who fell in the white warfare of the south and on the red fields of France and Flanders'.

162 Sir Tannatt David was largely responsible for the foundation of the Australian Mining Corps in the First World War, and became geographical adviser to the British Expeditionary Force in France. See *Western Mail*, 23 September 2005.

[163] Most notably in *Nostromo* (1904).

[164] For an excellent evocation of life aboard ship in the age of sail, see Derek Lundy, *The Way of a Ship: a Square-rigger Voyage in the Last Days of Sail* (London, 2002). For the Welsh context, see the superb works of Aled Eames (1921–96), such as *Ships and Seamen of Anglesey, 1558–1918* (1973), *Llongau a Llongwyr Gwynedd* (1976), *Meistri'r Moroedd* (1978), and *Machlud Hwyliau'r Cymry* (1984), mostly published by the Gwynedd Archives Franchise. For a brief note on women at sea, see Joanna Greenlaw, 'Uncommon Cape Horners: Women and Children at Sea', *Minerva*, 7 (1999), 38–40. For the nitrate trade, see David Burrell, *The Nitrate Boats* (London, 1995).

[165] J. Geraint Jenkins, *Welsh Ship and Sailing Men* (Llandysul, 2006) and *Maritime Heritage: the Ships and Seamen of Southern Ceredigion* (Llandysul, 1982).

[166] Owen Rhoscomyl, 'The Place of Wales in the Empire', *The Nationalist* (1912), 369–71; *Western Mail*, 15 August 1910. The most accessible account of Owen Rhoscomyl is in Hywel Teifi Edwards, *The National Pageant of Wales* (Llandysul, 2009), pp. 29–86. See also Bryn Owen, *Owen Rhoscomyl and the Welsh Horse* (Caernarfon, 1990) and John S. Ellis, 'Making Owen Rhoscomyl (1863–1919): Biography, Welsh Identity and the British World', *Welsh History Review*, 26/3 (2013), 482–511.

[167] G. A. Pocock, *Forgotten as Becomes a Frontiersman* (London, n.d.).

[168] A. R. Thurston, *The Legion of Frontiersmen: a Brief History* (London, 1975).

[169] H. G. Wells, *An Englishman Looks at the World* (London, 1914), p. 75.

[170] R. Pocock, *Chorus to Adventurers: Being the Later Life of Roger Pocock* (London, 1931), p. 177.

[171] John Humphries, *Gringo Revolutionary: the Amazing Adventures of Caryl ap Rhys Pryce*. His final appearance in a movie was as a leader of the Ku Klux Klan in the Welsh-descended D. W. Griffith's epic, though racist, masterpiece, *The Birth of a Nation*. Pryce appears to have been born into a family of adventurers. His father had business interests in Canada and the USA, his sister Gladys toured the USA and his elder brother, Henry, was general staff officer with the 38th (Welsh) Division.

[172] *Western Mail*, 15 August 1910. See also Owen Rhoscomyl, *Flame Bearers of Welsh History* (Merthyr Tydfil, 1905).

[173] *Western Mail*, 29 November 1919.

[174] Quoted in Michael Lieven, *Senghennydd: the Universal Pit Village* (Llandysul, 1984), p. 108.

[175] *The Nationalist* (January 1910). For another contemporary view of the role of heroes in history, see R. J. Derfel, 'Cymru yn ei Chysylltiad ag Enwogion', *Y Traethodydd*, 11 (1855), 322–59; W. Jenkyn Thomas, *Heroes*

of Wales (London, 1915); Alwyn D. Rees 'The Divine Hero in Celtic Hagiology', *Folklore*, 47/1 (1936), 30–41; and Marie Trevelyan, *The Land of Arthur: its Heroes and Heroines* (London, 1895).

176 *Western Mail*, 13 July 1911. For similar views of Wales's role alongside the English as the chosen people, see Owen Rhoscomyl, 'The Place of Wales in the Empire', *Wales*, 11 (1912), 369–71.

6 *'The Blood never Dried'*

1 *Trysorfa'r Plant*'s editor echoed the anti-English views expressed by Ieuan Gwynedd in the women's periodical *Y Gymraes* in 1850. Of the English he wrote: 'Carn lleidr y greadigaeth ydyw. Ymffrostai yn ei ddysg, ei wareiddiad a'i grefydd. Ei ddysg yw cigydd-dra, ei wareiddiad ydyw ysbail a'i dduw ydyw ei hun. Nid ydym yn darlunio personau ond ysbryd y cenedl, fel y mae yn ymddangos ar ddalennau yr oesoedd'. (He is the arch thief of creation. He boasts of his learning, his civilisation and his religion. His learning is butchery, his civilisation robbery, and his god is himself. We are not describing individuals, but the spirit of the nation as it manifests itself on the pages of history). Ieuan Gwynedd, 'Sais-addolaeth', *Y Gymraes* (1850), 75–6.

2 D. J. Williams, 'Y Tri Llwyth', *Hen Wynebau* (Llandysul, 1964), p. 15.

3 Waldo Williams, 'Y Tangnefeddwyr', *Dail Pren* (Llandysul, 1957). Bertrand Russell, *Freedom and Organisation, 1814–1914* (London, 1939). For a general survey that links British and imperial history and its opponents, see A. P. Thornton, *The Imperial Idea and its Enemies: a Study in British Power* (London, 1959) and *The Habit of Authority: Paternalism in British History* (London, 1966). Some of the most trenchant criticism of the empire has come from the actor and documentary film-maker Kenneth Griffith (1921–2006) of Tenby; see, for example, his *Soldiers of the Widow*, *Curious Journey* and *Hang up your Brightest Colours*. In his memoirs, *The Fool's Pardon* (London, 1994), he expresses sympathy for several independence movements, but oddly little support for the Welsh.

4 The story of the involvement of Wales and the Welsh in empire has only recently been studied. Amongst the most valuable works are Aled Jones and Bill Jones, 'The Welsh World and the British Empire, *c.*1851–1939: an Exploration', *Journal of Imperial and Commonwealth History*, 31/2 (2010), 51–81; John S. Ellis, 'Making Owen Rhoscomyl (1863–1919); Biography, Welsh Identity and the British World', *Welsh*

History Review, 26/3 (2013), 482–511. On the earlier involvement of Wales in the empire, see Huw Bowen (ed.), *Wales and the British Overseas Empire: Interactions and Influences, 1650–1830* (Manchester, 2012). For the wider context of the four nations of Britain, see John M. MacKenzie, 'Irish, Scottish, Welsh and English Worlds? A Four-nation Approach to the History of the British Empire', *History Compass*, 6 (2008), 1244–63, and 'Irish, Scottish, Welsh and English worlds? the historiography of a four-nations approach to the history of the British Empire', in Catherine Hall and Keith McClelland (eds), *Race, Nations and Empire: Making Historians* (Manchester, 2010), pp. 133–53. On the impact of the empire in Britain, see David Cannadine, *Ornamentalism: How the British Saw their Empire* (London, 2001). See also Stephen Howe's excellent review essay, 'British Worlds, Settler Worlds, World Systems and Killing Fields', *Journal of Imperial and Commonwealth History*, 40/4 (2012), 691–725.

5 Advertisements for Pears Soap claimed that it was 'the first step towards lightening the white man's burden in teaching the virtues of cleanliness. Pears soap is a potent factor in brightening the dark corners of the earth. As civilisation advances amongst the cultures of all nations it holds the highest place – it is the ideal toilet soap'. Chlorinol bleach also echoed the imperial theme of lightening the dark people with its claim, 'Be Like De White Nigger'. Love it or loathe it, Bovril ignored the alphabet and geography in a slogan which claimed that the route taken by Lord Roberts to Kimberley from Bloemfontein during the Boer War spelt out 'Bovril'. Niall Ferguson, *Empire: How the British Made the Modern World* (London, 2003), p. 254.

6 Eiluned Lewis, *The Captain's Wife*, ed. Katie Gramich (Dinas Powys, 2008), p. x.

7 Jeremy Black, *Maps and History: Constructing Images of the Past* (New Haven, 1997); Anne Godlewska and Neil Smith, *Geography and Empire* (Oxford, 1994).

8 To this day there is a Jones Street in the centre of Kimberley, South Africa, named after W. T. Jones, who turned his back on the traditional stereotype of the pious Welshman and opened the first pub in the city. For an interesting discussion of how exotic names were 'domesticated' and integrated, see David Young, 'East End Street Names and British Imperialism', *Local Historian*, 22 (1992), 17–28, and Robin Butlin, *Geographies of Empire: 1880–1960* (Cambridge, 2009). On the broader cultural impact of empire, see Catherine Hall (ed.), *Cultures of Empire: Colonizers in Britain and the Empire in the Nineteenth and Twentieth Centuries* (Manchester, 2000).

9 W. T. R. Pryse, *The Photographer in Rural Wales: a Photographic Archive of Llanfair Caereinion, Powys and its Region 1865–1986* (Llanfair Caereinion, 1991).

10 J. S. Bratton et al., *Acts of Supremacy: the British Empire and the Stage 1790–1930* (Manchester, 1991).

11 *Yr Herald Cymreig*, 2 May 1960. For music and the empire, see Peter Bailey, 'Custom, capital and culture in the Victorian Music Hall', in R. D. Storch (ed.), *Popular Culture in Victorian England* (London, 1982); Maurice Wilson Disher, *Victorian Song: from Live to Drawing Room* (London, 1955); and Jeffrey Richards, *Imperialism and Music: Britain* (London, 2001).

12 For the creation of a symbolism and the artistic expression of heroic masculinity, see Holger Hoock, *Empires of the Imagination: Politics, War and the Arts in the British World, 1750–1950* (London, 2010); see also F. Pearson, *Goscombe John at the National Museum of Wales* (Cardiff, 1979).

13 Many of his works can be seen in the magazine *Wales*, whilst his best political cartoons are in Beriah Gwynfe Evans, *Dafydd Dafis* (Carmarthen, 1898).

14 J. A. Mangan, 'Images of Empire in the late Victorian Public School', *Journal of Educational Administration and History*, 12 (1980), 31–9, *Athleticism in the Victorian and Edwardian Public School* (London, 1981) and *The Games Ethic and Imperialism* (London, 1986); Rupert Wilkinson, *The Prefects: British Leadership and the Public School Tradition* (London, 1964). For the Welsh context, see W. Gareth Evans, *A History of Llandovery College: the Welsh Collegiate Institution. A Study in Welsh Educational History* (Llandovery, 1981).

15 On the empire in literature, see Guy Arnold, *Hold Fast for England: G. A. Henty, Imperialist Boys' Writer* (London, 1980); Elleke Boehmer (ed.), *Empire Writing: an Anthology of Colonial Literature, 1870–1918* (London, 1998); Patrick Brantlinger, *Rule of Darkness: British Literature and Imperialism, 1830–1914* (Ithaca, NY, 1988); J. S. Bretton, *The Impact of Children's Fiction* (London, 1981) and 'British imperialism and the representation of femininity in girls' fiction, 1900–1930', in Jeffrey Richards (ed.), *Imperialism and Juvenile Literature* (Manchester, 1989), pp. 170–205; John Springhall, 'Healthy papers for manly boys: imperialism and race in the Harmsworth's halfpenny boys' papers of the 1890s and 1900s', in Richards (ed.), *Imperialism and Juvenile Literature*.

16 On some heroes of empire, see Edward Berenson, *Heroes of Empire: Five Charismatic Men and the Conquest of Africa* (University of California Press, 2010); Graham Dawson, *Soldier Heroes: British Adventure, Empire,*

and the Imagining of Masculinities; Michael Lieven, 'Heroism, Heroics and the Making of Heroes: the Anglo-Zulu War of 1879', *Albion: a Quarterly Journal Concerned with British Studies*, 30, 3 (Autumn 1998), 419–38.

17 Amongst Sir Charles Prestwood Lucas's published works are *The British Empire* (1915), *The Beginnings of English Overseas Enterprise* (1917), *The Partition and Colonization of Africa* (1922), *The Story of the Empire*, 2 vols (1924), *Religion, Colonising and Trade* (1930) and *The Empire at War*, 5 vols (1921–6).

18 On the role of the BBC in empire, see John MacKenzie, 'In touch with the infinite: the BBC and the Empire, 1923–53', in J. MacKenzie (ed.), *Imperialism and Popular Culture* (London, 1986), pp. 111–42.

19 John Barnes, *The Beginnings of the Cinema in England*, vols 5–6 (London, 1976) and *Filming the Boer War* (London, 1992).

20 C. L. R. James, *Nkrumah and the Ghana Revolution* (London, 1982), p. 36.

21 On the theme that the British unintentionally and unknowingly acquired an empire, see Bernard Porter, *The Absent-minded Imperialists: Empire, Society and Culture in Britain* (Oxford, 2004). The most evocative history of the empire is still Jan Morris's trilogy, *Pax Britannica: The Climax of an Empire* (London, 1968), *Heaven's Command: an Imperial Progress* (London, 1973) and *Farewell the Trumpets: an Imperial Retreat* (London, 1978); see also Richard Price, 'One Big Thing; Britain, its Empire, and their Imperial Culture', *Journal of British Studies*, 45 (2006), 602–27.

22 See also Robert Holland, *Blue-water Empire: the British in the Mediterranean since 1800* (London, 2013). On the general point of the empire's diaspora of people around the world, see Robert Bickers (ed.), *Settlers and Expatriates* (Oxford, 2010).

23 On the empire in Cyprus, see Andrekos Varnava, *British Imperialism in Cyprus, 1878–1915: the Inconsequential Possession* (Manchester, 2009).

24 During the First World War, Sir Evan Davies Jones attained the rank of major and his organisational skills were employed as the UK's first petrol controller. A loyal servant of the University of Wales and the National Library, a bust of him by W. Goscombe John graces the entrance to the latter establishment.

25 This was exceptionally profitable work, for when he died in January 1910 John Cory left £250,000 (almost £25 million in twenty-first century terms) to charitable organisations as well as substantial legacies to his children: *www.evangelical-times.org.archive/item/616* (accessed 1 November 2013).

[26] Elliot spent much of 1874 and 1875–6 in Egypt as a financial adviser to the insecure government of the Khedive; Elizabeth Phillips, *A History of the Pioneers of the South Wales Coalfield* (Cardiff, 1925).

[27] John Kent, *Egypt and the Defence of the Middle East* (London, 1998).

[28] Sir William Heneage Wynne-French served in the Egyptian army (1919–25) and in the Sudan Defence Force (1925–6), whilst Fitzroy Richard Somerset (1885–1964), fourth Baron Raglan, served in Egypt from 1913 to 1921. The posting gave Somerset sufficient opportunities to pursue his true vocations of archaeology and anthropology, especially his studies of the Nilotic Negroes. On the conflict in Egypt, see John Darwin, *Unfinished Empire: the Global Expansion of Britain* (London, 2012), pp. 86–7, 144–7, 310.

[29] On the concept of the British West, see James Belich, *Replenishing the Earth: the Settler Revolution and the Rise of the Anglo-World, 1783–1939* (Oxford, 2009), pp. 261–306.

[30] *The Times*, 3 January 1919.

[31] A. H. Milne's *Sir Alfred Lewis Jones, KCMG: a Story of Energy and Success* (Liverpool, 1914) is hagiographic, whereas Peter N. Davies's *Sir Alfred Jones: Shipping Entrepreneur Par Excellence* (London, 1978) is more impartial.

[32] *Y Genedl Gymreig*, 3 August 1909.

[33] Unsurprisingly, perhaps, given the swings in historical opinions and the nostalgia inherent in a nation still seeking a role in the world, after a period in which the empire has been criticised, several historians are now pressing the claims that it was a force for good. Most notable has been Niall Ferguson, *Empire: How Britain Made the Modern World* (London, 2003). There is also much relevant material in Andrew Thompson, *The Empire Strikes Back? The Impact of Imperialism on Britain from the Mid Nineteenth Century* (London, 2005); P. J. Cairn and A. G. Hopkins, *British Imperialism: Innovation and Expansion 1688–1914* (London, 1993); and Ronald Hyam, *Understanding the British Empire* (Cambridge, 2010).

[34] On the general themes in the emergence of imperialism and empire, see David B. Abernethy, *The Dynamics of Global Dominance: European Overseas Empires, 1415–1980* (New Haven, 2001); Ronald Hyam, *Britain's Imperial Century, 1815–1914* (Basingstoke, 1993); Lawrence James, *The Rise and Fall of the British Empire* (London, 1994); P. J. Marshall, *The Cambridge Illustrated History of the British Empire* (London, 2001); and Anthony Pagden, *Peoples and Empires: Europeans and the Rest of the World from Antiquity to the Present* (London, 2001).

[35] D. Myrddin Lloyd (ed.), *Detholiad o Erthyglau a Llythyrau Emrys ap Iwan* (Aberystwyth, 1940), p. 77.

36 Quoted in Huw Walters, *Canu'r Pwll a'r Pwlpud: Portread o'r Diwylliant Barddol Cymraeg yn Nyffryn Aman* (Denbigh, 1987), p. 163.

37 W. Nantlais Williams, *Murmuron Newydd: Telynegion Nantlais* (Ammanford, 1926) and *O Gopa Bryn Nebo* (Llandysul, 1967). On the general effect of religion on the empire, see Jane Samson, 'Are You What You Believe? Some Thoughts on Ornamentalism and Religion', *Journal of Colonialism and Colonial History*, 3/1 (2002), 214–39. For a succinct and eloquent criticism of the role of Welsh missionaries and religious leaders in the British Empire, see Jane Aaron, 'Slaughter and Salvation', *New Welsh Review*, 38 (1997), 38–46.

38 On Joseph Parry, see Dulais Rhys (ed.), *The Little Hero: the Autobiography of Joseph Parry* (Aberystwyth, 2004) and *Joseph Parry: Bachgen Bach o Ferthyr* (Cardiff, 1998); E. Keri Evans, *Cofiant Dr Joseph Parry* (Cardiff, 1921).

39 For the anthem, see a brief book with a very long title: Oswald Edwards, *A Gem of Welsh Melody: the Story of the Composition of 'Glan Rhondda' by Evan and James James and its Evolution as the Welsh National Anthem, 'Hen Wlad Fy Nhadau'* (Ruthin, 1989).

40 Sue Zemka, 'The holy books of empire': translations of the British and Foreign Bible Society, in Jonathan Arac and Harriet Ritvo (eds), *Macropolitics of Nineteenth-century Literature: Nationalism, Exoticism, Imperialism* (London, 1995), pp. 102–38; David Newsome, *Godliness and Good Learning* (London, 1961).

41 D. Brinley Pugh, *Triawd yr Ynys* (Denbigh, 1954).

42 For some studies of the Welsh missionaries, see the three volumes of *Hanes Cenhadaeth Dramor Eglwys Bresbyteraidd Cymru:* Ednyfed Thomas, *Bryniau'r Glaw, Cenhadaeth Casia* (Caernarfon, 1988); J. Meirion Lloyd, *Y Bannau Pell: Cenhadaeth Mizoram* (Caernarfon, 1990); and D. G. Merfyn Jones, *Y Popty Poeth a'i Gyffiniau: Cenhadaeth Sylhet-Cachar*, (Caernarfon, 1990); see also T. M. Basset, *The Baptists of Wales and the Baptist Missionary Society* (Swansea, 1991); E. Lewis Evans, *Cymru a'r Gymdeithas Genhadol* (London, 1945); Ioan W. Gruffydd, *Cludoedd Moroedd: Cofio Dwy Ganrif o Genhadaeth 1795–1995* (Swansea, 1995); G. Pennar Griffith, *Hanes Bywgraffiadol o Genhadon Cymreig i Wledydd Paganaidd* (Swansea, 1897); Jane Aaron, 'Slaughter and Salvation', *New Welsh Review*, 38 (1997), 38–46; Noel Gibbard, *Cymwynaswyr Madagascar, 1818–1920* (Bridgend, 1999).

43 Maurice Loader, *Capel Als Llanelli* (Swansea, 1980).

44 W. E. Soothill, *Timothy Richard of China, Seer, Statesman, Missionary and the Most Disinterested Adviser the Chinese ever Had* (London, 1924).

45 Timothy Richard, *Forty-five Years in China: Reminiscences* (London, 1916).

[46] H. M. Hughes, *Dr Griffith John, DD, Arwr China* (London, 1914).

[47] Noel Gibbard, *Griffith John: Apostle to Central China* (Bridgend, 1998). On the general role of missionaries in China, see Robert Bickers, *The Scramble for China: Foreign Devils in the Qing Empire, 1832–1914* (London, 2011).

[48] Pugh, *Triawd yr Ynys*, pp. 9–32.

[49] *North Wales Chronicle*, 19 October 1956.

[50] Norman Etherington, *Missions and Empire* (Oxford, 2008); Stephen Neill, *A History of Christian Missions* (London, 1986). If you can forgive the message, there is much valuable material in C. Gordon Olson, *What in the World is God Doing?* (London, 2003). One of the most interesting and inventive presentations of a missionary and his impact on a country and a family is the novel by Barbara Kingsolver, *The Poisonwood Bible* (London, 1998). Catherine Hall, *Civilizing Subjects* (Oxford, 2002) is a big, rich, wonderful recreation of missionary culture in the nineteenth century.

[51] Pugh, *Triawd yr Ynys*, p. 170.

[52] Jones and Jones, 'The Welsh World and the British Empire', 71.

[53] G. Wynne Griffith, *Cofiant cenhades, Miss J. Helen Rowlands MA, DLitt (Helen o Fôn)* (Caernarfon, 1961).

[54] Laurel Gray, *Sinabada Woman among Warriors: a Biography of the Rev. Sue Rankin* (Adelaide, 1988).

[55] Obituary in *Welsh Congregationalists Year Book, 1992* (Swansea, 1992).

[56] E. Lewis Evans, *Cymru a'r Gymdeithas Genhadol* (Swansea, 1945).

[57] Evans, *Cymru a'r Gymdeithas Genhadol*.

[58] The most famous of such medical missionaries, of course, was David Livingstone; see Michael Gelfand, *Livingstone the Doctor, his Life and Travels: a Study in Medical History* (Oxford, 1957).

[59] Gelfand, *Livingstone the Doctor, his Life and Travels*; Pugh, *Triawd yr Ynys*, pp. 55–79; *Bye-Gones, Relating to Wales and the Border Counties* (1892), p. 300.

[60] Quoted in Nigel Jenkins, *Gwalia in Khasia: the Biggest Overseas Venture ever Sustained by the Welsh* (Llandysul, 1995), p. 302.

[61] *Bye-Gones, Relating to Wales and the Border Counties* (1892), p. 300; *The Times*, 17 January 1950.

[62] Gwyn Campbell, *An Economic History of Imperial Madagascar* (London, 2002).

[63] *The Times*, 17 January 1950; *www.wbo.llgc.org.uk/en/s2-JONE-CLE01875.htm* (accessed 1 November 2013).

[64] Dafydd Meirion, *Cymru Gwyllt y Gorllewin* (Talybont, 2002), pp. 77–9.

[65] See *www.wbo.llgc.org.uk/en/s2-JONE-CLE01875.htm* (accessed 1 November 2013).

[66] P. G. Williams, *Y Parch Bowen Rees, Pant-teg ac Affrica* (London, 1939); Ioan Bowen Rees, 'Surviving the Matabele Rebellion', *Planet*, 120 (1996–7), 82–91.

[67] John Harrison, *Where the Earth Ends: a Journey beyond Patagonia* (Ceredigion, 2000), pp. 250–1.

[68] *Trysorfa'r Plant*, June 1880.

[69] W. J. Gruffydd, *Hen Atgofion: Blynyddoedd y Locust* (Llandysul, 1964), p. 131.

[70] Meirion, *Cymru Gwyllt y Gorllewin*, 71.

[71] Meirion, *Cymru Gwyllt y Gorllewin*, 73.

[72] Meirion, *Cymru Gwyllt y Gorllewin*. Many travel writers who are usually praised in historical studies appear on closer reading of their work to be less open-minded and tolerant than bigoted and racist. T. H. Parry-Williams, on a journey to South America in the early twentieth century, noted, 'Yr oedd haid o dagoes – fel arfer – yn dadlwytho trwy'r dydd heddiw . . . Yr oedd golwg arw ar rai o'r giwed a ddaeth i'r llong, yn enwedig rai o'r taclau sy'n mynd i'r trydydd dosbarth.' (There was a gang of dagoes – as usual – unloading throughout the day . . . There was a rough look to some of the crowd who boarded the ship, especially some of the creatures who entered third class); quoted in Leusa Fflur Llewelyn, 'T. Ifan Rees ac ysgrifennu taith yn y Gymraeg' (unpublished MPhil thesis, Aberystwyth University, 2010), p. 127. There is a valuable discussion of the racist and anti-Semitic attitude of writers such as T. H. Parry-Williams, O. M. Edwards, Saunders Lewis and T. Gwynn Jones, in this work, especially on pp. 125–31.

[73] Joseph Conrad, quoted in Pankaj Mishra, *From the Ruins of Empire: the Revolt against the West and the Remaking of Asia* (London, 2012), p. 7; see also his article in *The Guardian*, 28 July 2012. On the role of Nonconformists, see C. Kidd, *The Forging of Races: Race and Scripture in the Protestant Atlantic World, 1600–2000* (Cambridge, 2006) and Jeffrey Cox, 'Were Victorian Nonconformists the Worst Imperialists of All?, *Victorian Studies*, 46/2 (2004), 243–55.

[74] William Griffith, *Anturiaethau Cymro yn Affrica*, 2 vols (Denbigh, 1894, 1895). The quotation is from *Barn*, June 2009, p. 15.

[75] Sir Samuel Walker Griffith retained a strong pride in his origins, for his lavish home in Brisbane was named Merthyr. On his policies, see David Cannadine, *The Undivided Past: History Beyond our Differences* (London, 2013), p. 191; see also M. Lake and H. Reynolds, *Drawing the Global Colour Line: White Men's Countries and the International Challenge of Racial Equality* (Cambridge, 2008); J. Bryce, *The Relations of the Advanced and the Backward Races of Mankind* (Oxford, 1902).

[76] Stanley has attracted several biographers. Amongst the best are Emyr Wyn Jones, *Sir H. M. Stanley: the Enigma* (Denbigh, 1980); Alan Gallop, *Mr Stanley, I Presume?* (Sutton, 2004); Frank McLynn, *Stanley: Dark Genius of African Exploration* (London, 2004); see also Tim Jeal, *Explorers of the Nile* (London, 2011) and *Stanley: the Impossible Life of Africa's Greatest Explorer* (London, 2007).

[77] On the complexity of his character, see Emyr Wyn Jones, *Henry M. Stanley: Pentewyn Tân a'i Gymhlethdod Phaetonaidd* (Denbigh, 1992) and Richard Hull, *Stanley: an Adventurer Explored* (London, 1974).

[78] Stanley wrote with the speed and power with which he explored Africa. Amongst his writings are Dorothy Stanley (ed.), *The Autobiography of Sir Henry Morton Stanley: the Making of a Nineteenth-century Explorer* (Santa Barbara, CA, 2001); Henry Morton Stanley, *In Darkest Africa or the Quest, Rescue, and Retreat of Emin Governor of Equatoria* (Santa Barbara, CA, 2001) and *How I Found Livingstone: Travels, Adventures and Discoveries in Central Africa, Including Four Months' Residence with Mr Livingstone* (Amsterdam, 1884). For a graphic account of his techniques and determination, see Daniel Liebowitz and Charlie Pearson, *The Last Expedition: Stanley's Fatal Journey through the Congo* (London, 2005); for one of many examples of his 'Jungle Justice', see pp. 228–31.

[79] Stanley himself was aware of this: see his own self-defensive works, *H. M. Stanley and the Slave Trade in Africa* (London, 1893) and *Africa, its Partitions and its Future* (London, 1898).

[80] Thomas Pakenham, *The Scramble for Africa: 1876–1912* (London, 1991), pp. 24–8, 37–8, 59–60, 161–2, 316–21, 325–7, 332–3.

[81] Characteristically Stanley, once a journalist always a journalist, sought to influence his contemporaries and historians with his monumental, thousand-page *The Congo and the Founding of the Free State*, 2 vols (London, 1885). Even more characteristically, he wrote this massive work with a speed that Balzac might have envied, in just eighty-nine days. Despite his efforts, historians have proved unreceptive to his views. The controversy over his involvement in Africa continues into the twenty-first century. When plans to host a statue of him in his home town of Denbigh were unveiled, a storm of protest ensued (see the *Telegraph*, 25 July 2010). Nevertheless with a persistence that characterised the man, the statue stands today in the town, somewhat incongruously caught almost in mid-step along the main street.

[82] Joseph Conrad's *Heart of Darkness* was first included in *Youth: a Narrative and Two Other Stories* (London, 1902). For Conrad's links with Cardiff, see John Stape, *The Several Lives of Joseph Conrad* (London,

2008), pp. 36, 46–8, 97–8. He lived in the social ferment of the Sailors' and Fishermen's Home in Tiger Bay.

83 Quoted in Mario Vargas Llosa, *The Dream of the Celt* (London, 2012), p. 32. Casement later prepared a scathing report on the atrocious conditions in the Congo under King Leopold and Stanley's role in establishing the Free State. The atrocities included the murder of children, cutting off people's hands in order to claim reward money and the sexual abuse of women. One of those who worked to discredit Casement's report was Sir Alfred Jones, a close collaborator of King Leopold; one of the few who assisted Casement was E. D. Morel, who was also an eyewitness to the atrocities in the Congo and who lived at Hawarden, north Wales in 1904; see Adam Hochschild, *King Leopold's Ghost: A Story of Greed, Terror and Heroism in Colonial Africa* (London, 1998), pp. 204, 206.

84 On the Welsh in Edwardian India, see D. E. Lloyd Jones, 'David Edward Evans: a Welshman in India, *Transactions of the Honourable Society of Cymmrodorion* (1967), 132–41.

85 Lloyd Jones, 'David Edward Evans', 132–41.

86 *The Times*, 3 September 1932.

87 Welsh Biography Online, *www.wbo.llgc.org.uk/en/s20THOM-ROG-1886.htm* (accessed 4 November 2013).

88 There is an autobiographical memoir in *Annals of Tropical Medicine and Parasitology* (1907 and 1918).

89 John Hughes Morris, *The Story of our Foreign Mission* (London, 1930), pp. 54–5.

90 *British Medical Journal*, 20 October 1923.

91 Frances Bostock, *Oxford Dictionary of National Biography*, *www.oxforddnb.comm/view/article/48882*. On imperial networks, see David Lambert and Alan Lester (eds), *Colonial Lines across the British Empire: Imperial Careering in the Long Nineteenth Century* (London, 2001).

92 On these themes, see William D. Rubinstein, *Who were the Rich? A Biographical Dictionary of British Wealth-holders* (London, 2009).

93 William D. Rubinstein, *Men of Property: the Very Wealthy in Britain since the Industrial Revolution* (London, 1981).

94 *The Times*, 3 October 1928.

95 J. Beverly Smith, 'Thomas Peter Ellis (1873–1936), Lawyer and Historian', *Journal of the Merioneth Historical and Record Society*, 15/1 (2006), 89–117, and M. O'Dwyer, *India as I knew it, 1885–1925* (London, 1925).

96 H. B .E. Frere, 'On the Laws Affecting the Relations between Civilised and Savage life, as Bearing on the Dealings of Colonists with Aborigines', *Journal of the Anthropological Institute of Great Britain and Ireland*,

11 (1882), 313–54, and 'On Systems of Land Tenure among Aboriginals in South Africa,' *Journal of the Anthropological Institute of Great Britain and Ireland*, 12 (1883), 258–76. See also Shaunnagh Dorsett and Ian Hunter (eds), *Law and Politics in British Colonial Thought: Transpositions of Empire* (London, 2011) and B. R. Nanda, *Gokhale: the Indian Moderates and the British Raj* (London, 1977).

97 *Welsh Dragon*, 1, 483–93.

98 *The Times*, 12 January 1954.

99 *The Times*, 3 October 1928.

100 *Western Mail*, 11 November 1943.

101 J. Casson, *Lewis and Sybil: a Memoir* (London, 1972)

102 *The Times*, 3 December 1918.

103 *Western Mail*, 16 April 1952.

104 Mortimer Wheeler, *Still Digging* (London, 1958); Ronald William Clark, *Sir Mortimer Wheeler* (New York, NY, 1960). Wheeler's move was rivalled only by the transfer of the Egyptologist Iorwerth Eiddon Stephen Edwards (1909–96) to Cairo in 1942; the posting enabled Edwards to revisit all the major pyramid sites and do research for his magnum opus, *The Pyramids of Egypt* (London, 1947).

105 Patrick French, *India: a Portrait* (London, 2012), pp. 1–7.

106 John Darwin, *Unfinished Empire: the Global Expansion of Britain* (London, 2012), pp. 202–12.

107 G. Wynne Griffith, *Cofiant Cenhades* (Caernarfon, 1981); Robert Eric Frykenberg, 'Modern Education in South India, 1784–1854: its Roots and Role as a Vehicle of Integration under Company Raj', *American Historical Review*, 9/1 (February 1986), 37–65.

108 Lloyd Jones, 'David Edward Evans', 132–41.

109 Edward Blunt, *The I. C. S. – the Indian Civil Service* (London, 1937); Evan Maconochie, *Life in the Indian Civil Service* (London, 1926); and more recently Chris Poullaos and Suki Sian (eds), *Accountancy and Empire: the British Legacy of Professional Organisation* (New York, 2010).

110 Stephen Howe, *The New Imperial Histories Reader* (London, 2013); Robert Johnson, *British Imperialism* (Basingstoke, 2003); Bernard Porter, *The Lion's Share: a History of British Imperialism 1850 to the Present* (London, 2012); and Douglas M. Peers, 'Is Humpty Dumpty Back Together Again? The Revival of Imperial History and the Oxford History of the British Empire', *Journal of World History*, 13/2 (2002), 451–67.

111 This complexity and indeed paradox was not lost on J. B. Seeley, who noted as early as 1883 that the British Empire could simultaneously support despotism in India and democracy in Australia. On the themes

of the complex and contradictory legacy of the empire, see Kwasi Kwarteng, *Ghosts of Empire: Britain's Legacies in the Modern World* (London, 2011).

112 Jones and Jones, 'The Welsh World and the British Empire'. For an excellent portrait of how diverse and disordered the people involved in the empire were, see Margery Harper and Stephen Constantine, *Migration and Empire* (Oxford, 2010). On the complexities of identities, see Ian Baucom *Out of Place: Englishness, Empire and the Locations of Identity* (Princeton, NJ, 1999); Steve Attridge, *Nationalism, Imperialism and Identity in Late Victorian Culture: Civil and Military Worlds* (Basingstoke, 2003).

113 MacKenzie, 'Irish, Scottish, Welsh and English Worlds? The historiography of a four-nations approach to the history of the British Empire'. This four-nations approach was emphasised by the late Professor Sir R. R. Davies; see, for example, *Dominion and Conquest: the Experience of Ireland, Scotland and Wales, 1100–1300* (Cambridge, 1990); *Celts and Saxons: Historical Perceptions* (Aberystwyth, 1978); and *Beth yw'r Ots gennyf i am Brydain?* (Aberystwyth, 1999).

114 Gwyn A. Williams, 'Imperial south Wales', in *The Welsh in their History* (London, 1982), pp. 171–83.

115 See, for example, the special issue on Wales and the empire in *Wales*, July 1912; Harry Jones, 'Glimpses of Welsh History and Character', *Welsh Review*, 1 June 1906; and D. Wynne Evans, 'Cambria's Part in Empire Building', *Wales*, August 1911. For a scathing criticism of Wales's search for world importance, see Hywel Teifi Edwards, *Codi'r Hen Wlad yn ei Hôl, 1850–1914* (Llandysul, 1989), pp. 12–17. See also Jodie Kreider, '"Degraded and Benighted": Gendered Constructions of Wales in the Empire, *c*.1847', *North American Journal of Welsh Studies*, 2/1 (2002), 24–35.

116 *Western Mail*, 14, 18 February 1942.

117 Porter, *The Lion's Share*, p. 89.

118 Frank Richards, *Old Soldier Sahib* (Eastbourne, n.d.). In a chapter entitled 'Native and Servants', Frank Richards recalled the ubiquitous nature of sex in India for a British soldier: 'they were wicked little devils and at the early age of eight they knew more about sexual matters than the majority of grown-up men' (p. 185). On the theme of the empire as a zone of sexual liberation, see Ann Laura Stoler, *Carnal Knowledge and Imperial Power: Race and the Intimate in Colonial Rule* (Berkeley, CA, 2002); Philippa Levine, *Prostitution, Race and Politics: Policing Venereal Disease in the British Empire* (New York, NY, 2003) and *Gender and Empire* (Oxford, 2004).

[119] R. Hyam, 'Empire and Sexual Opportunity', *Journal of Imperial and Commonwealth History*, 14 (1986), 29–39, and *Empire and Sexuality: the British Experience* (Manchester, 1990).

[120] *Cambrian*, 5 May 1898.

[121] Lloyd Jones, 'David Edward Evans', 136–40.

[122] For a discussion of the characters (many of whom were Welsh or of Welsh origin) who 'ruled' the empire, see Stephanie Williams, *Running the Show: the Extraordinary Stories of the Men who Governed the British Empire* (London, 2011); see also Douglas Hay and Paul Craven (eds), *Masters, Servants and Magistrates in Britain and the Empire, 1562–1955* (Chapel Hill, NC, 2004).

[123] David Jenkins, *Thomas Gwynn Jones: Cofiant* (Denbigh, 1973), pp. 71–3.

[124] See, for example, Vyvyen Brendon, *Children of the Raj* (London, 2005).

[125] *Who's Who in Wales* (Cardiff, 1937).

[126] Harriet Tuckey, *Everest, the First Ascent: the Untold Story of Griffith Pugh, the Man Who Made it Possible* (London, 2013), pp. 87–9.

[127] Anne de Courcy, *The Fishing Fleet: Husband-Hunting in the Raj* (London, 2012).

[128] On the stereotypical images of women in the Raj, see Marion Amies, 'The Victorian Governess and Colonial Ideas of Womanhood', *Victorian Studies*, 31/4 (1988), 537–65; see also A. James Hammerton, *Emigrant Gentlewomen* (London, 1979).

[129] Edith Picton Turbervill, *Life is Good: an Autobiography* (London, 1939). Mary Eliza Isabella May Frere was the daughter of the imperious Henry Bartle Frere, who helped the British to gain revenge for the Indian 'mutiny' and led them to an unnecessary war against the Zulus. William Dalrymple has edited a study of Fanny Parkes; see *Begums, Thugs and White Mughals: The Journals of Fanny Parkes* (London, 2002).

[130] Quoted in Hywel Teifi Edwards, *Codi'r Hen Wlad yn ei Hôl*, p. 143.

[131] Edward Besly, *For Those in Peril: Civil Decorations and Lifesaving Awards at the National Museums and Galleries of Wales* (Cardiff, 2004).

[132] On the complexity of the Welsh identity in South Africa, see the insightful study by Heather Hughes, 'How the Welsh Became White in South Africa: Immigration, Identity and Economic Transformation from the 1860s to the 1930s', *Transactions of the Honourable Society of Cymmrodorion*, 7 (2000), 112–27.

[133] Baruch Hirson and Gwyn A. Williams, *The Delegate for Africa: David Ivon Jones, 1803–1924* (London, 1995).

[134] Edgar H. Brookes, *R. J. – in Appreciation of the life of John David Rheinallt Jones and his Work for the Betterment of Race Relations in Southern Africa* (Johannesburg, 1953).

[135] On the move from empire into the commonwealth of colonies, see Denis Judd and Peter Slinn, *The Evolution of the Modern Commonwealth, 1902–80* (London, 1982); Duncan Bell, *The Idea of Greater Britain: Empire and the Future of World Order, 1860–1900* (Princeton, NJ, 2007); and P. J. Cain and A. G. Hopkins, *British Imperialism: Crisis and Deconstruction, 1914–90* (London, 1993). See also the very valuable study by Andrew Ladley, *The Britannic Vision: Historians and the Making of the British Commonwealth of Nations, 1907–48* (Basingstoke, 2009).

[136] John Charmley, *Lord Lloyd and the Decline of the British Empire* (New York, 1987). A dapper, manacled little misogynist, with oiled hair and an olive complexion, Lloyd was one of those who could not accept that the empire he so loved was, by the 1920s, in decline, for his mission in life, most clearly seen when he was an authoritarian governor of Bombay, was to advance himself and prevent an imperial retreat. Transferred to Egypt in 1925, he noted at the bosky fifteenth hole of the Gezira golf course, 'when I see those jacarandas in bloom . . . I know it is time to send for a battleship'; quoted in Piers Brendon, *The Decline and Fall of the British Empire* (London, 2007), p. 325.

[137] M. Meredith, *Diamonds, Gold and War* (London, 2007). As the title suggests, neither Bartle Frere or the earl of Caernarvon is treated well in A. Parker, *Fifty People who Stuffed Up South Africa* (Cape Town, 1910).

[138] Thomas Keneally, *Australians: Origins to Eureka* (London, 2009), pp. 237–9.

[139] *Obituaries from The Times* (London, 1975), p. 350.

[140] Andrew Thorpe, 'J. H. Thomas', *Midland History*, 15 (1990), 111–28; Gregory Blaxland, *J. H. Thomas: A life for Unity* (London, 1964). For a tongue-in-cheek evaluation of J. H. Thomas, see Piers Brendon, *The Dark Valley: a Panorama of the 1930s* (London, 2000), pp. 44–6, 50, 153–6, 161–2. Winthorp Young was a close confidant and collaborator of T. E. Lawrence during the Arab campaigns and he was warmly referred to in the latter's *Seven Pillars of Wisdom.* Young's views on the Near East were set out in *The Independent Arab* (London, 1933).

[141] For an evaluation, see Kenneth O. Morgan, *Labour People: Leaders and Lieutenants, Hardie to Kinnock* (Oxford, 1987), pp. 197–204. See also J. Beverly Smith (ed.), *James Griffiths and his Times* (Ferndale, 1978) and James Griffiths's autobiography, *Pages From Memory* (London, 1969).

[142] England Commonwealth Development Corporation, *Report on the Gambia Egg Scheme* (London, 1952); *http://2ndlook.wordpress.com/2009/*

12/30/1945-britain-imperial-ambitions-of-a-starving-nation (accessed 1 December 2013).

143 *The Times*, 11 May 1994.

144 The historian of empire, Sir Charles Prestwood Lucas (1853–1950), was also influential in the Colonial Office in the late nineteenth century; B. L. Blakely, *The Colonial Office, 1868–1892* (London, 1971); T. R. Reese, *The History of the Royal Commonwealth Society* (London, 1968).

145 There are good overviews in Douglas Porch, *Wars of Empire* (London, 2000); Philip J. Haythornthwaite, *The Colonial Wars Source Book* (London, 1997); Ian Hernon, *Britain's Forgotten Wars: Colonial Campaigns of the Nineteenth Century* (Stroud, 2003); and Saul David, *Victoria's Wars* (London, 2006). For an entertaining study of British involvement overseas, see Stuart Laycock, *All the Countries We've Ever Invaded: and the Few We Never Got Round To* (London, 2012).

146 Jeffrey Bloomfield, *The Making of the Commissioner* (London, 1886). For one of Warren's adrenalin-charged adventures, see *On the Veldt in the Seventies* (London, 1902).

147 David, *Victoria's Wars*.

148 David, *Victoria's Wars*.

149 Arthur Abraham, 'Bai Bureh, the British and the Hut Tax War', *International Journal of African Historical Studies*, 7/1 (1974), 99–106.

150 *The Times*, 4 March 1908.

151 *The Times*, 15 February 1956.

152 Lynne Milne, 'Lloyd Mathews', *Dictionary of National Biography, www.oxforddnb.com/view/article/34936* (accessed 9 November 2013).

153 Francis Wallace Grenfell, *Memoirs of Field Marshall Lord Grenfell, PC, GCB* (London, 1925). On the theme of the ongoing brutalities of empire, see Richard Gott, *Britain's Empire: Resistance, Repression and Revolt* (London, 2011).

154 W. R. Owain-Jones, 'The Contribution of Welshmen to the Administration of India', *Transactions of the Honorable Society of Cymmrodorion* (1970), 258–9.

155 Quoted in Max Hastings, *All Hell Let Loose: the World at War, 1939–1945* (London, 2011), p. 434.

156 On the themes of how shameful episodes were transformed into heroic encounters, see John S. Ellis, '"The Methods of Barbarism" and the "Rights of Small Nations": War Propaganda and British Pluralism"', *Albion*, 30/1 (1998), 49–75.

157 John Pikoulis, *Alun Lewis: a Life* (Bridgend, 1991); Roy Pinaki, 'Poet in Khaki: Alun Lewis and his Combat Writings', *War, Literature and the Arts*, 24/1 (2012–13), 1–24.

[158] Frank Richards, *Old Soldier Sahib* (Eastbourne, n.d.); his other volume of memoirs is *Old Soldiers Never Die* (Eastbourne, n.d.). Other valuable experiences of the Welsh as the footsoldiers of empire are to be found in Gerald Morgan (ed.), *Lle Diogel i Sobri: Hunangofiant Capelulo* (Llanrwst, 1982); L. Wessels (ed.), *The Boer War Diary of Herbert Gwynne Howell* (Pretoria, 1986); Herbert Edwardes, *A Year on the Punjab Frontier* (London, 1850); and E. H. Jones, *The Road to En-dor* (London, 1955).

[159] On Bruce's links with Younghusband, see Patrick French, *Younghusband: the Last Imperial Adventurer* (London, 1995), pp. 102–4, 329–35, 342. On the successive wars in Afghanistan, the first in 1839–42, the second in 1878–80 and the third, largely forgotten, in 1919–20, see Michael Barhorp, *Afghan Wars and the North Western Frontiers, 1839–1947* (London, 1982); David Loyn, *Butcher and Bolt: Two Hundred Years of Foreign Engagement in Afghanistan* (London, 2009); and Alexander Rodger, *Battle Honours of the British Empire and Commonwealth Land Forces, 1662–1991* (Marlborough, 2003).

[160] Peter Hopkirk, *The Great Game: on Secret Service in High Asia* (Oxford, 1990) and *On Secret Service East of Constantinople: the Plot to Bring Down the British Empire* (London, 1994).

[161] Edmund Chandler, *The Unveiling of Lhasa* (London, 1905), p. 71.

[162] Chandler, *The Unveiling of Lhasa*, p. 71.

[163] Chandler, *The Unveiling of Lhasa*, p. 71.

[164] Chandler, *The Unveiling of Lhasa*, p. 71.

[165] Arnold Henry Savage Landor, *Tibet and Nepal Painted and Described* (London, 1905), p. 49.

[166] F. Emery, 'Geography and Imperialism: the Role of Sir Bartle Frere, 1825–1884', *Geographical Journal* (1984), 342–50; Phillida Brooke Simons, *Apples of the Sun: Being an Account of the Lives, Visions and Achievements of the Molteno Brothers, Henry Bartle Frere and Henry Anderson* (Cape Town, 1999).

[167] N. Mostert, *Frontiers: the Epic of South Africa's Creation and the Tragedy of the Xhosa People* (New York, NY, 1992).

[168] Saul David, *Zulu: the Heroism and Tragedy of the Zulu War of 1879* (London, 2004); Michael Lieven, 'Heroism, Heroics and the Making of Heroes: the Anglo-Zulu War of 1879', *Albion*, 30/3 (1998), 419–38.

[169] Ron Lock, *Blood on the Painted Mountain: Zulu Victory and Defeat, Hlobane and Kambula, 1879* (London, 1995); Ron Lock and Peter Quantrill, *Zulu Victory: the Epic of Isandlwana and the Cover-up* (London, 2002).

[170] The most creative description of the fighting can still be found in Donald R. Morris, *The Washing of the Spears: the Rise and Fall of the Great Zulu Nation* (London, 1966).

[171] Frank Emery (ed.), *The Red Soldier: Letters from the Zulu War* (London, 1977), p. 137, and 'Soldiers' Letters from the Zulu War', *Natalia*, 8 (1978), 54–60.

[172] Emery (ed.), *The Red Soldier*, pp. 204–5. See also Ian Knight, *The National Army Museum Book of the Zulu War* (London, 2003).

[173] Emery (ed.), *The Red Soldier*, pp. 204–5.

[174] *South Wales Daily Telegram*, 8 March 1879.

[175] *South Wales Daily Telegram*, 8 March 1879.

[176] Saul David, *Zulu: the Heroism and Tragedy of the Zulu War of 1879.*

[177] Ian Knight, *Rorke's Drift 1879: 'Pinned like rats in a hole'* (London, 1996) and Edmund Yorke, *Rorke's Drift, 1879* (Stroud, 2001).

[178] Most famously in the 1964 film *Zulu*, which starred Michael Caine and Ivor Emmanuel. Confronted by the basso profundo chanting of thousands of Zulu warriors, Emmanuel's character, Private Owen, a baritone, offers the criticism 'no top tenors'. It is a moment of pure bathos, evidence, perhaps, that the Welsh too had the sangfroid and stiff upper lip that was supposedly a characteristic of the imperialistic and imperious English.

[179] Barry C. Johnson, *The Life of Henry Hook, VC* (London, 1986); Walter Wood, 'An Account by Private Alfred Henry Hook, 2/24th regiment', *Royal Magazine*, February 1905. See also *www.rorkesdriftvc.com/vc/hook/htm* (accessed 1 December 2012).

[180] To right this outrageous insult, a campaign was launched on the centenary of Pte Robert Jones's death in 1998 to turn his headstone so that it faced the same way as all the others in Peterchurch cemetery. His descendants refused to support the campaign, arguing that the dishonour reflected badly not on Robert, but on the locals.

[181] Michael Asher, *Khartoum: the Ultimate Imperial Adventure* (London, 2006), p. 357.

[182] National Library, *Casglu'r Tlysau / Gathering the Jewels* (accessed 8 January 2009).

[183] The best account of the Boer War remains Thomas Pakenham, *The Boer War* (London, 1982).

[184] Pakenham, *The Boer War*, pp. 508–9. For the development of technology and the Welsh press, see above, chapter 2.

[185] *Liverpool Daily Post*, 12 October 1935.

[186] M. E. Chamberlain, 'Lord Aberdare and the Royal Niger Company', *Welsh History Review*, 3 (1996–7), 45–62.

[187] Colin Baker, *Sir Glyn Jones: a Proconsul in Africa* (London, 2000).

[188] Even T. E. Lawrence, the flamboyant hero of the Desert War, had a breakdown. To avoid the publicity generated by the film *With Allenby*

in Palestine and his best-selling book, *Seven Pillars of Wisdom,* Lawrence rejoined the RAF and was posted to Karachi, before retiring to Dorset. He was killed in a meaningless, somewhat mysterious, motorcycle accident in 1935. For the prevailing sense of doom and despair, see Richard Overy, *The Morbid Age: Britain between the Wars* (London, 2009).

189 Quoted in Brendon, *The Decline and Fall of the British Empire,* p. 321.

190 For Amritsar, see Derek Sayer, 'British Reaction to the Amritsar Massacre, 1919–22', *Past and Present,* 131 (1991), 130–64, and Nicholas Lloyd, *The Amritsar Massacre: the Untold Story of One Fateful Day* (London, 2011).

191 David Hein, 'Vulnerable: HMS *Prince of Wales* in 1941', *Journal of Military History,* 77/3 (2013), 955–89.

7 'Ha! Ha! among the Trumpets' – a Century of Warfare

1 The historiography of the First World War is vast and varied. So much has already been published that it would be impossible for one person to read it all. The centenary of the war (2014–18) promises that even more material will pour from the presses and the documentary production houses. The brigade has become an army of books. Two useful websites which have been launched are *www.cymruww1.llgc.org.uk* (Y Rhyfel Byd Cyntaf a'r Profiad Cymreig / The Welsh Experience of World War One 1914–18) and Welsh voices of the Great War online *www.cardiff.ac.uk/school/research/projectreports/welshvoices*. Sisyphus's cursed task of endlessly rolling a rock up a hill seems more achievable than attempting to read or view all the material published or broadcast on the war. Some Stakhanovites of the historical profession such as Martin Gilbert have produced books at a rate that Dickens would envy. In the Welsh context, Robin Barlow's *Wales and the War* (Llandysul, 2014) provides a valuable overview of the ways the war impacted on Welsh lives. On the war's origins, there is still much to learn from the old masters; see Fritz Fischer, *Germany's Aims in the First World War* (London, 1961); A. J. P. Taylor, *War by Timetable* (London, 1969), *The Struggle for Mastery in Europe* (Oxord, 1954) and 'Fritz Fischer and his school', *Journal of Modern History,* 47/1 (1975), 211–41. Amongst most successful studies are Barbara W. Tuchman, *The Guns of August* (London, 1962); Max Hastings, *Catastrophe: Europe Goes to War 1914* (London, 2013); and Chris Clark, *The Sleep-Walkers: How Europe went to War in 1914* (London, 2012). As with her book on the war's contentious ending,

The Peacemakers: Six Months that Changed the World (London, 2001), Margaret MacMillan's study of the war's controversial commencement, *The War that Ended Peace: How Europe Abandoned Peace for the First World War* (London, 2013), is superb. The greatest visual presentation of the war is still the twenty-six episodes of *The Great War* (1963). Like the conflict itself, this was a colonial project involving the BBC, the Canadian Broadcasting Corporation and the Australian Broadcasting Corporation. This truly was path-breaking television, made stronger by the fact that fifty years ago many of the participants in the war were still alive and contributed interviews.

It appears that the giant cogwheels of historical studies have turned full circle. The view that it was a futile war, best emphasised by satirical presentations such as *Oh! What a Lovely War* and the BBC's magisterial *Blackadder*, which memorably described British war aims as 'moving General Haig's drinks cabinet six feet closer to Berlin', are slightly out of fashion. Increasingly, in 2014/15, authors such as Max Hastings have argued that it was a war essential to safeguarding British freedom and values. Of the early centenary studies, of particular value is David Reynolds, *The Long Shadow: the Great War and the Twentieth Century* (London, 2013), which tries to show that our view of the war has been hopelessly skewed by seeing it solely through the prism of the war poets – our perspective stuck in Poet's Corner. The year 2014 opened with an unedifying spat between the historian Richard Evans and the education secretary, Michael Gove, over the 'true' nature of the Great War. Like the Treaty of Versailles, their 'debate' was fractious, a discreditable carve-up of the past with everyone claiming to speak for the dead. The dead deserve better than this.

2 On the deployment of some Welsh troops around the world see: *www.1914-1918.net/welshhorse.htm* (accessed 29 March 2011). On the issue of global war, see Hew Strachan, *The First World War: a New History* (London, 2006), pp. 65–95.

3 An excellent study of the contradictions and complexities of the First World War is Gordon Corrigan, *Mud, Blood and Poppycock: Britain and the First World War* (London, 2004).

4 Amongst the major creative works by members of the Royal Welsh Fusiliers are Robert Graves, *Goodbye to All That* (1929), Wyn Griffith, *Up to Mametz and Beyond* (1931), Frank Richards, *Old Soldiers Never Die* (1938), Siegfrid Sassoon, *Counter-Attack and Other Poems* (1918), *Memoirs of a Fox-hunting man* (1928) and *Memoirs of an Infantry Officer* (1930), and perhaps greatest of all, a work which captures the diversity and dislocation of war, David Jones, *In Parenthesis* (1937). Of the anthologies

of war poetry and prose, two in particular deserve close attention from the historian of Wales: Alan Llwyd (ed.), *Out of the Fire of Hell: Welsh Experience of the Great War 1914–1918, in Prose and Verse* (Llandysul, 2008); and Alan Llwyd and Elwyn Edwards (eds), *Gwaedd y Bechgyn: Blodeugerdd Barddas o Gerddi'r Rhyfel Mawr* (Llandybïe, 1989). There is much insight to the way the war changed culture in Samuel Hynes, *A War Imagined: the First World War and English Culture* (London, 1990).

5 Lieutenant R. St John Richards, Ernie Williams and Frank Richards claimed to have witnessed the football match. Lieutenant Richards later wrote home to Llangerniew rectory, 'I must say that to a casual onlooker it would have appeared we were friends, not foes. Some of the more sportive even got out a football, and we had a sort of friendly match. They were a Saxon corps.' Quoted in Stanley Weintraub, *Silent Night: the Remarkable Christmas Truce of 1914* (London, 2001), p. 121.

6 Paul Mainwaring Jones, *War Letters of a Public-school Boy* (London, 1918).

7 The phrase 'a Duw ar drau ar orwel pell' (God is ebbing on a far horizon) is from the poem 'Rhyfel' by Hedd Wyn (Ellis Evans, 1887–1917).

8 Ifor Leslie Evans (1897–1952), a student in France and in Germany, later principal at Aberystwyth, was totally unprepared for the war. He was captured in 1914 and spent four years as a prisoner of war in Ruhleben prison camp. It was there that he learnt Welsh and changed his first name from Ivor to Ifor.

9 Cyril Parry, 'Gwynedd and the Great War', *Welsh History Review*, 14/1 (1988), 81.

10 C. Hughes, 'Army Recruitment in Gwynedd 1914–18' (unpublished MA thesis, University of Wales, Bangor, 1983), pp. 90–2; I. Nicholson and T. Lloyd Jones, *Wales: its Part in the War* (Cardiff, 1919).

11 I am grateful to Dr Robin Barlow for this information, published in his work *Wales and World War One* (Llandysul, 2014).

12 Parry, 'Gwynedd and the Great War', 91, ff.72.

13 For two contradictory yet complementary views, see Dewi Eirug Davies, *Byddin y Brenin: Cymru a'i Chrefydd yn y Rhyfel Mawr* (Swansea, 1988) and J. D. Davies, *Britannia's Dragon: a Naval History of Wales* (Stroud, 2013). On the pacifist tradition in Wales, see Deian Hopkin, 'Patriots and Pacifists in Wales 1914–1918', *Llafur* (1974), 30–42; and K. O. Morgan, 'Peace Movements in Wales, 1889–1945', *Welsh History Review*, 10/3 (1981), 400–19.

14 On the problems of recruitment from Welsh farms in the Marches, see Nick Mansfield, 'The Persistence of Anti-Welshness in the Marches',

Llafur (2010), 120–2. The headline is from the *Western Mail*, 12 January 1915.

15 Bertrand Russell, *Why Men Fight* (New York, NY, 1916), p. 7.

16 *Western Mail*, 20 August 1914.

17 *Western Mail*, 19 and 22 March 1915.

18 *Western Mail*, 3 May 1915.

19 *Y Genedl Gymreig*, 1 June 1915.

20 *Western Mail*, 19 June 1915.

21 For the 1915 strike, see Anthony Mór-O'Brien, 'Patriotism on Trial: the Strike of South Wales Miners, July 1915', *Welsh History Review*, 12/1 (1984), 76–104. Complaints about profiteering by the coal companies outweighed any ideological issues.

22 On these themes, see Brock Millman, *Managing Domestic Dissent in First World War Britain* (London, 2000), pp. 7–29, 36, 138–66.

23 On David Watts Morgan, see the *Western Mail*, 23 February 1933. Andrew Thomas Griffiths of Haverfordwest joined up with his son Frederick in 1915. Both lied about their ages, for Frederick was only 15.

24 For a report of such a meeting, see the *North Wales Chronicle*, 2 October 1914.

25 Such claims were made in *Y Dinesydd Cymreig*, 16 September 1916. On Grace Williams, see *www.oxforddnb.com/view/article/55453* (accessed 27 January 2014).

26 Morgan Watkin-Williams, *From Khaki to Cloth: the Autobiograohy of Morgan Watcyn-Williams* (London, 1948), p. 7.

27 *Y Genedl Gymreig*, 1 June 1915.

28 John Terraine, *The Western Front, 1914–1918* (London, 2003); John Keegan, *The Face of Battle: a Study of Agincourt, Waterloo and the Somme* (London, 1976); see also Thomas Dilworth, *David Jones in the Great War* (London, 2012).

29 There was a substantial advertising campaign in the newspaper press across Wales in both English and in Welsh. See, for example, the advertisement for *Y Fyddin Newydd* (the New Army) in *Y Genedl Gymreig*, 25 August 1914. Though it was not published bilingually, the Kitchener poster was also extensively circulated. *Y Genedl Gymreig* reported the distribution of 30,000 leaflets at hiring fairs in Caernarfonshire and Anglesey, resulting in the somewhat disappointing enlistment of twenty-three recruits. January 1915 saw 3,000 leaflets distributed to schools in Caernarfonshire and Anglesey and 1,000 to schools in Merioneth, whether to entice the young or to get them to put pressure on older siblings or relatives was not clear. Later in the war such pressure from younger siblings was effective, for it was to

prevent his younger brother going to war that the poet Hedd Wyn went to fight and famously die.

30 On the Swansea battalions, see Bernard Lewis, *Swansea Pals: a History of the 14th (Service) Battalion, Welsh Regiment in the Great War* (Barnsley, 2004); and J. R. Alban, 'The Formation of the Swansea Battalion, 1914–15', *Gower*, 25 (1974), 21–32. In the north, too, Pals battalions were formed. Sir Henry Lewis, for example, wrote of a typical recruiting march when 250 soldiers from the Pals Brigade marched from Penrhyndeudraeth to Llandudno via the Llŷn Peninsula, Bangor, Bethesda and Caernarfon; quoted in Parry, 'Gwynedd and the Great War', 82.

31 For an evocative photograph of the Swansea Pals, including Tawe their bulldog and the infamous Willie Williams of the Cuba Hotel, see Lewis, *Swansea Pals*, p. 58 (see also p. 281 above). One gets the feeling that this was quite literally a band of brothers in arms, as the comments by Wyn Griffith on the loss of his brother at Mametz Wood so eloquently show. The Swansea Pals letters are highly evocative on the loss of close friends; see for example, the reaction of Private William Williams of Law Street, Morriston, to the loss of Private J. Lewis, an old friend. At the start of the war, Welsh newspapers were more prone, or free, to publish such experiences. For example, here is Lieutenant Strange on the death of Private Austin:

> his death was as noble as his life. He was hit very badly when out with me on . . . and his mate was hit beside him. Though in pain he forced himself to keep quiet, and so enabled us to rescue both himself and his wounded mate. The last words I heard him say were, 'Stick it the Welsh'.
>
> *South Wales Daily Press*, 24 June 1916,
> quoted in Bernard Lewis, *Swansea Pals*

Emlyn Davies recalled that 'in our battalion, five Jones brothers from the Ffestiniog area served. Four of them were killed; a father and son suffered similarly all in the same day'; quoted in Keith Strange, *Wales and the First World War* (Cardiff, n.d.), p. 31.

32 Ernest Jones, *Free Associations: Memoirs of a Psycho-analyst* (London, 1959), pp. 71–2.

33 Strange, *Wales and the First World War*, p. 17.

34 Peter Parker, *The Old Lie: the Great War and the Public-school Ethos* (London, 1987).

35 E. L. Ellis, *The University College of Wales, Aberystwyth, 1872–1972* (Aberystwyth, 1972), p. 41; Parry, 'Gwynedd and the Great War', 78–117. For an account of a recruitment meeting in the university, see *Y Genedl Gymreig*, 1 June 1915.

36 Another iconic painting is J. P. Beadle's of the meeting between the 2nd Worcestershires and the 1st South Wales Borderers in the grounds of the chateau in Gheluvelt. The battle was, uncharacteristically for the Western Front, one of fast flowing movement. See *www.news.bbc.co.uk/today/hi/today/newsid-91300/913207/stm* (accessed 1 November 2010).

37 Mainwaring Jones, *War Letters of a Public-school Boy*.

38 On these themes, see Richard van Emden, *Boy Soldiers of the Great War* (London, 2012).

39 Davies, *Byddin y Brenin*; D. Densil Morgan, *Cedyrn Canrif: Crefydd a Chymdeithas yng Nhgymru'r Ugeinfed Ganrif* (Cardiff, 2001), especially chapter 1, 'Ffydd yn y ffosydd: D. Cynddelw Williams (1870–1942)', pp. 1–28.

40 R. W. Jones, *J. Puleston Jones* (Caernarfon, 1929).

41 Davies, *Byddin y Brenin*, p. 17.

42 Davies, *Byddin y Brenin*, pp. 82, 92, 98, 103–5.

43 Davies, *Byddin y Brenin*; see also Gerwyn Wiliams, *Y Rhwyg: Arolwg o Farddoniaeth Gymraeg ynghylch y Rhyfel*, p. 29.

44 Penry Jones, *Peter Price* (Swansea, 1949), p. 39.

45 See also David A. Pretty, *Rhyfelwyr Môn: y Brigadydd-Gadfridog Syr Owen Thomas, AS, 1858–1923* (Denbigh, 1989), pp. 23–7.

46 J. Lambert Rees, *Timothy Rees of Mirfield and Llandaff. A Biography* (London and Oxford, 1945).

47 Davies, *Byddin y Brenin*, pp. 29–35.

48 Davies, *Byddin y Brenin*, pp. 29–35.

49 *Y Geninen*, January 1915.

50 *Cymru*, 1 November 1914, 202.

51 For the impact of the sinking of the *Lusitania*, see Diana Preston, *Wilful Murder: The Sinking of the Lusitania* (London, 2002). Two who survived were the Liberal politician D. A. Thomas, later Lord Rhondda, and his daughter, Margaret. See Viscountess Rhondda, *This was my World* (London, 1933), pp. 24–50, for her rescue from the sea. Another who survived was William Gwynn Parry Jones, who floated in the water for eight hours before being rescued.

52 *Y Brython*, 17 September 1914.

53 Llwyd and Edwards (eds), *Gwaedd y Bechgyn*, p. 71.

54 Tecwyn Lloyd, 'Welsh Public Opinion and the First World War', *Planet*, 10 (1972), 25–37, 'Pan fu "gwaedd y bechgyn lond y gwynt", 1914–18', *Y Faner*, 31 August 1984, and 'Welsh Literature and the First World War', *Planet*, 11 (1972), 17–23; Aled Eurig, 'Agweddau ar y Gwrthwynebiad i'r Rhyfel Byd Cyntaf yng Nghymru', *Llafur*, 4/4 (1987), 58–68.

[55] Quoted in James Joll, *The Origins of the First World War* (London, 1984), p. 184; see also Alan Ryan, *Bertrand Russell: a Political Life* (London, 1988), p. 56.

[56] *Cymru*, November 1914, 202; David French, 'Spy Fever in Britain, 1900–1915', *Historical Journal*, 21 (1978), 71–82.

[57] *Cymru*, November 1914, 153.

[58] *Cymru*, November 1914, 202.

[59] On the general paranoia, see James Hayward, *Myths and Legends of the First World War* (Stroud, 2002), pp. 1–32 for the spymania and pp. 32–47 for the Russians in Britain.

[60] Lewis Valentine's *Dyddiadur Milwr* contained the following phrases and appeals to God: 'Uffern aflan', 'diawlineb', 'cigfa', 'cythreuliaid digwylydd', 'Uffern! Uffern! Uffern!', 'Y mawr drugarod Dduw beth yw dyn?', 'Gwae – gwaed – gwallgofrwydd!', 'cnawd drylliedig', 'esgeiriau yn ysgyrion', 'Atal, Dduw y dwymyn wallgof, atal boeredd y mallgwn'. *Seren Gomer* (Gaeaf, 1970), 96.

[61] It is hard to provide a starker, darker portrait of the impact of the war on the soldier than in David Jones, *In Parenthesis*. Set in the period December 1915 to July 1916, the poem has its climax at Mametz Wood during the Battle of the Somme, when so many Welsh troops went to hell. For the quotation about the ravens, see Gwyn Thomas, *Y Traddodiad Barddol* (Cardiff, 1976), p. 37.

[62] One of the most graphic of war books is the superb compendium compiled by Captain J. C. Dunn, *The War the Infantry Knew, 1914–19, a Chronicle of Service in France and Belgium with the Second Battalion His Majesty's Twenty-Third Foot, the Royal Welsh Fusiliers* (London, 1938). Dunn's experience as RMO of the Welsh Fusiliers was moving and remained a living thing for him throughout his life and his work is a useful corrective to Robert Graves's *Goodbye to All That*. Dunn, a literal type, despaired of the literary Graves, who often allowed his poetic licence free rein. See also Emlyn Davies, *Taffy Went to War* (Knutsford, 1975) and Lord Silsoe, *Sixty Years a Welsh Territorial* (Llandysul, 1976).

[63] On Cynddelw Williams, see Morgan, *Cedyrn Canrif*, pp. 1–27.

[64] Davies, *Byddin y Brenin*.

[65] Siegfried Sasson, *Memoirs of an Infantry Officer* (London, 1937), p. 71.

[66] Quoted in Strange, *Wales and the First World War*, p. 22.

[67] I am grateful to Dr Robin Barlow for this information.

[68] Colin Hughes, *Mametz: Lloyd George's 'Welsh Army' at the Battle of the Somme* (London, 1979), p. 213.

69 Llewelyn Wyn Griffith, *Up to Mametz and Beyond* (London, 1931), p. 218.
70 Griffith, *Up to Mametz and Beyond*, p. 218.
71 Quoted in Morgan, *Cedyrn Canrif*, p. 11.
72 Albert Evans-Jones (Cynan), *Cerddi Cynan: y Casgliad Cyflawn* (Liverpool, 1959), p. 39.
73 Frank Richards, *Old Soldiers Never Die* (Eastbourne, n.d.), p. 162.
74 Ira Jones, *Tiger Squadron* (London, n.d.), *passim.*
75 T. H. E. Travers, *The Killing Ground* (London, 1987); and Ernest Thurtle, *Shootings at Dawn* (London, 1922).
76 J. Vyrnwy Morgan, *The War and Wales* (London, 1916), p.103; see also Gerard J. DeGroot, *Blighty: British Society in the Era of the Great War* (London, 1996), p. 163.
77 Dunn, *The War the Infantry Knew*, pp. 1–49.
78 Ernest Thurtle, *Time's Winged Chariot* (London, 1945). Thurtle's greatest achievement in parliament was to bring about the abolition of the death penalty for cowardice or desertion in the British Army.
79 Dunn, *The War the Infantry Knew*. Ford Madox Ford evokes this spirit of entertainment in his four-volume novel, *Parade's End* (1924–8).
80 Jon Stallworthy, *Wilfred Owen: a Biography* (London, 1974), p. 160; Dominic Hibberd, *Wilfred Owen: The Truth Untold* (London, 2002), p. 337.
81 P. Griffith, *Battle Tactics of the Western Front* (London, 1994), *passim.*
82 Edward Wagenknecht and Anthony Slide, *The Films of D. W. Griffith* (New York, NY, 1975); William M. Drew, *D. W. Griffith: his Life a nd Work* (New York, NY, 1972). Essential reading for the impact of the silent movies is Kevin Brownlow's evocative and emotional *The Parade's Gone By* (New York, NY, 1968). There is also much of value in N. Reeves, 'Film Propaganda and its Audience: the Example of Britain's Official Films during the First World War', *Journal of Contemporary History*, 18 (1983), 117–31.
83 C. H. Dudley Ward, *History of the Welsh Guards* (London, 1920); Ian Beckett and Keith Simpson (eds), *A Nation in Arms* (Manchester, 1985); Tim Cross (ed.), *The Lost Voices of World War One*; D. G. Phillips, 'Dai Bach y Soldiwr: Welsh Soldiers in the British Army, 1914–18', *Llafur* (1993), 94–105.
84 Morgan, *Cedyrn Canrif*, p. 9.
85 Jones, *In Parenthesis*. See also Paul Fussell, *The Great War and Modern Memory* (Oxford, 1975), pp. 150–2.
86 Richard Holmes, *Tommy: The British Soldier on the Western Front, 1914–1918* (London, 2005), p. 116.

[87] Holmes, *Tommy*, p. 503. See also Joseph Persico, *Eleventh Month, Eleventh Day, Eleventh Hour: Armistice Day 1918, World War I and its Violent Climax* (London, 2005), pp. 127–30.

[88] Richards, *Old Soldiers Never Die*, p. 117.

[89] Parry, 'Gwynedd and the Great War', 84.

[90] *Y Goleuad*, 11 September 1914.

[91] Alan Llwyd, *Bob: Cofiant R. Williams Parry, 1884–1956* (Llandysul, 2013), pp. 123–74.

[92] Captain G. C. Wynne, *If Germany Attacks: the Battle in Depth in the West* (London, 1940), p. 273.

[93] Alexander Barrie, *War Underground: the Tunnellers of the Western Front* (Staplehurst, 2000).

[94] Sir Tannatt William Edgeworth David (1858–1934) of St Fagans, the geologist and explorer who had reached the South Magnetic Pole during Shackleton's Nimrod expedition in 1907–8, served in the Australian Mining Corps (or Tunnellers). His geological expertise was vital to advise on the construction of dugouts, trenches and tunnels and in the provision of pure drinking water from underground supplies. David fought at the Battle of Messines and received the Distinguished Service Order; see David Branagan, *T. W. Edgeworth David: a Life. Geologist, Adventurer, Soldier and 'Knight in the Old Brown Hat'* (Canberra, 2005).

[95] The Marquess of Anglesey, *A History of the British Cavalry, 1816–1919, Vol. 8: the Western Front* (Barnsley, 1997).

[96] *www.oxforddnb.com/view/printable31892* (accessed 25 July 2006).

[97] Brian Glover, *Prince of Ales: a History of Brewing in Wales* (Stroud, 1993), p. 106.

[98] Weintraub, *Silent Night*.

[99] Robert Graves, 'Christmas Truce', in Lucia Graves, *Robert Graves: Complete Short Stories* (New York, NY, 1995).

[100] Richards, *Old Soldiers Never Die*, pp. 65–70.

[101] Richards, *Old Soldiers Never Die*, pp. 65–70.

[102] Holmes, *Tommy*, pp. 502–4.

[103] Ward, *History of the Welsh Guards*, p. 393.

[104] Holmes, *Tommy*, p. 503.

[105] Eric Hiscock, *The Bells of Hell Go Ting-a-ling-a-ling* (London, 1976). The definitive history of Gallipoli is Alan Moorehead, *Gallipoli* (London, 1956), but Carlyon, *Gallipoli* (London, 2002), now runs it close.

[106] For Welsh involvement, see Robin Barlow, 'The Gallipoli Campaign 1915: Experiences of two Carmarthenshire Men', *Carmarthenshire Antiquarian*, 27 (1992), 79–86. One, Cecil Phillips, earned the Military Cross for rescuing four wounded men on 15 August 1915. The Welsh

Fusiliers also fought at Gallipoli; see Carlyon, *Gallipoli*, p. 359.

[107] Barlow, 'The Gallipoli Campaign 1915'. For the Goya quotation, see George Panichas and Sir Herbert Read, *Promise of Greatness: the War of 1914–1918* (New York, NY, 1968), pp. 72, 84.

[108] Edward J. Erickson, *Ordered to Die: a History of the Ottoman Army in the First World War* (London, 2001).

[109] Erickson, *Ordered to Die*.

[110] Elias Henry Jones, *The road to En-dor: a True Story of a Cunning Wartime Escape* (London, 1930).

[111] For a recent reproduction of the painting, see Tony Curtis (ed.), *Wales at War: Critical Essays on Literature and Art* (Bridgend, 2007).

[112] T. E. Lawrence's 'Welshness' is often a matter of dispute. He was born in Tremadog in 1888, a fact which made him eligible for the Meyricke Scholarship at Jesus College, Oxford. His ancestors, on his mother's side, were from Swansea and Chepstow. Alan Llwyd was sufficiently persuaded to include Lawrence in *Out of the Fire of Hell: Welsh Experience of the Great War 1914–18 in Prose and Verse* (Llandysul, 2008), pp. 22–3. See also Michael Korda, *Hero: the Life and Legend of Lawrence of Arabia* (London, 1835).

[113] Especially promoted in Lawrence's monumental memoir, *Seven Pillars of Wisdom* (London, 1927), and in Robert Graves, *Lawrence and the Arabs* (London, 1935).

[114] See *www.telstudies.org/* (accessed 11 January 2014).

[115] John Buchan, *Pilgrim's Way* (London, 1940), p. 111.

[116] T. E. Lawrence, *Seven Pillars of Wisdom* (London, 1935), pp. 524, 527. Young later worked for the Foreign Office, where his Arabic and expert knowledge of the Arab world helped to form the policy eventually adopted in the 1920s and 1930s towards Iraq. A cultured, musical intellectual as well as a man of action, Young wrote exceptionally well, especially in his *The Independent Arab* (London, 1933).

[117] For the war across Africa, see Edward Paice, *Tip and Run: the Untold Tragedy of the Great War in Africa* (London, 2007); In *Black Laughter* (New York, NY, 1924), Llewelyn Powys provides an eyewitness account of many of the deaths through famine rather than fighting.

[118] N. A. M. Rodger, *The Price of Victory: a Naval History of Britain, 1815–2007* (London, 2014).

[119] Robert K. Massie, *Dreadnought: Britain, Germany and the Coming of the Great War* (London, 1991).

[120] J. J. Sumida, 'British Naval Operational Logistics 1914–18', *Journal of Military History*, 57/3 (1993), 447–80.

121 A. Gordon, *The Rules of the Game: Jutland and British Naval Command* (London, 1996).

122 On Sir Hugh Evan-Thomas, see Davies, *Britannia's Dragon*, pp. 197–8.

123 Davies, *Britannia's Dragon*, pp. 197–8. See also Robert Havard, 'Thomas Picton and Sir Thomas Picton: two Welsh Soldiers in Spain', *Transactions of the Honourable Society of Cymmrodorion* (2000), 164–81.

124 In the words of *Y Tyst*, 12 May 1915,

> 'ni bu trychineb mwy ellyllaidd a chreulon yn hanes unrhyw ryfel . . . Ac i wneud ei haerllugrwydd pen chwiban yn gan mil gwaeth, beiddia ddadleu ei bod hi'n ddiniwed am ei bod wedi rhybuddio pawb mai dyna a wnai. Mae llofruddiaeth yn gyfreithlon os ymostynga'r llofrudd i anfon 'post card' ymlaen llaw at ei ysglyfaeth i'w hysbysu o'i fwriad.'
>
> (There has never been a more devilish or cruel outrage in any war. To make her heinousness even worse, she argues innocence on the basis that she had forewarned everyone of her intentions. Murder is legal just so long as the murderer sends a postcard to his prey announcing his intentions.)

Y Goleuad, 29 June 1917, considered it the result of 'dichell satanaidd' (devilish conspiracy). *Seren Cymru* and *Y Brython* were united in outraged anger at the act.

125 Gerwyn Wiliams, *Y Rhwyg* (Llandysul, 1993), p. 67. See also Diana Preston, *Wilful Murder: the Sinking of the Lusitania* (London, 2002). For the ballad 'Suddiad y Lusitania', see the *Casglu'r Tlysau / Gathering the Jewels* website, item GTJ18704.

126 Viscountess Rhondda, *This was my World*. See also Angela V. John, *Turning the Tide: the Life of Lady Rhondda* (Cardigan, 2013), pp. 121–36, 407–8.

127 J. S. Breemer, *Defeating the U-Boat: Inventing Anti-submarine Warfare* (Newport, RI, 2010), *passim*.

128 W. A. Williams, *Heart of a Dragon: the VCs of Wales and the Welsh Regiments, 1914* (Wrexham, 2008), pp. 132–43.

129 Alfred Noyes discusses this issue in *The Accusing Ghost* (London, 1953); see also W. Jerrold, *Alfred Noyes* (London, 1930).

130 W. S. Chalmers, *Max Horton and the Western Approaches* (London, 1954).

131 Ralph Barker, *The Royal Flying Corps in World War I* (London, 2002), especially pp. 3–14.

132 Basil Collier, *Heavenly Adventurer: Sefton Brancker and the Dawn of British Aviation* (London, 1959). Brancker later became a pioneer of civil Aviation and having been taunted into joining its maiden flight, he died aboard the airship R101 when it crashed in flames in 1930.

133 N. Macmillan, *Sir Sefton Brancker* (London, 1935).

134 M. Izzard, *A Heroine in her Time* (London, 1969); the pains were still sharp when Douglas-Pennant wrote *Under the Searchlight* (London, 1922).

135 A. G. D. Alderson, *The First War in the Air, 1914–1918* (privately printed, 1990) gives something of a noble, Biggles-style-heroic portrait of the RAF, as does John Hammerton, *War in the Air, Aerial Wonders of our Time* (London, 1936).

136 See *www.firstworldwar.com* (accessed 23 October 2008).

137 R. Collishaw and R. V. Dodds, *Air Command: a Fighter Pilot's Story* (London, 1973).

138 Byron Rogers, *The Bank Manager and the Holy Grail* (London, 2004), pp. 118–20.

139 Jones, *Tiger Squadron*, p. 170.

140 *London Gazette*, 3 August 1918; 21 September 1918.

141 Rogers, *The Bank Manager and the Holy Grail*, p. 181.

142 Gwilym H. Lewis, *Wings over the Somme* (London, 1976), p. 109.

143 Barker, *The Royal Flying Corps in World War I*, p. 199.

144 One of the most succinct explanations of the impact of war on the accelerated development of technology is provided in Graham Greene's script to the film *The Third Man*:

> In Italy for 30 years under the Borgias, they had murder, terror, bloodshed. They produced Leonardo da Vinci, Michaelangelo and the Renaissance. In Switzerland, they had five hundred years of peace, brotherly love and democracy, and what did they produce? The cuckoo clock.

Airplanes, submarines, tanks, armoury and a host of items were developed but the First World War was, in a real sense, 'the chemists' war', as a host of poison gases were created. In contrast, the Second World War would be claimed as the physicist's war. See Robert Harries and Jeremy Paxman, *A Higher Form of Killing: the Secret History of Chemical and Biological Warfare* (London, 2002). See also Barton C. Hacker, 'The Machines of War: Western Military Technology, 1850–2000', *History and Technology*, 21/3 (2005), 255–300; and John Ellis, *The Social History of the Machine Gun* (London, 1986).

145 J. Casson, *Lewis and Sybil: a Memoir* (London, 1972).

146 *The Times*, 6 August 1974.

147 See *www.oxforddnb.com/view/printable31892* (accessed 25July 2006).

148 *The Times*, 4 February 1955.

149 See *www.oxforddnb.com/view/article/36476* (accessed 14 January 2014).

150 See *www.oxforddnb.com/view/article/36476* (accessed 14 January 2014).

151 See *www.oxforddnb.com/view/article/34465* (accessed 14 January 2014).

152 *Dictionary of Welsh Biography*, article on the Hanbury-Williams family.

153 For cartoons of the war, see M. Bryant, *Illingworth's War in Cartoons: One Hundred of his Greatest Daily Mail Drawings* (London, 2009) and W. Feaver, *Masters of Caricature: from Hogarth to Gilray to Scarfe and Levine* (London, 1981).

154 M. Bryant, '"Crusader, White Rabbit or Organ Grinder's Monkey?" Leslie Illingworth and the British Political Cartoon in World War II', *Journal of European Studies*, 31 (2001), 345–66.

155 M. Bryant and S. Heneage, *Dictionary of British Cartoonists and Caricaturists, 1730–1980* (London, 1994).

156 E. Andrews, *A Woman's Work is Never Done* (Rhondda, 1956), p. 20; see also S. Minwel Tibbott and B. Thomas, *O'r Gwaith i'r Gwely / Cadw Tŷ, 1890–1960* (Cardiff, 1994).

157 Angela V. John, *Turning the Tide: the Life of Lady Rhondda* (Cardigan, 2013), pp. 161–82; Lisa Snook, '"Out of the cage"? Women and the First World War in Pontypridd', *Llafur*, 8/2 (2001), 75–88.

158 Deirdre Beddoe, *Out of the Shadows: a History of Women in Twentieth-century Wales* (Cardiff, 2000), pp. 69–72.

159 Deirdre Beddoe, 'Munitionettes, maids and mams: women in Wales, 1914–39', in Angela V. John (ed.), *Our Mother's Land: Chapters in Welsh Women's History* (Cardiff, 2011), pp. 189–209; I. Hay, *HM Factory Queensferry, 1915–1918* (Queensferry, 1948).

160 A. Marwick, *Women at War 1914–1918* (London, 1977), *passim.*

161 G. Braybon, *Women Workers in the First World War* (London, 1981).

162 *Welsh Outlook*, July 1917; Beddoe, 'Munitionettes, maids and mams', 67–9.

163 Joyce Mollet, *With a Camera in my Pocket: the Life and Times of a First World War Nurse* (Baddeley, 2005). During her time working in the military capital in Cairo, Mary Jane Hughes cared for several Welsh soldiers from her native Llanelli. She then worked in horrific conditions on a series of hospital ships. In addition to the usual cases of measles, scarlet fever, diphtheria, chicken pox, smallpox, and venereal disease, she also had to work against typhoid and paratyphoid, typhus, cholera, blackwater fever, malaria, amoebic dysentery and tetanus. However, the illnesses she found most unsettling were the 'mental cases' caused by the atrocities of the war (p. 40).

164 Peter Lord (ed.), *Between Two Worlds: the Diaries of Winifred Coombe Tenant* (Aberystwyth, 2011), p. 228.

165 Lord, *Between Two Worlds*, p. 231.

166 One of the best studies of the emotional trauma of the First World War is Pat Barker's novel *Regeneration* (Harmondsworth, 1991). Joanna Bourke's *Dismembering the Male: Men's Bodies, Britain and the Great War* (London, 1996) was a pioneering study of how men began to suffer hysteria, a disease which until the war had been perceived to be endemic to women. Since her pathbreaking, others have followed; see for example, Michael Roper, *The Secret Battle: Emotional Survival in the Great War* (Manchester, 2009); Jessica Meyer, *Men of War: Masculinity and the First World War in Britain* (Basingstoke, 2009); Paul Lerner, *Hysterical Men: War, Psychiatry and the Politics of Trauma in Germany, 1890–1930* (Ithaca, 2003); Fiona Reid, *Broken Men: Shell Shock, Treatment and Recovery in Britain, 1914–30* (London, 2010); and Peter Barham, *Forgoten Lunatics of the Great War* (New Haven, 2004).

167 Eighteen years on night shifts suggests strongly that David Morgan Williams must have upset someone in authority in the mine. See *www.oxforddnb.com/article64683* (accessed 6 September 2005).

168 Miranda Seymour, *Robert Graves: Life on the Edge* (London, 1995), pp. 98–100.

169 Ivor Gurney's experiences with Welsh troops during the war were sufficient reason for Alan Llwyd to include him in his anthology of 'Welsh' war writing, *Out of the Fire of Hell* (Llandysul, 200), p. 13. On Gurney, see Michal Hurd, *The Ordeal of Ivor Gurney* (London, 2008). On these themes, see Malcolm Brown, *The Imperial War Museum Book of 1918* (London, 1999); see also the special issue of the *BBC History Magazine*, November 2004.

170 Herbrandston is the only doubly thankful village in Wales, for all of its people returned after the Second World War.

171 I am grateful to Dr Robin Barlow for this information.

172 D. Hibberd, *Wilfred Owen: the Last Year, 1917–1918* (London, 1992), p. 177. For the poems, see J. Stallworthy (ed.), *Wilfred Owen: the Complete Poems and Fragments*, 2 vols (London, 1983).

173 On Saunders Lewis's reaction, see T. Robin Chapman, *Un Bywyd o Blith Nifer: Cofiant Saunders Lewis* (Llandysul, 2006), pp. 39–45, and for Lewis Valentine see Arwel Vittle, *Valentine: Cofiant i Lewis Valentine* (Talybont, 2006).

174 Michael Holroyd, *Augustus John: the New Biography* (London, 1997), pp. 439–41, 454.

175 Margaret MacMillan, *Peacemakers: Six Months that Changed the World* (London, 2003), p. 480, provides useful studies of the three great north Walians and the outcome of the peace treaties. Much to the Welsh nation's disappointment, Charles Evans Hughes, a descendant of the

eighteenth-century religious leader Howel Harris, failed by a whisker to be elected president of the United States in 1917. The historian and literateur Emyr Humphreys notes that 'if that had happened the two great English-speaking empires would have been led by two Welsh-speaking Welshmen and it is alarming to contemplate the paroxysms of joy with which such a divine event would have been greeted in Wales'; Emyr Humphreys, *The Taliesin Tradition* (Bridgend, 2000), p. 191. See also Manfred Boemeke et al. (eds), *The Treaty of Versailles: a Reassessment after 75 Years* (London, 1998).

176 R. F. Harrod, *The Life of John Maynard Keynes* (London, 1951), p. 257.

177 Quoted in MacMillan, *Peacemakers*, p. 48.

178 James Barr, *A Line in the Sand: Britain, France and the Struggle that Shaped the Middle East* (London, 2011) and *Setting the Desert on Fire: T. E. Lawrence and Britain's Secret War in Arabia (1916–18)* (London, 2012).

179 Giles Milton, *Paradise Lost: Smyrna 1922, the Destruction of Islam's City of Tolerance* (London, 2009).

180 MacMillan, *Peacemakers*, p. 54.

181 MacMillan, *Peacemakers*, p. 54.

182 C. Seymour, *Letters from the Paris Peace Conference* (London, 1965), p. 144; Harold Nicolson, *Peacemaking, 1919* (London, 1933; 2009 edn); Anthony Lentin, *Guilt at Versailles: Lloyd George and the Pre-history of Appeasement* (London, 1985) and *Lloyd George and the Lost Peace: from Versailles to Hitler, 1919–40* (London, 2004).

183 L. F. Fitzhardinge, *The Little Digger 1914-1952: William Morris Hughes, a Political Biography*, 2 vols (London, 1979).

184 L. F. Fitzhardinge, 'W. M. Hughes and the Treaty of Versailles, 1919', *Journal of Commonwealth Political Studies*, 5 (1967).

185 S. Bonsall, *Suitors and Suppliants: the Little Nations at Versailles* (London, 1946), p. 229.

186 L. F. Fitzhardinge, 'Hughes, Borden and the Dominions Representation at the Paris Peace Conference', *Canadian Historical Review*, 49 (1968).

187 MacMillan, *Peacemakers*, p. 352; Naoko Shimazu, *Japan, Race and Equality: the Racial Equality Proposal of 1919* (London, 1998), pp. 80–96. The Japanese were also aggrieved by the activities of the Welsh-descended Charles Evans Hughes, the US secretary of state, who forced them into acceptance of the humiliating naval treaty which gave a 5:5:3 advantage to the US and Britain over Japan. It was referred to disparagingly as the 'Rolls-Royce, Rolls-Royce, Ford' formula.

188 Malcolm Brown, *Lawrence of Arabia: the Life, the Legend* (London, 2005) and *T. E. Lawrence in War and Peace: an Anthology of the Military Writings of Lawrence of Arabia* (London, 2005).

189 John. E. Mack, *A Prince of our Disorder: the Life of T. E. Lawrence* (Cambridge, MA, 1998), p. 170; see also Scott Anderson, *Lawrence in Arabia: War, Deceit, Imperial Folly and the Making of the Modern Middle East* (London, 2014).

190 Elie Kedourie (with introduction by David Pryce-Jones), *The Chatham House Version and other Middle Eastern Studies* (London, 1970).

191 T. E. Lawrence, *Seven Pillars of Wisdom* (London, 1935 edn). It is interesting to note that the lure of the lore and legend of Lawrence lives on. In January 2014, a signed first-edition of *Seven Pillars of Wisdom* was sold at auction for £42,000.

192 Lawrence, *Seven Pillars of Wisdom*, p. 340.

8 'Once more unto the Breach' – Wales and the Welsh go to War, Again

1 Alan Sharp, *The Peace Conferences 1919–23 and their Aftermath* (London, 2011); see also Niall Ferguson, *War of the World* (London, 2007) and Zara Steiner, *The Lights that Failed, European International History, 1919–1933* (Oxford, 2007).

2 E. H. Carr, *The Twenty Years' Crisis 1919–1939: an Introduction to the Study of International Relations* (London, 1939); see also Stéphane Audoin-Rouzeau and Christophe Prochasson, 'Aftershocks: Violence in Dissolving Empires after the First World War', *Contemporary European History*, 19/3 (2010), 183–284.

3 Piers Brendon, *The Dark Valley: a Panorama of the 1930s* (London, 2001); Mark Mazower, *Dark Continent: Europe's Twentieth Century* (Harmondsworth, 1998).

4 K. O. Morgan, *Consensus and Disunity: the Lloyd George Coalition Government, 1918–1922* (Oxford, 1979).

5 Giles Milton, *Paradise Lost: Smyrna 1922, the Destruction of Islam's City of Tolerance* (London, 2011).

6 John Humphries, *Gringo Revolutionary: the Amazing Adventures of Caryl ap Rhys Pryce* (St Athan, 2005), pp. 228–30.

7 The involvement of the Welsh in the battles in Russia following the revolution of 1917 is a story that still awaits its historian. On the reaction in Wales, see David Egan, 'The Swansea Conference of the British Council of Soldiers' and Workers' Delegates, July 1917: Reactions to the Russian Revolution of February 1917 and the Anti-War Movement in South Wales', *Llafur*, 1/4 (1975), 12–37. Gwyn A. Williams and Baruch Hirson's *The Delegate for Africa: David Ivon Jones 1883–1924*

(London, 1995) gives some attention to one figure. The historiography, such as it is, seems to portray the Red Bolshevik forces in heroic terms, those of the White troops as reactionary.

8 Byron Rogers, *Three Journeys* (Llandysul, 2011), p. 230.

9 Paul Ferris (ed.), *Dylan Thomas: the Collected Letters* (London, 1985), p. 90.

10 Craig Brown, *One on One: 101 True Encounters* (London, 2011), pp. 1–3.

11 Norman P. Grubb, *Rees Howells: Intercessor* (Cambridge, 1973).

12 Two contrasting, conflicting views of Welsh involvement in the Spanish Civil War can be found in Hywel Francis, *Miners against Fascism: Wales and the Spanish Civil War* (London, 1984) and Robert Stradling, *The Dragon's Dearest Cause? Wales and the Spanish Civil War* (Cardiff, 2004).

13 On these themes see J. M. Sanchez, *The Spanish Civil War as a Religious Tragedy* (Notre Dame, IN, 1987).

14 Eric Linklater, *The Impregnable Woman* (London, 1938).

15 Stradling, *The Dragon's Dearest Cause?*, pp. 113–16, 164–5, 205, 227, 231.

16 *North Wales Observer*, 20 August 1936.

17 Stradling, *The Dragon's Dearest Cause?*, pp. 46–7, 143–4, 197–8, 217, 223.

18 Brendon, *The Dark Valley*, p. xviii; David Steeds, 'David Davies, Llandinam and International Affairs', *Transactions of the Honourable Society of Cymmrodorion*, 9 (2003), 122–34; John Graham Jones, 'Lord Davies and *The Problem of the Twentieth Century*' (1930), *Llafur*, 2/1 (2012), 63–82.

19 On 'Terfysgoedd Daear', see Alan Llwyd, *Rhyfel a Gwrthryfel: Brwydyr Moderniaeth a Beirdd Modern* (Llandybïe, 2003), pp. 267–70; see also Caradog Prichard, *Afal Drwg Adda: Hunangofiant Methiant* (Denbigh, 1973), p. 117.

20 Peter Lord, *Winifred Coombe Tennant: a Life through Art* (Aberystwyth, 2007), pp. 159–60.

21 Alun John, *Alun Lewis* (Cardiff, 1970), p. 55.

22 Ambrose Bebb, *Dydd-lyfr Pythefnos, neu y Ddawns Angau* (Bangor, 1939).

23 A. N. Wilson, *After the Victorians, 1901–1953* (London, 2005), p. 176; L. Merricks, *The World made New: Frederick Soddy, Science, Politics and Environment* (London, 1976).

24 Michael Foot, *Aneurin Bevan: A Biography. Volume 2, 1945–60* (St Albans, 1975), *passim*.

25 Donald Thomas, *An Underworld at War: Spivs, Deserters, Racketeers and Civilians in the Second World War* (London, 2003); Edward Greeno, *War on the Underworld* (London, 1960).

[26] Mari A. Williams's *A Forgotten Army: Female Munitions Workers of South Wales, 1939–45* (Cardiff, 2002) relates the story of four female 'pests' from Penarth, who were imprisoned for six months in 1943 for harassing American troops (p. 203).

[27] On some of these themes, see Michael Burleigh, *Moral Combat: A History of World War II* (London, 2010).

[28] For opposition to the war in Wales, see Stuart Broomfield, *Wales at War: the Experience of the Second World War in Wales* (Stroud, 2009), pp. 42–53. As with the First World War, the Second World War has been the subject for armies of books and broadcasts. Over the forty years during which this author has been reading about the war, histories, said to be definitive, of the conflict have appeared with a regularity which negates that claim. Probably more trees have been felled in producing the paper for these works than fell during the fighting. The works of particular value include, in alphabetical order, not in order of merit: Michael Burleigh, *Moral Combat* (London, 2010); Lizzie Collingham, *The Taste of War: World War Two and the Battle for Food* (London, 2009); I. C. B. Dear and M. R. D. Foot, *The Oxford Companion to the Second World War* (Oxford, 1998); Paul Fussell, *The Boys' Crusade* (London, 2004); Max Hastings, *All Hell Let Loose: the World at War 1939–1945* (London, 2011); John Kennedy, *The Business of War* (London, 1957); Norman Lewis, *Naples '44: an Intelligence Officer in the Italian Labyrinth* (London, 1983); Richard Overy, *Why the Allies Won* (London, 1995)and *Russia's War, 1941–1945* (London, 1997); Geoffrey Perrett, *Days of Sadness, Years of Triumph* (Madison, WI, 1973); Martin Poppel, *Heaven and Hell: the War Diary of a German Paratrooper* (London, 1988); Andrew Roberts, *The Storm of War* (London, 2009); Gerhard Weinberg, *A World at Arms* (Cambridge, 1994); Chester Wilmot, *The Struggle for Europe* (London, 1997). As with the First World War, one of the best documentary presentations of the war was produced a long time ago in the iconic *The World at War* (1973–4), one of the few occasions when independent television triumphed over the BBC in documentaries.

[29] The title, typical of Little Englanders, is a grave offence to Wales and the other nations of the UK, but the content is fascinating: Colin Smith, *England's Last War against France: Fighting Vichy, 1940–42* (London, 2010).

[30] Roald Dahl, *Going Solo* (London, 1986), p. 21.

[31] Smith, *England's Last War against France*, p. 70.

[32] Gwyn A. Williams, *Fishers of Men – Stories towards an Autobiography* (Llandysul, 1996), p. 17.

[33] David Gilmour (ed.), *Richard Cobb: Paris and Elsewhere: Selected Writings* (London, 1998), p. 3.

[34] Sue Roe, *Gwen John: a Life* (London, 2002), p. 304.

[35] David Roberts, *Swansea's Burning: Remembering the Three Night's Blitz* (Swansea, 2011).

[36] J. R. Alban, *The Three Night's Blitz: Select Contemporary Reports relating to Swansea's Air Raids of February 1941* (Swansea, 1994).

[37] Alban, *The Three Night's Blitz*. For other local studies of the impact of war, see Sally Bowler, *Swansea at War* (Sutton, 2006); Kate Elliot, Carol Powell and John Powell, *Memories of Mumbles at War, 1939–45* (Mumbles, 2005); Dennis Morgan, *Cardiff: a City at War* (Cardiff, 1998); Don Powell, *Pontypridd at War, 1939–45* (Pontypridd, 1999); John Tipton, *Tenby during World War Two* (Tenby, 1986); and June Morris, 'Morale under attack: Swansea 1939–1941', *Welsh History Review*, 11/3 (1983), 358–87.

[38] John O'Sullivan, *When Wales Went to War, 1939–45* (Stroud, 2004), pp. 24–6, 34–5, 39–52.

[39] J. Hayes, *The Art of Graham Sutherland* (London, 1980).

[40] 'Ceremony after a Fire Raid', in Ralph Maud and Walford Davies (eds), *Dylan Thomas: Under Milk Wood, the Definitive Edition* (London, 1995), p. xxxi.

[41] O'Sullivan, *When Wales went to War*, pp. 58–61.

[42] D. R. Davies, *In Search of Myself* (Bridgend, 1961).

[43] The Hugh Dalton quote is in Paul Fussell, *Wartime: Understanding and Behaviour in the Second World War* (Oxford, 1989), p. 102.

[44] Bertrand Russell, *Which Way to Peace?* (London, 1936).

[45] O'Sullivan, *When Wales Went to War*, p. 48.

[46] O'Sullivan, *When Wales Went to War*, pp. 31, 42.

[47] Gwyn Thomas, *A Welsh Eye* (London, 1964), p. 170.

[48] Ivor Wynne Jones, *Hitler's Celtic Echo* (Llanrwst, 2006), pp. 17–21.

[49] Morine Krissdóttir, *Descents of Memory: the Life of John Cowper Powys* (London, 2007), pp. 363–96.

[50] Gwyn Thomas, *A Welsh Eye* (London, 1964), p. 170. On the general reaction to the bombing of Britain, see Angus Calder, *The Myth of the Blitz* (London, 1991).

[51] Byron Rogers, *Three Journeys* (Llandysul, 2011), p. 116; Herbert Williams, *Nice Work If You Can Get it* (Llandysul, 2004), pp. 113–14.

[52] Ernest Jones, quoted in Richard Overy, *The Morbid Age: Britain and the Crisis of Civilization* (London, 2009), p. 71.

[53] Herbert Hughes, *An Uprooted Community: a History of Epynt* (Llandysul, 1998), pp. 21–5.

[54] Herbert Hughes, *Come Out, Wherever You Are: the Great Escape in Wales* (Llandysul, 2004), pp. 113–14.

[55] Williams, *A Forgotten Army*; Brian Roberts, 'A Mining Town in Wartime: the Fears for the Future, *Llafur*, 6 (1992), 82–95, and '"The Budgie Train": Women and Wartime Munitions Work in a Mining Valley', *Llafur*, 7 (1998–9), 143–52.

[56] Williams, *A Forgotten Army*, p. 31.

[57] Leigh Verrill-Rhys (ed.), *Iancs, Conshis a Spam: atgofion menywod o'r Ail Ryfel Byd* (Aberystwyth, 2001); Virginia Nicholson, *Millions Like Us: Women's Lives in War and Peace, 1939–1949* (London, 2009).

[58] Constantine Fitzgibbon, *The Life of Dylan Thomas* (Boston, 1965), p. 256. On the problem of food in war, see Lizzie Collingham, *The Taste of War* (London, 2011), and Daniel Smith, *The Spade as Mighty as the Sword: the Story of World War Two's 'Dig for Victory' Campaign* (London, 2013).

[59] See also John Costello, *Love, Sex and War: Changing Values 1939–45* (London, 1986).

[60] Roderick Bailey, *The Wildest Province: SOE in the Land of the Eagle* (London, 2008); *The Times*, 23 and 26 January 1956.

[61] *The Times*, 16 November 1960.

[62] *The Times*, 23 and 26 January 1956.

[63] Alan Jeffreys, 'Slim's Welsh General: Major-General 'Pete' Rees in the Burma Campaign', *Transactions of the Honourable Society of Cymmrodorion*, 12 (2006), 147–60.

[64] Lewis, *Naples '44*, pp. 71–2.

[65] Caradog Prichard, *'Rwyf innau'n Filwr Bychan* (Denbigh, 1943).

[66] *The Times*, 10 September 2007.

[67] Hugh Sebag-Montefiore, *Dunkirk: Fight to the Last Man* (London, 2006), p. 552; John Ellis, *The Sharp End of War* (London, 1980), p. 103.

[68] Ifan Gruffydd, *Gŵr o Baradwys* (Denbigh, 1963).

[69] Bickam Sweet-Escott, *Baker Street Irregular* (London, 1965); *The Times*, 14 November 1981.

[70] Ben Pimlott, *Hugh Dalton: a Life* (London, 1995). On the SOE, see M. R. D. Foot, *SOE: an Outline History of the Special Operations Executive, 1940–1946* (London, 1984).

[71] David Fisher, *The War Magician: the Man who Conjured Victory in the Desert* (London, 2004), pp. 20, 100.

[72] Ewen Montagu, *The Man Who Never Was: World War II's Boldest Counter-Intelligence Operation* (Oxford, 1996).

[73] Nicholas Rankin, *Churchill's Wizards: the British Genius for Deception, 1914–1945* (London, 2008).

74 Robert Waller, *Prophet of a New Age: the Life and Thoughts of Sir George Stapledon, FRS* (London, 1962).

75 J. G. Crowther and R. Whiddington, *Science at War* (London, 1947). The best study is David Edgerton, *Britain's War Machine: Weapons, Resources and Experts in the Second World War* (London, 2011).

76 See *www.bletchleypark.org.uk* (accessed 14 January 2014); see also Michael Smith, *Station X: the Codebreakers of Bletchley Park* (London, 2007); and F. H. Hinsley and A. Strip, *Codebreakers: the Inside Story of Bletchley Park* (Oxford, 1993).

77 *Western Mail*, 14 July 2006; Gwen Watkins, *Cracking the Luftwaffe Codes: the Secrets of Bletchley Park* (private printing, 2006). There is an excellent new biography of the superior socialite and occasional socialist Roy Jenkins by John Campbell, *Roy Jenkins: a Well-rounded Life* (London, 2014).

78 B. Randell, 'The Colossus', in N. Metropolis, J. Howlett and G. C. Rota (eds), *A History of Computing in the Twentieth Century* (New York, 1980); Paul Gannon, *Colossus: Bletchley Park's Greatest Secret* (London, 2009); and Jack Copeland et al., *Colossus: the Secrets of Bletchley Park's Codebreaking Computers* (London, 2006).

79 *The Times*, 26 February 1972.

80 *The Times*, 29 May 1991.

81 See *www.oxforddnb.com/view/36476* (accessed 29 June 2005).

82 *The Times*, 22 March 1996.

83 See *www.oxforddnb.com/view/34465* (accessed 8 March 2007).

84 Stephen Budiansky, *Air Power: a History of the People, Ideas and Machines that Transformed War in the Century of Flight, from Kitty Hawk to Gulf War II* (Harmondsworth, 2003), pp. 247–8.

85 *The Times*, 12 August 1974.

86 J. Tysul Jones (ed.), *Yr Athro Evan James Williams* (Llandysul, 1967).

87 E. Linklater, *The Man on my back* (London, 1941); M. Parnell, *Eric Linklater* (London, 1984).

88 Ian McLaine, *Ministry of Morale: Home Front Morale and the Ministry of Information in World War II* (London, 1979), p. 41.

89 *Dylan Thomas: a War Films Anthology* (Imperial War Museum Archive DVD).

90 For thumbnails of Illingworth's wartime cartoons, visit the British Cartoon Archive, University of Kent, *www.cartoons.ac.uk/search/cartoon_item/illingworth?page=3* (accessed 11 January 2011). See also M. Bryant, 'Crusader, White Rabbit or Organ Grinder's Monkey? Leslie Illingworth and the British Political Cartoon in World War II', *Journal of European Studies*, 31 (2001), 345–66.

[91] D. Hill, *Cartoons and Caricatures by Bert Thomas* (London, 1974).

[92] Richard Overy, *The Morbid Age: Britain between the Wars* (London, 2009).

[93] John Toland, *Infamy: Pearl Harbour and its Aftermath* (London, 1982); Robert Lyman, *Slim, Master of War: Burma and the Birth of Modern Warfare* (London, 2004); Field Marshal William Slim, *Defeat into Victory* (London, 1956); Jeffreys, 'Slim's Welsh General', 147–60; Hastings, *All Hell Let Loose*, pp. 201–68; Colin Smith, *Singapore Burning: Heroism and Surrender in World War II* (London, 2006).

[94] Cecil Brown, 'World Battlefronts: *Wales, Repulse*: a Lesson', *Time Magazine*, 22 December 1941; H. G. Thursfield, 'Sir Tom Spencer Vaughan Phillips', *Oxford Dictionary of National Biography*.

[95] Sebag-Montefiore, *Dunkirk*; Gregory Blaxland, *Destination Dunkirk: the Story of Gort's Army* (London, 1973).

[96] Sebag-Montefiore, *Dunkirk*, pp. 132–7, 520.

[97] Sebag-Montefiore, *Dunkirk*, pp. 366–7.

[98] Major L. F. Ellis, *The War in France and Flanders, 1939–1940* (London, 1953) and *Welsh Guards at War* (Aldershot, 1946).

[99] Lewis, *Naples '44*, pp. 49, 77.

[100] Patrick Hannan (ed.), *Wales on the Wireless: a Broadcasting Anthology* (Llandysul, 1988), p. 113. Wynford Vaughan Thomas, *Trust to Talk* (London, 1980), p. 70; *www.oxforddnb.com/articles/40/40169* (accessed 8 January 2009).

[101] Ron Berry, *History is What you Live* (Llandysul, 1998), p. 30.

[102] Harry Secombe, *Arias and Raspberries* (London, 1989), pp. 61–80.

[103] Spike Milligan, *Where Have All the Bullets Gone?* (Harmondsworth, 1985), pp. 231–2.

[104] C. Blair, *Hitler's U-boat War: the Hunters, 1939–1942* (London, 1997) and *Hitler's U-boat War: the Hunted, 1942–195* (London, 1999); Richard Woodman, *The Real Cruel Sea: the Merchant Navy in the Battle of the Atlantic, 1939–1943* (London, 2004); Bernard Edwards, *The Quiet Heroes: British Merchant Seamen at War, 1939–1945* (Stroud, 2010); Martin Middlebrook, *Convoy: the Greatest U-boat Battle of the War* (London, 2013).

[105] Phil Carradice and Terry Breverton, *Welsh Sailors of the Second World War* (Cowbridge, 2007), pp. 7–10, 239–41.

[106] The losses started swiftly. The first Welsh ship to be sunk was the *Winkleigh*, lost just five days after the outbreak of war. Thereafter, the ships of companies like Reardon Smith, Tatem, and Evan Thomas and Radcliffe went to their watery graves in Davy Jones's locker with distressing regularity. The last Welsh ship to go down was the *Filleigh*,

after being torpedoed in the North Sea by U-245 on 18 April 1945. Of a fleet of 164 at the beginning of the war, no fewer than 123 were sunk (Carradice and Breverton, *Welsh Sailors*, p. 12).

107 Carradice and Breverton, *Welsh Sailors*, p. 210.

108 Carradice and Breverton, *Welsh Sailors*, pp. 274–5.

109 Carradice and Breverton, *Welsh Sailors*, pp. 276–87.

110 O'Sullivan, *When Wales Went to War*, pp. 80–4.

111 J. D. Davies, *Britannia's Dragon: a Naval History of Wales* (Stroud, 2013).

112 *The Times*, 3 April 1993.

113 C. Messenger, *'Bomber' Harris and the Strategic Bombing Offensive, 1939–1945* (London, 1984).

114 104842 P/O G. Anthony, *Letters from Iraq, 1942–1945* (private printing, n.d.), p. 19.

115 Dahl, *Going Solo*, p. 33.

116 *The Times*, 18 September 1998.

117 *Western Mail*, 14 April 2009.

118 *Western Mail*, 15 September 2011.

119 See *www.oxforddnb.com/view/printable/60404* (accessed 19 July 2006).

120 *The Times*, 16 March 1986.

121 *The Times*, 7 January 2000.

122 Kenneth Griffith, *The Fool's Pardon* (London, 1994), pp. 139–49.

123 O'Sullivan, *When Wales Went to War*, p. 79.

124 Personal knowledge.

125 Brian MacArthur, *Surviving the Sword: Prisoners of the Japanese, 1942–1945* (London, 2005), pp. 193–200.

126 MacArthur, *Surviving the Sword*, pp. 124–5.

127 While still at school, Wilfred Wooller played in the first rugby victory for Wales at Twickenham in 1933 and was an important part of the Welsh team that defeated the All Blacks in 1935. He also won the county cricket championship with Glamorgan in 1948 and played football for Cardiff City; Andrew Hignell, *The Skipper: a Biography of Wilf Wooller* (Cardiff, 1995); *Western Mail*, 24 March 1995.

128 Jack Edwards spent much of his life working to bring Japanese war criminals to trial.

129 Anton Gill, *The Great Escape: the Full Dramatic Story* (London, 2001), pp. 188, 190.

130 See *Western Mail*, 17 March 2004, and Ken Rees, *Lie in the Dark and Listen: the Remarkable Exploits of a WWII Bomber Pilot and Great Escaper* (private printing, 2004).

131 Guy Griffiths also fought in the Spanish Civil War and took up flying in 1938. His brother was killed in the Indian Army in that year.

Guy piloted a Skua bomber in the first British naval bombing mission of the war. The Royal Marines Museum, Portsmouth, held an exhibition in April–October 2010 entitled, 'Griff: Thinker, Painter, Forger, Spy?'

132 Eric Williams, *The Wooden Horse* (London, 1949), *The Escapers* (London, 1953) and *More Escapers* (London, 1968).

133 Midge Gillies, *The Barbed-Wire University – the Real Lives of Allied Prisoners of War in the Second World War* (London, 2012).

134 Laurens van der Post, *The Night of the New Moon* (London, 1970), pp. 10–12.

135 MacArthur, *Surviving the Sword*, pp. 241–56.

136 The issues of the remarkable newsletters are to be found online: *www.llgc.org.uk/digitalmirror/cyl/CYL00001/25/unigol.html?lng=cy* (accessed 3 September 2009).

137 *Daily Mirror*, 13 September 1945. Quoted in *http://martinjohnes.wordpress.com/201207/04welshness* (accessed 7 February 2014).

138 MacArthur, *Surviving the Sword*, pp. 241–56.

139 *Western Mail*, 27 January 2005.

140 *Wales on Sunday*, 12 November 2011; Ron Jones with Joe Lovejoy, *The Auschwitz Goalkeeper: a Prisoner of War's True Story* (Llandysul, 2013).

141 Paul Weindling, '"Belsenitis": Liberating Belsen, its Hospitals, UNRRA and Selection for Re-emigration, 1945–1948', *Science in Context*, 19/3, 401–18.

142 Weindling, '"Belsenitis"', 44.

143 Raymond and Olwen Daniel, *Llyfr Mawr Llanddewi Brefi* (Aberystwyth, 2011), p. 60. I am very grateful to Olwen for this reference.

144 On the end of the war see Ben Shephard, *The Long Road Home: the Aftermath of the Second World War* (London, 2010); and Keith Lowe, *Savage Continent: Europe in the Aftermath of World War II* (London, 2012).

Conclusion: L'Heure Bleue

1 Jean Rhys (1890–1979) was the daughter of William Rees Williams, a Welsh doctor and Minna Williams, a Creole from Dominica. She is most famous as the author of *Wide Sargasso Sea* (London, 1966), a postcolonial novel and a prequel to Charlotte Bronte's *Jane Eyre*. Her novel *Quartet* (1929) chronicles the breakdown of her relationship with Ford Madox Ford. For an excellent biography, see Lillian Pizzichini, *The Blue Hour: a Portrait of Jean Rhys* (London, 2009).

Index